Wisdom and Holiness, Science and Scholarship

Essays in Honor of Matthew L. Lamb

Wisdom and Holiness, Science and Scholarship

Essays in Honor of Matthew L. Lamb

Edited by Michael Dauphinais
& Matthew Levering

Sapientia Press
of Ave Maria University

Requests for permission to make copies of any part of the work should be directed to:

Sapientia Press
of Ave Maria University
1025 Commons Circle
Naples, FL 34119
888-343-8607

Cover Image:
Masolino da Panicale (1383–1447)
St. Peter Preaching to the Multitude (Post-restoration)
Brancacci Chapel, S. Maria del Carmine, Florence, Italy
Photo: Scala/Art Resource, NY

Cover Design: Eloise Anagnost

Printed in the United States of America.

Library of Congress Control Number: 2007926235

ISBN-10: 1-932589-42-2

ISBN-13: 978-1-932589-42-9

Table of Contents

Foreword . . . . Archbishop Charles J. Chaput   vii

Introduction . . . . Michael Dauphinais & Matthew Levering   ix

1   The Idea of a University . . . . Don Briel   1

2   *Tanquam spiritualis pulchritudinis amatores*
    The Consecrated Vocation of Matthew Lamb . . . Romanus Cessario, O.P.   17

3   Knowledge Possessed and Desired:
    Aquinas and the Catholic University . . . . Michael Dauphinais   47

4   Wisdom as the Source
    of Unity for Theology . . . . Avery Cardinal Dulles, S.J.   59

5   Set Free by First Truth: *Ex corde Ecclesiae*
    and the Realist Vision of Academic Freedom
    for the Catholic Theologian . . . . Paul Gondreau   73

6   St. Thomas's Commentary on Philippians 2:5–11:
    A New Translation with Introduction and Notes . . . . Jeremy Holmes   109

7   Hierarchy and Holiness . . . . Matthew Levering   143

8   The Voices of the Trinity in Scripture . . . . Guy Mansini, O.S.B.   173

9   Revelation as Disclosure: Creation . . . . Francis Martin   205

10   A Thomistic Contribution to Ecumenism . . . . . . CHARLES MOREROD, O.P.   249

11   The Coming Middle Ages . . . . EDWARD T. OAKES, S.J.   273

12   What Use Is Kant for Theology? . . . . GIOVANNI B. SALA, S.J.   293

13   A Speyrian Anthropology: The Expansion of
     Human Liberty to the "Measure"
     of the Divine . . . . MICHELE M. SCHUMACHER   315

14   The Augustinian Foundations of a Nuptial
     Theology of the Body: "He Who Created
     Both Sexes Will Restore Both" . . . . LAWRENCE J. WELCH   353

15   Finality, History, and Grace: General and Special
     Categories in Lonergan's Theory of History . . . . JEREMY D. WILKINS   375

     General Index   403
     Index of Scriptural Citations   423

For Father Lamb

A FRIEND ASKED me recently: What kind of bishops does the Church need now and in the immediate future—good pastors, good preachers, good administrators? Obviously, the men God calls to be bishops in the years ahead will need all these skills, and a lot more. Pressures on the faithful, those who actually live and practice their Catholic beliefs, will grow in the coming decades, not decrease. So maybe the core virtue of tomorrow's bishop will need to be courage.

That would be a good answer. But there is an even better one. My answer is that for today and the foreseeable future we need theological bishops. Not necessarily bishops who are theologians, but bishops who understand the central theological issues facing the Church, and in the light of God's wisdom, act on them. Courage is a great quality, but without good intellect and insight guiding it, courage goes nowhere. And that is where the fraternal collaboration of bishops and faithful theologians becomes so crucial to the life of the Church, and so fertile.

I have been an admirer of Father Matthew Lamb for many years. For those who know him, I do not need to spend time praising his character and intellect. These qualities are obvious in every aspect of his life. They speak for themselves. But what I respect most deeply in the man are the simple qualities of his love for Jesus Christ, his obedience to the mind and heart of the Church as a scholar, and his gratitude for his own priesthood.

It is a privilege to call him my friend, and to wish on the bishops of the century ahead the good counsel of men like Father Lamb. May God grant him another fruitful seventy years. The Church needs him.

Most Reverend Charles J. Chaput, O.F.M. Cap.
Archbishop of Denver

Introduction

JUST BEFORE his fifteenth birthday, Matthew Lamb entered the Trappist Abbey of the Holy Spirit in Conyers, Georgia. In addition to the daily prayer and farmwork of the monks, young Matthew Lamb read the Fathers and St. Thomas Aquinas in the original languages and met such Catholic luminaries as Dorothy Day and Flannery O'Connor, and also translated Aquinas's *Commentary on Ephesians*. Ordained a priest, Father Lamb traveled to Rome to study theology with Bernard Lonergan, S.J., at the Gregorian University. After experiencing the final sessions of the Second Vatican Council, he moved to Germany to study with many of the leading theologians of the day, including Karl Rahner, S.J., and Johann Baptist Metz, under whom he wrote his dissertation. Returning to America in the early 1970s, he taught at Marquette University and then at Boston College, guiding the work of numerous doctoral students with his typical wisdom and generosity of spirit. In addition to the over one hundred articles he has published, his *History, Method and Theology* compared and contrasted the work of Wilhelm Dilthey and Bernard Lonergan, indicating the importance of intellectual conversion and metaphysics for a theology of history. His *Solidarity with Victims* demonstrated the inseparability of orthopraxy and orthodoxy.

His publications in the past two decades on history, eschatology, Americanism, Catholic theological formation, and sapiential theology have confirmed his significance for our time; see most recently his *Eternity, Time, and the Life of Wisdom*. For his unceasing efforts to renew Catholic theology in the United States, Franciscan University in Steubenville awarded him an honorary doctorate, and he has served on the boards of St. John Vianney Major Seminary in Denver, Colorado, and Blessed John XXIII seminary in Weston, Massachusetts. In 2004 he assisted in founding the M.A. and Ph.D.

programs in theology at Ave Maria University, where he presently teaches theology and directs the graduate programs. The esteem in which he is held is reflected in Archbishop Chaput's foreword to this Festschrift.

On behalf of his many friends and colleagues, we are delighted to present him with this Festschrift in honor of his seventieth birthday. Father Lamb took Matthew Levering under his wing at Boston College and served on the board of his doctoral dissertation. At Ave Maria University, Fr. Lamb has worked closely with Michael Dauphinais in order to develop a Catholic graduate program that addresses the needs of the contemporary Church, in particular the need for a sapiential retrieval of the traditions of philosophical and theological reflection. We have also worked closely with Fr. Lamb in planning theological conferences, in research projects, and in a myriad of other ways. His generous friendship is an ongoing gift and blessing in our lives.

The scholars who have contributed to this Festschrift have likewise done so out of deep admiration for Fr. Lamb's life and work. Due to the need to publish this volume by Fr. Lamb's birthday, many who wanted to contribute an essay were unable to do so. While this Festschrift therefore represents just the tip of the iceberg, nonetheless it manages to convey the unusually wide range of Fr. Lamb's thought.

A brief survey of the essays exhibits their particular fittingness for a Festschrift honoring Father Matthew Lamb. Don Briel, Michael Dauphinais, Avery Cardinal Dulles, S.J., and Paul Gondreau examine from different angles the nature of the Catholic university and in particular Catholic theological formation, a topic to which Fr. Lamb has devoted much labor both in writings and in action. Romanus Cessario, O.P., explores the consecrated vocation, thus recalling the Cistercian roots of Fr. Lamb's sapiential theology. Jeremy Holmes engages St. Thomas Aquinas's *Commentary on Philippians* in a way that accords with Fr. Lamb's lifelong interest in the theological fruitfulness of Aquinas's biblical commentaries; similarly Guy Mansini, O.S.B., and Francis Martin take up issues in theological biblical interpretation by extending insights of St. Augustine and St. Thomas. Matthew Levering and Charles Morerod, O.P., reflect upon ecclesiological concerns—the nature of ecclesial hierarchy, the task of ecumenism—that have informed Fr. Lamb's theological commitment to the magisterial teaching of the Church. Edward T. Oakes, S.J., identifies challenges to the relationship of faith and reason in the twenty-first century, and argues, as Fr. Lamb has done, that retrieving the philosophical and theological resources of the medieval period will prove to be decisive. Michele Schumacher sets forth a Christian anthropology rooted in the work of Adrienne von Speyr and Hans Urs von Balthasar, whose awareness of the Marian "Yes" to God informs Fr. Lamb's understanding of the Christian vocation; and Lawrence Welch also takes up a key issue in Christian anthropology from the Augustinian perspective that so enriches Fr. Lamb's work. Giovanni Sala, S.J., and Jeremy Wilkins delve into the Thomistic critique of Kant and into Bernard Lonergan's theological achievements in a manner that echoes Fr. Lamb's own indebtedness to Fr. Lonergan.

In short, the essays presented here in honor of Father Matthew Lamb both reflect the sources and goals of his theological labors, and constitute in their own right important contributions to contemporary theology. Given the fruitfulness of Fr. Lamb's vocation, this is to be expected. We speak for the contributors and for so many others in praising God for the abundance of blessings that he continues to bestow upon us through the labors and love of Matthew Lamb.

—Michael Dauphinais
& Matthew Levering

CHAPTER 1

The Idea of a University

Don Briel

For Father Matthew Lamb whose long dedication to Catholic higher education has been an inspiration to more than one generation of students and colleagues.

J. M. CAMERON insisted, in many ways rightly, that "Modern thinking on university education is a series of footnotes to Newman's lectures and essays";[1] nonetheless, *The Idea of a University* is a classic that is today both systematically neglected and widely misunderstood. Newman himself thought that it was one of his two most perfect works artistically, but he also noted that it was the most difficult to write and the one that had given him the least immediate satisfaction. He complained to a correspondent of his difficulties in preparing the discourses: "I am lost on the ocean with them, out of sight of land, with nothing but the stars."[2] Despite Pater's claim that the work embodied the perfect handling of a theory, many today remain confused about its basic arguments and assumptions.

There are a number of sources of this confusion. Some reflect aspects of the contemporary situation that Newman could not have anticipated fully in the middle of the nineteenth century. In "A Form of Infidelity of the Day," he had argued that one of the great advantages of the Church in his own time was its doctrinal clarity and the renewed vitality of papal authority. In contrast, in earlier periods both the patristic debates and the seemingly endless

---

[1] J. M. Cameron, *John Henry Newman* (London: Longmans, Green and Co., 1956), 25.
[2] John Henry Newman, *The Letters and Diaries of John Henry Newman*, vol. 15, ed. Charles Stephen Dessain (London: Nelson, 1964), 133.

disputations of the medieval schools demonstrated the consistent force of theological dissent within the Church. In the modern era, he insisted, theological dissenters have alternative forums for the expression of their views and as a result they are more likely to be found outside rather than inside the Church. This is, in itself, a gain, for the theological debates could now be waged with greater coherence and clarity. However, despite the increased prestige of the papacy in the last twenty-five years, the contemporary situation more often resembles that of the medieval period than that of the nineteenth century. The Catholic university shares in this more complex and ambiguous situation.

In his accounts both of the Church and of the university Newman assumed that theologians, whether clerical or lay, understood themselves in terms of an ecclesial vocation rather than a mere academic profession. This, too, has changed dramatically since 1852. Although he was keenly aware of the unprecedented extension of secularization in the nineteenth century, the full effects of that process could not have been taken fully into account in his description of the university and its relations to the Church. Newman could still have assumed a basic biblical literacy among his students and a generally pervasive religious culture. In addition, Newman was writing in a time in which higher education had a very restricted audience, and he surely could not have anticipated the sheer complexity and scale of the contemporary university with its remarkable diversity of functions and programs.

Finally, throughout his work, but perhaps most notably in the *Apologia Pro Vita Sua* and "Christianity and Physical Science," one finds an emphasis on the importance of a slow ventilation of ideas and a careful and deliberate reflection on their implications and applications. He insisted that the authority of the Church was very slow to intervene to resolve intellectual and doctrinal debates and that this process secured both an appropriate liberty for scholars and a careful and deliberate development of magisterial teaching for the Church. He pointed to the medieval Church, marked by its vital tensions and debates as an indication of the nature of this careful working out of the energy and dynamic tension of human thought. However, in contemporary Western cultures, media often enter into these theological debates, reduce the complexity of their terms, and distort and oversimplify their nature, forcing the Church to enter the debate prematurely in order to defend traditional teaching and to protect against scandal. This new situation further complicates the nature of university teaching and research and its relationship to the authority of the Church.

The question of university education was not by any means new to Newman. He said repeatedly that his chief interest in life was education, and he had written to Ambrose St. John that "the battle in Dublin will be what it was in Oxford twenty years ago."[3] But, as a Catholic, Newman recognized the nature of the battle with greater clarity and increasing alarm. However, the very terms of that battle are no longer clear to many today and as a result his claims may often seem merely antiquarian.

The most central difficulty lies in the simple fact that Newman asserts at the same time what he claims to be two obvious facts that are by no means self-evident today: that knowledge is an absolute good in itself and the equally clear claim that it is not the highest good. Most commentators would affirm the former but largely ignore the latter; others stress the importance of the latter and ignore the former. The tension between the two assertions accounts for the remarkable vitality and relevance of Newman's educational work as a whole. In order to explore that tension between what Ian Ker called "Newman's sustained eulogy of a liberal education" and one that "is systematically qualified by a reminder of its limitations,"[4] I will attempt to summarize briefly the arguments of *The Idea of a University*, and to provide some consideration of their contemporary significance. In doing so, I can only offer a sketch or outline of a complex work of Christian humanism that continues to define the basic nature of the modern Catholic university.

The complex history and ultimate failure of the Catholic University of Ireland has recently been treated well by Colin Barr in *Paul Cullen, John Henry Newman, and the Catholic University of Ireland*,[5] although this work can be supplemented by Newman's own accounts of his campaign in Ireland and his reflections on the project in his letters and diaries. Newman does say that in his effort to found the Irish university, especially in his description of it in the discourses that were intended to provide a view of its character, that he had two principal targets in mind. The first was the view of those critics of liberal education who complained of its inutility and its remoteness from the occupations and duties of daily life. The second was the view of those who argued against the religious exclusiveness of any university committed to an ecclesial tradition who were at this time celebrating the promised emancipation of Oxford and Cambridge from religious tests, the creation of the non-sectarian University of London, and the realization of the secular Queen's College system in Ireland. He had in mind then both the increasing strength of the claims that a university education should be practical and useful and at the same time that it ought not be subject to any dogmatic claims of religious faith. But in addition, he had to contend with the bishops of Ireland who in differing ways emphasized the apparently mutually exclusive

---

3 Ibid., vol. 14, 389.

4 Ian Ker, *John Henry Newman: A Biography* (Oxford: Clarendon Press, 1988), 385.

5 Colin Barr, *Paul Cullen, John Henry Newman, and the Catholic University of Ireland* (Notre Dame, IN: University of Notre Dame Press, 2003).

priorities of catechetical instruction, the promotion of Irish nationalism, and a cautious political expedience.

Newman was attempting to navigate among a variety of contending positions; and in the first sections of the work, he sought to make a number of distinctions in order to identify the specific character of university education and its relation to the Church. In the preface Newman stated directly that

> the view taken of a university in these discourses is the following: that it is a place of teaching universal knowledge. This implies that its object is, on the one hand, intellectual, not moral; and on the other, that it is the diffusion and extension of knowledge rather than its advancement. If its object were scientific and philosophical discovery, I do not see why a university should have students; if religious training, I do not see how it can be the seat of literature and science.
>
> Such is a university in its essence and independent of its relation to the Church. But practically speaking, it cannot fulfill its object duly, such as I have described it, without the Church's assistance, or to use the theological term, the Church is necessary for its integrity. Not that its main characters are changed by this incorporation: it still has the office of intellectual education, but the Church steadies it in the performance of that office.[6]

Newman's insistence that the Church is necessary for the integrity of the university results both from his assumptions about the nature of knowledge itself and its relation to virtue, as well as his awareness of the divisions among the Irish bishops about the nature and task of the new university. In the preface, he had to confront a pervasive Irish suspicion about the foreign background of its English rector, and he reminded his audience that the inspiration for the new university came not primarily from the Irish bishops themselves or from the English rector but from the pope, and he also reminded them that their own common Catholic inheritance, either as Saxon or Celt, had the same historical source. He then considered the question of the pope's motives in creating a Catholic university in Ireland and asked whether he had any legitimate concern in or responsibility for secular knowledge at all. "Is the vicar of Christ bound," he asked, "by office or by vow to be the preacher of the theory of gravitation, or a martyr for electromagnetism?"[7] He then proceeded to insist on the rational character of faith in rather sharp contrast to the tendencies of nineteenth-century liberal

---

6 John Henry Newman, *The Idea of a University* (Notre Dame, IN: University of Notre Dame Press, 1982), xxxvii.

7 Ibid., xxviii.

Protestant thought in which faith had come to be described as a mere sentiment or feeling. He insisted that the pope "rejoices in the widest and most
philosophical systems of intellectual education, from an intimate conviction
that truth is his real ally, as it is his profession, and that knowledge and reason are sure ministers to faith."[8]

This emphasis on the ultimate complementarity of faith and reason, that
truth cannot contradict truth, led Newman to insist that a university, to be a
university, must teach universal knowledge because all knowledge is connected
and mutually interdependent. He refers to a circle of knowledge in which all
the disciplines depend on a certain mutual correction and completion—in
which the absence of any discipline weakens all disciplines. He has in mind, of
course, the increasing tendency to exclude theology from university teaching.
In the second discourse, he asks on what grounds such an exclusion can be justified; and in a remarkably prophetic passage, Newman granted that

> divine truth differs in kind from human, but so do human truths differ
> in kind from one another. If the knowledge of the Creator is in a differ-
> ent order from knowledge of the creature, so in like manner metaphys-
> ical science is in a different order from physical, physics from history,
> history from ethics. You will soon break up into fragments the whole
> circle of secular knowledge, if you begin the mutilation with divine.[9]

The often decried Balkanization of the curriculum of the modern university had its origins in this apparently benign exclusion of theology, for as
Newman noted: "The systematic omission of any one science from the cata-
logue prejudices the accuracy and completeness of our knowledge altogether,
and that in proportion to its importance."[10] He later added: "In a word, religious truth is not only a portion, but a condition of general knowledge. To
blot it out is nothing short, if I may so speak, of unraveling the web of university teaching."[11]

In the fifth discourse, Newman argued that the knowledge appropriate to
a university is not a means to something beyond itself, but is its own end.
Such knowledge is liberal rather than servile, and it is not immediately useful
or practical. In this sense a university is a place for education rather than
instruction, and Newman insisted that university education, as such, does not
directly intend the moral improvement of its students. The goal of liberal
education is the gentleman, not the saint.

---

8 Ibid.
9 Ibid., 19–20.
10 Ibid., 39.
11 Ibid., 52–53.

Newman argued that a student is drawn into a "pure and clear atmosphere of thought," in which

> he apprehends the great outlines of knowledge, the principles on which it rests, the scale of its parts, its lights and its shades, its great points and its little, as he otherwise cannot apprehend them. Hence it is that his education is called liberal. A habit of mind is formed which lasts through life, of which the attributes are freedom, equitableness, calmness, moderation, and wisdom, or what in a former discourse I have ventured to call a philosophical habit.[12]

Such liberal education has as its aim neither practical application nor virtue; its aim is intellectual excellence. And so in one of the most famous passages of the work, Newman argued that

> it is as real a mistake to burden it with virtue or religion as with the mechanical arts. Its direct business is not to steel the soul against temptation or to console it in affliction, any more than to set the loom in motion, or to direct the steam carriage; be it ever so much the means or the condition of both material and moral advancement, still, taken by and in itself, it as little mends our hearts as it improves our temporal circumstances. And if its eulogists claim such a power, they commit the very same kind of encroachment.[13]

He then continued to draw out the implications of this central distinction:

> Knowledge is one thing, virtue is another; good sense is not conscience, refinement is not humility, nor is largeness and justice of view, faith. Philosophy, however, enlightened, however profound, gives no command over the passions, no influential motives, no vivifying principles. Liberal education makes not the Christian, not the Catholic, but the gentleman. It is well to be a gentleman, it is well to have a cultivated intellect, a delicate taste, a candid, equitable, dispassionate mind, a noble and courteous bearing in the conduct of life; these are the connatural qualities of a larger knowledge; they are the objects of a university . . . but still, I repeat, they are no guarantee for sanctity or even for conscientiousness, they may attach to the man of the world, to the profligate, to the heartless,—pleasant, alas, and attractive as he shows when decked out in them. Taken by themselves, they do but seem to be what they are not; they look like virtue at a distance, but they are

---

[12] Ibid., 76.
[13] Ibid., 90–91.

detected by close observers. . . . Quarry the granite rock with razors, or moor the vessel with a thread of silk; then may you hope with such keen and delicate instruments as human knowledge and human reason to contend against those giants, the passion and the pride of man.[14]

Newman then distinguished liberal knowledge from mere learning. Liberal or philosophical knowledge is integrated knowledge; it knows the mutual and true relations of things, not simply things themselves. Such knowledge is not confinable to the classroom. In fact Newman claimed that if he had to choose between a university with comprehensive final examinations but without a residence requirement and a tutorial system and one with these characteristics but no professors or examinations at all, he would choose the latter. "I am but saying that that youthful community will constitute a whole, it will embody a specific idea, it will represent a doctrine, it will administer a code of conduct, and it will furnish principles of thought and action."[15] Such a community would

> at least recognize that knowledge is something more than a sort of pas-sive reception of scraps and details; it is a something, and it does a something, which never will issue from the most strenuous efforts of a set of teachers, with no mutual sympathies and no intercommunion, of a set of examiners with no opinions which they dare profess and with no common principles, who are teaching or questioning a set of youths who do not know them, and do not know each other, on a large num-ber of subjects, different in kind, and connected by no wide philoso-phy, three times a week, or three times a year, or once in three years, in chill lecture rooms or on a pompous anniversary.[16]

It will be important to return to Newman's emphases on the importance of the residential character of a university and the personal relations of faculty and students, not only in terms of their capacity to develop the conversa-tions and character that form the fundamental basis of a liberal education but also because it is here, within the residential college, that Newman argues that the Church must be most direct and active in forming the moral life of university students.

In the seventh discourse Newman contrasted liberal knowledge and pro-fessional skill, a distinction often misunderstood today. For Newman the pro-fessions must be situated within the whole of the university's general

---

[14] Ibid., 91.
[15] Ibid., 111.
[16] Ibid., 111–12.

curriculum; and although liberal education cannot be immediately practical for "good indeed means one thing and useful another," still it must be said "though the useful is not always good, the good is always useful."[17] Nonetheless he insisted that nothing can be more absurd than to neglect in education those matters that are necessary for a young man's future calling, and he argued that professional disciplines had an appropriate place within the university's curriculum.

Still, liberal knowledge supplies a context as well as a corrective for the specialization of professional skill in the modern world for, as Newman pointed out:

> Society itself requires some other contribution from each individual, besides the particular duties of his profession. And if no such liberal intercourse be established, it is the common failing of human nature, to be engrossed with petty views and interests, to underrate the importance of all in which we are not concerned and to carry our partial notions into cases where they are inapplicable, to act, in short as so many unconnected units, displacing and repelling each other.[18]

Newman reminds us of a particularly pressing truth in our day—that "a man who has been trained to think upon one subject or for one subject only, will never be a good judge even in that one: whereas the enlargement of his circle gives him increased knowledge and power in a rapidly increasing ratio."[19] And so Newman claimed that liberal knowledge is the great ordinary means to a great but ordinary end:

> It is the education which gives a man a clear conscious view of his own opinions and judgments, a truth in developing them, an eloquence in expressing them, and a force in urging them. It teaches him to see things as they are, to go right to the point, to disentangle a skein of thought, to detect what is sophistical, and to discard what is irrelevant. It prepares him to fill any post with credit, and to master any subject with facility. It shows him how to accommodate himself to others, how to throw himself into their state of mind, how to bring before them his own, how to influence them, how to come to an understanding with them, how to bear with them. He is at home in any society, he has common ground with every class; he knows when to speak and when to be silent; he is able to converse, he is able to listen; he can ask a question pertinently, and gain a lesson seasonably, when he has nothing to

---

17 Ibid., 124.
18 Ibid., 127–28.
19 Ibid., 131.

impart himself; he is ever ready, yet never in the way; he is a pleasant companion, and a comrade you can depend upon; he knows when to be serious and when to trifle, and he has a sure tact which enables him to trifle with gracefulness and to be serious with effect.[20]

Newman's great eulogy to liberal knowledge is disclosed in his description of the gentleman, the highest good of the natural order of knowledge. But in the eighth discourse Newman cautioned against a religion of intellectual culture that threatens to become merely an artificial religion of self-respect. In the civilized age of the gentleman, conscience is no longer the word of a lawgiver but "the dictate of their own minds and nothing more," a mere taste or sentiment. "They look not out of themselves to their maker but are engrossed in notions of what is due to themselves, to their own dignity, and their own consistency. Their conscience has become mere self-respect."[21] It is here that Newman insisted on the fundamental distinction between modesty and humility as habits of mind and heart.

When they do wrong they do not sin, for "they feel, not contrition of which God is the object, but remorse and a sense of degradation. They call themselves fools, not sinners; they are angry and impatient, not humble. They shut themselves up in themselves. . . . They are victims of an intense self-contemplation."[22] Newman insisted that a philosopher's, a gentleman's, religion is of a liberal and generous character. It insists on honor and tolerance and pleasantness, but this does not make it Christian.

> This was the quarrel of the ancient heathen with Christianity, that instead of simply fixing the mind on the fair and pleasant, it intermingled other ideas with those of a sad and painful nature; that it spoke of tears before joy, a cross before a crown; that it laid the foundation of heroism in penance.[23]

The paradoxical character of the relations between humility and hope, in contrast to the civilized age's emphasis on the relations of modesty and optimism, led Newman to stress the distinctive Christian anthropology that he recognized as a perennial scandal to the world:

> The notion of an all perfect, ever present God in whose sight we are less than atoms, and who while He deigns to visit us, can punish as well

---

[20] Ibid., 134–35.
[21] Ibid., 146.
[22] Ibid.
[23] Ibid., 147.

as bless, was abhorrent to them; they made their own minds their sanctuary, their own ideas their oracle, and conscience in morals was but parallel to genius in art and wisdom in philosophy.[24]

This led Newman to a lengthy reflection on the pattern-man of philosophical virtue, Julian the Apostate, whose intellectual and military accomplishments define the highest expression of natural virtue. Newman summarized the events leading to Julian's death and then concluded:

> Such, gentlemen, is the final exhibition of the Religion of Reason: in the insensibility of conscience; in the ignorance of the very idea of sin, in the contemplation of his own moral consistency, in the simple absence of fear, in the cloudless self-confidence, in the serene self-possession, in the cold self-satisfaction, we recognize the mere philosopher.[25]

The eighth discourse concludes with Newman's celebrated description of the gentleman in which he makes clear that philosophical education is compatible with Christianity but is no guarantee of it, and is in fact often its unrelenting foe. Later in the *Apologia Pro Vita Sua,* Newman would remind us of the moral ambiguity of the intellect, describing Catholic Christendom as "a vast assemblage of human beings with willful intellects and wild passions . . . , the raw material of human nature, so excellent, so dangerous, so capable of divine purposes."[26]

This led Newman to clarify the point that although it is good in itself to be a gentleman, to have refined habits and to be freed from the temptations of mere prejudice and vulgarity, such a condition is no guarantee of sanctity.

> Such are some of the lineaments of the ethical character, which the cultivated intellect will form, apart from religious principle. They are seen within the pale of the Church and without it, in holy men, and in profligate; they form the *beau-ideal* of the world; they partly assist and partly distort the development of the Catholic. They may subserve the education of a St. Francis de Sales or a Cardinal Pole; they may be the limits of the contemplation of a Shaftesbury or a Gibbon. Basil and Julian were fellow students at the schools of Athens; and one became the Saint and Doctor of the Church, the other her scoffing and relentless foe.[27]

---

[24] Ibid.

[25] Ibid., 149.

[26] John Henry Newman, *Apologia Pro Vita Sua,* ed. Ian Ker (London: Penguin Books, 1994), 225.

[27] Newman, *Idea,* 160–61.

In the last discourse Newman considered the relations of the university and the Church. In the preface, Newman had argued that the Church was necessary for the integrity of the university, not so much to impose an external corrective claim but rather to fulfill its deepest inclinations and pretensions, to draw out its most central insights and provide natural knowledge with the supernatural complement of faith. This is what Newman meant when he argued that it was the task of the Church to steady the university, but this steadying may on occasion reflect a general tension that is essential to intellectual activity in general. In the *Apologia Pro Vita Sua*, Newman had argued that "the energy of the human intellect 'does from opposition grow'; it thrives and is joyous, with a tough elastic strength, under the terrible blows of the divinely fashioned weapon, and is never so much itself as when it has lately been overthrown." He does not hesitate, in fact, to employ the language of combat to describe the ongoing tension of reason and faith: "It is the vast Catholic body itself, and it only, which affords an arena for both combatants in that awful, never dying duel. It is necessary for the very life of religion, viewed in its larger operations and its history, that the warfare should be incessantly carried on."[28] Here Newman was speaking of the necessary tensions between theology and the infallible authority of the Church, in which he pressed the claim of interdependence but also on occasion, real collision of distinct authorities. He underlined the point in arguing that

> if the Catholic faith is true, a university cannot exist externally to the Catholic pale, for it cannot teach universal knowledge if it does not teach Catholic theology. This is certain; but still, though it had ever so many theological chairs, that would not suffice to make it a Catholic university; for theology would be included in its teaching only as a branch of knowledge, only as one part of many constituent portions, however important a one, of what I have called philosophy. Hence a direct and active jurisdiction of the Church over it and in it is necessary, lest it should become the rival of the Church with the community at large in those theological matters which to the Church are exclusively committed.[29]

It is not enough that the whole system of Catholicism be recognized and professed, for without the direct presence and active authority of the Church, such an institution is not Catholic.

Ian Ker has pointed out the remarkable analogy between Newman's well-known description of the infallible authority of the Church in the fifth

---

[28] Newman, *Apologia*, 225.

[29] Newman, *Idea*, 163.

chapter of the *Apologia Pro Vita Sua* as essential to restrain and direct the passions of the human intellect and the intellectual authority of the university, which, in Newman's words, not only

> occupies the whole territory of knowledge. . . . It professes much more than to take in and to lodge as in a caravanserai all art and science, all history and philosophy. In truth, it professes to assign to each study, which it receives, its own proper place and its own just boundaries; to define the rights, to establish the mutual relations, and to effect the intercommunion of one and all; to keep in check the ambitious and encroaching, and to succor and maintain those which from time to time are succumbing under the more popular or the more fortunately circumstanced; to keep the peace between them all, and to convert their mutual differences and contrarieties into the common good. . . . It is pledged . . . to give full play to thought and erudition in their most original forms, and their most intense expressions, and in their most ample circuit. Thus to draw many things into one, is its special function.[30]

As Ker noted, both the university and the Church are described as political organisms in which individuals are brought into

> unity not uniformity, and where the conflict of the various parts ensures and enhances their own vitality. Both paradoxically bring peace and harmony out of the very rivalry they encourage, by fostering "private judgment" in the one case, and the different branches of knowledge in the other. Both preserve and promote freedom of thought, not in spite of, but by virtue of the authority which each exercises in defense of the whole circle of truth against individual aberrations and excesses.[31]

But of course how skeptical we have become, if not of this infallible authority of the Church, surely of the powerful authority of a coherent, integrated and confident Catholic university. Such skepticism is perhaps natural in an age in which the university has been reduced to a bureaucratic proceduralism that seeks merely to mediate competing and often incoherent disciplinary and ideological perspectives and pretensions.

Newman was not naïve about the inherent limitations of universities and reminded us that they have perhaps an inevitable tendency to become hostile to revealed truth. "Liberal knowledge has a special tendency, not necessary or rightful but a tendency in fact, when cultivated by beings such as

---

[30] Newman, "Christianity and Scientific Investigation," in *Idea*, 344.

[31] Ian Ker, introduction to John Henry Newman, *The Idea of a University* (Oxford: Clarendon Press, 1976), lxxv.

we are, to impress us with a mere philosophical theory of life and conduct, in the place of revelation."[32] For

> truth has two attributes—beauty and power; and while useful knowledge is the possession of truth as powerful, liberal knowledge is the apprehension of it as beautiful. Pursue it, either as beauty or as power, to its furthest extent and its true limit, and you are led by either road to the Eternal and Infinite, to the intimations of conscience and the announcements of the Church. Satisfy yourself with what is only visibly or intelligibly excellent, as you are likely to do, and you will make present utility and natural beauty the practical test of truth, and the sufficient object of the intellect. It is not that you will at once reject Catholicism, but you will measure and proportion it by an earthly standard. You will throw its highest and most momentous disclosures into the background, you will deny its principles, explain away its doctrines, rearrange its precepts, and make light of its practices, even while you profess it. Knowledge viewed as knowledge, exerts a subtle influence in throwing us back on ourselves, and making us our own center, and our minds the measure of all things. . . . A sense of propriety, order, consistency, and completeness gives birth to a rebellious stirring against miracle and mystery, against the severe and terrible.[33]

The result, he later said, would be to "put an end in the schools of learning to the long reign of the unseen, shadowy world, by the mere exhibition of the visible. . . . For thanks to the new Philosophy, sight is able to contest the field with faith."[34] This reduction to a materialist view of life is perhaps a necessary consequence of the loss of the organic unity of the university in removing theology and ultimately the influence of the Church from its life. It was, as Newman said about the modern world in general, a vision to dizzy and appall.

In a sermon delivered at the University Church in Dublin on the feast of St. Monica, 1856 ("Intellect, the Instrument of Religious Training"), Newman reflected upon the nature of the Catholic university as an *alma mater*. He began with a reflection on Monica's motherly concern for the intellectual and moral formation of her son, Augustine, and Newman gives a remarkably realistic account of the ways in which young men, marked by original sin and formed in an increasingly secular culture, are prone to come to accept as necessary the fundamental separation between the intellectual and the moral life,

---

[32] Newman, *Idea,* 165.
[33] Ibid.
[34] Ibid., "A Form of Infidelity of the Day," 298.

which might at first be lamented. In consequence, however, faith begins to seem merely a sentimental dream, a sort of childhood remnant of innocence, and they now begin to form their own ideas of things, then change them, then perhaps decide that because of such changes, nothing is true, nothing certain. Newman argued that, within a university, youth need "a masculine religion, if it is to carry captive their restless imagination and their wild intellects, as well as touch their susceptible hearts." In one of his most well-known passages, a reminder of T. S. Eliot's claim that Newman was one of the two greatest homilists in the English language, he described the object of the Church in founding universities:

> to reunite things which were in the beginning joined together by God and have been put asunder by man. Some persons will say that I am thinking of confining, distorting, and stunting the growth of the intellect by ecclesiastical supervision. I have no such thought. Nor have I any thought of a compromise, as if religion must give up something, and science something. I wish the intellect to range with the utmost freedom and religion to enjoy an equal freedom; but what I am stipulating for is that they should be found in one and the same place and exemplified in the same persons. I want to destroy that diversity of centers, which puts everything into confusion by creating a contrariety of influences. I wish the same spots and the same individuals to be at once oracles of philosophy and shrines of devotion. It will not satisfy me, what satisfies so many, to have two independent systems, intellectual and religious, going at once side by side, by a sort of division of labor and only accidentally brought together. It will not satisfy me if religion is here and science there, and young men converse with science all day and lodge with religion in the evening. It is not touching the evil, to which these remarks have been directed, if young men eat and drink and sleep in one place and think in another. I want the same roof to contain both the intellectual and the moral discipline. Devotion is not a sort of finish given to the sciences; nor is science a sort of feather in the cap, if I may so express myself, an ornament and a set-off to devotion. I want the intellectual layman to be religious and the devout ecclesiastic to be intellectual.[35]

But how, in fact, is this to be achieved in our own time?

In some measure, this passage helps to clarify some of the confusion about Newman's treatment of the specific aims of the university and his claim that within a university, liberal knowledge is both its own end and yet

---

[35] John Henry Newman, *Sermons Preached on Various Occasions* (London: Longmans, Green and Co., 1921), 12–13.

no guarantee of virtue. However, Newman was describing the university in the abstract, in its idea; and as such its object is knowledge. But in a later discarded preface to the sixth discourse (now the fifth), he insisted that insofar as it is a Catholic university, it will recognize Catholicism in all aspects of its life and discipline and, in order to ensure this recognition, it is invested with a coercive power of enforcement of its views. This would involve, at a minimum, if we follow Newman's line of thought, a distinctive role for the Church and Revelation within the university curriculum, an active superintendence of the residential life of the associated colleges of the university, a careful selection and supervision of faculty and staff, and a sustained and effective relationship with the pope and bishops. However, Newman is insistent on the fact that the role of the Church and that of the university are distinct, if ultimately complementary and interdependent, and his earlier cited analogy between the authority of the Church and the authority of the university is here instructive.

Newman's prophetic critique of the reductionist tendencies of contemporary culture, a culture that he rightly suggested would eventually lead to very serious deformations but perhaps on a scale that he himself could not have fully envisioned, continues to be of central importance. In his *biglietto* speech in 1879, Newman indicated that he had spent his entire life combating liberalism, but, as Christopher Dawson pointed out several decades later, liberal culture's passing cannot for the Catholic be seen to be an unmixed blessing: What has replaced it is something even more threatening, a technological culture that has succeeded in instrumentalizing all of reality, even those elements that seemed least susceptible to its claims. Among them he listed the family, sexuality, religion, and economic exchange. But surely we should also include education. It is, perhaps, this cultural shift that makes it so difficult for many today to grasp Newman's central claims about the nature and promise of university education.

In 1966, Joseph Ratzinger reflected on the power of the emerging technological culture and warned of the consequences of its cultural triumph, for it inevitably produces, he said, a

> new orientation toward human existence, based on the opportunity to make things functional in the service of man. But this alters the basic relation of man to reality. He now views reality essentially from a functional point of view. He no longer approaches the world from the viewpoint of contemplation and wonder, but as one who measures, weighs, and acts.[36]

---

[36] Joseph Ratzinger, *Theological Highlights of Vatican II* (New York: Paulist Press, 1966), 162.

And so we encounter the triumph of the "merely visible." But surely New-man's basic principles are reaffirmed with a new sense of urgency in Pope John Paul II's *Ex Corde Ecclesiae* in which he reminded us of the distinctive identity of the Catholic university. Here he also insisted, as had Newman, on the com-plementary but distinct authorities of Church and university in a unity, rather than uniformity of expression and relation. John Paul cited Newman's claim in *The Idea of a University* that the Church has "an intimate conviction that truth is [its] real ally . . . and that knowledge and reason are sure ministers to faith."[37] Newman's careful distinction between the two, as well as his ultimate insistence on their interdependence, is perhaps the most important achieve-ment of the work as a whole, and constitutes a central critique of the func-tional imperatives of contemporary higher education and of technological culture as a whole. It supplies a reminder of the remarkable but long neglected promise of Catholic higher education for contemporary culture.

---

[37] See Ker, introduction to Newman, *Idea,* xxxviii.

CHAPTER 2

Tanquam spiritualis pulchritudinis amatores
The Consecrated Vocation of Matthew Lamb

ROMANUS CESSARIO, O.P.

> *Donet Dominus ut observetis haec omnia, tanquam*
> *spiritualis pulchritudinis amatores, et bono Christi*
> *odore de bona conversatione fragrantes, non sicut*
> *servi sub lege, sed sicut liberi sub gratia constituti.*
>
> —*Regula B. Augustini Episcopi in fine*[1]

Introduction

THE LITERARY GENRE of a festschrift ordinarily requires that colleagues honor a fellow scholar of great eminence by composing an essay that contributes to the general field of learning in which the honoree enjoys acknowledged mastership. On the occasion of his seventieth birthday, I take the liberty of saluting Father Matthew Lamb by writing principally about his person not his thought. There is a reason, a *logos*, for this option. What distinguishes the scholarship of Matthew Londergan Lamb lies in his lifelong pursuit of and personal commitment to spiritual beauty. Indeed, this dedicated priest-scholar rightfully belongs in the company of those lovers of spiritual beauty that St. Augustine, in the *Regula* that bears his name, strongly exhorts each of us to embrace.

As the epigraph indicates, the theme of spiritual beauty comes from the thought of St. Augustine, whom Father Lamb acknowledges as a preferred master and special guide in his lives, both theological and theologal. *The Rule of St. Augustine* still animates the consecrated life of various religious institutes,

---

[1] This text of the *Rule of St Augustine* is taken from the received text within the Dominican Order as it appears in *Liber Constitutionum et Ordinationum Ordinis Fratrum Praedicatorum* (Rome: Curia Generalitia, 1984).

including my own, the Order of Friars Preachers. Although not a Dominican, religious consecration best describes the vocation of the priest whom this collection of essays celebrates. This consecration began the moment when, as a very young man, his parents allowed Matthew to place himself under the Rule of St. Benedict as observed by the Trappist monks in the Monastery of [Our Lady of] the Holy Spirit located at Conyers, Georgia. It continues to the present moment when, as a senior scholar and distinguished professor, Father Matthew Lamb fulfills his monastic and intellectual vocation within the enclosure of the new Ave Maria University campus in Naples, Florida. Throughout his adult life, this priest, scholar, and friend has inspired countless Catholics, students, and folks in general to become "lovers of spiritual beauty."

If one were to inquire what constitutes "spiritual beauty," no more concise answer may be found than that set down by another of Matthew Lamb's spiritual masters and theological guides, St. Thomas Aquinas (whom Father Lamb likes to describe as the best Augustinian of the Middle Ages). In his discussion of cardinal temperance, St. Thomas writes in terms that are persuasively Augustinian in tone: "Beauty of spirit *[pulchritudo spiritualis]* consists in conversation and actions that are well proportioned in accord with the spiritual clarity of reason."[2] The following pages aim to illustrate the importance that religious institutes play in preserving a love of spiritual beauty among Christian believers and in developing an authentic appreciation for spiritual beauty among persons of all credences and cultures.

My contribution consists of two parts, which I believe correspond to the principal moments in the intellectual élan of Father Lamb. First, I comment on the present state of religious life, with reference to North America in general, and especially to women religious in the United States. This moment represents one of critical reflection and, therefore, invites further statistical and other research that would ensure the ongoing correctness of the analysis, which as it now stands represents an admittedly negative picture of the evolution of religious life after the Second Vatican Council (1962–65). Secondly, I turn to a positive or constructive moment, which aims to illustrate how at least one major religious institute proposes to maintain its spiritual charism and vigor, thereby ensuring that its members become and remain lovers of spiritual beauty.

It is not my place to comment on the Trappist monks who gave Father Lamb his initiation into the great tradition of religious rules and observances

---

[2] In *Summa theologiae* II–II, q. 145, a. 2, Aquinas compares spiritual beauty with physical beauty: "Unde pulchritudo corporis in hoc consistit quod homo habeat membra corporis bene proportionata cum quaedam debiti coloris claritate. Et similiter pulchritudo spiritualis in hoc consistit quod conversatio hominis sive actio ejus sit bene proportionata secundum spiritualem rationis claritatem."

(and to whose company, upon his retirement, he hopes to return).[3] However having been one for more than forty years, I can speak about the Dominicans. Aquinas, it is well-known, holds that Dominicans occupy the highest rank among religious institutes, even higher than contemplative institutes such as the Trappists, "just as it is better to illumine than merely to shine."[4] The Dominicans, moreover, are dedicated to preaching and teaching and so merit, in Aquinas's view, the highest rank among consecrated clerics inasmuch as they "are closest to the perfection of bishops, [and] because here, as in other things, 'the limits of the lower grade are joined to the beginnings of the highest grade,' as Dionysius says."[5] The second part of this essay examines seven features of Dominican spirituality, and answers the question: What are the qualities required for Dominicans to uphold the "highest place" among those Christians who fulfill their Baptismal commitments by following an approved rule of life?

In his foreword to this commemorative volume, Capuchin Archbishop Charles Chaput of Denver honors Father Lamb by pointing to the present-day, strongly felt need for bishops who have developed the virtues of the intellectual life. Perhaps the Holy Father one day would choose Father Lamb to fill an episcopal office in the Church. At the same time, one may argue that Father Lamb in this active period of his life, which includes his early teaching at Jesuit universities—first Marquette University and then Boston College—and now at the new and renewing Ave Maria University, both fulfills the Dominican vocation as Aquinas describes it and embodies in an eminent way the qualities that distinguish Dominican spirituality.

One thing is sure: Matthew Lamb's teaching ministry proceeds from the fullness of contemplation, about which Pope Gregory the Great comments: "It is said of perfect men returning from their contemplation: They shall publish the memory of thy sweetness *[suavitatis]*."[6] This text from Gregory's commentary on the prophet Ezekiel, which Aquinas uses to support his argument about the superiority of the mixed life, that is, the active and contemplative life, includes a reference to verses in Psalm 145.[7] Gregory reads the Psalmist as affirming that the one who meditates on the glorious splendor of

---

[3] See the faculty directory for Ave Maria University: "Before his studies in Rome, Fr. Lamb spent fifteen years in a contemplative Trappist monastery, where he hopes to return when he retires from the university."

[4] See *ST* II–II, q. 188, a. 6: "Et hoc [work that proceeds from the fullness of contemplation] praefertur simplici contemplationi. Sicut enim majus est illuminare quam lucere solum, ita majus est contemplata aliis tradere quam solum contemplari."

[5] *ST* II–II, q. 188, a. 6.

[6] *Homilies on Ezekiel* II, 5 (PL 76, 826).

[7] See Ps 145, vv. 4–7.

the divine majesty will declare out loud the greatness of God. No one who has been in the presence of Father Matthew Lamb for more than a few minutes could fail to recognize that he represents that man who is not afraid to declare out loud the greatness of God and of his Church. To put it otherwise, Matthew Lamb remains one whom, I suggest, both Gregory the Great and Thomas Aquinas would recognize as a true lover of spiritual beauty and of its surpassing suaveness. What else would have driven Father Matt to devote his productive life to the proclamation and publication of divine truth? *Contemplata et aliis tradere.* This phrase has become the motto of the Dominicans. It should rightly be inscribed over the door of the modest quarters where Father Matthew Lamb today fulfills his chosen vocation, which is consecrated to the promotion of sound Catholic theology and practice.

The Present-Day State of Consecrated Life

We begin with a question. What is the present-day state of consecrated life, especially in North America? In particular, what are the realizations of consecrated life, the challenges that face institutes of consecrated life, and the signs of hope that exist for new but as yet fully unrealized initiatives? These reflections on the actual situation of consecrated life in North America follow upon the recent celebration of the fortieth anniversary of the Decree on the Renewal of Religious Life, *Perfectae caritatis,* that the fathers of the Second Vatican Council promulgated on October 28, 1965.[8]

What follows below makes no pretense to report exhaustively on the statistics or even on the names of every form or institute of consecrated life that exists in North America. Reliable and recent statistics are readily available from the Roman dicastery that is concerned with the majority of religious institutes that enjoy official standing in the Church: the Congregation for Institutes of Consecrated Life and Societies of Apostolic Life. Some forms of consecrated life that the Second Vatican Council reinstituted or reinvigorated have found fruitful realizations in North America. In many dioceses in the United States, there are consecrated virgins and even diocesan hermits. It is therefore a fair generalization to say that those forms of consecrated life that do not fall under the definition of religious institutes are represented here and there in North America. At the same time, their realizations and prospects for further growth remain, at this juncture, a matter of speculation. One negative indication about their future growth may be gleaned

---

[8] The Congregation for Institutes of Consecrated Life and Societies of Apostolic Life will publish the proceedings of an international colloquium that was held in Rome to commemorate this anniversary. See note 10 below.

from the fact that several secular institutes that traditionally have found members in North America today experience the same difficulties in recruitment that will be examined below in connection with declining membership in religious life. In any case, knowledgeable persons estimate that religious properly so-called make up about 90 percent of the consecrated persons who remain active in North America. So what follows focuses on realizations of religious life, such as the Cistercians and the Dominicans.

Religious after Vatican II

It would be difficult to chart the post-*Perfectae caritatis* history of religious institutes in the United States without reference to a study of these same bodies that was commissioned by the Holy See in the early 1980s.[9] By that time, about twenty years after the promulgation of the conciliar decree, it had become apparent that renewal of religious life would not be reflected in increased numbers of religious vocations. In fact, the sharp decline in applicants, especially to congregations of religious women, and particularly to those communities engaged in active or apostolic life, drew the attention of the Holy See and thus of the bishops of the United States. Archbishop John R. Quinn, then of San Francisco, was asked to chair a committee among whose tasks included inquiring into the causes for this sharp decline in vocations to many sisterhoods that until the Second Vatican Council had formed an integral part of what some observers still consider a remarkable witness to the power of consecrated life in the world.

A brief historical retrospect will help. It is important to evaluate the status of religious institutes in North America today by reference to the circumstances of these communities before 1962. Their accomplishments still impress us. From about the beginning of the nineteenth century (and earlier in Canada), North American religious women built the largest private systems of education, health care, and social assistance that the world has known. In countless Catholic schools, hospitals, and social agencies, religious women enacted the evangelization of culture *ante nomen*. Catholic women, many of whom were the daughters of European immigrants to North America, almost singlehandedly reversed the Enlightenment secularization of the very works of mercy that, before the start of the modern period, had been considered the proper competence of the Church. To do justice to the history of religious life in North America, and to its accomplishments, would require mention of the various contributions of religious men, diocesan bishops and priests, and others, including the laity, who helped to realize this remarkable witness to the Church's place in human

---

[9] The three-member commission was appointed by Pope John Paul II in June 1983.

society. The fact remains, however, that without the consecrated lives of countless religious women, the magnitude and the success of these caritative works would not have achieved the proportions that they in fact attained. The expansive growth of the Church in the United States in many ways remains a testimony to the noble generosity of these religious women.

Historians and sociologists have reported on the influence that the institutional commitment of the Church exercised on certain regions of the United States. Something analogous occurred in Canada, although the silent revolution of the 1960s affected Canada in a way that up to this point has not occurred dramatically in the United States. In any case, it is well-known that in North America evangelization before the Second Vatican Council occurred within the triangular structure of parish Church, sisters' convent, and parochial school. The neighborhood became the center of evangelization. Nothing parallel developed in Europe. At the peak of Catholic schools in the 1950s, 11 percent of the school-age population in the United States was educated in parochial schools where all the teachers were nuns.[10]

To return to the announced theme: Given this amazing testimony to the power of both ecclesial life and religious consecration, what factors, during the twenty-year period following the close of the Second Vatican Council, led to the sharp decline in persons interested in continuing this remarkable success story? This question and the scarcity of credible explanations that had been proffered by Church leaders in North America both prompted and directed the work of Archbishop Quinn's commission. The summary report by this committee prepared for the bishops of the United States is a matter of public record.[11] It suffices to remark that the report did not offer an articulated plan for altering the putative course of renewal that religious institutes had pursued in the United States, and so the hemorrhaging continued.

After the submission of the Quinn Committee Report, applications to the majority of religious sisterhoods continued to decline, sharply. Statistics for the forty-year period after the close of the Second Vatican Council confirm this erosion. The number of religious sisters fell from 180,000 in 1965 to 68,000 in 2005. That is, the number of sisters dropped by half.[12]

The Quinn Commission Report did observe one new development. It mentioned that a small, revisionist group of institutes of women had stepped

---

[10] See Seán Patrick O'Malley, O.F.M., Cap., "Present Reality Regarding Consecrated Life: Its Realization, Challenges, Perspectives: North America," in the forthcoming *Proceedings of the Symposium Organized on the Occasion of the 40th Anniversary of the Conciliar Decree Perfectae Caritatis* (September 26–27, 2005).

[11] Both a preliminary and final reports appeared in *Origins* 14 (1984): 91–93 and 16 (1986): 467–70.

[12] See O'Malley, "Present Reality."

away from the major leadership conference and were forming their own support structures. It was also noted that communication between the two groups of religious women, the mainline institutes, represented by the Leadership Conference of Women Religious (LCWR),[13] and the revisionist ones—as they were then viewed—was strained. One anecdote may help to explain the reported tension. By the early 1980s, it was commonly asserted, and with approximate correctness, that 20 percent of the institutes of religious women were receiving about 80 percent of the new candidates for religious formation. What later became evident is that these high-recruitment congregations represented by and large the so-called revisionist sisterhoods who had withdrawn (at least, psychologically) from the LCWR. In fact, the communities attracting novices were those that, for a variety of reasons, had refused to follow the trends in religious life that by the mid-1980s had become firmly enshrined in the day-to-day lives of most of the LCWR sisterhoods. That is, the 80 percent.

Other informal and non-authoritative studies were done in the late 1980s and early 1990s. Again, it remains safe to generalize that those institutes of religious women that had been considered traditionalist or even retrogressive in the mid-1980s continue to prosper at the start of the new millennium. During the first decade of the twentieth-first century, it is clear that these institutes of religious life have maintained or adopted what, for lack of a better term, one may describe as the classical elements of religious life. These classically minded communities today enjoy corporate representation in the Council of Major Superiors of Women Religious, which was recognized by the Vatican in 1995.[14]

It is easy to speculate about the causal factors that led to a sharp decline in the numbers of religious women in the United States and Canada. Some observers point to societal factors, and even cite findings of the social sciences: for instance, the preference of many couples for smaller families, the growth of non-traditional families that eschew accepted religious affiliation and ideals, such as single-parent homes and same-sex couples living together as spouses. There also exists speculation of a theological kind: for example,

---

[13] "The Leadership Conference of Women Religious (LCWR) is the association of the leaders of congregations of Catholic women religious in the United States. The conference has approximately 1,000 members, who represent about 95 percent of the 75,000 women religious in the United States. Founded in 1956, the conference assists its members to collaboratively carry out their service of leadership to further the mission of the Gospel in today's world." Statistics from the LCWR website.

[14] For a brief account of the history of the two groups, see the news report, "2 Different Organizations for Women Religious Take Distinct Paths," *National Catholic Register,* August 3, 2006.

about the adequacy of instruction in and adherence to the Catholic faith among North American Catholics. When it is agreed that a majority of young people do not know about the Eucharistic Real Presence, it is unlikely to expect that these same persons will dedicate themselves entirely to adoring or teaching others about the Blessed Eucharist.

Other observers remark on a general decline in the practice of the virtue of religion, which at the same time may not entail a flagging display of religious sentiment. It is important to observe that whereas many people, including young people, are wont to view religion as an instrument of social cohesion and even of social usefulness, not all who share this utilitarian outlook are ready to commit themselves to God in an authentically religious way. Instead, many persons look upon God through the typically modern lenses that make the divine instrumental to human well-being. These points of view are not those that encourage the kind of dedication that is required of consecrated persons, especially of religious. To put this observation another way, Durkheim and Weber may have left their mark on the religious sensibility of the modern soul more than some Catholic leaders are given to acknowledge. However, sociologists cannot teach authoritatively that God is worth a life of total self-giving.[15] There exists a certain urgency to address this deficient view of what constitutes the religious person, whether consecrated or not.

Causal explanations aside, the fact remains that the vast majority of congregations of religious women in North America display radically declining populations. Consider as a case in point one institute of religious women. The Sisters of St. Joseph of Boston exemplifies a congregation that had been among the principal elementary and secondary school teachers in the archdiocese of Boston, as were their sister congregations elsewhere throughout the United States. Today the Boston Josephites number only a few members under the age of forty. At the same time, the community buries elderly sisters weekly at the former novitiate now turned into an infirmary-rest home. A properly conducted actuarial study would reveal that these Boston sisters represent what has transpired in similar institutes of religious life elsewhere throughout North America. The bishops in the United States long ago instituted a special collection for elderly religious, and they continue to distribute the collected funds on a need basis. Without new members, other means of support are insufficient to ensure that consecrated women will receive the care that they deserve at the end of long years—sometimes sixty and even seventy-five years—of dedicated service to the local Church.

It would be rash to project what a study team such as the one headed by Archbishop Quinn in the 1980s would report if, today, the members of the

---

[15] See my "The Sacred, Religion, and Morality," *Doctor Communis* VII, n.s., Atti della V Sessione Plenaria, 24–26 Giugno 2005 (Vatican City: 2006): 173–86.

team again were asked to conduct an investigation. Likewise, it would be difficult to conclude that the renewal of consecrated life that some had expected from the Second Vatican Council has been realized among those communities of women that before 1962 had flourished, at least insofar as membership numbers provide a measure. I also believe that it would be difficult to infer from our actual circumstances that a pruning has taken place: A smaller, leaner, more authentic group of "Vatican Two" consecrated women replaces an inflated body of women religious whose vitality and sense of purpose was compromised by ghetto Catholicism and the questionable values that some contend this sociological reality generated and enshrined. Although there are notable and individual exceptions, both those who have remained in the old-line sisterhoods and those who, during the past twenty years, have entered secularized religious communities of women reflect in their own dispositions and attitudes the same theological uncertainties that in fact have influenced the direction of the religious institutes themselves.

How Did Religious Get Where They Are?

A complete account of the causal factors that have left religious life in North America, especially institutes of women religious, in the depleted and unpromising state that they find themselves goes beyond the scope of this essay. It should be noted for the sake of theological precision, however, that insofar as sinful departure from God's law has contributed to the decline of a given institute, no positive cause can be assigned inasmuch as sin always remains a privation. One can only point to a series of historical intersections within which sin emerges. So, for example, where practices of gross unchastity or deep-seated impurity or complaisance with these sins have become accepted within religious communities, the consequent decline of membership in the community should be considered the result of the disintegration that sin leaves behind in sinners and their social structures.

What is true of congregations of religious women also applies to institutes of non-ordained religious men. The number of religious brothers fell from 12,000 in 1965 to 5,000 in 2005. The case of the ordained religious is somewhat different, in large measure because of the vocational identity and canonical status that attaches to the priesthood. At the same time, the effervescence of religious priestly vocations may be noted, and the same above-mentioned observations *(mutatis mutandis)* about the causes would apply. The number of religious priests fell from 23,000 in 1965 to 14,000 in 2005. To see an account, for instance, of the decline in Jesuit vocations, see Joseph Becker, S.J., *The Re-Formed Jesuits: A History of Changes in Jesuit Formation During the Decade 1965–1975.* The author lists in an appendix the Jesuits whom he mentions in the book, with an asterisk by the names of those who have departed the Society.[16]

There is one factor, albeit occasional in nature, which merits further consideration. In the United States and Canada, the rapid disintegration of many institutes of consecrated life has not occurred because powerful external forces appeared on the scene and sought to exterminate religious women and men. The situation in the United States is not that of England in the sixteenth century or France in the eighteenth and nineteenth centuries or of Mexico and Spain in the twentieth century. No one forced consecrated persons to leave their convents. The religious left on their own initiative. Since 1962 in North America, no anti-Catholic tyrant systematically exiled or murdered religious. It rather remains the case that the religious themselves, especially those charged with leadership positions, espoused strategies for renewal that conduce to their own self-diminution. As noted below, author Ann Carey documents this imposed estrangement from classical forms of religious formation and life. Many North American religious women followed renewal programs that had been concocted by theological and canonical experts who interpreted the documents of the Second Vatican Council without reference to the anterior tradition, or interpreted them with what we call today the hermeneutics of discontinuity.

How best to interpret the reception of the Second Vatican Council in Anglophone countries remains a matter of dispute among historians and theologians. Father Matthew Lamb has argued that the Second Vatican Council was introduced to the Catholics of North America by media-supported "popularizers" and other pundits. He considers this unfortunate circumstance a key one to explain why so much that one may have expected from the conciliar documents fell short of the mark. Instead, as Father Lamb likes to remind us, many proposals in theological studies were acted upon without proper scrutiny in order to determine their conformity with the plain meaning of the conciliar documents and their continuity with what had been taught by earlier councils and other magisterial authorities.

Father Lamb mentions popularizing at the end of a published response to Religious Sister of Mercy Margaret Farley, who had complained publicly about Vatican oversight of Catholic theologians: "Any effort," responds Father Lamb,

> to spin papal and Vatican concern for Catholic theological orthodoxy as "stifling scholarship" is just plain false. The dissent is not based upon serious theological scholarship but on superficial popularized distortions.

---

[16] Joseph Becker, S.J., *The Re-Formed Jesuits: A History of Changes in Jesuit Formation During the Decade 1965–1975* (San Francisco: Ignatius Press, 1992).

Orthodox Catholic faith enlightens human intelligence. Dissent weakens both faith and intelligence.[17]

Religious life in North America was severely weakened indeed by the postconciliar theology of the popularizers and the dissent that it engendered. A clarifying and well-researched exposition of how popular dissenting theologians were involved in deconstructing what had been a flourishing of consecrated life among women religious appears in *Sisters in Crisis: The Tragic Unraveling of Women's Religious Communities* by American author Ann Carey.[18]

Let me offer two examples that may illustrate the Lamb-Carey thesis: The early proponents of the hermeneutics of discontinuity argued that supplementing the study of theology with heavy doses of the empirical life sciences (for example, psychology, sociology, and anthropology) formed a necessary part of the updating that the Fathers of the Council had mandated. These same sciences today enjoy a strong influence in the actualization of religious life. In many instances, findings from the life sciences trump magisterial teaching when it comes to the directions taken by religious institutes of women, especially. There have been studies done and reports written about the number of religious women who promote the practice of the parapsychological (for example, the enneagram). Other secular therapies are common among the offerings that some religious women provide at religious community-sponsored centers of spirituality. In sum, new age and liberationist attitudes and outlooks enjoy support among religious women and their collaborators, especially those who remain persuaded of 1970s ideological feminism, as Mary Ann Glendon explains it.[19]

Other popular interpreters of the council, including those who had discovered for the first time the Italian word *aggiornamento*, claimed that an integrated or correlative approach to theology is the only way of responding to the council's suggestion that Catholic studies should become more open to the world than had been allegedly the case in the theological programs of the preconciliar period. During the decade of the 1970s, the codeword used in English was "secularity." Today, the policies that have been developed under the rubric of "openness to the world" are to be found illustrated even in melodramas and television sitcoms. The caricature of the "modern nun" is well-known to the contemporary audience, but not the religious values that she stands or stood for. The most noticeable indication of secular encroachment into the daily lives of religious women is, alas, their attire. In general,

---

17 See Father Lamb's remarks in *Fellowship of Catholic Scholars Quarterly* 21 (1998): 2–5.

18 Ann Carey, *Sisters in Crisis: The Tragic Unraveling of Women's Religious Communities* (Huntington, IN: Our Sunday Visitor Publishing, 1997).

19 See Mary Ann Glendon, "The Pope's New Feminism," *Crisis* 15.3 (March 1997): 28.

the members of those institutes that find themselves in a precarious membership situation are the ones least likely to appear in a recognizable habit and veil, the ancient visible sign of a woman's consecration to the Lord. If there is a group of Catholics who embody the hermeneutics of discontinuity as the preferred way to implement the documents of the Second Vatican Council, dissident religious women in the United States rank among the leading candidates.[20]

Let me summarize: The general ecclesial and cultural atmosphere that colors Catholic life in predominantly Anglophone countries (as well as French-speaking Canada) affects profoundly the state of religious life in North America. Pope Benedict XVI has reminded us that the 68ers, *les soix-antehuitards*, failed to keep their promises for renewal.[21] Essential elements of religious life did not so much fall into desuetude; rather they were deliberately put aside. The fundamentals of religious life as the Church enshrines them gave way to the opinions and viewpoints of persons who were touted as announcing the authentic path to renewal, but in fact were possessed of some other beguiling spirit. They did not keep their promises. In a word, theoreticians dismantled religious life in North America. The theologically defective arguments advanced for espousing this or that novelty were enhanced by the influences of a secular culture that confuses ersatz humanism for Christian witness. No wonder that dissent embedded in cynicism and feminism, to cite only two pronounced cultural factors that dominate Anglo-American-Germano popular thought, became influential—to various degrees and in various ways—on religious congregations of women. It is not uncommon, for example, to discover among religious women attitudes toward the public expression and approval of male and female homosexuality that depart dramatically from what one may prudently describe as a posture of ensuring "no unjust discrimination." All in all, the situation among a large percentage of religious congregations of women is not a promising one. To make the same kind of generalization about the institutes of consecrated men would be more difficult and would require further nuance. The main reason for this qualification, as I have suggested, is that the large majority of

---

[20] See the forthcoming *Vatican II: Renewal Within Tradition*, ed. Matthew Lamb and Matthew Levering, especially the article on *Perfectae caritatis* by Sr. Prudence Allen, R.S.M. and Sr. Mary Judith O'Brien, R.S.M.

[21] "But we see that '68 did not keep its promises, and there is a rebirth of the awareness that there is another way, one that is more complex because it demands these transformations of our heart, but one that is also more genuine." The complete text, in Italian, of Benedict XVI's address and his responses to the questions from the priests of the diocese of Aosta is available on the Vatican website: "Incontro con il clero della diocesi di Aosta, 25 luglio 2005."

religious men are also ordained priests. The oversight of the Church is more direct on clerics, for whom Canon Law provides sanctionable parameters within which they can operate.

Challenges and New Expectations

The first and most obvious challenge that consecrated life faces in North America is theological in kind. There needs to be a concerted effort to supply sound theological instruction for religious and other consecrated persons that reflect what the Church teaches about the nature of their special consecration. This effort should address issues in ecclesiology and sacramental and moral theology inasmuch as these disciplines govern many of the ecclesial values in which religious have been ill-formed. Perhaps a useful initiative would be to propose that the Holy See consider publishing a "Catechism of Consecrated Life." Such a text would provide a sort of handbook of elementary but necessary instruction in the theological and canonical aspects of religious and other forms of consecrated life.

A second challenge that faces consecrated life is the failure of bishops and priests to preach adequately on the nobility and significance of this vocation within Christian life and community. Many Catholic priests remain reluctant to acknowledge the "objective superiority" of consecrated life, or find themselves at a loss to explain what this teaching of the Catholic tradition means.[22] Pastoral care for people who are considering a vocation provides another challenge. The Church needs not only to encourage priests to preach about consecrated life, but also to train them to serve persons in the consecrated state. This applies especially to the office of the confessor and spiritual director. A special caution needs to be raised: mistaken views on the distinction of vocations within the Church, on the nature of the sacred power *(sacra potestas)* of the priest, and on the need for sacramental ministrations have infiltrated many institutes of religious women as well as of men. The residual revolutionary ideologies of the 1970s still pump feminist distortions of the Gospel into many communities of consecrated women. To meet the second challenge that threatens the promotion of consecrated life will require an adequate address of the misgivings that many consecrated women and non-ordained men hold about the priesthood and the sacrament of Holy Orders that confers it. These misgivings generated by the proliferation of ill-formed and even erroneous theological opinions are

---

[22] See the 1996 postsynodal apostolic exhortation of the Holy Father John Paul II, *Vita consecrata,* no. 18: "This is why Christian tradition has always spoken of the *objective superiority of consecrated life*" (original emphasis).

supported by popular misunderstandings about the nature of collaboration in the care of souls between laity and clerics.[23]

The third challenge that faces all specialized vocations within the Church is one that the late Holy Father, Pope John Paul II, remarked on at various instances, namely, the parlous state of the Catholic family. Family life is the seedbed of consecrated and priestly vocations. When the Catholic family is diminished, it is unlikely that young people will consider the nobility of a life specially dedicated to the Lord. Children learn obedience from parents. Absence of authentic examples of paternity affects the capacity of young people to live a life of obedience within a religious context. Without the experience of a true and loving paternity, future religious will be less inclined to exercise and to follow authority in a way that conforms to the requirements of evangelical consecration.

A fourth challenge that faces consecrated life, especially when it is lived in community, is the rampant individualism that characterizes the modern ethos. Sometimes too much personalism can work against upholding Christian values. This challenge is not one that is easily addressed. Pope Benedict XVI, however, has pointed to the role of St. Benedict in cultivating human and social values in Europe. We need more Benedicts to teach us about the human foundation that is required for making it possible for individuals to live in common. This work precedes, in my estimate, the initiatives that men like St. Francis and St. Dominic emphasized in establishing their thirteenth-century mendicant foundations. Mendicant fraternities assumed that community life would flourish among men and women who had learned within the boundaries of a natural family how to live in ordered though unequal relationships with one another. A judicious use of sound social psychology can illuminate the difficulties that face young people who today want to assume the burdens of community life.

A fifth challenge that faces consecrated life, inasmuch as this form of ecclesial consecration entails a lifelong commitment to chastity, is the widespread ignorance about what constitutes the chaste and pure life. This challenge, in my view, opens up an enormous area of research and study that would serve the Church in North America. The Institute for the Psychological Sciences in Alexandria, Virginia, already has begun to study in an interdisciplinary mode and under the guidance of the Magisterium the important themes of chastity and natural law. Distinguished specialists in the fields of psychology and other life disciplines join philosophers and theologians to

---

[23] For an expression of the Church's concern about this matter, see the interdicasterial instruction, *Ecclesiae de mysterio* (On Certain Questions Regarding the Collaboration of the Non-Ordained Faithful in the Sacred Ministry of the Priest), issued by eight dicasteries of the Holy See on August 15, 1997.

discover ways to present the classical truths about human sexuality and the virtues of the Christian life in a way that responds to the challenges of modern culture.

The recent time of crisis through which the Church in North America has passed affords one example of the legacy of the sexual revolution of the 1960s and 1970s. There is no indication that present-day, secular Western culture will help the Church instill in young people a respect for chastity. Abusive relationships will be punished, but consensual unchastity among persons of legal age and autosexuality among persons of whatsoever age are abetted, if not promoted, by secular authorities, including educators and other agents of social formation. This pattern will occur without anyone stopping to ask whether there is a connection between "lawful unchastity" and the unlawful perpetration of abuse that is so deplored by the representatives of secular authority.[24] The Church must work consciously and actively to teach the full truth about chastity. Bishops cannot assume that young people have maintained their innocence, and this means that some persons who enter consecrated life will have to be helped to achieve what spiritual authors describe as the "purification of memory."

A sixth challenge to consecrated life remains the uncertain state of reflection—psychological, sociological, and theological—about homosexuality. This subject was aired during the 2005 apostolic visitation of Catholic seminaries and houses of formation in the United States. The findings of this visitation will form the basis for an eventual pronouncement from the Holy See. It is expected that an eventual statement will complement what already has been prescribed in the 2005 instruction on vocational discernment issued by the Congregation for Catholic Education.[25] Suffice it to remark that the cultural incursions of gay and lesbian lifestyles into institutes of consecrated life should not be overlooked when answers are sought as to why the number of consecrated persons is dwindling.

Seventh, a final challenge to the development of consecrated life in North America arises from the special demands that evangelical poverty poses for many young people who have grown up during a period of economic and technological prosperity. The effects of the consumer society and everything that the Church warns about the high-risk dynamics of unbridled capitalism shapes the native ethos of young people in North America,

---

[24] For a development of this subject, see my "Person & Being: Theological and Psychological Considerations," *Doctor Communis,* Atti della IV Sessione Plenaria 25–27, Giugno 2004 (Vatican City: 2006): 75–84.

[25] Congregation for Catholic Education, "Instruction Concerning the Criteria for the Discernment of Vocations with Regard to Persons with Homosexual Tendencies in View of Their Admission to the Seminary and to Holy Orders," November 4, 2005.

perhaps more than in any other region in the world. Religious institutes need to discover ways to live poverty realistically in the age of mobile phones and of computers and of other technology that without beckoning can intrude into silence. And what are we to say about travel and the opportunity for business class accommodations that at times are offered to religious by benefactors or by those who think that granting perks to clerics is still good for business? Because a second story was not customary for the houses of the poor, St. Dominic ordered his friars to remove the one that they were about to add to a priory that they were constructing in Bologna.[26] His first followers—some of whom are now beatified—had opined otherwise. It is not easy even for holy persons to agree on the actual dimensions that poverty should take.

There are signs of new commitment to religious life that are apparent among communities of both men and women. An elenchus of new or breakaway religious institutes founded since the Second Vatican Council would surprise some Catholics in the United States. Then there are the 20 percent mentioned in the Quinn Commission Report. These women are religious who have maintained the classical features of religious life and follow the Magisterium of the Church's pastors. Their sustained growth remains the best sign of hope for consecrated life in North America. This group of sensitively renewed religious women include: (1) sisterhoods (both of diocesan and pontifical right) that have been founded by North Americans, even as early as in the nineteenth century; (2) sisterhoods of pontifical right that came to the United States from Europe or South or Central America who have benefited from the support they receive from international governance; and (3) newly formed sisterhoods that have achieved, in some cases even after a relatively short period of time, a certain stability. As mentioned above, the majority of these institutes belong to a recognized national body, the Council of Major Superiors of Women Religious, which ensures their mutual support.[27]

To conclude this first section, it is useful to return to the theme of the virtue of religion. The real crisis in religious life stems from an erosion among North American Catholics of the virtue of religion. All that has been lost during the postconciliar period is difficult to enumerate. One lost value, however, remains the classical understanding of what it means to be a religious person, one who acknowledges, even on the basis of reason alone, that God is an Object of dutiful veneration. The practice of some theologians to include

---

[26] For an account of Dominic's distinctive love of poverty, see Guy Bedouelle, O.P., *The Grace of the Word,* trans. Sister Mary Thomas Noble, O.P. (San Francisco: Ignatius Press, 1987), ch. 8, and for a reference to the Bologna complaint, 152.

[27] See above, note 14.

religion among the theological virtues sets the stage for the shift from thinking about religion as a natural-law relationship to God that reason itself can
identify to presenting religion only as a private world of individual beliefs and
personal values. Furthermore, there is the historical fact—for which there are
more than several explanations—that in the nineteenth century the industri-
alized countries of Europe lost all sense of religion as an obligation imposed
on the creature precisely by reason of his creaturely nature.

At the present time, the debates surrounding the place that religion and
Christianity hold in the proposed Constitution for Europe should be sufficient to indicate that giving a historical explanation for the apostasy is less
important than discovering a remedy for the disappearance of God in the
West.[28] Pope Benedict XVI enlarged on this point in his September 12,
2006, address at the University of Regensburg: "A reason which is deaf to
the divine and which relegates religion into the realm of subcultures is incapable of entering into the dialogue of cultures. . . . The West has long been
endangered by this aversion to the questions which underlie its rationality,
and can only suffer harm thereby."[29] It is difficult to imagine how there will
be a renewed flourishing of vocations to consecrated life without a renewed
appreciation of what it means to be a plain religious person. Obviously the
Church cannot repose trust in the political order to generate this fundamentally spiritual renewal. No return to throne and altar. The task then falls to
bishops and theologians. Whatever instruction, moreover, is given about the
nature of religious persons must attain the status of the fully theological and
not sink to the level of the "subcultures." To counteract the modern penchant to confuse religious expression of what, in fact, are the hypothetical
claims of sociology or psychology or anthropology with sound Catholic theology requires that those who instruct in sacred doctrine return to the
sources of the acknowledged religious traditions or charisms.

What it means to be religious finds its best illustration in the founding
charters of the great monastic and capitular and conventual traditions: The
Rule of St. Benedict, the Rule of St. Augustine, the Rule of St. Francis.
These documents teach us about the true nature of religious consecration.
Religious rules insist that those who follow a rule of life submit themselves
entirely to God through the human instruments that the Church puts at our
disposal. God is worth a life. Become a lover of spiritual beauty. This is the
message that needs to be announced to the young people of the present generation, and there are signs already that they will respond generously.

---

[28] See the "Draft Treaty Establishing a Constitution for Europe" drawn up by the
European Parliament Delegation and adopted on June 18, 2004.

[29] See "Faith, Reason, and the University: Memories and Reflections," *L'Osservatore
Romano* (English) (September 20, 2006): 11.

It should be clear from the challenges and history recounted above that the task of promoting the renewal of religious life in the United States will require magnanimity. This great-heartedness is required not only on the part of those who seek admission to consecrated life but also on the part of those who now profess it and on the part of the bishops of the Church to whom the charge of promoting and sustaining consecrated life is given by reason of their episcopal consecration.[30] Again, what is required entails a renewal of the call to become lovers of spiritual beauty. This call is more easily addressed within a climate of sound Catholic theology. Perhaps that is why Archbishop Chaput contemplates Father Lamb among the great Bishop-Doctors of the Church. It should not take long to assess the influence that Father Matthew Lamb has exercised on the students who come to Ave Maria University to pursue their studies. It will only require counting the number of men and women who pursue a vocation in some form of religious or other consecrated life.

"The Grace of Dominican Spirituality"

In the second part of this essay, I borrow from some unpublished notes compiled by Peter John Cameron, O.P., playwright, spiritual author, and the editor-in-chief of *Magnificat*. Father Cameron identifies and gives the rationale for seven essential elements that he considers distinctive of Dominican spirituality. The spiritual heritage described below is something from which all Catholics may draw inspiration. Dominican spirituality is a mode of Christian spirituality. At the same time, this synopsis of Dominican spirituality will help those consecrated men and women who follow in the footsteps of Dominic de Guzmán (1170–1221) to fulfill the mandate of the Second Vatican Council that requires religious persons to follow the "original genius" of their founder.[31] St. Dominic's genius, as Father Guy Bedouelle proposes, is fittingly called "The Grace of the Word."[32] In addition, observing the qual-

---

[30] See the October 28, 1965, Vatican Council II decree, "Pastoral Office of Bishops in the Church" *(Christus Dominus)*, no. 15: "As those who lead others to perfection, bishops should be diligent in fostering holiness among their clerics, religious, and laity according to the special vocation of each." See also, idem, "Dogmatic Constitution on the Church" *(Lumen Gentium)*, nos. 44 and 45.

[31] See Second Vatican Council, "Decree on the Sensitive Renewal of Religious Life," *Perfectae caritatis*, no. 2: "The sensitive renewal of religious life involves: the constant return to the sources of Christian life in general, and the original genius of religious foundations in particular; together with the modifications of such foundations to accommodate new circumstances."

[32] For the standard biography, see M.-H. Vicaire, *Saint Dominic and His Times*, trans. Kathleen Pond (New York: McGraw-Hill, 1964).

ities below should help Dominicans to avoid the precipitous decline that has become the woeful lot of so many institutes of religious women.

Realism

Dominican spirituality is rooted in realism. St. Dominic was a supreme realist—he saw Jesus Christ, the Eternal Logos, in everything and everyone. It should come as no surprise to discover that the blazon of his Order is *Veritas*—Truth. Dominicans find themselves committed to the practice of divine Truth and to the universal irradiation of the Light of Life.[33] Specifically, Dominic de Guzmán lived his life within the acute realization that Jesus Christ alone stands at the center of every human life.[34] As St. Paul says in his Epistles, which St. Dominic carried (along with the Gospel of Matthew) with him at all times, "Christ is everything in all of you" (Col 3:11). No wonder it is said that St. Dominic "spoke only to or about God." Because St. Dominic recognized that there is nothing that is ultimately perfective and good in the human race apart from Jesus Christ, he established a "Holy Preaching." In other words, the Dominican Order finds its original inspiration in the universal mandate of the Church to preach the Gospel of Jesus Christ, which by its own divine grace resists all human efforts rationalistically to reduce it or mythologically to recount it. The Gospel of Jesus Christ is served neither by overscripted narratives that do not reflect sound doctrine nor by facile reductionisms that are trimmed to fit the contours of here-today-gone-tomorrow social acceptance. Instead, "Christ is everything in all of you."

One may inquire, how does the Order of St. Dominic differ from other religious institutes committed to the expansion of the Gospel? In principle, the "real" should control every institute dedicated to Truth. How do Dominicans characteristically safeguard the real? One of the early Dominican saints, Catherine of Siena (1347–80), sought to understand the difference between the Friars Minor (the Franciscans) and the Friars Preachers (the Dominicans). The text from her *Dialogue* helps us to discover something of what is specific about the Dominicans. St. Catherine reports what Our Lord himself explained to her:

> See with what perfection and order of poverty Francis ordered his ship. . . . Each order excels in a particular virtue . . . although all possess charity

---

[33] Reginald Garrigou-Lagrange, O.P., "Character and Principles of Dominican Spirituality," in *Dominican Spirituality*, trans. Anselm M. Townsend (Milwaukee: The Bruce Publishing Company, 1934), 63. This little volume contains essays that were originally published in the early twentieth century in France. It supplies a rich source for material on classical Dominican spirituality.

[34] For a good introduction, see Bedouelle, *Saint Dominic: The Grace of the Word.*

which is the principle of all the virtues. . . . Poverty belonged especially to my poor man Francis who placed the principal foundation of his order in love for this virtue. . . . Thy Father, Dominic, my son, wished that his sons would apply themselves only to my honor and the salvation of souls by the light of knowledge, which light he laid as his principal foundation . . . in order to extirpate the errors which had arisen in his time, thus taking upon him the office of my only begotten Son, the Word. . . . He was a light which I gave the world by means of Mary. . . . At what table does he feed his sons with the light of knowledge? At the table of the Cross. . . . Look at my glorious Thomas who gazed with the gentle eye of his intellect at my Truth whereby he acquired supernatural light and knowledge infused by grace, for he obtained it rather by means of prayer than by human study.[35]

The text serves as an admirable compendium of the elements that comprise Dominican spirituality, while at the same time reporting a source that is impeccable. The message is clear: The realism of St. Dominic is ordered to embracing the Word of Truth that St. Thomas Aquinas, for one, expounded.

Consider the central claim made to St. Catherine of Siena: They take upon themselves the office of my only begotten Son, the Word. Dominicans prefer to root their Christocentrism in the identity of the Second Divine Person, the *Logos* or the Word of God. This means that Dominicans are wont to seek the truth about reality in both its natural and supernatural instantiations. The basic intelligibility of the created order prompts Dominicans toward the pursuit and embrace of the light of knowledge or *scientia*, that is, toward seeking reasoned explanations about the truth of all that exists. Once the Word becomes flesh in the womb of the Blessed Virgin Mary, this pursuit takes on a new and utterly supernatural dimension that is made possible by the definitive communication of Divine Revelation. It is a kind of sanctified intelligence that informs the spirit of the Dominicans, and explains why the characteristic act of Dominican life remains the contemplation of divine things. In order to arrive at this contemplation, the Dominican requires tools. Natural philosophy and metaphysics are required of the theologian. As, Santiago Ramirez, a great Thomist commentator of the twentieth century puts it, the theologian is "a master of reason and a disciple of faith."[36]

---

[35] *The Dialogue of the Seraphic Virgin, Catherine of Siena: Dictated by Her, While in a State of Ecstasy, to Her Secretaries, and Completed in the Year of Our Lord 1370: Together with an Account of Her Death by an Eye-Witness,* trans. Algar Thorold, (London: Kegan Paul, Trench, Trubner & Co., Ltd., 1907), ch. 139, "Treatise on Obedience," 312.

[36] Jacobus M. Ramirez, O.P., from *De Hominis Beatitudine Tractatus Theologicus,* in the *Edicion de las Obras Completas,* vol. 3, ed. Victorino Rodriguez, O.P. (Madrid: Instituto

Contemplation of divine Truth leads us to appreciate that God is the Creator "of all things visible and invisible." Harmony of life and the tranquility of order that defines peace characterize the contemplative person. Indeed, all that transpires in the course of life should be directed toward that divine contemplation which itself is ordered to the greatest charity.[37] Thus, the Dominican motto, *Contemplare et contemplata aliis tradere.* St. Dominic learned this lesson firsthand. Because of his unshakable conviction about the unity of all that exists, St. Dominic was keenly sensitive to the errors of dualism, especially the metaphysical dualism of the thirteenth-century Cathars, whom he met while traveling though the Languedoc. The Cathars held that the material world is intrinsically evil and that it remains at war with the spiritual world, although at the same time they gave license to the movements of the flesh. St. Dominic recognized that all moral disorders adversely affect the person's capacity to contemplate.

It is commonly asserted that Dominican and Thomist theology favors theocentrism over Christocentrism. There is truth to the claim. Only God unites. *Deus semper maior.* At the same time, St. Thomas acknowledged that the existential plan for our salvation centers on the Incarnation of the Son of God. Dominican spirituality is Christ-centered. One may see this visually represented in the fresco that hangs in the chapter room of the fifteenth-century former Dominican convent in Florence that now houses the Museo di San Marco. There Blessed Fra Angelico, Giovanni da Fiesole (ca. 1395–1455), painted several Dominican saints whose postures express their distinctive personalities, even as they stand united around the cross of Christ. Each one centers his contemplation on the crucified Lord of Glory.

This large depiction and other smaller frescoes that Fra Angelico painted in the cells of the former Dominican convent exhibit the unrivaled primacy that the Incarnation holds in Dominican spirituality; better put, the redemptive Incarnation. The Dominican saints gather around the mysteries of Christ's life and death. It is not easy to recount the ways that Dominican saints have found their personal center in the incarnate Word. One clear sign of this dominant feature of Dominican spirituality is the order's devotion to

---

de Filosofia, 1972), 103: "Theologus tamen in hoc medio inveniendo se habere debet ut discipulus fidei et ut magister rationis naturalis" ("Yet the theologian should discover in this the mean that he requires as a disciple of faith and a master of natural reason").

37 Today the sense of contemplative unity is missing in many Christians, in whom it has been replaced with a new kind of dualism that leads people to attempt to separate God from what they consider "real life." This pernicious outlook manifests itself in moral choices ("pro-choice Catholics"), politics, the lack of a religious spirit, and the espousal of relativism.

the Holy Name of Jesus, beautifully exemplified in the life of the Rhineland mystic, Blessed Henry Suso (1296–1366). His *Book of Eternal Wisdom* was once the most widely read spiritual book in Germany. "It is considered," reports Father Raymond M. Martin, "to be the fairest fruit of German mysticism."[38] Earlier, Blessed John of Vercelli (d. 1283) preached ardently devotion to the Holy Name of Jesus. The Dominican Order is credited with both founding, in the fifteenth century, the Holy Name societies as well as beginning the practice of bowing the head at the mention of the Holy Name of Jesus. When done in faith, this simple action produces a contemplative moment, which supplies the most effective way of uniting the one who says the Name of Jesus with that which is the most Real.

Providence

Dominican spirituality is expressed in a profound abandonment to and dependence on Divine Providence and grace. Because he recognized only the present moment as an expression of God's will, St. Dominic was also a realist in terms of starting with the actual situation: the reality placed before him at a given moment and the taking of things as they were. St. Dominic, seeing the presence of Christ in everyone and everything, accepted each moment in accord with the designs of Divine Providence. Today many people are frightened at the prospects of God taking an effective hold of their lives. The general spirit of rebelliousness that manifests itself in both society and the Church mistrusts a directive principle of Dominican life: Grace perfects nature. Many people rather fear that divine grace will destroy a man's human nature. They reject not only the enactment of moral truth, but, what is more pernicious, the teaching of moral truth. Married couples, for example, are persuaded that to stop sterilizing their procreative acts will ruin both their marriages and their lives. Almost everybody is persuaded that without some form of sexual gratification, whether autosexual, heterosexual, or homosexual, their human psyches will develop deep neurosis or other forms of mental unbalance. Businessmen believe that the observance of justice will destroy, not perfect, their enterprises and themselves. And so on. In short, most people are persuaded that grace destroys nature rather than elevates and perfects it. This circumstance, in my view, forms a principal challenge to realizing the growth of Christianity in the present day, at least in the developed countries.

Dominicans preach something different than "Be on your guard lest the Church ask too much in the name of God." They rather seek to examine the

---

38 Fr. Raymond M. Martin, "The Historical Development of Dominican Spirituality" in Townsend, *Dominican Spirituality*, 51.

root causes of the particularly contemporary malaise that leaves the belea-
guered individual we call modern man so much at the mercy of harmful ideologies, such as gay rights movements and anti-life political initiatives.
Dominicans like to begin by showing why the Truth matters. They explore,
especially in matters of moral theology, the arguments of reason and of
grace, of the natural law and of the Sermon on the Mount. Father Reginald
Garrigou-Lagrange (1877–1964), another great Thomist and spiritual
author of the twentieth century, puts it well: "Dominican spirituality coun-
sels the full development of the natural gifts which we have received from
God, the study of human wisdom, which is the perfect use of natural reason,
in union with the divine wisdom drawn from prayer."[39] In other words,
Dominicans discover the truth about nature and supernature, and from this
personal discovery unmask all pretensions to the truth that can cause so
much harm to human persons, both here below and in the sweet hereafter.
To put this another way, the purpose of those spiritual exercises that legiti-
mately can claim the title "Dominican" is to discover the rhythms of divine
benevolent love as these take hold of the fragile world of human freedom.

The confidence that develops from believing in God's love assured St.
Dominic that God was in charge in every moment, in every trial, contradiction, frustration, conflict, and humiliation. The catalyst for St. Dominic
finding his vocation was a failure—his aborted participation in a mission to
arrange a royal marriage for the Castilian crown prince. In 1203 or 1204 he
accompanied the bishop of Osma, Diego de Acebo, on a diplomatic mission
for Alfonso VIII, king of Castile, in order to secure a bride in Denmark for
crown prince Ferdinand. The mission made its way to Denmark via the
south of France, where Dominic de Guzmán remained, establishing the first
convent of Dominican nuns near Prouilhe in 1206.[40] Dominicans do not
harbor an unhealthy fear of failure. They, on the other hand, recognize that
God permits sin to occur in the world for a purpose: to move Christians to
cling more firmly to the person of Jesus Christ. Because we know about the
living alternative to sinful disorder, we are not tempted to rationalize sin or
to make excuses for it.

Dominican spirituality delights in the present moment, singing "the
things that happen one by one are just the way they ought to be." This joyful sentiment does not of course encourage passive acceptance of sinful conduct or—to use a theological term—a quietistic attitude toward spiritual
alertness and energy. Rather it is a way of expressing what is set down in the
Song of Songs about the existential immediacy of the relationship between

---

[39] Garrigou-Lagrange, "Principles," 70.

[40] See Jordan of Saxony, *Libellus de principiis,* 14–20, and Gérard de Frachet, Chron-
ica prima, in *Monumenta Ordinis Praedicatorum Historiae,* 1.321.

God and the creature: "I am my beloved's and my beloved is mine; he pastures his flock among the lilies" (Song 6:3). Dominicans are reluctant to see even a germ of the supernatural life in human nature unaided by divine grace. They rather appreciate that the bestowal of divine grace entails "a real and formal participation in the intimate life of God." This means that the immediacy of the God-creature relationship that exists in the life of grace reaches its perfection in the Eucharist. About this Sacrament, Thomas Aquinas sings, *"O res mirabilis, manducat Dominum/Pauper, servus et humilis."* O wonderful thing! A humble, poor servant consumes his Lord.

The providential bestowal of the gift of divine friendship shapes the way that Dominicans look at everyday occurrences. How else can we explain what is reported about St. Dominic's distress over Brother John of Navarre, who demanded from St. Dominic money for the trip he was about to make to Paris. St. Dominic responded: "Have confidence in the Lord since nothing is lacking to those who fear God." John would not give in; his disobedience reduced the patriarch to tears, though St. Dominic compromised and gave him some money. Dominicans also know how to go easy. Dispensation lies at the heart of implementing the *Constitutions*. St. Dominic was too much of a realist to suppose that any document, even one that he inspired, would be able to capture all of the unforeseen contingencies of the future. So Dominicans live with an alert attentiveness to the moment. "I am my beloved's and my beloved is mine" (Song of Songs 6:3).

Dominican spirituality is lived in the concrete and personal assurance that grace builds on nature. No matter what nature may throw our way at the moment, grace can and will make the best of it, transforming it to the benefit and purpose of Divine Providence. Without this optimism associated with Dominican spirituality, we fall either into a dour moralism or espouse a compromising moral relativism. These are the bad spirits that inform many Christian people today.

Truth

Dominican spirituality reverences and proclaims the Truth. The Dominican heart cannot abide compromise. When St. Dominic met, again in the Languedoc, in southern France, and converted an unidentified Albigensian innkeeper, what horrified the saint was the way this ordinary man had been seduced by half-truths. Every heresy contains a semblance of truth, after all. There is no surer indication of Dominican presence than the black and white of the habit. When they are faithful to their spiritual and intellectual birthrights, holy Dominicans can be trusted to see things clearly. They succumb neither to rationalization nor mythologizations. In his book, *In the Image of Saint*

Dominic, Dominican Guy Bedouelle sketches the lives of several well-known Dominicans who demonstrate this feature of Dominican spirituality across several centuries of the order's life.[41]

Dominican *Veritas* means a total commitment to Jesus who is the Truth and to the integrity of life possible through virtuous union with him. Only the Truth can set us free—symbolized again in the Dominican habit. The black cloak represents what we are in ourselves, apart from the transformative power of divine grace, and the white tunic represents what we become insofar as we abide in the life of divine grace that is supremely and uniquely realized in the person of Jesus Christ. But in order to counteract the deceptions of the world, the Dominican soul has to remain devoted to the Word of God—not as a book to learn, but as a Person to love.

The defining activity of all Dominicans is expressed in a phrase that St. Thomas Aquinas penned: "Contemplate and then share with others the fruit of contemplation."[42] From this comes the impulse of friendship, which among intelligent creatures is the only way that they can realize the divine dynamic of being, namely, that goodness is diffusive of itself. Hidden in the very nature of the supreme Goodness that is God, we discover the pattern for the core Dominican desire to draw others into that sort of relationship with Jesus Christ that saves whomsoever comes to him with sincerity. So Dominican preaching aims to declare out loud the Word of God, the Person of Christ. It is doctrinal, geared toward the integrity of thought and belief, making plain how the Incarnation transforms the world and how all Truth is one. It enables people to love the Truth and inflames them to want to live in the Truth.

Study is crucial to this process. The discipline of study serves as a source of insight, illumination, integration, filtering, purification; study helps to make connections between things, to know what people are thinking, to refine thought. While Father Lamb was tending sheep in a Trappist monastery, Dominicans of my generation were told to find their crosses in the wood of the desk. Today, I suppose that we would need to adapt the metaphor to allow for the plastic of the computer keyboard. In any case, the Dominican must be ready to stay nailed to his work. It creates the environment in which he discovers the distinctively Dominican ascesis. Without this spiritual discipline (which can cut more deeply than the discipline used for flagellation), the Dominican becomes hollow, given to cynicism, especially.

In a special way, virtue occupies a central place in Dominican commitment to the Truth, and it permeates Dominican preaching. Virtue recognizes

---

[41] Guy Bedouelle, O.P., *In the Image of Saint Dominic: Nine Portraits of Dominican Life,* trans. Sr. Mary Thomas Noble, O.P. (San Francisco: Ignatius Press, 1994).

[42] See *Summa theologiae* II–II q. 188, art. 6: "ita maius est contemplata aliis tradere quam solum contemplari."

our God-ordered destiny and provides the means for the human creature to attain it and so to gain happiness through human flourishing. Virtue-centered spirituality forms the backbone of Dominican life and obedience. Voluntarism, with its half-forms of continence and perseverance, finds no welcome among Dominicans. In fact, sound Dominican theologians, such as Belgian Dominican Servais Pinckaers, have labored mightily to eschew the pernicious, modern preoccupation with human willing and striving that has crept into expositions of Christian ethics.[43]

Mercy

Dominican spirituality remains focused on the cross and is confident in God's mercy. When all thought of God disappears from the mind of a man, the concept of sin becomes meaningless, although the effects of sin still erode the good of human nature. The negligence and presumption that forgetfulness of God generates are more deadly than the sins that made us forget God. Today especially, people find it easy to fall into presumption. St. Dominic, on the other hand, was overwhelmed by his penetrating insight into the horror of sin. So he spent his nights praying in church and imploring God's mercy for sinners. There is nothing to fear when we find little to appreciate in ourselves. The Eternal Father spoke these comforting words to St. Catherine of Siena: "You are the one who is not; I am the one who is."[44] Dominicans always return to the basic truth that God loves us because he is good not because we are. Thereby they escape the vicious blackmail of the devil, who by contrast always stands ready to accuse. Mercy empowers Christian believers to face the truth about themselves and to entrust themselves to the compassion of God revealed in the Blood of Christ. That is why during Mass the corpus of the processional cross according to Dominican usage faces the priest—it is there for him to focus on. And further, that is why the Sacrifice of Jesus Christ— the Eucharist—stands at the very heart of Dominican life and Dominican spirituality. Christians find there the daily renewal of spirit that confirms their gradual transformation into the Body of Christ.

Dominican spirituality is penitential, but the penance remains ordered toward promoting deep loving. There is nothing of the calculative in the Dominican spirit. They do not measure. They do not store up points. But

---

[43] For further information on Fr. Pinckaers and his work, see my "Hommage au Père Servais-Théodore Pinckaers, O.P. The Significance of His Work," *Nova et Vetera,* English Edition 5:1 (2007): 1–16

[44] See Raymond of Capua, *The Life of Catherine of Siena,* trans. Conleth Kearns (Wilmington, DE: Glazier, 1980), I, X, 92.

their commitment to Truth imposes on us the most severe penance: The obligation to love, deeply.

Obedience

Dominican spirituality is distinguished by its devotion to holy obedience. Since Dominicans are realists, they are also realistic about the inner daily rebellion whereby fallen man finds himself torn between remaining true to the Gospel and giving in to the absolute exaltation of self. What pacifies that struggle and fills our daily living with peace? The evangelical counsel of obedience. Obedience is the way Dominicans overcome themselves in the heart. Obedience means living everything for the reasons of an Other—an Other who can complete us. Obedience and the Dominican understanding of freedom are intimately linked. Dominicans understand freedom to be the complete adherence of self to that which satisfies our deepest desires. Dominicans profess obedience to a person, not to a rule. That is why community remains so crucial to healthy Dominican spirituality: It is easy to live obedience when there are no people around to obey. Obedience is best realized when one is surrounded by a world of other wills, all vying to be first, best, most important.

Choral office and prayer for the dead are crucial aspects of Dominican spirituality. Faithful obedience to these practices bears witness to the act of love that testifies to the universal reconciliation in Christ. Obedience is helped by structures. The monastic or conventual observances distinguish Dominican life from other forms of religious life, including the Benedictine monastery and the Carthusian charterhouse. Suffice it to remark that the great reformers of the order during the modern period, that is, after the French Revolution, insisted variously and variously on the regular rhythms of conventual life. The wearing of the Dominican habit ranks foremost among them. Two nineteenth-century Frenchmen, Henry Dominic Lacordaire (1802–61) and Vincent Alexander Jandel (1810–72), gave an impulsion to the Dominican Order that lasted more than a century. It is not at all clear that what has developed since the General Chapter of Affairs held at River Forest in 1968 will match the effectiveness of the Lacordaire reform. This general chapter was called in response to the instructions of the Second Vatican Council to begin renewal.

The Dominican Friars also hold local chapters or regular meetings of the brethren to discuss different points of view so that a common understanding about those things that are non-gainsayable with respect to the life of the order may take hold among the members. Among those elements that are non-gainsayable is the choral recitation of the Liturgy of the Hours. The Dominican needs time to ponder what is said in the official worship of the Church. There he learns to arrange in a hierarchy the most varying elements of nature and supernature because he sees everything from a universal point of view, *"in Deo, sicut in summo rerum vertice,"* to quote St. Thomas Aquinas.[45] That is, the Dominican contemplative in choir comes to view everything in God, from the vantage point of the highest point where things turn.[46]

Humor

Dominican spirituality is imbued with a healthy sense of humor. The Dominican capitular form of government requires a sense of humor. Dominicans know how dangerous it is to take themselves too seriously. A sense of humor keeps them humble. So many of the stories about St. Dominic and the lives of the brethren highlight their quirks and eccentricities as well as the delight they took in life. Consider, for instance, St. Dominic's would-be response to the men who wanted to murder him.[47] Risibility is one of the properties of being human. It is Dominican to delight in good comedy and humor. As a result, Dominican spirituality is not rigid. The Dominican sense of humor keeps us fixed on what really matters; it reinvigorates our realism and renews our sense of hope. So too the Dominican innovation of "dispensation" endows Dominican spirituality with a certain holy flexibility.

Mary

Dominican spirituality is deeply joined to the Blessed Virgin Mary. Jesus comes to us through Mary, therefore Dominicans can never overestimate the indispensable role of the Mother of God. Saint Louis Grignon de Montfort associated himself with the Dominicans in order to ground his *True Devotion* in a tradition that is solidly Christocentric and Marian. At the same time, the Blessed Virgin Mary keeps Dominicans humble, reminding them that each of them and each Christian believer remains a child in need of her

---

[45] *ST* I, q. 57, a. 1: "Et ideo in Deo, sicut in summo rerum vertice, omnia supersubstantialiter praeexistunt secundum ipsum suum simplex esse, ut Dionysius dicit, in libro De div. nom 1."

[46] M.-V. Bernadot, O.P., "The Place of the Liturgy in Dominican Spirituality," in Townsend, *Dominican Spirituality,* 95.

[47] "I should have asked them [he replied] not to wound me mortally at once, but to prolong my martyrdom by mutilating all my limbs one by one. Then to display the pieces of these hacked limbs before my eyes and next to pluck out my eyes, finally to let the trunk steep in its own blood or finish it off completely. Thus by a more lingering death I should earn the crown of a more glorious martyrdom." See M.-H. Vicaire, *Histoire de saint Dominique,* vol. 1, *Un homme evangélique* (Paris: Les Éditions du Cerf, 1982), 318.

maternal care and protection. The concrete sign of this protection is the white scapular that was given to Blessed Reginald of Orleans, an early disciple of St. Dominic who died before him in 1220. Without devotion to the Mother of God, the temptation grows to demote the Word of God into the idea of God. The Rosary keeps Dominicans and everyone centered in the Incarnation; in praying it, the mystery of Christ is regenerated in us through Mary's maternal mediation. The Immaculate Conception is the supernatural assurance of divine mercy and the possibility of Redemption. God reveals in her what we could never know on our own.

De Maria numquam satis. This should be the attitude of everyone who embraces what I have described as Dominican spirituality. Never too much about Mary! In the woman who embodies the truth of our original call to beatitude, the Dominican finds the exemplar of his contemplation, his apostolate, and his spiritual life. In the Fair Daughter of Sion, we all discover the preeminent human exemplar of spiritual beauty. No wonder Father Matthew Lamb has found in a place dedicated to the Virgin Mother of God a fruitful setting in which to pursue his consecrated vocation. Ave Maria! Hail Mary, often. Those who follow this salutary practice will find themselves drawn to the spiritual beauty that transforms human beings created in the image of God into adopted sons and daughters filled with divine charity.

This transformation takes place preferably within an environment where sound Catholic theology flourishes. Catholics in the United States owe Father Matt Lamb a huge debt of gratitude for declaring out loud during the postconciliar period the need to reform the practice of theology. To the extent that he has dedicated himself to this mission, he has in his own way realized the spirituality that derives from St. Dominic de Guzmán. At the same time, Matt Lamb radiates the special graces that belong to a devoted follower of St. Augustine of Hippo, of St. Benedict of Nursia, and to be sure, of his first spiritual father, the manly, love-filled, twelfth-century, crusade-preaching, and monk-reforming St. Bernard of Clairvaux.

CHAPTER 3

Knowledge Possessed and Desired:
Aquinas and the Catholic University

MICHAEL DAUPHINAIS

Introduction

IN THE 1992 Apostolic Constitution *Ex Corde Ecclesiae*, Pope John Paul II addressed the dynamic tension between knowledge possessed yet desired: "A Catholic university's privileged task is 'to unite existentially by intellectual effort two orders of reality that too frequently tend to be placed in opposition as though they were antithetical: the search for truth, and the certainty of already knowing the fount of truth.'"[1] *Ex Corde Ecclesiae* admits the tension between seeking knowledge and security in its position, while refusing the opposition. Were such an opposition to exist, so would an opposition between the rigorous intellectual inquiry characteristic of a university and the Catholic Church's recognition of herself as the recipient of the deposit of faith from Christ.

In his recent article, "Aquinas and Catholic Universities," Brian Davies presents certain themes from Aquinas concerning teaching, learning, and theology in light of their contribution to contemporary Catholic universities. Unfortunately, it must be asked whether Davies suggests an oppositional relationship between the search for and the possession of knowledge. He ends his article with the following claim:

> In conclusion, though, I have to add that I do not think that Aquinas would favour a ghetto-like approach to Catholic education today. I have been reading and writing about Aquinas for years, and it seems to me to be perfectly clear that he would have had little time for educational institutions unwilling to engage with views opposed to its basic

[1] An earlier version of this essay was presented at the Center for Ethics and Culture's conference "Joy in the Truth: Catholic Higher Education in the Third Millennium," University of Notre Dame, September 29, 2005.

tenets, or unwilling to expose their students to such views. When George Bernard Shaw visited Washington, D.C., he was told that the Catholic University of America was located in the city. Shaw then said that a Catholic university is a contradiction in terms. I presume that he was expressing an aversion to places in which non-Catholic thinking is not taken seriously. Yet some of the most approvingly quoted authors in Aquinas's writings are not even Christians. So Aquinas clearly thought that people who disagreed with him could help him to learn. And maybe that is one of the chief thoughts he would have wished to bequeath to those concerned with Catholic education today.[2]

It is a questionable assertion that there are such Catholic schools that do not discuss non-Christian or non-Catholic philosophers. There may be some, however, that teach that such seminal figures as Kant and Nietzsche arrived at false conclusions. The central assertion in Davies' article appears to be the character of engagement with the modern world and its philosophies and sciences broadly conceived. The warning with which he concludes seems to suggest that, for Davies, "engagement" requires a willingness on the part of Catholic universities actively to bracket (ultimately, not merely initially by the very act of questioning) the conviction that those with whom adherents of the Catholic faith disagree are in fact wrong concerning certain key claims about God and humankind. Davies assumes an antinomy between the search for truth and resting in truth already possessed.

On which side would St. Thomas Aquinas fall? Where would he place his *sic* and *non* were he faced with the apparent antinomy? This essay will show that St. Thomas Aquinas presents an integrated and balanced approach to the search for and the possession of knowledge.

This essay proceeds in three steps. First, it will provide a summary of Davies' presentation of Aquinas's views on education and Catholic universities. Second, it will offer a criticism of Davies' account. Third, the essay will present some other significant components of Aquinas's understanding of education and learning. Davies' article is noteworthy because of the erudition it displays as well as its somewhat typical attempt to adduce Aquinas's authority in support of a moderate position among the issues confronting the Catholic Church, in this case, Catholic colleges and universities.[3]

---

[2] Brian Davies, O.P., "Aquinas and Catholic Universities," *New Blackfriars* 86 (2005): 290.

[3] This follows a common, albeit dubious, interpretation of the "progressive" Thomists versus the "conservative" Augustinians penned by Joseph Komonchak. See his "Dealing with Diversity and Disagreement: Vatican II and Beyond," *The Annual Catholic*

Davies' Account of Aquinas on Education:
A Survey and Critical Response

In his article, Davies begins with a presentation of Aquinas's views of learning and the acquisition of knowledge or *scientia*. Although teachers play an irreplaceable role in helping one to know, "they cannot *make* you know."[4] True knowledge or scientia takes place when learners see for themselves how the effects flow from the causes or the conclusions from the premises. Davies summarizes Aquinas's thesis here as follows: *"While recognizing that nobody can cause another person to know, also recognize that one can help people to know by training them in certain ways and by presenting them with what can lead them to know on their own."*[5]

Davies subsequently observes Aquinas's distinction between faith, or *fides*, and *scientia*: *Scientia* sees for itself whereas *fides* trusts in the authority of another. In this life we need *fides* to know the truths of divine revelation.[6] According to Davies,"[Aquinas] thinks that we need faith in order to be united with God."[7] Davies identifies Aquinas's phrase *sacra doctrina* with the presentation of the truths of faith.[8] Davies clarifies that this is not theology in the sense of what theologians teach: "[F]or Aquinas, however, *sacra doctrina* is what *God* has to offer."[9] More specifically he writes, "The teaching of *sacra doctrina* is, for Aquinas, an attempt to set out what Christ taught."[10]

Davies presents well here the two necessary modes of knowing the truth: *scientia* and *fides*. As thus far discussed, learning will require seeing for oneself in *scientia* as well as trusting in the Church's creedal proclamation of Christ in *fides*. The balanced interplay between *scientia* and *fides*, however, is short-lived for Davies. In further comments, Davies progressively weakens the role of *fides* to such an extent that it is oddly absent from his concluding remarks about what we most need to learn from Aquinas today. Consequently, the positive role of reliance on the Church for her presentation of *sacra doctrina* also fades. The process in Davies' article is as follows. Both *scientia* and *fides*

Common Ground Initiative Lecture 2003, published online at www.nplc.org/common ground/lecture/komonchak2003.htm.

[4] Davies, "Aquinas and Catholic Universities," 277.

[5] Ibid., 279.

[6] Ibid., 281

[7] Ibid.

[8] As has been observed, *sacra doctrina* is difficult to translate. It is often rendered "sacred doctrine", but this expression leaves aside its meaning that includes the activity of teaching. With this in mind, Fr. Victor White, O.P., offered "holy teaching" as a more adequate translation.

[9] Davies, "Aquinas and Catholic Universities," 282.

[10] Ibid.

are necessary for Aquinas. *Fides* relies on *sacra doctrina*. As *scientia* progressively makes *sacra doctrina* more unknowable, *fides* cedes the field of intellectual activity. Knowledge possessed cedes to knowledge desired.

Davies progressively emphasizes the role of *scientia* or the search for knowledge in his comments on philosophy and biblical studies. Both disciplines interact directly with theology. In this manner they provide an example of how knowledge interacts with faith.

With respect to Aquinas and philosophy, Davies observes, "There is a school of thought which sees philosophy, especially philosophy hostile to or incompatible with Catholicism, as something from which students should be protected. Yet it is hard to imagine Aquinas endorsing such an approach. The ways in which he discusses philosophers in general, and those with whom he disagrees in particular, show him to be acutely sensitive to the opportunities for learning and understanding provided by them."[11] In this context of philosophical education, Davies presents Aquinas as being open to and interested in erroneous philosophical positions for the opportunities for learning that they provide.

These views of philosophy correspond to views about biblical scholarship. Davies notes that Aquinas held that *sacra doctrina* was revealed by Christ and recorded in Sacred Scripture. He then questions whether Aquinas would have maintained such a position in light of contemporary biblical scholarship. Citing Beryl Smalley's work on biblical interpretation in the Middle Ages, Davies observes that Aquinas was more interested in the literal meaning of the Old Testament than other patristic and medieval theologians who were content with allegorical readings of obscure scriptural passages.[12] From the premise that Aquinas displays genuine interest in the literal meaning of the Old Law, Davies draws the conclusion that "Aquinas would be more than interested in engaging with, and getting students to engage with, the best that is now on offer when it comes to biblical scholarship—just as he would clearly be interested in engaging with, and getting students to engage with, the best available philosophical writings."[13] The latest in biblical studies and philosophy will have pedagogical pride of place.

These comments about Aquinas's interest in the latest philosophy and the latest biblical scholarship develop into Davies' major thesis about Aquinas and Catholic universities. It is not entirely clear what Davies envisions when he speaks about protecting students from "philosophy hostile to or incompatible with Catholicism." According to his assumed rhetorical paradigms, "pro-

---

[11] Ibid., 285.

[12] Henri de Lubac, S.J.'s four-volume *Exégèse médiévale* provides an alternative account of patristic and medieval exegesis.

[13] Davies, "Aquinas and Catholic Universities," 284.

tecting students" has bad connotations; whereas "getting students to engage with the best available philosophical writings" has good ones. Yet would it not be possible to "protect students"—in other words, lead them to be able to apprehend truth—by engaging philosophical writings with a concern, among other things, to show where and how philosophies hostile to Catholicism have missed the mark? Surely Davies would not support a view of engagement that required the student to begin from a point of Cartesian neutrality with respect to the truths about the world, the human being, and God.

Further, Davies juxtaposes Aquinas's strong interest in engaging the best and latest biblical scholarship with Aquinas's conviction "(a) that [Christian doctrines] come to us from Christ as reported in Scripture, and (b) that they cannot be established philosophically (that we cannot come to know that they are true by using our powers of reason)."[14] Davies, however, leaves open the question of whether we can inherit Aquinas's conviction here. He writes, "so justified skepticism when it comes to what is often called 'the problem of the historical Jesus' would be very damaging to the core of Aquinas's teaching."[15] Davies' purported emphasis on engagement still remains here, but it is now separated from the conviction that we have firm access to the teachings of Christ through *fides*. This inversion of *scientia* and *fides* crucially alters the notion of "engagement" since it is through *fides* that the Catholic intellectual tradition possesses its privileged access to the revealed truth. The search for knowledge now trumps its possession. Or, to put the matter differently, because the possession of Christ's revelation now runs through the philosophical, social, and historical sciences, Christ's revelation no longer forms the center of the intellectual inquiry of a Catholic University according to Davies' train of thought.

The shift away from the possession of truth from revelation becomes apparent when Davies' distills what contemporary Catholic universities can learn from Aquinas. Davies earlier stated, "For if Aquinas is right, then what people need to be instructed in above all is *sacra doctrina*, considered as equivalent to the teachings of Christ as recorded in the Gospels—from which it would seem to follow that a Catholic university should be a place in which special attention is given to ensure that students are exposed to people who expound the recorded teachings of Christ as historical and authoritative."[16] It is worth observing that Davies writes "if Aquinas is right" and then "it would seem to follow." Later in the article when Davies speaks of Aquinas's implications for Catholic universities, he does not return to Christ's teachings as "historical and authoritative," but instead asserts two central themes from

---

[14] Ibid., 285.
[15] Ibid.
[16] Ibid.

Aquinas: "The first is 'Strive to see connections.' The second is 'Recognize that both teaching and learning have ethical dimensions.'"[17] Although these are both laudable goals that work against the fragmentation of learning and the claims to moral neutrality of many contemporary universities, they both elide the specificity of Christian revelation.

Developing the implications for contemporary Catholic universities, Davies writes that "It seems to me clear that [Aquinas] would not be a paradigm of what I take to be political correctness."[18] Davies does have some guidelines for professors at Catholic universities today: "I take it that he would be urging that Catholic universities should be staffed by people who are drawn to what the Catholic Church takes to be good. I also take it that he would think of a Catholic university as a place in which students are actively helped to like and become attracted to this."[19] Davies also emphasizes his commitment to values: "I take it that, were he alive today, he would be encouraging administrators and teachers in Catholic universities to be doing what they can to help their students to develop ways of acting and reacting valued by Catholics."[20] It appears that for Davies, "ways of acting and reacting valued by Catholics" have replaced the intellectual appropriation of knowledge through *fides*.

Davies thus attempts to present Aquinas as an advocate for a "moderate" position within contemporary debates in higher education. Against the extreme secularists, Davies' Aquinas insists on (1) seeing connections, (2) recognizing ethical implications of teaching and learning, and (3) eschewing political correctness as the paradigm of education by encouraging Catholic values. Yet, his Aquinas also opposes those "educational institutions unwilling to engage with views opposed to the basic tenets [of Catholic education], or unwilling to expose their students to such views." Too holistic to be taken in by the secularists, too engaged to be taken in by conservatives, Davies' Aquinas stands as the beacon of "moderate" Catholic higher education.

Is Davies' portrait of Aquinas accurate?

First, engagement requires the presence of theological professors who assent to the teachings of the Catholic Church. As Davies knows, Aquinas begins with the authoritative character of divine revelation as given in Christ, recorded in Scripture, and summarized in the teaching of the Church. Revelation always has the last word. For instance, when Aquinas considers the question of whether the universe was created in time or whether it always existed, he shows that philosophically both options are reasonable. But that matters

---

[17] Ibid.
[18] Ibid., 289.
[19] Ibid.
[20] Ibid., 290.

not in determining the truth of the matter: We know that the universe had a temporal beginning because Scripture reveals it so. Accordingly, *sacra doctrina* engages other views either to show that they are false or to elucidate the truth already known by human reason. Aquinas often includes heretical viewpoints in his writings, but he always presents them as heresy. He engages the views of the Arians, the Manichees, and the Nestorians in order to illumine more deeply the truth of the ecclesial *sacra doctrina*. There is no question of an equal engagement as though the teacher and learner must consider both sides with an open mind. Such an even-handed approach necessarily would close off both the teacher and the learner from knowing the ultimate truth about God, man, and the universe that is accessible only through revelation.

Revelation must be received by *fides*, specifically faith in the revelation of the Trinity in Jesus Christ. In treating the virtue of *fides*, Aquinas says, "Christ is the first and principle teacher of spiritual teaching and faith."[21] When Aquinas treats the *doctrina Christi*, the teaching of Christ, he says, "The greater the teacher, the greater should be the manner of teaching. And therefore to Christ the greatest teacher belonged this manner, namely, He impressed his teaching on the hearts of His listeners. For this reason it is said in Matthew that 'He was teaching them as one having authority' (7:29)."[22] Only Christ can teach this way because he is the incarnate Word. A human teacher "signifies things to his disciples through spoken signs, and cannot illumine interiorly, as God can do."[23] Aquinas teaches that "it was fitting that the perfect law of the New Testament be given directly by God himself made man."[24] Christ is the consummate teacher: As God he illumines interiorly impressing his teaching directly on the hearts of his listeners; as man he uses external signs and language to lead his disciples to share in his perfect actualization of understanding. *Fides* assents to the teaching of Christ and, more specifically, to Christ as the teacher. Aquinas says that "the act of the believer does not terminate in a proposition, but in a reality *(res)*."[25] *Fides* consequently opens up a horizon of truth otherwise inaccessible to human beings— the Triune God and his actions toward man's salvation through Jesus Christ. This revealed truth does not come as one probable argument among others.

Sacra doctrina is God's holy teaching and yet Davies has posed a problem about how we have access to that divine teaching. Access to God's holy teaching comes through the mediation of the latest philosophy and biblical

---

[21] *Summa theologiae* III, q. 7, a. 7: "Spiritualis autem doctrinae et fidei primus et principalis Doctor est Christus. . . ."

[22] *ST* III, q. 42, a. 4.

[23] *ST* II–II, q. 173, a. 2.

[24] *ST* I–II, q. 98, a. 3.

[25] *ST* II–II, q. 1, a. 2, ad 2.

scholarship. When Davies actually draws his own conclusion from Aquinas's understanding of *sacra doctrina*, it does not include teachers of theology who faithfully adhere to Scripture, Tradition, and the Magisterium. Unity of knowledge and ethical implications require a connection to Christian revelation. Unity of knowledge and ethical implications are also present in *Ex Corde Ecclesiae*, alongside the concrete requirement of the *mandatum* for teachers of Catholic theology.

The omission of the *mandatum* for professors of Catholic theology stems from an omission in the presentation of Aquinas's understanding of *sacra doctrina*. Davies' summary of *sacra doctrina* omits the role of the Magisterium of the Catholic Church. For instance, Aquinas teaches that the pope possesses the authority to publish creedal statements.[26] It will not do to say that Aquinas understood *sacra doctrina* to be only Christ's teachings as recorded in Scripture without reference to the ongoing authority of the Church. This would introduce a false biblicism into Aquinas's theological practice, which frequently made use of the authoritative creeds of the Church's tradition. Aquinas teaches that faith assents to revealed realities through the articles of the creed, summaries of Scripture as defined by the Church.[27] Biblical studies and non-Catholic philosophies are illuminating, but they cannot determine the content of faith's assent. It would be more accurate to say that Aquinas considers *sacra doctrina* as equivalent to the teachings of Christ as recorded in the Gospels and authoritatively taught through the creeds and Magisterium.

Following Aquinas in this manner, Catholic educational institutions would engage, and expose students to, views opposed to Catholic truth, but would not engage these opposed views on an equal footing. Aquinas thus offers a model of cultural dialogue compatible with the Catholic faith. Here we come to a second implication of engagement: Engagement requires professors who are firmly rooted in the Catholic tradition in its intellectual aspects, not merely in its ethical implications. Aquinas, for instance, draws upon the pre-Christian authors—Aristotle, Plato and Cicero. He draws upon the Jewish thinker Maimonides and the Islamic philosopher Avicenna. He engages them because he is a bold seeker of truth. Employing the weapons of reason and revelation, Aquinas engages thinkers in order to distinguish the true from the false, both in terms of those views that contradict reason and those that contradict revelation. Engagement does not seek engagement for its own sake, but rather seeks truth in the admittedly imperfect manner in which we can grasp it in this life.

Third, engagement requires that professors have knowledge, however imperfect, of truth in the disciplines based on divine revelation and human

---

[26] *ST* II–II, q. 1, a. 10.
[27] Cf. *ST* II–II, q. 1, aa. 6–9.

reason in order to lead students into the truth. I would suggest that Aquinas offers a deeper understanding than Davies allows of the teaching and learning that should inform Catholic universities. It is clear that Davies offers many helpful insights from Aquinas's views on education. Davies is certainly correct when he emphasizes that Aquinas taught that a student must learn for himself if learning truly is to take place. "[Teachers] cannot *make* you know. And yet, so Aquinas thinks, they can *help* you to know."[28] Davies distinguishes three modes of such assistance: First, teachers can provide us with the ability to use language; second, teachers can teach skills of deductive argumentation; and, third, teachers can speed up the learning process by laying out the path to knowledge more clearly for their students.[29] As far as it goes, this presentation of Aquinas's thought is accurate, and conforms to the general understanding of the interplay between teacher and learning. Aquinas says that "the teacher leads the pupil to knowledge of things he does not know in the same way that one directs himself through the process of discovering something he does not know."[30] The way of learning by instruction imitates the way of learning by discovery, a point Davies explicates well.

Nonetheless the manner in which teachers can assist students in their learning by "laying out the path to knowledge more clearly" requires further attention. It is here that we see that Aquinas has something to say that many contemporary universities need to hear—a point that Davies obscures. Davies explicates this manner of assisting the student along the path of knowledge as follows: "For example, [Aquinas] thinks that they can present information which you might not yet have come across—information which might help you to extend the range of your learning."[31] Yet, this example defines teaching down, by reducing the knowledge possessed by the teacher to mere information. The role of the teacher in leading the student to truth depends not simply upon the greater experience or the larger data set of the teacher, but on the *habitus* of mind that sustains a more adequate understanding of the world, man, and God. In "On the Teacher," from his *Disputed Questions on Truth*, Aquinas says that, "teaching implies the perfect activity of knowledge in the teacher or master. Hence, the teacher or master must have the knowledge which he causes in another explicitly and perfectly, as it is to be received in the one who is learning through instruction."[32] This is in the context of Aquinas's denial that human beings can be said to teach themselves. Learning by instruction cannot be reduced to learning by discovery. Other human beings

---

[28] Davies, "Aquinas and Catholic Universities," 277.

[29] Ibid., 278.

[30] *De veritate,* q. 11, a. 1.

[31] Davies, "Aquinas and Catholic Universities," 278.

[32] *De veritate,* q. 11, a. 2, reply.

as teachers are necessary. Moreover, human teachers must have at least in some sense "the perfect activity of knowledge" in order to instruct a student.

Developing the parallel between the art of teaching and the art of medicine, Aquinas shows the secondary, but nonetheless real, character of human healing and human teaching. "Since all human teaching can be effective only in virtue of [the light of reason], it is obvious that God alone teaches interiorly and principally, just as nature alone heals interiorly and principally."[33] Human teaching is secondary insofar as it relies upon the interior light of reason instilled in the human creature by God; and yet human teaching nonetheless acts as a true cause of learning. We can summarize two conclusions. First, human teachers must have a true actualization of knowledge—not mere information—in order to instruct students. Second, it is this actualization that acts as a cause of learning in the students.

Aquinas thus gives a more necessary role to the teacher than does Davies in terms of the student's ability to pursue truth. Aquinas excludes the human teacher only from the interior illumination that God alone can cause: "When Augustine proves that only God teaches, he does not intend to exclude man from teaching exteriorly, but intends to say that God alone teaches interiorly."[34] The inability to teach interiorly does not exclude the active role of human teacher. Aquinas states that teachers can truly be said to teach: "Man can truly be called a true teacher inasmuch as he teaches the truth and enlightens the mind. This does not mean, however, that he endows the mind with light, but that, as it were, he co-operates with the light of reason by supplying external help to it to reach the perfection of knowledge. This is in accordance with Ephesians (3:8–9): 'To me, the least of all saints, is given this grace . . . to enlighten all men.'"[35]

Let us now consider an ambiguity in Davies' closing comments. He states that "Aquinas clearly thought that people who disagreed with him could help him to learn."[36] Learning, however, can be either direct or indirect. If I show a student that $2 + 2 = 4$, the student learns directly. If I show a student that $2 + 2 = 5$, the student does not learn, but might discover that $2 + 2 = 4$. If I show a student that $2 + 2 \neq 5$, then the student does not learn from the error directly, but can learn indirectly by reinforcing his primary understanding of numbers. Aquinas did not learn directly from others in the areas they disagreed with him, but rather in the areas in which they agreed with Catholic teaching and could lead him further. When he considered areas in which they disagreed with him, he could only learn indirectly from those areas of dis-

---

[33] Ibid., q. 11, a. 1.

[34] Ibid., q. 11, a. 1, ad 8.

[35] Ibid., a. 11, a. 1, ad 9.

[36] Davies, "Aquinas and Catholic Universities," 290.

agreement to strengthen the philosophical acuity with which he presented his arguments. From the error he could show that we can learn an implication of the faith or why—absent revelation—the error seems reasonable. For example, he learned from Maimonides's understanding of the distinction between the Creator and the created world and in a certain attention to the literal meaning of the Old Law; but he did not learn from Maimonides's teaching that all affirmative statements about God are really negations nor from his views on Jesus Christ, except by employing those views as a means for illumining the accurate view. In the case of language about God, the mistakes of Maimonides were used to state more precisely and carefully the truth of the analogous character of such language. The goal is not to learn from people with whom we disagree in general, but to seek truth where it is to be found even when one finds it among those who do not possess the fullness of the revelation of God in Jesus Christ. True learning requires learning from teachers who have actualized their potential understanding of the truth. Moving from ignorance to knowledge *(scientia)* requires learning from those who share in some actualization of knowledge—specifically in those areas in which they possess that true actualization.

Learning from those with whom Catholic faith disagrees in the way Davies recommends, qua disagreement, is not engagement with the philosophers of the world, but ultimately capitulation. Davies holds that learning from those with whom Catholic faith disagrees "is one of the chief thoughts he would have wished to bequeath to those concerned with Catholic education today."[37] I would suggest, instead, that we can draw upon the generally insightful comments by Davies on the centrality of the student's own search for truth, the learning that leads the student to see for himself the truth as true. That process, however, requires that the teachers have some hold on the truth. The search for knowledge takes place in relation to knowledge possessed. *Sacra doctrina,* the Scriptures, Tradition, and the Magisterium of the Church, provide the norms by which theological truths can be assented to by the teachers. Such teachers of Catholic theology, with the confirmatory mandatum, can be the occasion for the students at Catholic universities to share in the truths about God and his creation and redemption. Likewise in the broader areas of philosophy, the humanities, and the natural sciences, teachers can only be the occasion for leading students toward the acquisition of knowledge insofar as they are oriented toward the truth themselves and have actualized the particular insights common to their discipline. In human teachers, the acquisition of knowledge of course always remains incomplete. Learning at Catholic universities thus aims at the quest for truth, rooted in

---

[37] Ibid.

the recognition that our complete appropriation of knowledge is beyond our present capacities in this life. Engagement seeks truth. Consequently, the most important thing contemporary Catholic universities have to learn from Aquinas is not that we can learn from those with whom we disagree, but rather that we must seek out professors who have appropriated wisdom from *scientia* and *fides* and entrust them with the noble, albeit secondary, art of human teaching.

CHAPTER 4

Wisdom as the Source of Unity for Theology

AVERY CARDINAL DULLES, S.J.

FATHER MATTHEW LAMB, to whom this volume is dedicated, has written extensively and well on the negative effects of fragmentation in the university curriculum today.[1] Without renouncing the benefits of specialization, he maintains, Catholic universities are challenged to cultivate human wisdom, strengthened and enlightened by the wisdom that comes from God. In the present essay I shall reflect upon the prospects for such a program in the study of theology.

The Fragmentation of Theology

Over the past fifty years we have all heard the repeated complaint, amounting sometimes to a lamentation, that theology has lost its unity. Like Humpty Dumpty it has suffered a great fall, and all the pope's theologians have not succeeded in putting it together again. Theology is splintered into subdisciplines that insist on their own autonomy without regard for one another. Biblical studies go in one direction, historical scholarship goes in another, ethics in a third, and spirituality in a fourth.

In addition to this fragmentation of disciplines, there is a growing breach between past and present. The classic statements of the faith are studied historically, in relation to the circumstances in which they arose. If their contemporary relevance is not denied, they are reinterpreted for today in ways that preserve little if anything of their original content. The Magisterium, which has traditionally been the guardian of theological orthodoxy,

---

[1] Matthew L. Lamb, "Challenges for Catholic Graduate Theological Education," in *Theological Education in the Catholic Tradition*, ed. Patrick W. Carey and Earl C. Muller (New York: Crossroad, 1997), 108–30.

is simply ignored by some theologians and bitterly criticized by others. Dogmatic theology, which seeks to ground itself in official Catholic teaching, is shunned as being servile and unprogressive. In many Catholic faculties dogmatic theology has been replaced by the traditionally Protestant discipline of "systematic theology"—a discipline that seeks to synthesize the results of religious experience and positive historical research in the light of some freely chosen philosophical system, be it idealist, existentialist, phenomenologist, pragmatist, or whatever. Each theologian is expected to be creative and is encouraged to say something novel and surprising. A theologian who reaffirms the tradition and fails to challenge the received doctrine is considered timid and retrograde.

The current fragmentation of theology is occasioned by a variety of sociocultural factors such as democratization, individualism, and the mobility of populations. The ever-accelerating progress of technology has brought different cultures and ideologies into close contact. The slow-moving, culturally unified traditional society seems to be a thing of the past. In the current situation it is easy to fall into historical and cultural relativism and abandon the quest for permanent and universal truth. Theology, which used to pride itself on its perennial validity, has become unsure of its own heritage. Some are inclined to speak of the death of theology, if not the death of God.

Fortunately, however, there are countervailing forces. The high incidence of future shock and culture shock testifies that the human spirit is resistant to agnosticism and provisionality. It reaches out ineluctably toward universally valid truth that is able to withstand the vicissitudes of time and circumstance. From the "eternal city" of Rome, we have heard a fresh summons to hope and courage.

Pope Benedict XVI, some years before assuming his present office, maintained that the strength of philosophy is "Eros, that openness of man that compels him to transcend again and again the limits of the merely knowable and to move toward the eternal."[2] Only the wise can see reality as a whole and, from God's perspective, grasp the true order in which each element of reality receives its due. Peace and unity, he concludes, are unattainable without the wisdom that comes from on high. He praises Pope John Paul II for having sought "to rehabilitate the question of truth in a world characterized by relativism."[3]

John Paul II in his encyclical *Fides et Ratio* analyzed what he called the "fragmentation of knowledge," which makes it so difficult for our contem-

[2] Joseph Cardinal Ratzinger, *Principles of Catholic Theology* (San Francisco: Ignatius Press, 1987), 360.

[3] Joseph Cardinal Ratzinger, *Truth and Tolerance* (San Francisco: Ignatius Press, 2004), 184.

poraries to escape the pitfalls of relativism and skepticism. He called for a recovery of the sapiential dimension of human knowledge, which answers to the quest for ultimate meaning innate in every person (*Fides et Ratio*, no. 81). Philosophy and theology, he contends, must take up anew the search for authentic wisdom.

In the section of the encyclical dealing with Thomas Aquinas, the pope notes that the Angelic Doctor discusses three distinct types of wisdom: philosophical wisdom, which is based on the natural capacity of the human intellect to explore reality; theological wisdom, which explores reality in the light of Revelation; and infused wisdom, the gift of the Holy Spirit that enables one to formulate right judgments by means of a divinely given connaturality (*Fides et Ratio*, no. 44). With the aim of setting theological wisdom in its proper context, I shall analyze the concept of wisdom in each of these three modalities.

Philosophical Wisdom

Wisdom is something different from technical or calculating reason or artistic creativity. It differs likewise from erudition, which consists in a well-stocked memory of facts and figures. To be wise is to understand the real connections between things and to be able to answer broad speculative and practical questions.

Specialists may have a certain limited wisdom if they have succeeded in mastering some particular discipline. An investment counselor, for example, is considered wise if he is able to make prudent judgments about how to handle a client's portfolio by grasping the joint significance of economic variables that might seem meaningless or unrelated to the non-expert. A farmer is called "weather wise" if he knows how to judge from a variety of indications what kind of day it will be tomorrow. But wisdom in the full and unrestricted sense of the word belongs to those who can discourse about reality in general, seeing all things in their mutual interrelationships, and assigning to each its proper place within an intelligible whole. To be able to perceive the similarities and differences, the mutual dependences and orientations of a vast multitude of distinct realities is a superlative exercise of intellectual power.[4]

According to St. Thomas Aquinas, intelligences may be classified as higher or lower according to their respective powers of synthesis. God, as the

---

[4] John Henry Newman devotes considerable attention to the theme of wisdom in his Oxford University Sermons, sermon 14, in his *The Idea of a University*, esp. ch. 6; and at various points in his *Grammar of Assent*. The preceding paragraph is partly dependent on these works.

supreme intelligence, is able to comprehend all things in a single Word, through whom everything was created. The angelic minds are ranked according to their ability to grasp larger portions of reality under fewer intelligible species. Applying this principle to human beings, St. Thomas adds:

> Concerning this we can find a kind of example in ourselves. Some people are not able to understand intelligible truth unless it is explained to them in detail by individual cases, and this happens because of the weakness of their intelligence. But others, who have stronger minds, are able to understand many things from a few principles.[5]

Although he was not presumably thinking of himself, St. Thomas was outstanding in his ability to articulate general principles and apply them by adducing examples from many different fields including Scripture, philosophy, law, biology, and physics.

Aristotle maintained that wisdom in the true sense of the word is knowledge of the first principles or causes that belong to reality as such, rather than those confined to some particular segment of reality. The wise man, he says, knows all things, not in detail, but in their most fundamental characteristics. The possession of such knowledge, he admits, might seem to be beyond human power. He cites the objection of Simonides, who contended that it is unfitting for human beings to seek knowledge far above them, which properly belongs to God alone. In so doing they might excite the "jealousy of the gods"—a common theme of poets and dramatists. Aristotle, rejecting the claim that God can be jealous, replies that no other science is so honorable as that which approximates the wisdom of God, who has comprehensive understanding of the causes and ends of everything that exists.[6]

Philosophy, as the Greek etymology of the term implies, is a loving pursuit of wisdom (*philos* + *sophia*). The whole enterprise presupposes that the human intellect is not confined to any particular spatiotemporal standpoint. As the faculty of being, the intellect has the capacity to transcend its subjective limitations and to attain eternal and universal truth. But the task involves much toil. The human mind, since it is conjoined with a body, can arrive at universal truth only by abstraction from sensible phenomena, to which it must continually make reference.

Because of this limitation, the objection of Simonides should not be lightly dismissed. The practice of metaphysics is analogous to the ascent of Mount

---

[5] Thomas Aquinas, *Summa theologiae* I, q. 55, a. 3, c. References to this work will henceforth be given in the text within parentheses in briefer form; for example, *ST* I, q. 55, a. 3, c.

[6] Aristotle, *Metaphysics* I, 2.

Everest. Those who hope to succeed must have an unusually strong constitution; they must undergo a long period of training under skilled masters, and they must make use of excellent equipment. Failures are more common than successes in this difficult field. When they claim to include the whole of reality, including God himself, within their own conceptual schemes, philosophers fall into the kind of arrogance against which Simonides was warning.

The weakness of philosophy is especially apparent when it directs its attention to the divine. Although in principle it is possible for the human intelligence, from its experience of finite reality, to discover the existence of God as a single, eternal, personal being who created all things, few have achieved this goal by philosophical tools alone. Even at its ideal best philosophy can attain only those aspects of God that are knowable from created things. Since God is infinite, it is evident that some aspects of his being must elude human inferential knowledge. The human quest for wisdom, therefore, cannot be satisfied by philosophy alone.

Theological Wisdom

Believing that there is a God who called all things into being by his free and generous action, religious persons yearn for a deeper and more intimate knowledge of the Creator. They plead with him to emerge from his mystery and show his face. That prayer has not remained unanswered. In the course of time, Christians believe, God has expressed himself through words and deeds, manifesting far more of himself than could be inferred by reasoning from the data of ordinary experience.

Revelation, accepted in faith, gives a new and deeper access to God and his intentions in our regard. Tenets of faith are not mere opinions but firm and solid convictions grounded in the infallible wisdom of God himself. Faith itself, however, falls short of deserving the name of wisdom insofar as it does not provide a synthesis or causal account of its own contents. Although one may have good reasons for believing, faith is in some sort a sacrifice of reason. It submits to the Word of God in spite of its failure to understand how things can be as Revelation says they are.

The contents of Christian Revelation include mysteries that defy all human understanding. The ideas that God eternally exists as three persons, that the eternal Son could enter time as a man, that a man could be virginally conceived, that the God-man could be allowed to die on a cross, that his dead body could be raised from the grave to eternal glory, that he could give himself as food and drink to the community of his disciples—these and other articles of faith are so mysterious that some regard faith as an affront to reason. Christian Revelation seems calculated to confound and humiliate reason rather than satisfy its native dynamism to fashion a harmonious, all-embracing synthesis.

The Apostle Paul was keenly aware of the tension between faith and reason. He warns the Christians at Colossae against being taken in by humanly concocted "philosophy and vain deceit" (Col 2:8). The pagan philosophers, in his view, have become futile in their thinking. "Claiming to be wise," he writes, "they became fools and exchanged the glory of the immortal God for images resembling mortal man or birds or animals or reptiles" (Rom 1:22–23). To the Corinthians he writes: "Not many among you were wise according to worldly standards, . . . but God chose what is foolish in the world to shame the wise . . . so that no human being might boast in the presence of God" (1 Cor 1:26–29). Paul abstains from lofty arguments because he does not want the faith of his converts to rest on "plausible words of wisdom," but rather on "demonstration of the Spirit and power" (1 Cor 2:4).

This negative judgment on wisdom, however, is not Paul's final word. He goes on to declare: "Yet among the mature we do impart wisdom, although it is not a wisdom of this age or of the rulers of this age, who are doomed to pass away. But we impart a secret and hidden wisdom of God" (1 Cor 2:6–7). Paul expects the message he preaches to mature into wisdom, a wisdom schooled by what he calls "the word of the cross" (1 Cor 1:18). Thus he writes to the Colossians that in proclaiming Christ the hope of glory he is "teaching every man in all wisdom, that we may present every man mature in Christ" (Col 1:28).

The wisdom that comes from faith is in many ways unique. Unlike philosophical truths, articles of faith need not be, and normally are not, demonstrable by cogent arguments. Some truths of faith, as I have suggested, seem so unlikely as to verge on absurdity. In accepting them, we allow our minds to be governed by God, whose Revelation, we trust, cannot in the end be contrary to anything we know from other sources to be true.

Theologians must always be warned against rationalism. Anxious to win others to the faith, they are tempted to make the Christian Revelation more plausible by whittling away at its hard doctrines. We are all familiar with this misguided apologetical strategy. Some, offended at the orthodox teaching on the Trinity, reduce it to the doctrine that there are three aspects or modalities of the divine being viewed from our human perspective. Others reduce the momentous wonder of the Incarnation to an assertion that Jesus was a man gifted with exceptional holiness and grace. They look upon the Crucifixion not as a divinely intended sacrifice but an unforeseen catastrophe that was foreign to God's redemptive plan. They present the Resurrection as a metaphor by which the disciples expressed their conviction that Jesus could not have perished totally. The sole mediatorship of Jesus Christ is for them an instance of the "love language of the early Church." By treating the dogmas of the faith as metaphor or hyperbole, they hope to make Christianity more credible, but in fact they make it less interesting and attractive. Since God is so far beyond human comprehension, we should be prepared to expect that his self-revelation would contain mysteries. Why should we believe in a God who cannot tell us anything that exceeds our own powers of discovery?

Reductive styles of apologetics fail to reckon with the distinction made by Paul between worldly wisdom and Christian wisdom. Instead of allowing human rationality to be expanded and transformed by Revelation, such methods imprison the Word of God within the horizons of merely human opinions and patterns of thought. As John Henry Newman asserted, "a rationalistic spirit is the antagonist of faith; for faith is, in its very nature, the acceptance of what our reason cannot reach, simply and absolutely upon testimony."[7]

Newman, however, goes on to speak of a legitimate exercise of reason within faith. It is not rationalism, he holds, to inquire into the grounds for believing that God has revealed what is claimed as his word, nor is it rationalism to combine the data of Revelation with our previous knowledge so as to achieve an integral Christian vision. Nor is it rationalism to trace the mutual relations among revealed truths and to pursue them to their ultimate implications. By virtue of such efforts the simple assent of faith flowers into Christian wisdom. This development corresponds to what Paul may have meant by the mysterious wisdom of God that he imparted to believers who were mature in faith (cf. 1 Cor 2:6–7).[8]

Thomas Aquinas, in the first question of his Summa theologiae, poses the question squarely: Is sacred doctrine wisdom? In response he quotes Aristotle to the effect that wisdom is achieved by considering the first and highest cause of all things. Theology, he concludes, since it treats of God, the universal supreme cause, deserves to be called wisdom by a stronger title than any other human science. Sacred doctrine is superior to philosophy because it knows God not merely by inference from created realities but on the basis of his own self-knowledge communicated through Revelation (*ST* I, q. 1, a. 6).

When we call theological knowledge wisdom, we must be conscious of two limitations. The first is that the principles from which we reason are not self-evident to us, but are received by Revelation and accepted in trustful submission to God's word. In view of this, St. Thomas calls theology a subalternate science. He compares it with optics, which receives its principles

---

7 John Henry Newman, "On the Introduction of Rationalistic Principles into Revealed Religion," tract 73, in *Essays Critical and Historical*, vol. 1 (London and New York: Longmans, Green, 1895), 31.

8 Ibid., 32.

from geometry. Optics, he says, is a science because its principles are self-evident, not indeed to the optician but to the geometer. So too, he argues, the principles of theology, though not self-evident to us, are so to God and to the blessed in heaven. These principles can therefore provide grounds for an authentic science (*ST* I, q. 1, a. 2). But since no human being on earth has command of its principles, theology does not fit the usual definition of science or wisdom.

Secondly, theology falls short of the ideal of wisdom because Revelation contains mysteries that, in the words of Vatican I,

> so far excel the created intellect that, even when they have been communicated in Revelation and received in faith, they remain covered by the veil of faith itself and shrouded as it were in darkness so long as in this mortal life "we are away from the Lord; for we walk by faith, not by sight" (2 Cor 5:6–7). (Denzinger-Schönmetzer, *Enchiridion Symbolorum*, (*DS*, no. 3016)

Theology therefore falls short of fully satisfying the innate quest of the human mind. It operates by a borrowed light, that of Revelation received in faith—a light that, moreover, does not dispel the darkness in which mysteries are enveloped when seen from below. To quote Newman again: "No Revelation can be complete and systematic, from the weakness of the human intellect; so far as it is not such, it is mysterious. . . . A Revelation is a religious doctrine viewed on its illuminated side; a mystery is the selfsame doctrine viewed on the side unilluminated."[9] Newman goes on to explain that Revelation does not come as a system. It consists of a number of detached and incomplete truths belonging to a vast system unrevealed. To organize revealed doctrines into something resembling a system is precisely the task of theology.

According to Vatican I, reason illuminated by faith can, by God's grace, attain a certain understanding of revealed mysteries—an understanding that is indeed very fruitful. The council suggests three strategies for theology: to make use of the analogy of objects of natural knowledge; to discern the interconnections among the various revealed mysteries; and to see how these mysteries help us to fulfill our inbuilt drive toward our ultimate end (*DS*, no. 3016). In the course of centuries, the great theologians have brilliantly shown forth the compatibility of Revelation with all that we know from reason and experience, its inner unity and coherence, and its power to give shape and substance to our inarticulate aspirations. Under these three aspects theology surpasses the achievements of philosophy and eminently deserves the name of wisdom.

---

[9] Ibid., 41.

Wisdom as a Gift of the Holy Spirit

Philosophy and theology, as I have so far described them, give only a theoretical knowledge of the divine, seen as it were from a distance. Divine grace, however, makes it possible to achieve intimate familiarity with God. It involves the indwelling of the three divine persons—they in us and we in them. The virtue of charity, as a gift from God, unites us to God and makes us become one spirit with him, as Paul says in 1 Corinthians 6:17. In a certain sense we know God by loving him. Sharing in the divine nature, persons living by the grace of God know him through a kind of interior instinct, which inclines them to adhere to what is genuinely divine. Thomas Aquinas speaks in this connection of wisdom as a gift of the Holy Spirit. The indwelling Spirit enables us to judge rightly concerning divine things by virtue of our connaturality with the divine (*ST* I, q. 1, a. 6; I–II, q. 68, a. 1; II–II, q. 45, aa. 1–2).

St. Thomas also notes that the word *sapientia* in Latin is derived from *sapere*, meaning to taste (*ST* II–II, q. 45, a. 2, obj. 2). This verbal connection is enlightening because it suggests that wisdom involves having a taste for the things of God, so that we delight in them. While theology does not argue from the theologian's personal feelings or inclinations, an interior sense of the divine will greatly help the theologian to judge rightly concerning the things of God. For this reason, perhaps, the Church has insisted that only saints can be Fathers and Doctors of the Church. Thanks to their close union with the Holy Spirit, the saints were able to speak with special power and unction and to detect the fallacies in spurious presentations of Christian doctrine. In memorable prose Newman has illuminated how this Christian tact operates in practice:

> We know that it is the property of life to be impatient of any foreign substance in the body to which it belongs. It will be sovereign in its own domain, and it conflicts with what it cannot assimilate into itself, and is irritated and disordered till it has expelled it. Such expulsion, then, is emphatically a test of uncongeniality, for it shows that the substance ejected, not only is not one with the body that rejects it, but cannot be made one with it; that its introduction is not only useless, or superfluous, or adventitious, but that it is intolerable.[10]

Saintly theologians, then, have a kind of wisdom that is lacking to mere academicians in the field. They know the divine not only through the discipline acquired by study but more directly through the gift of the Holy Spirit.

---

[10] John Henry Newman, *On Consulting the Faithful in Matters of Doctrine* (Kansas City, MO: Sheed & Ward, 1985), 74.

For them the contemplation of revealed truth is a mode of loving communion with God himself. All of us who pursue theology should aspire to this union with God that will give power and unction to our utterances.

The Recovery of Unity

It remains for me to explain how the retrieval of the sapiential dimension can serve to overcome the fragmentation of theology to which I alluded in the first portion of this essay. My response, very concisely, will be that theology has its unity from its formal object and its principal theme, which is God inasmuch as he reveals saving truth. Theology is true to its nature when it focuses its attention on God and does so in the light of God's self-revelation.

It is often said that theology underwent a seismic shift at the beginning of the nineteenth century, when it relinquished its focus upon God and turned to human questions as its primary theme. This shift could be acceptable, since in the Christian understanding the divine and the human are intimately related. The human person is made in the image and likeness of God; the God-man, Jesus Christ, is God's perfect image; all men and women are called to union with God in eternal life. Theologically, therefore, it is necessary to speak both of God and of humanity in order to speak properly of either. But theology would denature itself if it cultivated anthropology at the expense of its primary object, which is God.

By focusing our attention on God, we can give due consideration to historical contingencies without losing sight of what is constant. God, who comprehends all time in his eternity, is Lord of all ages. "Jesus Christ is the same yesterday and today and forever" (Heb 13:8). The theologian can study the changes of time in the light of the eternal. The Word of God is always conveyed through fragile human vessels, but by the help of the Holy Spirit, human language can become a medium of God's self-disclosure. In some contemporary literature, the name of theology is improperly applied to miscellaneous religious studies, in which disciplines such as history and philosophy, psychology and sociology seem to have the upper hand. Not infrequently, divine Revelation is subjected to purely human standards rather than the reverse.

If theology is to recover its unity, all theological disciplines must be presented in relation to God as their primary reference point. Biblical studies, while they should make use of auxiliary disciplines such as philology and archaeology, must not get lost in textual, historical, and literary analysis. Instead of treating Holy Scripture as a merely human document, theological exegesis must approach it as the Word of God—a word that lives on in Christian tradition. Biblical studies become theological at the point when they illuminate what God is saying to the Church through these inspired texts.

So it is likewise with historical studies. Historical theology is not just Church history or the history of doctrines. If theology is faith seeking understanding, historical theology is faith seeking understanding by reference to faith's own past. The historical theologian must treat the documents of tradition with reverence inasmuch as they transmit the Word of God from generation to generation. Historical theology, like all theology, must submit to the norm of living tradition, but it has a certain normative value of its own, since past expressions of the Church's faith are authoritative for the present.[11]

Patristic theology is a privileged segment of historical theology, since the orthodox teachers of the early centuries have exercised a formative influence upon all later generations. Patristics, then, cannot be reduced to a generalized study of ancient Christian writers. It deals with the holy witnesses to the faith who deserve the name of Fathers because of their enduring formative influence. The Catholic Church today is not simply an offspring of the patristic Church; it is and remains the Church of the Fathers, just as the Church never ceases to be apostolic even though the apostles have long since died.[12]

While responsible hermeneutics can always throw useful light on the deeper meaning of the texts, the interpretation of biblical, patristic, and magisterial documents must not disregard what the writers actually said with the assistance of the Holy Spirit. In the absence of duly authenticated new Revelation, we are not entitled to substitute what we might think they ought to have said for what they did actually say. Biblical and historical theologians, like all believers, stand under God's word as given and transmitted in human words. Systematic or dogmatic theology, seeking to rise above the unaided capacities of human reason, must draw its content from the testimony of Scripture and tradition under the authoritative guidance of the Magisterium. It cannot be satisfied with simply studying the opinions of theologians, interesting as these may be. Dogmatic theology must of course go beyond catechetics, but it cannot do so unless its students have been thoroughly catechized in the doctrine of the Church. Much of the chaos in contemporary theology stems from a lack of familiarity with Catholic doctrine or from failure to accept that doctrine.

Moral theology, in recent years, has tended to degenerate into a merely ethical discipline heavily dependent on the methodologies of social and behavioral sciences. As Pope John Paul II insisted in *Veritatis Splendor*, it

---

11 See Joseph T. Lienhard, "Historical Theology in the Curriculum," in Carey and Muller, *Theological Education in the Catholic Tradition,* 266–79.

12 Yves Congar, *Tradition and Traditions* (New York: Macmillan, 1966), 440–43.

needs to retain its character as theology by acknowledging "that the origin and end of moral action are found in the One who 'alone is good' and who, by giving himself to man in Christ, offers him the happiness of divine life" (*Veritatis Splendor,* no. 29). Faithful to the supernatural sense of the faith, moral theology must take account of the "spiritual dimension of the human heart and its vocation to divine love" (*Veritatis Splendor,* no. 112). In so doing moral theology retains its authentic links with Scripture and tradition in its various expressions.

The desired unity of theology should not be confused with uniformity. Although the system of Thomas Aquinas is justly praised above all others, it should not be allowed to eclipse the contributions of Gregory of Nyssa, Augustine, Anselm, Bonaventure, and Duns Scotus. Among the moderns, Johann Adam Möhler, Matthias Joseph Scheeben, John Henry Newman, Réginald Garrigou-Lagrange, Henri de Lubac, and Hans Urs von Balthasar, to mention only a few, provide examples of how different approaches can all be authentically Christian and Catholic. A healthy variety of systems is to be welcomed, since no one theological system can do justice to the richness of revealed truth.

Finally, something must be said about the gift of infused wisdom, which the Holy Spirit imparts with special intensity to the saints. Divine grace, which unites the soul to God in love, does not by itself make its recipient a theologian, but it can greatly help the properly trained theologian speak rightly of God.

The sense of the faith is not a purely individual attainment. If theologians wish to avoid an unhealthy individualism and be attuned to the mind of the Church, it is important for them to participate in the Church's prayer and worship. An intense life of prayer, nourished by the liturgy, gives intelligibility to the doctrines of the Church and in so doing assists theological speculation. As I have already pointed out, a well-ordered love gives rise to an instinctive recognition of the harmony or discord between theological theories and the deposit of faith. Theology matures under the sunlight of the Holy Spirit, who gives joy and ease in assenting to the truth of Revelation.[13]

The wisdom of theology, like that of philosophy, is rarified and abstract. It is the special vocation of a dedicated minority. As the Christian people, individually and in groups, strive to find God's will and work out their salvation, they should be able to receive some helpful guidance from the theological community. Theologians, as a responsible order within the Church, have

---

[13] The Second Council of Orange taught that the Holy Spirit, by illumination and inspiration, "dat omnibus suavitatem in consentiendo et credendo veritati" (*DS,* no. 377). See also Vatican II, *Dei Verbum,* no. 5. This influence of the Holy Spirit sustaining faith is at work in generating the *habitus theologiae.*

an obligation not to mislead the People of God. They must be modest in their claims and faithful in their performance. Giving full scope to the Word of God, they can, I believe, help the body of the faithful not to be carried to and fro by every wind of doctrine but to advance toward that solidarity and maturity according to what Paul described as "the measure of the stature of the fullness of Christ" (Eph 4:13).

CHAPTER 5

Set Free by First Truth: *Ex corde Ecclesiae* and the Realist Vision of Academic Freedom for the Catholic Theologian

PAUL GONDREAU

THE PURPOSE of this essay is to give a public hearing to a debate over competing notions of academic freedom touched off, especially, by the release of Pope John Paul II's 1990 landmark apostolic constitution on Catholic universities, *Ex Corde Ecclesiae*.[1] This debate, I shall argue, stems from two fundamentally divergent visions of freedom: the one that we find currently widespread in Catholic academia—a voluntarist view; and the other—a realist one—that we see favored by the Church and implied in such documents as *Ex Corde Ecclesiae* and the *Instruction on the Ecclesial Vocation of the Theologian* issued by the Congregation for the Doctrine of the Faith (CDF) also in 1990.

While the following remarks will have applicability to a general consideration of the principle of academic freedom as it relates to most any scholar—and, by extension, to the larger issue of Catholic identity—the more particular concern of this essay centers on the manner by which the Catholic theologian can lay authentic claims on this principle. In sum, I shall argue that dissent from the teaching of the Magisterium, in most instances, constitutes an irresponsible abuse of academic freedom, and, correspondingly, that adherence to magisterial teaching gives to the theologian his true academic freedom. My argument shall draw its chief inspiration from St. Thomas Aquinas, adapting the principles of his thought to address this contemporary issue. If the line of argument I take will be found objectionable by certain theologians, for whom nothing is more sacrosanct than academic freedom, it

[1] I would like to express my gratitude to the Centre for Philosophical Psychology of the Institute for the Psychological Sciences (Arlington, Virginia) at Blackfriars Hall, University of Oxford, England, which made the writing of this essay possible. I am also grateful to my colleagues Paul Keller, O.P., Gary Culpepper, and James F. Keating for their comments on an earlier draft of this essay, which helped to improve its quality.

can induce a much needed discussion at a time when we should consider the place of the theologian in the Church of the twenty-first century.

The Dilemma: A Polarized Contest of Wills

Freedom versus Authority?

To set the context for this debate, let us consider for a moment how today many Catholic theologians work from the mindset that the enjoyment of academic freedom and complete adherence to the teaching of the Magisterium represent mutually exclusive options. Often it is assumed that fidelity to the Magisterium requires the theologian to check his claims on academic freedom at the door. Theologians often react to interventions by Church authorities, especially those that impinge upon academic activity, as heavy-handed intrusions that ask for the sacrifice of academic autonomy and theological creativity at the altar of magisterial authority.

As a result, Vatican attempts at affirming in the same breath both the principle of academic freedom *and* the theologian's duty to adhere to the teaching of the Magisterium often land like a thud on the professional theological community. Besides *Ex Corde Ecclesiae*, a good example of such a Vatican attempt comes from *Sapientia Christiana*, Pope John Paul II's 1979 apostolic constitution on ecclesiastical universities and faculties. Reminding theologians that "true freedom in teaching [and research] is contained *within the limits* of God's Word, as it is constantly taught by the Church's Magisterium," this document concludes that genuine academic freedom operates only "upon firm adherence to God's Word and deference to the Church's Magisterium."[2]

However, since many theologians hold tenaciously to a rugged autonomous or individualistic approach to their discipline, and thus to a minimalist notion of academic limit, they can only shake their heads incredulously at *Sapientia Christiana*'s suggestion that God's Word and the teaching of the Magisterium either "limit" the reach of academic freedom or establish the conditions under which such freedom authentically operates. Is such a suggestion, at bottom seemingly oxymoronic, not simply code word for "submission to ecclesiastical control" or for "theological servitude"? In a climate of mistrust and suspicion on the part of so many theologians, we should hardly be surprised that what we find besetting the Catholic academy in America

---

[2] *Sapientia Christiana*, Article 39, §2; emphasis added. For its part, *Ex Corde Ecclesiae*, no. 29, affirms that it is "intrinsic to the principles and methods" of theological teaching and research that theologians "assent to Catholic doctrine."

now is a veritable contest of wills. One could characterize it as an adversarial relationship pitting the autonomous conscience of the theologian—or, more generally, of the Catholic university—against higher ecclesiastical authority.

A Voluntarist Notion of Academic Freedom

What accounts for this state of affairs, which Pope Benedict XVI, when he was Cardinal Prefect of the CDF, termed "a mistaken and unacceptable opposition between theologian and Magisterium"?[3] While arising, no doubt, from a complex variety of factors, I would suggest it marks a consequence in many ways of the way in which the philosophical notion of voluntarism has sunk deep roots in Western thought, and thereby impacted the modern conception of academic freedom.[4]

Without treating the matter extensively—which has been done sufficiently by other scholars—we shall simply underscore how voluntarism stresses the central role that obligations and prohibitions imposed by a higher authority hold for moral action.[5] Rejecting as well the realist account of the human person as ordered to and determined by the true (perfective of the mind) and the good (perfective of the will), voluntarism instead espouses a view of the human person as indifferent to whatever set of choices, to whatever set of goods (or evils), stand before him. This results in a view of freedom as pure

---

3 Cardinal Ratzinger offered this remark at a press conference in Rome on June 26, 1990, announcing the release of the CDF's *Instruction on the Ecclesial Vocation of the Theologian* (found in Origins 20 [July 5, 1990], 117–26, with Ratzinger's remarks on p. 119 [margin]).

4 William J. Hoye ("The Religious Roots of Academic Freedom," *Theological Studies* 58 [1997]: 409–28, at 409) rightly observes that "[t]he idea of academic freedom is the result of a long historical development, indeed longer than is commonly imagined." Hoye's principal objective in his essay is to trace the roots of the notion of academic freedom to Christian ideas that predate the Renaissance or the Age of the Enlightenment. For a historical survey of the relationship between theologian and Magisterium, cf. Francis Sullivan, *Magisterium: Teaching Authority in the Catholic Church* (New York: Paulist Press, 1983), 181–84.

5 One can find an in-depth treatment of voluntarism, which is traditionally traced back to the fourteenth-century Franciscan William of Ockham, and its impact on moral theology well chronicled in Servais Pinckaers's classic study, *The Sources of Christian Ethics,* trans. Mary T. Noble (Washington, DC: Catholic University of America Press, 1995), especially 240–353. Pinckaers's study is recapitulated by Romanus Cessario, with an emphasis on casuistry, in *Introduction to Moral Theology* (Washington, DC: Catholic University of America Press, 2001), 229–42. Also, John Grabowski details an insightful overview of the influence of voluntarism and other historical trends on Catholic moral theology in his *Sex and Virtue: An Introduction to Sexual Ethics* (Washington, DC: Catholic University of America Press, 2003), 1–22.

willing, that is, as the raw ability to choose whatever one wishes, whether it be a good or an evil. It views freedom as unconstrained choice. Instead of looking upon freedom as inscribed in our natural inclination to a determinable, if still complete, fulfillment (the realist view), voluntarism opts for an a priori freedom grounded in the pure autonomy of the individual.

Grafting on to the voluntarist conception of freedom and authority are other close relatives, if not derivatives, of it. These include a casuistic-like stress on private, subjective morality and on the governing role of conscience in teasing out the limits of personal autonomy.[6] Included as well would be the existentialist conception of the human person as a completely autonomous individual, as his own god, to quote Rousseau, with little or no grounding in a fixed human nature. Nietzsche's infamous "will to power" has also elevated voluntarism to newfound heights. By this phrase many interpreters think Nietzsche means a kind of sublime, creative force of will that allows us to raise our humanity, which issues from no preexisting order, above its mediocrity to attain the higher goals on which we set our sights.[7] No doubt other factors have contributed to voluntarism's ongoing evolution, but the central idea behind its view of freedom (or autonomy) and authority has remained constant.

When confronting the notion of academic freedom today, then, one is faced, I think, with a veritable academic voluntarism. I would argue that it is this voluntarist notion of freedom and authority that accounts for the two extremes we see currently widespread in the Church: either absolute voluntaristic obedience to Church authority on the one side; or, especially in academic circles, the jealous guarding of autonomous free choice coupled with wary uneasiness, even outright hostility, toward such authority on the other. Among Catholic intellectuals one certainly need not search far for reactions to documents like *Ex Corde Ecclesiae* that evince the latter extreme, and which give evidence of what one may call an academic voluntarist mindset.[8]

---

6 The CDF's *Instruction on the Ecclesial Vocation of the Theologian*, no. 28, notes how in the modern view, conscience is often looked upon as "an autonomous and exclusive authority for deciding the truth of a doctrine." For a detailed consideration of the casuist system, cf. Romanus Cessario, *Introduction to Moral Theology*, 229–42, esp. 232–41.

7 I am indebted to Gary Culpepper for this insight (in personal communication).

8 In the following sample of reactions to *Ex Corde* (one is a reaction to the CDF's *Instruction*), we see a kind of implied academic voluntarism "on parade." Daniel Maguire ("Academic Freedom and the Vatican's *Ex Corde Ecclesiae*," *Academe* 88, 3 [2002]: 46–50 [online version]) argues that every theologian owns "the right and the obligation to dissent from hierarchical teaching when necessary." Robert J. Egan ("The 'Mandatum': Now What?," *Commonweal* 129 [April 5, 2002]; online version) worries that the implementation of *Ex Corde* "will violate what has, for the last thirty years or more, been considered the legitimate autonomy of these [American Catholic]

In the universe of academic voluntarism, academic freedom is construed, at least implicitly, as the ability to say or teach whatever one chooses (provided it *somehow* relates to one's discipline or to the subject matter at hand). Though most academics, theologians included, would probably deny they simply "teach whatever they please," the principle of academic freedom is typically invoked by them as if it entitles them to this right.[9] And, in any case, the pedagogy they employ often amounts to a heralding of willing, or creativity, ahead of truth, whereby the main goal is to stoke a sense of creativity and autonomy in their students in order to raise them above the dangers of a prevailing herd-like mentality (the academic equivalent of the Nietzschean "will to power"). In this voluntarist universe, academic freedom is often looked upon as providing the scholar with protection. This is especially the case for the theologian, whose appeals to academic freedom often imply a kind of sanctuary from the Magisterium's encroaching efforts to force theologians to teach what it tells them to teach.

An Alternative Vision

The purpose of this essay, however, is not so much to explore the many complexities of academic voluntarism, but to highlight the fact that there exists

---

universities and their freedom from interference by external authorities of any kind, civil or religious." J. Donald Monan and Edward A. Malloy (" 'Ex Corde Ecclesiae' Creates an Impasse," *America* [January 30, 1999]; online version), who were, respectively, presidents of Boston College and the University of Notre Dame when *Ex Corde* was issued in 1990, express concern over what *Ex Corde* will mean for the "institutional self-governance or autonomy" and "academic freedom in teaching and research" that are "written into their [i.e., U.S. Catholic universities] governing documents and statutes." Commenting on the CDF's *Instruction on the Ecclesial Vocation of the Theologian*, Francis Sullivan ("The Theologian's Ecclesial Vocation and the 1990 CDF Instruction," *Theological Studies* 52 [1991]: 51–68, at 51) describes a voluntarist-like "face-off" when he writes: "[I]t seems inevitable that on this question [of teaching authority in the Church] statements by members of the hierarchy will tend to stress the authority of the magisterium and the obligation on the part of theologians to follow its directives, while statements by theologians will tend to stress the freedom of theological research and publication."

[9] That said, in one ironic case I know of a theologian who was summoned before an official administrative body at the Catholic institution where he teaches and interrogated by feminists, who otherwise championed the principle of academic freedom, to make sure he was covering politically correct issues in the classroom, in particular the role of women in the Church. This case is not an isolated one. How often do we see avid, vocal proponents of the principle of academic freedom do what they can to make others think like them, even should this mean exerting authoritative pressure on those with views that differ from their own?

an alternative to the voluntarist conception of academic freedom, namely, a realist one. More specifically, for the remainder of this essay I wish to argue that, in the final analysis, the only authentic vision of academic freedom is the realist one; it is the mantle of academic realism, not academic voluntarism, which best protects and advances the freedom of the scholar. This holds for the Catholic theologian in a particularly privileged way.

As already indicated, both *Ex Corde Ecclesiae*, the self-proclaimed "magna carta" of Catholic higher education, and the CDF's *Instruction on the Ecclesial Vocation of the Theologian*, which was released just two months before *Ex Corde* in 1990, appeal to a realist notion of academic freedom (the latter document does so more directly in relation to the theologian). In so doing, these two documents, in my estimation, advance a coherent and sound view where academic freedom and adherence to the Magisterium can be seen sitting amicably at the same table together.[10] If Catholic theology in America is to emerge from the quandary of academic freedom in which it is currently mired, it is my contention that retrieval of this realist notion of freedom will play an essential role.

The Case for a Realist Account of Academic Freedom

Realism grounds its notion of freedom in a proper metaphysics of human nature, that is, in an objective order of being, in the objective nature of the human person, including especially the faculties of mind and will.[11] It is a view where free choice proceeds from the nature of the human person (*natura ut voluntas*), or, more specifically, from the operations of mind and will (working always in synergy with each other). And for the realist, the operation of the will follows upon that of the mind (choice follows upon knowledge). The operation of the mind must therefore frames the realist discussion of academic freedom.

---

[10] *Ex Corde* has, of course, been the subject of countless articles and editorials; only a few will be cited in this essay. An important source for the CDF's *Instruction* is the 1975 report by the International Theological Commission, *Theses on the Relationship between the Ecclesiastical Magisterium and Theology,* in Francis Sullivan, *Magisterium: Teaching Authority in the Catholic Church,* 178–216 (with commentary). For examples of negative reaction to the CDF's *Instruction,* cf. Ladislas Orsay, "The Limits of Magisterium," *Tablet* (August 25, 1990): 1066–69; and Christian Duquoc, "The Curia Sews It Up," *Tablet* (September 1, 1990): 1097–98. For the various ways in which *Ex Corde* has been received and implemented at the institutional and diocesan level, cf. Alice Gallin, ed., *Ex Corde Ecclesiae: Documents Concerning Reception and Implementation* (Notre Dame, IN: University of Notre Dame Press, 2005).

[11] For works that outline a realist vision of the moral life in general, cf. Servais Pinckaers, *The Sources of Christian Ethics,* and Romanus Cessario, *Introduction to Moral Theology.*

Academic Study and the "Search for Truth"

The mind, of course, is a power or faculty of the human soul. As with any power or faculty of the soul, it does not operate in a vacuum. Rather, it is ordered to a specific kind of act that its proper object determines: intelligible truth (or simply being itself).[12] This means that truth is the proper object of academic study, as it marks the proper object of knowledge in general. With this in mind, *Ex Corde* defines the university as a place of "searching for, discovering and communicating truth in every field of knowledge" (no. 1); as a place that pursues "a continuous quest for truth" (no. 30). What distinguishes the various academic disciplines from each other is the formally distinct ways each examines the truth. While biology studies truth under the formality of natural life, theology studies truth under the formality of God himself, as he is known through divine revelation.

By any reading the word truth stands out at the operative term of both *Ex Corde* and the CDF's *Instruction*.[13] It appears no less than sixteen times in the introductory section alone of *Ex Corde*, while the CDF's *Instruction* begins with the opening line, "The truth which sets us free," and devotes its first section to "The Truth, God's Gift to His People." *Ex Corde* prefers to use the term in the locution "search for truth" (or the identical "quest for truth"), which appears twelve times, and appeals to the following moving passage from Augustine's *Confessions* in order to set the tone for the role that truth holds in the academic life: "[T]he happy life consists in the joy that comes from the truth, since this joy comes from You, O God, who are Truth, my light, salvation of my face, my God."[14]

Whether in his teaching or in his research, then, the academic is by the very nature of his profession engaged in a speculative, even contemplative-like

---

[12] Cf. Aquinas, *Summa theologiae* (hereafter cited as *ST*) I, q. 77, a. 3 and I, q. 79, a. 1 (English translations of the *ST* are, with minor modifications, taken from the Dominican Fathers of the English Province [New York: Benziger Bros., 1947]); cf. as well *De veritate*, q. 15, a. 2 (English translations of the *De veritate* are, with minor modifications, taken from *Truth. St. Thomas Aquinas,* trans. Robert Mulligan and James McGlynn [Chicago: Henry Regnery, 1952–53]). For passages in Aquinas explaining why one may consider both being and truth as the object of the mind, cf. *ST* I, q. 16, aa. 1, 3 (*corpus* and ad 1) and 5; and *De veritate*, q. 1, a. 1 (*corpus* and ad 3) and 2. For an exhaustive treatment of Aquinas's account of human knowledge, cf. Jacques Maritain, *The Degrees of Knowledge* (or *Distinguish to Unite*), translation from the 4th French edition under the supervision of Gerald B. Phelan, presented by Ralph McInerny (Notre Dame, IN: University of Notre Dame Press, 1995).

[13] While this present essay takes Thomas Aquinas as the representative voice of realism, this is not meant to suggest the comments on academic freedom in *Ex Corde* and the CDF's *Instruction* are particularly Thomist-inspired ones.

[14] *Confessions,* X, 23.

enterprise, no matter the practical ends of his discipline. By this we mean it is an activity ordered to knowledge of the truth for its own sake (practical ends notwithstanding), especially in the case of theology, which examines First Truth. (St. Thomas explains how theology is primarily speculative and secondarily practical, in that it is speculatively "concerned with divine things," which has the practical benefit of "ordering man to . . . eternal happiness.")[15] If the academic does not see himself as a pursuer or considerer of the truth (in the scholastic sense of the term), he fails to grasp the ultimate significance of his profession.

A Realist Definition of Academic Freedom

The operation of the mind in its grasp of truth is not the only matter of concern for academic freedom. Because the proper act of freedom (or free-will) is choice, any free choice, academic free choice included, engages an act of the will as well.[16] Just as the mind does not operate in a vacuum, neither does the will, but it is ordered to a specific act: to the choosing of the good (its object). As the mind is ordered to and perfected, governed, by truth, so is the will ordered to and perfected, governed, by the good.[17] This explains why the realist position holds that the human person is ordered to and determined, perfected, by the true and the good.

When it concerns the specific freedom, then, that functions in relation to academic study—that is, academic freedom—the object of choice is of an academic kind, namely, a good of the mind: truth.[18] With this in mind, we may formulate a realist definition of academic freedom (academic free choice) in the following way: *the will's election of the object of intellectual knowledge,*

---

[15] *ST* I, q. 1, a. 4. For speculative knowledge in general, cf. *ST* I, q. 14, a. 16; q. 79, a. 11; and *De veritate*, q. 11, a. 4.

[16] "Two things concur in free choice [free-will]: one on the part of the cognitive power [the mind], the other on the part of the appetitive power [the will]" (*ST* I, q. 83, a. 3).

[17] Anticipating a voluntarist-like position, Aquinas explains in *ST* I, q. 82, aa. 2 and 3: "The will does not desire of necessity whatsoever it desires . . . [since] the appetible good is the object of the will."

[18] "[T]ruth is itself the good of the intellect, since it is its perfection." *ST* II–II, q. 4, a. 5 ad 1. Previous to this Thomas writes that "truth and good include one another *(se invicem includunt),* since truth is something good, otherwise it would not be desirable, and good is something true, otherwise it would not be intelligible." *ST* I, q. 79, a. 11 ad 2; cf. q. 82, a. 4 ad 1. On the subject of truth and goodness as convertible properties of being, Thomas explains in *ST* I, q. 5, a. 1: "Goodness and being are really the same, and differ only in idea . . . [inasmuch as] goodness presents the aspect of desirability [i.e., goodness adds the aspect of desirability to being, whereas truth adds to being the notion of relation to the intellect]."

namely, the truth, chosen as a good for the mind, indeed, as a good for the entire human person. Recognizing, with Aquinas, that free choice marks a power that "regards not the end, but the *means* to the [determinable] end,"[19] we can see that academic freedom is *properly* exercised *only* when we choose to say or teach that which orders us to the truth, as a means ordering us to a higher end, namely, the end of academic study (truth).

Because it grounds its discussion of academic freedom in a realist perspective, *Ex Corde* never fails to link such freedom to "the truth and the common good" (nos. 4, 12, 21, 29, and Article 2, §5). Affirming an inherent relation linking academic freedom with the "common good," *Ex Corde* underscores the fact that the will's choice of truth is elected not only as a good for the mind and not merely as a good for the human individual as such. It is chosen as a good for the entire academic community as well, and, indeed, as a good for all (a common good). In serving the truth, academic freedom serves the common good of human culture, since all desire knowledge of the truth.[20]

For the realist freedom does not operate blindly; it is *informed*, nourished, supplied by something *prior* to it: the mind's grasp of truth. Freedom *follows*, and is thus dependent, upon the truth as the mind grasps it, upon what the mind learns is authentically good for the human person. The academic mind cannot remain indifferent in the face of truth. In its ordering to its object, the mind yearns, longs for the truth, just as the will longs for the good.[21] Without the truth, the mind does nothing, and academic free choice (academic freedom) fades as an empty illusion.

What all this leads to is that the academic finds his *real* freedom not in some supposed blind, indifferent power of choice, in an entitlement to teach whatever one chooses (tantamount to a kind of intellectual indifferentism), but in that which governs and perfects the mind: truth. Since the human mind has natural limits (the limits placed on it by truth), so does academic thought, and so should, by consequence, academic freedom. *Authentic* academic freedom targets the light of truth, not the autonomy or creative self-expression of the scholar. *All* are set free by the truth, academics included.

---

[19] *ST* I, q. 82, a. 1 ad 3; emphasis added.

[20] For its part, the CDF's *Instruction* places the stress on the will's role in choosing truth, in pursuing truth, in assenting to truth once the mind is confronted with it. Defining academic freedom as "an openness to accepting the truth that emerges at the end of an investigation" (no. 12), or, later, as "the free self-determination of the person in conformity with his moral obligation to accept the truth" (no. 36), this document reminds the academic of his duty to assent, through an act of the will, to the truth attained by the mind.

[21] *ST* I, q. 16, a. 1: "As the good denotes that towards which the (will) tends, so the true denotes that towards which the intellect tends."

We live in an age when many academics who teach at Catholic institutions think that academic rigor and excellence is not served, and indeed is menaced, by a strong commitment to the Catholic faith (or to Catholic identity). However, just the reverse is correct. Since Catholic institutions, at least in principle, work from the standpoint that the fullness of truth resides in the Catholic faith (as the Second Vatican Council affirms), the stronger the adherence to the Catholic faith, the more academic excellence will thrive.[22] The academic life attains its highest culmination when the pursuit of truth occurs under the full light of Catholic truth.

Freedom as an a priori Power in the Voluntarist View

In contrast to the realist conception of freedom, the voluntarist view holds that free choice marks an a priori power *(voluntas ut voluntas)* that *precedes*, stands before, the operations of mind and will (I am free to know the truth or not, I am free to choose the good or not); it is not a power inscribed in our natural inclination to our determinable perfection *(natura ut voluntas)*.[23] Positioning autonomous freedom before all else, voluntarism seems to look upon free choice as a power that allows the autonomous agent to choose or determine his own end, rather than as a power that regards the means to our determinable end.

---

[22] As Vatican II's Decree on Ecumenism, *Unitatis redintegratio*, no. 3, affirms: "[T]he very fullness of grace and truth is entrusted to the Catholic Church." In his work, *Theology in the Public Square: Church, Academy and Nation* (Oxford: Blackwell, 2005), 216, Gavin D'Costa argues that "[t]he Christian Church [he has in mind especially the Catholic Church] at the heart of the university will facilitate such genuine developments that can only enrich intellectual and cultural life, facilitate real pluralism and dialogue, and serve the common good."

[23] This insight is indebted to the remarks of Servais Pinckaers from his oral presentation "Réflexions sur mes sources," offered on October 29, 2005, at a conference in Fribourg, Switzerland, honoring his 80th birthday. It is indebted as well the comments of Romanus Cessario (*Introduction to Moral Theology*, 230) on how the "freedom of indifference" that voluntarism leads to and that holds that the human person remains radically indifferent or undetermined when confronted with a judgment of reason about a good to be pursued: "The liberty of indifference is not to be identified with *natura ut voluntas* and the distinctive ordering to an end ('velle, intendere, frui') that governs the realist view of the moral life. On the contrary, the liberty of indifference expresses a sort of pure willing *(voluntas ut voluntas)* that remains inherently unrelated to the goods of excellence that perfect the human person." Cf. as well Bernard Schumacher, *A Philosophy of Hope: Josef Pieper and the Contemporary Debate on Hope,* trans. D. C. Schindler (New York: Fordham University Press, 2003), 6.

We can see why, then, the CDF's *Instruction* (no. 33) employs the term "positivist" to categorize the voluntarist view of academic freedom. By this the *Instruction* means such a view prescinds from the mind's duty to conform to the truth (the *Instruction* has in mind specifically the theologian who thinks he is unbound to any "non-infallible" magisterial teaching). More generally, we could say it is positivist because it pays no heed to the objective nature of the human person. That is, it discounts the fact that free choice flows from the mind's natural ordering to the truth and the will's natural ordering to the good. We might also call it nominalist, since, by compartmentalizing freedom and severing it from the guiding hand of truth, it adheres to a rugged individualistic autonomy of the most radical kind.[24]

Academic Freedom and the Theologian

We come, then, to the crux of the issue, at least in regard to the principal concern of this essay: applying the foregoing analysis of a realist account of academic freedom to the specific case of the Catholic theologian. In so doing, we shall establish the grounds on which the theologian can lay authentic claims on such freedom. Since the notion of truth frames the realist view of academic freedom, so must we first turn to a consideration of truth, insofar as it relates to theology, in making our realist case for the theologian's entitlement to academic freedom.

First Truth (Revealed Truth) as the Object of Theology

Among all the academic disciplines, theology enjoys an exalted status, as theology examines First Truth, that is, God himself.[25] And since proper knowledge of a thing follows upon the conformity of that thing to the mind, theological knowledge of God consists in the conformity of the mind to the very being of God in himself. Divine revelation, of course, makes this conformity possible.

---

[24] It is noteworthy that in his criticism of *Ex Corde*, Daniel Maguire ("Academic Freedom and the Vatican's *Ex Corde Ecclesiae*") appeals to the "trailblaz[ing]" thought of the founder of modern nominalism and voluntarism, William of Ockham, and to his struggle "for the freedoms relished in every modern Western university today."

[25] "[I]n sacred science [i.e., theology], all things are treated under the aspect of God *(sub ratione Dei)*, either as they concern God himself, or inasmuch as they relate to God as their beginning and end." Aquinas, *ST* I, q. 1, a. 7. For a detailed examination of First Truth as the object of faith, cf. Romanus Cessario, *Christian Faith and the Theological Life* (Washington, DC: Catholic University of America Press, 1996), 49–83.

As a discipline, theology concerns a body of knowledge proper to God (the knowledge God possesses of himself) but which he has imparted to us through his revelation. Revealed truth is thus the pivotal term in any discussion on the life and work of the theologian.[26] Furthermore, because the theologian is bound to teach what God teaches (reveals), we can say that theology, as a discipline, operates in obedience to authority, to God's authority. Aquinas reminds us that the argument of authority reigns in theology because theology reflects upon truths accepted on the authority of God's revelation.[27] In virtue of their task of communicating First Truth, theologians sit in a privileged position of satisfying what Aristotle, in the memorable opening line of the *Metaphysics*, calls "the natural desire of all men to know."[28]

Yet today one often looks in vain for Catholic theologians to draw clear reference to revealed truth when describing the meaning and purpose of their work.[29] Not infrequently theologians assume, even if implicitly, that their discipline has little or nothing to do with the confessional contemplation of revealed truth and of its relation to the Three-Personed God. One need only point to the religious studies craze endemic of so many Catholic colleges and universities as evidence of this.

---

[26] *Sapientia Christiana* (no. 3) is clear on theology owning "a special link with Christian revelation," since this discipline aims at gaining "a deeper grasp of revealed truth"; cf. as well Article 3, §1, and Article 66, for more of the same.

[27] "[Sacred] doctrine [i.e., theology] is especially based upon arguments from authority, inasmuch as its principles [or starting points, sources] are obtained by revelation." *ST* I, q. 1, a. 8 ad 2. Earlier in a. 2, Thomas writes: "[J]ust as the musician accepts *on authority* the principles taught him by the mathematician, so sacred science is established on principles revealed by God" (emphasis added).

[28] Thus, St. Thomas, *De malo*, q. 9, a. 1 (cited in *Ex Corde*, no 1): "[I]t is natural for man to desire knowledge of the truth."

[29] A good case in point is seen in the mission statement of sorts posted by the Board of Directors of the Catholic Theological Society of America (CTSA) on its website in February, 2005: "Our purpose, within the context of the Roman Catholic tradition, shall be to promote studies and research in theology, to relate theological science to current problems, and to foster a more effective theological education, by providing a forum for an exchange of views among theologians and with scholars in other disciplines. In this way the Society seeks to assist those trusted with a teaching ministry of the Church to develop in the Christian people a more mature understanding of their faith, and to further the cause of unity among all people through a better appreciation of the role of religious faith in the life of human society." While innocuous enough, the language in this statement is yet vague and generic and lacks any explicit reference to God or to divine revelation, to the truth, or certainly to the Magisterium's guidance. The *telos* of the Catholic theologian, it appears, is simply to cultivate a "forum for an exchange of [theological] views" for its own sake.

Further, the foregoing analysis of truth as the object of intellectual inquiry should not sound a merely abstract ring to the ear of the theologian. It should carry a profoundly *personal* resonance for the one who studies God himself, the Truth that unites and is the source of all other truths. For the theologian, truth is not merely the object of his study. Truth has a name, it bears a face. It is Jesus Christ, who is himself First Truth incarnate and who calls himself the Truth (Jn 14:6).[30] Fully revealed in Christ is the truth of God as three Persons, Father, Son, and Holy Spirit, united in a communion of eternal self-subsisting love. Given this personal nature of the discipline of theology, truth acts not only as the object of the theologian's study, it is also (or at least *should* be) the object of his deepest affective love.

Revealed Truth and the Magisterium

Acknowledging the role of revealed truth in theology simply marks the first step. The question remains as to how divine revelation is made accessible to the theologian, as to any believer. Addressing this very concern, the Second Vatican Council's Dogmatic Constitution on Divine Revelation, *Dei Verbum* (no. 10), famously decrees that divine revelation is offered both in "sacred tradition and sacred Scripture," with the result that both "form one sacred deposit of the word of God, committed to the Church."[31]

This last clause, "committed to the Church," is key, since it accounts for the very *raison d'être* of the Magisterium: "the task of authentically interpreting the word of God, whether written or handed on," *Dei Verbum* (no. 10) continues, "has been entrusted exclusively to the living Magisterium of the Church *(soli vivo Ecclesiae Magisterio)*, whose authority is exercised in the name of Jesus

---

[30] "[T]he object of theology is the truth which is the living God and his plan for salvation revealed in Jesus Christ." CDF, *Instruction*, no. 8. In its Thesis 11, the International Theological Commission's 1975 report *Theses on the Relationship between the Ecclesiastical Magisterium and Theology* (in Francis Sullivan, *Magisterium: Teaching Authority in the Catholic Church*, 214) writes: "[T]his truth [of the faith] is not something we have forever to search for, as though it were doubtful or quite unknown. Rather, it is truth that has been truly revealed and has been entrusted to the Church to be faithfully preserved."

[31] By sacred tradition *Dei Verbum* (no. 9) means the entrusting of the Word of God to the apostles "by Christ the Lord and the Holy Spirit" and the subsequent handing on of this Word of God "in its full purity" to the apostles' successors, the bishops. Earlier in no. 8, in fact, the same document states: "[T]he apostolic preaching, which is expressed in a special way in the inspired books, was to be preserved by an unending succession of preachers until the end of time." English translations of the texts from Vatican II are, with minor modifications, by the Holy See.

Christ." *Dei Verbum* immediately follows with a clear distinction between the authority of the Word of God and that of the Magisterium, however, in that the "Magisterium is not above the word of God, but serves it."[32] This suggests the teaching authority of the Magisterium, while indispensable, is not simply interchangeable with that of the Word of God, as if the two occupied the same rung. If the Magisterium *draws from* the Word of God, it does not *impart* it, as do sacred tradition and the inspired texts of Scripture.

At the same time, we need to underscore *Dei Verbum*'s unequivocal affirmation that the way the Magisterium "serves" revealed truth is through the "authentic interpretion" it offers of the Word of God, "in accord with a divine commission and with the help of the Holy Spirit." This constitutes the Magisterium as the guarantor of revealed truth, as the faithful guardian of the "one deposit of faith," which links it inseparably to sacred Scripture and sacred tradition.[33] For this reason Vatican II's Dogmatic Constitution on the Church, *Lumen Gentium* (no. 25), speaks of the Magisterium's "vigilant warding off of any errors" that threaten the faith of the Church, and of its task to "preserve religiously and expound faithfully" divine revelation.

With this teaching in mind, we can see how magisterial pronouncements play a vital role in the work of the theologian. Following this teaching of Vatican II and echoing the CDF's *Instruction, Ex Corde Ecclesiae* provides us with a fuller definition of the study of theology, one that takes into account the requisite role of the Magisterium: "(Theologians) seek to understand better, further develop and more effectively communicate the meaning of Christian Revelation *as transmitted in Scripture and Tradition and in the Church's Magisterium.*"[34]

---

[32] According to the CDF's *Instruction* (no. 35), the Magisterium acts in "obedience to the Word of God."

[33] "The Magisterium . . . listens to (the Word of God) devoutly, guards it religiously and explains it faithfully *(sancte custodit et fideliter exponit)* in accord with a divine commission, and with the help of the Holy Spirit it draws from this one deposit of faith *(uno fidei deposito)* everything which it presents for belief as divinely revealed. It is clear, therefore, that sacred tradition, Sacred Scripture and the Magisterium of the Church, in accord with God's most wise design, are so linked and joined together that one cannot stand without the others *(unum sine aliis non consistat)*. . . ." *Dei Verbum,* no. 10. Cf. as well *Lumen Gentium,* no. 24: "Bishops, as successors of the apostles, receive from the Lord, to whom was given all power in heaven and on earth, the mission to teach all nations and to preach the Gospel to every creature. . . . "

[34] *Ex Corde,* no. 29; emphasis added. The wording of the CDF's *Instruction* (no. 6) reads: "(The theologian's) role is to pursue in a particular way an ever deeper understanding of the word of God found in the inspired Scriptures and handed on by the living tradition of the church. He does this in communion with the Magisterium, which has been charged with the responsibility of preserving the deposit of faith."

The Magisterium as Auctoritas for Theological Reflection

So crucial is the role of magisterial teaching in theology that we can say it occupies a seat of authority—in the sense, noted above, of how theology operates in obedience to God's authority—in theological reflection. For when *Dei Verbum,* and *Lumen Gentium* before it, affirm that the Magisterium speaks with the voice of Christ, a position of authority not unlike that of God himself is implied.[35]

We should be aware, however, that when the term "authority," *auctoritas,* is employed by Aquinas in his description of the study of theology, it does not suffer the voluntarist baggage it often does in modern parlance, where it can carry a pejorative, domineering sense. In Aquinas's vocabulary, *auctoritas* holds a rich, dynamic significance, particularly in reference to the discipline of theology. When he says God's authority sits at the foundation of the study of theology, St. Thomas takes authority, *auctoritas,* to mean source, well-spring or font, starting point, from which the radiance of theological truth burgeons forth. And since the mind's thirst for knowledge achieves its deepest satisfaction, and freedom, only when it possess this truth, *auctoritas* (in theology) can be taken to mean source of life-giving truth ("infallible truth," as Aquinas calls it).[36]

Benefiting from the promised assistance of the Holy Spirit, then, the Magisterium acts as the God-willed (or Christ-instituted)—and *infallible*—guardian or guarantor of revealed truth.[37] Mindful of Aquinas's notion of *auctoritas,* we can say this makes the Magisterium's teaching a veritable *source* of life-giving theological knowledge, a font or well-spring of theological reflection.

That said, we should immediately clarify that the teaching of the Magisterium does not act as font in the same manner as do Scripture and sacred tradition. Scripture and tradition communicate the Word of God in a qualitatively superior way. While Scripture, for instance, "is the word of God

---

[35] *Lumen Gentium,* no. 25, professes: "[B]ishops are preachers of the faith, who lead new disciples to Christ, and they are authentic teachers, that is, teachers endowed with the authority of Christ. . . . In matters of faith and morals, the bishops speak in the name of Christ *(in nomine Christi prolatam)."*

[36] *ST* I, q. 1, a. 8.

[37] For the infallibility of the Magisterium, *Lumen Gentium,* no. 25, famously writes: "[The Church's bishops] proclaim Christ's doctrine infallibly whenever, even though dispersed through the world, but still maintaining the bond of communion among themselves and with the successor of Peter, and authentically teaching matters of faith and morals, they are in agreement on one position as definitively to be held. . . . [T]his is the [same] infallibility which the Roman Pontiff, the head of the college of bishops, enjoys in virtue of his office."

inasmuch as it is consigned to writing" (*Dei Verbum,* no. 9), the Magisterium is but the "servant" of the Word of God. Whereas Scripture is "inspired," the teaching of the Magisterium, as Cardinal Newman so carefully noted, is merely "preserved from error," as it receives the deposit of faith in its fullness and safeguards it from corruption and contamination (for which reason Newman considered "rest" to be the "better thing" for the Church to do).[38] The Magisterium enjoys the role not of imparting revealed truth per se (Scripture and tradition do this), but of clarifying what belongs to revealed truth (some use the term "proximate norm" of faith for the Magisterium). For his part, Aquinas holds that the "Sovereign Pontiff" (we can say the Magisterium) owns the task of making "more explicit" the "truth of faith that is sufficiently expounded in the teaching of Christ and the apostles," especially as doctrinal errors arise that threaten to pervert the truth of faith.[39] In short, we might simply say revealed truth has one unique "source"—the Word of God—which is communicated in three distinct yet interconnected ways.

We can see, then, that since the Magisterium acts as the infallible guardian of revealed truth, the theologian is bound to teach what the Magisterium teaches (or at least is bound not to dissent from the Magisterium), just as he is bound to teach what God teaches. What the theologian discharges, in other words, is not so much his own mind as the mind of the Church, the mind of God, whether communicated through Scripture,

---

38   In his *Letter Addressed to the Duke of Norfolk,* ch. 9, no. 6 (in *Certain Difficulties Felt by Anglicans in Catholic Teaching,* vol. 2 [New York: Longmans, 1900], 175–378, at 327–28), John Henry Cardinal Newman distinguishes the inspiration enjoyed by the apostles from the way the Magisterium acts as guardian of revealed truth: "[W]e [must] consider that neither Pope nor Council are on a level with the Apostles. To the Apostles the whole revelation was given, by the Church it is transmitted; no simply new truth has been given to us since St. John's death; the one office of the Church is to guard 'that noble deposit' of truth, as St. Paul speaks to Timothy, which the Apostles bequeathed to her, in its fulness and integrity. Hence the infallibility of the Apostles was of a far more positive and wide character than that needed by and granted to the Church. We call it, in the case of the Apostles, inspiration; in the case of the Church, *assistentia.* . . . I speak of the special and promised aid necessary for (the Church's) fidelity to Apostolic teaching; and, in order to secure this fidelity, no inward gift of infallibility is needed, such as the Apostles had, no direct suggestion of divine truth, but simply an external guardianship, keeping them off from error. . . ." Thus Francis Sullivan's equivocal and misleading remark ("The Theologian's Ecclesial Vocation," 58) that the "inspired Scriptures have God as their author, but this is not true even of the most solemn pronouncements of the Magisterium." Newman's comment on rest being the better course of action is quoted in Ian Ker, *John Henry Newman: A Biography* (Oxford: Clarendon Press, 1988), 652.

39   *ST* II–II, q. 1, a. 10 ad 1.

sacred tradition, or magisterial pronouncements.[40] No theologian has the "freedom" to depart from this mind, to lay it aside, even should he want to. For from this mind flows the truth that sets free.

Now there are distinctions to be made as to the precise ways by which the Magisterium acts as the infallible guardian of revealed truth: For example, there are the extraordinary and ordinary teaching functions of the Magisterium, and there is definitive and non-definitive teaching. These are not always evident, at least in certain concrete instances, even to the theologian, which can give rise to some rather thorny dilemmas about specific positions to present in one's teaching or research. Because practically important, this issue shall receive consideration in the final section of this essay (section IV). But for the moment, we must address the notion of academic freedom as it relates to the teaching authority of the Magisterium.

Academic Freedom and the Magisterium

Having just asserted that the theologian lacks the "freedom" to depart from the mind of the Church, including the way that mind is expressed in magisterial teaching, we are of course appealing to a realist notion of freedom: a freedom that is limited by, because inscribed in, the human person's natural inclination to a determinable perfection; a freedom that is ordered, as a means to an end, to the mind's grasp of truth and will's love of the good. This is a view of freedom that is difficult to grasp in a voluntarist climate where theologians, overprotective of their autonomy (read: freedom), stand perpetually on guard against the slightest hint of magisterial encroachment.

Yet if this essay has attempted to establish one thing, it is to show that the realist vision of academic freedom offers a much more attractive, nay (at the risk of pun) "freeing," alternative to the voluntarist one that otherwise often restricts theological discourse to less than constructive musings. The realist account of academic freedom, it seems clear to me, offers theologians a viable way to overcome the merely minimalist and begrudging regard by which they frequently heed magisterial direction.

As we saw above, the realist notion of academic freedom places the primary focus on the light of truth rather than on the autonomy or creative self-expression of the scholar, rather than on some blind indifferent power of choice. This focus allowed us to define academic freedom as the will's election of the truth (the object of academic study), chosen as a good for the mind—as a good, in fact, for the entire human person. In the case of the

---

[40] Gavin D'Costa (*Theology in the Public Square,* 216) argues that "[i]f theology is to be theology, it must be ecclesial, and this involves prayer and careful attention to various polyphonic sources of authority."

theologian, we could define academic freedom as the will's election of First Truth, revealed truth, the object of theological study.

As a result, the theologian *best* exercises his academic freedom when he chooses to say or teach that which conforms to First, revealed truth. Since revealed truth is properly (infallibly) understood (among other ways) in light of the teaching of the Magisterium, the theologian makes responsible use of his academic freedom when he adheres to the teaching of the Magisterium. Conversely, to dissent from the teaching of the Magisterium is to allow one's academic freedom to suffer abuse.

Here we would do well to keep in mind what was stated above about *auctoritas* in theology, applicable to the Magisterium (in a qualified way), constituting a source or wellspring of life-giving truth. The mind's thirst for knowledge of the truth is satiated when it is allowed to drink from this well-spring, and the soul as a result is set free from the shackles of ignorance and pride. To say, then, that academic freedom thrives under the auspices, the guidance, of the truth is to assert its theological counterpart: The theologian's academic freedom thrives under the guidance of the teaching authority of the Magisterium. Because the Magisterium ensures that theologians remain ordered to revealed truth in their teaching and research, this organ of the Church plays an indispensable role in *safeguarding*, not threatening or undercutting, the theologian's authentic entitlement to, and subsequent enjoyment of, academic freedom. Hence, the apostolic constitution *Sapientia Christiana*'s insistence, as seen earlier, that genuine academic freedom operates only "upon deference to the Church's Magisterium."

We should recall as well *Ex Corde*'s insight that a proper exercise of academic freedom serves the common good, since teaching or writing in conformity with the truth is good not only for the academic himself, but for all who seek the truth. Just as the theologian enjoys the eminent role of communicating First Truth, so as a consequence is he charged with the highest of responsibilities: promoting the common good of the Church through the probing and elucidating of revealed truth. The CDF's *Instruction* (nos. 22 and 37) specifies that the theologian accomplish this by "presenting and illustrating the doctrine of the faith in its integrity and with full accuracy," as this sustains the faithful in their perseverance in the "unity of faith." For this the theologian must rely closely upon the Magisterium's delineation of the parameters of the deposit of faith. To suppose such delineation is per se potentially stifling or suffocating of theological creativity, if not actually so, is to misread grossly the role of the Magisterium in theological reflection.[41]

---

[41] In this sense, Jean Porter ("Misplaced Nostalgia: 'Ex Corde' and the Medieval University," *Commonweal* 128 [April 20, 2001]: 12–15, at 14–15) shows how difficult it is even for someone who knows well the thought of Aquinas to resist voluntarist

Now we can see why Pope Benedict XVI (then Cardinal Ratzinger) deplored, as quoted above, the "mistaken and unacceptable opposition between theologian and Magisterium." *Sapientia Christiana* and *Ex Corde* instead envision a Church where theologians stand out as "examples of fidelity to the Church" on account of their adherence to the "full doctrine of Christ, whose authentic guardian and interpreter has always been the Magisterium."[42] The CDF's *Instruction* in its turn appeals to the celebrated maxim *sentire cum ecclesia* when reminding theologians of *Lumen Gentium*'s famous call for a "religious submission *(religiosum obsequium)* of mind and will" to the Magisterium's teaching.[43] Roused by their love for the object of their discipline, First Truth, *and* for its guardian the Magisterium, theologians ought to be, in principle and in practice, shining examples of such an interior submission of mind and will. The faithful should be able to see in theologians what a living model of *sentire cum ecclesia* looks like.

Freedom and Obedience to Authority

The CDF's *Instruction* goes further by appealing repeatedly to *obedience*—hardly a popular notion among academics—as an appropriate ideal for the

---

trappings and to rise above the suspicion that magisterial teaching is of its very nature potentially choking: "Very few Catholic theologians would deny the legitimacy and importance of the teaching function of the magisterium, that is, the formulation of doctrines that express the essential elements of Christian belief. These doctrines serve to set the boundaries that preserve our integrity as a community of faith. *Yet if drawn too tightly, boundaries can strangle the community life they are meant to preserve.*" (Emphasis added.) In his historical survey of the relationship between theologian and Magisterium, Francis Sullivan (*Magisterium: Teaching Authority in the Catholic Church,* 181–84) fails to take into account the shift from a realist notion of freedom to a voluntarist one.

[42] *Sapientia Christiana,* no. 4. Fidelity to the Magisterium is a favorite theme of *Sapientia Christiana*: "Faculties [of theology must] . . . ceaselessly promote their fidelity to the Church's doctrine" (no. 4); "Those who teach matters touching on faith and morals are to be conscious of their duty to carry out their work in full communion with the authentic Magisterium of the Church, above all, with that of the Roman Pontiff" (Article 26, §2); "In studying and teaching the Catholic doctrine, fidelity to the Magisterium of the Church is always to be emphasized" (Article 70). According to *Ex Corde*, Article 4, §3, "Catholic theologians, aware that they fulfill a mandate received from the Church, are to be faithful to the Magisterium of the Church as the authentic interpreter of Sacred Scripture and Sacred Tradition."

[43] CDF, *Instruction,* nos. 23 and 35; and *Lumen Gentium*, no. 25, which also says: "To these [infallible] definitions [of the Magisterium] the assent of the Church *(assensus Ecclesiae)* can never be wanting, on account of the activity of that same Holy Spirit, by which the whole flock of Christ is preserved and progresses in unity of faith."

theologian, namely, obedience to the authority of Christ, obedience to the truth, obedience to the Magisterium.[44] While obedience to authority may rub against a voluntarist spirit of freedom and autonomy, in the realist account obedience, when correlating with truth, frees the mind from the shackles of ignorance and error, which in turn allows one's freedom to *flourish*. For the realist, obedience to the authority of the truth, including the truth safeguarded by the teaching of the Magisterium, liberates the human spirit to excel at creative self-expression.

While paradoxical, obedience to authority as a means to freedom and creative self-expression, to creative excellence, exists all around us if we but recognize it. Human thought, indeed, human life, thrives whenever there is obedience to regulated order, structure, and authority. Most forms of the martial arts, for instance, stress hierarchy, authority, obedience, respect, self-restraint, discipline, directed order. Without submitting to these, excellence in the respective martial art form remains ever elusive. In the literary field, the more a gifted writer observes, respects, and obeys the structured rules of grammar and logic, the more his literary creativity takes flight. And nearly any virtuoso musician knows that strict obedience to regulated order is the font from which genuine musical freedom and creativity flow. Few individuals would pay good money to see the "performance" of a person who knows nothing of the rules governing music and yet, wishing to express his "freedom and creativity" on the piano, offers a concert in which he brutishly bangs away at the keyboard. While good music might expand established conventions, these conventions are never eclipsed or abandoned in their expanded form. Musical authorities such as Nadia Boulanger (mentor to Leonard Bernstein and Aaron Copeland) have noted, for instance, how J. S. Bach's compositions, like his *Well-Tempered Clavier*, stand as a model for the way obedience to authoritative rules or conventions that can be explained in clear terms allows musical creativity to take flight and soar to unprecedented heights.

Theological thought is no different. The theologian begins by obeying magisterial teaching. But within that obedience, the theologian is absolutely free. Until he cultivates a spirit of *religiosum obsequium* toward the authority of the Magisterium, even in its "non-definitive" teaching, the theologian will

---

[44] In no. 7 the *Instruction* speaks of the theologian's duty to be "[o]bedient to the impulse of truth," and that theology "constitutes an integral part of obedience to the command of Christ." In no. 23 this document explains how the religious submission of mind and will called for by *Lumen Gentium* "cannot be simply exterior or disciplinary, but must be understood within the logic of faith and under the impulse of obedience to the faith." For this reason, in no. 29 the *Instruction* appeals to theologians to adhere to the teaching of the Magisterium "by reason of the obedience of faith."

never taste the freedom of being released from the seductive illusion that one's own views represent the most reliable source of knowledge. In his obedience to the Magisterium's authority, the theologian secures his freedom in a way analogous to the way he gains his freedom when he obeys Christ's authority, since Christ takes away nothing genuinely human (as Pope Benedict XVI reminded us in his inaugural homily).[45]

We can say more. Within the frontiers of theological reflection demarcated by obedience to magisterial teaching, the theologian has more room to roam than can ever be exhausted. The truth of the mystery of the living God, the object of magisterial teaching, lies utterly beyond any purely human conceptualization.[46] No human explanation or formulation (the Magisterium's included) can exhaust our understanding of the revealed truth of God. No human set of words can adequately capture God's essence. At the same time, this does not mean that just any wording will suffice, as the Church of the patristic age learned in such markedly painful ways. Paradoxically, the theologian's task is never ending and, literally, open-ended to the Infinite, all the while remaining obedient to the Magisterium's demarcation of the parameters of the deposit of faith.

Of course, obedience to magisterial teaching, expressive of a dutiful spirit of *religiosum obsequium*, does not mean all potential conflict between theologian and Magisterium becomes reduced to nothing more than phantom threat. Some theologians, in fact, might object that the general principles outlined above forecast nothing but happy harmony between theologian and Magisterium, at least in the abstract, while glossing over conflicts that are sure to arise *in the concrete* even under a spirit of obedience. They might object that the realist vision of academic freedom, as far as I have presented it at any rate, cannot avoid cases where obedience to the Magisterium would demand a purely willful, that is, voluntaristic-type submission. This would happen when, say, a theologian is asked to give assent to a magisterial pronouncement

---

[45] In that homily the Pope implored the youth, and, indeed, the world, to throw open wide the doors to Christ, since in Christ "nothing is taken away" and "everything is given to us." It is the same for the freedom of the scholar who gives his obedience to the Magisterium, since he gives it to Christ himself. As the CDF's *Instruction*, no. 17, puts it: "[A]ll acts of the Magisterium derive from the same source, that is, from Christ, who desires that his people walk in the entire truth."

[46] Thus Cardinal Ratzinger's remark, issued at the press conference announcing the release of the CDF's *Instruction* (in *Origins* 20 [July 5, 1990]: 120 [margin]): "The panorama is much wider and much more beautiful than (the simple alternative of either confirming or dissenting from the statements of the Magisterium)." To quote the *Instruction* itself, no. 34: "The ultimate reason for plurality [of theologies] is found in the unfathomable mystery of Christ, who transcends every objective systematization."

against his own best judgment. These are worthy objections and will be addressed in the final section (section IV) of this essay.

Academic Freedom and the Mandatum

No one would deny that the greatest perceived threat to academic freedom coming from *Ex Corde* is this document's reminder to theologians that they "fulfill a mandate *(mandatum)* [to teach] received from the Church."[47] This reminder has certainly incited a firestorm of debate, much of it not without easy caricaturing or unfair criticism. More than anything else, this debate exposes the wide chasm separating a realist notion of academic freedom from a voluntarist one, since criticism of the *mandatum* has issued almost exclusively from an implied voluntarist mindset.[48]

Yet if the *mandatum* requirement is to be properly understood, we need to see it, I think, in close relation to the Magisterium's role as "authority" *(auctoritas)* argued above. That is, the *mandatum* testifies to the theologian's reliance upon magisterial teaching as a genuine well-spring and guidepost for theological reflection. We should see the *mandatum*, then, not as the Vatican's

---

[47] *Ex Corde*, Article 4, §3, which simply reiterates canon 812 of the *Code of Canon Law*, states: "It is necessary that those who teach theological disciplines in any institute of higher studies have a mandate from the competent ecclesiastical authority." On May 3, 2001, the U.S. Conference of Catholic Bishops ruled that canon 812 would have "the force of particular law for the United States" (though, in the sequel, the bishops have refrained from vigorously implementing this law). For its part, *Sapientia Christiana*, Article 27, §1, says: "Those who teach disciplines concerning faith and morals . . . do not teach on their own authority but by virtue of the mission they have received from the Church."

[48] For just a few examples of such criticism, one can cite the following. Claiming to hold the middle ground between "both popular Catholic conservatism and popular Catholic liberalism," Robert J. Egan ("The 'Mandatum': Now What?") warns that the *mandatum* requirement will have "a chilling effect on the academic freedom of Catholics . . . working in the field of theology" and will be "injurious to Catholic intellectual life, to the Catholic character and future prospects of Catholic universities." Jean Porter ("Misplaced Nostalgia: 'Ex Corde' and the Medieval University," 15) has "serious concerns" the *mandatum* requirement will wreak "negative consequences on Catholic theology" and will "undermine the freedom of the individual scholar." The former university presidents J. Donald Monan and Edward A. Malloy (" 'Ex Corde Ecclesiae' Creates an Impasse") assert that the *mandatum* requirement constitutes an "obvious threat to academic freedom" and that the Church "cannot conceal the fact that it is an instrument, however ineffective, to control what is taught and written." And Daniel Maguire ("Academic Freedom and the Vatican's *Ex Corde Ecclesiae*") sees in the *mandatum* a sorry attempt by the Vatican to implement "a system of oversight and control that would chill and even negate . . . theological duties and freedoms."

attempt to keep theologians on a leash. Rather, we should appreciate it for the positive signal it sends about the intimate bond linking the theologian to the heart of the Church's teaching mission. The CDF's *Instruction* (no. 22) even hails the *mandatum* as evidence of the theologian's "participation in the work of the Magisterium." To take a cynical line on the *mandatum* evincing such participation would simply make one's own bias on the issue transparent.

I am convinced, in fact, that the *Instruction* means participation in its most vibrant and robust sense. In the very least, the *mandatum* does not intend the theologian to take a distant, "third person," or "agnostic" approach to his discipline. I once heard a theologian say (somewhat voluntaristically) that he considered it his duty not to teach at all what he thinks, but only what the "Catholic Church" thinks. While it is true theologians discharge more the mind of the Church than their own mind per se, this does not mean the theologian's own mind is irrelevant. On the contrary, explaining and elucidating the faith *hinges directly* upon the theologian's own intellectual grasp of the matter. And since this grasp can never adequately measure up to the mystery of God, the theologian's probing of the faith (the faith proclaimed by the Magisterium), no matter how eloquent or brilliant, can always expand.

Furthermore, we need to recall, with Aquinas, that no discipline calls into question its starting points, or "argues in proof of its principles [or starting points]," least of all theology, whose starting points "are the articles of faith."[49] This means that the theologian, committed to First Truth as the object of his academic inquiry should, in the very least be presumed to accept the deposit of faith *as true*. Otherwise, if judgment is suspended on these articles of faith, the very nature of the discipline is radically altered. No longer is theology taught as predicated on a supernatural type of knowledge, as a human participation in God's own knowledge of himself, made possible by the gift of faith. Instead, it is taught as a purely human, natural type of knowledge. It is taught as a kind of "religious studies" (or "history of religions") discipline, since it assumes no intellectual assent on anyone's part, least of the professor, to the truth of the religious doctrines it examines.

Also problematic is when a theologian (in fact, another I know) thinks the *mandatum* allows him to teach both what the Catholic Church holds on the one side and what he himself holds (including dissenting views) on the other, provided that when he does this he makes it clear it is his "own opinion" and "not the Church's" he is presenting. Only under these conditions,

---

[49] *ST* I, q. 1, a. 8: "As other sciences [or disciplines] do not argue in proof of their principles, but argue from their principles to demonstrate other truths in these sciences, so this doctrine [i.e., theology] does not argue in proof of its principles, which are the articles of faith, but from them it goes on to prove something else."

as he confessed, did his "conscience" assure him he was teaching "Catholic theology in communion with the Church" as required by the *mandatum*.[50]

Leaving aside the confusion this can cause in the minds of undergraduates, such an approach borders on the attempt to set up "a parallel magisterium of theologians" warned against in CDF's *Instruction* (no. 34). After all, why insist on presenting one's own opinion alongside the Church's unless one is convinced the former is true (or at least more probable) and the latter is not (an undertone we can be sure is not lost on the students)? Is it not a misleading, disingenuous project when a professor professes to be teaching Catholic theology, which takes as its starting point the truth of the deposit of Catholic faith (of which the Magisterium serves as guardian), all the while making it clear he keeps this truth (as taught by the Magisterium) at an arm's distance? On this point, Aquinas insists that since revealed truth is made known and explained by those who understand it better, "those who have the task of teaching others are under the obligation to have fuller knowledge of matters of the faith, *and to believe them more explicitly.*"[51]

In its fullest sense, then, the *mandatum* ought to signify a committed believer who actively participates in the sacramental and moral life of the Church and who engages in the academic exercise of "reasoning in the faith": *fides querens intellectum.*

Complementary Roles for the Common Good of the Church

Before proceeding to the final section of this essay, there remains one matter for our consideration that touches on the relationship between the theologian's freedom and the Magisterium's authority, namely, the distinct yet complementary roles each exercise for the common good of the Church. This relationship is not merely one-sided, as if only the theologian depended upon the teaching authority of the Magisterium. The Magisterium, too, benefits from the invaluable service provided by the theologian. Devoting an entire section to the matter, the CDF's *Instruction* speaks of the "collabora-

---

50 To be fair, one could argue this theologian was simply observing what the American bishops, in their agreed-upon implementation of the *mandatum* requirement, decided to ask theologians: [N]amely, that they "refrain from putting forth as *Catholic teaching* anything contrary to the Church's Magisterium" (emphasis added). Still, it is ironic that such an obedience to the letter of the law (i.e., the law stipulated by the implementation document of the bishops) should come from a mindset determined to find a way to air dissenting theological views in the classroom. Furthermore, the Church in its *mandatum* requirement hardly intends theologians to adopt a minimalist mindset.

51 *ST* II–II, q. 2, a. 6; emphasis added.

tive relations" between Magisterium and theologian (nos. 21–31): Both share the same goal, namely, "preserving the people of God in the truth which sets free" (no. 21).[52]

The Magisterium works toward this goal by "authentically teach[ing] the doctrine of the apostles," as the *Instruction* (no. 21) puts it. One of preservation, the Magisterium's task is more "defensive" or "protective" in nature, since the Magisterium acts as guardian of revealed truth. As noted earlier, it receives the deposit of faith in its fullness and safeguards it from corruption and contamination. In its teaching this organ of the Church takes a more descriptive approach, as it relies heavily upon the witness of Scripture and tradition.

The theologian, on the other hand, takes the deposit of faith and seeks to clarify and explain it.[53] This makes the theologian's task less protective and more "constructive," inasmuch as it advances our understanding of the Christian faith to new levels. Often the theologian employs not merely a descriptive approach but a more abstract and speculative one. That is, theologians often pursue a distinctly deductive reasoning process, aided especially by the light of philosophical wisdom.

From this we can see how the Magisterium and the theologian share a natural kinship. They exercise complementary, not competitive, roles (the CDF's *Instruction* [no. 40] speaks of how the two should "interpenetrate and enrich each other"). The faithful expositor and guardian of revealed truth, the Magisterium acts as *auctoritas*, that is, source or font of theological thought (among other, greater fonts). Theologians take their cue from magisterial teaching as from a point of departure and as with a constant marker of the frontiers of their reflection. At the same time, if theologians depend upon the Magisterium to know what belongs to the deposit of faith, it is no exaggeration to say the Magisterium depends upon theologians to help the faithful better understand this same deposit. Moreover, the Magisterium often relies upon the insights, speculations, discussions, and debates of theologians in the formulation of its own teaching. Nothing could be more unnatural than theologians working without, or, worse, against, the Magisterium.

---

[52] Thesis 2 of the 1975 International Theological Commission's report *Theses on the Relationship between the Ecclesiastical Magisterium and Theology* (in Sullivan, *Magisterium,* 185) states: "This service [of Magisterium and theologian provided to the Church] must first of all maintain the certainty of the faith; this is done differently by the magisterium and by the ministry of theologians, but it is neither right nor possible to establish a hard and fast separation between them."

[53] "Theology, for its part, gains by way of reflection an ever deeper understanding of the word of God found in Scripture and handed on faithfully by the Church's living tradition under the guidance of the Magisterium." CDF, *Instruction,* no. 21.

Some Practical Concerns and Implications

As noted earlier, encouraging theologians to surrender their minds and hearts to the authority of the Magisterium out of a spirit of obedience may sound fine in principle, but some theologians might object that its practical payoff remains questionable. Take, for instance, the dilemma of making judgments on matters where the position of the Magisterium remains unclear, or where the theologian is convinced sound reason lies with the opposing argument, such as on the issue of artificial contraception, or on the question of women's ordination. Would obedience to the Magisterium under these conditions not look like the blind obedience that stifles individual creative thought? Would it not epitomize the other voluntaristic extreme, namely, an act of pure willing by assenting to magisterial judgment on the sole grounds such a judgment is imposed by a higher authority, an attitude that Ignatius of Loyola sums up well in his famous line: "[I]f (the Church) shall have defined anything to be black which to our eyes appears to be white, we ought in like manner pronounce it black"?[54]

Distinguishing a Non-Voluntaristic Act of Obedience from a Voluntaristic One

Without calling into question the edifying fruits that Ignatius of Loyola's directive can produce—after all, voluntaristic obedience to Church authority is better than no obedience at all—or suggesting that this great saint was consciously espousing a less than ideal form of obedience (voluntarism was after all deeply imbibed in the culture of his day, let alone in his experience as a Spanish soldier), we need to distinguish carefully a voluntaristic type of obedience from a non-voluntaristic kind (call it a realist type of obedience). This is all the more important for a contemporary audience, since the argument of authority in general, not to mention authoritative judgments proceeding from the Magisterium in particular, have come under assault in the modern period. For this period has witnessed, largely as a consequence of the success of the experimental method in the natural sciences, a special concern over what can be called critical rationality or "evidentialism."[55] According to this view all truth claims must be based on evidence, or at least on the probable weight of evidence, rather than on appeals to authority. How this

---

[54] Ignatius of Loyola, *The Spiritual Exercises,* trans. Charles Seager (London: Dolman, 1847), the thirteenth point under the heading, "Some Rules to Be Observed in order that We May Think with the Orthodox Church."

[55] I am grateful to James F. Keating and Gary Culpepper for bringing this point to my attention (in personal communication).

squares with the reasonableness of the act of faith, or with the reasonableness of theological truth claims, remains debated. Certainly, it has led some theologians, mindful that strict evidentialism would equate any final reliance upon authority with irrational belief, to search for probabilistic evidence in order to bolster the reasonableness of faith (à la Newman).

If we transpose this to the case of the theologian who, say, before the release of *Humanae Vitae* in 1968 had proposed probabilistic reasons in favor of the use of artificial contraceptives, we would seem to be left with but one conclusion: [H]is submitting to the Magisterium's judgment on this matter, expressed in *Humanae Vitae* (and in subsequent documents), would constitute not only a voluntaristic act of obedience but an irrational, fideistic-type one as well. The same would hold for the theologian advancing probabilistic evidence in favor of women's ordination at the time of the release of *Ordinatio Sacerdotalis* in 1994 and of the CDF's *Responsum ad Dubium* that followed in 1995.

Without wishing to launch into a discussion whose adequate treatment, including a detailed formulation of a position along Thomist lines, would require another essay altogether, we can at least say the following in the immediate interests of this essay.

The Act of Faith Flows from the Ordering of Higher Wisdom

We need to stress that, for the realist, the argument of authority in theology does not operate along voluntarist lines, as if revealed truth issued primarily from a supreme command of God's will. Instead, the authority that sits at the ultimate basis of all theological argument is identified with a supreme *wisdom*, that is, with an ordering of God's *mind*, and from this wisdom all else flows, including God's willful commands. A realist recognizes a higher wisdom, and thus a higher (intelligible) coherence—not simply a higher will—as the oracle of divine revelation.

To term such wisdom higher is to admit that the human mind cannot grasp it perfectly and that its truths can never be perfectly demonstrated: Theology, or sacred doctrine, "is wisdom above all human wisdom," to quote St. Thomas.[56] But to identify it with a wisdom and with an intelligible coherence is to affirm that the mind has access to a partial, imperfect, but meaningful grasping of it. Believing in this higher wisdom, in which the

---

[56] *ST* I, q. 1, a. 6. Also, in II–II, q. 1, a. 5 ad 2, Aquinas explains the nature of theological reflection: "The reasons employed by holy men to prove things that are of the faith are not demonstrations. They are either persuasive arguments showing that what is proposed to our faith is not impossible [this equates with the probabilistic weight of evidence characteristic of modern 'evidentialism' in theology], or else they are proofs drawn from the principles of faith, i.e., from the authority of sacred Scripture."

act of faith consists, is therefore never purely willful, or fideistic. It is an informed assent—faith is always "thinking with assent"—that is, a choice of the will to push the mind to accept as true that which the mind, despite the lack of demonstrative evidence, is drawn.[57] Ordering the mind to First Truth, the act of faith implies a coherence and a wisdom—which the very discipline of theology, for its part, attempts to show.

The coherence and wisdom inherent in the deposit of faith is guaranteed to rest, by virtue of its office as infallible guardian of revealed truth, upon the Magisterium's definitive teaching (though on the *content alone* of this teaching, and not on the circumstances surrounding its formulation). Of course, divine protection only extends to the Magisterium's teaching on faith and morals. But the latter includes, as *Humanae Vitae* famously affirms, matters of the natural moral law, that is, truths pertaining to the moral order that are otherwise accessible to human reason alone.[58] The higher wisdom, which is the oracle of revealed truth, is at the same time the Author of the natural order with its inscribed moral laws.[59] With legitimate—and infallible—authority, then, does the Church make definitive pronouncements on matters of the natural law (e.g., artificial contraception, same-sex unions, stem-cell research). In a world where no human mind is guaranteed an infallible grasp even of truths relating to the natural moral order, but where human flourishing hinges directly upon good moral conduct, such unerring teaching authority that is inclusive of both supernatural and natural truths marks one of God's greatest gifts to the Church.

When the Church, therefore, invites the theologian to adopt a spirit of obedience (or of *religiosum obsequium*) toward the Magisterium, it is not

---

[57] "Faith implies assent of the intellect to that which is believed. . . . [This happens] through an act of choice." Aquinas, *ST* II–II, q. 1, a. 4; cf. as well q. 2, a. 1; and q. 2, a. 2, which states: "'[T]o believe' is an act of the intellect, insofar as the will moves it to assent."

[58] *Humanae Vitae*, no. 4, writes: "[T]he Church is competent in her Magisterium to interpret the natural moral law. . . . (Christ) constituted (the Apostles) as the authentic guardians and interpreters of the whole moral law, not only, that is, of the law of the Gospel but also of the natural law. For the natural law, too, declares the will of God and its faithful observance is necessary for men's eternal salvation." Later in no. 18, the encyclical affirms that the Church is the servant of the natural law, in a way that echoes *Dei Verbum*'s statement that the Magisterium serves the Word of God: "Of such [natural] laws the Church was not the author, nor consequently can she be their arbiter; she is only their guardian and their interpreter. It could never be right for her to declare lawful what is in fact unlawful, since that, by its very nature, is always opposed to the true good of man." English translation: *The Pope Speaks* 13 (1969): 329–46.

[59] As Aquinas writes in *ST* I, q. 1, a. 6 ad 1: "Sacred doctrine [theology] derives its principles . . . from the divine knowledge, through which, as through the highest wisdom, all our knowledge [including that of the natural moral order] is set in order."

simply asking for a submission to a higher will per se (the voluntarist view), or for a submission of pure willing. Rather, a realist spirit of obedience implies an assent to the wise ordering of First Truth, albeit communicated through a human medium composed of very fallible individuals but whose definitive pronouncements on matters of faith and morals enjoy infallible protection. In a passing comment, Aquinas notes how the act of faith "proceeds from the will obeying God."[60] Put in other terms, the act of faith of its very nature implies an act of obedience (which is an act of the will), all the while consisting first and foremost in an assent of the mind. Since the Magisterium is divinely protected in what it declares conforms to the object of faith, First Truth, we should see obedience to the Magisterium as a participation in the obedience to God that is integral to the act of faith itself.

Concrete Application: Obedience Not at Odds with Intellectual Engagement

Let us apply the foregoing to the problematic case of the theologian who has employed his reason to reach one judgment (via a probabilistic form of reasoning), only to have the Magisterium judge for the other side. Again, on the surface any act of obedience under these conditions might seem like a blind, voluntaristic submission of calling black what appears as white. The theologian is asked to give assent against his own best judgment and to surrender his mind, as if heeding the ordering of a supreme will.

But a non-voluntarist act of obedience, even under these conditions, marks a different reality altogether, as it flows from a distinctly, if subtly, different undercurrent. It flows from an ordering that draws the mind, enlightened by faith, into a higher wisdom beyond itself. The realist universe is wisdom-centered, not will-centered, even if a supreme will owns its rightful place in it. At all points the theologian is invited, in his very act of obedience, not just to "will" with the Church (the voluntarist way), but to "think" (*and* will) with the Church (the realist way). Here is how such "thinking and willing" with the Church might look concretely in the dilemma at hand.

At the outset, said theologian should recognize that the reasoning process he pursues is never guaranteed of being divinely protected, whether on matters concerning the natural law (e.g., artificial contraception) or on matters of faith that reason can never purely demonstrate anyway (e.g., women's ordination). Since the act of faith draws the mind into a wisdom beyond itself, theologians must accept the fact that they are never assured of an unerring grasp of this higher wisdom, even if they think the "probabilistic evidence" supports their

---

[60] *ST* II–II, q. 4, a. 2, obj. 2; cf. as well q. 2, a. 5 ad 3: "The act of obedience consists in the promptness of the will subject to authority."

own judgment. This is not to deny, of course, the real possibility that any given judgment a theologian reaches might very well correspond to the truth. But it also means the probabilistic evidence a theologian might put forward in favor of some position is hardly immune from criticism or correction, particularly from that authority whose definitive judgments are infallible.

And even where the definitive nature of the Magisterium's teaching remains debated or unclear, it is better to trust that authority whose definitive judgments, including those that issue from its *ordinary* teaching, enjoy divine protection.[61] As we all know, theologians continue to debate whether the judgments of such documents as *Ordinatio Sacerdotalis* or *Humanae Vitae* constitute definitive teaching. But this should matter little in the concrete, for it does not follow that we can regard such teaching as if it were *non-definitive* while its definitive nature remains open to debate. Recall how the CDF's *Instruction* (no. 33) rightly denounces as "positivist" the opinion by which theologians think they are not bound to any "non-infallible" magisterial teaching.

In its teaching, then, and because of the divine assistance standing behind it, the Magisterium is always inviting the theologian into the higher wisdom of the faith (even on matters where this organ of the Church leans upon the assistance of theologians). So when a theologian comes to learn that his position stands at odds with the Magisterium's, he can rest assured that the intelligibility of God's higher wisdom has been presented to him by the Church's infallible guide (again, insofar as the *content* of magisterial teaching is concerned, and not in the way it is worded or *how* it is pre-

---

[61] It is precisely the infallibility of the Magisterium's ordinary teaching (what theologians call the "ordinary Magisterium") that *Lumen Gentium*, no. 25, is talking about when it writes: "[The Church's bishops] proclaim Christ's doctrine infallibly whenever, *even though dispersed through the world,* but still maintaining the bond of communion among themselves and with the successor of Peter, and authentically teaching matters of faith and morals, they are in agreement on one position as definitively to be held" (emphasis added). The pope, for his part, shares in the infallibility of the ordinary Magisterium in a unique fashion, precisely as head of the Church. With this in mind, the CDF's *Instruction*, no. 18, notes how "the documents issued by this Congregation [for the Doctrine of the Faith] expressly approved by the Pope participate in the ordinary Magisterium of the successor of Peter" (a reference is offered to Pope Paul VI's Apostolic Constitution *Regimini Ecclesiae*, nos. 29–40). CDF documents approved by the pope *may* therefore (though not necessarily) share in such infallibility, no matter Francis Sullivan's curious remark ("The Theologian's Ecclesial Vocation," 59) that "it is true that documents issued by the CDF participate in the ordinary (but never the infallible) magisterium of the Pope." This seems to assume that the pope is never infallible when his teaching (including the documents he approves) issues from the ordinary Magisterium of the Church.

sented).[62] Though such intelligibility had hitherto eluded him, said theologian should at this point open his mind and consider anew, even radically if need be, the argument. Cognizant of his duty to judge theological truth (or even natural truth when it falls under the purview of Christian doctrine) in light of magisterial teaching, he should reevaluate his thinking on the matter and consider where it may have gone astray. Then an informed, enlightened obedience ordered by the wisdom of First Truth can fall into place—a truly intellectual engagement.

If we think about it, such a reasoning process, whereby authoritative judgment triggers a radical reconsideration and eventual revision of one's views, happens to all of us quite regularly in many areas. For example, consider a current debate on economic reform taking place among the countries of the European Union. Many economists are convinced that the way to boost the sagging economies of various European nations (such as France) is to adopt the so-called "Anglo-Saxon way" of reform. This proposes free-market reform in the interests of an expanding global economy, but at the expense of many generous social subsidies and welfare programs. Let us suppose that one of these economists then speaks to a higher authority on the matter, such as the former prime minister of Finland, who had instituted free-market reform in the mid-1990s without sacrificing Finland's generous social subsidies and welfare programs. Such reforms acted as the spark that ignited Finland's now-booming economy. This opens the economist's eyes and he recognizes the viability of another way of reform (the so-called "Nordic way"), one that safeguards generous social subsidies and welfare programs. Instigated by an authoritative claim, he is led, through a critical reasoning process, to hold a position he had previously dismissed as untenable.

Is it naïve to expect the same could happen to the theologian who, say, favored women's ordination before *Ordinatio Sacerdotalis*, or who favored the use of artificial contraceptives before *Humanae Vitae*? For the realist, or for the one who does not look upon the authority of the Magisterium as an inherent menace to his autonomy as a theologian, the answer is no.

Of course, such reevaluation and eventual revision of one's views may take time, depending on the theologian and the specific issue in question, during which time said theologian "withholds assent" (a viable option, especially in

---

62 Often, such intelligibility is offered with tightly reasoned argument, as in the case of *Humanae Vitae* on the issue of artificial contraception, or, on the issue of women's ordination, in the CDF's "Declaration on the Question of the Admission of Women to the Ministerial Priesthood," *Inter insigniores,* issued on October 15, 1976 (in *Origins* 6,33 [1977]: 518–31). On the former, demonstrative reasoning is advanced, since it concerns a matter of the natural law, on the latter "probabilistic reasoning" (to use the modern terminology) or reasons of "fittingness" are given.

extraordinary cases). Perhaps he fails within any set time frame to recognize where his reasoning went astray, so that he continues indefinitely in his "withholding of assent." This is still viable, though not ideal, provided he adhere to magisterial teaching in the classroom, particularly at the undergraduate level, and when speaking to the public. Such adherence is still *reasonable* and not purely willful, in that he knows the judgment of the Magisterium shares in a supreme wisdom and coherence that is clear to God (at least), just not to him at the moment. If he wishes to dialogue over the matter—though "remaining silent without assent" (à la De Lubac) is certainly acceptable—this should be conducted in the appropriate scholarly journals and/or other professional or ecclesiastical fora.

In any case, we know "loyal dissent" (à la Charles Curran) is no option, since this verges on the attempt to set up "a parallel magisterium of theologians," which, as we saw, the CDF's *Instruction* excludes. And, besides, there stand many matters theologians either do not understand adequately or remain uncomfortable with. This does not mean they should "dissent" or even "withhold assent" from any one of them. For theologians, obedience to Church teaching means theologizing about the faith of the Church, as taught by the Magisterium, even when they do not understand it perfectly themselves.

The Role of the Will in Cases of Conflict

Whereas I have carefully distanced a realist or non-voluntaristic act of obedience from an act of pure willing, it is not as if the will plays no role in such obedience—obedience is, after all, an act of the will, and for the realist the goal is both to think *and* to will with the Church. Recall, too, that the very act of faith, while consisting primarily in an assent of the mind, implies an act of the will, indeed, an act of obedience (to God). For this reason Aquinas teaches that charity (a virtue pertaining to the will) informs and perfects faith.[63] Put in other terms, the degree of one's love for God—and for the Church—will largely shape the kind of faith one has, and, as a result, the type of theologizing one does.

As a result, we should not underestimate the role of the will in cases of conflict between theologian and Magisterium. There is always a voluntary side to every theological opinion one holds; as Aquinas says in a key passage, more than a propos here: In the act of faith (inclusive of the act of theological belief), "the intellect turns willingly to one side rather than to the other."[64] More to the point, we should not cast a blind eye to the way one's will often determines what one "wants" to hold theologically. We might won-

---

[63] *ST* II–II, q. 4, a. 3.
[64] *ST* II–II, q. 1, a. 4.

der, in fact, how many theologians refuse to accept the definitive judgment of *Ordinatio Sacerdotalis* on the question of women's ordination because they simply do not want to accept it, and turn to probabilistic evidence for cover. The same holds for theologians who withhold assent, let alone actually dissent, from *Humanae Vitae* or from other magisterial pronouncements.

Allowing Room for a Responsible Critical Regard for the Magisterium

After differentiating a voluntaristic spirit of obedience from a realist one, we should introduce further distinctions in order to show how the realist spirit of obedience does not require one to adopt a completely uncritical regard for the Magisterium. There is a distinction to be drawn, for instance, between particular judgments on specific matters (such as whether a particular war is just, or whether circumstances warrant a particular nation's use of the death penalty) from universal norms and principles that touch on essential matters of doctrine (such as the very principle that war does not constitute an intrinsic evil and can be just under certain conditions, or the very principle that capital punishment is not an intrinsic evil and that every state has a right to exact it).

Whereas the teaching of the Magisterium on the latter enjoys divine protection, the judgment of the pope and bishops on the former does not. (Indeed, an informed judgment on some particular war would in many cases require access to classified information that falls under the purview not of the head of a religious institution that transcends all national boundaries, but of the governmental officials of the respective nations involved in the war.) Cardinal Ratzinger, just before becoming pope, implied this important distinction when he affirmed, "there may be a legitimate diversity of opinion even among Catholics about waging war and applying the death penalty, but not however with regard to abortion and euthanasia."[65] What the theologian, as with any Catholic, is bound to accept as *de fide* are only those elements of magisterial teaching that are essential to Christian doctrine (including matters of the natural law). Aquinas calls them "those things which are clearly contained in the doctrine of faith."[66]

Does this mean that theologians, mindful of this distinction, should simply ignore what the pope proclaims, say, about Western military intervention in Iraq? By no means, since in his (fallible) judgment on this particular situation

---

[65] Cardinal Ratzinger offered these remarks in July 2004, in "Worthiness to Receive Holy Communion," which was a response to the dilemma raised by Catholic politicians who take positions on key moral issues, like abortion, in opposition to magisterial teaching and yet who present themselves for reception of holy communion when attending mass.

[66] *ST* II–II, q. 2, a. 5.

he may appeal to (infallible) universal principles binding on all Christians, such as the obligation to strive for peace and to love one's enemy.[67] In any case, the pope always speaks in the name of the Church, whether officially or not, and whether or not in his infallible teaching capacity. In the instance of military intervention in Iraq, a spirit of *religiosum obsequium* would demand that the theologian give proper deference to the pope's teaching, especially insofar as it bases itself on binding, univeral principles and norms, without necessarily accepting the particular conclusion the pope draws from such principles and norms.

As suggested above, we need also to distinguish the *content* of magisterial teaching from the *circumstances* surrounding its formulation. The gift of infallibility is of a very restrictive kind and only safeguards *what* the Magisterium teaches (i.e., its content), not *how* it formulates its teaching, *whether* it formulates it in the best manner possible, *when* it teaches it, or under all the other circumstances *by which* it issues it. This means the door remains open to the possibility of "inopportune" action on the Magisterium's part, to quote Cardinal Newman, who thought this about projected plans to have the doctrine of papal infallibility proclaimed at the soon-to-be convened ecumenical council (namely, the First Vatican Council). While he thought this doctrine was true, and that if decreed would be divinely protected, he feared its proclamation would cause more harm than good because it would dredge up past scandals of the papacy and because the doctrine was being handled more "as a move in ecclesiastical politics."[68] Whereas we can debate whether Newman's fears proved true, most theologians would agree the history of the Church does provide other examples of "inopportune," and thus imprudent, action on the Magisterium's part.

---

[67] In point of fact, in his message for the January 1, 2006, World Day of Peace, Pope Benedict XVI, while not addressing the particular situation in Iraq, noted that peace "cannot be reduced to the simple absence of armed conflict, but needs to be understood . . . as a harmonious coexistence of individual citizens within a society governed by justice, one in which the good is also achieved, to the extent possible, for each of them." The pope also reminds "the many soldiers engaged in the delicate work of resolving conflicts and restoring the necessary conditions for peace" that they should see themselves "as guardians of the security and freedom of their fellow-countrymen" and that "they too contribute to the establishment of peace."

[68] Newman, quoted in Ian Ker, *John Henry Newman: A Biography,* 652–54; this whole issue is well chronicled from 651–61. Ker additionally notes (655) that Newman feared that the definition of papal infallibility would incite "skepticism" and "secret infidelity as regards all dogmatic truth" among educated Catholics. Certainly this fear has proved true, though some theologians hardly "keep secret" their dissent from various doctrinal matters.

The theologian has legitimate grounds, therefore, to adopt a responsibly critical attitude (in scholarly journals and/or other professional or ecclesiastical fora, but not in the undergraduate classroom and never in public) regarding the wording and/or circumstantial nature of magisterial teaching. But the theologian never has justifiable grounds on which to object to, that is, dissent from, the content of such teaching, particularly when it is definitive.

Conclusion

In this essay I have attempted to show that from a realist perspective, central to *Ex Corde Ecclesiae* and the CDF's *Instruction*, academic freedom means not the scholar's autonomous right to say or teach whatever he wishes (a voluntarist view), but the scholar's responsibility to speak or teach in conformity with the truth. It means exercising one's duty to lead the mind to a firmer grasp of the truth, chosen as a good for the mind and as a good for the entire academic community. In the realist view, freedom is limited by, because inscribed in, the human person's natural inclination to a determinable perfection, namely, the human person's inclination to the truth (perfective of the mind) and to the good (perfective of the will). It is not a view where freedom stands before all else in some a priori manner, indifferent to truth as the object of academic study.

For the theologian this duty of teaching or speaking in conformity with the truth reaches a privileged rank, as the theologian is charged with the task of clarifying First Truth, revealed truth. The theologian best exercises his academic freedom, then, when he chooses to say or teach that which conforms to First, revealed truth. Since revealed truth is infallibly understood in light of magisterial teaching, the theologian makes responsible use of his academic freedom when he adheres to the teaching of the Magisterium, and abuses it when he dissents from this teaching. But such adherence, far from choking one's freedom, truly liberates the theologian's mind to excel at creative self-expression and to soar unto unprecedented heights.

Only when this realist vision of academic freedom becomes a reality can we hope to move beyond a polarizing contest of wills. Only then can we attain what *Ex Corde* and the CDF's *Instruction* herald as Magisterium and theologian exercising in concert their essential and complementary roles for the common good of the Church. Only then can theologians truly accomplish their invaluable work "from the heart of the Church" and know what it means to be both vigorously Catholic and rigorously academic. This theologian, for one, longs to see this day.

CHAPTER 6

St. Thomas's Commentary on Philippians 2:5–11: A New Translation with Introduction and Notes

Jeremy Holmes

VERY FEW STUDIES have been devoted to Thomas Aquinas's commentary on the letters of Paul.[1] This is a pity, because although the finest of Thomas's commentaries are those on the Gospel of John, Job, and the Letter to the Romans, after these masterworks it is without doubt the commentary on the Pauline corpus that holds the most value for theologians and exegetes. The present study seeks to imitate and extend the work done by Fr. Matthew Lamb in his translation of and introduction to Aquinas's commentary on the Letter to the Ephesians.[2] In the introduction, Fr. Lamb argues that Thomas's primary contribution to biblical studies was in the area of presuppositions rather than exegetical techniques; he then goes on to draw a portrait of Thomas as an exegete first in terms of his presuppositions and then in terms of his techniques.[3] I will attempt to extend Fr. Lamb's investigation of Thomas's

---

[1] Christopher Baglow, *Modus et Forma: A New Approach to the Exegesis of Saint Thomas Aquinas with an Application to the* Lectura super Epistolam ad Ephesios (Rome: Pontifical Biblical Institute, 2002); Wanda Cizewski, "Forma Dei, Forma Servi: A Study of Thomas Aquinas' Use of Philippians 2:6–7," *Divus Thomas* 92 (1989): 3–32; Otto Herman Pesch, "Paul as Professor of Theology: The Image of the Apostle in St. Thomas' Theology," *The Thomist* 38 (1974): 584–605; Waclaw Swierzawski, "God and the Mystery of his Wisdom in the Pauline Commentaries of St. Thomas Aquinas," *Divus Thomas* 74 (1971): 466–500; and idem, "Faith and Worship in the Pauline Commentaries of St. Thomas Aquinas," *Divus Thomas* 75 (1972): 389–412; and also idem, "Christ and the Church: Una Mystica Persona in the Pauline Commentaries of St. Thomas Aquinas," in *S. Tommaso Teologo*, ed. A. Piolanti (Rome: Libreria Editrice Vaticana, 1995), 239–50.

[2] Thomas Aquinas, *Commentary on Saint Paul's Epistle to the Ephesians,* trans. Fr. Matthew Lamb (Albany, NY: Magi, 1966).

[3] Lamb, intro., in Aquinas, *Commentary,* 3–36.

presuppositions and add some further detail to our picture of his techniques as an introduction to a fresh translation of Thomas's commentary on Philippians 2:5–11.

Christopher Baglow has argued that, due to his particular theory of inspiration, Thomas is more at home in argumentative texts such as Paul's letters than in narrative material such as the Gospel of Matthew.[4] While I would register some disagreement with Baglow's reasoning,[5] his observation is a real insight into Thomas's work: It is the argumentative format of Job that draws Thomas's attention and makes his commentary on that book a great one, and within the commentary on the Gospel of John one can observe a qualitative change between passages where Thomas must comment on the narrative and those passages where he can analyze the argumentative discourses of Jesus. Extending this principle, one can expect that the commentaries on Isaiah, the Psalms, and the Gospel of Matthew will not exhibit Thomas's strengths so clearly as will those on the letters of Paul.[6] One has only to compare Thomas's commentary on Matthew with Bonaventure's superior commentary on Luke to confirm this.[7]

Most immediately striking to the modern reader is the way in which Thomas treats the Pauline corpus as exactly that—a single corpus that can be commented upon as such. While there is little certainty about the dating of the Pauline commentaries, the consensus among scholars seems to be that Thomas commented on most or all of the letters of Paul earlier in his career, some time between the two Parisian periods, and then commented on Romans and possibly some of 1 Corinthians during his second Parisian regency. Despite the temporal spread of his effort, his preface to the (later) commentary on Romans clearly supposes that all of his commentaries on Paul are one work, and the prefaces to the (earlier) lectures on the individual letters

---

[4] Baglow, *Modus et Forma*, 23–29, 80–88.

[5] Even as Baglow describes it, Thomas's theory of inspiration is entirely compatible with a view of the evangelists (for example) as "narrative theologians," as thinkers who express their insights in narrative form. I rather suspect that the true reason for Thomas's comfort with argumentative texts was simply personal habit of thought: He was not a storyteller and did not think like one.

[6] Marcia L. Colish sees a similar, if not so pronounced, preference in medieval scholastic exegesis generally. See Colish, *Peter Lombard*, vol. 1 (Leiden: Brill, 1994), 188–90. Colish's discussion of medieval Pauline exegesis (189–225) provides an excellent historical framework within which to appreciate Aquinas's work.

[7] For the strengths of Bonaventure's commentary on Luke, see Robert J. Karris, "Bonaventure and Talbert on Luke 8:26–39: Christology, Discipleship, and Evangelization," *Perspectives in Religious Studies* 28 (2002): 57–66.

carry out the task proposed in the preface to the commentary on Romans. In that preface, Thomas offers a *divisio* of the entire Pauline corpus:[8]

I. All of the letters are about the grace of Christ. Nine letters consider the grace of Christ as it exists in the mystical body itself:

    A. This grace is considered in three ways. First, in itself, and this is how it is treated in the letter to the Romans.

    B. Second, in the sacraments which communicate it:

        1. In 1 Corinthians, the sacraments themselves are considered;

        2. In 2 Corinthians, the ministers of the sacraments are discussed;

        3. In Galatians, certain sacraments (namely those of the Old Law) are excluded;

    C. Third, in its effect, namely the unity of the mystical body, the Church:

        1. First, the unity itself is discussed:

            a) In Ephesians, the foundation *(institutio)* of the Church's unity is considered;

            b) In Philippians, the progress and confirmation of the Church's unity is set forth;

        2. Second, its defense:

            a) Against error, in the letter to the Colossians;

            b) Against persecution:

                (1) In the present in 1 Thessalonians;

                (2) In the future (and chiefly at the time of the Anti-Christ) in 2 Thessalonians

II. Four letters consider the grace of Christ as it exists in the chief members of the Church, namely the prelates:

    A. First, in the spiritual prelates, in 1 and 2 Timothy and Titus;

    B. Second, in temporal prelates, and this is how it is considered in the letter to Philemon;

III. One letter, that to the Hebrews, considers the grace of Christ as it exists in the head of the body, Christ himself.

---

[8] See *In Rom., prologus* 11.

Quoting this division in full, Otto Pesch remarks:

> The modern reader cannot believe his eyes: the medieval commentator stresses a picture according to which the most spirited and least systematic author of the New Testament sits at his writing table, far from the world, and meditates on the suitable division of a dogmatical monograph about the grace of Christ. The results were fourteen chapters which treat the whole topic in an exhaustive way and in a definite sequence. Only an unimportant accident diffused his monograph over the whole world in the form of fourteen letters. But that is Paul in the eyes of Thomas Aquinas![9]

Also quoting this division in full, Jean-Pierre Torrell comments in a similar vein:

> Today's reader, used to an entirely different approach to the Bible, whether scientific or pastoral, cannot help but be surprised at this systematic exposition. Thomas does not seem to realize that Paul's letters are nothing more than occasional writings and that nothing was further from the apostle's thinking than to wish to transmit so strongly constructed a teaching about Christ's grace.[10]

But Torrell adds a caution: "We must, nonetheless, not think Thomas more naïve than he was, nor that he imagined himself to have discerned all the richness of Paul's text."[11] Torrell's warning is a sound one, given the text immediately following Thomas's division of the Pauline corpus—a text quoted by neither of the above authors. Thomas raises an objection to his division to the effect that, from internal evidence, it would appear that 1 Corinthians was written before the letter to the Romans. So why is 1 Corinthians not placed first?

> The letter to the Corinthians is prior in time of writing. But the letter to the Romans is put first, both because of the dignity of the Romans, who ruled over the other nations, since in this letter Paul restrains pride, which is the beginning of every sin . . . and because

---

9 Pesch, "Paul as Professor," 585.

10 Jean-Pierre Torrell, *Saint Thomas Aquinas,* vol. 1, *The Person and his Work,* trans. Robert Royal (Washington, DC: The Catholic University of America Press, 1996), 256.

11 Ibid.

the order of teaching requires that grace be considered in itself before being considered as it exists in the sacraments.[12]

Thomas agrees that 1 Corinthians was indeed written prior to Romans, but argues that it is fitting for the letter to the Roman church to be placed first, and that the "order of teaching" required that Romans come first. Clearly, Thomas is aware that the letters were written at various times, and that Paul did not sit down at a desk and deliberate about how to organize a treatise. He even argues (in agreement with contemporary scholars) that Paul wrote a letter to the Corinthian church that never made it into the canon.[13] The ordering of the Pauline corpus is not something Thomas attributes to Paul at all, but to those who assembled the books in their canonical order.[14]

However, there is more to Thomas's *divisio* than the order of the letters: There is also the fact that these various letters *admit* of being arranged in the form of a treatise, a feat not possible with just any collection of letters. For this, one can only suppose that Thomas would appeal to the inspired nature of the Scriptures. This supposition is borne out by the fact that, in his inaugural lecture as a master at Paris, Thomas offered a comprehensive *divisio* of the entire Bible, and he was quite aware that no one human mind was responsible for the organization of both the Old and the New Testaments.[15]

---

[12] *In Rom.*, prologus, 12: "Sed videtur quod epistola ad Romanos non sit prima. Prius enim videtur scripsisse ad Corinthios secundum illud Rom. 16: commendo autem vobis Phoeben, sororem nostram, quae est in ministerio ecclesiae quae est Cenchris, ubi est portus Corinthiorum. Sed dicendum quod epistola ad Corinthios prior est in tempore Scripturae. Sed epistola ad Romanos praemittitur, tum propter dignitatem Romanorum qui aliis gentibus dominabantur quia hic confutabatur superbia quae est initium omnis peccati; ut dicitur Eccli. 10:14; tum quia etiam hoc exigit ordo doctrinae ut prius gratia consideretur in se quam ut est in sacramentis."

[13] *In II Corinthians* 1:15–16, 36. Thomas held that our 1 and 2 Corinthians were actually the second and third letters written, the first having been lost. Modern scholars have theorized beyond this that 2 Corinthians may be a conflation of more than one Pauline letter. For a summary of this discussion, see Raymond E. Brown, *An Introduction to the New Testament* (New York: Doubleday, 1997), 548–51.

[14] Current scholarship suggests that the principle used to order the letters of Paul may have been relative length. That is to say, allowing for groupings such as the Corinthian correspondence, for example, or the advantages of keeping the letters to Timothy and Titus together, the Pauline corpus proceeds from longest letter to shortest. For a detailed but easily understood discussion, see Jerome Murphy-O'Connor, *Paul the Letter-Writer: His World, His Options, His Skills* (Collegeville, MN: Liturgical Press, 1995), 120–26.

[15] *De Commendatione et partitione sacrae Scripturae*, in *Opuscula theologica*, vol. 1 (Rome: Marietti, 1954), 436–39. Cf. the translation by Ralph McInerny in *Thomas Aquinas: Selected Writings*, ed. and trans. idem (London: Penguin Books, 1998), 7–12; the

In other words, the hyper-organization Thomas perceives in the Pauline corpus is not due to an image of Paul as professor of theology but to an understanding of the Bible as an inspired whole.[16]

The import of this fact can only be grasped by following Paul's *divisio* at a more detailed level. We may take as an example the commentary on the letter to the Philippians. In his major division in the preface to Romans, Thomas describes the letter to the Philippians as setting forth the progress and strengthening *[confirmatio]* of the unity of the Church. In the preface to the commentary on Philippians, he clarifies this by stating that Philippians offers an example of the unity of the Church, due to the fact that the Philippians had progressed beyond other congregations with regard to unity.

As Thomas provides the divisions within the letter, it becomes clear that "example" is a major theme. Once past the greeting (1:1–2), Paul treats the past in 1:3–11, offering prayers for them, and so on. Then he offers his own past as an example for the Philippians in 1:12–24. After describing what is expected of himself in verses 25–26, he then lays out what is expected of the Philippians in 1:27–30. Pursuant of this expectation, he exhorts them to future progress in the rest of the letter, and first in chapter 2 by offering the

---

same is presented as a schematic chart in Michael Waldstein, "On Scripture in the *Summa theologiae*," *Aquinas Review* 1 (1994): 73–94. Note how the divisio of Paul's letters given above fits into the overall scheme of the New Testament in Aquinas's mind: The Gospels treat the *origin* of grace, Jesus; Paul of the power of grace (that is, as witnessed in the Church and the sacraments); Acts, the Catholic letters: and Revelation of the *working out* of grace in the world.

16 Nowhere does Thomas explicitly take up the question of whether the order of the canon is itself a subject of inspiration. *Which* books are in the canon is clearly a matter of inspiration and God's providence, whence one would expect the Bible as a whole to demonstrate some unity and coherence of content, but other features of the canon—the names of the books attributing them to this or that author, for example—are clearly not taken by the Church as inspired. The question is complicated by the fact that there are differing orders of the canon in differing traditions: The Septuagint, for example, does not have the same order as the Old Testament found in the Vulgate. Once the Christian canon was settled, the order of the New Testament remained fairly constant, but then again, the order of the books cannot have been determined until well after the death of the last apostle, making inspiration a difficult concept to apply. Brevard Childs, while an advocate of "canonical criticism," says in his book *The New Testament as Canon: An Introduction* (Philadelphia: Fortress Press, 1985) that "No great theological weight can be attached to the order [of the Pauline epistles] which continued to fluctuate within different textual traditions" (425). However, given the connection between context and meaning, I would urge from a Catholic perspective that the Church's role as primary interpreter of the Scriptures lends credence to the idea that the end product of the fluctuation of orders was subject to Divine Providence.

example of others: Christ (2:5–18), then Timothy and Epaphroditus (2:19–30). In chapter 3, Paul speaks of what they should avoid, offering himself again as an example of how to do that. Chapter 4 concludes with a moral admonition (4:1–9) and a thanksgiving for the Philippians' past kindness (4:10–23).

This internal division of the letter is remarkably coherent with Thomas's overall division of the Pauline corpus. For example, Thomas treats the Christological hymn in Philippians 2:5–11 more strictly as an example than his patristic and medieval predecessors[17] by seeing verse 6 as setting out the majesty of Christ "that his humility may be all the more commended" to the reader. Philippians 2:6, then, is ordered to 2:5–11 as rendering Christ's example of humility more striking and attractive; 2:5–11 is ordered to the whole of Philippians as an example meant to persuade the reader to follow the exhortation to unity in 1:27–30; the whole of Philippians is meant to offer an example of progress and strengthening in church unity to complement the discussion of the foundation of ecclesiastical unity in Ephesians; these two letters together set forth the unity of the church as the effect of grace; this consideration of the effect of grace is subordinated to the overarching topic of "the grace of Christ" in the Pauline corpus. From the whole corpus to a single verse, Thomas's *divisio* is a seamless garment.[18]

Clearly Thomas sees Paul's intention at work with regard to the internal divisions of the letter to the Philippians. Yet these internal divisions mesh perfectly as one whole with the larger divisions of the Pauline corpus, which Thomas must have attributed in some way to divine providence working by way of inspiration. Hence we can see an overlap of divine and human intentions in the internal divisions of the letter, which were obviously intended by Paul but must also have been ordered by a divine agent to the larger whole.

---

[17] See the historical review in Cizewski, "Forma Dei," 3–11.

[18] In addition to being rigorous and in a way beautiful, at unsuspected points Thomas's division seems to work! For example, Thomas takes Romans as treating "grace in itself." From the viewpoint of history, Romans is the one letter Paul wrote to a community he did not found in any way. By writing to them and explaining his teaching, he hoped to gain their support for his missionary work beyond Rome in Spain. In other words, Romans is in fact the one letter in which Paul lays out his "gospel" in a quasi-systematic way without addressing his thoughts to a particular error or practical need. He explains his gospel "in itself," to borrow Thomas's phrase. Another example is the letter to the Philippians, where Thomas's brief description of the purpose of the letter is almost exactly what modern commentator Peter T. O'Brien says about Paul's purpose in writing. See O'Brien, *The Epistle to the Philippians* (Grand Rapids, MI: Eerdmans, 1991), 36–37. O'Brien lists a few auxiliary purposes as well, such as the need to reassure the Philippians as to Epaphroditus's health.

It appears that Thomas does not stop to distinguish what the human author intended from what the divine author added to that intention.

This fact is all the more striking when we consider that the *divisio textus* is in fact an exegetical method.[19] To divide the text and discover the ordering of the parts to the whole is in fact to interpret the text's *meaning*; one can always get an overview of Thomas's interpretation of a book of Scripture simply by collecting into outline form his division of the text. If Thomas does not separate out the divine and human authors with regard to the structure of Paul's letters, it follows that he does not separate out the divine and human authors with regard to the meaning of the letters as well.

John F. Boyle has recently argued this same point from what Thomas says in the disputed questions *De potentia*.[20] Faced with the question of how to decide between various interpretations of a biblical text, Thomas offers two criteria: First, an interpretation must not contradict known truth; second, it must fit more or less with the context. If these two criteria are met, there is no reason why a single passage of Scripture cannot have any number of legitimate meanings. Thomas does not suggest that one must attempt to discern the author's meaning—*sensus auctoris* is a phrase Thomas uses only once, and then he argues that multiple meanings are possible.[21] The reason is that, as Fr. Lamb points out, Thomas sees God not only as inspiring the sacred author but also as disposing men and history precisely so that they might communicate his word as they did.[22] Paul's intention with regard to the letter to the Ephesians is only a part of God's overarching providential design into which the occasions of Paul's writing, his dispositions and thoughts while writing, and indeed all the circumstances surrounding the production of all the books of Scripture are subsumed. The divine intention encompasses and surpasses the human.

---

[19] Margherita Maria Ross, "La 'divisio textus' nei commenti scritturistici di S. Tommaso d'Aquino: Un procedimento solo esegetico?" *Angelicum* 71 (1994): 537–48, esp. 540–44.

[20] John F. Boyle, "Authorial Intention and the *Divisio textus*," in *Reading John with St. Thomas Aquinas*, ed. Michael Dauphinais and Matthew Levering (Washington, DC: The Catholic University of America Press, 2005), 3–8.

[21] *De potentia*, 4.1, resp.: "Whence it is not beyond belief that to Moses and the other authors of sacred Scripture it may have been divinely granted to know the various things which men are able to understand and to indicate them under one sequence of writing, such that any one of them would be the author's meaning" (Unde non est incredibile, Moysi et aliis sacrae Scripturae auctoribus hoc divinitus esse concessum, ut diversa vera, quae homines possent intelligere, ipsi cognoscerent, et ea sub una serie litterae designarent, ut sic quilibet eorum sit sensus auctoris).

[22] Lamb, *Commentary*, 8–9.

Boyle goes on to suggest that Thomas sees, not the human author's *sensus*, but the human author's *intentio* at work in the division of the text.[23] While agreeing with Boyle's fundamental thesis, I would argue on the basis of my analysis above that in practice Thomas simply does not stop to distinguish the divine and human authors either with regard to the meaning or with regard to the structure of the text. It is not that he perceives a distinction between them but chooses to ignore it; rather, such a distinction is not a mental habit operative for Thomas. As Pierre Benoit points out, Thomas and his contemporaries distinguished clearly between the literal sense of Scripture, which can be attributed to a human author, and the spiritual senses of Scripture, which can only be attributed to God, but they did not make our modern distinction *within* the literal sense between what Benoit calls the "primary" meaning of the text and the *sensus plenior*.[24] There are hints of this distinction in Thomas's discussions of Augustine's famous passage in the *Confessions* about Moses' meaning in Genesis, but it is not developed.

If Thomas assumes that the biblical text is divine, he also treats Paul's letters as human texts that proceed according to human methods. A comparison with contemporary scholarship is helpful here. Modern research into Paul's rhetorical strategies have yielded helpful insights into the text, in particular by revealing the essentially argumentative or persuasive nature of ancient discourse. There was a period earlier this century when scholars thought of Philippians as "artless" and "stream of consciousness," but more recent research based on ancient rhetorical practices has uncovered how carefully constructed is the entire letter.[25] Rhetorical analysis demonstrates that Paul's letters are organized around a *propositio*, the "thesis," so to speak.

According to a study by Duane F. Watson, the letter to the Philippians can be outlined in light of classical rhetoric as follows:[26] Philippians 1:1–2 is the standard letter greeting; 1:3–26 is the *exordium*, designed to capture the

---

[23] Boyle, "Authorial Intention," 7–8.

[24] Paul Synave and Pierre Benoit, *Prophecy and Inspiration,* trans. Avery Dulles (New York: Desclee Company, 1961), 147–51. While the spiritual sense is a meaning of the realities to which the words of Scripture refer, the *sensus plenior* refers to a deeper meaning of the words themselves, intended by God but not clearly intended by the human author. Some authors exclude the *sensus plenior* from the literal sense, choosing to call "literal" only what Benoit calls the "original sense." This difference in terms does not affect the point made in the present article. See Raymond E. Brown, "The *Sensus Plenior* of Sacred Scripture," (Ph.D. diss., St. Mary's University, 1955), 2–5.

[25] Duane F. Watson, "A Rhetorical Analysis of Philippians and Its Implications for the Unity Question," *Novum Testamentum* 30 (1988): 57–88; for his comment on scholarship of the recent past, see p. 57.

[26] Ibid., 57–88.

audience's attention and goodwill; 1:27–30 is both the *narratio*, relating the chief concerns to be addressed, and the *propositio* at the same time, as was allowed in the manuals. Philippians 2:1–3:21 is the *probatio*, in which the thesis is argued, using example and comparison as is typical of deliberative rhetoric. This long section is subdivided into 2:1–11, in which the *propositio* is revisited and the example of Christ is set forth; 2:12–18, containing further development of the thesis; 2:19–30, an extended *digressio* that provides further examples of the thesis in Timothy and Epaphroditus; and 3:1–21, in which verse 2 offers negative example and verses 3–21 positive example, the example of Paul himself. Philippians 4:1–20 is the *peroratio*, which is designed both to summarize the main points of the letter (4:1–9) and make a final emotional appeal to the audience (4:10–20).

If we return to Thomas's division in more detail, it is remarkable how closely it resembles Watson's modern analysis:

Salutation 1:1–2

Epistular Narration *(epistolaris narratio)*

   I. First, he treats of the past;

      A. He prefaces a thanksgiving for them 1:3–4

      B. He talks about the matter of what he has just said: the matter

         i. of the thanksgiving 1:5;

         ii. of his joy about the future 1:6–7;

         iii. of his prayer 1:8–11

   II. Second, he exhorts to future progress 1:12ff;

      A. He sets out examples to be followed and avoided;

         i. He shows what should be imitated;

            a) He puts himself forward as an example with regard to

- his progress 1:12–17
- the joy he has over his progress 1:18
- the fruit of his progress 1:19ff.
  - He sets out the fruit itself 1:19–21;
  - He raises a difficulty 1:22–24.
  - He solves the difficulty 1:25ff.

- He shows what is required on his part 1:25–26;
- He shows what is required on the part of the Philippians 1:27–30

  b) He puts others forward as examples chapter 2;
  - the example of Christ;
    - He prefaces an exhortation 2:1–4;
    - He brings in the example 2:5–11;
    - He draws conclusions from the example 2:12–18;
  - the example of his disciples, whom he hopes to send to strengthen the Philippians 2:19;
    - Timothy
    - Epaphroditus

ii. He shows what should be avoided chapter 3;

  a) He sets out those who are to be avoided 3:1–3;
  b) He shows how they are avoided by the saints 3:3;
  - how all the saints avoid them 3:3;
  - how Paul himself avoids them 3:4ff;

B. He offers a moral admonition chapter 4;

  i. He shows how they should conduct themselves in the future;

  a) He admonishes them to maintain what they have 4:1–3;
  b) He admonishes them to progress to what is better 4:4–9;

  ii. He commends them for the past 4:10ff;

  a) He sets out the commendation 4:10–18;

He concludes the epistle with a prayer and a salutation 4:19ff.

The similarity of the divisions made is remarkable, but perhaps the most important point of similarity between Thomas's division and Watson's is the role played by 1:27–30. Thomas sees these verses as expressing "what is required on the part of the Philippians," which accordingly will form the thesis to be supported by all the following examples and exhortations, just as it stands in Watson's outline.

That Thomas should have arrived at an outline so strikingly similar to an analysis based on ancient rhetoric is less surprising when we consider that Thomas, like all educated men of his age, was himself well versed in ancient rhetoric. Cicero's rhetorical treatises were standard fare in the thirteenth century, and Thomas also had the opportunity to study Aristotle's Rhetoric. In fact, the rhetoric current in Paul's day was familiar to all educated men until the nineteenth century, when the study of rhetoric fell out of style. Modern rhetorical criticism is not so much a discovery of new insight as a recovery of the old.[27]

However, Thomas does not rely directly on Ciceronian rhetoric for his division of Paul's letters, but on a newer medieval art which applied Ciceronian rhetoric specifically to letter writing: the *ars dictaminis*. The invention of this branch of rhetoric is usually attributed to Alberic of Monte Cassino in the eleventh century, but works on the subject proliferated between then and the thirteenth century.[28] In his work *Rationes dictandi*, written between 1119 and 1124, Hugo of Bologna makes the following interesting comment:

> We divide [prose orations] by a similar and suitable classification, for we say that plain prose is one thing, while that which is both prose and epistle is another. Examples of plain prose are the *dictamen* of Salust and Cicero. Examples of that which is both prose and epistle are [the letters] of Paul.[29]

As I am suggesting Thomas did, Hugo sees in Paul's letters an exemplar of the art of letter writing, closely related to Ciceronian rhetoric.

According to the medievals, a letter should follow a standard outline:[30]

1. *Salutatio.* The salutation expresses a greeting, conveying a friendly sentiment while not inconsistent with the social rank of the persons involved.

---

[27] The story of rhetoric from its beginnings in ancient Greece to its decline in the nineteenth century can be found in George A. Kennedy, *Classical Rhetoric and Its Christian and Secular Tradition from Ancient to Modern Times* (Chapel Hill, NC: University of North Carolina Press, 1980); for the middle ages in particular, see pp. 173–94.

[28] For an overview of the *ars dictaminis*, see James J. Murphy, *Rhetoric in the Middle Ages: A History of the Rhetorical Theory from Saint Augustine to the Renaissance* (Tempe, AZ: Arizona Center for Medieval and Renaissance Studies, 2001), 194–268.

[29] Ludwig Rockinger, *Briefsteller und Formelbücher des eilften bis vierzehnten Jahrhunderts* (New York: Burt Franklin, 1863, 1961), 55: "Quod particione tali congrue diuidimus, cum alius tantum prosam, aliud prosam et epistolam dicimus. Tantum prosa, ut dictamen Salustii et Ciceronis. Prosa et epistola, ut Pauli."

[30] For my research I used the texts in Rockinger, *Briefsteller*. This fundamental collection is quite useful for the number and variety of texts included, but the introductions are not always accurate and the texts not always critical. For a listing of critical

2. *Captatio benevolentiae* or *exordium*. After the greeting, the author had immediately to secure the attention and goodwill of his reader.

3. *Narratio*. The narration presents an orderly account of the matter under discussion, and an explication of the author's intention.

4. *Petitio*. The "petition," as its name implies, requests something, but under this heading also fall didactic, exhortatory, admonitory, or even menacing discourses.

5. *Conclusio*. The conclusion need not be anything more than a brief closing line, but is often used as an occasion to sum up the points made in the letter and point out their advantages and disadvantages.

An author did not have to include every part of the outline, nor was it always necessary to follow precisely this order of parts. For example, the author of the *Rationes dictandi* says that a letter can consist of a *salutatio* and *narratio* alone, or of a *salutatio* and *petitio* alone, the *exordium* and *conclusio* being more dispensable.[31]

This outline explains some of the differences between the classical terminology in Watson's outline, drawn from ancient rhetoric, and Thomas's description of the *divisio textus*. While the *narratio* in ancient usage referred to a statement of the thesis with perhaps a short explication of the meaning of the thesis, Thomas's *epistolaris narratio* is much broader, encompassing as well the arguments for the thesis. The *probatio* in Watson's outline has become the *petitio* (exhortation) in Thomas's division, comprising exhortation and admonition. Thomas's outline of 4:1–9 captures the same insight as Watson's label *peroratio* inasmuch as he sees the moral admonition presented there as built on the preceding examples, but for Thomas the letter conclusion is the brief paragraph at 4:19–23.[32]

---

editions, see James J. Murphy, *Medieval Rhetoric: A Select Bibliography,* 2nd ed. (Toronto: University of Toronto Press, 1989), 82–96.

Of the texts in Rockinger, seven discussed the parts of a letter: *Alberici cassinensis rationes dictandi,* 9–28 (the attribution to Alberic is mistaken); *Hugonis bononiensi rationes dictandi prosaice,* 53–88; *Ars dictandi aurelianensis,* 103–14; *Summa prosarum dictaminis,* 208–346; *Ludolfi magistri summa dictaminum,* 359–400; *Conradi summa de arte prosandi,* 417–82; *Baumgartenberger formularius de modo prosandi,* 725–834. The list I have provided of the parts of a letter is identical to those given by all but Hugh, who omits the *petitio*.

[31] Rockinger, *Briefsteller,* 22–23.

[32] Watson depends quite heavily on Quintillian, but substantially the same outline for a speech can be found in texts Thomas read and cited: see Pseudo-Cicero's *Rhetorica ad Herrenium,* bk. 1, ch. 3; and Aristotle's *Rhetoric,* bk. 2, chs. 13–19.

Treatises on the *ars dictaminis* focused on the *salutatio* and the *captatio benevolentiae*, mostly treating of the remaining parts of the letter in terms of stylistic ornamentation, so it is difficult to discern any influence on Thomas's commentaries within these sections.[33] The particular concern in the *salutatio* that the social rank of the persons involved be taken into account can be seen in his commentary on Philippians 1:1: "Paul and Timothy, servants of Jesus Christ, to all the saints in Christ Jesus who are at Philippi, with the bishops and deacons." Thomas notes that the congregation is mentioned before the bishops, and asks why the lesser have been named before the greater. He responds that the people are prior to the prelate, the flock to the shepherd, insofar as the notion of a shepherd presupposes that of a flock.[34]

Thomas does not follow the standard letter outline of the medieval *ars dictaminis* in a mechanical way. He does not always give an explicit label to each part of the letter; for example, he does not call the last part of Philippians the *conclusio*, but describes how it functions within the letter: "Paul ends [*finit*] the letter with a prayer."[35] With his penchant for divisions into two and three parts, he often describes everything after the salutation as the *epistolaris narratio* instead of distinguishing the exhortation and the conclusion as parts outside of the narration. In his division of the letter to the Ephesians, however, Thomas follows the standard outline more closely:

First he sets out the salutation, in which he demonstrates his affection for them [1:1–2];

Second, the narration, in which he strengthens them in good habits . . . [1:3–23];

Third, the exhortation, in which he urges them to further good things [4:1–6:9];

Fourth, the conclusion of the epistle, in which he fortifies them for spiritual combat. . . . [6:10–24][36]

---

[33] Cf. Murphy, *Rhetoric in the Middle Ages*, 225.

[34] In Phil. 1:1, no. 6: "Quaestio est quare minores praeponit maioribus? Quia prius est populus quam praelatus. . . . Greges enim pascendi sunt a pastoribus, non e converso."

[35] *In Phil.* 4:19, no. 180.

[36] *Super ad Ephes.* 1:1, no. 3. "Primo ergo ponit salutationem, in qua suum affectum ad eos demonstrat; secundo narrationem, in qua eos in bonis habitis confirmat, ibi benedictus deus, etc., usque ad IV cap.; tertio, exhortationem, in qua eos ad ulteriora bona provocat, a cap. IV usque ad locum illum cap. VI de caetero, fratres, confortamini in domino, etc.; quarto epistolae conclusionem, in qua eos ad certamen spirituale confortat a loco isto de caetero, usque in finem."

Apart from the optional *captatio benevolentiae*, each part of the standard outline is given here by its proper name (note the conveyance of a friendly sentiment in the salutation). In modern terms, we would say that Thomas is analyzing the text according to its literary genre: While familiar with the rhetoric of Cicero, he has chosen to use the conventions proper to letter writing (as he knew it) in his division of the text.

As we proceed to a more detailed look at the commentary on Philippians 2:5–11, we find some areas in which Pesch's criticisms may be more justifiable. Thomas appears to assume that Paul was versed in the philosophy of Aristotle and that he wrote in the manner of an Aristotelian. For example, commenting on 2:6 [54], "though in the form of God," Thomas remarks that a thing falls into a genus or species by reason of its form, so that the form can be called the nature of a thing; to be "in the form of God" is to be in the nature of God. But then he wonders why Paul did not simply say "nature" if he meant nature. The reason, he suggests, is that "form" fits more neatly with certain names given to Christ: For example, Christ is called the Son of God, that is, the one begotten by the Father, and the terminus of *generatio* is the form. In other words, Thomas takes the Aristotelian analysis of generation in terms of matter and form to be at play in Paul's choice of words. To this extent, he does seem to envision Paul as a professor, learned in philosophy and speaking the language of the schools. While the *sensus plenior* explains how Paul could speak more of the truth than he realizes, it does not seem that inspiration would cause a human author to employ the technical terms of particular schools of philosophy. Thomas's error is more understandable if we recall that he had a justifiable sense of continuity with Paul's intellectual world, as was established above with respect to the rhetorical traditions—a world that was shaped in some respects by Aristotle, if not in the ways in which Thomas assumed.

A closer examination of the text in question exposes the difficulty, while at the same time opening the way to a partial solution. The word translated in Philippians 2:6 by the Latin *forma* is μορφή, which in its root meaning refers to that which is exteriorly perceptible, and is difficult at times to distinguish from the related words εἶδος and σχῆμα. Although μορφή is a word Aristotle used to mean "form" in the technical sense of the term of generation,[37] contemporary scholarship has shied away from seeing Paul's use of the word in Philippians 2:6 as informed by Aristotelian philosophy. By Paul's day, the word had largely fallen out of use among the schools of philosophy, and in any case no longer carried the technical sense Aristotle had given it.[38] More probably, in the opinion of many researchers, the word

---

[37] See J. Behm, morfh, in *TDNT*, vol 4, 744–45.

[38] Ibid., 745 and 751–52.

bore its Septuagintal nuance of God's "exterior appearance," that is, the glory of God; Christ was "in the glory of God," as though the glory of God were a garment in which he was clothed.[39]

This view is often framed in opposition to J. B. Lightfoot's argument that μορφή is used "in a sense substantially the same which it bears in Greek philosophy" (that is, Plato and Aristotle), but Lightfoot's position deserves consideration:

> In accepting this conclusion we need not assume that St Paul consciously derived his use of the term from any philosophical nomenclature. There was sufficient definiteness even in its popular usage to suggest this meaning when it was transferred from the objects of sense to the conceptions of the mind.[40]

In other words, Paul may have gravitated to words like μορφή to express the inner reality of a thing for the same reason Aristotle did, because such a usage is not foreign to the common meaning of the word but a natural sharpening of it. Even those who interpret μορφή as "glory" go on to say that the glory of God is, of course, expressive of his being, and that to share in the glory of God is to share in God's being.[41] Thomas himself makes this point in his commentary on Philippians 2:11, number 73.[42]

It is not my intention to engage all the vast literature on Philippians 2:6, one of the most hotly debated verses in the New Testament.[43] I have chosen

---

[39] See the history of research in Ralph P. Martin, *A Hymn of Christ: Philippians 2:5–11 in Recent Interpretation & in the Setting of Early Christian Worship* (Downer's Grove, IL: Intervarsity, 1997), 99–133; and especially O'Brien, *The Epistle to the Philippians,* 206–11.

[40] Lightfoot, *St. Paul's Epistle to the Philippians* (Peabody, MA: Hendrickson, 1987), 132–33.

[41] See O'Brien, *The Epistle to the Philippians,* 210–11.

[42] While modern translations render Philippians 2:11 as "all tongues confess that Jesus Christ is Lord, to the glory of the Father," Thomas's Latin text offers the (grammatically plausible) rendering "all tongues confess that Jesus Christ the Lord is in the glory of the Father." Thomas notes that to be "in the glory" of the Father is to be in his nature, but draws out a contrast between the Latin word *forma* in v. 6 and the word *gloria* in v. 11: *forma* points the nature as it is in itself, while *gloria* adds the idea of being known by others. This, Thomas argues, fits with the progression of the story, because 2:5 refers to the point when Christ's divinity was unknown to others while 2:11 describes how Christ was exalted by having his divinity made known to all, so that "what he had from eternity, he will make known to all, as it says in John 17:5, 'Glorify me, Father, with the same glory which I had from You before the world began.'"

[43] See the histories of research in Martin, *A Hymn of Christ,* and O'Brien, *The Epistle to the Philippians.*

one mainstream interpretation of μορφή to illustrate the possibilities of Thomas's philosophical approach to Paul's letters. It must be admitted that his implicit investment of Paul with the training and vocabulary of an Aristotelian scholastic is unfortunate. But because scholastic philosophy is a "common-sense philosophy" grounded in the senses and the common usage of words, taking Paul's words in an Aristotelian sense does not always lead one too far astray. Another example of this is Thomas's commentary on Philippians 2:7 [58], "taking the form of a servant." Why does Paul not say "taking a servant"? Because, Thomas explains, "servant" is the name of a hypostasis or supposit: To say "taking a servant" would be to suggest some form of adoptionism. This is a valid insight even if Paul did not think of it in those terms. We do not need to see Paul as employing Aristotelian "form" and Nicene "hypostasis" to suppose he would have shied away from a phrasing that would in fact suggest that Christ was a glorified man rather than a humbled deity.

As the above discussion has illustrated, Thomas was entirely dependent on Latin translations of the Bible. Unless he found linguistic comments in the glosses or in one of the Fathers' commentaries, he worked with the Latin text as it stood and with all the nuances carried by the Latin words.[44] A good example is his comment on 2:5, number 52. Modern translations often render this verse "have this mind among yourselves which was also in Christ Jesus": Thomas's Latin text read *hoc sentire in vobis*, literally "sense this in yourselves." The semantic domains of Greek φρονέω and Latin *sentire* overlap inasmuch as each refers to an interior act, "to think" or "to feel," but the connotation of φρονέω is exclusively interior while *sentire* is rooted in the world of the exterior senses. Thomas lights on the bodily connotation of *sentire*, thus straying from the underlying Greek text, but the result is a moment of mystical theology well worth the loss in linguistic precision. We must "sense" Christ by each of the five senses, seeing his glory, hearing his wisdom, smelling the grace of his meekness, tasting the sweetness of his tenderness, and touching his power, that we may be enlightened, beatified, attentive, beloved of God, and saved. To each mystical "sensing" of Christ corresponds

---

[44] Hugh Pope shows that Thomas was familiar with a larger number of Greek words than one might at first suppose, and was acquainted with a handful of transliterated Hebrew phrases, but admits that, like most of his contemporaries, he relied on the Vulgate for his knowledge of Scripture. See Pope, "St. Thomas as an Interpreter of Holy Scripture," *St. Thomas Aquinas, Being Papers Read at the Celebrations of the Sixth Centenary of the Canonization of Saint Thomas Aquinas* (Oxford: Basil Blackwell, 1925): 111–44. For more on Aquinas's Greek vocabulary, see Adriana Caparello, *Esegesi aristotelico-tomista e terminologia greca* (Vatican City: Libreria Editrice Vaticana, 1979).

a conformity to Him: "And thus 'sense,' as though touching [Christ] by the imitation of his deed."

An outline of Thomas Aquinas as an interpreter of Paul begins to emerge from all that has been said to this point. He worked comfortably with Paul's letters as authored by God, but treated them simultaneously as achievements of human artifice. His acquaintance with ancient rhetoric coupled with his strong sense of the flow of an argument gave him a sound grasp of the division of the text. His perception of Paul as an Aristotelian philosopher turns out to have been historically mistaken, but the nature of the "common-sense philosophy" mitigates the damage done by his error. Like many of his contemporaries, he depended on translations for his exegetical work, and this sometimes led him astray; but so profound are his theological reflections that even these moments of linguistic misfortune can make for profitable reading.

A few remarks are in order about the translation below. F. R. Larcher already translated the entire commentary on Philippians, but a new translation of this section seemed desirable for several reasons.[45] Larcher's translation has no notes of any kind. According to the convention of the series in which he published the volume, he bound himself to using the RSV for all Scripture quotations instead of translating the citations as they stand in Thomas's text. This makes it impossible to see the verbal connections between text and comment; when the translation available to Thomas differs significantly from the RSV, it can be difficult to understand his comments. Last and most important, my hope is that republishing this commentary on an important doctrinal text, and in a format more useful to scholars, will stimulate further research into Thomas's commentaries on the Pauline corpus.

As there is no critical text of the commentary on Philippians, I used the Marietti edition as my base text.[46] The formatting of the translation duplicates the helpful numbering and paragraph breaks of the Marietti edition. I also compared the Marietti text with the Parma edition, which has some footnotes about variant manuscripts. Where the Marietti and Parma editions differ, I have mentioned it in a footnote; when both editions agree but the Parma edition indicates that there are manuscript variants, I include the variants in a footnote with the phrase, "Some manuscripts say. . . ."

---

[45] Thomas Aquinas, *Commentary on Saint Paul's First Letter to the Thessalonians and the Letter to the Philippians,* trans. F. R. Larcher and Michael Duffy (Albany, NY: Magi, 1969).

[46] *Super epistolas sancti Pauli lectura,* vol. 2, ed. P. Raphaelis Cai (Turin/Rome: Marietti, 1953).

Aquinas on Philippians 2:5–11

Chapter 2, Lecture 2

v. 5 [n. 51] *Sense this* [hoc sentite][47] *among yourselves which was also in Christ Jesus.*

v. 6 [n. 53] *Who, though he was in the form of God, did not judge it robbery to be himself equal to God;*

v. 7 [n. 56] *But emptied himself, taking the form of a servant, being made to the likeness of men, and in habit*[48] *found as a man.*

v. 8 [n. 63] *He humbled himself, being made obedient even to death, even the death of the cross.*

51. Having set out his exhortation, here the apostle exhorts [the Philippians][49] to the virtue of humility, by the example of Christ. And

first, he leads [them] to imitating the example of Christ;
second, he sets out his example, there [n. 53] at *Who, while in the form,* etc.

52. He says therefore: Be humble, as I have said, and so *Sense this,* that is, grasp by experience what was *in Christ Jesus.*

Note that one should sense this in five ways, namely by the five senses. First to see his radiance[50] so that, being enlightened, we may be conformed

---

47 The Parma edition has the word *enim* between *hoc* and *sentite*. The Greek text has φρονεῖτε, which has an exclusively mental semantic domain, but Thomas exploits the more physical connotation of *sentire* to arrive at a marvelous set of metaphors, worth having whether or not they reflect the original intention of Paul.

48 *Habitus* refers to one's condition or state, or outward appearances such as one's clothing or demeanor. The Greek word used by Paul (σχῆμα) has roughly the same span of meaning, although the primary referent in this case is the outward appearance of a thing. But the Latin *habitus* is also the perfect passive participle of the verb *habeo,* "to have," so Thomas—following Augustine—pursues the various ways *habitus* could refer to "a thing had." For Thomas, *habitus* would also have referred to one of Aristotle's ten categories of being. Because no English word covers all these possibilities, and because students of Thomas are accustomed to seeing *habitus* or "habit" used in English, I have simply left the Latin word as it stands in Thomas's biblical text.

49 Larcher supplies "them" in this sentence and in the next. In all such cases, however, I have put brackets around my suggestions, because it is not clear that Aquinas thinks of Paul as addressing "them." He may well experience the text as speaking directly to the reader and the reader's time, despite certain points in the text that require him to notice for a moment that the original audience was in the past.

50 "Radiance"—following the Parma text, *claritatem.* The Marietti edition reads *charitatem.*

to him. Isaiah 33:17, "Your eyes shall see the king in his splendor," and so on. 2 Corinthians 3:18, "But we all, with unveiled face, beholding the glory of God," and so on. Second, to hear his wisdom, that we may be made blessed. 1 Kings 10:8, "Blessed are your men, and blessed your servants, they who stand before you and hear your wisdom." Psalm 17:45, "As soon as they heard with their ears, they obeyed me." Third, to smell the grace of his meekness,[51] that we may attend to him. Song 1:3, "Draw me after yourself, we will run in the fragrance of your ointments." Fourth, to taste the sweetness of his tenderness *[pietas]*, that we may always be beloved[52] in God. Psalm 33:9, "Taste and see that the Lord is pleasant *[suavis]*." Fifth, to touch his power, that we may be saved. Matthew 9:21, "If I but touch the fringe of his garment, I will be saved."[53] And thus Sense, as though touching [him] by the imitation of his deed.[54]

53. Then when he says, *Who, though in the form of God,* and so on, he sets out the example of Christ. And

> first, he sets out Christ's majesty as a preface;
> second, he sets out his humility, [n. 56] at the words *But emptied himself,* etc.
> third, his exaltation, [n. 67] at the words *Because of this,* etc.

And first he sets out Christ's majesty as a preface, that his humility may be commended all the more.[55] And he sets down two things relating to Christ's dignity: first, the truth of his divine nature; second, his equality [with the Father], [n. 55] at the words *did not judge it robbery.*

54. He says therefore, *Who,* namely Christ, *though in the form,* and so on. For any given thing is said to be in the nature of a genus or a species through its form, whence the form is called the nature of a thing. And thus to be in the form of God is to be in the nature of God, by which one may understand that [Christ] is truly God. 1 John 5:20, "That we may be in his true son Jesus Christ."[56] But one must not think that the

---

[51] Some manuscripts omit "of his meekness" *[suae mansuetudinis]*.

[52] Some manuscripts omit the word "beloved" *[dilectus]*, as does the Parma text.

[53] Working from memory, Aquinas imports the word "fringe" from the previous verse of Matthew.

[54] Larcher omits this sentence altogether. It forms a powerful *inclusio* with the first sentence of the paragraph.

[55] "Commended" as an example: cf. the *Glossa ordinaria* (PL 114: 603C), *Praemittit alta de Christo, ut hi in quibus est locus abjectionis non dedignentur humiliari.*

[56] Thomas's biblical text matches neither the Greek original nor any version of the Vulgate available to us. It is unfortunate that we have not yet recovered the Latin Bible from which Thomas would have been working. See Weisheipl's comments on the text

form of God is one thing and God himself another: for in simple things and immaterial[57] things the form and that of which it is the form are the same, and [this is true] most of all in God.

But why does he say *in the form* rather than "in the nature"? Because this fits with the special names of the Son, in three ways. For he is called Son, and Word, and Image. Now a "son" is one who is begotten *[generatur]*, and the end of begetting *[generatio]* is the form. And therefore, to show that he is the perfect Son of God, he says *in the form*, as though [to say], having perfectly the form of the Father. Similarly, a word is only perfect when it leads one to knowledge of the nature of a thing; and thus the Word of God is said to be *in the form of God* because he has the whole nature of the Father. Similarly, an image is only called perfect if it has the form of that[58] whose image it is. Hebrews 1:3, "Being the radiance of his glory, and the figure of his substance," etc.

55. But does he not have [the form of God] perfectly? Yes, for *he did not judge it robbery*, etc.[59] This can be understood in two ways.

One way is in reference to his humanity, but Paul did not understand it this way, because this would be heretical; for it *would* be robbery, if it were understood with reference to his humanity.[60]

Therefore one must explain it another way, namely as said of Christ according to his divinity.[61] It flies in the face of reason to say otherwise, because the nature of God is not apt to be received in matter; the fact that something existing in some nature participates [in the nature of God] more or less is due to matter, but there is no [matter in the divinity]. Therefore one must say that *he did not judge it robbery*, namely *to be*

---

of Isaiah used in the preface of the commentary on John, in Thomas Aquinas, *Commentary on John*, trans. James A. Weisheipl and Fabian R. Larcher (Albany, NY: Magi Books, 1980), vol. 1, 447–49.

57 The Marietti text reads *materialibus*, but the correct reading is surely the Parma text: *immaterialibus*.

58 Marietti text lacks "of that" *[eius]*, present in the Parma edition.

59 *Sic, quia **non rapinam**, etc.* The Marietti edition mistakenly puts *quia* in bold print, as though it were part of the text of Philippians.

60 cf. the *Glossa ordinaria* (PL 114:603C), Vel, non est arbitratus se aequalem Deo esse secundum humanitatem, quod esset rapinam facere, id est, non suum praesumere.

61 Some manuscripts insert a few extra sentences at this point: "In one way, thus. *He did not judge it robbery*, etc., because it *would* have been robbery if it were referred to the humanity; but it is not speaking about this; but if it is said of the humanity, this is heresy, because John 5 [says]: 'making himself equal to God,' therefore He judged himself equal to God." This extra material seems to be a confused scribal repetition of material in the text above.

himself equal to God, because he is in the form of God, and knows his own nature well. And it is because he knows this[62] that John 5:18 says "he makes himself equal to God";[63] but this was not robbery, as it was when the devil or a man wished to be made equal to him. Isaiah 14:14, "I will be like the Most High," for example, and Genesis 3:5, "You shall be as gods."[64] But this was robbery; it was for this that Christ came to make satisfaction.[65] Psalm 68:5, "What I did not steal, I then paid for."

56. Then when he says *But emptied himself*, etc., he points out Christ's humility.

> First, as regards the mystery of the Incarnation;
> Second, as regards the mystery of the passion, there [n. 63] at
> he *humbled himself*, etc.
> Concerning the first,[66] he sets out Christ's humility;
> Second, its manner and form.

57. He says therefore *but emptied himself*, etc. But since he was full of divinity, did he not empty himself of divinity? No, because he remained what he was, and what he was not, he took up. But one must understand this with reference to his taking on what he did not have, not with reference to his taking on what he had. For just as he descended from heaven, not because he ceased to be in heaven, but because he began to be on earth in a new way, so also he emptied himself, not by setting aside the divine nature, but by taking on a human nature.[67]

---

62 Some manuscripts lack the word *ideo*, found in the Marietti and Parma texts, but this difference does not appear in my translation.

63 John 5:18, "This was why the Jews sought all the more to kill him, because he not only broke the Sabbath but also called God his Father, making himself equal with God."

64 The reference to Adam and Satan, with the attendant citations of Isaiah and Genesis, comes originally from Augustine's tractates on the Gospel of John, whence it passed into most later commentaries on Philippians, including the *Glossa ordinaria*. See Augustine, *Sancti Aurelii Augustini in Johannis evangelium tractatus CXXIV*, CCSL 36: Aurelii Augustini opera pars 8 (Turnhout: Brepols, 1954), 178, and the *Glossa*, PL 114: 603C; for further discussion, see Cizewski, "Forma Dei," 6–10.

65 Elsewhere (*In Sent.* 3, dist. 20, q. 1, art. 3), Thomas uses Philippians 2:7 to raise an objection: If Adam's sin was one of pride, then would not Christ's Incarnation alone atone for Adam's sin, without the cross? Thomas responds that Adam's sin included not only pride but also carnal delight, and so Christ's atonement fittingly included not only the humiliation of the Incarnation but also the bodily torment of the cross.

66 Following the Marietti text: *circa primum ponit*, etc. The Parma text reads *circa primum, primo ponit*, etc., while noting the absence of *primo* in some manuscripts.

67 In a disputed question on the Incarnation, Aquinas quotes Philippians 2:6–7 in the context of answering this same difficulty. There he notes that the person of the Word is the supposit of the divine nature, and so cannot extend itself to anything further. How

Yet beautifully does he say *emptied*. For the "empty" is opposed to the "full." Now the divine nature is plenteously full, because every perfection of goodness is there. Exodus 33:19, "I will show you every good thing."[68] A human nature, and the soul, is not full, but in potency to fullness; for it is made like a blank slate *[tabula rasa]*. Therefore human nature is empty. He says therefore *emptied*, because he took on a human nature.[69]

58. Hence he touches first on the assumption of a human nature, saying *taking the form of a servant*. For man is God's servant from his creation, and human nature is the form of a servant. Psalm 99:3, "Know that the Lord, he is God, he has made us and we are his."[70] Isaiah 42:1, "Behold my servant, I will uphold him," etc. Psalm 3:4, "But You, Lord, are my protector, my glory," etc.

Why is it more fitting to say *the form of a servant* than "a servant"? Because "servant" is the name of a hypostasis or supposit, which was not assumed—a nature was assumed.[71] For what is taken up is distinguished from the one who takes it up. Therefore the Son of God did not take up a man; for one would be led to think that the man was something other than the Son of God, when in fact the Son of God became a man. Therefore he took the nature up in his person, that the Son of God and the son of man might be the same in person.

59. Second, he touches on the conformity of [his] nature [to ours], saying *being made to the likeness of men*, namely according to species.[72] Hebrews 2:17, "It was fitting for him to be made like his brothers in all things."

---

ever, because the divine nature is infinite, and comprehends in itself all finite nature, the person of the Word was able to take on a human nature without extending himself beyond the divine nature. See *S. Thomae Aquinatis quaestiones disputatae* (Rome: Marietti, 1953), *Quaestio disputata de unione Verbi incarnati,* a. 1, vol. 2, 422 and 425.

[68] Larcher omits this scriptural citation.

[69] Cf. Aquinas's comment on Romans 9:28, *quia Dominus faciet super terram verbum breviatum*. As a second interpretation of the phrase, he says that the Lord will make over the earth a *verbum abbreviatum*, "that is, an incarnated [word], because the Son of God emptied himself, taking on the form of a servant. And it says 'emptied' or 'abbreviated' not because anything is subtracted from the fulness or magnitude of his divinity, but because He accepted our poverty and our littleness." *In Rom.* 9:28, no. 805.

[70] We hear "Lord" used for Yahweh so often that we tend to forget that it is a correlative of "servant." Aquinas stops his citation short at *Know that the Lord, He is God*, omitting the following words that actually make his point—a good example of how brief citations in medieval texts are meant to be understood by the reader in fuller form.

[71] Quia servus est nomen hypostasis vel suppositi, quod non est assumptum sed natura.

[72] The word *species*, from a lexical point of view, could mean either "species" or "appearances." The latter meaning is clearly not Aquinas's intention, as it would give a docetistic slant to the Philippians Hymn. He quotes Philippians 2:7 in *ST* III,

And if you say that it was not fitting for the Lord Jesus Christ to take on a species, this is true of what[73] would result from the divinity and the humanity, if the divinity and the humanity were to come together so to speak in one common nature. It would follow from this that the divine nature (if I may speak thus) would be changed.[74]

60. Third, he sets out the conditions of the human nature, saying *and in habit found as a man*, because he took up all the defects and properties accompanying[75] the species, except for sin. And this is why it says "in habit found as a man," namely in the exterior conduct of life, because he thirsted as a man, was tired, and so on. Hebrews 4:15, "One tempted in all things just as we are, without sin." Baruch 3:38, "Afterwards he was seen upon earth, and lived among men."

And in this way we can refer "habit" to exterior conditions.[76]

---

q. 5, a. 1, obj. 1 and reply, to point out that the "likeness" Paul speaks of is a likeness in human nature and not simply in outward appearance.

73 Following the Parma text, *verum est quae resultet,* etc. The Marietti text reads *verum est qua resultet,* etc.

74 Aquinas labors in this paragraph to find words to express the absurd, and his grammar shows the strain. Et si dicas quod in Domino Iesu Christo non convenit speciem accipere, verum est, qua resultet ex divinitate et humanitate. . . . The phrase *non convenit speciem accipere* lacks any grammatical subject. Larcher takes *convenit* as an impersonal verb: "It is not fitting to speak of a species in the Lord Jesus Christ." However, given the context of the commentary on Philippians 2:7, it seems preferable to think of *speciem accipere* as applying somehow to Christ. But in reality, were the proposed amalgamation of human and divine natures to take place, the person of Christ would cease to exist and some new hypostasis would take his place. Hence Aquinas leaves "the Lord Jesus Christ" dangling in a modifying phrase, suggesting itself as a grammatical subject but not actually playing the part. Both translations have something to commend them.

75 Following the Parma text, *consequentes,* instead of the Marietti text, *continentes.* The Marietti reading, noted by the Parma edition, is possible, and could be translated as follows: "properties making up the species."

76 Aquinas appealed to this verse in many different situations wherein the true humanity of Christ was at stake. In the *Summa* alone, he refers to this verse (often together with v. 8) with regard to whether there is a union of soul and body in Christ (III, q. 2, a. 5), whether the Son of God ought to have assumed a true body (III, q. 5, a. 1), whether it was fitting that the Son of God should assume defects of the body (III, q. 14, a. 1), whether we may say that Christ is subject to the Father (III, q. 20, a. 1), and whether it pertains to Christ to pray according to his sensuality (III, q. 21, a. 2).

61. Or *in habit*, because he took up humanity itself like a habit. Now there are four kinds of habit.[77] One changes the one who has it, and is not changed itself, as a fool is changed by wisdom. Another kind both changes and is itself changed, like food. Yet another kind neither changes nor is changed, like a ring placed on a finger. And there is another kind which is changed and yet does not change, like an article of clothing.[78] And by likeness to this [last] kind the human nature in Christ is called a habit, because it came to the divine person in such a way that it did not change him, but was itself changed for the better, because it was filled with grace and truth.[79] John 1:14, "We have seen his glory, glory as of the only begotten of the Father, full of grace and truth."

He says therefore *being made in the likeness of men*, yet in such a way that he was not changed, because he was *in habit found as a man*.

62. But one should be aware that some have erred because of this phrase *in habit*, etc. Hence three opinions are discussed in book 3, distinction 6 of the *Sentences*.[80]

---

[77] Larcher (80) adds here a gloss on *habitus*: "four kinds of habit, or ways of being 'had.'" See note 48 above. This discussion of four kinds of *habitus* originates with an exegesis of Philippians 2:6–7 in question 73 of Augustine's *De diversis quaestionibus* 83, which later became the chief text supporting the "third opinion" discussed in Peter Lombard's *Sentences*, bk. 3, dist. 6. According to this opinion, not only were Christ's soul and body not joined to form a single substance, but these elements of humanity related to Christ's divinity as accidents, being put on by the Word after the manner of an article of clothing. Thomas will take up these difficulties below.

[78] An article of clothing "is changed" inasmuch as it conforms itself to the shape of the one who wears it, but "does not change" the shape of the wearer.

[79] In the *Summa contra Gentiles*, bk. 4, ch. 37, Aquinas points out that this *habitus* text and its exposition in terms of an article of clothing has led some to think that Christ's humanity is attached to the divine person in the manner of an accident. Against this error, Aquinas stresses that habitus is used here metaphorically. In *Sent.* 3.6.2, ad 1; *De Unione Verbi*, a. 1; and *ST* III, q. 2, a. 6, obj. 1 and reply, he works out carefully the way in which the hypostatic union does and does not resemble an accidental union. See his discussion of the "three opinions" below.

[80] Larcher (81) drops the reference to the *Sentences*, attributing the discussion of the three opinions to Paul: "Hence he touches on several opinions."

Thomas appears to be launching into a discussion of the "three opinions" in order, but having begun he digresses into a refutation of all the famous Christological heresies. Often in Thomas's commentaries a pause in the lecture in order to discuss one question becomes an occasion for discussing any number of more–or–less related issues. In this case, the litany of refutations offered here serves as a "rough draft" for many arguments in the *Summa contra Gentiles*, bk. 4. For particular comparisons, see Cizewski, "Forma Dei," 17–21.

The first is that Christ's humanity belongs to him as an accident, which is false: The supposit of the divine nature was made the supposit of the human nature; so the humanity does not belong to him as an accident, but substantially, not because the divinity does not belong to him naturally, but [because the humanity] is predicated of him substantially.[81] And this also excludes the error of Photinus, who said that Christ was merely a man and not from the Virgin, because it says *though he was in the form of God*. Therefore he was in the form of God before he took on the form of a servant, because of which he is less than the Father, because he *did not judge it robbery*, etc. Therefore [the opinion] that he merited [divinity] through the form of a servant is vanquished.[82]

Likewise excluded is the error of Arius, who said that he was less than the Father, because he *did not judge it robbery*, etc.

And similarly the error of Nestorius, who said that the union [of divine and human natures] should be understood as an indwelling, inasmuch as God dwelt in a man,[83] and that the son of man is one thing and the Son of God another. But Rabanus says that the apostle names the

---

[81] This is an ambiguous and difficult sentence, due to Aquinas's multiple indefinite pronouns and unspecified grammatical subjects: Suppositum divinae naturae factum est suppositum humanae naturae; ed ideo accidentaliter non advenit ei, sed substantialiter; non quod divinitas naturaliter non advenit ei, sed substantialiter praedicetur de ipso. Larcher's translation (82) is rather free here, and understandably so: "The person existing in the divine nature became a person existing in the human nature; therefore, it [the humanity] is present not as an accident, but substantially: not that the humanity is united to the Word in his nature, but in his person." However, if one takes the indefinite pronouns as referring in every case to the person of Christ, the translation I have given emerges as the only alternative.

The difficulty posed by this sentence is reflected in the manuscripts. The Parma edition, while noting that some manuscripts offer the text I have followed, reads: Suppositum divinae naturae factum est suppositum humanae naturae; ed ideo accidentaliter non advenit ei, sed substantialiter: non quod divinitas naturaliter, sed substantialiter praedicetur de ipso. The distinction made in this variation between predicating the divinity of Christ *naturaliter* and predicating it *substantialiter* makes even less sense than manuscript tradition reflected in the Marietti text.

The sense of the text as I have rendered it is this: Because of the hypostatic union, the Word is human in his very substance; this does not deny that he is also divine in his very substance, but affirms the real substantiality of his humanity.

[82] Vincitur ergo quod per formam servi meruit. Larcher omits this sentence. According to Aquinas, Photinus argued that Christ merited a share in the divine nature by his obedience and suffering on the cross. The argument against Photinus's use of Philippians 2:5–11, sketched briefly here in the commentary, is more clearly set out in *SCG*, bk. 4, ch. 4.

[83] Larcher adds a gloss: "So that God dwells in the Son of man as in a temple" (82).

Incarnation "emptying." Now it is agreed that the Father and the Spirit dwell in [Christ];[84] therefore[85] they too were emptied, which is false. Again, he says: He *emptied himself,* therefore the one who was emptied and the one who did the emptying are the same. But the one like this is the Son of God, because he emptied himself, and therefore the union is a union in person.

Likewise the error of Eutyches, who said that one nature results from the two. Therefore he did not take on the form of a servant, but some other thing, which is contrary to the text.

Likewise the error of Valentinus, who said that he brought a body down from heaven.

Likewise that of Apollinarus, who said that he did not have a soul. For if this were true he would not be *made in the likeness of men.*[86]

63. Then when he says *he humbled himself,* etc., he points out Christ's humility as regards the mystery of his passion. And

> First, he shows Christ's humility;
> Second, the manner of his humility, there [n. 65] at *being made obedient,* etc.

64. He is therefore a man, but wondrously great, and still he humbled himself. Sirach 3:18, "The greater[87] you are, the more you must humble yourself in all things."[88] Matthew 11:29, "Learn from me, for I am meek and humble of heart."

65. The operative mode of self-abasement[89] and the sign of humility is obedience, because the attribute proper to the proud is that they seek their

---

84 Based on the present tense of *inhabit,* Larcher (82) renders the sentence this way: "Now it is evident that the Father and the Holy Spirit are involved in every indwelling." This translation requires shifting the discussion from one particular indwelling (in Jesus) to every indwelling, a move which is not required for the *reductio* of Arius's position.

Aquinas offers an interesting variation on this *reductio* in *SCG,* bk. 4, ch. 34. There he argues that, since the Word dwells in all the saints without being said thereby to empty himself, the phrase "emptied himself" must point to a mode of union beyond that of mere indwelling.

85 Some manuscripts omit "therefore," but this would complicate the sense of the text.

86 This argument forms the *sed contra* of *ST* III, q. 2, a. 5.

87 Some manuscripts read *magnus* for *maior,* but *maior* agrees with the Vulgate text as we know it.

88 This is Sirach 3:18 in the Vulgate, but 3:17 in the LXX and modern translations.

89 *Modus humilationis,* "the mode of humiliation." Adding the word "operative" specifies that "humilation" is an active process rather than something passively suffered. Prefixing "self" to "abasement" *[humiliatio]* makes the same point. Both of these

own will: The proud man seeks height, and it is characteristic of what is high not to be ruled by something else but to rule others, and so obedience is contrary to pride. Hence [Paul], desiring to show the perfection of Christ's humility and passion, says that he was *made obedient*, because if he had not suffered out of obedience he would not have been as recommendable,[90] for obedience gives merit to our sufferings.[91]

But how was he made obedient? Not in his divine will, for that is itself the measure; but in his human will, which was ruled in all things in accord with the Father's will.[92] Matthew 26:39, "Nevertheless not as I will, but as you will."

66. And it is fitting that he brings up obedience in connection with the passion, because the first sin was committed through disobedience.[93] Romans 5:19, "For as through the disobedience of one man many were made sinners, so also through the obedience of one man many are made righteous." Proverbs 21:28, "An obedient man will speak of victories."

It is clear that this obedience is great and commendable: Obedience is great when[94] someone follows the command of a higher [authority] contrary to one's own inclination *[motum proprium]*. Now the human

---

changes are in keeping with the context of the sentence, which speaks of the differing behaviors of the humble and the proud.

90 *Commendabilis* can mean "commendable" or "praiseworthy," but the context clearly shows that Aquinas means "able to be used as an example for behavior," or as I have rendered it, "recommendable."

91 Cf. *ST* II–II, q. 124, a. 3, ad. 2: "Martyrdom embraces the highest possible degree of obedience, namely obedience unto death; thus we read of Christ (Phil 2:8) that He became 'obedient unto death.' Hence it is evident that martyrdom is of itself more perfect than obedience considered absolutely."

92 Aquinas quotes Phil 2:7 in connection with the question of Christ's subjection to God in *ST* III, q. 20, a. 2, sed contra (cf. a. 1). There he argues that Christ in the form of a servant is subject to himself in the form of God. While this is Thomas's favored response to the question of Christ's obedience, in some places he develops a more nuanced position that would allow for an "obedience" of the Word inasmuch as the Word receives all from the Father; see Michael Waldstein, "The Analogy of Mission and Obedience: A Central Point in the Relation Between *Theologia* and *Oikonomia* in St. Thomas Aquinas's *Commentary on John*," in Dauphinais and Levering, *Reading John*, 92–112.

93 Larcher's rendering (83) is worth mentioning: "And it is fitting that He bring obedience into his passion." Whereas my translation has Paul or the text bringing up the subject of obedience in his discussion of Christ's passion, Larcher's interpretation has Christ bringing the element of obedience into the passion. Both translations are grammatically possible, although the idea of Christ "introducing" *[introducit]* obedience into the passion strikes me as awkward.

94 Some manuscripts read "because" *[quod]* instead of "when" *[quando]*.

will tends toward two things: to life and to honor. But Christ did not refuse[95] death. 1 Peter 3:18, "Christ died once for our sins," etc. Likewise, he did not flee from ignomy. Hence he says, *even the death of the cross,* which is most ignominious. Wisdom 2:20, "Let us condemn him to a most shameful death." Thus he fled neither from death nor from the most ignominious[96] kind of death.[97]

Chapter 2, Lecture 3

v. 9 [n. 67] *For which reason God also exalted him, and gave him the name which is above every name.*

n. 10 [n. 72] *That at the name of Jesus every knee may bend, in heaven, on earth, and in the depths.*

v. 11 [n. 73] *And every tongue confess that the Lord Jesus Christ is in the glory of the Father.*

67. Above, he pointed out Christ's humility [n. 53]; here he points to his reward, which is exaltation and glory. Luke 14:11, and 18:14, "Everyone who exalts himself shall be humbled, and he who humbles himself shall be exalted." Job 22:29, "The one who has been humiliated shall be in glory."[98]

> Note that there are three exaltations of Christ, namely as regards his rising to glory, there [n. 68] at *For which reason,* etc.
> As regards the public manifestation of his divinity, there [n. 69] at *and gave him the name,* etc.
> And as regards the reverence of the whole of creation,[99] there [n. 72] at *that at the name,* etc.

68. He says therefore *For which reason God also exalted Him,* namely that he might rise again from death, and likewise from mortality to immortality. Romans 6:9, "Christ rising from the dead does not die now, death no longer has power over him." Psalm 117:16 ff, "The right hand of the Lord exalted me, I shall not die, but live." He also exalted him by establishing

---

[95] Some manuscripts have "does not refuse" *[non recusat]* instead of "did not refuse" *[non recusavit].*

[96] Some manuscripts omit "the most ignominious *[ignominiosae].*

[97] Interestingly, Aquinas does not bring out the implications of this text for the doctrine of Christ's true humanity, as he does in *ST* III, q. 5, a. 1, ad 1.

[98] This is the Vulgate rendering, which reflects neither the MT nor the LXX.

[99] Larcher's rendering of *totius creaturae* as "every creature" misses a nuance that Aquinas caught: The three-part sequence "heaven, earth, and under the earth" is a biblical commonplace for "the whole of creation."

him at his right hand. Ephesians 1:20 ff., "Establishing him at his right hand in the heavenly places, above every principality, and power, and virtue, and domination, and every name," etc.

69. It is true that others are exalted in glory, and in immortality, but this one is exalted more, because *he gave him the name*, etc. Now a name is given to signify something, and a name is loftier according as[100] the thing it signifies is loftier, and so the name of the divinity is the highest [name]. Psalm 8:2, "O Lord, our Lord, how wonderful is Your name in all the earth," etc. Therefore the Father gave to him—namely to Christ, as to the true God—this name, that he should be called and should be God.

70. But Photinus says that this is set down here as the reward of Christ's humility: And he says that he is not truly God, but that a certain eminence among creatures is given to him, and a likeness of the divinity. This is not true, because it was said above [v. 6], "Though he was in the form of God," etc.

Therefore one should say that there are two natures in Christ and one supposit, for this person is God and man. So the [text] can be explained in two ways: in one way, that the Father gave this name to him insofar as he is the Son of God, and this he did from eternity by an eternal begetting; this "giving" is nothing other than his eternal begetting. John 5:26, "As the Father has life in himself, so he has given the Son also to have life in himself," etc.

In another way the text can be explained as about the man Christ, and in this way the Father gave this man a name, that he should be God—not by nature, because the nature of God is one thing and the nature of man another—but that he should be God by the grace, not of adoption, but of a union by which he should be at the same time God and man. Romans 1:4, "Who was predestined the Son of God in power, *namely the one Who was* descended from David according to the flesh" (Rom 1:3).

And this is Augustine's explanation in accordance with the apostle's intention. A similar thing[101] is found in Acts 2:36, "Therefore let all the house of Israel know most certainly that God hath made both Lord and Christ, this same Jesus, whom you have crucified," etc. The first explanation is Ambrose's.

---

[100] Some manuscripts read "because" *[quod]* here instead of "according as" *[quanto]*.

[101] Both the Marietti and the Parma texts have "similarly" *[similiter]*, but some manuscripts read "a similar thing" *[simile]*. For smoothness of translation at least, I have followed this variation.

71. But objecting to both explanations, you may ask why *For which reason* comes after "he humbled himself," when a reward does not precede the deserving of it *[meritum]*.[102] Therefore neither the eternal generation nor the Incarnation is the reward of Christ's passion, because they precede it.[103]

But one should say that in Sacred Scripture a thing is said to occur when it becomes known. So he *gave*, that is, he made it manifest to the world that Christ has this name.

It was made manifest at the resurrection, for before this Christ's divinity was not so known. And this fits well with the text that follows, [which reads] not as though he gave Christ what he did not have, but rather gave [the outcome] that all should venerate that [which he had].[104]

72. And two kinds of veneration are set down, namely subjection in deed and confession by mouth, there [n. 73] at *And every tongue*, etc.

He says therefore, *And gave him the name which is above every name*, even according as he is a man. This is why he adds *that at the name of*

---

[102] Some manuscripts offer a garbled text here: *quantum ad utrumque expositionem*, Humiliavit *etc., et* Propter hoc *etc., praemium non praecedit meritum. Non ergo aeterna generatio et incarnatio etc.* ("You ask, with regard to both explanations, *He humbled*, etc. and *For this reason*, etc., a reward does precede merit. Therefore the eternal generation and the Incarnation is not, etc.")

[103] The full force of this objection can perhaps be brought out by rephrasing it. The exaltation of Christ's humanity surely took place at the Incarnation, when it was elevated to divinity. But the phrase *For this reason* seems to suggest that Christ was exalted because of his crucifixion. If so, then the reward of exaltation came before the deed that earned it!

[104] Philippians 2:8 constitutes the *sed contra* of *ST* III, q. 49, a. 6. In the reply to the first objection, Aquinas points out that the hypostatic union resulted in a glorification of Christ's soul from conception, but the glorification of his body was given as a result of the merit he acquired by the passion: "The source of meriting comes of the soul, while the body is the instrument of the meritorious work. And consequently the perfection of Christ's soul, which was the source of meriting, ought not to be acquired in him by merit, like the perfection of the body, which was the subject of suffering, and was thereby the instrument of his merit."

Aquinas turned to Philippians 2:8–9 in many circumstances wherein the merit of Christ's passion was at stake. In the *Summa*, he uses these verses to address the questions of whether by his death on the cross Christ merited to be exalted (III, q. 49, a. 6), whether the human action of Christ could be meritorious for him (III, q. 19, a. 3), whether Christ's judicial power corresponds to the voluntary poverty he undertook (III, q. 89, a. 2), and whether Christ's Passion brought about our salvation by way of merit (III, q. 48, a. 1). In an interesting application of the passage, he argues that Christ wished to preach only to Israel during his earthly ministry because it was through the passion that he merited exaltation in the sight of all nations (III, q. 42, a. 1).

Jesus, which is the name of a man, *every knee should bend*. Isaiah 45:24, "To me every knee shall bend," etc.

But Origen erred here, because when he heard that *every knee should bend*, which is a sign of reverence, he thought that at some future time every rational creature, whether angels, men, or demons, would be subject to Christ with the subjection of charity.

Against this is Matthew 25:41, "Depart, you accursed, into the eternal fire," etc.

But one should say that there are two kinds of subjection, one voluntary and the other involuntary.[105] And it will happen that all the holy angels will be voluntarily subjected to Christ; and this is why he says, *Every knee shall bend*. And the sign is put down for the thing signified. Psalm 96:7, "Adore him, all his angels."[106] And all blessed men, both the saints and the righteous, will be subjected in this way.[107] Psalm 85:9, "All the nations You have made shall come, and shall adore before You, Lord, and shall glorify Your name." However, the demons and the damned will not be subjected in this way, but involuntarily.[108] James 2:19, "The demons believe, and tremble," etc.

73. Then when he says *And every tongue confess*, etc., he sets down the demonstration of reverence by confession with the mouth: *Every tongue,*

---

[105] Commenting on Ephesians 1:22, "He has subjected all things under his feet," Aquinas refers to the doctrinal issue at stake here (*Super Ephesios* ch. 1, lect. 8): "One should recall here that something can be subjected to Christ in two ways, either voluntarily or involuntarily. Failing to understand this, Origen took an occasion for error from these words of the Apostle, saying that all things subject to Christ partake of salvation. . . . And so he said that all the demons and the damned will be saved one day, when they are subjected under Christ's feet."

[106] This citation of Psalm 96:7 only works in the Vulgate translation. In the Hebrew (reflected by modern translations), the Psalm refers to gentile gods by the ambiguous *elohim*, not to angels or messengers, which would be *malakim*.

[107] *Homines beati, et sancti ac iusti hoc modo subiicientur.* Larcher (86) translates this as, "Holy and just and beatified men will be subject in this way." But it seems to me that "saints" refers to those already in heaven, while "just" or "righteous" refers to holy men and women still on earth, and "blessed men" is a general category embracing both those in heaven and those on earth. In his discussion of voluntary subjection, Aquinas naturally mentions those in heaven and those on earth because these are the first two groups mentioned in Philippians 2:10, the text under discussion. He will speak of those "in the depths" when he discusses involuntary subjection.

Some manuscripts read here simply "and that men" *[item quod homines]* and proceed directly to the quotation from Psalm 85.

[108] Some manuscripts read here simply, "And that the demons, although involuntarily" *[et quod daemones, licet involuntarie]* and proceed directly to the quotation from James.

namely *in heaven, on earth, and in the depths.* With respect to those in the depths this does not mean the confession of praise, but the forced confession that comes from the recognition of God. Isaiah 40:5, "All flesh together shall see, that the mouth of the Lord has spoken," etc. Psalm 98:3, "Let them confess to Your great name, for it is terrible and holy," etc.[109]

And [they will confess] this, *that the Lord Jesus Christ,* etc., namely this man, *is in the glory,* etc.[110] He does not say "in a similar [glory]," because it is the same [glory].[111] John 5:23, "That all may honor the Son as they honor the Father."[112]

And one should note that he says in the beginning [of this passage], *Who, though he was in the form,* etc., and here he says *is in the glory,* because it will happen that, what he had from eternity, he will make known to all, as it says in John 17:5, "Glorify me, Father, with the same glory which I had from You before the world began."

---

[109] Correcting *confiteatur* to *confiteantur,* to agree both with the Vulgate and with the context.

[110] Larcher's custom of using the RSV for biblical texts is particularly problematic here. His translation (86) has this important sentence as "And this confession will recognize *that Jesus Christ is Lord [in] the glory of the Father.*" This glosses over a key difference between the RSV and the Vulgate. While the RSV says "Jesus Christ is Lord to the glory of the Father," the Vulgate says *Dominus Iesus Christus in gloria est Dei Patris,* "the Lord Jesus Christ is in the glory of the Father." Both the RSV and the Vulgate are possible renderings of the Greek from a grammatical perspective, but the difference between the two translations is considerable. All things considered, the RSV is a better translation and would fit better with Aquinas's interpretation of the Hymn, but to import the RSV translation into Aquinas's commentary does not promote a clear understanding of his comments.

[111] For a discussion of the meaning of "glory" in Aquinas's commentaries on Paul, see Swierzawski, "God and the Mystery of his Wisdom," 484–87. Swierzawski does not bring up this brief comment on Phil 2:11, but the texts he assembles are helpful for fleshing out its meaning.

[112] As he alludes to John 5:23 here, so Aquinas alludes to Philippians 2:6–7 in his commentary on John 5:23.

CHAPTER 7

Hierarchy and Holiness

MATTHEW LEVERING

FATHER MATTHEW LAMB'S life as a devoted follower of Christ Jesus and man of the Church well expresses St. Paul's injunction, "whatever you do, do all to the glory of God" (1 Cor 10:31). It is with joy that I dedicate this essay as a token of gratitude and love to Fr. Lamb, a dear teacher, colleague, and friend.

In his *Church, World and the Christian Life: Practical-Prophetic Ecclesiology*, the Catholic theologian Nicholas M. Healy makes a case for "theodramatic" ecclesiology as opposed to what he calls the "epic" ecclesiologies that have predominated. Healy defines "epic" ecclesiologies as those that, seeking to affirm the Church's holiness, depict an idealized Church that does not exist in this world and avert their gaze from the sins and weaknesses of the concrete Church.[1] By contrast, "theodramatic" ecclesiologies witness to "the

---

[1] For explanation of this terminology, see Nicholas M. Healy, Church, *World and the Christian Life: Practical-Prophetic Ecclesiology* (Cambridge: Cambridge University Press, 2000), 150–51, and elsewhere. He refers to "epic" ecclesiologies also as "blueprint" ecclesiologies. After emphasizing the distinction between the concrete sinful Church and the eschatological perfect Church, he remarks, "Blueprint ecclesiologies thus foster a disjunction not only between normative theory and normative accounts of ecclesial practice, but between ideal ecclesiology and the realities of the concrete Church, too. They undervalue thereby the theological significance of the genuine struggles of the Church's membership to live as disciples within the less-than-perfect Church and within societies that are often unwilling to overlook the Church's flaws. As a consequence, blueprint ecclesiologies frequently display a curious inability to acknowledge the complexities of ecclesial life in its pilgrim state. To take just one instance, we noted how Tillard believes that the Eucharist is the most perfect expression of 'communion.' While that may well be true, eucharists are concretely and frequently divided by race, class, gender, and political ideology, to say nothing of denominational divisions" (37).

Church's belief that all people and institutions, itself included, should humbly acknowledge their sinfulness, finitude, and dependence upon the grace and mercy of God."[2] For Healy, the holiness of the Church belongs not to the concrete or pilgrim Church, but to the "eschatological Church of the saints who can no longer sin and whose lives together no longer need continual reformation."[3] Healy affirms that the pilgrim Church and the eschatological Church are related, but he thinks that ecclesiology must carefully distinguish what can be affirmed about the former from what can be affirmed about the latter:

> The eschatological Church should continue to be the subject of theological inquiry since the pilgrim Church proleptically participates in the eternal Church and so an account of the latter bears upon what we say about the former. But the two forms of the Church are not the same and cannot be treated in the same manner. An ecclesiological method that is appropriate for describing the ideal, eternal Church is not broad enough to deal adequately with the Church on earth. We must say far more about the Church *in via* than about the heavenly Church, and say it in a different and more complex way.[4]

On the basis of this distinction, Healy seeks to get out from under a number of difficulties that have troubled Catholic ecclesiologists. For instance, he finds that the call of all humankind to be united to the one Church (the Church's unity and catholicity) can be referred simply to the eschatological Church. Thus he states, "We can follow Rahner and the tradition generally in claiming that salvation requires at least an orientation to the Church; but we are not thereby obliged to understand this as an orientation to the Church on earth."[5] Similarly, he interprets the holiness of the

---

2 Ibid., 151. Earlier Healy explains that in his book "the word 'church' refers to all those diverse Christian groups who accept what is sometimes cumbersomely called the Niceno-Constantinopolitan creed" (6), although he expects that sometimes his Roman Catholic perspective will show through, as for instance "when I discuss the issue of ecclesial arrogance, my primary reference is, as it must be, to the Roman church, although the problem clearly arises in different forms within other denominations" (6).

3 Ibid., 150.

4 Ibid. Healy observes that "in general, ecclesiology in our period has become highly systematic and theoretical, focused more upon discerning the right things to think about the Church rather than orientated to the living, rather messy, confused, and confusing body that the Church actually is. It displays a preference for describing the Church's theoretical and essential identity rather than its concrete and historical identity" (3).

5 Ibid., 151.

Church as pertaining to the eschatological Church, and so he affirms that the Catholic Church has erred in fundamental ways. He has in mind in particular the Church's "misuse of power and authority, its tolerance of slavery, its treatment of women, Jews, and non-Christians, and its other failures to conform to its Lord."[6] In this regard he decries the fact that "Charles Journet's formula, asserting that 'the Church is not without sinners, but she herself is sinless,' has been accepted as if it were doctrine."[7] Granted that the Church flows from the activity of Christ's Holy Spirit, it still does not follow, Healy argues, that "when the Church is truly itself, or when considered at its most profound level, it is something that is fundamentally free of sin."[8] His strong distinction between the concrete Church and the eschatological Church—related solely "proleptically"—makes it possible avoid claims about the holiness of the Church on earth. As he puts it, "Sin and error, in short, are part of the Church's theological and concrete identity prior to the eschaton."[9] It follows, one supposes, that all doctrines and structures of the Church are changeable until the Second Coming of Christ.

Healy identifies the Church's understanding of ecclesial power as a particular locus of the Church's sinfulness. As he puts it, "The power of sin is manifested not only in the actions of individuals but in the Christian communal body, when the latter fosters practices, valuations, and beliefs in its membership that are incompatible with the Gospel. One of the more obvious examples of this is the failure of the Church's leadership to avoid the corruptions of power."[10] Thus Boniface VIII's papal bulls *Clericis laicos* (1296) and *Unam sanctam* (1302) sinfully taught false doctrine, inflated accounts of papal authority, although the sin may well reside not in Boniface but in the common assumptions, built up over centuries, of the Church of his time that was "corrupted by the ideology and practices of worldly power."[11]

Healy's critique extends, of course, beyond the medieval Church. He repeatedly suggests that similar corruptive "practices of worldly power" are still sinfully marginalizing groups of people within the Catholic Church:

---

6 Ibid., 8.

7 Ibid., 9.

8 Ibid., 10.

9 Ibid., 11; cf. 175. He adds, "God is the solution to the problems of the world, not the church. The church, although oriented to, and governed by, the solution, still remains part of the problem" (12). He is careful to say that he does not mean to condemn the Church in a hypocritical fashion: "I try to discern the speck in my church's eye so that it may pluck it forth and then more readily help me discern the beam in my own" (13).

10 Ibid., 7.

11 Ibid., 8.

Laypeople, women, majorities, and minorities of various kinds may be marginalized within some forms of the Christian Church. They may not only have a different perspective upon the Church and its interaction with other traditions, they may have clearer insights into its sinfulness and inadequacies, into the challenges it faces, and perhaps as to how it should be reformed.[12]

Similarly "it may well be that the more a Christian grows into her unique role, the more she will find herself having to challenge certain ecclesial cultural patterns, even if she has no leadership role."[13] Contrasting his view on women in the Church with Jean-Marie Tillard's call for calm reflection on the topic, he notes that "the history of the Church indicates that serene reflection is the perquisite of those in power. Reforms, like doctrinal agreements, are usually the result, not of serenity, but of struggle and eventual compromise."[14] A key task of Healy's "practical-prophetic" and theodramatic ecclesiology is therefore "actively seeking out and bringing to light anti-Christian practices and beliefs and . . . proposing suitable reforms,"[15] although Healy leaves this task to another book.

It seems to me that Healy's approach to the Church lacks the sacramental and Christological depth needed for appreciating the presence of the Holy Spirit in the pilgrim Church. Paradoxically, his approach is not "theodramatic" enough.[16] Yet his approach taps into and expresses a widespread feel-

---

[12] Ibid., 178.

[13] Ibid., 179.

[14] Ibid., 38.

[15] Ibid., 185.

[16] For a better approach that attempts to integrate Healy's concerns, see Frederick Christian Bauerschmidt, " 'That the Faithful Become the Temple of God': The Church Militant in Aquinas's *Commentary on John*," in *Reading John with St. Thomas Aquinas*, ed. Michael Dauphinais and Matthew Levering (Washington, DC: Catholic University of America Press, 2004): 293–311, although Bauerschmidt's treatment of the sinfulness of the Church according to Aquinas needs a more nuanced explication. Bauerschmidt writes, "Thomas believes, of course, in the holiness of the Church: that the Church lives by grace and the promise of Jesus that the gates of hell shall not prevail against her. But this is something different from the view, heard these days in certain ecclesiastical circles, that, while *Christians* may sin, the *Church* cannot, because she is objectively holy in her structures and sacraments" (309). The question is, What would it mean for the "Church" to "sin"? One supposes this would require that the Church, acting qua Church, teach false doctrine or bestow objectively graceless sacraments. On Aquinas's ecclesiology in the contemporary context, see also Charles Morerod, O.P., "John Paul II's Ecclesiology and St. Thomas Aquinas," in *John Paul II and St. Thomas Aquinas*, ed. Michael Dauphinais and Matthew Levering (Naples, FL: Sapientia Press, 2006): 45–73.

ing of discontent regarding the role of hierarchical authority in the Catholic Church. For many, hierarchical authority, lacking the leveling influence of democratic structures, belongs to the corruptive "ideology and practices of worldly power" that formed Boniface VIII and that "epic" ecclesiologies, with their misguided attribution of eschatological marks to the pilgrim Church, continue to foster. Proposals to weaken hierarchical authority in the Church, generally by putting in place a democratic substratum that would bind hierarchical authority closely to congregational opinion, regularly appear.[17]

[17] See, e.g., Paul Lakeland, *The Liberation of the Laity: In Search of an Accountable Church* (New York: Continuum, 2003); Eugene C. Bianchi and Rosemary Radford Ruether, eds., *A Democratic Catholic Church: The Reconstruction of Roman Catholicism* (New York: Crossroad, 1993); Stephen J. Pope, ed., *Common Calling: The Laity and Governance of the Catholic Church* (Washington, DC: Georgetown University Press, 2004); Ghislain Lafont, *Imagining the Catholic Church: Structured Communion in the Spirit,* trans. John J. Burkhard, O.F.M. Conv. (Collegeville, MN: Liturgical Press, 2000). Even Christopher Ruddy's *The Local Church: Tillard and the Future of Catholic Ecclesiology* (New York: Crossroad, 2006)—which concentrates in large part upon the ecclesiology of Jean-Marie Tillard, O.P., whose approach Healy criticizes as "epic" ecclesiology—decries "papal maximalization" under John Paul II and finds hope instead in increasing democratization: "although it might seem counterintuitive in light of [Pope] Benedict's support for the priority of the universal church to the local churches, his unassuming, self-effacing exercise of the papacy may help to foster decentralization and to strengthen the life of the local churches. His dislike for bureaucracy is well-known, as is his desire to simplify the Church's administration. Benedict surely has shown little desire to create new synodal and collegial bodies, but he also seems—at least in the early stages of his pontificate—to be more willing to allow local bishops a greater role in the Church's governance and perhaps to rein in some of the papal maximalization that occurred in recent decades" (154). For his part, Lakeland wishes to get away from the two-tiered hierarchical system and return to a "servant leadership" in which priests and bishops make decisions with the community. In so doing, he hopes to return the Church to its roots: "[T]he picture of ministries outlined here approximates that which seems to have marked the early Church. A clergy/lay distinction was foreign to the consciousness of the early Christians. . . . Some were undoubtedly called to leadership positions that the majority would not occupy, but this in no way introduced a hierarchical distinction among Christians, still less two separate orders of life. Only later, when secular models of leadership and the holiness of the monastic vocation came to cloud the picture, did something like the lay/clerical divide become a reality in the Church" (Lakeland, *The Liberation of the Laity,* 285). He proposes therefore reintegrating the community into the Church's decision-making: "When the time comes for the community to have new servant leaders, or when the community is so moved by the qualities of one of its members that it wishes to have that person called to servant leadership, the bishop becomes part of the mix. The Church is not just the local church but also the universal church, and the role of the bishop here is as the symbolic focus of unity of the Church and leader of the diocese. It is the bishop who confirms the calling of the

Underlying these proposals, on the theological level, is the question of whether the Church's hierarchical structures of authority are truly fit to express the mutually self-subordinating love that Christians are called to manifest. Does not hierarchical authority tend to elevate some Christians above other Christians in a manner better suited to royal and aristocratic courts than to Christian brotherhood? Put another way, when organized in a hierarchical fashion, can the Church as a whole be transparent to the cruci-fied One? Does hierarchical authority, by its very nature, hinder the Church's mission of manifesting to the world—and forming within the Christian community itself—the mutual self-subordination that should characterize Christians?

Indeed, certain passages from the Gospels make this question even more pressing. In reply to the disciples' question "Who is the greatest in the king-dom of heaven?," Jesus brings forward a little child and says to the disciples that "unless you turn and become like children, you will never enter the kingdom of heaven. Whoever humbles himself like this child, he is the greatest in the kingdom of heaven" (Mt 18:3–4). Does not the very posses-sion of hierarchical authority, the possession by some Christians of a perma-nently elevated status vis-à-vis other Christians, militate strongly against the ability of the one in authority to "humble himself like this child"? Likewise, when the two sons of Zebedee strive to obtain a particular position of emi-nence among the disciples, Jesus tells the disciples,

> You know that the rulers of the Gentiles lord it over them, and their great men exercise authority over them. It shall not be so among you, but whoever would be great among you must be your servant, and whoever would be first among you must be your slave; even as the Son of man came not to be served but to serve, and to give his life as a ran-som for many. (Mt 20:25–28)

But do not the bishops and the pope—if not all priests—possess offices that make them seem much more like "the rulers of the Gentiles" than like a "slaves"? Given that the disciples possess authority in the early Church, surely their authority would not have been conceived along hierarchical

---

new servant leader in the laying on of hands, but he should never take this step except in response to the expressed will of the community that this particular indi-vidual be appointed to minister as a servant leader in their midst. This two-sided process preserves the responsibility of the local community and of the bishop for protecting the genuineness of the calling" (284). Similarly, Ghislain Lafont calls for the election of bishops by the congregations, to be confirmed by the presiding bishop: see Lafont, *Imagining the Catholic Church,* 174–75.

lines, given that Jesus wished them to humble themselves like children and servants? How can mutual self-subordination truly be normative for a hierarchical relationship in which power is not equal?

The present essay takes up this question of whether and, if so, why Christ's saving acts require a hierarchical priesthood, not just a universal priesthood whose leadership could be organized in a variety of ways. I will look first at some recent historical accounts that place into question whether hierarchical ecclesial authority in fact has an intrinsic historical/theological place in the community of Christ. Second, I will examine some of the New Testament evidence that suggests that hierarchical authority is intrinsic to the kind of communion that Christ establishes for believers. I will argue that hierarchical authority belongs to the "theodrama" in which divine power—the power of Christ's saving work—is mediated through mere human beings.

Hierarchical Authority in the Earliest Church: Recent Historical Expositions

Teaching mutual self-giving love, could the incarnate Son of God have also taught his disciples to organize the Church in a hierarchical manner? Contemporary historical research generally concludes that hierarchical authority is not intrinsically embedded in the Church's structure, although the later development of hierarchical authority may well have had functional benefits for the early Church's survival. I will here discuss three examples of such conclusions, by the biblical exegete Raymond Brown, the Church historian and theologian James Burtchaell, and the ecclesiologist Francis Sullivan, respectively.

Raymond Brown separates the bishops' hierarchical authority, which developed some time after Christ, from Christ's own activity. Brown argues that various forms of authority arose in the Christian communities after Christ's death and resurrection. In his view, the claim that the bishops' hierarchical authority can be traced back to Christ's commissioning of the apostles cannot be sustained. He finds this claim to be at odds with the evidence found in the New Testament and early theological writings. As he concludes:

> The presbyter-bishops described in the NT were not in any traceable way the successors of the Twelve apostles. . . . And so the affirmation that all the bishops of the early Christian Church could trace their appointments or ordinations to the apostles is simply without proof—it is impossible to trace with assurance any of the presbyter-bishops to the Twelve and it is possible to trace only some of them to apostles like Paul.[18]

---

[18] Raymond E. Brown, S.S., *Priest and Bishop: Biblical Reflections* (New York: Paulist Press, 1970), 72–73. He observes in a footnote, "The claims of various sees to

Instead, the most that can be said about the bishops' hierarchical authority is that the Holy Spirit inspired the early Christian communities to move in this direction. As Brown states,

> The affirmation that the episcopate was divinely established or established by Christ himself can be defended in the nuanced sense that the episcopate gradually emerged in a Church that stemmed from Christ and that this emergence was (in the eyes of faith) guided by the Holy Spirit.[19]

For Brown, the denial of the bishops' "apostolic succession," their direct link with Christ's commissioning of the apostles, does not pose a problem for the Church's hierarchical structure. He assumes that the Holy Spirit has simply guided a development of doctrine—although admittedly one based for centuries upon a false claim. As he puts it, "Personally, I do not think that tracing the appearance of the episcopate more directly to the Holy Spirit than to the historical Jesus takes away any dignity from bishops." Anticipating sharp criticism, however, he adds a barb directed toward those who might disagree: "I suggest that, upon reflection, these conclusions [of Brown] will be scandalous chiefly to those who have never understood the real import of our oft-repeated boast that Christianity is a historical religion."[20] It is antithetical to Christianity itself to cling to the vision of a timeless Church—what Healy might term "epic" ecclesiology.

Yet, once the episcopate has been separated from Jesus Christ, and linked instead to the Holy Spirit, one might ask whether the Holy Spirit could implement in the future a non-hierarchical Church structure. Put succinctly, if Jesus Christ did not directly intend the structure of hierarchical authority that later formed, then could other forms of authority be more clearly intrinsic to the community that Jesus directly intended? Could episcopal hierarchical authority be done without, as it was in the earliest Church? Although hierarchical authority may have functioned well in the early days of the Church and thus have been approved by the Holy Spirit, perhaps now hierarchical authority's weaknesses may be more apparent—especially in light of the difficulty of squaring hierarchy with a community of mutual self-subordination—and the Holy Spirit may move the Church in another direction.

descend from particular members of the Twelve are highly dubious. It is interesting that the most serious of these is the claim of the bishops of Rome to descend from Peter, the one member of the Twelve who was almost a missionary apostle in the Pauline sense—a confirmation of our contention that whatever succession there was from apostleship to episcopate, it was primarily in reference to the Pauline type of apostleship, not that of the Twelve" (72, n. 53).

[19] Ibid., 73.
[20] Ibid.

Brown does not draw this conclusion, but it does not seem an illegitimate one once "apostolic succession" loses its direct link with Christ.

Taking up a similar range of issues, James Burtchaell's *From Synagogue to Church: Public Services and Offices in the Earliest Christian Communities* attempts to set forth and evaluate the traditional debate between Catholics and Protestants over the structure of the earliest Church. He summarizes the traditional "Catholic" position as holding that "certain offices were established by apostolic authority, and that the apostles in doing this were acting as plenipotentiaries of the Lord."[21] Scholarly opinion, he observes, generally accords with the "Protestant" position, namely that the "appearance of ordered authoritarian offices has its warrant, not from Jesus or the apostles, but from men like Clement and Ignatius, in defiance of the authentic egalitarianism they squelched."[22] Burtchaell calls for a third position, a *via media*. He criticizes both the Catholic and the Protestant traditional positions for ignoring portions of the historical evidence:

> The "Catholic" theory projects backward a scenario of dominating clergy who are simply not to be found in the first documents. The "Protestant" theory has had to shrug off the exhibits in evidence—few but unequivocal—that they are unhappy to accept as precedents. For instance, they discount the *episkopoi* and *diakonoi* greeted by Paul in the address of his letter to the Philippians; Paul's call for deference to those put in charge of the Church when they give admonitions; the primacy of the Jerusalem church presided over by James, a non-apostle, with a bench of elders; and the assertion by Clement to the Corinthians who still remembered their earliest days as Church, that in their memory apostles had provided their churches with governing officers whose successors were to be chosen by due process (giving credibility to similar texts in Acts).[23]

Burtchaell argues, then, that there were authoritative offices, including presiding bishops, in the earliest Church, but not "dominating clergy" or carefully

---

[21] James Tunstead Burtchaell, *From Synagogue to Church: Public Services and Offices in the Earliest Christian Communities* (Cambridge: Cambridge University Press, 1992), 348.

[22] Ibid., 349.

[23] Ibid. Regarding Clement, Raymond Brown states in a footnote, "The picture is simplified even further by Clement of Rome who asserts that the apostles who received the Gospel and their commands from Jesus Christ went forth to preach and appointed their first converts to be bishops and deacons, with the condition that if these should die, other approved men should succeed to their ministry (42:1–4; 44:1–2). Clement has combined the Twelve with Paul. The contention that this must be historical because it was written in 96, relatively few years after the events, is naïve in its evaluation of historical memory." Brown, *Priest and Bishop,* 72, n. 52.

organized apostolic succession. He proposes that scholars seek to understand the role of authoritative positions in the earliest Church by attending to how authority functioned in the synagogue. As he says, "It was a Jewish view, not a Christian view, that Jesus tore away from the people and traditions of Abraham, Isaac, and Jacob. And if this be so in so many other usages, might it not be worthwhile to investigate whether and to what extent community organization among the earliest Christians might display and even be illuminated by continuities with its past?"[24]

Turning therefore to the structure of the synagogue, Burtchaell finds a variety of offices as well as a line of authority among the various synagogues. With regard to the latter point, he notes, "The mother of mothers, of course, was Jerusalem, and all synagogues looked to the great council there as to an ultimate authority."[25] This parallels the position of the earliest Christian community in Jerusalem, and later the position of the church of Rome. Among the officers of the synagogue, Burtchaell first treats elders, *presbyteroi*: "Their precise function was to give wise counsel and to legitimate community policy, whether they actually formulated it or only ratified it. Elders were collegial."[26] How people became elders, Burtchaell notes, remains unclear, but he suggests that the elders "expected to enjoy that dignity throughout their lifetimes."[27] Secondly, Burtchaell discusses "the notables" of the synagogue, *archontes,* an elite group emerging out of the council of elders. Thirdly, the council of elders (*gerousia*) possessed a "senior elder" or "president," the *gerousiarches.*[28] Among the various synagogues in a large city such as Rome, there could also be an *archigerousiarches* distinguished above the other senior elders.[29] In addition, an *archisynagogos,* or "community chief," had charge of the liturgical worship and, under the guidance of the elders and the notables, "he presided over the community, he convened it for its activities, he superintended its staff."[30] Burtchaell compares this position to the presiders, *episkopoi,* of the earliest Christian communities. Other offices include assistant, commissioner, scribe, and reader.

Lastly, there were the priests, although they presided only at the Temple in Jerusalem, not in the synagogues. Burtchaell comments, "It is striking how decisively the priesthood vanished from the scene of power after the fall of Jerusalem in 70"[31] and the destruction of the Temple. Justifying his down-

---

[24] Burtchaell, *From Synagogue to Church,* 192.

[25] Ibid., 217.

[26] Ibid., 228.

[27] Ibid., 231.

[28] Ibid., 237.

[29] Ibid., 239.

[30] Ibid., 244.

[31] Ibid., 253.

playing of the priesthood in his list of offices, he explains that well before A.D. 70, "the local synagogues had already chosen to deny priests any special privileges or position." Despite respect for the priesthood evident in the time of the Maccabean revolt and the elevated position of the priests in Jewish sects, such as the one at Qumran, Burtchaell says, the laity had almost entirely decided that the priesthood no longer mattered outside Jerusalem: "[I]n the villages and towns and cities, where priests in plenty dwelt and were available, a totally lay synagogue organization had long since decided it needed no legitimacy which the priests could give."[32] He sees this viewpoint as persisting in the earliest Christian communities, where "it is not that there are no longer any priests: there are no longer any who are not priests."[33] The earliest Christian churches, according to Burtchaell, did not have ordained "priests" in the later sense of the word, associated with the celebration of the sacraments.

Comparing Christianity to "contemporaneous sectarian movements" within Judaism, Burtchaell observes that even radical critique of mainstream Judaism often went together with profound indebtedness to the synagogue's institutional structure.[34] With bishops, presbyters, and deacons in mind, he states, "The presiding officer, the college of elders, and the assistant appear to carry over from synagogue to church."[35] He points out, however, that as in the Jewish synagogue, the most important role in the earliest Church did not belong to the "presiding officer" or *episkopos*. Rather, the "apostles and prophets," and the charismatics, stood at the center of the earliest Church, although they did not preside. Burtchaell remarks, "The people who bore most powerfully in their persons the force of divine conviction and transformative impetus were people who, without community screening or authorization, did God's work. They spoke with authority."[36] Thus while the standard "Protestant" position is mistaken that there were no stable offices in the earliest Church, this position is right to accord emphasis to the charismatic leaders.[37] Similarly, the "Protestant" position is wrong to suppose that Jesus led his disciples away from the structure of communal offices, but the "Catholic" position is wrong to suppose that Jesus instituted offices. According to Burtchaell, "Jesus instigated no characteristic new organization or anarchy among those who shared faith in him. They proceeded from where they found themselves. And they found themselves in the synagogue."[38] Jesus' apparent

---

[32] Ibid., 254.
[33] Ibid., 323.
[34] Ibid., 344.
[35] Ibid., 339.
[36] Ibid., 350.
[37] Cf. ibid., 351.
[38] Ibid., 352.

lack of interest in organizing his disciples made the synagogue context the inevitable starting point.

On the basis of his reconstruction, Burtchaell provides an evaluation that also aims to chart terrain between the "Catholic" and "Protestant" evaluative standpoints. In his view, it is indisputable that a large organizational shift, as the "Protestant" position holds, occurred in the Church in the late first and early second centuries A.D. The officers overtook the charismatic leaders, and the bishops overtook the presbyters.[39] Rome replaced Jerusalem as the center of Christianity. But whether these shifts were a development or a retrogression cannot be determined historically. On the historical evidence alone, one cannot say that had the shift never taken place, the Church would have survived and developed as well as it did. Just as the authority of bishops can and has been used both well and ill, so authority arising from a more egalitarian community can also be used both well and ill; and there are strengths and weaknesses associated with both approaches to authority.

Like Brown's rejection of apostolic succession, Burtchaell's emphasis on the determinative role of the synagogue (freed from the priestly cult of Jerusalem) thus would seem, in part, to support doubts about the exercise of hierarchical authority within a community of mutual self-subordination. Those who immediately followed Jesus, at least, emphasized according to Burtchaell more egalitarian and diverse modes of leadership in their pursuit of *caritas*. Furthermore, they devoted themselves to teaching and service, rather than cultic/priestly ministry that mediated the saving power of Christ's Paschal mystery.

The view of the Catholic ecclesiologist Francis Sullivan points in generally the same direction. With "the consensus of scholars," Sullivan finds that "the church of Rome was led by a college of presbyters, rather than by a single bishop, for at least several decades of the second century."[40] According to Sullivan's reading of the First Epistle of Clement, written from Rome to the church at Corinth in the 90s, the letter gives no indication either that the Corinthian church has a bishop, or that the church in Rome has one. Instead, Clement always uses plural terms to refer to the leaders of the Corinthian

---

[39] Ibid., 347, 353.

[40] Francis A. Sullivan, S.J., *From Apostles to Bishops: The Development of the Episcopacy in the Early Church* (New York: Paulist Press, 2001), 221–22. Sullivan observes earlier, "The question dividing the churches is not whether or how rapidly the development from the leadership of a college of presbyters to that of a single bishop took place, but whether the result of that development is rightly judged an element of the divinely ordered structure of the Church. This is a question of the theological significance of a post-New Testament development, and history alone cannot give the answer" (218).

church. Similarly *The Shepherd of Hermas*, composed in the first half of the second century in Rome, always uses plural terms when speaking of leadership in the Church. Sullivan, however, does envision a certain kind of "apostolic succession," although he grants that the available documents cannot demonstrate such an occurrence. Sullivan affirms that there is "New Testament evidence that the apostles shared their mandate with both their missionary coworkers and with the leaders in the local churches and that when the apostles died both of these groups carried on their ministry."[41] So long as the "mandate" and "ministry" do not require the transmission of a particular power specifically from Jesus Christ, "apostolic succession" is uncontroversial, since it comprises only the idea that the apostles did not refuse to share the function of teaching and leadership when they could not be present. When in the second century the "monoepiscopate" developed, it would not have been illegitimate, Sullivan suggests, for the local churches in which these bishops emerged to "establish his link with the apostles either through earlier coworkers or through a succession of presbyters in their church."[42] Some link, it would seem, could inevitably be found, given this broad definition of "apostolic succession."

Sullivan goes beyond Burtchaell somewhat by adding, in order to "justify the assertion of Vatican II that 'bishops have by divine institution taken the place of the apostles as pastors of the Church' (*Lumen Gentium,* no. 20),"[43] a brief section defending the affirmations that "the post-New Testament development is consistent with the development that took place during the New Testament period," and that this development is both functionally necessary for the post-New Testament Church's "unity and orthodoxy" and guided by the Holy Spirit.[44] Drawing here upon Brown's work, Sullivan proposes that Jesus left the disciples with a mandate to teach, but not much instruction about organization. Perhaps unaware of Burtchaell's view that the disciples therefore took up the synagogue's structure, Sullivan suggests that the New Testament demonstrates the ad hoc character—aimed at meeting emerging needs—of development in Church structure during the New Testament period. Without denying the continuance of "charismatic ministry,"[45] he finds in "the parts of the New Testament written during the subapostolic period, especially 1 Peter, Acts, and the Pastorals," an increasing concern for such tasks as "selecting the right persons for ministry in the local churches and ordaining them by the laying on of

---

[41] Ibid., 223.
[42] Ibid.
[43] Ibid., 218.
[44] Ibid., 225.
[45] Ibid., 227.

hands."[46] While he notes that only James, "the 'brother of the Lord,'" is described "as having been left in charge of a local church," he suggests that the development in this direction, toward more defined leadership for local churches, allows us to recognize the rise of the episcopate as a legitimate development of doctrine, present already *in nuce* in the concerns of the earliest Christian communities.[47]

He goes on to emphasize that this second-century rise of the episcopate can be recognized historically as preserving the unity of the Church against the Gnostics in the second century, and can be recognized as the work of the Holy Spirit due to the Church's "reception" of the episcopate, a reception that paralleled the Church's reception of the canonical books of the Bible rather than the Gnostic books: "We have just as good reason for believing that the Spirit guided the Church in recognizing its bishops as successors of the apostles and authoritative teachers of the faith as we have for believing that the Spirit guided it in discerning the books that comprise the New Testament."[48] Since the Spirit is the Spirit of Jesus Christ, the Spirit enacts Christ's will for the Church.

As it stands, Sullivan's defense of the episcopate seems to be an ecclesiological functionalism (the need to preserve orthodoxy and unity) ratified by the Holy Spirit—a ratification made known, crucially, by the "reception" accorded to the episcopate's authority by the various communities of believers, thereby locating the center of Christian authority ultimately in the people's own authorization of the arrangement. By raising the issue of the apostles' "mandate" and "ministry," Sullivan helps us to ask what the apostles thought that they were doing. Were they merely teaching the Scriptures (enlightened by Christ) and serving the community? Or were they also sharing a sacramental power, a participation in Christ's Pasch?

In other words, did the mandate and ministry of the apostles contain a communication of the power of the Cross and Resurrection, a power that flowed through the apostles because of Christ's direct commissioning of them? Did the apostles share this power with those who presided over the Eucharistic gatherings of the Church? If so, then one could not speak, with Burtchaell, of a situation after Christ in which there were no "priests" because "there are no longer any who are not priests."[49]

The claim that the apostles received from Christ and transmitted to others a unique power rests at least in part upon the New Testament evidence. Does

---

[46] Ibid., 226.

[47] Ibid., 227.

[48] Ibid., 230.

[49] Burtchaell, *From Synagogue to Church*, 323.

this evidence point to anything more than teaching and service as comprising the essential apostolic "mandate" and "ministry"? In what follows, I will examine Paul's First Letter to the Corinthians and the Gospel of Matthew.

The Apostolic Mandate: Paul's First Letter to the Corinthians

The distinctions that Paul makes as he writes to the Corinthians illumine his view of the apostolic mandate. On the one hand, he distinguishes between Jesus Christ and all Christians. The "church of God which is at Corinth" is "sanctified in Christ Jesus, called to be saints together with all those who in every place call on the name of our Lord Jesus Christ" (1 Cor 1:2). Christ, not Christians, is the source of this sanctifying power. The Corinthian believers receive "the grace of God . . . in Christ Jesus," a grace that enriches them "with all speech and all knowledge" (1 Cor 1:5) so that they receive every "spiritual gift" (1 Cor 1:7) and are enabled by Christ to remain "guiltless" (1 Cor 1:8) on the day of judgment.[50] Christ's power of sanctifying those who believe in him comes from his Cross. Paul warns the Corinthians against relying upon any other source than Christ crucified for "our wisdom, our righteousness, and our sanctification and redemption" (1 Cor 1:30), "lest the cross of Christ be emptied of its power" (1 Cor 1:17). The sanctifying power of the Cross is the mystery that Paul calls "a secret and hidden wisdom of God, which God decreed before the ages for our glorification" (1 Cor 2:7).

When Paul instructs the Corinthians about how human beings receive the power of the Cross, he distinguishes between ordinary believers and the apostles, along with those who share their mandate.[51] At first glance, he

---

[50] James W. Thompson observes that God's grace here has a "corporate dimension," building up the community as opposed to "Corinthian factionalism." Thompson, *Pastoral Ministry According to Paul: A Biblical Vision* (Grand Rapids, MI: Baker Academic, 2006), 123.

[51] Hans Urs von Balthasar's comments are pertinent here: "It is significant that though the difference in rank between the Apostle and his coworkers persists even when he names them in addressing a letter ('Paul, called as an apostle of Jesus Christ and Sosthenes, our brother' [1 Cor 1:1], Paul wants his 'fellow workers' (that word again! [2 Cor 8:23]), Titus and Timothy, to be just as highly esteemed by the congregation as he is himself. When Timothy comes to Corinth, he is to be treated like the Apostle, 'for he is doing the Lord's work, as I also am. Let no one therefore despise him' (1 Cor 16:10–11). If Paul is his congregation's bishop, then his fellow workers may be designated as auxiliary bishops. The pastoral letters make it clear that they have the necessary authority (in Crete, Titus is instructed to 'appoint elders in every city as I directed you' [Titus 1:5]). . . . Precisely because the (fellow) workers are promoters *(auctores)* of the building, they have the right to exercise the determining influence *(auctoritas)*. Despite what is sometimes claimed nowadays, there is no trace of Church

appears to locate this distinction solely in the relationship between teacher and learner, which need not require any particular power in the teacher beyond the ability to communicate the Gospel. Paul makes clear that faith, the work of the Holy Spirit in us, establishes believers' contact with the power of the Cross: "Now we have received not the spirit of the world, but the Spirit which is from God, that we might understand the gifts bestowed on us by God. And we impart this in words not taught by human wisdom but taught by the Spirit, interpreting spiritual truths to those who possess the Spirit" (1 Cor 2:12–13). Faith illumines believers' minds with "the mind of Christ" (1 Cor 2:16). The apostles and those who share their mandate—Paul here names himself, Apollos, and Peter (1 Cor 1:12)—are teachers of faith. Their authority comes from "the will of God" (1 Cor 1:1); they have been sent by Christ (1 Cor 1:17). While the apostles and those who share their mandate are not the primary agents causing faith in believers, they are instrumentally agents. The faith of the Corinthian believers is owed not to Paul but to "the power of God" (1 Cor 2:5). Paul is the teacher who has delivered the good news to the Corinthians; thus for those whom God calls, Paul's words inspire faith: "[W]e preach Christ crucified, a stumbling block to the Jews and folly to the Gentiles, but to those who are called, both Jews and Greeks, Christ, the power of God and the wisdom of God" (1 Cor 1:23–24).

Paul cautions against valuing the teachers over what they are teaching, namely "Jesus Christ and him crucified" (1 Cor 2:2). As he puts it, "Is Christ divided? Was Paul crucified for you? Or were you baptized in the name of Paul?" (1 Cor 1:13). Vis-à-vis Christ, Paul and those Paul teaches are on an equal level. They all serve Christ: "What then is Apollos? What is

---

democracy in Paul's writing. Instead there is *koinonia*, 'fellowship' (1 Cor 1:9, 10:16; 2 Cor 13:14) based on, and called for, by Christ's love. *Koinonia* requires us to live for one another, which means being open and transparent in mutual love. This will turn out to be exactly what Paul demands of the pastoral office, This *mutual openness*, which should banish all mistrust, is the reason why Paul has no difficulty in uniting love and obedience in the Church (2 Cor 7:15). The paradigm of this unity is Christ's obedience, even unto death; therefore the Corinthians, too, must be 'obedient in all things' to the Apostle" (Von Balthasar, *Paul Struggles with His Congregation: The Pastoral Message of the Letters to the Corinthians,* trans. Brigitte L. Bojarska [San Francisco: Ignatius Press, 1992 [1988], 25–26). Von Balthasar goes on to say, "*The unity between the authority of the Church and the community of the Church* finds its ultimate expression in the delicate decisions which Paul, as the pastor in charge, has to make alone but doesn't want to make without the congregation's consent" (26–27). He concludes, "In the final analysis, the unity between the pastoral office and the congregation becomes tangible in *the pastoral office's need for the congregation's prayer,* in order to carry out its work in accordance with God's will" (28).

Paul? Servants through whom you believed, as the Lord assigned to each. I planted, Apollos watered, but God gave the growth. So neither he who plants nor he who waters is anything, but only God who gives the growth" (1 Cor 3:5–7). Yet, Paul also participates in Christ's power in a way that sets him apart from those whom he teaches. Paul has received a position of authority within "the kingdom of God" (1 Cor 5:20). He thus can warn the Corinthian believers, "Some are arrogant, as though I were not coming to you. But I will come to you soon, if the Lord wills, and I will find out not the talk of these arrogant people but their power. For the kingdom of God does not consist in talk but in power" (1 Cor 5:19–20). Paul's distinctive participation in that power enables him to speak with authority to people who are otherwise his equals. He asks, "What do you wish? Shall I come to you with a rod, or with love in a spirit of gentleness?" (1 Cor 5:21).

Paul describes himself and those who share the apostolic mandate as the "stewards" of Christ's saving power: "This is how one should regard us, as servants of Christ and stewards of the mysteries of God" (1 Cor 4:1). As a "steward," Paul possesses "a rod" to enforce his pedagogical authority. Indeed, this "rod" can be active in the Corinthian church without Paul being physically present. Paul can speak in the Lord's name, with the Lord's power: "For though absent in body, I am present in spirit; and as if present, I have already pronounced judgment in the name of the Lord Jesus on the man who has done such a thing. When you are assembled, and my spirit is present, with the power of our Lord Jesus, you are to deliver this man to Satan for the destruction of the flesh, that his spirit may be saved in the day of the Lord Jesus" (1 Cor 5:3–5). Paul's power as "steward of the mysteries of God" thus extends over the community for the exercise of judgment, as part of his task of building up the community of believers.

To this point, we have shown that Paul, by his own description, participates uniquely in the cruciform power that he proclaims, the sanctifying power of Christ's Cross and Resurrection. We have noted that Paul identifies faith as the portal through which believers participate in this power. Paul is a "steward" of this faith. Believers also participate in the sanctifying power of Christ by means of baptism and the Eucharist. Although Paul says that "Christ did not send me to baptize but to preach the Gospel" (1 Cor 1:17), among the Corinthians Paul baptized at least Crispus, Gaius, and the household of Stephanas. With respect to the Eucharist he asks rhetorically, "The cup of blessing which we bless, is it not a participation in the blood of Christ? The bread which we break, is it not a participation in the body of Christ?" (1 Cor 10:16). The message of faith, baptism, and the Eucharist all unite believers to the sanctifying power of Christ crucified. Regarding this union with Christ's power, Paul states, "Because there is one bread, we who are many are one body, for we all partake in the one bread" (1 Cor 10:17). Their common participation in "the one bread," which itself is "a participation in the body of Christ," makes them "one body."

As one of the "stewards of the mysteries of God," Paul possesses authority over the modes of participating in Christ's sanctifying power. Put another way, these modes of sharing in Christ's sanctifying power flow through Paul (and through the other men who share the apostolic mandate). Not only does Paul assert his authority over the faith and morals upheld by the Corinthian community, but he also asserts his authority over the celebration of the Eucharist. Thus, he observes that in common understanding, "those who eat the sacrifices" are "partners of the altar" (1 Cor 10:18), and concludes from this that those who partake of the Eucharist may not partake of other sacrificial meals: "You cannot drink the cup of the Lord and the cup of demons. You cannot partake of the table of the Lord and the table of demons" (1 Cor 10:21). Similarly, he warns that the Corinthian mode of celebrating the Eucharist has not built up the Church's unity in the way that proper celebration of the Eucharist does. Although the Corinthians should be eating "the Lord's supper" (1 Cor 11:20), in fact when they gather together each eats his own supper, so that some go hungry. In this regard, Paul solemnly recalls the words of the Lord about the Eucharist as a warning against the Corinthians:

> For I received from the Lord what I also delivered to you, that the Lord Jesus on the night when he was betrayed took bread, and when he had given thanks, he broke it, and said, "This is my body which is for you. Do this in remembrance of me." In the same way also the cup, after supper, saying, "This cup is the new covenant in my blood. Do this, as often as you drink it, in remembrance of me." For as often as you eat this bread and drink the cup, you proclaim the Lord's death until he comes. (1 Cor 11:23–26)

Paul's apostleship or stewardship includes both watching over the Corinthians' faith, and instructing them on how to "remember" and "proclaim" the Lord in the Eucharist, and thereby participate in the power of his Pasch.

In short, Paul mediates between Christ and the Corinthians. Christ and the Corinthians are connected through the mediation of Paul, and yet the Corinthians are directly united with Christ. How can a mediated connection be direct? In a relationship of participation, mediation need not impede direct participation. By faith, baptism, and the Eucharist, the Corinthians participate directly in Christ's Cross and Resurrection. Yet this direct participation does not occur without apostolic mediation. Paul's (apostolic) participation in Christ's power nourishes and safeguards the Corinthians' (all Christians') participation in Christ's power. Christ's power flows through Paul, as apostle, precisely so that it might flow through the Corinthians.

Hierarchical authority in this way is not opposed to mutual self-subordination. The apostolic power that Paul receives from Christ is entirely subordinated, given over, to the power that the Corinthian believers thereby gain in Christ. Paul says in this regard, "I try to please all men in everything I do, not seeking my own advantage, but that of the many, that they may be saved" (1 Cor 10:33). Paul must be transparent to Christ: "For no other foundation can any one lay than that which is laid, which is Jesus Christ" (1 Cor 3:11). Paul passes on this apostolic authority to his collaborators: "Therefore I sent to you Timothy, my beloved and faithful child in the Lord, to remind you of my ways in Christ, as I teach them everywhere in every church" (1 Cor 4:17). In turn, the Corinthian believers receive Christ's power by subordinating themselves to Paul's power to mediate Christ's saving power. As Paul remarks, he is their "father in Christ Jesus through the Gospel" (1 Cor 4:15). No more than Paul can they claim any power that originates in themselves. Paul asks them, "What have you that you did not receive? If then you received it, why do you boast as if it were not a gift?" (1 Cor 5:7).

Paul employs the human body as an image of this mediated unity with Christ. He writes, "For just as the body is one and has many members, and all the members of the body, though many, are one body, so it is with Christ. For by one Spirit we were all baptized into one body—Jews or Greeks, slaves or free—and all were made to drink of one Spirit" (1 Cor 12:12–13). In the unity of the body, there is a hierarchy of parts, but this hierarchy does not place the parts in opposition. Each part of the body participates in the others, so as to constitute a hierarchical unity: "For the body does not consist of one member but of many" (1 Cor 12:14), and "there are many parts, yet one body" (1 Cor 12:20). As Paul points out, the relationship among the members of the body is not therefore one of competition: "If the foot should say, 'Because I am not a hand, I do not belong to the body,' that would not make it any less a part of the body" (1 Cor 12:15). Similarly, although in a rightly functioning body the "lower" parts of the body are subordinated to the "higher" parts, nonetheless this subordination does not constrict the lower parts but rather enables them to share in fulfilling the purposes of the entire body. In this regard Paul observes that "the parts of the body which seem to be weaker are indispensable" (1 Cor 12:22) and that "God has so adjusted the body, giving the greater honor to the inferior part, that there may be no discord in the body, but that the members may have the same care for one another" (1 Cor 12:24–25). The unity of the body does not negate the hierarchical ordering of the parts, but rather the hierarchy of the parts serves the flourishing of the one body. Paul concludes, "If one member suffers, all suffer together; if one member is honored, all rejoice together" (1 Cor 12:26).

For Paul, then, mediated union with Christ through the Holy Spirit is like the hierarchical mediation and participation that marks human bodiliness. Christ's power, the sanctifying power of the Cross and Resurrection, flows through the entire body and each part of the body participates in it directly by the Holy Spirit. As Paul puts it, "Now there are varieties of gifts, but the same Spirit; and there are varieties of service, but the same Lord; and there are varieties of working, but it is the same God who inspires them all in every one. To each is given the manifestation of the Spirit for the common good" (1 Cor 12:4–7). Yet, Christ's power, as the cruciform power of self-giving "weakness," is participated through self-subordinating love. Thus Christians directly receive Christ's power as mediated by self-subordinating relationships with others, founded upon love. In addition, because of the kind of power that it is—the power of sanctification in the Crucified One—this power must always have its source in Christ. It is not the kind of power that one can appropriate for oneself; only Christ can give it through his Holy Spirit. Christ does so through a hierarchical structure of participation and mediation that Paul describes as constituting the unity of the Church: "Now you are the body of Christ and individually members of it. Now God has appointed in the Church first apostles, second prophets, third teachers, then workers of miracles, then healers, helpers, administrators, speakers in various kinds of tongues" (1 Cor 12:27–28).

In this "body of Christ," the hierarchical organization of offices is one way in which Christ mediates to believers his self-subordinating love. Each member of the "body" must depend upon and serve the other members. Paul asks rhetorically, "Are all apostles? Are all prophets? Are all teachers? Do all work miracles? Do all possess gifts of healing? Do all speak with tongues? Do all interpret?" (1 Cor 12:29–30). The fact that the believers possess distinct vocations provides the opening for self-subordinating love, which Paul calls the "still more excellent way" (1 Cor 12:31) that belongs at the heart of every vocation. As Paul depicts the primacy of love:

> If I speak in the tongues of men and of angels, but have not love, I am a noisy gong or a clanging cymbal. And if I have prophetic powers, and understand all mysteries and all knowledge, and if I have all faith, so as to remove mountains, but have not love, I am nothing. If I give away all I have, and if I deliver my body to be burned, but have not love, I gain nothing. (1 Cor 13:1–3)

As he puts it elsewhere with specific regard to his own mandate, "I do not run aimlessly, I do not box as one beating the air; but I pommel my body and subdue it, lest after preaching to others I myself should be disqualified" (1 Cor 9:26–27).

The apostolic mandate gives a special power with respect to the communication of Christ's sanctifying power, but it does not *guarantee* that its possessor will abide in cruciform love. Yet, it does *assist* in configuring Paul to the self-subordination of Christ's Cross. As Paul says:

> For I think that God has exhibited us apostles as last of all, like men sentenced to death; because we have become a spectacle to the world, to angels and to men. We are fools for Christ's sake, but you are wise in Christ. We are weak, but you are strong. You are held in honor, but we in disrepute. To the present hour we hunger and thirst, we are ill-clad and buffeted and homeless, and we labor, working with our own hands. When reviled, we bless; when persecuted, we endure; when slandered, we try to conciliate; we have become, and are now, as the refuse of the world, the offscouring of all things. (1 Cor 4:9–13)

Paul's hierarchical authority leads to opposition and "disrepute" because his authority opposes the pride of other believers. Paul finds himself having to warn the Corinthians, "What! Did the word of God originate with you, or are you the only ones it has reached?" (1 Cor 14:36). Such exercise of hierarchical authority inevitably involves offense, and yet it affirms the crucial principle of Christian receptivity in contrast to pride. Receptivity is the key to Christian wisdom. As Paul states, "If any one thinks that he is a prophet, or spiritual, he should acknowledge that what I am writing to you is a command of the Lord. If any does not recognize this, he is not recognized" (1 Cor 14:37–38).

Paul shares his apostolic mandate with certain members of the Corinthian community, as well as with others whom he instructs the Corinthians to hear with obedience. Timothy is an important example: "When Timothy comes, see that you put him at ease among you, for he is doing the work of the Lord, as I am. So let no one despise him" (1 Cor 16:10–11). Apollos, too, "will come when he has opportunity" (1 Cor 16:12). From within the Corinthian community, Paul identifies Stephanas: "Now, brethren, you know that the household of Stephanas were the first converts in Achaia, and they have devoted themselves to the service of the saints; I urge you to be subject to such men and to every fellow worker and labor" (1 Cor 16:15–16). Mentioning Stephanas, Fortunatus, and Achaicus, Paul again emphasizes that they participate in his authority: "Give recognition to such men" (1 Cor 16:18).

For Paul, then, hierarchical authority in the Church belongs to Christ's mode of communicating, in the Holy Spirit, the power of Christ's self-subordinating love. Hierarchical authority befits Christ's Church because it makes manifest the fruitfulness of subordinating oneself to others in love, rather than placing oneself first. Paul is well aware of how difficult it is for believers to obey other Christians, but he insists upon it. He does so because such obedience expresses love (against the temptation of pride, the temptation to cling to oneself) and because of the very nature of the union of believers with Christ's sanctifying power as a direct and mediated union. As Paul says to the Corinthians, "Be imitators of me, as I am of Christ" (1 Cor 11:1; cf. 4:16).[52]

Hierarchical authority in the Church serves the mediation of Christ's self-subordinating love. No merely human teaching or merely human sacramental symbolism could mediate the saving power of Christ's Cross and Resurrection. Christ has chosen to give believers this saving power by requiring them to receive it from other believers. In its very nature, then, Paul's mandate and mission to communicate Christ's saving power to others sets Paul apart from other believers whom he serves. Christ alone can give what Paul (mediating Christ's gift) gives; thus Paul and his generation stand at the beginning of the "apostolic succession" by which the unique apostolic participation in Christ's power is passed down through the generations. Does this hierarchical authority, hierarchical mediation, disfigure the Church's witness to mutual self-subordinating love? No, because receiving from others is the very opposite of pride, and because those who give in the name of Christ must themselves become cruciform. Paul must be configured to Christ's self-

---

[52] Joseph Ratzinger likewise points to the Corinthian correspondence as indicating an apostolic power, given by Christ, to communicate the power of the Cross in a manner that other believers cannot communicate it. Commenting on 2 Cor 5, Ratzinger observes, "This text displays quite plainly that representative and missionary character of the apostolic ministry that we have just come to understand as the essence of a 'sacrament'; the God-given authority originating precisely in self-dispossession, in not speaking in one's own name, emerges clearly in this passage" (Joseph Cardinal Ratzinger, *Called to Communion: Understanding the Church Today,* trans. Adrian Walker [San Francisco: Ignatius Press, 1996], 118). He goes on to say that the "God-given authority" is to communicate "reconciliation with God, which springs from the Cross of Christ. . . . Since as a historical happening it [the Cross] belongs to the past, it can be appropriated only 'sacramentally'" (118). To understand this appropriation Ratzinger turns to 1 Corinthians: "[W]hen we listen to 1 Corinthians, we perceive that baptism and the Eucharist, which are inseparable from the word of preaching that produces faith and thus brings us to new birth, are essential for this event. Accordingly, it also becomes quite clear in Paul that the 'sacramental' authority of the apostolate is a specific ministry and in no wise describes Christian life as a whole, though many have wanted to draw this conclusion from the fact that the Twelve represent at the same time the future office and the Church as a whole" (118–19).

subordinating love so as to fulfill, in its fullest dimensions, the apostolic vocation of spending his life in giving Christ to other believers.[53]

The Apostolic Mandate: The Gospel of Matthew

Does the Gospel of Matthew add to this understanding of the relationship of hierarchical authority and self-subordinating Christian love? We have already noted two passages in Matthew that seem to militate against the fittingness of hierarchical authority in the Church: "[U]nless you turn and become like children, you will never enter the kingdom of heaven. Whoever humbles himself like this child, he is the greatest in the kingdom of heaven" (Mt 18:3–4), and:

> You know that the rulers of the gentiles lord it over them, and their great men exercise authority over them. It shall not be so among you,

---

[53] Pheme Perkins agrees that Paul's understanding of authority in the Church merits imitation, but she interprets his view in a different manner than I do. She begins by noting, "Accustomed to the authoritarianism of today's hierarchy, most Catholics presume that Paul exercised apostolic authority in the same way" (Perkins, " 'Being of One Mind': Apostolic Authority, Persuasion, and *Koinonia* in New Testament Christianity," in *Common Calling: The Laity and the Governance of the Catholic Church*, ed. Stephen J. Pope [Washington, DC: Georgetown University Press, 2004], 25). For Paul, she says, "The true apostle was not to be found in the royal entourage of a triumphal parade, but among the condemned captives at its end, mere garbage in the world's estimation" (31). She presents his understanding of apostolic authority as grounded in an authenticity recognized by the community: Paul's "principle remains fundamental to authority within the Christian churches: there must be a discernable 'fit' or coherence between the concrete words and deeds of leaders (apostles, preachers, teachers) and the Gospel they proclaim" (30). Due to this principle, Paul's exercise of authority passes muster even today. Perkins states, "In Paul's case, the imitation of Christ crucified engendered a pastoral practice that acknowledged the need for local flexibility in preaching the Gospel and building up the community of faith" (33). While criticizing Paul's practice and doctrine on some points, she finds that for Paul, "The cross negates every form of human self-assertion and domination (2 Cor 13:3–4)" (35). Her praise of Paul, however, depends upon the idea that Paul claims no authority other than the insight into the Gospel, and thus his ability to teach the Gospel, that his sufferings have given him: "The local leaders and teachers of Paul's time had no 'office' that gave them the right to determine belief or action. Rather, the authority of communal prophets and teachers was a consequence of their activities in the Church, encouraging, exhorting, and instructing others" (34; she cites here Troels Engberg-Pedersen, "1 Corinthians 11:16 and the Character of Pauline Exhortation," *Journal of Biblical Literature* 110 [1991]: 679–89). It is this limited view of apostolic authority as rooted solely in their teaching abilities that I am contesting in this essay.

but whoever would be great among you must be your servant, and whoever would be first among you must be your slave; even as the Son of man came not to be served but to serve, and to give his life as a ransom for many. (Mt 20:25–28)

Again one might ask: Can Paul's strong sense of his own apostolic authority—recall his claim that "if anyone does not recognize this, he is not recognized" (1 Cor 14:38)—be squared with Jesus' teaching in the Gospel of Matthew that Jesus' followers must humble themselves like children and must be the slaves of all? In order to gain insight into this question, I will identify seven characteristics that belong to the "mandate" of the disciple/apostle in the Gospel of Matthew.

First, the disciples/apostles are those who share Jesus' last Passover supper with him, and who thus bear responsibility for sharing it with the world. As Matthew describes it:

Now as they were eating, Jesus took bread and blessed and broke it and gave it to the disciples and said, "Take, eat; this is my body." And he took a cup, and when he had given thanks he gave it to them, saying, "Drink of it, all of you; for this is my blood of the covenant, which is poured out for many for the forgiveness of sins." (Mt 26:26–28)

Earlier Jesus feeds the crowds with his miraculous food through the mediation of the disciples/apostles. Thus Jesus "took the seven loaves and the fish, and having given thanks he broke them and gave them to the disciples, and the disciples gave them to the crowds" (Mt 15:36).

Second, the disciples/apostles receive the mission to communicate Jesus' sanctifying power to the entire world. The risen Lord appears on a mountain in Galilee only to the eleven disciples, Judas having committed suicide: "And Jesus came and said to them, 'All authority in heaven and on earth has been given to me. Go therefore and make disciples of all nations, baptizing them in the name of the Father and of the Son and of the Holy Spirit, teaching them to observe all that I have commanded you'" (Mt 28:18–20). Their mission depends upon their ongoing sharing in the presence of the risen Jesus, who tells them, "Lo, I am with you always, to the close of the age" (Mt 28:20). During his earthly ministry, too, Jesus calls the twelve and sends them on mission. In calling them to follow him, Jesus promises them, "'Follow me, and I will make you fishers of men'" (Mt 4:19). He gives them the mission to proclaim, by words and deeds, the coming of the kingdom of God in the towns of Israel (at first not entering any gentile or Samaritan town). Foreseeing their later journeying throughout the world, Jesus promises them that in bearing witness to him they will suffer, but that the Holy Spirit will speak through them: "When they deliver you up, do not be anxious how you are to speak or what you are to say; for what you are to say will be given to you in that hour; for it is not you who speak, but the Spirit of your Father speaking through you" (Mt 10:19–20).

Third, Jesus gives his disciples/apostles special explanations of his teachings. For example, after teaching the crowds at length in parables, Jesus interprets for his disciples/apostles alone the key parable, that of sower. As Matthew tells us,

> Then he [Jesus] left the crowds and went into the house. And his disciples came to him, saying, "Explain to us the parable of the weeds of the field." He answered, "He who sows the good seed is the Son of man; the field is the world, and the good seed means the sons of the kingdom; the weeds are the sons of the evil one, and the enemy who sowed them is the devil; the harvest is the close of the age." (Mt 13:36–39)

His disciples/apostles have a unique authority, therefore, to proclaim his teaching: "[teach] them to observe all that I have commanded you" (Mt 28:20).

Fourth, while all the disciples/apostles have a special share in Jesus' authority, Simon Peter stands out. He is the first one of the disciples to confess in faith that Jesus is "the Christ, the Son of the living God" (Mt 16:16). This faith comes not from Peter's own strength, but has been given Peter by "my [Jesus'] Father who is in heaven" (Mt 16:17). Jesus gives Peter a unique share in Jesus' authority,

> And I tell you, you are Peter, and on this rock I will build my Church, and the powers of death shall not prevail against it. I will give you the keys to the kingdom of heaven, and whatever you bind on earth shall be bound in heaven, and whatever you loose on earth shall be loosed in heaven. (Mt 16:18–19)

Yet Jesus' praise of Peter hardly means that Jesus does not recognize Peter's profound weakness. Peter cannot as yet imagine a Messiah who would suffer and die, and Peter rebukes Jesus for saying that this is what will happen. Jesus responds, "Get behind me, Satan! You are a hindrance to me; for you are not on the side of God, but of men" (Mt 16:23). Peter's strength is not his own. Likewise when Jesus commands him to walk on water, Peter does so but then begins to falter and begs Jesus to save him. Matthew relates, "Jesus immediately stretched out his hand and caught him, saying to him, 'O man of little faith, why did you doubt?'" (Mt 14:31). He is one with the rest of the disciples/apostles in this weakness of faith, and yet he receives authority that goes beyond theirs.

Fifth, the disciples/apostles leave everything to follow Jesus. The twelve, more than any others of those who followed Jesus during his earthly ministry, abandoned their earlier pursuits so as to serve the Lord. Because of this, they have a special share in Jesus' authority, a share that Jesus describes in eschatological terms: "Truly, I say to you, in the new world, when the Son of man shall sit on his glorious throne, you who have followed me will also sit on twelve thrones, judging the twelve tribes of Israel" (Mt 19:28). Others too will share in the reward given to the followers of Jesus. Thus Jesus continues, "And every one who has left houses or brothers or sisters or father for my name's sake, will receive a hundredfold, and inherit eternal life" (Mt 19:29).

Sixth, their power depends entirely upon Jesus. When they try to act on their own, they are repeatedly shown to be incompetent. For instance, when a man whose son suffers from epilepsy reports that the disciples could not cure the child and begs Jesus for a cure, Jesus answers, "O faithless and perverse generation, how long am I to be with you? How long am I to bear with you?" (Mt 17:17). After Jesus has healed the child, the disciples ask him why they could not do it. He answers, "Because of your little faith" (Mt 17:20). This same lack of faith appears when they wake Jesus out of fear that their boat will capsize. Jesus responds, "'Why are you afraid, O men of little faith?' Then he rose and rebuked the winds and the sea; and there was a great calm" (Mt 8:26). Yet their devoted following of Jesus suggests, at their best, a childlike faith in him. Indeed, Jesus rejoices that some people have understood him:

> I thank thee, Father, Lord of heaven and earth, that thou hast hidden these things from the wise and understanding and revealed them to babes; yea, Father, for such was thy gracious will. All things have been delivered to me by my Father; and no one knows the Son except the Father, and no one knows the Father except the Son and any one to whom the Son chooses to reveal him. (Mt 11:25–27)

When Jesus calls them, they do not hesitate: "Immediately they left their nets and followed him" (Mt 4:20), and "Immediately they left the boat and their father, and followed him" (Mt 4:22).

Seventh, having sworn not to abandon Jesus in his hour of trial, the disciples abandon him. Quoting Zechariah's messianic prophecy, Jesus tells them that they will fall away and then be gathered again. Led by Peter, they all deny that they will ever fall away:

Peter declared to him, "Though they all fall away because of you, I will never fall away." Jesus said to him, "Truly, I say to you, this very night, before the cock crows three times, you will deny me three times." Peter said to him, "Even if I must die with you, I will not deny you." And so said all the disciples. (Mt 26:33–35)

One of the disciples, Judas, betrays Jesus to the Roman authorities and in his guilt kills himself (Mt 27:5). They abandon Jesus even though three of them, Peter, James, and John, earlier witness the transfigured Lord beside Moses and Elijah (Mt 17:1–7).

The Gospel of Matthew presents these seven ways (no doubt among others) that Jesus sets apart the apostles from his other followers. The disciples/apostles have a unique share in the Passover meal and the distribution of Jesus' food to the world; they are called by Jesus to undertake the mission of communicating Jesus' sanctifying power to the world; they receive fuller explanations of Jesus' teachings and thereby have unique authority to teach in his name; Peter stands out among the disciples/apostles as sharing above the others in Jesus' authority; they leave everything to follow Jesus and receive authority accordingly; their power depends entirely upon Jesus; they all abandon Jesus in his hour of trial.

The Gospel of Matthew ends with the risen Lord's commissioning of the apostles; the Gospel does not tell us whether the apostles' unique power in the Church can be or is passed down to others so as to establish a permanent hierarchical leadership in the Church. However, the Gospel does indicate that the apostolic office in the Church is more than that of teachers of faith, requiring simply zeal and divine call. While the apostles possess unique authority to teach faith in Jesus, their unique mission is rooted in their sharing in the sanctifying power of the Cross and Resurrection by which Christ establishes the kingdom of God. Their share in this sanctifying power includes their mandate to baptize in the name of the Father, the Son, and the Holy Spirit and their unique participation in Jesus' own Paschal meal, the Eucharist. Peter's sharing in Jesus' authority is particularly striking. It should also be noted that Peter's authority is never separated from that of the other apostles, which provides its context.

It seems to me, then, that the hierarchical structure of participation and mediation that we saw in St. Paul also appears in the Gospel of Matthew. Does this hierarchical mediation assist or obscure the primacy of self-subordinating love in the Church? That hierarchical mediation can be abused is not news to the evangelist Matthew: Peter himself abuses his role, placing himself in front of Jesus rather than remaining transparent to Jesus. Nonetheless, Jesus wills to give Peter this role—and the rest of the apostles their role—even while knowing that all the apostles, and especially Peter, will abandon Jesus in his time of trial, and even despite the fact that Jesus has to rebuke Peter immediately after bestowing upon Peter his role. The mandate Jesus gives the apostles is not, then, based on expectations that those who share this mandate will be particularly holy in how they exercise hierarchical mediation.

Why then did Jesus choose hierarchical mediation as the structure for the communication in his Church of his sanctifying power? The disciples/apostles leave everything to follow Jesus, and their power (as participated power) depends entirely upon Jesus, without whom they are exposed as incompetent at best and enemies of Jesus at worst. So long as Jesus is in charge, then, hierarchical mediation teaches Christians that they cannot rely upon themselves. Just as it is through learning to depend upon Christ for salvation that we learn that we cannot depend upon ourselves, so also the Church becomes a school that teaches us how radically we must receive salvation from outside ourselves. Since Adam and Eve's sin consists precisely in refusing to receive (the prideful desire for self-sufficiency), sin's remedy in Christ must teach us to receive. If we cannot humble ourselves in front of the neighbor we see, then we will not be able to humble ourselves in front of the God whom we cannot see (cf. 1 Jn 4:20). The Church forms a school for self-humbling, because the Church compels us to receive not only from God, but even from fellow human beings whom we might otherwise proudly disdain.

What about, however, the persons at the "top" in terms of hierarchical authority—the bishops, and especially the pope? Do they receive? Does not their exalted position teach them the very opposite lesson, namely, that their power is their own, that their word is sufficient? Bishops and popes have not moved beyond the Church's structures of mediation. They are people formed in receiving, their lives spent in receiving Christ's teachings through the Church and receiving sacramental grace. Indeed, their lives are not their own, but are devoted to giving to the Church these very things that they receive.

Yet those who share the mandate of the apostles are often, like the disciples/apostles, publicly revealed to be what they are, weak human beings. Jesus lifts them up so as to fulfill his promises that "the powers of death shall not prevail" against the Church (Mt 16:18) and that the Holy Spirit "will teach you all things" (Jn 14:26). The "peace" and "freedom" in Christ that the Church enjoys (cf. Jn 14:27; Jn 8:32) is owed to the work of the holy Trinity. Those who share the mandate of the apostles are, as Paul and Barnabas say, merely "men, of like nature with you" (Acts 14:15). Ultimately the efficacy of hierarchical mediation in the Church rests on the Father, Son, and Holy Spirit's will to work out the salvation won by Christ, in and through the lives of sinful human beings. Recall Peter's words after hauling up "a great shoal of fish" (Lk 5:6) through Christ's instructions, after spending the night catching nothing: "Depart from me, for I am a sinful man, O Lord" (Lk 5:8). Jesus responds, "Do not be afraid; henceforth you will be catching men" (Lk 5:10). Why does Jesus take this risk, the terrible risk of allowing his sanctifying power to be mediated to others through sinful human beings? By means of participating in this structure of mediation and receptivity, human beings are formed in Christ's image.

But could not the structure of mediation and receptivity be radically deformed by sinful human beings so as no longer to mediate Christ's saving truth and power? To this there can only be one answer, namely Jesus' abiding presence in his Church: "Lo, I am with you always, to the close of the age" (Mt 28:20).

Concluding Reflections

Recall Healy's remark:

> The power of sin is manifested not only in the actions of individuals but in the Christian communal body, when the latter fosters practices, valuations, and beliefs in its membership that are incompatible with the Gospel. One of the more obvious examples of this is the failure of the Church's leadership to avoid the corruptions of power.[54]

The question before this essay has been whether the strong role of hierarchical authority in the Church "fosters practices, valuations, and beliefs in its membership that are incompatible with the Gospel." We have noted that many Catholic ecclesiologists today, following in the footsteps of many others through the course of Church history, believe that hierarchical authority in the contemporary Church should be changed to serve and validate democratic congregational decision-making. Similarly the mainstream of Catholic scholars of the earliest Church have argued that hierarchical authority, understood sacramentally, does not arise in a manner that could constitute theologically significant "apostolic succession" until well after the apostolic generation.

By examining 1 Corinthians and the Gospel of Matthew, I have tried to show that a sacramental sense of hierarchical authority belongs to the "theodrama" from the very beginning. Theologically, such hierarchical authority is intrinsic to the Church because the Church's mediation of Christ's saving power requires forming a receptive people. Many of the Corinthians clearly did not wish to receive Christ's saving power from Paul. They wished to go

---

[54] Healy, *Church, World and the Christian Life*, 7.

their own way, and one can hardly blame them. Why should disciples/apostles who abandoned Jesus, let alone those who came later such as Paul, be entrusted with communicating the power of Christ's Cross and Resurrection? Why not entrust this power to the whole community or entrust it to one-on-one encounters with Christ? Why hierarchical mediation of Christ's saving power? I have suggested both that Paul saw himself as possessing hierarchical power to mediate Christ's power, and that the Gospel of Matthew depicts the apostles in the same role.

Why then does this special power of the apostles and their successors not disfigure the Church's mission to manifest Christ's self-subordinating love? Simply put, as an antidote to pride, which desires autonomy, Christ calls his followers to receive him from others, just as "being found in human form, he humbled himself and become obedient unto death, even death on the cross" (Phil 2:8). Only such self-subordinating receptivity configures the Church to Christ's own humility, which is revealed to be true power: "Therefore God has highly exalted him and bestowed on him the name which is above every name" (Phil 2:9).

CHAPTER 8

The Voices of the Trinity in Scripture

GUY MANSINI, O.S.B.

IN THE INTRODUCTION to his translation of St. Thomas's commentary on the Letter to the Ephesians of some forty years ago, the preoccupying contemporary issue Fr. Lamb addressed was the openness of St. Thomas's exegetical principles to modernity's more or less exclusive attention to the literal sense of Scripture, understood as defined by authorial intention.[1] It is a measure of the thoroughness, objectivity, and theological insight with which he presented those principles of St. Thomas, however, that his introduction remains, forty years later, on the other side of Hans Frei and for those of us evermore preoccupied with the unity of the Testaments, a helpful resource and a reliable guide.[2] This is so because he shows us not only the openness to the new but the continuity with the old in which St. Thomas's principles stand. We see that, whether one suppose a humanly unintended spiritual sense to the Old Testament on the one hand, or a humanly intended literal but for all that Christological sense of the Old Testament on the other, the Bible cannot otherwise be one and the Old Testament cannot otherwise be Christian. In what follows, both issues, the nature of the literal sense and the

---

[1] Matthew Lamb, Introduction, in St. Thomas Aquinas, *Commentary on Saint Paul's Epistle to the Ephesians,* trans. Matthew L. Lamb (Albany, NY: Magi Books, 1966), 15–17; and see also the link to the contemporary treatment of the subject of inspiration, 256–57, n. 18.

[2] I mean Frei's *The Eclipse of Biblical Narrative: A Study in Eighteenth and Nineteenth Century Hermeneutics* (New Haven and London: Yale University Press, 1974). The question of the unity of the Testaments takes us either to Brevard Childs, canonical criticism, and biblical theology, or better, to retrievals of patristic exegesis. For the latter, see the splendid study of John J. O'Keefe and R. R. Reno, *Sanctified Vision: An Introduction to Early Christian Interpretation of the Bible* (Baltimore and London: Johns Hopkins University Press, 2005).

unity of the Testaments, are prominent, and it is a great honor to dedicate this essay to Fr. Lamb.

• • • • •

In the Bible, God speaks to us; in the Bible, God speaks to us about God. But God is Triune. So, the Triune God speaks to us in the Bible, revealing the Trinity. If there are three persons revealed, are there three voices speaking and revealing? And if there are, do the persons speak individually, or all together in chorus, or sometimes individually and sometimes in chorus?

St. Augustine addresses this question in Book II of the *De Trinitate*, asking about the theophanies of the Old Testament. He says it is natural to take the divine speaker of Genesis 2 who speaks to Adam as the same divine speaker of Genesis 1. That speaker, however, is God the Father. For since he is said to create by his speaking, he is creating by his Word, and the one who speaks the Word is the Father.[3] "However," he says, "there is nothing to prevent us from taking those voices which Adam heard as not only being produced by the three, but also as manifesting the person of the same three [*sed etiam personam demonstrantes eiusdem Trinitatis*]."[4] He thinks that we have to consider each scene of the Old Testament on its merits. So, in Genesis 18, the whole Trinity seems to appear in the figures of the three visitors to Abraham, and all three persons likewise speak from the burning bush in Exodus 3.[5] At Sinai, it seems to be the Holy Spirit (for Sinai is like Pentecost).[6] In Genesis 33, the back of God would seem to be the humanity of Christ, so it is Christ that Moses sees, and in Daniel, the Ancient of Days and the Son of Man are Father and Son.[7]

St. Augustine thinks we should not be "dogmatic in deciding [*ut temerere non dicemus*] which person of the three appeared in any bodily form or likeness to this or that patriarch or prophet."[8] Notwithstanding this advice, I aim in this essay to offer a rather more determinate answer to the question of who speaks to us in the Bible than St. Augustine thinks wise.

There can also be a question about whether and in what sense God speaks in all created speaking, and not just prophetic and apostolic speaking, allied with the question of whether and in what sense God teaches in all

---

[3] St. Augustine, "The Trinity," in *The Works of Saint Augustine*, ed. John R. Rotelle, O.S.A. (Brooklyn, NY: New City Press, 1991), bk. II, ch. 4, 17 [= 10, 17, in the older division], 109.

[4] Ibid., ch. 4, 18 [= 10, 18], 110.

[5] Ibid., ch. 4, 20 [= 11, 20], 111–12; ch. 5, 23 [= 13, 23], 113.

[6] Ibid., ch. 5, 26 [= 15, 26], 115.

[7] Ibid., ch. 6, 28 [= 17, 28], 117; ch. 7, 33 [18, 33], 120.

[8] Ibid., ch. 7, 35 [= 18,35], 121–22.

human teaching. In general, the creator can be said to speak in all created speaking when the truth of what God has made is declared.[9] The question of who is speaking is more complicated, however, when we consider the revelation of the Trinity and how that is accomplished, by what voices—by *whose* voices.

Robert Sokolowski has addressed this question in part in an article titled "The Revelation of the Holy Trinity: A Study in Personal Pronouns."[10] He shows us the necessity of the Incarnation for the revelation of the Trinity. "The Holy Trinity could only have been revealed 'from within,' by a speaker who indicates the differentiations within the Trinity not only by what he says but also by his very act of speaking."[11] This speaker is the incarnate Son. Through Moses and the prophets, Sokolowski says, God can speak of his relation to the world but not of "his own internal life."[12] "God has to accomplish this revelation [of the Trinity] by himself, in his own voice, through a speaker who was part of the divine life and not someone chosen to speak about it."[13] This seems to mean that, broadly, we can say that in the Old Testament we hear the Father, and in the New the Son. But Sokolowski does not deal with the question of the voices of Scripture comprehensively. Hans Urs von Balthasar relates the words of Scripture variously and always insightfully to the persons of the Trinity in an essay on the Word of God, but does not aspire to the strictness and consistency of usage to which this essay (perhaps unwisely) aspires.[14]

I propose to answer the question about who is speaking in the Bible as follows. I think St. Augustine's first idea should not be abandoned, and that, in general, the God who speaks in the Old Testament (and who is spoken to by men) is the God who first speaks in Genesis 1. Therefore, in the first place, God the Father speaks to us in the Old Testament. It is he who speaks, either in his own voice or through the voices of the hagiographers; it is generally him,

---

[9] See my "Doing and Speaking, Created and Uncreated," to appear in *Logos.*

[10] Robert Sokolowski, *Christian Faith & Human Understanding: Studies on the Eucharist, Trinity, and the Human Person* (Washington, DC: The Catholic University of America Press, 2006), 131–48.

[11] Ibid., 134–35.

[12] Ibid., 135.

[13] Ibid.

[14] Hans Urs von Baltasar, "The Word, Scripture and Tradition," *Explorations in Theology I The Word Made Flesh,* trans. A. V. Littledale with Alexander Dru (San Francisco: Ignatius Press, 1960, 1989), 11–26. Part 1 of Telford Work's *Living and Active: Scripture in the Economy of Salvation* (Grand Rapids, MI: Eerdmans, 2002) also touches on the question of this essay in various ways.

not the Spirit and not the Son, saving the more complicated question of the psalms and certain prophetic texts, which will be dealt with in due course.[15]

Second, in the New Testament, when the incarnate Son is represented as speaking to us, then it is indeed the Son, and not the Father or Spirit, who speaks.[16] Within the Trinity, only the Father speaks; of course, he speaks the Word, who cannot himself properly speak.[17] The Son can have no voice with which to speak to us or to the Father except as Incarnate.[18] And to think of the persons speaking to one another within the Trinity seems ineluctably tritheistic.

Should we not say, however, that when the incarnate Word speaks, the Father also speaks, since it is the Father who speaks the Word who is speaking? Yes. Moreover, in John's gospel, Jesus says he speaks what he hears, and St. Augustine tells us that he is "hearing" in the sense of being spoken, being the Word.[19] Still, the humanity of Jesus is assumed by the Word, the Son alone, and not by Father or Spirit, and it is therefore the Son who speaks in and through this humanity, this created mind and voice, although, to be sure, he speaks only what he hears from the Father.[20] The Father therefore speaks through him rather as one quoted can be said to speak when he is quoted by another. On the other hand, and third, when in the New Testament the apostle or some evangelist speaks in his own voice, not quoting or paraphrasing the words of Jesus, then we will say that it is both the Father and the Son who speak. The Father speaks through them in the New just as in the Old he speaks through the prophets. The intelligibility of taking things this way will be indicated shortly. But also, when the New Testament writers and speakers are speaking about Christ and speaking from their experience of him, the incarnate Son continues to speak through them. "When they wrote what he

---

[15] Broadly, therefore, this essay follows the line of Origen; see Manlio Simonetti, *Biblical Interpretation in the Early Church: An Historical Introduction to Patristic Exegesis,* trans. John A. Hughes (Edinburgh: T&T Clark, 1994), 41. Note the distance Balthasar puts between himself and Origen, in "The Implications of the Word," *Explorations in Theology I,* 49–51.

[16] St. Augustine, "The Trinity," bk. II, ch. 4, 18 [= 10, 18], 110.

[17] Bernard J. F. Lonergan, S.J., *De Deo Trino II. Pars systematica* (Rome: Gregorian University, 1964), q. 20, 196.

[18] See on this, Robert Sokolowski, *Eucharistic Presence: A Study in the Theology of Disclosure* (Washington, DC: The Catholic University of America, 1993), 75: "It seems that the Incarnation allowed a kind of response by God to God himself to take place, a response that could not have occurred in any other way."

[19] St. Augustine, *Homilies on the Gospel of John,* vol. 7 of *Nicene and Post-Nicene Fathers,* ser. I (Edinburgh: T&T Clark, 1988), on John 5:30, tractate 22, 14, p. 150.

[20] See Gilles Emery, O.P., "The Personal Mode of Trinitarian Action," *The Thomist* 69 (2005): 62: The action of the incarnate Son, because of the hypostatic union, is proper to the Son, where the humanity is the principle of the action.

showed them and said to them, it ought by no means to be said that he himself did not write it," St. Augustine says, "since his members wrote what they knew at the dictation of the Head."[21] Here, the reality of the Head–Body relation grounds the recognition of the voice of, say, James, as the voice also of Christ.

What of the Holy Spirit? Does not the Holy Spirit, of whom the ecumenical Creed says "he has spoken though the prophets," speak always and everywhere in the Bible? The Church from the outset attributed the hagiographers' inspiration to the Spirit, following 2 Peter 1:21.[22] But inspiring to speak is not speaking, or at least it is speaking in another sense. I will follow St. Thomas, who in commenting on John 14:26 holds that the Spirit speaks as a teacher in the sense that he makes the apostle or evangelist able to receive what another divine person says. We will visit this important text in due course, as also the few times in the New Testament where the Spirit is said to speak. But it can be observed here immediately that, though the Spirit is said in the Creed to speak "through the prophets," when the prophets speak, they say "thus saith the Lord...," and as will be argued, this must be understood to be the Father.

There is also the matter of authorship. We may well say that God or the Spirit is the "author" of the Bible.[23] But an author is not a voice, immediately, unless he writes in the first person. If by author we mean efficiency, the making of the minds and the thoughts that make the Book, then all three Persons are the author, since every exercise of efficiency *ad extra* is common to the three.[24] But we are interested in voices. If causing to know is speaking, and that is all we mean by it, then all three speak always in Scripture. But if we make speaking include an identifying and manifesting of the very person or persons causing, then within the book, of which the triune God is author,

---

[21] St. Augustine, *De consensu evangelistarum* I, 35, 54: cum illi scripserunt quae ille ostendit et dixit, nequaquam dicendum est quod ipse non scripserit; quandoquidem membra eius id operata sunt, quod dictante capite cognoverunt.

[22] See ch. 1, "Inspiration and Prophecy: The Second Century," in J. Patout Burns and Gerald M. Fagin, *The Holy Spirit*, vol. 3 of *Message of the Fathers of the Church* (Wilmington, DE: Michael Glazier, 1984). Formulae are various: The Holy Spirit speaks in Scripture, Christ speaks to us in Scripture through the Holy Spirit, Scripture is inspired of the Holy Spirit, the Holy Spirit fills a prophet who then speaks, the Spirit shows the Word to the prophets, etc. Robert Louis Wilkin, *The Spirit of Early Christian Thought* (New Haven, CT: Yale University Press, 2003), 62, quotes Cyril of Alexandria: "The entire Scripture is one book and was spoken by one Holy Spirit."

[23] St. Thomas, *Expositio super Isaiam ad literam*, prooemium: *Auctor enim Scripturae sacrae spiritus sanctus est.*

[24] As St. Augustine notes precisely in this context, *The Trinity*, bk. II, ch. 4, 18 [= 10, 18], 110; see St. Thomas, *Summa theologiae* I, q. 45, a. 6.

sometimes one or the other of the persons speak distinctly from the others, as with the voice of the Father from heaven: "This is my beloved Son . . ." or as with the voice of the Son incarnate, where the Word speaks through his humanity. True, "he who hears me hears the one who sent me." So, the Father is speaking, too, but again, rather as one quoted.[25]

Closely related to, indeed, inseparable from, the question as to who is speaking is the question of what the persons speak, what they speak about. So, what Father and Son speak of in the Bible is the Trinity; what is revealed—by their speaking—is the mystery of the three distinct persons who are each the one God. In trying to throw light on this it is important to identify the Son also as Word, as I hope to show.[26] In the Old Testament, where the God who speaks there, the one whom Jesus calls "Father," is spoken of, then naturally he is what the discourse is about. But the entire meaning of everything else spoken of in the Old Testament—about the kingdom and the temple and the people and the covenants, and so on—is Christ, so that *what* the Father speaks, through prophets and hagiographers inspired of the Spirit, is Christ.[27]

What is spoken in the Old Testament is always "words," or we may say, the Word as articulated in the many words of God spoken by God the Father through the prophets and, more anonymously, through the hagiographers.[28] What is spoken about are all the many things comprising the history of patriarchs and people, exodus and entry into the promised land, sacrifice and law, covenant and kingdom, exile and return, law and wisdom. But insofar as all these things are fulfilled in Christ, each and every one, what is spoken of is the incarnate Word. This can be called the "spiritual sense," and by it we can

---

[25] So, when the Son speaks to us, the Father speaks to us too. When the Son speaks to the Father, and this in virtue of his human mind, shall we then say that only he speaks? No; what he offers to the Father in prayer is a returning of what he has received.

[26] Sokolowski discusses the distinction as of the Son from the Father, not as of Word from Speaker.

[27] See here the important analyses of John Behr, *Formation of Christian Theology*, vol. 1, *The Way to Nicea* (Crestwood, NY: St. Vladimir's Seminary Press, 2001), 25–28, 116–29 (Irenaeus), 169–84 (Origen), 239, on the identity of the word of Scripture and the Word made flesh. For medieval expressions of this point, see Henri de Lubac, *Medieval Exegesis*, vol. 2, *The Four Senses of Scripture,* trans. E. M. Macierowski (Grand Rapids, MI: Eerdmans, 2000), 89–98.

[28] Louis Bouyer, *The Eternal Son: A Theology of the Word of God and Christology,* trans. Sr. Simone Inkel and John F. Laughlin (Huntington, IN: Our Sunday Visitor Press, 1978), 59: "[T]he Word the prophets had been prompted to transmit at a given time was nonetheless a unique Word, and moreover the Word that had been spoken to Moses and Abraham, ultimately the Word that created Israel's history, as well as universal history and even all of creation."

mean a sense intended by God, if not by the human author.[29] If the Father is the original speaker of what means the incarnate Word in the Old Testament, moreover, then the same is so for the New. When evangelist or apostle speaks of Christ, and Christ is the meaning of their words, then it is the Word spoken, and therefore, it is the Father who is the original speaker.

If the Word is spoken of in terms of kings and covenants and other Old Testament realities, may it not be objected that Word and Spirit are sometimes spoken of quite directly and as the very topic of the discourse in the Old Testament as in the New? In the New, this is certainly so. For the Old, we will also answer affirmatively, but understand that this occurs only given that the New has been written and the spiritual sense of the Old declared. Then Sirach and Proverbs can tell us of the Word, and Isaiah of the Spirit.

Furthermore, that what the Father speaks through prophets and hagiographers inspired of the Spirit is Christ turns out to be important for the very recognition of the Son as Word and as fully divine. Because we hear them speak to and about one another in the New Testament, we know the real distinction of Father and Son; but because Christ's speech and action fulfill what the Father spoke in the Old Testament, showing us that he is that "spoken," we know that he is Word, and we know the unity of substance, the identity of essence, of Father and Son.

The Trinity cannot be something that is just known about; we must share in it in order to know it. That is, we know it only by faith and love, a function of the Spirit dwelling in our hearts. As the Holy Spirit first moved prophets and hagiographers to speak and write, so he enables us to hear and read the words and to recognize the Word, and to repeat the words in praise and evangelizing and catechizing and within the contemplation of theology.[30] The Holy Spirit also brings us joy when we see how we get to the knowledge

---

[29] Notoriously, the spiritual sense is variously defined, but for St. Thomas, it does not necessarily mean a sense not known, not intended, by the human author; see Daniel E. Flores, "Thomas on Theodore of Mopsuestia, Exegete," *The Thomist* 69 (2005): 268–69, 270–71, 272. It is also necessary to recall here that for St. Thomas, the *literal* sense of substantial portions of the Old Testament, a sense intended by the human author, is expressly Christological. According to his inaugural sermon, the subject of Isaiah is the advent of Christ, of Jeremiah his passion, of Ezekiel his resurrection, and of Daniel his divinity. Moreover, the matter of the psalms is Christ and the members of his body. It is hard, but necessary, to recover the supposition of such places as Acts 3:24, where "all the prophets" proclaim the days of Christ; namely, that they proclaimed them knowingly, just as at Acts 2:31 it is said that David "foresaw and spoke of the resurrection of Christ" in Psalm 15.

[30] See here Lamb's summary of St. Thomas on prophecy, whose grace includes last but not least the interpretation of Scripture, in his Introduction to St. Thomas Aquinas, *Commentary,* 7.

of the Trinity, which is to say how it is revealed, for knowledge increases love and love makes joy abound.

• • • • •

Let us return again to St. Augustine's first suggestion as to who is speaking in the Old Testament. In chapter one of Genesis, the Lord God creates and furnishes the world by his word—"God *said,* let there be light," and so on. According to John's gospel, this word is the Word by whom all things were made. Therefore, the one speaking in Genesis 1 is the Father, who calls the world and the things therein to existence by his Word. But, St. Augustine observes, there is no indication of a shift of speaker from the first to the second and third chapters of Genesis. Therefore, it is God the Father whose words we hear, whose actions we observe, and who is spoken to in turn by Adam and Eve. We add, however, that this seems to be the case not just through Genesis, but throughout the Old Testament: The God speaking, witnessed to, spoken of, spoken to, is the Father; there is never a shift of divine speaker, and the God of the Old Testament is therefore the Father.

There are also strong New Testament reasons for taking things so. The beginning of the Letter to the Hebrews informs us that "[i]n many and various ways God spoke of old to our fathers by the prophets; but in these last days he has spoken to us by a Son." Therefore, it is the Father that we hear in the Old Testament.[31] There is also the speech of Stephen in Acts. The "God of glory" who appeared and spoke to Abraham and to Moses, who settled Israel in Canaan, for whom Solomon built the Temple, this is the God beside whom Stephen sees standing the Son of man, Jesus (7:56). Therefore, the God of the Old Testament is the Father, whose Son, Jesus, we see in the New.[32]

Even so, we will want to make some distinctions with regard to the "voices" we hear. In his inaugural sermon on the "Commendation of and Division of Sacred Scripture," St. Thomas divides the Old Testament into Law, Prophets, and Writings.[33] In the first two, God speaks. In giving the Law,

---

[31] It is to be noted that the Son is addressed in the words of Ps 44 at Hebrews 1:8–9, and of Psalm 101 at Hebrews 1:10–12, and of Psalm 109 at Hebrews 1:13. The Son is spoken of in Psalm 8 at Hebrews 2:5–8, and he speaks in the words of Psalm 21 at Hebrews 2:12 and of Isaiah 8 at Hebrews 2:13, as also of Psalm 39 at Hebrews 10:5–7. The Holy Spirit speaks in the words of Psalm 94 at Hebrews 3:7–11, and in the words of Jeremiah 31 at Hebrews 10:16–17. The problem raised by these passages is dealt with below.

[32] Without necessarily agreeing that *"theos" means* "Father" (rather than merely supposing for the Father), it remains profitable to read Karl Rahner, "Theos in the New Testament," *Theological Investigations,* vol. 1 (Baltimore: Helicon, 1961), 79–148.

[33] De Commendatione et Partitione Sacrae Scripturae, in *Opuscula Theologica I. De Re Dogmatica et Morali,* ed. R. A. Verardo, O.P. (Rome: Marietti, 1954), no. 1204.

he himself speaks. Second, he speaks through heralds, the prophets, who speak "in his person" (*ex persona Dei*). And for the third part, hagiographers "inspired by the Holy Spirit" (*Spiritu Sancto inspirati*) spoke about him.

If "God" supposes here for the Father, as according to the first suggestion of St. Augustine, and according to the Acts of the Apostles, then:

1. The Father speaks in the Old Testament, in his own voice, as it were, to Adam, to Noah, to Abraham, to Moses It is not that Adam and Moses and the rest know the one speaking as Father. We know this, however, because we have both Testaments.

2. The Father also speaks to the people through the prophets, his heralds, who speak "in his person," in the phrase of St. Thomas. What the Father says can be mediated. It can be repeated, quoted by another, and as by one who is commissioned to do so.

3. The hagiographers speak about the Father and his works and his words, in their own voices, in their own persons, but do so inspired of the Holy Spirit. These words, too, however, are to be ascribed ultimately to the Father, as has already been briefly argued.

Analogously, for the New Testament, we could then say:

1. The Word made flesh speaks in the New Testament in his own voice, the voice he has in virtue of his assumed humanity, to disciples, to Pharisees, to scribes and priests.

2. The Word made flesh also speaks to people in towns and villages and ultimately the world through the apostles, his heralds, speaking "in his person" (for example, Mt 10, 28). What the Word says can be mediated. It can be repeated, quoted, by others, and as by those commissioned to do so.

3. The writers of the New Testament speak about the Word made flesh and his works and words, in their own voices, in their own persons, but inspired of the Holy Spirit. Since they speak of Christ, himself spoken by the Father, what they are saying is first spoken by the Father. But as in Christ and as members of his body, they possess another and special relation to Christ, as we have seen St. Augustine to teach, and are moved as members by him, the Head.

There is a new translation of this text in *Thomas Aquinas: Selected Writings*, ed. and trans. Ralph McInerny (London: Penguin Books, 1998); see p. 8. As to the division itself, see Jer 18:18—"the law shall not perish from the priest, nor counsel from the wise, nor the word from the prophet," and cf. Ez 7:26.

It has been pointed out that the Word speaks in virtue of his assumed humanity. The second person can speak straightforwardly and properly only as incarnate. Is he not said to teach and so speak insofar as, according to St. Augustine, he is the interior teacher of every human acquisition of knowledge? Yes, but in that way he teaches not so much as speaking a word but as being the Word, the Expressed Intelligibility, of which every interior word is a participation.[34] Strictly, *dicere* is proper to Father.[35] Again, if speaking means "the expression of a conceived word," then a speaker has to have concepts to manifest in order to speak.[36] The Father can speak; he has his Word. But for the Word to have words, he must have an assumed humanity.

As for the Spirit, neither does the Holy Spirit speak within the Trinity. The Spirit does not have the Word as does the Father, since he rather proceeds from the Word, and so he does not speak him. Does he speak within the economy? Since all Scripture is inspired of the Spirit, we might say that we always hear the Holy Spirit in some way. It is not, however, in his own voice or only rarely so. So in the Letter to the Hebrews, he is said to speak in the words of Psalm 94 at 3:7–11 and in the words of Jeremiah 31 at 10:16–17. There are some few other passages where what is said seems proper to him. In Revelation 14:13 and 22:17, the Spirit voices the finality of things in Christ. In both cases, however, one might still take what the Spirit says as the prayer of the Church. So, in 22:17, where "the Spirit and the Bride say 'Come,'" this might as well mean "the Spirit through the Bride, as inspiring her, says 'Come.'" In Acts 10:19–20 and 13:2 the Spirit speaks in the first person of disciples who have a mission in Christ. And in Matthew 10:20, Jesus says that the Spirit of the Father will speak through those whom he, Christ, sends. For these places, an observation of Robert Sokolowski is especially appropriate, when, following Anscar Vonier, he would have us remember that the Spirit completes but does not add to the Incarnation. He points out as well that the Spirit is more often

---

[34] St. Augustine, *De magistro*, 11, 38; St. Thomas, *Lectura super evangelium S. Ioannis*, ed. R. Cai, O.P. (Rome: Marietti, 1952), at 13:13, no. 1775. At 7:16, no. 1037, however, St. Thomas says that all truth, no matter who speaks, is also to be attributed to the Holy Spirit. In *ST* I, q. 117, a. 1, ad 1, the interior teacher of men can be said to be simply God, according as God creates the intellect. We will see later how the persons can be distinguished within this one activity. See especially Gilles Emery, *Trinity in Aquinas* (Ypsilanti, MI: Sapientia Press, 2003), 288–91; and "Personal Mode," 62–65.

[35] See note 17 above.

[36] St. Thomas, *Super Epistolam ad Hebraeos Lectura*, in *Super Epistolas S. Pauli Lectura*, II, ed. R. Cai, O.P. (Rome: Marietti, 1953), at 1:2, no. 15: tria requiruntur ad locutionem nostrum. Primo, verbi conceptio, qua scilicet praeconcipiatur in mente id quod ore loquendum est; secundo ipsius verbi concepti expressio; tertio ipsius rei expressae manifestatio, qua res expressa evidens fiat.

represented as force and breath relative to the voiced word of some other speaker than as speaking in his own voice. So, where St. Paul says the Spirit intercedes, it is with "inexpressible groanings" (Rom 8:26), "that is, without syntax and without any first-person pronouns."[37] Rather than his own, the Spirit makes us hear the voices of Father, or Son, or hagiographer and those men whom the hagiographers quote.[38]

More important than the few places where the Spirit is represented as speaking the word are those places where he is represented as enabling the conception of the word. This is directly related to our topic. The Spirit enables the prophets to conceive the Word of God (for example, Nm 11:25; 1 Sam 10:10; Is 61:1; Ez 2:2); the same Spirit enables Mary to conceive the Word (Mt 1:18; Lk 1:35).[39] In both cases, it is the same word, the prophetic word as part of the single Word; and in both cases it is therefore the same speaker. And so, in the Old Testament, it is the Father whose voice is principally heard.

We cannot identify the speaker of the Old Testament as the Father until the New, until Jesus speaks in such a way and tells us such things as to inform us both that he is the Word, spoken by the Father, by the God who now appears to us as his Father, and that he is the meaning of the Old Testament. In fact, it can be argued that he does the former by way of doing the latter. That is, he reveals to us that he is the Word precisely by showing himself to be the meaning of the Old Testament, to be there already spoken and spoken of. From the vantage of the New Testament, the word that God speaks in the Old Testament and what he speaks about is identically the Word made flesh.[40] Once Christ is revealed as Word in this way, it follows of course that we know not just the dominant and new voice of the New Testament, but at the same time the dominant voice of the Old Testament. To know the Son is to know the Father, and to know where the one speaks is to know where the other speaks. Nor should we be surprised, at the end of the day, to see that when God speaks, even to us, he can speak only divine things. When the Father speaks, even to us, all he can say is his Son. "Whatever the Father says to us," St. Augustine explains, "he says by his Word: the Word of the Father is the Son; is there another word by which he speaks to the Word? God is one; he has one Word; he contains all things in the one Word."[41]

[37] Sokolowski, "Revelation of the Holy Trinity," 145.

[38] Ibid., 146; see St. Irenaeus, *Proof of the Apostolic Preaching,* trans. Joseph P. Smith, *Ancient Christian Writers,* vol. 16 (Westminster, MD: Newman Press, 1952), 80 (no. 49).

[39] This is commonly noted. See, for instance, Yves Congar, *I Believe in the Holy Spirit,* vol. 1, *The Experience of the Spirit,* trans. David Smith (New York: Seabury, 1983), 6.

[40] See again the work of Behr, cited above at note 27.

[41] *Homilies on the Gospel of John,* tractate 22, 14, p. 150: I have altered the translation slightly (quidquid nobis Pater dicit: Verbo suo dicit: Verbum Patris Filius est, ipsi

· · · · ·

The communication that Jesus is the Word can be seen to begin with his claims to fulfill the Law and the prophets. Once this is made good, then he can be identified with the Word–Wisdom that the later writers of the Old Testament themselves sometimes identified with the Law and associated with prophecy. That is, he first tells us that he has not come to abolish but to fulfill the Law and prophets (Mt 5:17). This includes but is not just a matter of a teaching that completes and perfects the teaching of the Old Testament. Additionally, he claims to be and is ever increasingly appreciated in the New Testament as in himself the fulfillment of Scripture. The Old Testament canon is established precisely as these writings and not others are seen to be about him, to speak of him, and they become "old" words only by contrast to the novelty of the Word made flesh (see Lk 24; 2 Cor 3:14). As St. Paul says, "all the promises of God find their Yes in him" (2 Cor 1:20). This is the hinge. For if he is the fulfillment of Scripture in this personal and comprehensive sense, then he is the meaning, the single "word" spoken in the many words of the Scriptures throughout their breadth, the wisdom of God expressed in Law and prophet, whose presence in the history of Israel is witnessed throughout the prophets and the writings. As incarnate, he is truly the *verbum breviatum* of the Scriptures (Rom 9:28 Vulg.). To be the fulfillment of the words of the Law and the prophets is to make them true, as being their truth, their actuality. Thus he shows himself the Word, the actuality of all the words of the Old Testament (for example, in John 5:39). And since God's word and wisdom are always with him, as St. Athanasius pointed out, he will be the Word by whom in the beginning the heavens and the earth were made.

In the rest of this section, synoptic material is briefly reviewed, and in the next, Paul and John and Revelation. We begin by collecting some of the claims, explicit and implicit, that our Lord is represented as making to fulfill the Law and the prophets, beginning with the most obvious and transparent

In Mark's gospel, Jesus applies the words of Psalm 117 to himself, "the very stone which the builders rejected has become the head of the corner" (12:10). His prediction of his passion at 10:45 recalls both Daniel 7 and Isaiah 53. At 14:27, he makes himself the shepherd who is struck according to the prophecy of Zechariah 13:7. In both the eschatological discourse of chapter 13 and at 14:62, during the trial, he is again the Son of man of Daniel 7. He claims to fulfill Psalm 21 ("my God, my God . . .") from the cross (15:37), as earlier Psalm 109 (14:62).

Such employment of particular texts alerts us to look for more comprehensive claims. Jesus' career begins with the announcement of the fullness of time and the advent of the eschatological kingdom (Mk 1:15), the *telos* of the previous trajectory of word and deed in the Old Testament. He calls the people to a repentance and renewal that will prepare them to be the eschatological Israel, and everything unfolds within this encompassing program, such as his identification of the Baptist with the Elijah who was to come (9:11; cf. Mal 4:5), and his provision of a new ethic for an eschatologically renewed people, as with the teaching on divorce (10:2–9).[42] The execution of that program very much involves the interpretation of Scripture, and under the overarching claim of the presence of the kingdom, his authoritative interpretation of the Scriptures enacts a claim to be or to provide for their fulfillment. This is so with the teaching on divorce (10:2–9; cf. Gen 2:24 and Dt 24:1–4), with the teaching on the resurrection within which we learn what it means to say that God is the "living God" (12:26–27; cf. Ex 3:6 and Dt 25:5), with the question of the ordering of the Law (12:28), and with the interpretation of David's Lord in Psalm 109 (12:35). Then there are such implied fulfillments as that of the Parable of the Vineyard in chapter 12 (cf. Is 5), and the grand entry into Jerusalem and the cleansing of the Temple (Is 56), both in 11, and both made explicit in Matthew.

Many individual Old Testament passages are evoked as finding their fulfillment in Jesus. Also, there is a claim to fulfill the whole, to be the meaning of the whole of the "Scriptures." This lies just under the surface of the teaching on the resurrection, already mentioned. Jesus says to the Sadducees, ignorant of the resurrection, "you know neither the Scriptures nor the power of God" (Mk 12:24). But ignorance of the Scriptures is here equivalent to ignorance of Jesus, since he has come to reveal the resurrection. In John 11, of course, he will be identified as "the resurrection and the life" and in 1 Corinthians as "the power of God" (1:24).[43] The same equivalence of the resurrected one, on the one hand, and Moses and the prophets, on the other, is proposed by the parable of Dives and Lazarus (Lk 16:29–31), where failure to comprehend and believe one is failure to grasp the other. Then there is the Transfiguration, where Moses and Elijah appear with Jesus in a sort of enactment of the saying of Matthew 13:10 that "many prophets and righteous men longed to see what you see." What Jesus' contemporaries see is

---

Verbo quo alio verbo dicit? Unus est Deus, unum Verbum habet, in uno Verbo omnia continet).

[42] Ben F. Meyer, *The Aims of Jesus* (London: SCM Press, 1979), 139–42.

[43] On Mk 12:18–27, see Richard B. Hays, "Reading Scripture in the Light of the Resurrection," in *The Art of Reading Scripture*, ed. Ellen F. Davis and Richard B. Hays (Grand Rapids, MI: Eerdmans, 2003), 224–29; the power of God is linked with the Son of man in Dan 7 and the Son of man is linked with the general resurrection in Dan 12.

him; and Moses and Elijah witness to the passing of Law and prophecy into the glory of the gospel, the glory specifically of the cross, which here, more manifestly, shows up as the meaning of the Scriptures, the key to the book.[44]

That Jesus is the fulfillment of the whole of Scripture is not merely implied but very fully stated in many places of the non-Markan material common to Matthew and Luke.[45] I count five.

First, there is the statement of Matthew 13:10 just referred to. In its Lukan form (10:24), we read: "many prophets and kings [Mt: "righteous men"] desired to see what you see, and did not see it, and to hear what you hear, and did not hear it." But the "prophets and kings" are those whose words and deeds are recorded in the Scriptures, and their longing for Christ is expressed there, in the record of what they said and did, which is equivalent to saying Christ is the fulfillment of Scripture.

Second, in Jesus' condemnation of the scribes and Pharisees, there is a sort of reverse form of the statement just considered. As Jesus is the end of the line of the prophets and the just, the scribes and Pharisees who persecute Jesus are the end of the line of those who persecuted them.[46]

> For you build the tombs of the prophets whom your fathers killed [Mt: "and adorn the monuments of the righteous"]. So you are witnesses and consent to the deeds of your fathers; for they killed them, and you build their tombs. Therefore also the Wisdom of God said, "I will send them prophets and apostles [Mt: "prophets and wise men and scribes"], some of whom they will kill and persecute," that the blood of all the prophets, shed from the foundation of the world, may be required of this generation, from the blood of Abel the just to the blood of Zechariah, who perished between the altar and the sanctuary. Yes, I tell you, it shall be required of this generation. (Lk 11:47–51 = Mt 23:29–31 and 34–36)

So, from the story of Abel onward, with prophets and kings and wise men, the whole of the Scriptures are indicated, and in suffering persecution, Jesus fulfills them all.

Third, and in the same vein, there is the lament over Jerusalem.

> O Jerusalem, Jerusalem, killing the prophets and stoning those who are sent to you! How often would I have gathered your children together. . . . Behold, your house is forsaken [Mt: "and desolate"]. And I tell you,

---

[44] See again Behr, *Way to Nicea,* 118.

[45] I follow the order of the material assembled in Ben Witherington III, *Jesus the Sage: The Pilgrimage of Wisdom* (Minneapolis: Fortress Press, 1994), 219–21.

[46] This argument is repeated by Stephen, Acts 7:52.

you will not see me until you say, "Blessed is he who comes in the name of the Lord." (Lk 13:34–35 = Mt 23:37–39)

In this text (1) Jesus fulfills Jeremiah 22:5 (the house desolate), (2) is the fulfillment of Psalm 117:26 ("blessed is he"), (3) as it were, closes the history of election and prophecy recounted in the Old Testament, and (4) most strikingly suggests his own agency within the Old Testament, when he says, "how often I would have gathered your children," for the meaning is, "how often I would have gathered them those many times in which the prophets were sent to you."

Fourth, speaking of judgment, Jesus makes it equivalent to his recognition of men on the last day (13:25–27), and adds:

> There you will weep and gnash your teeth, when you see Abraham and Isaac and Jacob and all the prophets in the kingdom of God and you yourself thrust out. And men will come from east and west, and from north and south, and sit at table in the kingdom of God." (Lk 13:28–29 = Mt 8:11–12)

The geographic comprehensiveness of the kingdom is matched by the breadth of the time of its preparation, from the patriarch to all the prophets, and in this way, again, Jesus is the term of Scripture and what is recorded in Scripture.

Last, there is Jesus' saying about John the Baptist and the turning of the age.

> The Law and the prophets were until John [Mt: "for all the prophets and the law prophesied until John"]; since then the good news of the kingdom of God is preached, and every one enters it violently. But it is easier for heaven and earth to pass away, than for one dot of the law to become void. (Lk 16:16–17 = Mt 11:12–13 and 5:18)

Thus, the Law and the prophets culminate in the kingdom that Jesus preaches and brings and in that way his mission is the fulfillment of the Scriptures.

It is not in my competence to determine what precisely of the above material goes back directly and explicitly to Jesus and what does not. What is not in doubt is the great amount of it, and the variety of forms in which Jesus and his career are cast as fulfillment. That this effort of interpretation begins with Jesus, however, is certain, as Ben Meyer shows with regard to the self-understanding of Jesus as eschatological herald in terms of Isaiah 52 and 61.[47] So to

---

[47] Ben F. Meyer, "Jesus Christ," in *The Anchor Bible Dictionary* (New York: Doubleday, 1992), III, 780.

speak, that he fulfills and is the fulfillment is multiply attested, in many forms, by many voices.[48]

When we turn to Matthew, as we know, the number of explicit claims to fulfillment increases.[49] Also, however, we should think of the large framework the evangelist gives us within which to view Jesus. The Sermon on the Mount is a fulfillment of the Law, especially at its core, the Decalogue, and the five discourses of the gospel as a whole recall the five books of the Law. Matthew also makes it explicit that the form of Jesus' teaching brings forward the ancient writings, as in chapter 13 (vs. 35) he reminds us of Psalm 77, "I will open my mouth in parables." When Jesus claims to fulfill the messianic task of building the eschatological temple of God (Mt 16:18; 26:61), then all the material about the Tent in the wilderness and the Temple of Jerusalem, the abiding question of how God effects his presence to his people—all that is seen to culminate in Jesus, Emmanuel, "God with us" (Mt 1:23 with Is 7:14).[50]

The Last Supper, furthermore, presents a fulfillment of the covenants, as of the sacrifices. The "blood of the covenant" by which the disciples share in Christ is as the blood of the Sinai covenant in Exodus 24, which unites God and the people. A covenant sacrifice, the Eucharist is also a Passover sacrifice (Ex 12) and as well a sacrifice for sin, for the blood is shed "so that sins might be forgiven," recalling the Day of Atonement of Leviticus 16.

The presentation of Jesus as the fulfillment and meaning of Scripture, and the whole of it, comes to especial clarity in Luke-Acts. The parable of the Rich Man and Lazarus has already been mentioned. The gospel begins in this key, set by the angelic messages to Zechariah and Mary and their own prophetic response to events in the first chapter. In Luke 4, this reading of the Old Testament is seen to have dominical authority, as Jesus himself declares the meaning of Isaiah 61 to be himself. Climactically, in Luke 24, the risen Lord tells the disciples on the road to Emmaus, and then his chosen and designated witnesses, "all the things" in the Law and the prophets that concern him.[51] Furthermore, the speeches of Peter and Stephen and Paul in Acts make it clear that "all the things" in the Law and the prophets concerning him is all the Law and the prophets (Acts 3:18, 22, 24; 7:52; 10:43; 13:27–29, 32; 26:6, 22; 28:23).

---

[48] See Meyer, Aims, 85–87, on indices of historicity.

[49] See the tables in Krister Stendahl, *The School of St. Matthew and Its Use of the Old Testament* (Philadelphia: Fortress Press, 1968), 43–45.

[50] See Meyer on messianic cleansing and building of the eschatological temple, *Aims*, 181–202, And Bouyer, *Eternal Son*, 55–56, 269–70, on the shekinah and the presence of God in tent, tabernacle, and Temple.

[51] This handling continues in Acts, as the nascent Church repeats the interpretation received from her Lord in the speeches of Peter and Stephen (2:14–36; 7:2–53), in the conversion of the Ethiopian Eunuch (8:25), in Paul's speech in Antioch in Pisidia (13:27).

Is this Luke or is it Jesus who claims this? It is at least implicitly the claim of Jesus. To confess him is to have eschatological salvation, according to Luke 12:8—so, it is not just taking what he says, but taking him, as the final message of God, and so as the eschatological, final, and fulfilling word. For the final word is the telos—that for which all the other words were said, as sharing in which they find their ultimate meaning.

Now if the Scriptures speak of Jesus and he is their meaning, then it is a short step to identifying him as the Wisdom of God and the Word of God. Baruch 4:1 has it that "[s]he [wisdom] is the book of the commandments of God, and the law that endures for ever." If Jesus is the meaning of the book, which is wisdom, then he, too, should be called wisdom.

Like Baruch, Sirach 24 also identifies wisdom with the book of the Law. "All this [= the regime and ordering of wisdom in both the life of the Israelite and Israel; see vs. 8] is the book of the covenant of the Most High God, the law which Moses commanded us" (24:23). Prophecy also is attached to wisdom (24:33). More strikingly, the last part of Sirach recounts the career of wisdom, as it were, from creation (42:15ff.) and the natural order (43) through the famous men of the nation to the day of Simon, son of Onias (44–50). This parallels the appreciation of wisdom in the Book of Wisdom. She is present when God made the world (9:9), but then also accompanies the patriarchs and prophets, from Adam to Noah and Abraham and Jacob to Joseph and Moses (cc. 10–11). The order and intelligibility of the history of Israel, recorded in the Scriptures, is the wisdom by which the world is made; it is the wisdom that is recorded in the Law (cf. 6:17–18) and the words of the prophets (7:27). Insofar as the Wisdom of God is displayed throughout the course of history and is its intelligibility and meaning, as described in the Scriptures, and insofar as Jesus is the meaning of these Scriptures, then he is also "wisdom."

As just presented, this is a conclusion from beholding Jesus as the meaning and fulfillment of the Scriptures. But it is a conclusion in continuity with his word as attested to especially but not exclusively by the non-Markan synoptic material common to Matthew and Luke.[52] "What is the wisdom given to him?" his unbelieving countrymen ask in Mark (6:2); but

---

[52] I have been arguing from the apprehension of Jesus as the meaning of the Scriptures to the apprehension of him as Wisdom, but the development could be the other way around, or indeed, the ideas could be coeval, as they seem to be in the material common to Matthew and Luke. For the treatment of Jesus as sage and as wisdom, see Witherington, *Jesus the Sage,* 221–36. This material is commonly dated from A.D. 40 to 80; Witherington puts it in the 50s or 60s (236), which would make it available to Paul (332). In any event, and considering the evidence of early Christian hymns, Witherington thinks that Wisdom Christology is early, not late (292), and explains this ultimately as an explicit dominical claim (204).

at least they recognize that he has a wisdom to offer. Giving the new commandments of God, a refurbished Law, as in the Sermon on the Mount, which is a wisdom teaching (Mt 7:24), Christ shows himself as a teacher of wisdom.[53] As Messiah, he must be not just another teacher, but the last and perfect teacher of wisdom (Mt 23:8, 10, "one teacher . . . one master, the Christ"). In fact, he also presents himself as the wisdom to be learned. The "come to me" of Matthew 11:28, promising rest to the weary (cf. Jer 31:25), echoes the call of wisdom in Sirach 24:19. The yoke the disciples of Jesus are to take upon themselves answers to the yoke of wisdom in Sirach 51:26, and the yoke of the Law in Jeremiah 2:20 and 5:5. Learning "of me," of Christ, is thus more directly to learn him, and instruction in that wisdom, in him, will give the rest spoken of in Sirach 51:17. Challenged to justify his actions, which is to say, challenged to justify himself, Jesus replies in Matthew 11:19: "Wisdom is justified by her children"—that is, I, Jesus, am the wisdom justified by my works. At Matthew 12:42, he says that "one greater than Solomon is here." But Solomon is the preeminent man of wisdom, the only greater-than-which would be the Wisdom by which Solomon was wise; and if he replaces the Law, fulfills it, as according to Matthew 5:17 he does, it is because he is the Wisdom of which the Law was an expression.[54]

· · · · ·

St. Paul knows Christ as the meaning of Scripture, for it was already part of what was "delivered" to him, namely, that the death and resurrection of Christ were "in accordance with the Scriptures" (1 Cor 15:1–3).[55] It is enough to advert to the structural role Christ's fulfillment plays in Paul's thought, expressed in the great parallel between the first and second Adams in First Corinthians and Romans, and in the relation of Christ to Abraham and Moses (the Law) in Romans and Galatians. It is this structural role that provides the framework for more textually precise reminiscences, such as those of the Akadah in Romans 8 or of Genesis 3 in Romans 5.

---

[53] Ibid., 155–56: "By even a conservative estimate, at least 70 percent of the Jesus tradition is in the form of some sort of Wisdom utterance such as an aphorism, riddle, or parable."

[54] Martin Hengel, *The Son of God: The Origin of Christology and the History of Jewish-Hellenistic Religion* (Philadelphia: Fortress Press, 1976), 74: "The connection between Jesus and Wisdom had thus been prepared for by Jesus' own preaching during his ministry, the form of which was very much in the wisdom tradition."

[55] For the demonstration that this text does not mean accordance with some few texts, for example, Hosea 6:2 or Psalm 15:10 but all the Scriptures, see Christopher Seitz, "Creed, Scripture and 'Historical Jesus' ('in accordance with the Scriptures')," in *The Rule of Faith: Scripture, Canon, and Creed in a Critical Age*, ed. Ephraim Radner and George Sumner (Harrisburg, PA: Morehouse Publishing, 1998), 126–35.

It is noteworthy that Paul presents himself to the Romans as an apostle of that gospel that "God promised beforehand through his prophets in the Holy Scriptures" (1:2). More particularly in Romans, Christ is said to fulfill the Law, inasmuch as dying he makes the "just requirements of the law" be fulfilled in us (8:4). Fulfilling it, Christ is the "end (telos) of the law" (Rom 10:4).[56] As Deuteronomy remarks that we need neither ascend to the heaven or go across the sea to find the Law of God (30:12f.), so Paul says the "word" of God, the Law is close to us, too, for Christ has both come down from heaven and ascended from the abyss (10:6–8). So, Christ is the Word. And just as the crucifixion of the Lord of glory is according to the Law and is its fulfillment, so is it accomplished according to the wisdom of God (1 Cor 2:7), now manifest in Christ, who is our wisdom (1:30).

In 2 Corinthians 1:20, Christ is the "yes" to all the promises of God—the promises contained in the Book. This is developed in chapter three (vv. 12ff.), where the Scriptures are said to be veiled as was the face of Moses coming from the Tent of Meeting. This veil is taken away "through Christ," so that we see the meaning of Scripture and at the same time behold the glory of the Lord. The manifestation of the meaning of Scripture is the showing of Christ as its meaning: The shining of the face of Moses, the shining of Scripture, is Christ. But if Christ is the meaning of the Book, how is he not the Book? The meaning of a book is "in" it, we say, meaning that it is the book.[57]

Entirely in accord with this, Paul is represented in 2 Timothy 3:15 as recalling to Timothy his acquaintance "with the sacred writings which are able to instruct you for salvation through faith in Christ Jesus." So much is the Old Testament's witness to Christ integral to the Gospel that in Ephesians the prophets are paired with the apostles as the foundation of the Church (2:20).

The claim of fulfillment is well developed in John. Jesus says in John's gospel that the Scriptures which the Jews search and in which they think to find eternal life bear witness to him, Jesus, the one sent by the Father, whom they do not believe and do not believe in as the Son sent by the Father (Jn 5:37ff). Eternal life is still to be found in the Scriptures, presumably, but now by finding Jesus there, whom to know is to have eternal life (17:3). To know

---

[56] On Romans 10:4, see Richard B. Hays, *Echoes of Scripture in the Letters of Paul* (New Haven, CT: Yale University Press, 1989), 75–77.

[57] On 2 Corinthians 3:1–4–6, see Hays, *Echoes*, 122–53. Summing up, Hays says: "The reader who turns to the Lord and finds the veil taken away will return to the reading of Moses to discover that all of Scripture is a vast metaphorical witness to the lived reality of the new community of Christ" (151), a community which is being transformed into the image of Christ (3:18).

him as Son is to know the Scriptures—to know what their words mean—and vice versa, and this is to know the eternal life the Scriptures promise. So already in 2:45, Philip says "we have found him of whom Moses in the law and also the prophets wrote." As Jesus says that Moses wrote of him (5:46), so the evangelist says that Isaiah "saw his glory and spoke of him" (12:41).

Since whoever hears the word of Jesus has eternal life (5:24; 8:51), and Abraham rejoiced to see his day (8:56), it can be said that he fulfills the promissory words of the Old Testament, that he is the promise kept, the presence of the Word of God as fulfilled, and therefore is the Word, for word and the accomplished word, word and deed come together in God's word (Is 55:10–11). His word is the Father's word, and if the disciples keep it, he and his Father will dwell in them (14:23–25) in the way wisdom dwelt in the just (Prov 8:12).

The connections with the Old Testament teaching about wisdom are developed at length.[58] In chapter six, Jesus is the Bread of Life come down from heaven. This harks back not just to the manna of Exodus 16:4, and the reprise of Exodus 16 in Wisdom 16, but also to Sirach 24 and to Proverbs 9:5, where wisdom itself is the bread that sustains life. Then there is "the spring of water welling up to eternal life" that Christ will give to those who believe in him (4:14), which water is the Spirit (7:38–39), and which recalls Baruch 3:9ff, according to which Israel would not have been exiled had she not forsaken wisdom. "You have forsaken the fountain of wisdom" (3:12; cf. Jer 2:13, "they have forsaken me, the fountain of living waters"). Faith in Christ gives the wisdom spoken of by the prophets, the wisdom of which he is the principle, which flows from him, and which is the Spirit. Last, according to Sirach 24:8, wisdom has pitched her tent in Jacob, and according to Wisdom 18:15, the Word has leapt down from his throne to save Israel (which is styled in this book as Son of God at 18:13, with God as Father at 14:3), both of which places are in play in John 1:14, according to which the Word has pitched his tent among us by taking flesh.

Already in the Old Testament, the principle is established that the final Word of God is the founding Word of God, that the Omega is the Alpha.[59] Or, as Martin Hengel has it, the eschatological word must be the protological word; only the word that arranges the beginnings can determine the end of things.[60] So, already with Mark 1:15 or Luke 12:8, it is all there: Speaking and guaranteeing the eschatological word by his presence, he is the sacra-

---

[58] For a compact presentation, see Raymond E. Brown, *An Introduction to New Testament Christology* (New York: Paulist Press, 1994), 204–10.

[59] Paul Beauchamp, "Scripture, Fulfillment of," in *Encyclopedia of Christian Theology*, vol. 3, ed. Jean-Yves Lacoste (New York: Routledge, 2005), 1456–57.

[60] Hengel, *The Son of God*, 69.

ment of that word, and so also the wisdom by whom all things came to be according to Proverbs 8 and Wisdom 9.

The same apprehension of the relation of Christ to the Scriptures is suggested in Revelation in the figure of the sealed scroll. Jesus, the Lamb, is the one most suited to unlock the meaning of history; he can break the seals of the scroll, for he is the key to its meaning (Rev 5:1–5). He is the Alpha and the Omega, the beginning and the end (21:6, 22:13), perceived as the Beginning because declared and vindicated as the End. It is suggestive that the beginning and the end are the first and the last letters of the alphabet, as comprising between themselves the meaning of all that could be written by God. John is bidden to write what he sees in a book (1:11), to write to the churches (2:1, etc.), to write other things (14:13, 19:9), and there are other writings spoken of (14:1, 17:8). But if Christ is Alpha and Omega, all that is written is contained in him. It is important, too, that the Lamb is the Lamb slain from the foundation of the world. It is the cross, especially, as finishing the history of Jesus of Nazareth, that is the key.

There is also the theology of inspiration of 1 and 2 Peter, for which the spirit of prophecy is the Spirit of Christ (1 Pt 1:10–11). The prophets predict the sufferings of Christ (11), and serve us "in the things which have now been announced" in the gospel (12). "The prophetic word" of 2 Peter 1:19 is to be interpreted by the same Spirit. And this means, again, that Christ is the meaning of the Scriptures.[61]

The Letter to the Hebrews concludes this entire trajectory of thought in the New Testament, but as it were from the vantage point of the confident possession of the identity of Jesus as Word. That is, there is a route from Jesus' fulfillment of Scripture to beholding him as Word. This is to read Christ in the light of Scripture. But then there is the reverse route, from Jesus beheld as Word to seeing his fulfillment of Scripture. This is to read Scripture in the light of Christ. It is the route of the Letter to the Hebrews, and we note the following high points. According to Hebrews, with Christ we have a mediator more glorious than Moses (3:3), a better priesthood (7:11–18), a better hope (7:19) founded on better promises (8:6), a better covenant (7:22), a better sacrifice (9:12), a better sanctuary (9:24). All this is seen in the tightest relation to Scripture, which is constantly recalled in speaking of priests, promises, covenants, and sacrifice, so that we might see its fulfillment in Christ. Because he fulfills in this way, the Letter can present him from the outset as the "reflection of the glory of God," and the "stamp of his nature," just as wisdom was said to be an "emanation" of God's glory, the "reflection of eternal light" (Wis 7:25–26).

---

[61] There is also an argument to be made from the correspondence of baptism to the flood; see 1 Peter 3:18–22.

• • • • •

Let us take stock of things. In fulfilling the Scriptures, Christ turns out to be the thing constantly spoken of, the meaning spoken out, in the Old Testament. Because of this, the speaker too is revealed. Just as the inspiration of the Scriptures could not be fully manifest before Christ, and just as apart from Christ, neither could its unity be evident, as deriving from and repeating some aspect of the Word, so also neither could the personal identity of the speaker of Scripture show up prior to Christ.[62] But now, if Christ fulfills the prophecies, then the prophets spoke of him. And speaking through the prophets we will discern—we will hear—the Father. If the Son is there the spoken, then it is the Father who is there the speaker. What is spoken is always the Wisdom and Word of God accompanying Israel (cf. 1 Cor 10:4), a wisdom embedded in history, a word partially expressed in covenant and promise, in law given by God and worship ordained by him. According as it is the same incarnate Word, but now, openly spoken of and explicitly in the New, then again, except where the Word in his humanity speaks, it is the Father who speaks. As the Father eternally speaks the Word, and as he sends at the Incarnation, so also, in the Old Testament, he speaks the words whose meaning is Christ, the Word incarnate, the Son sent. The economy reflects the Trinity.

In another way, too, we can see how the Old Testament prepares the New. God is represented in the Old Testament as speaking in his own voice (as in creating and giving the Law). He is represented as speaking also through the prophets, for what he says, like any saying, is "portable," and can be quoted, repeated, by another. Last, he speaks to us through his Son (Hebrews), and this is a sort of blend of the Father speaking both in person and via another. Here, what he says is not just the message that some other, the prophet who speaks for him, will say, but what he says is the very other. He speaks through another, and the person through whom he speaks to us is himself the spoken. Moreover, the incarnate Word speaks human words to the one who is represented as speaking in his own voice and being spoken about in the Old Testament. They must be distinct as persons. And yet, since what one speaks is in another sense the very understanding of things one is, God and the person whom God speaks must be united in some closer unity than that of united minds and united hearts. It must be the unity of one mind and one heart, the unity of one *ousia*.

---

62 For Christ and the recognition of inspiration, see Origen, *Philocalie 1–20: Sur les Écritures, Sources chrétiennes* 302, trans. Marguerite Harl (Paris: Éditions du Cerf, 1983), I, 6 (paraphrased by Harl), and for Christ and the unity of Scripture, its being one book, see *Philocalie* V, 4; and VI, 2.

In John's gospel, the Lord says to the disciples: "I have yet many things to say to you, but you cannot bear them now" (16:12). St. Thomas, in his commentary on John, tries to imagine what these things were the disciples could not bear, but which the Holy Spirit would teach them later.

> The Lord proposed to them all things that belonged to faith, but not in the way he later revealed, and especially in eternal life. Thus therefore the things they were not able to bear are the full knowledge of divine things, which they did not have then, as for instance the equality of the Son to the Father, and things of that kind. Whence Paul, 2 Corinthians 2:4—"I have heard the secret words which it is not permitted to a man to speak," which were not about some other truth than the faith, but in a higher mode. Again, the spiritual understanding of all the Scriptures, which they did not then have, but [only] when "he opened to them the sense so that they might understand the Scriptures," Luke 24:45. Again, the sufferings and dangers which they were going to suffer which they then were not able to bear, because their minds were weak; Sirach 6:26—"Lower your shoulder, and carry it." Thus therefore instruction was necessary for them.[63]

The list of things they could not bear is the full doctrine of the Trinity, the spiritual interpretation of the Scriptures, the Old Testament, and their share in the cross. Elsewhere, St. Thomas suggests that it was not just the spiritual sense of the Scriptures, but the literal sense of the prophets and as speaking of him that the Lord gave to the disciples.[64] St. Thomas does not point it out, but it is possible to think that these three things—namely the Trinity, the Cross, and the Christological sense of the Scriptures—form a kind of unity. The full doctrine of the Trinity depends on the illumination of the Spirit in entering into the experience of the cross at baptism and in life, and on the interpretation of Scripture. For the distinction of persons is shown

---

63 *Lectura in evangelium S. Ioannis,* no. 2101: Omnia ergo quae fidei erant, Dominus proposuit eis, sed non eo modo quo postea revelavit, et praecipue in vita aeterna. Sic ergo quae portare non poterant, sunt plena cognitio divinorum, quam non habebant tunc, puta aequalitatem Filii ad Patrem, et huismodi. Unde Paulus II Cor 2:4: "Audivi arcana verba, quae non licet homini loqui," quae non erant de alia veritate quam fidei, sed altiori modo. Item spiritualis intellectus omnium Scripturarum, quem tunc non habebant, sed quando "aperuit eis sensum ut intelligerent Scriptures": Lc. ult. 45. Item passiones et pericula quae passuri erant quae tunc non poterant, quia animi eorum imbeciles erant; Eccli 6:26: "Subiice humerum tuum, et porta illam." Sic ergo necessaria erat eis instructio.

64 *Lectura in evangelium S. Matthaei,* ed. Raphael Cai, O.P. (Rome: Marietti, 1951), at 1:23, no. 148. On this and similar passages, see Flores, "Thomas on Theodore of Mopsuestia, Exegete."

unsurpassably on the cross (cf. Heb 9:14), and the understanding of the Scriptures, as has just been argued here, shows both the identity of the Son as Word and his consubstantial equality with the Father.

• • • • •

Commenting on John 14:25, St. Thomas says, "this is indeed the greatest benefit, that the Son himself speaks to us and teaches us," and he quotes Hebrews 1:1.[65] In the Incarnation, the Word becomes a speaker. The Incarnation itself, however, is true, divine speaking, just as much—more—than God's speaking through the prophets, according to St. Thomas in his commentary on Hebrews.

> The publication of [intelligible] species in the angelic or human mind [as in prophecy] is ordered exclusively to the cognition of the divine wisdom, and therefore can be said to be a speaking. The [Incarnation] . . . on the other hand, which is through the assumption of flesh, is ordered to being [as is also the "speech" that creates in Genesis 1] and to cognition [like prophetic illumination], and to express manifestation, because through the assumption of flesh, the Word both became man, and leads us into the perfect cognition of God, as John 18:37 [has it]—"For this I was born, to bear testimony to the truth"; and he expressly manifested himself to us. Baruch 3:38— "After these things he has been seen on the earth, and has conversed with men."[66]

Christ is in his reality for us, in his history and career, the Word made flesh. That is, he is the Word of the Father, spoken eternally, now also spoken to us via the assumed humanity. For both St. Augustine and St. Thomas, the relation of the eternal Word to the humanity is like that of concept to a voiced word of the mouth. Since speaking this Word to us fulfills the prior prophetic words, those words too are most fittingly seen as spoken by the Father.

In the introduction to the *Compendium theologiae*, the Word made flesh is said to have taken on our smallness *(brevitas)*, and what he, the Word, "handed

---

[65] *Lectura in evangelium S. Ioannis*, no. 1953: et hoc quidem maximum beneficium est ut ipse Filius nobis loquatur et nos doceat.

[66] *Lectura super epistolam ad Hebraeos*, at 1:2, no. 15: Secunda vera expressio, quae est editio specierum in mente angelica, vel humana, ordinatur tantum ad cognitionem sapientiae divinae, et ideo potest dici locutio. Tertia vero, quae per assumptionem carnis, ordinatur ad esse, et ad cognitionem, et ad expressam manifestationem, quia per assumptionem carnis, et Verbum factum est homo, et nos in cognitione Dei perfectam. (Io. 18:37: "Ad hoc natus sum, ut testimonium perhibeam veritati.) Et se nobis expresse manifestavit. Bar. 3:38: "Post haec in terris visus est, et cum hominibus conversatus est."

on widely and plainly through the various books of Sacred Scripture to the studious," this same Word, now shortened, passed on in the short form of the Creed, the Law of Love, and the Our Father to those burdened with work.[67] Commenting expressly on the "abbreviated word" of Romans 9:28, moreover, St. Thomas identifies three ways to take it. In the first place, it is the gospel that can be considered an abbreviation of "the multitude of figures and precepts of the Law," for the sacrifices of the old Law are comprehended by the one sacrifice of Christ, and the moral precepts of the Law are included in the two precepts of charity. Second, there is the word spoken by the incarnate Lord, "more perfect and of greater power" than the words spoken through the prophets. Last, the abbreviated word is the Word as incarnate, taking on "our weakness and poverty."[68] Now, an abbreviation maintains the same sense and meaning of the first edition; it is in that sense the same word or Word, spoken by the same Speaker, whether in the Old Testament or the Incarnation.

The gospel, too, therefore, cannot be other than this one word or Word. The Word spoken in the Incarnation speaks many human words, conversing with men, manifesting himself to us as Word. He speaks that we may hear him, as a whole, as spoken. What he says and what he delivers, subsequently gathered, preached, and written, is the gospel. These words that he speaks, words that are original relative to apostle and evangelist, are not, he says, absolutely originally his. The words he speaks, the Lord expressly says, are not his but the Father's (14:24). They are his as pronounced by him, but they are the Father's as coming from the Father, St. Thomas says.[69] And following

---

67 *Compendium theologiae,* in *Opuscula Theologica* I, no. 1: *Aeterni Patris Verbum* sua immensitate universa comprehendens, ut hominem per peccata minoratum in celsitudinem divinae gloriae revocaret, breve fieri voluit nostra brevitate assumpta, non sua deposita maiestate. Et ut a caelestis verbi capessenda doctrina nullus excusabilis redderetur, quod pro studiosis diffuse et dilucide per diversa Scripturae sanctae volumina tradiderat, propter occupatos sub brevi summa humanae salutis doctrinae conclusit. And the *doctrina* is explicated in Creed, Command, and Our Father.

68 *Lectura super epistolam ad Romanos,* no. 803, dicit "abbrevians" . . . quia nihil est praetermissum de multitudine figurarum et praeceptorum legis; no. 804, perfectius enim debet esse verbum et maioris virtutits quod ipse Dominus Deus carnem indutus locucutus est per semetipsum, quam verba quae locutus est per prophetas; no. 805, dicitur . . . exinanitum vel breviatum, non quia aliquid subtractum sit plenitudini vel magnitudini divinitatis ipsius, sed quia nostrum exilitatem et parvitatem suscepit. Moreover, such abbreviation is a fulfillment of an explicit prophetic text, Isaiah 10:22: consummationem enim et abbreviationem Dominus Deus exercituum faciet in medio omnis terrae.

69 *Lectura,* no. 1950: "that is, [the word you have heard me speak] is not mine as from myself, but it is mine as from another, namely from the Father who sent me. . . . the word which you heard, pronounced by me, a man, is indeed mine, insofar as I pronounce it, and it is not mine insofar as it is mine from another" (idest, non mihi a

St. Augustine, St. Thomas also remarks the difference between the singular Word and the plural words in the gospel.

> When he speaks of his own words, he uses the plural, "my words"; but where he speaks of the word of the Father, he speaks in the singular, saying "And the word which you have heard, is not mine"; because by "word of the Father," he wants himself to be understood, who is the Father's unique Word. Whence neither does he say he is his own, but the Father's, because neither is he his own Image, nor his own Son, but the Father's. But all the words in our hearts are from the unique Word of the Father.[70]

The words of Jesus are both his and his Father's. Passing to John 14:26, we have also the Holy Spirit, who Jesus says will teach us. Does the Spirit then speak? Throughout the commentary, as occasion gives warrant, St. Thomas will say that God, or Christ or the Holy Spirit teaches us. But now St. Thomas delays to provide some precision.

> Next he treats of the effect of the Holy Spirit, saying, "He will teach you all things." For just as the effect of the mission of the Son was to lead to the Father, so the effect of the mission of the Holy Spirit is to lead the faithful to the Son. The Son, however, since he is begotten wisdom itself is the truth itself; above, 15:6—"I am the way, the truth, and the life." And therefore the effect of a mission of this kind is to make men sharers in the divine wisdom, and knowers of the truth. Therefore the Son gives us doctrine, since he is the Word; but the Holy Spirit makes us able to receive [capaces] his teaching.[71]

---

meipso, sed est mihi ab alio, scilcet a Patre qui me misit. . . . sermonem, sive sermo, quem audistis, a me homine prolatum, est quidem meus, inquantum ipsum pronuntio, et non est meus, inquantum est mihi ab alio). Thomas directs us to Jn 7:16.

[70] *Lectura,* no. 1951: ubi autem loquitur de sermone Patris, loquitur in singulari, dicens Et sermonem quem audistis, non est meus; quia per Verbum Patris seipsum intelligi voluit, qui est unicum Verbum eius. Unde nec suum se esse dicit, sed Patris, quia nec sua imago est, nec suus Filius, sed Patris. Sermones autem omnes in cordibus nostris sunt ab unico Verbo Patris.

[71] *Lectura,* no. 1958: Consequenter agit de effectu Spiritus sancti; dicens, "Ille vos docebit omina." Nam, sicut effectus missionis Filii fuit ducere ad Patrem, ita effectus missionis Spiritus sancti est ducere fideles ad Filium. Filius, autem, cum sit ipsa sapientia genita, est ipsa veritas; supra 14:6: "Ego sum via, veritas et vita." Et ideo effectus misionis huiusmodi est ut faciat homines participes divinae sapientiae, et cognitores veritatis. Filius ergo tradit nobis doctrinam, cum sit Verbum; sed Spiritus sanctus doctrinae eius nos capaces facit. Remember that in this way, as Emery says, "all natural human knowledge is a participation in the Word," *Trinity,* 288; see the *Lectura* at 1:26, no. 246 and at 8:55, no. 1284. So also, *Summa contra Gentiles* IV, 13, 11.

The Son gives doctrine, as being the subsistent truth and wisdom of which doctrine is a participation. The Holy Spirit gives it as making us able to hear it. And the Father? "Since someone's teaching is nothing else than his word, and since the Son of God is his Word, it therefore follows that the teaching of the Father is the Son himself."[72] Obviously, the Father gives doctrine as speaking the Word, working in the work and mission of Word and Spirit. There is, then, an articulation according to the persons, all three, for the teaching of the one God.[73] The commentary at 14:26 continues:

> Therefore he says "He will teach you all things," because whatever a man may teach from the outside, unless the Holy Spirit give understanding interiorly, he labors in vain: because unless the Spirit be present to the heart of the hearer, the word of the teacher will be useless, Job 32:8—"let the inspiration of the Almighty give understanding;" and insofar as even the Son himself speaks by the instrument of his humanity, it has no effect unless he work interiorly through the Holy Spirit.[74]

The Holy Spirit "speaks" not from the outside and in a bodily way, St. Thomas says at 16:13, "but interiorly in the mind by illuminating it *[illuminando]*." And he invokes Hosea 2:14, where God will speak "to the heart," and Psalm 84:9, where the psalmist hears what the Lord says "in" him.[75]

---

72 *Lectura,* at 7:16, no. 1037: cum doctrina uniuscuisque nihil aliud sit quam verbum eius, Filius autem Dei sit Verbum eius: sequitur ergo quod doctrina Patris sit ipse Filium.

73 See Emery, "Personal Mode," 63–64, on how for St. Thomas the three persons can act in one action according to their personal mode.

74 *Lectura,* no. 1958: Dicit ergo "ille vos docebit omnia," quia quaecumque homo doceat extra, nisi Spiritus sanctus interius det intelligentiam, frustra laborat: quia nisi Spiritus adsit cordi audientis, otiosus erit sermo doctoris, Iob 32:8: "Inspiratio Omnipotentis dat intelligentiam;" et intantum, quod etiam ipse Filius organo humanitatis loquens, not valet, nisi ipsemet interius operetur per Spiritum sanctum. Also at 17:26, no. 2269, Christ teaches exteriorly and interiorly, this last by the gift of the Holy Spirit. Christ is interior teacher both (1) by giving Spirit and (2) by being the Word of which all words and concepts are participations. For the last, see at 13:13, no. 1775. Cf. also at 3:2, no. 428.

75 *Lectura,* no. 2103. Sometimes St. Thomas just says simply that the Spirit teaches. For instance, at Jn 7:16, no. 1037, "every truth, no matter by whom it be spoken, is from the Holy Spirit." But the more precise delimitation of the role of the Holy Spirit is elaborated at length at 14:26, no. 1959: "the Holy Spirit makes us know all things by interiorly inspiring, directing, and raising up to spiritual things." And at no. 1960: "[the Holy Spirit] secretly helps by supplying *[subministrat]* the powers for knowing. Or, he teaches, insofar as he makes us partakers in the wisdom of the Son. He suggests, in as much as he impels us, insofar as he is love. Or 'he will suggest to you all things'; that is, he will bring [everything] back to memory."

• • • • •

There remains the difficult problem of the psalms, which are texts for many voices according as they are used in the Church's praise and worship. It is not just that many voices are heard within the psalms, but the same text can be mouthed by several voices. Let us first recall the teaching of St. Athanasius and the practice of St. Augustine.

The teaching of St. Athanasius is compactly rendered in his *Letter to Marcellinus*.[76] The Holy Spirit presides over the composition of all the Scriptures (9), and arranges for the psalms especially to contain the emotions of the soul, such that use of the psalms heals our passions and installs equanimity in the soul (10). Some psalms speak about Christ, but in others Christ speaks (11). Excepting those psalms that prophesy of Christ and the nations, "he who recites the Psalms is uttering the rest as his own words, and each sings them as if they were written concerning him," such that "he handles them as if he is speaking about himself" (12). On the other hand, none of this prevents Athanasius from saying that "each psalm is both spoken and composed by the Spirit," and this "so that in these same words . . . the stirrings of our souls might be grasped, and all of them be said as concerning us" (12). Here, furthermore, the Lord presents himself as a model for us: "[I]t was indeed for this reason that he [Christ] made this resound in the Psalms before his sojourn in our midst, so that just as he provided the model of the earthly and heavenly man in his own person, so also from the Psalms he who wants to do so can learn the emotions and dispositions of the souls" (13). The Holy Spirit speaks the psalms, then, just so that they can be spoken by Christ, and Christ speaks them just so they can be spoken by us to the effect of "the therapy and correction suited for each emotion" (13).

The interpretive practice of St. Augustine in the *Ennarationes super psalmos* is canvassed by Michael Friedrowicz in his admirable introduction to the new translation by Maria Boulding.[77] "The fundamental point for Augustine's interpretation of the psalms is that he understood them as a prophecy of Christ."[78] Sometimes, the psalms are words to Christ; sometimes they are words about Christ or about the Church. The psalms can be voiced by Christ, speaking in his own name, or in our name. The psalms can

---

[76] In *Athanasius: The Life of Antony and The Letter to Marcellinus*, trans. Robert C. Gregg (New York: Paulist Press, 1980). I cite according to paragraph number.

[77] General introduction to *Expositions of the Psalms 1–32*, trans. by Maria Boulding, *The Works of Saint Augustine: a translation for the 21st century*, ed. John Rotelle (Hyde Park, NY: New City Press, 2000), 13–66.

[78] Ibid., 44. Note also, p. 24, that "the words of a psalm are often attributed immediately to the Holy Spirit as their proper speaker, without human agency."

be taken up by the voice of the Church, or by the voice of the whole Christ, head and members. They can also fill the voice of the heavenly Jerusalem.[79]

The patristic appreciation of the Psalms is grounded already in the New Testament.[80] For instance, an express Christological sense is imputed to the psalmist David, in Acts, where Peter takes David to be speaking of the resurrection in Psalm 15 and says of him that "he foresaw and spoke of the resurrection of the Christ" (2:25, 31).[81] If it be supposed to the contrary that David (and the other composers of the psalms) did not have an express understanding of Christ, then even so the ecclesiastical and liturgical understanding of the voices of the psalms can still be accounted for within the overall framework of this essay, where the Father is the speaker of the Old Testament, in the following way.

In the first place, if one makes the words of another one's own, then one is no longer quoting, but speaking as one's own person. If I sing to my beloved in the old words of love, handsome, and kind, then they become my words, and I am speaking them as my own person.

Second, the Lord Jesus prayed the psalms in synagogue and Temple and so, like any pious Jew, in making his prayer in the words of the psalms he made the psalms his own.

Third, Jesus is represented as the speaker of some psalms, as it were, as the prophesied speaker or original speaker. So, he speaks Psalm 109 during the trial at Mark 14:62, and Psalm 21 from the cross in Mark 15:37.[82]

But fourth, once it is realized that he made his relation to his Father and his work conscious and actual in the words of the psalms, then his speaking

---

[79] For St. Augustine on the therapeutic use of the psalms in healing the soul and its affections, ibid., 37–43.

[80] For the Psalms as spoken by Christ in the New Testament, see Richard B. Hays, "Christ Prays the Psalms: Paul's Use of an Early Christian Exegetical Convention," in *The Future of Christology: Essays in Honor of Leander E. Keck*, ed. Abraham J. Malherbe and Wayne A. Meeks (Minneapolis: Fortress Press, 1993), 122–36.

[81] This appreciation is shared by St. Thomas, who supposes a literal Christological sense for at least some psalms, and who appeals to Constantinople II for this teaching; see Flores, "Thomas on Theodore of Mopsuestia, Exegete," 251–58. St. Thomas is certainly in agreement with the express and clear teaching of Pope Vigilius on this matter, but it does not seem possible certainly to impute it to the council. For Vigilius, see *Epistula* 83, ll. 95–108, which is chs. 20–25 of his first *Constitutum*, *CSEL* 35, 256–60.

[82] Note Psalm 6:9 at Matthew 7:23, Psalm 8:3 at Matthew 21:16, Psalm 117:26 at Matthew 23:39. Jesus speaks the words of Psalm 21 at Hebrews 2:12 and of Psalm 39 at Hebrews 10:5–7. At Matthew 13:34, the evangelist understands Jesus to speak Psalm 78:21. In John 2:13–22, the disciples, in the light of the resurrection, understand Jesus to be the speaker of Psalm 69.

them acquires a certain preeminence and exemplarity. We should say of his praying of the psalms as of another Jew's praying of them not only that he is not really quoting the psalmist so much as making the words his own, but also that he is showing himself to be the preeminent or exemplary speaker of the psalms. Even among men, it may be that words originally formulated and spoken rightly by one speaker may be spoken more aptly and with more authority by another.

Fifth, when we pray the psalms, seeking to have the same mind as Christ Jesus (Ph 2), then it is not simply as if, making the words our own, we cease to quote. Rather, we make our voice to continue the voice of the Lord, and the Head can be said always to be moving his members to speak in these his words.

So, thinking about the psalms before Christ, we can say the psalmist's words are inspired of God through the Holy Spirit, and they remain the words of psalmist and God the Father until Christ. But with Christ, they become his words, words, as it were, prepared for him, prepared for his human voice by the Father through the psalmist. The words of the Father, already little partial words relative to the Word, become words of the incarnate Word.

At the time of composition, it is the Father who speaks all these things of the psalms; the Son has no distinct voice, cannot speak, until the Incarnation (or unless via a representation of the incarnate Word in the Old Testament).[83] With the Incarnation, psalms and certain prophetic texts can then be taken as spoken by him.

This is also true for other passages in the Old Testament that become taken up by Christ or attributed to Christ by the Church. For instance, St. Thomas, following patristic precedent, understands Proverbs 8 to be spoken in the person of the Word.[84] We might say that a sufficient condition of one speaking is that he be heard. When the Church, attentive to the voice of her spouse according to the Song of Songs (5:2), understands the psalms and such passages as Proverbs 8 to be spoken by Christ, then we can be sure that he speaks them. Such recognition on the part of the Church is dependent on the Incarnation, of course. Once Christ is recognized as the Word because of the summation of all the words of the Old Testament spoken by God, those places that speak explicitly of the word or wisdom of God can be thought, like the psalms, to have been prepared by God especially for the speaker who is the Son.[85]

---

[83] Of course, the Son is not in time, so strictly, we should say that, although he eternally speaks in the discourse of Jesus, he cannot be heard—by us—until *after* the Incarnation.

[84] *Summa contra Gentiles* IV, c. 11.

[85] See also the case of the Lukan transference of certain Old Testament uses of "Lord" to refer to Christ in C. Kavin Rowe, "The God of Israel and Jesus Christ: Luke, Marcion, and the Unity of the Canon," *Nova et Vetera* (English) 1 (2003): 359–79.

• • • • •

Asking who of the Trinitarian persons speaks in the Bible turns out to be a short way into the more theologically robust reading of the Old Testament of St. Thomas, of the Fathers, of the New Testament writers—dare we say, of the Lord? It involves us also in the difficult but crucial question of what the "literal sense" of Scripture is. Here, everything depends on whether the question is asked in a neutrally historical or a properly theological way. It is often pointed out that when St. Thomas discusses the spiritual sense of Scripture in the great *Summa*, he says that there is nothing necessary to faith contained in the spiritual sense that is not expressed elsewhere literally.[86] When it is a question of the meaning of this, that, and the other discrete passage of Scripture, we may take his point.[87] But we do not understand St. Thomas rightly if we think that everything necessary to faith can be found in reading Scripture in the manner of modern historical critics. They are not after a literal sense such as St. Thomas would recognize. Rather, if we moderns would mean by "spiritual sense" taking the Old Testament in its entirety as Christological, and this either literally or spiritually as the older theologians divided things, then this "spiritual sense" is absolutely indispensable for articulating the fullness of faith, for discerning the Trinity, for hearing the Word, and for identifying who of the Trinitarian persons speaks to us in the Bible and where.

---

[86] *ST* I, q. 1, a. 10, ad 1.

[87] This is the point of the place in Augustine St. Thomas sends us to, *Letter* 93, c. 2, 24: Quis autem non impudentissime nitatur aliquid in allegoria positum pro se interpretari, nisi habeat et manifesta testimonia, quorum lumine illustrentur obscura? It is a Question of the Rogatist (Donatist) interpretation of Song of Songs 1:6, Ubi pascis, ubi cubas in meridie.

CHAPTER 9

Revelation as Disclosure: Creation

FRANCIS MARTIN

I OFFER THIS STUDY in honor of Fr. Matthew Lamb, a good friend and gifted scholar, someone who has been true to his convictions during his whole scholarly life and has thus been an example of genuine Catholic scholarship.

In the late twelfth century, Alan of Lille composed a little poem that sums up a theme whose roots go back at least as far as Augustine:

Omnis mundi creatura
Quasi liber et scriptura
Nobis est, et speculum.[1]

I wish, in this study to return once again to this venerable tradition that sees creation as a book written by God and a source of revelation. This tradition often goes by the sobriquet "The Two Books of Revelation," or "Nature as a Book."[2] In any complete understanding of revelation there is, of course, the vast world of history, particularly that history of God's acts that has been taken up into language and needs to be revisited in our post-postmodern world. The events that have become word (and for Christians the Word that has become event) still manifest God as they reach us in the Sacred Text. We are now emerging from an era of non-transcendence in regard to both history and language. It seemed to me, therefore, that we should look first at the simpler

---

[1] Constant J. Mews, "The World as Text: The Bible and the Book of Nature in Twelfth-Century Theology," in *Scripture and Pluralism: Reading the Bible in the Religiously Plural World of the Middle Ages,* edited by Thomas J. Heffernan and Thomas E. Burman (Leiden: Brill, 2005), 95–122.

[2] For an older treatment of this theme, see Ernst Robert Curtius, *European Literature and the Latin Middle Ages,* trans. Willard Trask (New York: Harper & Row, 1953), 319–26.

"text," one that cannot bear witness on its own,[3] before approaching the more important topics such as the inspiration of the Sacred Text, the relation between revelation and language, the role of command in an understanding of revelation, and revelation in and through history. We need the light that an understanding of creation can bring to bear on the philosophical underpinnings of our reflection on these topics.

In the first part of the study I will consider the teaching of the biblical tradition on the revelatory nature of creation. I will preface this by citing a few texts from the Vatican II document *Dei Verbum* that will need reflection in the light of the ancient understanding of human capacity to "read" the message of revelation in the world of nature. In the second part I will reflect on how the biblical tradition and its ancient understanding can be recovered by confronting our modern understanding of "nature" and its message.

Creation as Revelation in the Present State of Catholic Teaching

Article 3 of *Dei Verbum* says that God, creating and conserving all things by his Word, offers to humankind a perpetual testimony to himself in created things. Moreover, intending to open the way to a supernal salvation, he manifested himself from the beginning to our first parents *(protoparentibus)*. The article thus clearly distinguishes between a "testimony" in created reality, which God constantly provides (the verbs are present participles), and a "self-manifestation" to the first humans. The text continues, referring to the traditional notion of God's care for the human race in the period between the original sin and the call of Abraham and then goes on to speak of Moses and the prophets.

Article 6, a sort of appendix to chapter 1, has to do with the truths that are revealed. Its last paragraph begins with a line that recalls and expands what was said in article 2: "By divine revelation God willed to manifest and communicate himself and the eternal decrees of his will concerning the salvation of humankind that is to say, in order to share *(ad participanda)* those divine goods which totally surpass human understanding." The text then goes on to cite Vatican I: "God as first principle and last end of all things can be known with certainty from created things by the natural light of reason," referring to Romans 1:20.[4] It then goes on to assert that, given the present

---

[3] St. Bonaventure once said: "The world was like a damaged *[deletes]* book which God brought to perspicacity *[illuminavit]* and rectified by the book of Scripture." *Collationes in Hexaemeron,* III 1.12 (Mews, "The World as Text," 18).

[4] In fact, the text goes on to cite Romans 1:20 according to the Vulgate. See Vatican I, sess. III, constitution *De Fide Catholica,* ch. 2, "De Revelatione" (Denziger-Schömetzer, 1785).

condition of the human race, God also reveals those things that can be known by reason so that they will be known by all "without great effort, with firm certainty, and without error entering in." A distinction is made, therefore, between the divine goods that "totally surpass human understanding" and the fact that God as first principle and last end of all things can be known by the natural light of reason. These latter truths are, however, also revealed in order to assure that all can know of them.

These two statements can serve as a preliminary summary of the position of the Catholic Church regarding God's knowability from creation. I wish now to institute a brief biblical reflection on this teaching in order to ascertain in what sense creation can be considered a revelation.

The Biblical Tradition

The Jewish Biblical Tradition

Creation in Narrative and Prayer

The notion that the God of Israel produced the world as we know it is a commonplace in the Bible, though the chronological determination as to exactly when this knowledge arrived at a reflexive monotheism is difficult to determine and will not be explicitly dealt with in this paper.[5] Given the fact that nearly all of Israel's neighbors and predecessors had grappled in their own way with the mystery of origins, it would have been surprising had Israel not attempted to integrate some account of origins into its understanding of itself as a people called and formed by its God. Of course, the more it had to reflect on its relation with other nations and to sustain for itself the claim that God had chosen them and was able to make good on his promises and covenants, the more clearly they saw that he had to be unique and all powerful.[6] Everyone agrees that this was achieved by the time of Deutero–Isaiah,[7] while some place it earlier,

---

[5] For a discussion of this issue and a bibliography, see Guy Mansini, "Error, Guilt, and the Knowledge of God: Questions About Robert Sokolowski's 'Christian Distinction,'" *Logos* 5 (2002): 116–36.

[6] Thus, Jeremiah 27:5: "It is I who by my great power and my outstretched arm have made the earth, with the men and animals that are on the earth, and I give it to whomever it seems right to me."

[7] For example, "Turn to me and be saved, all the ends of the earth! For I am God, and there is no other. By myself I have sworn, from my mouth has gone forth in righteousness a word that shall not return: 'To me every knee shall bow, every tongue shall swear.' Only in YHWH, it shall be said of me, are righteousness and strength; to him shall come and be ashamed, all who were incensed against him. In YHWH all the offspring of Israel shall triumph and glory" (Is 45:22–25).

and I agree with this, though it is difficult to determine when the "YHWH alone" view regarding Israel's worship actually matured into the "YHWH alone" view regarding the unique nature of YHWH in himself and his power over all else.[8] This latter view, whenever it became self-reflective in Israel, is well described by Claus Westermann: "The object of creation is without exception something outside the divine. The action of God as creator is directed exclusively to the world. God is outside creation; to be created means to be not-god."[9]

Several texts allude to a mythic theme of conflict in which YHWH triumphs over an enemy, usually associated with the sea or great waters, and thus guarantees stability for the world and for Israel. These texts are often expressive of a hope in YHWH's fidelity in time of suffering. We find, for instance, in Psalm 89, a lament over the disappearance of the kingship, not only verses that recall the promises made to David but also an allusion to a great victory of YHWH over hostile forces described in cosmic terms and perhaps also a reference to the victory over Egypt and other foes. Thus, the psalm begins with a celebration of YHWH's acts of loyal love (*hasdē* YHWH), goes on to speak of the everlasting covenant with David, and then of the authority and incomparability of YHWH and his might. This leads into the following account of his mighty deeds which are meant to recall to God's people and to God himself the awesome victories of old:

> YHWH, God of hosts, who is like you? Mighty YHWH, your abiding faithfulness is always present. You rule the raging sea; you still its swelling waves. You crushed Rahab with a mortal blow; your strong arm scattered your foes. Yours are the heavens, yours the earth; you founded the world and everything in it. Zaphon and Amanus you created; Tabor and Hermon rejoice in your name. Mighty your arm, strong your hand, your right hand is ever exalted. (Ps 89:9–14 NAB slightly revised)

There are several examples of this use of cosmic imagery to describe YHWH's mastery over the world where the mighty deeds of YHWH are recalled in a context of historical peril. Examples would be Psalm 74:12–17; Job 26:6–14; Isaiah 51:9.[10] Ezekiel 28:11–19 alludes to a mythic account of the first man, his glory, pride and fall, in the oracle against Tyre, but it does

---

[8] In Genesis 14, a text generally considered to be quite ancient, we read the expression, "the creator *(qonēh)* of heaven and earth" in vv. 19 and 22, with YHWH explicitly mentioned in the second of these verses.

[9] C. Westermann, *Genesis 1–11*, trans. John J. Scullion (Minneapolis: Augsburg, 1984), 26.

[10] For an extended discussion of this theme the reader may consult Jon D. Levenson, *Creation and the Persistence of Evil: The Jewish Drama of Divine Omnipotence* (San Francisco: Harper & Row, 1988).

not explicitly mention God's forming of the universe. There are also texts that, while they use many images, including that of YHWH as craftsman, evoke the overcoming of cosmic resistance. See for instance:

> Where were you when I laid the foundation of the earth? Tell me, if you have understanding. Who determined its measurements—surely you know! Or who stretched the line upon it? On what were its bases sunk, or who laid its cornerstone, when the morning stars sang together, and all the sons of God shouted for joy? Or who shut in the sea with doors, when it burst forth from the womb; when I made clouds its garment, and thick darkness its swaddling band, and prescribed bounds for it, and set bars and doors, and said, "Thus far shall you come, and no farther, and here shall your proud waves be stayed? (Job 38:4–11; see also Isa 40:12, 21–22)

The two most significant passages, however, that assert God's creative power and activity are to be found in the Priestly redactor's introduction to the whole of the Torah in Genesis 1:1–2:3, and the following text, Genesis 2:4–25, which forms the introduction to an earlier extended narrative formerly designated as source "J." These two texts were joined at the final redaction of the book of Genesis, probably after the exile. It is important to note that these texts are introductions; they lay the intellectual foundation for an understanding of the history of God's ways with Israel. They truly teach the uniqueness of God and the subordinate nature of everything else, but they do this in order to place God's choice of Israel in its proper context.

The first of these texts proceeds in a series of solemn formulae that move the action to a conclusion with the institution of the Sabbath. The high point of the text is in the center, the creation of *'ādām* as man and woman. The culmination is the institution of the Sabbath, that is, it grounds the observance of the Sabbath on the Word of God that imposes itself on what he has created,[11] and subtly teaches that the order of the universe is linked to obedience to that word, particularly in worship. To claim that this text teaches *creatio ex nihilo* is to transpose it to another thought world.[12] Whether the mention of

---

[11] This is reflected, for instance, in the motive given in Exodus 20:11, while in Deuteronomy 5:15 the motive links Sabbath to redemption: "You shall remember that you were a servant in the land of Egypt, and YHWH your God brought you out from there with a mighty hand and an outstretched arm; therefore YHWH your God commanded you to keep the Sabbath day."

[12] One of the earliest clear expressions of "creation from nothing" is to be found in 2 Maccabees 7:28 (ca. 100 B.C.): "I beg you, child, to look at the heavens and the earth and see all that is in them; then you will know that God did not make them out of existing things; and in the same way the human race came into existence."

"darkness" and "the Deep" allude to some sort of opposing presence is doubt-ful,[13] yet they are decidedly not *nihil,* any more than "the earth" that is also mentioned. Another aspect of this text besides its priestly order is the fact that both it and the following text, though their link with the cult and with God's relation to Israel is undoubted, actually are unique in the ancient world for their accent on *'ādām* as man and woman. Gerhard von Rad once remarked:

> The two presentations are alike in that they have as their chief end, though doing it in different ways, the creation of man, that is, mankind as male and female—with the result that the rest of the world is ordered round them as the chief work of YHWH in Creation. . . . The world and its fullness do not find their unity and inner coherence in a cosmologi-cal first principle such as the Ionian natural philosophers tried to dis-cover, but in the completely personal will of YHWH their creator.[14]

The second text, the introduction to the story of the origins of the world, of the nations and of Israel, is not a creation account in the same way as the text we have been considering. It sets the stage, rather, for an under-standing of how the chaos and violence that surrounds the human world and that YHWH has overcome, find their way into human history epito-mized by the shame, fear, domination, and animosity that begin to exist in the paradigm of all human relating: man and woman. The story moves from there to trace the progressive invasion of evil. After the story of Adam and Eve's transgression and a mysterious promise of an eventual victory, we are told of the murder of Abel, Lamech's song of vengeance, the generation of the flood, the tower of Babel. For each of these a divine remedy is provided until, after the scattering of the nations at Babel and an anxious period of waiting on the part of the audience, we are finally told of the call of Abra-ham: the beginning of a universal remedy for a universal disaster.[15]

---

13 For a discussion see Westermann, *Genesis 1–11,* 154.

14 Gerhard von Rad, *Old Testament Theology,* trans. D. M. G. Stalker, *The Theology of Israel's Historical Traditions,* vol. 1 (New York: Harper & Brothers, 1962), 141. Here, as elsewhere in this essay, I have changed the various renderings of the tetra-grammaton, even in quotations, to a form that is more acceptable to Jewish readers.

15 See G. von Rad, *Genesis,* trans. John H. Marks, *Old Testament Library* (Philadelphia: Westminster Press, 1961). The universal import of the blessing promised to Abraham is, as I understand it, the theological principle for the prayer and expectation on the part of Israel that, in one way or another, "All the nations you have made shall come to bow before you, Lord, and give honor to your name. For you are great and do won-drous deeds; and you alone are God" (Ps 86:9–10). For a treatment of this theme, see Norbert Lohfink and Erich Zenger, *The God of Israel and the Nations: Studies in Isaiah and the Psalms,* trans. Everett R. Kalin (Collegeville, MN: Liturgical Press, 2000).

We have seen how each of these fundamental texts speaks of YHWH's causality, mastery, if you will, and his care in regard to the world as we know it. The first text, which is more "cosmic," frames its material within the building of the universe whose stability is linked to the worship of YHWH given to Israel. The second text treats history and asserts that the redemption of the humanly dimensioned chaos we experience begins with the call of Abraham. All of the texts we have seen thus far consider God's creative power *functionally*, that is, God's mastery over all that exists forms the foundation, both in itself and in our understanding, for his authority and his exclusive right to worship. This can also be seen in texts that present his power in creating, echoing Genesis 1. An example would be Psalm 33:7–10. There, we have the fact of creation and God's authority over the nations presented in alternating lines:

> He gathered the waters of the sea as in a bottle; he put the deeps
> *(tᵉhômôt)* in storehouses.
> Let all the earth fear YHWH, let all the inhabitants of the world stand
> in awe of him!
> For he spoke, and it came to be; he commanded, and it stood forth.
> YHWH brings the counsel of the nations to nought; he frustrates the
> plans of the peoples.[16]

Two other examples of psalms that reflect the same viewpoint as Genesis 1 are Psalms 8 and 104. The first of these certainly sounds the theme of revelation by the mention of the "name" that, in the case of YHWH, implies a form of self-disclosure that makes him known even while concealing him. This name is majestic and it is "in all the earth," thus not exclusively in Israel. The mention of "the enemy and the avenger" implies some sort of opposition, but since these seem to be overcome by the praise of the little ones, they are not cosmic forces. The experience of nature's awesome grandeur is but part of the revelation that consists principally in a living experience of the reality of mankind in relation to nature (another universal theme) as this is presented in Genesis 1: an early instance of further revelation on the basis of a text.[17] It is significant that the question "what is man" can be found in at least three other contexts (Job 7:17;

---

[16] We may point as well to Psalm 24, which is, at least in its present form, an Entrance Liturgy whose central part, describing those who may ascend YHWH's mountain and stand in his holy place, is preceded by recalling the source of his authority: "The earth is YHWH's and what fills it, the world and those who dwell in it." It was because of this mention of creation that the b. Rosh. Hash. 31a prescribes this psalm for the day after the Sabbath.

[17] For a discussion of how one biblical text gives rise to another, more developed, revelation of a reality, see Francis Martin, "Sacra Doctrina and the Authority of its Sacra Scriptura in St. Thomas Aquinas," *Pro Ecclesia* 10 (2001): 84–102.

Ps 144:3; Sir 18:8), but only here is the response derived from the Genesis text and only here, in Psalm 8, do we find the note of awe and optimism.

Chapter 1 of Genesis also influences Psalm 104.[18] Classifications of the psalm vary, but it certainly contains wisdom motifs and is a hymn of praise. The material universe and man's place in it are revelations to the psalmist of YHWH's greatness, honor, and majesty (v. 1), as well as his wisdom (v. 24). These attributes of YHWH are a delight to the author of this psalm, but they are not conclusions of an inductive process of thought; they are rather like the reaction of a son who studies a statue made by his father and recognizes, rather than discovers, the "attributes" of his father. The psalm witnesses to this recognition and leads us to share in the revelation the author received so that we may join in the praise of the God we also know.

Psalm 19 is clearly to be classified as a wisdom hymn. It celebrates the glory of God made known by the heavens and sings of the firmament's witness that it is the work of his hands. It then goes on to listen to the voice of both day and night as they testify to all the earth and to the extremity of the world. The marvel of the sun is then singled out for admiration. Dwelling in the tent God has set for him, like a bridegroom he comes from his chamber and runs his course like an eager warrior. Abruptly the psalm changes and begins to praise the tôrat YHWH, listing its "attributes" and synonyms, and finally concludes with a prayer. Thus, though the first part of the psalm is the most explicit expression we have seen so far of revelation through nature, the second part of the psalm grounds or completes this with YHWH's instruction, a revelation of a different and higher order. Rashi states of the tôrâ: "she also gives light like the sun" in accord with what is stated at the end of the stanza (v. 9b) "making the eyes light up."[19] Since the final form of this psalm is a unity we need not discuss its possible multiple antecedents, if such there be. Psalm 8 also sounds the theme of nature, and especially man's place in it, as showing forth the majesty of YHWH's Name.

---

[18] For an argument that the direction of the dependence is from Ps 104 to Gen 1, see Levenson, *Creation and the Persistence of Evil*, 5, "Creation Without Opposition." Levenson carefully enumerates the commonality of vocabulary and order between the texts, but it is difficult to understand how a tightly structured report-narrative could be based on a poem, whereas the opposite seems much more likely.

[19] Translation from Rashi, *Rashi's Commentary on Psalms 1–89 (Books I–III). With English Translation and Notes,* ed. Jacob Neusner et al., trans. Mayer I. Gruber, *South Florida Studies in the History of Judaism 161* (Atlanta: Scholars Press, 1998), 118. Many ancient Jewish commentators already saw the intended counterpoint, sun—Torah, some pointing out that the Torah was just as necessary for existence as the sun. See Nahum Sarna, *On The Book of Psalms: Exploring the Prayers of Ancient Israel* (New York: Schocken Books, 1995), 75.

Creation in the Wisdom Tradition

Psalm 19:2–7 is the clearest example we have seen so far of the physical world being considered a revelation in a sense approximating a "discovery" rather than a "recognition." This line of thought is characteristic of the wisdom tradition that sees wisdom as something present in creation, "poured out" upon it by God (Sir 1:9), present at the creation (Prov 8:22–36), yet having a dwelling place in Jacob (Sir 24:1–23). Wisdom is fascinating and beckons to man, indeed calls to him (Prov 9) inviting companionship as a bride (Wis 8:2; Sir 20:14–10). Her company and help bring happiness, respect, and protection to a person (Prov 2), and yet, she is unattainable by human effort (Job 28), for the beginning, the source, of wisdom is fear of the Lord; it is acquired by heeding YHWH (Is 55:1–3).

It is in the light of this understanding that we must look at the teaching of Wisdom 13:1–14:31, the first part of a long excursus on idolatry.[20] The first section of this text is a discussion of nature worship that the author, along with Philo and others, considers less blameworthy than the worship of idols. The text then moves on to consider idolatry:

> Devoid of sense [are] all men by nature *(phusei)*, in whom is ignorance *(agnōsia)* of God; and from the good things seen, did not succeed in knowing Him who is *(ton onta* [Ex 3:14]), and from studying the works did not come to know *(epegnōsan)* the Artisan *(ton technitēn)*. Rather, either fire, or wind, or swift air, or the circuit of the stars, or the mighty water, or the luminaries of heaven, the governors *(prutaneis)* of the world, they considered gods. If through delight in the beauty of these things they took them to be gods, let them know how much superior is the Master *(Despotēs)* of these things; for the original source *(genesiarchēs)* of all beauty created *(ektisen)* them. Or if they were amazed at their power and energy *(dunamin kai energeian)*, let them understand *(noēsatosan)* from them how much more powerful is he who shaped them. From the greatness and beauty of created things *(ktismatōn)*, by analogy *(analogōs)*, their original author *(genesiourgos)* is seen *(theōreitai)*. Yet for these the blame is less; for they indeed have gone astray *(planōntai)* perhaps, seeking God and wishing to find him. For they search busily among his works, and place reliance on visual impressions *(peithontai tê opsei)*, for what is seen is beautiful. Yet even they are not to be excused *(suggnōstoi)*. For if they were so capable of coming to knowledge, that they were able

---

[20] I am following here the very informative commentary of David Winston, *The Wisdom of Solomon*, ed. William Foxwell Albright and David Noel Freedman (New York: Doubleday, 1979). Another late and somewhat Hellenized text is that of Sirach 17:1–24, which, however, does not speak of knowing God through creation.

to search out the Universe *(stochasthai ton aiōna)* how is it that they did not sooner find the Master of these things?

The next 21 verses [13:10–14:11] discuss the origin and sin of idolatry. This is followed by a conclusion that links sexual sin with idolatry.

> The beginning of wantonness *(porneias)* is the devising of idols, and their invention is the corruption of life. For in the beginning they were not, nor will they continue forever. By the empty illusion *(kenodoxia)* of men they came into the world *(eisēlthen eis ton kosmon)*, and therefore a sudden end is devised for them. (14:12–14)

The next 7 verses trace the way idolatry came about. And there then follows a "vice list" that mentions, among others, "child-slaying sacrifices," "frenzied carousals," "corruption, faithlessness, turmoil, perjury," "besmirching of souls, exchange of sex roles *(geneseōs enallagē)* disorder in marriage, adultery and debauchery *(aselgeia)*." Finally, in 14:27, the principle is stated: "For the worship of unspeakable idols is the beginning, end and cause of every evil." The section concludes with a consideration of what awaits people who worship and swear by idols.

Clearly, this text is speaking about a discovery of God rather than a recognition. The author describes the mental process by which this discovery could be made: knowing *ho Ōn* from the good things seen; knowing the Artisan from studying the works; understanding that the *Despotēs* is superior to and is the *genesiarchēs* of all the beauty we see and that he created it. The principle of this movement of thought is: "From the greatness and beauty of created things *(ktismatōn)*, by analogy *(analogōs)*, their original author *(genesiourgos)* is seen *(theōreitai)*." The term *analogōs* here has not the full connotation of the later Scholastic understanding of analogy, but it is describing the same movement of thought that is a comparison that can conjecture from beauty to Beauty.[21]

Our author goes further and asks why those who could advance so far as to conceive of the *Aion*, the Universe with temporal and spatial limits, could not go further. Why could they not step outside the closed system thus fashioned by Hellenistic thought and understand a Creator? No one outside the biblical tradition, or at least its influence, has ever done this. Many have arrived at a concept of a single principle governing the universe, but this is itself part of the closed system, the most noble and exalted part, but still part of a system considered to be eternal.[22] Still "Solomon" asks the question,

---

[21] For a brief history of the terms *metabasis* and *analogia*, see Winston, *The Wisdom of Solomon*, 252.

[22] See Robert Sokolowski, *The God of Faith and Reason. Foundations of Christian Theology* (Notre Dame, IN: University of Notre Dame Press, 1982).

one that will occupy us later in the study. Suffice it to say that the biblical tradition sees a moral dimension to the discovery of God. Speaking of our present text, James Reese observes:

> The Sage condemns every system of religious thought that confines man within the limits of the cosmic forces and the resources of purely human reasoning. Such a system cannot seek God "in sincerity of heart" (1.1: see 8.21) because it cuts itself off from the personal donor of divine Wisdom, "the initiate of the knowledge of God." (8.4)[23]

The line of thought found in the Book of Wisdom is characteristic of Hellenistic Judaism, which probably borrowed some of its arguments from Greek thinkers, particularly those who criticized the idolatry of their compatriots in the name of a single god who was the principle and governor of the universe: the world soul, the logos, and so on.[24] Certainly the Jewish author closest to the Book of Wisdom is Philo. David Winston adduces impressive indications of overlap in thought and vocabulary between these two that is probably due to a common thought world. Winston's late dating of Wisdom, however, in order to establish closer ties and even the dependence of Wisdom on Philo is more problematic. Let this text of Philo's represent several that could be adduced:

> The mind, having discerned through the faculty of sight what of itself it was not able to apprehend, did not simply stop short at what it saw, but, drawn by its love of knowledge and beauty and charmed by the marvelous spectacle, came to the reasonable conclusion *(logismon eikota)* that all these were not brought together automatically by unreasoning forces, but by the mind *(dianoia)* of God Who is rightly called Father and Maker *(patera kai poiēten)*. (*The Special Laws* 3, 189ff)[25]

---

[23] James Reese, *Hellenistic Influence on the Book of Wisdom and Its Consequences* (Rome: Pontifical Biblical Institute, 1970), 61.

[24] For a brief discussion and bibliography of the borrowing of Hellenistic arguments against idolatry and polytheism, see Jacques Dupont, *Gnosis. La Connaissance Religieuse dans les Épîtres de Saint Paul,* 2nd ed. (Louvain/Paris: Nauwelaerts/Gabalda, 1960), who concludes by saying, "Il n'est pas douteux que les thèmes de propaganda monothéiste que Paul reprend au judaïsme avaient assimilé bon nombre d'éléments hellénistiques" (23, n. 2). For a discussion of how even this Hellenistic "monotheism" was often an organized polity of forces or gods see Karl Rahner, "Theos in the New Testament," in *Theological Investigations I* (Baltimore: Helicon, 1961), 79–148.

[25] See also *Leg. All.* 3, 97; *De Spec. Leg.* 1, 30ff; 45; *De Opific. Mundi* 7; *De praem. et poen.* 38ff; *De vita contemp.* 3–8; De decal. 51ff.

A subsequent and very Hellenistic author, Josephus gives us this account of how Abraham came to his monotheism.

> [Abraham] was the first to venture to publish this notion, that there was but one God, the Creator of the Universe; and that as to other [gods], if they contributed anything to the happiness of men, that each of them afforded it only according to his appointment, and not by their own power. This, his opinion, was derived from the irregular phenomena that were visible both at land and sea, as well as those that happen to the sun and moon, and all the heavenly bodies, thus: "If, [said he] these bodies had power of their own, they would certainly take care of their own regular motions; but since they do not preserve such regularity, they make it plain, that insofar as they cooperate to our advantage, they do it not of their own abilities, but as they are subservient to him that commands them; to whom alone we ought justly to offer our honor and thanksgiving." [Note resemblance in this last line to Rom 1:21a.] *Antiquities* 1,7,1 (155–56)[26]

I will give but two other examples of this type of Jewish thinking since they illustrate the type of anti-pagan polemic that characterized both Jews and Christians in the early centuries. The first of these is the *Letter of Aristeas*, written perhaps 150–100 B.C.E., which purports to give an account of the translation of the "divine law" from Hebrew into Greek. The Eleazar mentioned in the text is presented as high priest at that time:

> Eleazar began first of all by demonstrating that God is one, that his power is shown in everything, every place being filled with his sovereignty, and that none of the things on earth which men do secretly are hidden from him, as well as that which is come to pass. . . . This was his introduction: He proceeded to show that all the rest of mankind ("except ourselves," as he said) believe that there are many gods, because men themselves are much more powerful than the gods whom they vainly worship; they make images of stone and wood . . . even though the insensibility (of the images) is close at hand to appreciate. (*Letter of Aristeas* 132–35)[27]

I will conclude this section with a later text whose roots may be earlier. It is a rabbinic tale about how Abraham heard the call of God. In one interpretation of the tale, there is an important insight to which we will refer

---

[26] A similar tradition is found in *Jubilees* 12, 17, which includes, however, a suggestion of revelation: "a word came into his heart."

[27] Translation by O. S. Wintermute, in *The Old Testament Pseudepigrapha, Volume 2*, ed. James H. Charlesworth (New York: Doubleday, 1985), 21–22.

later. The story and its interpretation are given by David Novak in his article, "Before Revelation: The Rabbis, Paul, and Karl Barth."[28] The text is a commentary on Genesis 12:1: God's sudden entrance into Abraham's life, his command and promise to Abraham.

> Rabbi Isaac said that it is like one who was travelling from place to place and who saw a palace burning *(doleqet)*. He said, "Could one say that there is a palace without an owner *(manheeg)*?" The master of the palace peered forth *(hetzeetz)* and said to him: "I am he who is owner of the palace!" So it is that because Abraham our father said, "Could one say that the world is without an owner?" that God peered forth and said to him, "I am the owner—the Lord *(Adon)* of the whole world."[29]

The first interpretation reads *doleqet* as "shining, illuminated," and portrays Abraham in wonder at the beauty of the palace (world) and enquiring after its "owner" (as in the story told by Josephus and *Jubilees* above). God rewards such earnest seeking by revealing himself. The second interpretation reads *doleqet* as "burning" and thus Abraham, seeing the disaster of the palace (world) and in danger himself, rather than succumb to the disaster or presume he can avoid or repair it, cries out not knowing if anyone will answer. God responds, announcing that he is the Lord of the whole world. This teaches that God's revelation of himself to Abraham was not the result of a peaceful inductive process but a gift provided to a man who continued to search for One greater than himself, and refused to practice idolatry. Thus, as in the sequel to the Babel narrative, the remedy to the universal disaster is the call of Abraham. This ideal of always seeking Someone greater will provide a solution to a question to be asked further on. Now we must turn to the New Testament teaching on creation as revelation.

The Christian Biblical Tradition

I intend here, as indicated by the title to include only the early centuries of Christianity, leaving the rest for Part II, where I will reflect on both traditions.

Most of the teaching on creation found in the New Testament is derived from the Prior Testament and its commentaries, though now creation is most often seen in a Christological focus. The fact of creation is stated in several texts, of which 1 Corinthians 8:4–6 may serve as an example:

---

[28] *Journal of Religion* 71 (1991): 50–66.

[29] Genesis Rabbah, 39,1; *Midrash Rabbah,* trans. H. Freedman and Maurice Simon, vol. 1 (New York/Jerusalem: Soncino Press, 1977), 313. I have retained Novak's system of transliteration as he placed it in the translation.

So about the eating of meat sacrificed to idols: we know that "there is no idol in the world," and that "there is no God but one." Indeed, even though there are so-called gods in heaven and on earth (there are, to be sure, many "gods" and many "lords"), yet for us there is one God, the Father, from whom all things are and for whom we exist, and one Lord, Jesus Christ, through whom all things are and through whom we exist (NAB).[30]

There are also texts that speak of God's witness to himself in and through creation.[31] The most well-known text, however, and the one most apposite for our study is Romans 1:18–23. I give here a literal translation, and then follow it with commentary that will give the understanding of this text from the patristic era up to the Middle Ages as summarized by Thomas Aquinas:

18   For the wrath of God is revealed from heaven upon all the ungodliness and injustice of men who, in injustice, suppress the truth.

19   Because what can be known about God is manifest among them: God has made it manifest to them.

20   For his invisible attributes, being understood from the creation of the world by means of what is made, are clearly perceived—his eternal power and divinity—so that they are without excuse.

21   Because, knowing God, they did not glorify him as God or give thanks, rather they became devoid of sense in their reasonings and their uncomprehending heart was darkened.

22   Claiming to be wise, they became foolish;

23   and they exchanged the glory of the incorruptible God for the likeness of the image of corruptible man, and of birds and four-footed animals and reptiles.

After asserting that the uprightness of God is revealed in the Good News (v. 17), Paul goes on to state that the wrath (orgē) of God ("the expected divine reaction to human sin and evil")[32] is revealed from heaven (= God) on all the ungodliness and injustice (asebeian kai adikia) of men. By describing God's wrath as "revealed," Paul implies that it requires faith to understand

---

[30] Some other texts are Matthew 11:25; John 1:3; Colossians 1:15–16; Hebrews 1:3.

[31] For example, Acts 14:15–17, 17:24–28.

[32] Joseph Fitzmyer, *Romans. A New Translation with Introduction and Commentary*, ed. William Foxwell Albright and David Noel Freedman (New York: Doubleday, 1992), 107.

what we see in a culture given over to the vices that follow upon idolatry. His lists of these at the end of this passage (vv. 24–31) bears many resemblances to that given at the end of the text from Wisdom considered above.

Suppression of the Truth

The primary act of ungodliness and injustice is that humans "suppress" or "impede" *(katechontōn)* the truth. The truth is the truth about God that they somehow recognize sufficiently to suppress it. The verb used here designates the source of all that follows, pointing as it does to the way of a culture that has designed itself to be impervious to the evidence of God. However, the expression speaks most of all of a subtle interior movement by which what is dimly grasped is prevented from growing into full knowledge. We will return to consider this verb at more length.

Manifestation

Paul goes on to explain why he accuses "men" of suppressing the truth: "Because what can be known about God is manifest among them: God has made it manifest to them."[33] The first statement addresses the question of the availability of what can be known about God: It is manifest among them, and can be understood by them. The second statement goes further and says that God himself has manifested what can be known about him. Thomas Aquinas, commenting on this second phrase, explains:

> He says that God manifested it to them as we read in Job 35:11: "He teaches us above the beasts of the earth." So we should consider that one man manifests something to another by explaining his concept through some external signs, either by speech or by writing; but God manifests something to man in a twofold manner. In one way, by infusing an interior light through which man knows: Psalm 42(Vg):3: "Send forth your light and your truth." In another way by setting forth external signs of his wisdom, that is creatures perceivable to the senses: Sirach 1:10(Vg): "He poured her (wisdom) out over all his works."

---

[33] This translation requires taking *gnōston* in a more classical and philosophical sense than would usually be found in this literature and milieu where it means "known" rather than "knowable." Most commentators accept the classical meaning here. See Stanislaus Lyonnet, "La connaissance naturelle de Dieu," in *Études sur L'Epître aux Romains*, ed. Stanislaus Lyonnet (Roma: Editrice Pontificio Istituto Biblico, 1989), 43–70. The translation "among them" represents *en autois*, while "to them" represents autois. The differentiation in Greek may be merely stylistic, but I wished to indicate that the first expression can mediate a communal notion while the second puts the accent on the individual.

Therefore, God manifested it to them either interiorly, by infusing light or exteriorly by setting forth visible creatures in which, as in a book, the knowledge of God might be read.[34]

By saying that what can be known about God is manifest because God made it manifest, Paul implies a certain action on the part of God. There is first of all the act of creating itself, which, of course, is durative: Creation is held in existence by the same power by which it was first given existence and is an expression of that power. Aquinas states above that the disclosure or manifestation has two dimensions: the created realities themselves and the light to read them correctly. He will say the same about the gift of prophecy, though he specifies that what is presented to the mind may also be divinely conferred and that the light given is superior to the light of reason.[35]

From the side of created realities we may infer from what Aquinas says elsewhere that they have the capacity to manifest themselves and, thus, play an active role in being known. Building upon his own understanding of the Platonic principle that "good is diffusive of itself," St. Thomas reasons that, since the act of existence is the foundation of all other perfections, indeed "the actuality of all acts and the perfection of all perfections,"[36] the diffusiveness of the good is rooted in the existence of a being; and it is thus that whatever exists manifests itself in the act of its existing.[37] Disclosure, therefore, involves both the created reality manifesting itself in and through the act of its existence and the creative receptivity of the mind that receives the act of the reality and gives

---

[34] *Ad Romanos, Lectura VI,* in *Super Epistolas S. Pauli Lectura* (Roma: Marietti, 1953), no. 116, I, 22.

[35] "Now by the gift of prophecy something is conferred on the human mind over and above the powers of its natural faculty in both respects, namely in respect of judgment by the infusion of intellectual light *[per influxum luminis intellectualis]*, and in respect of the acceptation or representation of realities which is done through certain species. In this second respect, but not in the first, human teaching *[doctrina]* can be likened to prophetic revelation, for a man furnishes his pupil with realities through word symbols, but he cannot illumine from within as God does. Of these two aspects of knowledge the first is more important *[principalius]* in prophecy: because judgment is the full fruit *[completivum]* of knowledge." *ST* II–II, q. 173, a. 2, c.

[36] *De potentia,* q. 7, a. 2, ad 9. Translation is from Walter Norris Clarke, "Action as the Self-Revelation of Being: A Central Theme in the Thought of St. Thomas," in *Explorations in Metaphysics,* ed. Walter Norris Clarke (Notre Dame, IN/London: Notre Dame University Press, 1994), 45–63.

[37] Later in the same essay (63, n. 11) Clarke cites Karl Rahner: "Our first statement which we put forward as the basic principle of an ontology of symbolism, is as follows: all beings are by their very nature symbolic, because they necessarily 'express' themselves in order to attain their own nature." Karl Rahner, "Theology of the Symbol," in *Theological Investigations,* vol. 4 (Baltimore: Helicon Press, 1966), 221–52.

it intelligibility, transposing it to the level of the knower. This energy, the capacity to receive and transpose, is what the ancient thinkers meant by the light of the mind. Aquinas says of this interior light of reason that it is itself a "certain participation in divine light" (*ST* I, 12, 11, ad 3); it is, in fact, "nothing else but the imprint of the divine light in us" (*ST* I–II, 91, 2). He also says that the intensification and elevation of this light, which is the heart of *sacra doctrina*, the reception and transmission of prophetic knowledge, is also "a certain imprint of the divine knowledge" (*ST* I, 1, 3, ad 2).

From the side of the mind itself, according to Aquinas, there are three dimensions of our knowing that can be manifestations of God. The first of these is the knowledge implicit in every act of knowing. That we know God implicitly in every act of knowing is stated in the treatise *De veritate*. In answering the question whether all things desire God himself, Aquinas confronts the objection that all things are ordered to God as knowable and desirable, but not all beings capable of knowledge actually know God, therefore neither do they actually desire him. This is his answer: "All knowing beings implicitly know God in whatever they know. For just as nothing is desirable except as it bears a likeness to the First Goodness, so nothing is knowable except as it bears a likeness to the First Truth."[38]

The second dimension of knowledge is intuition or *intellectus*. Its foundation is the presence of the thing known to the knower. In the very first article of *De veritate*, Aquinas, who is asking the question *"Quid sit veritas?"* discusses the relation of being to the intellect. He makes the following statement:

> True *(verum)* expresses the correspondence *(convenientia)* of being to the knowing power *(intellectus)*, for all knowing is produced by an assimilation of the knower to the thing known, so that assimilation is said to be the cause of knowledge *(assimilatio dicta est causa cognitionis)*.[39] Similarly, the sense of sight knows a color by being informed with a species of the color.
>
> The first reference *(comparatio)* of being to the intellect, therefore, consists in its agreement with the intellect *(ut ens intellectui correspondeat)*. This agreement is called "the conformity of thing and intellect" *(adaequatio rei et intellectus)* and in this conformity is found the formal constituent of the true *(et in hoc formaliter ratio veri perficitur)*, and this

---

[38] *De veritate*, 22, 2, ad 1.

[39] It is important to advert to another principle of Aquinas: *veritas fundatur in esse rei magis quam in ipsa quidditate* (*In I Sent*, d. 19, q. 5, a. 1, sol.) As David Bentley Hart remarks: "[T]he adequation that truth is consists in an assimilation of the esse of any given thing, whereby it accepts each thing as it is." David Bentley Hart, *The Beauty of the Infinite: The Aesthetics of Christian Truth* (Grand Rapids, MI: Eerdmans, 2003), 247.

is what the true adds to being, namely, the conformity or equation of thing and intellect *(conformitatem seu adaequationem rei et intellectus)*. As we said the knowledge of a thing is a consequence of this conformity *(ad quam conformitatem, ut dictum est, sequiter cognitio rei)*; therefore it is an effect of truth, even though the fact that it is a being is prior to its truth *(Sic ergo entitas rei praecedit rationem veritatis; sed cognitio est quaedam veritatis effectus)*.

"Assimilation is the cause of knowledge." And again, "knowledge of a thing is a consequence of the conformity of thing and intellect." And since truth is precisely the "assimilation of the knower to the thing known," it follows that "knowledge is a certain effect of truth." We may call the conformity or assimilation of the knower to what is known "ontological truth" and the knowledge that follows from this "epistemological truth." It is at the ontological level that the act of knowing imitates, in a created manner, the procession of the Word in the Trinity. A person is already modified by being or a being before he can articulate the conformity established through what Maritain calls "the basic generosity of existence."[40] Beings give themselves to us and modify us, thus establishing us in truth whose effect is knowledge. That knowledge that is the effect of truth must first be considered as *intellectus*, as Aquinas says in the *Summa contra Gentiles* (1, 57): "That which is supreme in our knowledge is not reason, but *intellectus* which is the source of reason."

Another mode of this type of knowledge is described in *ST* I–II, q. 2, a. 1, ad 1:

> To know that God exists in a general and confused way is implanted in us by nature, inasmuch as God is man's beatitude. For man naturally desires happiness, and what is naturally desired by man must be naturally known to him. This, however, is not to know absolutely that God exists; just as to know that someone is approaching is not the same as to know that Peter is approaching, even though it is Peter who is approaching; for many there are who imagine that man's perfect good which is happiness, consists in riches, and others in pleasures, and others in something else.

On one hand, the knowledge described here pertains to the first dimension since it is linked to the desire for happiness, the implicit desire for the good. Yet it shares in the nature of *intellectus* in that something is known not only implicitly but also, as it were, "symbolically" or as it fulfills the role of a "cipher." For it must be borne in mind that, of course, God is never directly or immediately known as an "object" of knowledge. It is rather that what can be

---

[40] Jacques Maritain, *Existence and the Existent* (New York: Doubleday, 1957), 90.

known bears within itself a tacit dimension (to use Michael Polanyi's term), an "aura" that can attract one beyond the immediate *intellectus* to the inferential pursuit of a more complete knowledge of what has been intuited. As Stanislaw Kowalczyk expresses it: "Whatever is real can be a cipher . . . the human being, consciousness, conscience, language, religion, art, the history of humanity . . . A cipher is something that lies between the Transcendent and existence; it is a sign pointing to a transcendent reality."[41] When the cipher or symbol is not allowed to make its full witness, when inferences are not drawn in a process of reasoning, there is the danger that the person will misconstrue the creature's role as witness to the transcendent and stop at the creature itself.[42]

The third dimension of knowledge is, then, reasoning *(ratiocinatio)*, which is a movement of the mind made in the power of the original intuition by which new truth is acquired and consciously assimilated in judgment. It is a movement from what is less determinate to what is more determinate; from a determination of actuality to a determination of form. But this must not be understood as a unidirectional movement. What is acquired by reasoning can itself become another *intellectus*, for, as Aquinas says elsewhere, *intellectus* is not only the principle of reason, but also its term or goal.[43]

If we return now to St. Paul's statement that suppression of the truth is an act of ungodliness and injustice *(asebeia kai adikia)*, we must ask at what dimension of knowledge this suppression takes place. First, however, it is important to realize that this suppression is initially personal, on the part of some leaders who shape the culture, and then also communal or cultural in that the resulting lack of the knowledge of God and the consequences of this become embodied in the institutions and thought world of the society. Paul is condemning a *culture* and is uncovering, with the help of what had already been revealed to God's people, the root cause of an aberration that is so mysteriously easy to generate and perpetuate and finally results in a culture that becomes a bondage. The following description of culture may help us enter into what Paul saw as he considered how suppression of the truth had become "inculturated" and produced, as it always does an anti-culture. The description is positive but it can be read as though negative by substituting

---

[41] "Ambiwalencja absolute Karla Jaspers" ["The Ambivalence of Karl Jaspers's Absolute"], *Zeszyty Naukowe* KUL 14.4 (1971): 32, cited in Karol Wojtyla (John Paul II), "The Problem of The Constitution of Culture Through Human Praxis," in *Person and Community: Selected Essays, Catholic Thought from Lublin 4* (New York: Peter Lang, 1993), 263–75.

[42] A masterful analysis of the illusions that follow upon a failure to reason from this confused knowledge, linked to desire, to a clear knowledge of man's last end can be found in *ST* I, q. 2, a. 2.

[43] *In III Sent.*, d. 35, q. 1, a. 3, sol. 2: *Intellectus est rationis principium et terminus.*

negative instances of the interaction of the four components of culture: beliefs, values, customs, and institutions, and realizing that an anti-culture is of its nature parasitic, even if it seems to be dominant. It is feeding off something more profound and more authentically human.

> Culture is an integrated system of beliefs (about God or reality or ultimate meaning), or values (about what is true, good, beautiful and normative), of customs (how to behave, relate to others, talk, pray, dress, work, play, farm, eat, etc.) and of institutions which express those beliefs, values and customs . . . which bind a society together and give it a sense of identity, dignity, security, and continuity.[44]

Not only is Paul considering the anti-culture as it confronts him, he is also aware of those who have, in whatever imperfect form, yielded to God's manifestation of himself in and through creation. Evidence of such piety abounds in Greek literature and is found in other literatures as well.[45] Paul himself in the next chapter speaks of those who, without the benefit of the revealed Law, nevertheless obey the precepts of the law:

> When Gentiles who have not the law do by nature what the law requires, they are a law to themselves, even though they do not have the law. They show that what the law requires is written on their hearts, while their conscience also bears witness and their conflicting thoughts accuse or perhaps excuse them on that day when, according to my gospel, God judges the secrets of men by Christ Jesus. (Rom 2:14–16)[46]

---

[44] From the Willowbank Report, Lausanne Committee for World Evangelization, 1978, as quoted in Michael Paul Gallagher, *Clashing Symbols: An Introduction to Faith and Culture* (London: Darton, Longman and Todd Ltd, 1997), 152.

[45] For examples of this literature, see André-Jean Festugière, *Personal Religion Among the Greeks* (Berkeley/Los Angeles: University of California Press, 1954, 1960). James B. Pritchard, ed., *Ancient Near Eastern Texts Relating to the Old Testament* (Princeton: Princeton University Press, 1969). For a discussion of religious intuition among non-historical religions, see Henri de Lubac, *The Discovery of God,* ed. David Schindler, trans. Marc Sebanc, Alexander Dru, and Cassian Fulsom, *Ressourcement* (Grand Rapids, MI: Eerdmans, 1996). See also Kenneth Schmitz, *The Gift: Creation, The Aquinas Lecture,* 1982 (Milwaukee, WI: Marquette University Press, 1982).

[46] We also read in the Acts of the Apostles words attributed to Paul by Luke in the Areopagus speech to Epicureans and Stoics, which reflects early Christian preaching to pagans and builds on whatever goodwill some of their religious practices may be interpreted to possess. So Paul, standing in the middle of the Areopagus, said: "Men of Athens, I perceive that in every way you are very religious. For as I passed along, and observed the objects of your worship, I found also an altar with this inscription, 'To an unknown god.' What therefore you worship as unknown, this I proclaim to

Before we return to consider the three dimensions of knowledge in the light of Paul's charge of "suppression," we should advert to one other aspect of knowledge, namely, that it is an act of the person and not only of the mind. This is clearly seen, for instance, when we compare various kinds of knowing. The lowest type is that enshrined by the positive sciences and unconsciously taken over in other disciplines, namely, knowledge caused by "compelling evidence." This knowledge strives for an ever-increasing elimination of the human factor, though the ideal has been subverted by the famous principle of indeterminacy. The second level is that of appreciating a work of art: Here the human factor is absolutely necessary since art demands of the receiver an active openness, a movement of receptivity. The third level is that of interpersonal knowledge, which is impossible without both active receptivity and self-gift. This last type reaches a unique level and intensity in the personal knowledge of God, something only achieved by divine initiative.

The principle is, therefore, that the higher forms of knowledge demand a greater self-involvement on the part of the knower, who must also finally become a lover. If we bear this in mind, I think we can understand Paul's indictment: He is not saying that God's self-manifestation in and through creation presents itself as "compelling evidence." It is rather an invitation to yield to the evidence and follow its lead. Refusal to do this is a form of human action, a praxis that can create an anti-culture. Furthermore, Paul is talking in general terms and makes no attempt to judge the presence or degree of culpability in an individual who is formed by the anti-culture and lacks the leisure and training to step outside its dynamism to reflect upon and challenge it. It was for this reason that Maimonides already taught that if mankind had only reason for a guide, "most people would die without having known whether there was a God or not, much less that certain things must be

---

you. The God who made the world and everything in it, being Lord of heaven and earth, does not live in shrines made by man, nor is he served by human hands, as though he needed anything, since he himself gives to all men life and breath and everything" (Acts 17:22–25). See also Acts 14:15–17: "Men, why are you doing this? We also are men, of like nature with you, and bring you good news, that you should turn from these vain things to a living God who made the heaven and the earth and the sea and all that is in them. In past generations he allowed all the nations to walk in their own ways; yet he did not leave himself without witness, for he did good and gave you from heaven rains and fruitful seasons, satisfying your hearts with food and gladness." It is also valuable to see how Paul describes the rhythm of the conversion of the Thessalonians: "For they themselves report concerning us what a welcome we had among you, and how you *turned to God from idols, to serve a living and true God,* and to wait for his Son from heaven, whom he raised from the dead, Jesus who delivers us from the wrath to come" (1 Thes 1:9–10).

asserted about Him and other things denied as defects. From such a fate not 'even one of a city or two of a family' (Jer 3:14) would have escaped."[47]

What is more, while hesitancy or confusion can result in the mistaken worship of cosmic forces, or of the world soul, and the like, refusal occurs when something else is substituted and worshipped as the ultimate determining factor of existence. Such is idolatry and it is this that Paul, along with the whole of the biblical tradition, excoriates because, as he will say shortly, it exchanges (substitutes) the glory of God (the revelation of his hiddenness) for something made by man, something, therefore, that while it demands sacrifice and even surrender, still leaves control in the hands of the worshipper: There is no self-gift on either side, whether the "other side" is an imaginative figment, a demon, or a totalitarian system of thought or government.

If we ask now after the place of the suppression in the various dimensions of knowledge distinguished previously, we see that it cannot take place in the dimension of implicit knowledge since that pertains to the nature of the mind and is present in the very act of knowing. In regard to *intellectus* we see that, since it is essentially an act of receptivity, suppression would consist in a refusal to be open to the witness of what is received, an inhibiting of its self-communicating. Such an act also suppresses the natural movement of the mind, the light that is the imprint of the divine light, so that there is no movement from what is indefinite to what is more defined and recognizable in both senses of this term.[48]

---

[47] Moses Maimonides, *The Guide for the Perplexed,* trans. M. Friedlander (New York: Dover Publications, 1956), XXXIV, 46. For a study of Maimonides on revelation, see Ben Zion Bokser, "Reason and Revelation in the Theology of Maimonides," *Hebrew Union College Annual* 20 (2000): 541–80. In *ST* I–II, q. 94, a. 6, Aquinas, perhaps in dependence upon Maimonides, asks whether the natural law can be obliterated *(deleri)* from the human mind. He replies by distinguishing between the general principles that cannot be altogether obliterated, though one or other may be obliterated as it applies to a particular action, and "secondary precepts" by which he means the Decalogue. These may be obliterated "either by evil persuasions, just as in speculative matters errors occur in respect to necessary conclusions; or by vicious customs and corrupt habits (anti-culture), as among some men theft and even unnatural vices, as the Apostle states, were not esteemed sinful." This state of affairs makes it necessary to reveal the natural law: "Because the law of nature had been destroyed by the law of concupiscence it was necessary that man be brought back to the works of virtue and withdrawn from vice: for which needful things there was the law of Scripture." *Expositio in duo praecepta caritatis et in decem legis praecepta,* Prologus, no. 1131, in *Opuscula Theological II* (Rome: Marietti, 1954). For a treatment of this theme and bibliography, see Guy Mansini and Lawrence J. Welch, "Revelation, Natural Law and Homosexual Unions," *Nova et Vetera* (English) 2 (2004): 337–66.

[48] Aquinas consistently teaches that God teaches by supplying the "subject matter" of the act of thought and the light by which this act is undertaken, for instance:

This brings us once again to a fundamental principle of Aquinas, namely, that knowledge is born of two lights: the light of *what* is known and the light *by which* it is known. Light, he tells us is that by which there is manifestation (read disclosure) of any kind. As we have seen, all beings manifest themselves by their act of being, and the power to receive that manifestation is the light of the mind itself, a participation in divine light.[49] This activity of the mind, however, must be applied by the person to the thing to be known and this at successive levels of engagement of the whole person, depending on the truth to be grasped. When the reality is God, he can only be known now in his effects, as the medieval adage expresses it. That is, created realities bear witness to their Source, but the person must be willing to follow their beckoning, and yield as well to the light given by God to grasp the true meaning of this witness, which, in the present order of things, leads to love and praise of God. I say "in the present order of things" to indicate that there is not any purely "natural order" in which the witness of creation can end with a knowledge of God divorced from his call to a personal relationship of obedience and trust.[50] I must return to this, but having placed the statement here enables me to end this section with a remarkable quote from Aquinas's commentary on the *De Trinitate* of Boethius, which points once again to the twofold light present even in the knowing that is faith, and to the fact that "something moves us to the assent."

> So also in the faith by which we believe in God there is not only the accepting of the object of assent, but something moving us to the assent. This is a kind of light—the habit of faith—divinely imparted to the human mind. It is more capable of causing assent than any demonstration. . . . It is clear, then, that faith comes from God in two ways: by way of an interior light that leads to assent and by way of the realities that are proposed from without and that had as their source divine revelation.[51]

"Therefore God so moves the created intellect, inasmuch as He gives it the intellectual power, whether natural, or superadded; and impresses on the created intellect the intelligible species, and maintains and preserves both power and species in existence" (*ST* I, q. 105, a. 3, c).

[49] This remark from earlier in the Summa: "And thus it is with the word light. In its primary meaning it signifies that which makes manifest to the sense of sight; afterwards it was extended to that which makes manifest to cognition of any kind. If, then, the word is taken in its strict and primary meaning, it is to be understood metaphorically when applied to spiritual things, as Ambrose says (*De fide,* ii). But if taken in its common and extended use, as applied to manifestation of every kind, it may properly be applied to spiritual things" (*ST* I, q. 67, a. 1).

[50] This is the famous Christian discussion of nature and grace.

[51] In *Boet. De Trin.*, 3, 1, ad 4. St. Thomas Aquinas, *Faith, Reason and Theology. Questions I–IV of his Commentary on the De Trinitate of Boethius,* Trans. Armand Maurer (Toronto: Pontifical Institute of Medieval Studies, 1987), 69.

What Can Be Known

Paul goes on to make explicit "what can be known about God." These are, "his invisible attributes" *(ta aorata autou)*, which are clearly perceived *(kathoratai)* because they can be "understood" *(nooumena)* from/since the creation of the world. These invisible realities are "his eternal power and divinity *(ē te aïdios dunamis kai theiotēs)*." Neither *aïdios* nor *theiotēs* are common words in the Septuagint, while *dunamis,* translating twenty-five different Hebrew words, occurs over 300 times, often with the notion of providence, sovereignty, and knowledge of men's deeds as in the *Letter of Aristeas* above. The terminology seems to be drawn from Hellenistic Judaism and Hellenistic philosophy in general.[52] We can only surmise that these "invisible attributes" are named here because they are most likely to inspire someone with awe, reverence, and gratitude. The very qualities, Paul says, successive cultures of humankind have lacked.

Failure to Glorify God

The consequence of this situation *(eis to einai)* is that they are without excuse *(anapologētous),*" a common Hellenistic term. Compare Wis 13:8 above: *syggnōstoi)*: "Because, knowing God, they did not glorify him as God or give thanks." The only way to understand how Paul can say that they knew God is to have recourse to what was said about implicit knowledge of God and the intuition into the witness created things make to their Creator (see verse 25, "the Creator"), producing a "general and confused" knowledge that, if yielded to, and the light-energy of the mind were allowed to follow out its dynamism, could have brought about an awareness of existence as gift. The anti-culture, the situation described by Aquinas above as one in which "the law of nature had been destroyed by the law of concupiscence," made such receptivity harder. The result is that this knowledge never matured into praise, obedience, and gratitude, and in that sense "the world with all its wisdom did not come to know God" (1 Cor 1:21). Lying behind Paul's oscillation in the use of the notion of "to know" is a biblical understanding of the Hebrew word *yd',* a word given profound theological significance by Hosea. It will be worthwhile, perhaps, to reflect on this significance.[53]

---

[52] See Ernst Käsemann, *Commentary on Romans,* trans. Geoffrey W. Bromiley (Grand Rapids, MI: Eerdmans, 1980), 39.

[53] The lines that follow are a modified form of part of an article already published and used here with the kind permission of the publisher: Francis Martin, "Israel as the Bride of YHWH: A Story of Sin and Renewed Love," *Anthropotes* 16 (2000): 129–54.

The notion of "the knowledge of God" is a central one in Hosea.[54] The root *yd'* occurs 17 times in the book with various nuances, some of which develop the linguistic potential of the term as he inherited it, and this can be seen in subsequent use, especially in Jeremiah. The English word that captures most of the developed semantic field is "recognize," which can mean both "perceive" and "acknowledge." "Perceive" extends to include not only "discern" but also "experience" and, in this sense, "know intimately." "Acknowledge," on the other hand, implies a movement of the will, a choice of someone or an acceptance of their authority. "To know God," therefore, means to discern his presence and action, to experience him and be in communion with him, but it also means to choose him and obey him.[55] Thus, the famous expression "knowledge of God," found in Hosea 4:1 and 6:6, refers to this lack of perceptual obedience caused by spiritual and bodily profligacy, and the same can be said of 5:4 ("they know not YHWH"). Israel's acknowledgment of YHWH as her only God is prescribed in Hosea 13:4,[56] while the following verse evokes more the sense of "choice" on the part of YHWH ("I knew you in the wilderness").[57] There are two texts in which the fullness of what it means to "know YHWH" are indicated: Both Hosea 2:2 and 6:3 are in the context of a renewed covenant.

Jeremiah well understood the significance of Hosea's teaching. In a denunciation of Jehoiakim's extravagant building program, and its concomitant manipulation of the poor, Jeremiah invokes the example of Jehoiakim's father, Josiah: "Because he dispensed justice to the weak and the poor, it went well with him. Is this not knowledge of me?—An oracle of YHWH" (Jer 22:16). More important still is Jeremiah's prophecy of a new covenant, "not like the covenant I made with their fathers." Because of the action of YHWH placing the principle of response in the hearts of his people, "all will know me from the least to the greatest." This prophecy, which forms the basis of the First Letter of John, is obviously dependent upon Hosea's prophecy of

---

54 See the fine article by Hans Walter Wolff, " 'Wissen um Gott' bei Hosea als Urform von Theologie," *Evangelische Theologie* 12 (1952–1953): 533–54.

55 It is interesting to observe how closely this understanding of knowledge is approximated by modern anthropology, which sees choice and reason as being the surface expressions of the spirit of man in which intuition *(intellectus)* and freedom are reciprocally active.

56 Hypocrisy in this matter is condemned in Hosea 8:2 (compare 1 John 2:4. "The one who claims: 'I have come to know him,' while not keeping his commandments, is a liar"), while acknowledgment is forced on Israel by the "days of punishment" mentioned in Hos 9:7.

57 Compare Amos 3:2, "You only have I known of all the families of the earth . . ." while the notion of acquiescence or acknowledgment is found in Hosea 8:4 ("They set up princes without my knowledge").

restoration in 2:22: "You will know YHWH," you will discern and experience him, you will have an intimacy with him of which marital intimacy can be but an icon, you will delight to obey him acknowledging what he has done for you and your gratitude to him. Perhaps the best way to sum up the full meaning of this prophecy of Hosea and Jeremiah (and Ezekiel 36:24–28) is to attend to Origen's definition of what "to know" means in the Bible: "Scripture says of those who are joined and at one with something, that they know that to which they are joined and in communion."[58]

There are two consequences of the failure to allow the receptive dynamism of the mind, its light, to follow the witness of creation and finally recognize God for who he can be perceived to be. The first of these is that "they became empty and futile *(emataiōthēsan)* in their thinking processes *(dialogismois)*, and their senseless heart was darkened."[59] And the second, which we will consider shortly, is idolatry itself. In regard to the first consequence, it is instructive to compare the text in Ephesians 4:17–19, noticing that there as well, and perhaps in dependence on the Pauline text, the pagan condition is portrayed as darkness of mind (described in six ways) and, thus, disordered sensuality:

> This, then, I declare and solemnly attest in the Lord: you must no longer walk as the pagans walk; in the empty futility of their minds *(en mataiōteti tou noos autōn)*, being darkened in their understanding, alienated from the life of God because of the ignorance that is in them caused by the hardness of their heart. Such people, devoid of any moral sensitivity, have given themselves over to unrestrained self-indulgence, carrying out every sort of impurity with a lust for more. (Eph 4:17–19)

Idolatry

We have arrived once again at the parable about Abraham and the burning palace since Abraham is presented to us as a man who continued to search above and beyond the chaos, rather than be content with his own thinking, until God spoke to him. A similar theme is presented in a passage from Irenaeus of Lyons:

> Abraham, desiring to know what should come to him through the blessing of his first father, inquired about the God for whom he was to wait. And, as following the inclination and tastes of his soul [the Thomistic "light"], he journeyed about the world, asking where God might be, and

---

[58] *In Joan.*, 19 (*Patrologia Graeca* 14, 529).

[59] Paul is using here the language of Jeremiah 2:5 (LXX): "They withdrew far away from me and went after futile things *(tōn mataiōn/hahebel)* and became futile themselves *(emataiōthēsan/wayyehĕbâlu)*.

as he grew faint, and ceased his inquiries, God took pity on him who sought him only in secret: he revealed himself to Abraham by means of the Word, as though by a ray of light, and made himself known.[60]

There are three aspects to idolatry: ceasing the search (suppressing the truth), remaining complacent in one's own knowledge (not acknowledging where it comes from or accepting the witness of creation), and substituting (exchanging) something else for God, that is, making something else the ultimate source of meaning and allegiance, and even the succor in one's life. There may be a fourth element as well, namely, the establishment of something as a symbol of one's choice of substitution: an image of an animal or a man, the expression, verbal or visual, of a nation or a movement or an ideology. All of these aspects or elements are present in Paul's description of what follows from futility of thought and darkness of heart: "Claiming to be wise, they became foolish; and they exchanged the glory *(kai ēllaxan tēn doxan)* of the incorruptible God for the likeness of the image of corruptible man, and of birds and four-footed animals and reptiles."(Rom 1:22–23)

In these words, Paul, following and making precise the biblical teaching, uncovers for us the root of the anti-culture's perversion: refusal to entrust oneself to God's leading and care, reliance on one's own arrested thinking, and finally, exchanging something else for God. In order to fix clearly the nature of this "exchange," Paul alludes here in verse 23 to Israel's "original sin" at Sinai. While the God who had rescued and cared for his people is giving them the Law through Moses, they are at the foot of Mt. Sinai fashioning a more domesticated god to whom they are willing to give worship and allegiance: "And they exchanged their Glory *(kai ēllaxanto tēn doxan autōn/wayyâmîru 'et kĕbodâm)* for the image *(en omoiōmati/bētabnît)* of a grass-eating bullock" (Ps 106:20).[61] Paul sounds the theme of "exchange" once again in verse 25, speaking of those who "exchanged the truth of God for a lie, and worshipped and

---

60 *The Demonstration of the Apostolic Preaching,* 24. Translation from de Lubac, *The Discovery of God,* 29.

61 This text is from Chrysostom's commentary on the Romans passage we are discussing. Note how he sees the beginning of the error in their overconfidence in their self-directed thought processes. (PG 60, 414): "And he names the cause through which they fell into such senselessness. What is it? They trusted everything to their reasonings. He does not say it this way, but in much sharper language: 'they became vain in their reasonings, and their foolish heart was darkened.' For if in a night without a moon someone were to go by a strange road or sail over a strange sea, he will wander so far from his intended destination so as to become lost. Thus, they, attempting to go the way leading to heaven, and having destroyed the light from their own selves, and in place of it, trusted themselves to the darkness of their own reasoning, and seeking in bodies and shapes for him who has no shape, suffered an awful shipwreck."

served the creature rather than the Creator—who is blessed for the ages, Amen!" The perversion of the human spirit consists in the fact that the natural movement toward acknowledging or recognizing God[62] has been twisted by the anti-culture and those who are its authors and victims. This leads to a perversion of activity, described by Paul three times as the result of God "handing them over" to their now aberrant drives.[63] Thus, the morass of societal perversion, from which some were able to preserve themselves, is attributed by Paul to the continuation of that movement by which the anti-culture turned from acknowledging God.

Summary

The biblical tradition is clear: God can be known in, by, and through his creation. For some, who first come to know God as Savior of his people, Source of instruction, and Respondent to their prayers, creation is a means by which God is *recognized* as also being the exclusive Author of the world. For those outside this dispensation, God and his uniqueness and rights can be *discovered* in his work of creation, in nature, and in the longings of the created heart. While it is true that this discovery can be made by the human mind, the "imprint of the divine light in us," it is also true that, in the present state of the human race, both individually and culturally, this *de jure* ability requires, as we have seen, a special help in order to arrive at its goal.[64] This is also attested to by the earliest Church Fathers. For instance, Origen: "We affirm that human nature is not sufficient in any way to seek God and find him with purity unless it is helped by the one who is the object of the search."[65]

---

[62] Verse 28: "And as they did not see fit to recognize God *(echein en epiginōsei)*, God gave them over to an unfit mind, to do that which is wrong."

[63] For a view that vices, particularly homosexuality, are unnatural one may consult Philo, On Abraham, 135 (the source of sin at Sodom was excessive wealth); *The Special Laws* 2, 50 (no specific mention of the source of this vice).

[64] For a discussion of this point, see Lyonnet, "La connaissance"; Hans Urs von Balthasar, *The Theology of Karl Barth,* trans. Edward Oates (San Francisco: Ignatius Press, 1992), pt. 3, "The Form and Structure of Catholic Thought."

[65] *Against Celsus,* 7, 42; 3, 47. In Robert Wilken, *The Spirit of Early Christianity: Seeking the Face of God* (New Haven, CT, and London: Yale University Press, 2003), 18. In the same place we find these words of Irenaeus: "The Lord taught us that no one is able to know God unless taught by God. God cannot be known without the help of God." (*Against Heresies,* 4, 6, 4). This is further developed by Aquinas when commenting on 1 Corinthians 1:21: ("For since, in the wisdom of God, the world did not know God through wisdom, it pleased God through the folly of what we preach to save those who believe"): "The divine wisdom when making the world, left his marks on the things of the world as it says in Sirach 1:10 'He poured her (wisdom) out over all his works.' Thus, creatures themselves, made through the wisdom of

It would seem that the *locus* of what St. Paul calls "suppression" is to be found in a disordered movement of the will, often influenced by the societal climate, the anti-culture. It consists in a refusal to allow creatures to make their total witness to their Origin and this is accomplished by a deviation in the movement of the mind caused by what the tradition has called variously "darkness," "concupiscence," and the like. However, according to Aquinas's account, "nothing is knowable except as it bears a likeness to the First Truth," and this means that the human being cannot stop looking for the Absolute even if the drive is diverted by substituting something else for God: This is idolatry, and it is not restricted to past ages.

Creation, Revelation, and the Situation Today

The texts of Vatican II, as well as those of Vatican I, had as their goal to defend the intrinsic ability of the mind to arrive at a knowledge of God. Their intent was to deny that the mind was so crippled that it has to rely on faith for certitude in religious and moral matters (fideism) and/or that all knowledge of God derives from a primitive revelation made to humanity and then subsequently obfuscated. As we have seen, this was a *de jure* statement: The mind is capable of knowing God since creation is a revelation of God as the biblical tradition asserts. On the other hand, the *de facto* situation is that human beings need divine help in order to exploit the full potential of their mind.

The Loss of Transcendence

The fact of the matter is that we now live in the first atheistic culture the world has ever known, and that our present discussion of creation as revelation takes place against a backdrop of widespread conviction that the mind moves within a closed system that makes the fact of creation at best an unknowable.[66]

God have a relation to God, whose marks they bear, like the words of a man relate to his wisdom which they signify. And as the disciple arrives at knowing the wisdom of the teacher through the words that he hears, so man can arrive at knowing God's wisdom through the creatures made by him as it says in Romans 1:20. . . . But man, because of the futility *[vanitatem]* of his heart, has gone astray from the rectitude of the knowledge of God as it says in John 1:10: 'He was in the world and the world was made by him and the world did not know him.' Therefore God led the faithful to a saving knowledge of himself by certain other means which are not found in the specific natures *[rationibus]* of creatures. For this reason these means are considered folly by worldly men who consider only the natures of human things. These other means are the teachings of the faith."

66 See Walter Kasper, *The God of Jesus Christ,* trans. Matthew J. O'Connell (New York: Crossroad, 1984), pt 1, "The God-Question Today." Also Henri De Lubac, *The*

Nearly all historians of Western thought place the origins of this journey in the fourteenth century.[67] Though preparatory stages can be discerned, the move became apparent and productive of consequences with the rise of the *via moderna* whose most salient characteristic was the search for the intelligibility of the existing concrete reality, not in a relation to a more universal relation but in terms of a network of equally concrete relationships. Western thought had appealed to ideas either as independently existing models for what we experience (Plato), or as intrinsic to what we experience (Aristotle). Still later, Christian antiquity understood that the things of this world are intelligible because they share in the eternal reasons existing in the Word of God through whom all things are made. William of Ockham, by denying that concrete individual things are intelligible because of relation to something greater, and by showing the inconsistencies in the superficial epistemology of his day, cut the human mind off from anything but itself in the search for intelligibility. The mind became the norm of the real, and intelligibility ultimately became identified with utility.

The problem was not the growth in understanding of the universe and history, much less the progress in epistemological sophistication; the problem lay in the fact that all of these advances of the mind were considered to have a mutually exterior relationship to faith. The "blindness" of faith no longer lay in the fact that what it considered far exceeded the powers of the mind, it was found rather in the fact that faith had no intelligible content: It could shed no light on what was being learned and could provide no integrating and healing power to the mind. The rising sciences and theology began, painfully, to agree on this one point: Reason and faith were extrinsic to each other in the elaboration of a vision of reality.

While none of what I have recounted above was apparent or even suspected by the original protagonists, the net result of this "turn to the subject," as it was later to be called, was an increasing mistrust in anything that, since it was not subject, became object. The first trust to be eroded was trust in God. The next trust to be weakened was trust in what was handed down by the Church and by the traditions of society. This began in the Renaissance with its independent and critical access to documents, its reliance on the findings of "modern science" (especially physics, history, and geography), and the resulting divergence between a sophisticated understanding of the world and history and the worldview of the Bible. The intrinsic intelligibility of the universe and

---

Drama of Atheist Humanism, trans. Edith M. Riley (San Francisco: Ignatius Press, 1950, 1995).

67 The paragraphs in this section are from my article, "The Psalms as a Particular Mode of Revelation," in *Nova et Vetera* 3 (2005) 279–94. They are used with the permission of the publisher.

of man's place in it became rather an independent intelligibility that had no need of revelation. Modern atheism arose when, because of a misguided understanding of "philosophy," religion appeared to need physics to establish its fundamental principle, that is, the existence of God, but physics did not need religion to return the favor. As Michael Buckley puts it: "Atheism came out of a turn in the road in the development and autonomy of physics."[68]

Next, trust was lost in the ability of our senses to bring reality's witness to itself into our consciousness, and with this any ability to account for the mystery of human communication. The isolated subject, trapped in a world of uncertain impressions, must have recourse to the immediate presence of individual consciousness (Descartes) and finally to the structures of that consciousness as it confronted an alien and rigidly determined cosmic system. Immanuel Kant's description of the isolated subject that must be determinative in the act of knowing bears eloquent witness to the penultimate stage in the journey toward a complete hermeneutics of suspicion.[69]

There are other aspects equally important to an understanding of the Kantian legacy, particularly the presupposition that what surrounds the tiny island of subjectivity is "nature," a foreboding, recalcitrant, and deceptive environment that refuses to yield to human effort though it continually invites it. Thus, we know only what we can dominate. The obverse is, then, Kant's image of human freedom: an area of retreat within a world of necessity. From this point there arose, via the immanent thinking of Hegel, the three "masters of suspicion": Marx, Freud, and Nietzsche, who, each in their own way, continued the movement toward an autonomous universe, but one that now was subject, at least in the case of Marx and Freud, to forces that are aberrant, unmastered, and unintelligible in themselves.[70]

---

[68] Michael Buckley, "The Newtonian Settlement and the Origins of Atheism," in *Physics, Philosophy, and Theology: A Common Quest for Understanding*, ed. W. Stoeger, R. Russell, and G. Coyne (Vatican: Vatican Observatory, 1988), 96.

[69] "We have now not merely explored the territory of pure understanding, and carefully surveyed every part of it, but have also measured its extent, and assigned to everything in it its rightful place. This domain is an island, enclosed by nature itself with unalterable limits. It is the land of truth—enchanting name!—surrounded by a wide and stormy ocean, the native home of illusion, where many a fog bank and many a swiftly melting iceberg give the deceptive appearance of farther shores, deluding the adventurous seafarer even anew with empty hopes, and engaging him in enterprises that he can never abandon and yet is unable to carry to completion." *Critique of Pure Reason,* trans. Norman Kemp Smith (New York: St. Martin's Press, 1929), 257.

[70] For an enlightening account of what I must examine rapidly here, see Louis Dupré, *Passage to Modernity: An Essay in the Hermeneutics of Nature and Culture* (New Haven, CT/London: Yale University Press, 1993). One may consult also Gallagher, *Clashing Symbols.*

The ultimate stage in the journey is arrived at in the postmodern suspicion of language itself, which, rather than an instrument of intersubjective communication, becomes the tool of power. While acknowledging the validity of this insight into the abuse of language, it must be borne in mind that an abuse is essentially the distortion of something by using it in a way that is contrary to its nature. In the realm of communication, suspicion becomes the way in which structures of power hidden in language are identified and unmasked. Where these are present, they must be understood for what they are, but this very unmasking presupposes that language is for the communication of truth and for the creation of community, not for the establishment of domination. A thoroughgoing sociocritical hermeneutics destroys, even while it uses, language as a means of communication.[71] A further step in the suspicion of language is taken by the Deconstructionists, who, were it not for their inconsistencies, would bring us into a morass of language without meaning, without subjects, without any personal communication: the climax of our journey to isolation.

Creation as a Light

An autonomous universe being regarded by isolated subjects can hardly be a witness to its Creator. We are faced with the same problem that faced the early Christian thinkers when they confronted the Greek philosophical tradition. With all its wealth and sophistication that tradition had inverted the order of importance in the scale of being. Because of their biblical vision of reality, most especially their understanding of God and creation, the Fathers of the Church performed the enormous task of turning the Greek system upside down while respecting its truths. What is important in reality is not the particular, as an instance of a more embracing category or law, but the individual, the *concretum*, whose mystery can only be grasped by seeing it in direct relation to God and thus possessing its own interior identity. It was from this perspective that the notion of person was born and applied, analogously, to human beings, to Christ, and to the Trinity.[72] Creation, in their thinking, was on the one hand a

---

71 "*Socio-critical hermeneutics* may be defined as an approach to texts (or to traditions and institutions) which seeks to penetrate beneath their surface-function *to expose their role as instruments of power, domination, or social manipulation.*" Anthony C. Thiselton, *New Horizons in Hermeneutics. The Theory and Practice of Transforming Biblical Reading* (Grand Rapids, MI: Zondervan, 1992), 379.

72 For an account of this work of the early Christian thinkers, see John D. Zizioulas, *Being As Communion* (Crestwood, NY: St. Vladimir's Seminary Press, 1985); Josef Ratzinger, "Concerning the Notion of Person in Theology," *Communio* 17 (1990): 439–54; Kenneth Schmitz, "The Geography of the Human Person," *Communio* 13 (1986): 27–48; David Schindler, "Norris Clarke on Person, Being, and St. Thomas," *Communio* 20 (1993): 580–92; Robert Spaemann, *Personen: Versuche über den*

revealed reality, which, once understood, could be grasped by reason, and on the other hand a light by which reality itself could be better understood.

I propose that in our day we are faced with a similar challenge. As I have just outlined, and as everyone knows, the philosophical climate augmented by the success of the empirical sciences has accepted the autonomous intelligibility of the universe, but has unnecessarily identified this with an *independent* intelligibility, thus making the universe once again a closed system whose "cause *(aitia)*" or "beginning *(archē)*" is somehow part of the system. No matter how one may try, it is impossible to grasp the nature of being without understanding creation, and thus all the modern systems of thought whether they be Kantian, Hegelian, Derridean, or Heideggerian fall into the same trap of creating a "system" of being within which is to be found reality's cause or beginning, all the while (certainly in the case of Heidegger) opposing an "onto-theology," which, they claim (sometimes justly) has made of being an overarching category that includes its origin within it.

I would like to suggest that Jewish and Christian thinkers, building on their own biblical traditions can, together, go far along the road of confronting these systems of thought. Using the fact of the createdness of the universe as a revealed light that can enshrine what is positive in these modern systems of thought, it will point beyond them to a true metaphysics and an understanding of God. Exposing the intellectual weaknesses of our modern anti-culture can strengthen the minds of believers, both Jewish and Christian, and it can provide some healing to the human tendency among believers and unbelievers (though in different degrees) to "suppress the truth." The revealed and revealing light provided by creation can be directed in at least two directions. It is first of all the foundation for understanding revelation itself. Second, it is the light by which we understand that God is infinitely Other, worthy of our awe, respect, worship, love, and also our docility: He can teach us who he is and lead us to delight in him.

Creation as the Foundation of Revelation

There seems to be a marked tendency among Jewish thinkers to develop this aspect of creation. Maimonides insisted on *creatio ex nihilo* since otherwise everything would take place by natural necessity and there would be no place for miracles, or God's acts for his people or for revelation:

> In short, the opinion of Aristotle is this: Everything is the result of management which is constant, which does not come to an end and does

not change any of its properties as e.g. the heavenly beings, and everything which continues according to a certain rule, and deviates from it
only rarely and exceptionally, as is the case in objects of Nature.[73]

Salomon Ludwig Steinheim bases his insistence on the need for an
understanding of creation on the same principle,[74] and Rosenzweig followed
him in this.[75] All of the Jewish thinkers I have consulted in regard to creation clearly hold for a universe totally dependent upon God, though some,
such as Abraham Heschel, make a strong distinction between the teaching of
Genesis and the tenets of philosophy.[76] In the section that follows, I will
attempt to show that a philosophical understanding of the consequences of
the biblical teaching is most useful in appreciating the strengths and weaknesses of many modern and postmodern theological positions.

Creation as the Foundation for Understanding Being

The biblical teaching about God and about creation can be expressed in philosophical terms by saying that only God is necessary: Everything else need not
be. This is so true that it is impossible to have a concept of being that does not
intrinsically include the note of "created." For, just as it is impossible to have a
genuine concept of "man" without including the notion of being able to laugh,
so it is impossible to have genuine concept of "being" that does not include the
notion of being created.[77] Or, to put it another way, it is impossible to have a

---

73 Maimonides, *The Guide,* III, 17, p. 283.

74 Joshua Haberman, "Salomon Ludwig Steinheim's Doctrine of Revelation," *Judaism*
17 (1968): 22–41.

75 Joshua Haberman, "Franz Rosenzweig's Doctrine of Revelation," *Judaism* 18 (1969):
320–36. Also Guy Petitdemange, "Existence et Révélation dans les Premières Oeu-
vres de Franz Rosenzweig," *Recherches de science religieuse* 60 (1972): 365–95.

76 Abraham J. Heschel, *God in Search of Man: A Philosophy of Judaism* (New York: Far-
rar, Strauss and Giroux, 1976), 15–17.

77 Ad primum ergo dicendum quod, licet habitudo ad causam non intret definitionem
entis quod est causatum, tamen sequitur ad ea qua sunt de eius ratione: quia ex hoc
quod aliquid per participationem est ens, sequitur quod sit causatum ab alio. Unde
huiusmodi ens non potest esse, quin sit causatum, sicut nec homo, quin sit risibile.
Sed quia esse causatum non est de ratione entis simpliciter, propter hoc invenitur
aliquod ens non causatum. "Though the relation to its cause is not part of the definition of a thing caused, still it follows, as a consequence, on what belongs to its
essence; because from the fact that a thing has being by participation, it follows that
it is caused. Hence such a being cannot be without being caused, just as man cannot be without having the faculty of laughing. But, since to be caused does not
enter into the essence of being as such, therefore is it possible for us to find a being
uncaused" (*ST* I, q. 44, a. 1, ad 1).

concept of "non-created being," though, of course such exists: He is God. It is significant to note that when this principle is not understood, badly understood, or outright denied, the result, both ancient and modern, is some form of totality thinking. "God" becomes the noblest part, but still a part of the Whole.

Those of us who accept the revelation that God has created everything that is not himself are challenged to justify our speaking about God, whom we cannot conceptualize and, thus, to justify the Bible's language about God and, in a reciprocal manner, our language about the world. It is a lamentable fact that the dominant tradition of late medieval Europe, namely the Christian tradition, failed for the most part to sustain the intellectual vigor of an earlier age and either succumbed to the objections made against their position or retreated into a defensive repetition of what they understood but partially (I gave a brief outline of this process above).[78] Recently there has been a willingness to consider and respond to the objections made to Christian speech about God that have been made in recent centuries. The first step is to restrain the incessant drive for isomorphic vocabulary, which, important as it is, represents but a fraction of the ways in which the human being understands and expresses reality. On the contrary, in the words of W. Norris Clarke:

> There is an indispensable role played in our thought and language by those systematically vague and elasti]c terms that alone can catch the similarities and affinities running all up and down and across the universe, especially between the realms of matter and spirit, cosmos and psyche. This is the secret life of the mind nourishing all metaphor, poetry, and art: the insight into authentic similarities and affinities across the universe.[79]

This basic understanding of language is expanded in reflecting upon analogy, which, in thinking about God, is linked to another insight, that of causality through participation.[80] This insight, one of the central contributions of

---

[78] Paul Ricoeur strongly faults Martin Heidegger for exploiting this weakness of late medieval thought and the neo-scholasticism that built upon it, using their inability to acknowledge in practice the inconceivability of God as a pretext for abolishing any metaphysics but his own. Paul Ricoeur, *The Rule of Metaphor: Multi-disciplinary Studies of the Creation of Meaning in Language,* trans. Kathleen McLaughlin, Robert Czerny, and John Costello (Toronto: University of Toronto Press, 1977), 311.

[79] William Norris Clarke, *The Philosophical Approach to God. A Neo-Thomist Perspective* (Winston-Salem, NC: Wake Forest University, 1979), 52.

[80] As Gregory Rocca puts it, paraphrasing Cornelio Fabro, "Participation is especially the ontology of analogy and analogy is the epistemology and semantics of participation." Gregory Rocca, "Analogy as Judgment and Faith in God's Incomprehensibility: A Study in the Theological Epistemology of Thomas Aquinas" (Ph.D. diss., Catholic University of America, 1989; Ann Arbor, MI: UMI Dissertation Services, 1994), 537. Rocca is condensing the thought of Cornelio Fabro, *Participation et*

Aquinas to metaphysical thought, was effected by combining a Plotinian interpretation of Plato's doctrine on participation with the Aristotelian teaching on
causality now opened to include the idea of creation. In order to grasp this we
must make the notion of cause "elastic" and unspecified enough to include
created causality, which we know, and uncreated causality of which we cannot
have a concept though its reality is undoubted. W. Norris Clarke offers a definition: A cause is that which fulfills the need for intelligibility by answering
the question, "What is effectively responsible for this datum x, which has
turned out to be non-self-explanatory?"[81] We must undertake a similar process
of "unspecification" with regard to participation as applied to God and creatures. Creatures owe both what they are and that they are to the fact that they
somehow share, participate, in the divine perfection: "To participate is to have
a part of something; we may speak of participation when something receives
or has that which belongs to another universally."[82]

Once we have clarified what we mean by analogy based upon causality
through participation, we are able to speak about God without ontotheol-
ogy, and we are able to bring this understanding to bear on our revealed
grasp on creation to the consideration of the modern understanding of subjectivity, history, and language. Obviously, I cannot develop these three areas
at this point, but a few general remarks may be in order, particularly in
regard to the fact that these aspects of human existence, once understood as
created by God, make it impossible that a human being be part of a Totality
rather than a member of a community.

Subjectivity

The light of creation moves us from the "the turn to the subject" to "the turn
to the person," with all that implies regarding being unique, having the dignity of being constituted by relation, primarily a relation to God, and, therefore, of being unsubordinatable. The deeper modern appreciation of the
person and its unique way of being has given rise to the proposal that a genuine consideration of being should be founded on a "meta-anthropology"

Causalité selon S. Thomas d'Aquin (Louvain: Publications Universitaires de Louvain,
1961), 634–40.

[81] W. Norris Clarke, "Analogy and the Meaningfulness of Language About God: A
Reply to Kai Nielsen," in *Explorations in Metaphysics* (Notre Dame, IN: University
of Notre Dame Press, 1994), 139.

[82] Aquinas, *In de hebd.*, l. 2, n. 24: "Est autem participatio quasi partem capere; et
ideo quando aliquid particulariter recipit id quod ad alterum pertinet universaliter,
dicitur participare aliquid." See Rudi A. te Velde, *Participation and Substantiality in
Thomas Aquinas,* ed. Jan A. Aertsen (Leiden: Brill, 1995), 11.

rather than a metaphysics.[83] This also means that "subjectivity" is not an inward reality as much as a relational reality: the uniquely human way of communicating from a mysterious incommunicable center that can never become merely a part of a larger whole. The revolt against collectivism was initiated early by thinkers such as Martin Buber, who, going beyond the later deconstructionist rejection of Totality, subverts Totality itself by the power of intersubjective truth.[84] Another dimension of personhood and relation, one equally opposed to the idea of Totality, is developed by Emmanuel Levinas whose work is well enough known not to need description here. I might dare to say that the thought of Levinas, and in a way that of Buber, will be deepened by an explicit consideration of the human person being constituted first and foremost by a relation to the Creator.[85] For just as a gift remains such by its relation to the giver, so, existence itself, the Gift beyond all gifts, is always such in its relation to the Giver. When this existence is human existence, then what is constituted by relation is a freedom by which the relation itself can become a relationship to God: This is the ground and possibility of every other relationship. The denial of Totality is accomplished by understanding the infinite distinction between God and everything else. Without this grounding the Other risks taking the place of God and, in addition, must remain "untouchable" for fear of the contamination of selfishness.[86]

Subjectivity may also be considered in terms of the Transcendental Ego, which is really not the fashioner of meaning but its recipient and is thus transcendental as person but not as mind. Despite its widespread acceptance, the

---

[83] Confer the excellent article by Martin Bieler, "The Future of the Philosophy of Being," *Communio* 26 (1999): 455–85.

[84] See Maurice S. Friedman, *Martin Buber: The Life of Dialogue* (New York: Harper & Row, 1960), 126–28. One of the most forceful modern proponents of the social consequences of personalism is Karol Wojtyla, Pope John Paul II, who also knew from experience the inhumanity of a totalitarian state. See, for instance, Karol Wojtyla, "The Person: Subject and Community," *Review of Metaphysics* 33 (1979): 273–308. Also see Aquinas, "persona significat id quod est perfectissimum in tota natura." (*ST* I, q. 29, a. 3).

[85] It would modify, for instance, statements like the following: "The visage of being that shows itself in war is fixed in the concept of totality, which dominates Western philosophy." Emmanuel Levinas, *Totality and Infinity. An Essay on Exteriority,* trans. Alphonso Lingis (Pittsburgh: Duquesne University Press, 1969), 21. The notion that totality thinking "dominates" Western philosophy reveals a lack of knowledge of a whole block of Catholic thinking, though it must be admitted that a certain amount of Christian philosophy was, at that time, oblivious of the fact that its understanding of Being made of it a Totality.

[86] For an appreciation as well as some trenchant criticism of Levinas, one may consult David Bentley Hart, *The Beauty of the Infinite: The Aesthetics of Christian Truth* (Grand Rapids, MI: Eerdmans, 2003), 75–92 et passim.

modern characterization of the one thinking as a subject, and thus perforce all else as an object, runs up against the problem of created being: Being can never be an object of thought divorced from the subject since both what is thought and who is thinking participate in the reality of being *(esse)*, which can never be "objectified." The obverse side of this truth, shown to us by the light of creation, is the fact that what is known is never an inert entity whose intelligibility is prescribed according to the structures of the mind, but rather something whose very act of being actualizes the knowing person who, by the mysterious alchemy of his own intellectual light, gives that something a new mode of existence: that of intelligibility. To recall what we considered previously: "[A]ll knowing is produced by an assimilation of the knower to the thing known, so that assimilation is said to be the cause of knowledge."

History

Creation is the irrefrangible obstacle to a dialectic of history since, no matter how exalted the dialectic envisaged may be, it still implies an "arena," a Totality within which the dialectic plays out, thus forming another closed system with "God" or "Spirit" as the most important component, but still a part.[87] The same may be said of most postmodern thought that bases itself, directly or indirectly, on the dialectic of Hegel, often described as "difference" and the violence of the Nietzschean and, in another way, the Heideggerian understanding of origins. This places not love and generous freedom at the origins of reality, but violence.[88]

> By turning from the Hegelian logic of negation to an ethos of pure affirmation Nietzsche at once demystified and forever consecrated violence: for *pure* affirmation, as could scarcely be otherwise within a discourse of defiant immanentism, must embrace the negative *as* the positive, being's *essential* positivity, its creative and wanton élan, in which violence participates not as dialectical negation—*Geist's* endless Sabbatarian probation—but as the world's essential, if atelic, creative power.[89]

I wish now to look at another aspect of the mystery of time and history, one that considers creation from the vantage point of Presence, and to suggest that, once the transcendent dimension of time is rescued from the modern

---

[87] "Ohne Welt is Gott nicht Gott." Hegel, *Begriff der Religion* (Leipzig: Felix Meiner, 1925), 148. See ibid., 256.

[88] I find it astonishing to see violence once more posited at the mystery of origins. This was the basis of all the myths of origins found in the ancient Near Eastern myths such as *Enuma Elish, The Epic of Gilgamesh,* and so on.

[89] Hart, *The Beauty,* 39–40.

study of history, the possibility of the integration with a biblical understanding is more attainable.[90] For modern history, time is succession, a dubious and uneven march toward an indeterminate future. The study of history, now capable of genuine reconstruction and insight, records this march. As we have seen, it resolutely eschews any consideration of transcendence, any search for a causality that exceeds the forces and resources of what is fundamentally a closed system.[91] For just as physics reduces the material universe to the "superior" language of mathematics, so critical history reduces the mystery of human temporal existence to the "superior" viewpoint of a certain understanding of causality and the attainability of knowledge of the past: Both are prisoners of the loss of transcendence of which I have spoken.[92]

I would propose that we use the term "temporality" to describe the nature of human existence: temporality includes succession in a vision of presence. I derive this understanding from St. Augustine. Insisting that the way to an understanding of eternity and transcendence lay in a conversion of life that rendered accessible an *experience* of Being, Augustine describes the fruit of his own conversion: "And in the flash of a trembling glance my mind came to That Which Is. I understood the invisible through those things that were created."[93] From this came an understanding of eternity as not being endless changelessness but rather infinite presence. This gives rise to an appreciation of the intrinsic reality of the *individuum* to which I referred earlier, not as a particular instance of a class but as a unique reality receiving its identity from a relation to its Creator.[94] God, the Creator, who is Eternity, is necessarily present in the action of sustaining all that is.[95] St. Augustine, responding to the opinion that, since God's will to create is eternal, creation itself must be eternal, answers in this manner:

---

[90] In the lines that follow, I am indebted to two studies delivered at a Symposium held at the Intercultural Forum of the John Paul II Cultural Center and published in *Nova et Vetera* 4:4 (2006). I am grateful to their authors to be able to utilize their material: Kenneth Schmitz, "The Ingathering of Being, Time and Word and the Inbreaking of a Transcendent Word,"; Matthew Lamb, "Temporality and History: Reflections from St. Augustine and Bernard Lonergan,".

[91] The relation between this view and the pre-Christian pagan view of reality can be seen in the study by Robert Sokolowski, *The God of Faith and Reason. Foundations of Christian Theology* (Notre Dame, IN: University of Notre Dame Press, 1982).

[92] For an admirable analysis of this reductive viewpoint, for good and ill, see Louis Dupré, *Passage to Modernity.*

[93] *Confessions* 7, 17. Translation by Matthew Lamb.

[94] I refer the reader to Kenneth Schmitz, "Created Receptivity and the Philosophy of the Concrete," *The Thomist* 61 (1997): 339–71.

[95] See note 32 above.

People who take that line do not yet understand you, O Wisdom of God and Light of our minds. They do not yet understand how things which receive their being through you and in you come into existence; but their heart flutters about between the changes of the past and future found in created things and an empty heart it remains. . . . [If they consider] they would see that in eternity nothing passes, for the whole is present (sed totum esse praesens) whereas time cannot be present all at once (nullum vero tempus totum esse praesens).[96]

In this deceptively simple presentation we have the way to recover transcendence in regard to human existence. Temporality, the proper mode of creation's existence, is not just succession; it is succession with the dimension of presence. In this sense *tempus*, is intrinsic to creation: "God, in whose eternity there is no change whatsoever, is the creator and director of time . . . the world was not created *in* time but *with time*."[97] To understand, therefore, time as intrinsic to creaturely existence,[98] and not an exterior and neutral "container" for the changes of the past and future, is to advance toward an understanding of history that includes what Jean Lacroix has already referred to as its "mystery."[99]

Augustine and many others have pointed to this dimension of the events narrated in the Bible. In the Christian viewpoint, the "mystery" is the eternally present Christological dimension of the events of salvation history as this moves through the succession of "before and after." The meaning is to be found, not in the discovery of an external resemblance of texts, but in the recognition of mutual participation in the plan of God. Let this text, one of a countless number that could be adduced, suffice to illustrate the ancient understanding of this principle: "Holy Scripture, in its way of speaking, transcends all other sciences because in one and the same statement while it narrates an event it sets forth the mystery."[100] The two words "event" and "mystery" refer, in turn, to the literal sense of the text, the original event

---

[96] St. Augustine, *The Confessions,* ed. John E. Rotelle, trans. Maria Boulding, vol. I/1, *The Works of St. Augustine* (Hyde Park, NY: New City Press, 1997). The passage is 11, 11.

[97] *De civitate Dei* 11, 6, translation is that of M. Lamb. "Cum igitur Deus, in cuius aeternitate nulla est omnino mutatio, creator sit temporum et ordinator . . . procul dubio non est mundus factus in tempore sed cum tempore."

[98] While succession, an aspect of time, is clearly present in material creation, created spirits also have succession in that they go from potency to act.

[99] Jean Lacroix, *Histoire et Mystère* (Tournai: Castermann, 1962).

[100] Gregory the Great, *Moralia in Job,* 20, 1 (PL 76, 135): "Sacra Scriptura omnes scientias ipso locutionis suae more transcendit, quia uno eodemque sermone dum narrat gestum, prodit mysterium." Augustine has much the same to say: "In ipso facto [the event itself], non solum in dicto [the text of the Prior Testament], mysterium [the plan of God revealed in Christ] requirere debemus." *On Psalm 68* (PL 36,858).

referred to, and then the same event as it is now seen to have been a participated anticipation of the mystery of Christ.

Language

Foundational to an understanding of language in the light of creation is the
fact that the human mind is "nothing else but the imprint of the divine light
in us." Another aspect of this reality is developed by St. Thomas in his commentary on the Gospel of John:

> Though there be many participated truths, there is but one absolute Truth
> which by its own essence is Truth, namely the Divine Being itself, by
> which Truth all words are words. In the same way there is one absolute
> Wisdom, raised above all, namely the Divine Wisdom by participation in
> whom all wise men are wise. And in the same way the absolute Word by
> participation in whom all who have a word are said to be speaking. This is
> the Divine Word, which in himself is the Word raised above all.[101]

The reality that links the mind's nature as a participation in divine light
to the fact of language is that of person, which is a relationally constituted
subjectivity that, in common with all being, is *diffusivum sui* and yet communicates in a unique manner. The classical definition of person, given by
Boethius and modified somewhat in the course of history, asserted basically
that a person is "an individual substance of a rational nature." When "substance" is seen in the light of creation, it becomes obvious that it is what it is
by its relation to God, that it subsists as what it is, and that it expresses what
it is by relation to other beings. Thus, of all being it is true to say that the
individuum, the *concretum*, seen in the light of its reality as created, is constituted by relation: to God, to itself, and to other beings.

If we understand "rational" in the above definition as an expression of
what is specifically human, we see that the unique and incommunicable reality of a person is also constituted by relation: It is *from* God, it relates *in* itself
and to itself, and it is a being *toward* others. What is unique in the instance of
person is that this threefold relation is actualized in the personal activity of
freedom by which the relation becomes *relationship*. Thus, the particular
property of a "rational" substance is that it is constituted by relation in such a
way that this is given properly human existence that take place in the free acts

---

[101] Thomas Aquinas, *Super Evangelium S. Joannis Lectura* (Rome: Marietti, 1952). A
consequence of this view was already enunciated by Aquinas's predecessor Hugh of
St. Victor: "The Word of God comes to man everyday, present in the human
voice." *The Word of God*, I, 2–3 (*Sources Chrétiennes* 155, 60).

by which the person realizes him- or herself. Such free activity takes place in the reciprocal rhythm of generosity and receptivity, that is, in communication. In an interpersonal relationship this rhythm, this communication between two beings who are constituted by what is incommunicable (their unique relation of from, in, and toward), takes place through language understood in the broadest sense possible but realized most humanly in words.

A corollary of this principle is simply this: "Wording," which includes the expression of both naming and syntax, is a relational act. It is public. Its medium is a commonly held possession, its destination, either implicitly or explicitly is communal, its expectation is that of a return. We think in the medium of this commonly held possession, and this affects the way we experience God and other realities, since experience takes place through contact and appropriated linguistic articulation. Language does not represent, it reveals, it discloses the virtualities of reality itself, and is thus not about other words but about consciousness, intentionality, and being, and thus of transcendence. As George Steiner expresses it:

> It is because Pindar and Augustine, Dante and Coleridge tell of language in ways consonant with our experience of consciousness and the poetic fact more immediately sensible than those of linguistic and logical positivism and "game theory" that the inference of "otherness" and of the transcendent, still commends itself to attention, to provisionality, a word in which the tentative and the visionary are so finely meshed.[102]

As is to be expected, Jewish thinking about language, which reflects three millennia of reflection, has used that perspective along with Western philosophy to advance the understanding of language and thought, especially in relation to revelation, in ways that have affected the discussion permanently.[103] In this brief study, I have wished merely to investigate how the fact of creation throws light on our understanding of language and transcendence. There is still much to work on jointly in this regard.

Conclusion

I began by invoking the ancient *topos* of creation as a book, and have reflected on how that book is a revelation from God, both manifesting God and serving as light by which modern thinking can be critically appropriated. One cannot help but notice, of course, that the reality of creation and the judgment

---

[102] George Steiner, *Real Presences* (Chicago: University of Chicago Press, 1989, 1991), 85.

[103] One immediately thinks of the work of Franz Rosenzweig and Martin Buber (who did not agree) and Emmanuel Levinas.

regarding its ability to reveal God come to us in a *text*. The next and most important step is to consider how the Scriptures, a text, are an instrument of revelation. If I understand correctly, most rabbinic and post-rabbinic thought considers the question of command as it is expressed in the *Tanak* as being the fundament of revelation, a personal address that challenges the modern recipient to interpret and obey. This is already an enormous challenge both linguistically and ethically: Which commands? What is the relation between command and law? Who or what is revealed? Is the oral Torah, ancient and modern, part of revelation? But there is another and, as I see it, more basic and more difficult question, that of narrative: How do the actions of God, which ground the Covenant,[104] assume a word dimension? How, in the light of critical historiography, do we understand the accounts we possess?[105] How are these events, as they reach us in word, a revelation of God?[106] I hope that in the future we can approach these questions even as, in the words of the Arab proverb, we leave a little work for our children.

---

[104] Ex 19:4-6: "You have seen what I did to the Egyptians, and how I bore you on eagles' wings and brought you to myself. Now therefore, if you obey my voice and keep my covenant, you shall be my treasured possession out of all the peoples. Indeed, the whole earth is mine, but you shall be for me a priestly kingdom and a holy nation."

[105] See, for instance, Marc Zvi Brettler, *The Creation of History in Ancient Israel* (London and New York: Routledge, 1995).

[106] There are also questions of convergence that should be investigated such as that between Levinas's understanding of freedom ("Freedom means, therefore, the hearing of a vocation which I am the only person able to answer-or even the power to answer right there where I am called." Emmanuel Levinas, "Revelation in the Jewish Tradition," in *The Levinas Reader*, ed. Seán Hand [Cambridge, MA: Blackwell, 1989, 1994], 210, n. 10) and von Balthasar's understanding of mission (Hans Urs von Balthasar, *Theo-drama: Theological Dramatic Theory*, trans. Graham Harrison, vol. 3, *Dramatis Personae: Persons in Christ* [San Francisco: Ignatius Press, 1983], II, B, "Christ's Mission and Person").

CHAPTER 10

A Thomistic Contribution
to Ecumenism

CHARLES MOREROD, O.P.

FR. MATTHEW LAMB is a master of a rare but very needed kind: His deep knowledge of theology in its best sources also shines through his own unified Christian life. Students can see in him the real possibility of a happy and meaningful life as a theologian. I am happy to present this essay to him in his honor.

The main Thomistic contribution to ecumenism is that it helps us understand theologically some controversial topics. On the one hand, Thomism is a unique help for an understanding of specifically Catholic doctrines, and this alone would be a useful ecumenical contribution. On the other hand, a Thomistic approach to non-Catholic doctrines is less likely to be biased by the prejudices of the Reformation and of the Counter Reformation, since Thomas's perspective was shaped before the sixteenth century. Such a theological and philosophical approach is complementary to historical studies.

It seems to me that it could be especially interesting to study three topics:

- The relation between divine action and human action and its impact, for example, on the understanding of the Church and sacraments;

- The light shed on Church authority and on the nature and purpose of ecumenical dialogue by Thomas's theology of faith (or preaching the Word of God); and

- The correspondence between Church and anthropology as a key to the question of salvation.

Since the third point would require development, I shall address the first two topics only.

Divine Action and Human Action

Traditional Protestant Questions

In 1518, at the very beginning of what was to become the Reformation, Martin Luther expressed his understanding of the sacrament of penance. His view of ministry leaves only a limited role to the action of the priest:

> Although the remission of the fault is done before the remission by the priest, nevertheless the infusion of grace is under the form of hidden wrath . . . , so that the human being to be unsure of grace. . . . Therefore generally speaking the remission of the fault is not certain to us, if not by the judgment of the priest.[1]

Seven years later, in his controversy with Erasmus about free will, the role of human actions in relation to God—and not only the actions of the minister in the sacraments—is reduced to nothing:

> You yourself [Erasmus] are aware that all the good in us is to be ascribed to God, and you assert this in your description of Christianity. But in asserting this, you are surely asserting also that *the mercy of God alone does everything, and that your will does nothing, but rather is passive; otherwise, all is not ascribed to God.*[2]

Luther sees that point as absolutely central: "I wish the defenders of free choice would take warning at this point, and realize that *when they assert free choice they are denying Christ.*"[3]

In spite of the differences between the two Reformers, Calvin also denies the weight of human actions in relation to God: "The sum is, that *man cannot claim a single particle of righteousness to himself, without at the same time detracting from the glory of the divine righteousness*"[4] and "to whatever extent any man rests in himself, to the same extent he impedes the

---

[1] Martin Luther, *Resolutiones disputationum de indulgentiarum virtute,* Concl. VII, WA 1, p. 541, my translation: "Licet remissio culpae fiat per infusionem gratiae ante remissionem sacerdotis, talis tamen est infusio gratiae et ita sub forma irae abscondita . . . , ut homo incertior sit de gratia. . . . Ideo ordine generali non est nobis certa remissio culpae nisi per iudicium sacerdotis."

[2] Martin Luther, *The Bondage of the Will* (*De servo arbitrio,* 1525), in *Luther's Works,* vol. 33 (Philadelphia: Fortress Press, 1972), 35, emphasis added.

[3] Ibid., 279, emphasis added.

[4] John Calvin, *Institutes of the Christian Religion* (Philadelphia: The Westminster Press;London: S.C.M. Press, 1967) (4), no. III.XIII.2, emphasis added.

beneficence of God."5 This view has an impact on Calvin's view of priesthood: "It was peculiar to him [Christ] alone to appease God and expiate sins by his oblation. When these men usurp it to themselves, what follows, but that they have an impious and sacrilegious priesthood?"6

There is a certain mindset in these texts that constantly implies a choice between divine action and human action: What is done by God cannot be done by human beings, because that would be a denial of the divine initiative and action of salvation. Such a mindset is still to be found in the official answers of many Protestant churches to the 1982 document of Faith and Order, *Baptism, Eucharist, Ministry* (BEM).7

That mindset appears, for instance, in a question asked by the Evangelical church in Baden (Germany): "Who is acting in the celebration of the Eucharist: Christ or the church?"8 The Salvation Army strongly opposes the human actions that are the rites to divine action: "The need for regeneration by the power of the Holy Spirit, through repentance towards God and faith in our Lord Jesus Christ. *We firmly reject the idea that any work or rite can accomplish what God has promised in response to faith.*"9 "The text . . . fails to make clear the crucial distinction between the sign and the truth signified, between the shadow and the reality. *It ascribes to the sacraments powers belonging to the Holy Spirit alone.*"10 The Italian and French Protestant churches refuse that the church or her ministries could be seen as *dispenser of grace.*11 The Presbyterian Church of Rwanda opposes some idea of apostolic

---

5 Ibid., no. III.XII.8.

6 Ibid., no. IV.XIX.28.

7 "Faith and Order," *Baptism, Eucharist and Ministry [BEM]*, Faith and Order paper no. 111 (Geneva: World Council of Churches Publications, 1982). The official answers have been published in *Churches Respond to BEM*, ed. Max Thurian, vols. 1–2 (Geneva: World Council of Churches, 1986); vols. 3–4 (1987); vols. 5–6 (1988).

8 Evangelical Church in Baden, in Thurian, *Churches Respond to BEM*, vol. 5, 46.

9 Salvation Army, in Thurian, *Churches Respond to BEM*, vol. 4, 235, emphasis added.

10 Ibid., 254, emphasis added.

11 Cf. the Waldensian and Methodist Churches in Italy, in Thurian, *Churches Respond to BEM*, vol. 2, 247: "Function of the church and of the ministries: church and ministries are at the service of God and his work of grace and cannot be presented as if they were proprietors, guarantors, and dispensers of the grace of God"; Standing Council of the Lutheran and Reformed Churches of France, in Thurian, *Churches Respond to BEM*, vol. 3, 144: "The role of the church: We maintain, with BEM, the necessity of structures for all ecclesiastical life. We think, however, that the church and its ministries are never in themselves dispensers or sole purveyors of grace. Every activity of the church and ministries has to be simply a means for the clear discernment of an activity which is God's alone."

succession to the gift of God: "As regard apostolic succession, we consider that it should not be tied to human persons because the gifts of God are not tied to human beings."[12]

In such a theological context, the different ministries are not really necessary, but they can be useful for the good order of the Church, as another German church says:

> Since Lutheran doctrine differentiates very carefully and concretely between the authority of the Lord who is himself present in the Supper and the authority of the ordained minister whom he authorizes to act, *we cannot possibly make the validity of a celebration of the Lord's Supper depend on its being conducted by an ordained minister, even though, in practice, in the interests of "due" order, we take great care to ensure that this is the case.*[13]

If the 1999 *Joint Declaration on the Doctrine of Justification* by the Lutheran World Federation and the Catholic Church clarifies the basic points of the doctrine of grace in both communions, it also says that some questions remain opened (this fact explains for a great part the negative public reaction of about 160 German-speaking, Protestant theologians to the declaration):[14]

> Our consensus in basic truths of the doctrine of justification must come to influence the life and teachings of our churches. Here it must prove itself. In this respect, there are still questions of varying importance which need further clarification. These include, among other topics, the relationship between the Word of God and church doctrine, as well as ecclesiology, authority in the church, ministry, the sacraments, and the relation between justification and social ethics. We are convinced that the consensus we have reached offers a solid basis for this clarification. The Lutheran churches and the Roman Catholic Church will continue to strive together to deepen this common understanding of justification and to make it bear fruit in the life and teaching of the churches.[15]

---

[12] Presbyterian Church of Rwanda, in Thurian, *Churches Respond to BEM,* vol. 3, 184.

[13] North Elbian Evangelical Church, in Thurian, *Churches Respond to BEM,* vol. 1, 50, emphasis added.

[14] Cf. *Materialdienst des Konfessionskundlichen Instituts Bensheim* 2 (1998): 33–35; 6 (1999): 114–15.

[15] Lutheran World Federation and the Catholic Church, *Joint Declaration on the Doctrine of Justification,* no. 43, www.vatican.va/roman_curia/pontifical_councils/chrstuni/documents/rc_pc_chrstuni_doc_31101999_cath-luth-joint-declaration_en.html.

Traditional Thomistic Answers

St. Thomas Aquinas and his disciples have their word to say about these questions. Historically, their first partial answer was written by Cardinal Cajetan, when he was preparing his meetings with Luther at Augsburg in October 1518. Addressing Luther's view of the sacrament of penance, he denies the necessity of a choice between the action of God and the action of the minister:

> But if words of the Lord when he gave the sacramental power are more clearly considered, one must have another opinion. Because the Lord did not say: "the ones whose sins you will have declared forgiven," but he said: "the ones whose sins you will have forgiven." . . . Therefore we must believe and confess that the effect of sacramental absolution correctly given . . . is the remission of sins, which is done with authority by God alone, but that the minister does ministerially through the sacrament of Christ.[16]

In a 1525 text about the Eucharist, the same Cajetan will express the same concern in more general terms. If the celebration of the Eucharist cannot really have an effect in regard to the remission of sins, then all other such actions are in the same situation, and the Creed of Nicea and Constantinople will have to be changed:

> [Objection] That faith according to which this sacrament destroys sins is wrong: because only the death of Christ destroys our sins. [Response] *From the fact that only Christ's death destroys our sins, the consequence is not that the application to us of Christ's death does not destroy sins. Likewise, the fact that only the worker makes the sphere does not exclude the worker's instruments.* The fact that only Christ's death destroys our sins does not exclude the sacraments of the Church, which are the instruments through which Christ's death is applied to us; otherwise, we should exclude from the Creed "I confess one baptism for the forgiveness of sins." Because *if it is so, that sacraments are excluded because only Christ's death destroys our sins, then also baptism is excluded from the*

---

16 Thomas de Vio/Cajetan, *De effectu absolutionis sacramentalis* (October 1, 1518), in Charles Morerod, *Cajetan et Luther en 1518,* vol. 1 (Fribourg: Editions Universitaires, 1994), 342–46, nos. XI.5–6: "Verum si domini verba diligentius perspecta fuerint quum potestatem sacramentalem dedit, aliter sentiendum est. Non enim dixit: 'Quorum declaraveritis remissa peccata,' sed dixit: 'Quorum remiseritis peccata.' . . . Credendum est igitur et confitendum, quod effectus sacramentalis absolutionis rite facte . . . est peccatorum remissio, quam auctoritative quidem solus deus facit; ministerialiter autem minister ipse christi sacramento mediante efficit."

destruction of sins. And because according to truth baptism is not excluded, neither are the other sacraments excluded from the destruction of sins.[17]

What Cajetan says here had been prepared two and a half centuries before by his master, St. Thomas. Aquinas was, of course, not trying to reply to the Reformation, but some objections to which Thomas had replied must have come back immediately to Cajetan's memory, and applied to the new situation:

> Some find it difficult to understand how natural effects are attributable at once to God and to a natural agent.
>
> For (Arg. 1) one action, it seems, cannot proceed from two agents. *If then the action, by which a natural effect is produced, proceeds from a natural body, it does not proceed from God.*[18]
>
> Arg. 2. When an action can be sufficiently done by one, it is superfluous to have it done by more: we see that nature does not do through two instruments what she can do through one. *Since then the divine power is sufficient to produce natural effects, it is superfluous to employ also natural powers for the production of those same effects.* Or if the natural

---

[17] Thomas de Vio, *De Erroribus contingentibus in Eucharistiae Sacramento,* cap. VIII: "Quomodo falsum non sit, sed verum, deleri & remitti peccata per hoc sacramentum Eucharistia," in *Opuscula omnia Thomae de Vio Caietani cardinalis Tit. S. Xisti,* in tres distincta tomos, variis quaestionibus, cum suis conclusionibus, ac utilissimis Annotationibus appositis, recens aucta ac locupleta (Lugduni, Sumptibus Philippi Tinghi Florentini, 1575), 145. My translation; emphasis added: "Falsa est fides sacramentum hoc delere peccata: quia sola mors Christi nostra delet peccata. Ex hoc enim, quod sola mors Christi nostra delet peccata, non sequitur, Ergo applicatio mortis Christi ad nos non delet peccata. Sicut namque ex hoc, quod solus artifex facit sphaeram, non excluduntur instrumenta artificis, quibus spheram operatur: ita ex hoc quod sola mors Christi delet nostra peccata non excluduntur sacramenta Ecclesiae, quae sunt instrumenta, quibus mors Christi applicatur ad nos, alioquin delere oportet ex symbolo, Confiteor unum baptisma in remissionem peccatorum. Si enim ex hoc, quod sola mors Christi delet nostra peccata, excluderentur sacramenta, Baptismus quoque excluditur a deletione peccatorum. Et sicut secundum veritatem non excluditur Baptismus, ita nec alia sacramenta excluduntur a deletione peccatorum."

[18] Emphasis added. This objection is quite similar to one of the two main objections St. Thomas mentions against the existence of God, *Summa theologiae* I, q. 2, a. 3, obj. 2: "It is superfluous to suppose that what can be accounted for by a few principles has been produced by many. But it seems that everything we see in the world can be accounted for by other principles, supposing God did not exist. For all natural things can be reduced to one principle which is nature; and all voluntary things can be reduced to one principle which is human reason or will. Therefore there is no need to suppose God's existence."

power sufficiently produces its own effect, it is superfluous for the divine power to act to the same effect.

Arg. 3. *If God produces the whole natural effect, nothing of the effect is left for the natural agent to produce.*

Upon consideration, *these arguments are not difficult. . . . The power of a lower agent depends on the power of the superior agent,* according as the superior agent gives this power to the lower agent whereby it may act; or preserves it; or even applies it to the action, *as the artisan applies an instrument to its proper effect,* though he neither gives the form whereby the instrument works, nor preserves it, but simply gives it motion. So, it is necessary for the action of a lower agent to result not only from the agent by its own power, but also from the power of all higher agents; it acts, then, through the power of all. And *just as the lowest agent is found immediately active, so also is the power of the primary agent found immediate in the production of the effect.* For the power of the lower agent is not adequate to produce this effect of itself, but from the power of the next higher agent; and the power of the next one gets this ability from the power of the next higher one; and thus the power of the highest agent is discovered to be of itself productive of the effect, as an immediate cause. This is evident in the case of the principles of demonstration, the first of which is immediate. So, *just as it is not unfitting for one action to be produced by an agent and its power, so it is not inappropriate for the same effect to be produced by a lower agent and God; by both immediately, though in different ways. Though a natural thing produces its own effect, it is not superfluous for God to produce it, because the natural thing does not produce it except in the power of God.* Nor is it superfluous, while God can of Himself produce all natural effects, for them to be produced by other causes: *this is not from the insufficiency of God's power, but from the immensity of his goodness, whereby He has wished to communicate his likeness to creatures, not only in point of their being, but likewise in point of their being causes of other things.* When the same effect is attributed to a natural cause and to the divine power, *it is not as though the effect were produced partly by God and partly by the natural agent: but the whole effect is produced by both, though in different ways,* as the same effect is attributed wholly to the instrument, and wholly also to the principal agent.[19]

For Thomas then, the fact that our actions can be also divine actions is not more impossible than the fact that a text can be completely written both by myself and by my pen: There is no reason to say that the pen writes only one-half of the text, or one-tenth . . . because I also write it. Of course the

---

[19] St. Thomas Aquinas, *Summa contra Gentiles* III, ch. 70, emphasis added.

same could not be said if I would write a text with another human author: Both could not claim to each have written 100 percent of the text. The difference is that both human authors are beings of the same kind, or at the same level, meanwhile a human being is not the same kind of being as God, or as a pen. The key to the question is the analogy of being, central to Aquinas and strongly rejected by Karl Barth (according to the Reformed pastor Henry Chavannes, Barth unconsciously rejected what he thought to be Aquinas's view with arguments in fact also used by Thomas himself).[20] In the line of St. Thomas, the analogy of being is important for many other questions; for instance, if God is the same kind of being as his creatures, just much bigger, then the existence of the world implies the impossibility of an infinite being "next to it." The analogy of being has been rejected after the rejection of the epistemological analogy in Duns Scotus's univocity, which Luther unconsciously kept from his nominalist theological studies and applied to his reading of Scripture.

What seems to be a very subtle question for specialists of medieval theology can in fact be a key to the dialogue between two different mindsets that permeate theology. It applies first to the relationship between God and his creatures: The importance of such a question does not need to be underscored. It also applies to the central question that is the inspiration of Scripture. Vatican Council II says that

> The books of *both the Old and New Testaments* in their entirety, with all their parts, are sacred and canonical because written under the inspiration of the Holy Spirit, they *have God as their author* and have been handed on as such to the Church herself. In composing the sacred books, *God chose men*; and while employed by Him they made use of their powers and abilities, *so that with Him acting in them and through them, they, as true authors,* consigned to writing everything and only those things which He wanted.[21]

God and men can then be, together, authors of the Bible. Not in the same sense as the human authors of the different parts of the Bible, because God and the human authors act at different levels. If they would act at the same level, the respect to divine Majesty would impose to choose between a simply divine Word and a merely human text. The first president of the Vatican's dicastery for ecumenism, Cardinal Bea, who was a Jesuit biblical scholar,

---

[20] Cf. Henry Chavannes, *L'analogie entre Dieu et le monde,* selon saint Thomas d'Aquin et selon Karl Barth (Paris: Cerf, 1969), 278–79.

[21] Vatican Council II, Constitution on Divine Revelation, *Dei Verbum,* no. 11, emphasis added.

attributed Vatican II's solution about biblical inspiration to St. Thomas Aquinas.[22] This delicate question could receive more clarity in ecumenical dialogue if the Thomistic insights were given more consideration.

Theology of Faith and Church Authority

The role and nature of authority in the Church is, of course, an important topic of ecumenical dialogue. I will try to show how St. Thomas Aquinas's theology of faith helps us understand questions of authority at a level far deeper than questions of personal ambition (which, of course, also exist), and even helps us understand the nature of ecumenism.

Authority in Ecumenical Dialogues

The fourth conference on Faith and Order, held in Montreal in 1963 addressed the burning ecumenical question of Tradition.[23] It wanted to overcome the difference on that question, and explained that the ecumenical movement itself recommends such a theological move for at least two reasons. The first reason is that ecumenical dialogue obliges all participants to realize that their different views (or different readings of Scripture) are due in part to their different histories, their different traditions:

> For a variety of reasons, it has now become necessary to reconsider these positions. We are more aware of our living in various confessional

---

[22] Cf. Augustine Cardinal Bea, *The Way to Unity after the Council* (London: Geoffrey Chapman, 1967), 92: "The second category of considerations forming a starting point for this doctrine of inspiration concerns God's manner of influencing the prophets. Here we turn to the Old Testament for guidance and are indebted to St. Thomas Aquinas for his assertion, after mature reflection, that the authors of the sacred books are God's instruments indeed, but living instruments who, even when being used by God, do not cease to be their complete selves and therefore act as intelligent and free agents, neither more nor less than would any other human authors. This concept of 'instrumentality' as an explanation for the mode of inspiration of the sacred books was expounded by Pius XII in *Divino afflante Spiritu*, which threw open to Catholic exegesis new avenues of study and made possible renewed research."

[23] Faith and Order, Fourth World Conference, "Scripture, Tradition and traditions" (Montreal, 1963), quoted according to the paragraphs of the text; the text can be found in *Faith and Order Findings: The Report of the Fourth World Conference on Faith and Order*, ed. Paul S. Minear, Faith and Order paper no. 37–40 (London: SCM Press, 1963); or in *Documentary History of Faith and Order*, ed. Günther Gassmann, Faith and Order paper no. 159, (Geneva: World Council of Churches Publications, 1993), 10–18.

traditions, for example, that stated paradoxically in the saying *"It has been the tradition of my church not to attribute any weight to tradition." Historical study and not least the encounter of the churches in the ecumenical movement have led us to realize that the proclamation of the Gospel is always inevitably historically conditioned.* We are also aware that in Roman Catholic theology the concept of tradition is undergoing serious reconsideration.[24]

The second reason is that the Gospel must be proclaimed in changing situations because the definitive mission of Christ is not limited to his own time:

> The Tradition in its written form, as Holy Scripture (comprising both the Old and the New Testaments), *has to be interpreted by the Church in ever new situations.* Such interpretation of the Tradition is to be found in the crystallization of tradition in the creeds, the liturgical forms of the sacraments and other forms of worship, and also in the preaching of the Word and in theological expositions of the Church's doctrine. *A mere reiteration of the words of Holy Scripture would be a betrayal of the Gospel* which has to be made understandable and has to convey a challenge to the world.[25]

"Tradition" means the transmission of the Gospel to all times.[26] In the present situation of Christians, it cannot not be seen that

---

[24] Ibid., no. 44, emphasis added.

[25] Ibid., no. 50. Cf. also no. 64: "The Church is sent by Christ to proclaim the Gospel to all men; the Tradition must be handed on in time and also in space. In other words, Tradition has a vital missionary dimension in every land, for the command of the Lord is to go to all nations"; or no. 66: "When the Word became flesh, the Gospel came to man through a particular cultural medium, that of the Palestinian world of the time. So when the Church takes the Tradition to new peoples, it is necessary that again the essential content should find expression in terms of new cultures. Thus in the great missionary expansion of the Eastern Church, the Tradition was transmitted through the life of the Church into new languages and cultures, such as those of Russia and the other mission fields. Just as the use of the Slavonic tongue was necessary for the transmission of the Tradition to the Slavs, so today it is necessary to use new languages and new forms of expression which can be understood by those to whom the good news comes. In order that this can be rightly done, it is necessary to draw together knowledge of the culture and language in question, along with a careful study of the languages of the Old and New Testaments, and a thorough knowledge of Church history."

[26] Cf. Ibid., no. 46: "What is transmitted in the process of tradition is the Christian faith, not only as a sum of tenets, but as a living reality transmitted through the operation of the Holy Spirit. We can speak of the Christian Tradition (with a capital T), whose content is God's Revelation and self-giving in Christ, present in the life of the Church."

This Tradition which is the work of the Holy Spirit is embodied in traditions (in the two senses of the word, both as referring to diversity in forms of expression and in the sense of separate communions). The traditions in Christian history are distinct from, and yet connected with, the Tradition. . . . This evaluation of the traditions poses serious problems. For some, questions such as these are raised. Is it possible to determine more precisely what the content of the one Tradition is, and by what means? *Do all traditions which claim to be Christian contain the Tradition?* How can we distinguish between traditions embodying the true Tradition and merely human traditions? Where do we find the genuine Tradition, and where impoverished tradition or even distortion of tradition? Tradition can be a faithful transmission of the Gospel, but also a distortion of it. In this ambiguity the seriousness of the problem of tradition is indicated. *These questions imply the search for a criterion.*[27]

The criterion is indispensable to ecumenism as such: How can we recognize whether any of the many "traditions" who claim to be Christian really transmit the faith Jesus Christ wanted his apostles to share? And how can we be united in the same Christian faith, nowadays? The Montreal conference explored many criteria:

- "The Tradition received from the apostles," in itself and then "embodied in the apostolic writings" (no. 49);

- "The Holy Scriptures rightly interpreted. But what is 'right interpretation'?" (no. 51);

- "[T]hat interpretation which is guided by the Holy Spirit" (no. 52);

- "[A]ny portion of Scripture is to be interpreted in the light of Scripture as a whole" or in relation to "what is considered to be the centre of Holy Scripture" or to "what Scripture says to the individual conscience, under the guidance of the Holy Spirit" or in the light of Fathers of the Church and of the ecumenical councils or of the Magisterium . . . (no. 53).

- "Modern biblical scholarship has already done much to bring the different churches," and "a common study of Scripture" should be encouraged (no. 55).

All these criteria have in common that their intention is not to substitute Scripture:

---

[27] Ibid., nos. 47–49.

In none of these cases where the principle of interpretation is found else-where than in Scripture is the authority thought to be alien to the central concept of Holy Scripture. On the contrary, it is considered as *providing just a key to the understanding of what is said in Scripture.*[28]

Nevertheless, although these criteria have already proved in part useful, the question remains: "How can we overcome the situation in which we all read Scripture in the light of our own traditions?"[29] In 1998, Faith and Order commissioned the document *A Treasure in Earthen Vessels,*[30] which deals with hermeneutics and states that *"Montreal helped to overcome the old contrast between 'sola Scriptura' and 'Scripture and tradition' and to show that the different hermeneutical criteria in the different traditions belong together,"*[31] but "Montreal left open the vital question of how churches can discern the one Tradition."[32]

Obviously, this question is central to ecumenism and directly linked to the dialogue on authority. Such dialogues happen because Christians disagree about the nature and purpose of authority in the Church. But more deeply they are necessary because of the hope for unity in faith itself: Who is going to say at a certain point that previously divided Christian communities are now united in a common faith, and that this will last? Such a question has been asked in many different ways. For instance, the American Lutheran George Lindbeck said in the 1970s that some kind of infallible authority would be indispensable, if unity matters, because it would the only way to limit the crisis of conscience.[33] In 1998, the Anglican-Roman Catholic International Commission published *The Gift of Authority*, that presents some authority—including the one of the bishop of Rome—as a condition for our answer to God's invitation to believe.[34] In 2005, the French ecumenical Groupe des

---

28 Ibid., no. 53, emphasis added.

29 Ibid., no. 54.

30 "Faith and Order," *A Treasure in Earthen Vessels: An Instrument for an Ecumenical Reflection on Hermeneutics,* Faith and Order paper no. 182 (Geneva: World Council of Churches Publications, 1998).

31 Ibid., no. 16, emphasis added.

32 Ibid., no. 18.

33 Cf. George A. Lindbeck, "The Infallibility Debate," in *The Infallibility Debate*, ed. John J. Kirvan (New York: Paulist Press, 1971), 149: "If this unity is . . . regarded as an ultimate value, an irrevocable gift of God whose loss is unthinkable, then, in a Christian context, the final adjudicator of controversies must be infallible, must be divinely protected against final error, even if not against preliminary falsity. This is necessary because otherwise believers would sometimes not be able in good conscience to remain in the Church when it decided against them."

34 Cf. (Second) Anglican-Roman Catholic International Commission, *The Gift of Authority*, Authority in the Church III (London: CTS, 1999).

Dombes highlighted the necessity of some authority for Christian unity,[35] not the least to make possible the reception of ecumenical documents.[36] The Groupe asked for more synodal elements within the Catholic Church,[37] and more decision-making possibilities within Protestant Churches:

> We ask the Churches of the Reformation to develop new processus of decision making, beyond regional and national Churches, within great denominational organizations. . . . It matters to the witness to be given to the Gospel in the world that Churches can visibly manifest their doctrinal communion and decide together on the highest possible number of matters.[38]

The question of authority is central to ecumenical dialogue, but it is also biased by historical controversies and by occurrences of badly used authority and so on. A theologian like Aquinas is not biased by the controversies of the Reformation and the Counter Reformation. He addresses the question of authority from a starting point that is not "political," namely the conditions for faith. Finally, he gives a theological justification to the role of human instances in our relationship to God.

The Role of Church Authority as a Service to Faith in Aquinas

Aquinas asks a question that can be accepted by all Christians: How can one come to have Christian faith? He sees two conditions:

> Two things are requisite for faith. *First, that the things which are of faith should be proposed to man*: this is necessary in order that man believe anything explicitly. The second thing requisite for faith is the assent of the believer to the things which are proposed to him. Accordingly, as regards the first of these, faith must needs be from God. Because those things which are of faith surpass human reason, hence they do not

---

35 Cf. Groupe Des Dombes, *"Un seul maître," L'autorité doctrinale dans l'Église* (Paris: Bayard, 2005).

36 Cf. Ibid., no. 440.

37 Cf. Ibid., nos. 457–59.

38 Ibid., no. 463, my translation: "Nous demandons donc aux Églises de la Réforme de développer des processus inédits de prise de décision au-delà des Églises régionales et nationales, au sein des grandes organisations, confessionnelles. Nous encourageons le développement de 'communions ecclésiales' d'Églises protestantes pleinement réconciliées, signe que les Églises autrefois séparées peuvent évoluer les unes vers les autres, en ayant le Christ pour centre. Il importe au témoignage à rendre à l'Évangile dans le monde que les Églises puissent manifester visiblement leur communion doctrinale et décider ensemble sur le plus de points possibles." Cf. also no. 392.

come to man's knowledge, unless God reveal them. To some, indeed, they are revealed by God immediately, as those things which were revealed to the apostles and prophets, while to some they are proposed by God in sending preachers of the faith, according to Romans 10:15: "How shall they preach, unless they be sent?"

As regards the second, namely, man's assent to the things which are of faith, we may observe a twofold cause, one of external inducement, such as seeing a miracle, or being persuaded by someone to embrace the faith: neither of which is a sufficient cause, since of those who see the same miracle, or who hear the same sermon, some believe, and some do not. Hence *we must assert another internal cause, which moves man inwardly* to assent to matters of faith.

The Pelagians held that this cause was nothing else than man's free will: and consequently they said that the beginning of faith is from ourselves, inasmuch as, to wit, it is in our power to be ready to assent to things which are of faith, but that the consummation of faith is from God, Who proposes to us the things we have to believe. But this is false, for, *since man, by assenting to matters of faith, is raised above his nature, this must needs accrue to him from some supernatural principle moving him inwardly; and this is God.* Therefore faith, as regards the assent which is the chief act of faith, is from God moving man inwardly by grace.[39]

In short, Christian faith must be announced and the person to whom it is announced must accept what is preached. None of that is possible without divine action: What is announced is first revealed by God, and the human assent is made possible by divine grace (which does not mean that grace suppresses the free will, it just makes its act possible in such a matter).[40] It appears that the weak points in these conditions are those that involve creatures: the preaching of the good news and its acceptance. The ecumenical movement

---

[39] *ST* II–II, q. 6, a. 1, emphasis added.

[40] Cf. *ST* I–II, q. 113, a. 3: "The justification of the ungodly is brought about by God moving man to justice. For He it is 'that justifieth the ungodly' according to Rm 4:5. Now God moves everything in its own manner, just as we see that in natural things, what is heavy and what is light are moved differently, on account of their diverse natures. Hence He moves man to justice according to the condition of his human nature. But it is man's proper nature to have free will. Hence in him who has the use of reason, God's motion to justice does not take place without a movement of the free will; but He so infuses the gift of justifying grace that at the same time He moves the free-will to accept the gift of grace, in such as are capable of being moved thus." Cf. also *ST* I, q. 62, a. 3, ad 2: "Every form inclines the subject after the mode of the subject's nature. Now it is the mode of an intellectual nature to be inclined freely towards the objects it desires. Consequently the movement of grace does not impose necessity; but he who has grace can fail to make use of it, and can sin."

arose in part from the fact that the divided preaching of the Gospel made its acceptance more problematic. The Thomistic school has been deeply aware of such a difficulty. Cardinal Cajetan comments on the conditions of faith:

> *As far as faith can depend on a created cause, it can have a created rule.* Obviously, two things interact in faith . . . namely [first] the assent and [second] the proposition and explanation of the things which must be believed; *on the point of view of the assent, faith depends only on God as agent, object end and rule. But on the point of view of the proposition of the things to be believed, it can depend on angels and human beings, through whom God proposes this or that to be believed;* on this point of view, "faith comes from hearing the word of God," as Rom. 10 says. And *so that no error might appear in the proposal or explanation of things to believe, the Holy Spirit provided a created rule, which is the sense and the doctrine of the Church, so that the authority of the Church is the infallible rule of the proposition and explanation of things which must be believed by faith.* Therefore, *two infallible rules concur to faith,* namely divine revelation and the authority of the Church; there is between them this difference: *divine revelation is the formal reason of the object of faith, and the authority of the Church is the minister of the object of faith.*[41]

Another Thomist, John of St. Thomas (1589–1644), shows that the mere fact that biblical texts are interpreted in different ways—sometimes complementary, sometimes incompatible—implies the necessity of some authority of interpretation. Without such an authority, the Bible alone does not achieve unity among human beings:

> Everybody cannot declare on a way which would resolve the question by a determination, and infallibly so, *because out of the mere fact that*

---

[41] Cajetan (1469–1534), *In ST* II–II, q. 1, a. 1, no. X: "inquantum fides potest dependere a causa creata, intantum potest habere aliquam regulam creatam. Constat autem quod, cum ad fidem concurrant duo, ut infra patet, scilicet assensus et propositio atque explicatio credendorum, fides ex parte assensus a solo Deo dependet ut agente, obiecto, fine et regula. Ex parte autem propositionis credendorum potest dependere ab angelis et hominibus, mediantibus quibus Deus proponit haec vel illa esse credenda: ex hac enim parte 'fides ex auditu est verbi Dei,' ut dicitur ad Rm 10. Et propterea quoad proponendum et explicandum credenda, ne possit accidere error, providit Spiritus Sanctus de infallibili regula creata, sensu scilicet et doctrina Ecclesiae: ita quod auctoritas Ecclesiae est infallibilis regula proponendi et explicandi ea quae sunt fide tenenda. Unde, duabus concurrentibus ad fidem infallibilibus regulis, scilicet revelatione divina et auctoritate Ecclesiae, inter eas tanta est differentia quod revelatio divina est ratio formalis obiecti fidei, auctoritas autem Ecclesiae est ministra obiecti fidei."

there is the whole controversy, about whether what the Church proposes and declares is contained in Scripture, and the fact that some deny and others affirm, therefore *if everyone could declare on that, everyone would pronounce for himself, and all would stay within the same confusion;* therefore it is necessary that the declaration and proposition by the Church be without any suspicion and fallibility; otherwise we would always have a doubt, on whether this is contained in Scripture.[42]

Created Means and the Economy of the Gospel, Sign of Divine Love

If some authority can be seen as useful for Church unity, it can also be seen as too human, not spiritual enough. Certainly, any minister as well as any Christian can sometimes be too human, and that harms the Church. But does God stop at that? The American Episcopalian R. R. Reno showed the connection of such a question to the Gospel:

> We ought to be careful, for the requirement of laying on of hands would seem to be exactly the sort of condition God chooses in Christ and for us. *The scandalous worldly features of the tradition of apostolical succession, the physical act of laying on of hands, echoes the much more scandalously worldly and physical features of Christ's obedience. Further, if we chuckle at the notion that God might use a bishop's hands to ensure the survival of his people, then we may all too easily chuckle when the gospel places demands upon our hands—to feed the hungry and cloth the naked.* Will we not dodge these gospel imperatives with some self-serving line about how God does not establish conditions, does not call human hands into action to do his work? Far, then, from corrupting the evangelical purity of the gospel, the requirement of historical succession is an intensification of the penetrating power of the gospel.[43]

---

[42] John of St. Thomas, *Cursus theologicus,* in *Summam theologicam D. Thomae,* nova editio, tomus primus, in *Primae Partis Quaestiones I–VII* (Paris: Vivès, 1883), I, q. 1, disp. I, a. 3, 433, emphasis added: "Non potest autem quilibet hoc declarare resolutorie determinando, et infallibiliter, cum de hoc ipso sit tota controversia, an contineatur in Scriptura id quod Ecclesia sic proponit et declarat, et quidam negent, alii affirment, unde si quilibet posset hoc declarare, quilibet pro sua parte pronuntiaret, et manerent omnes in eadem confusione; ergo oportet, quod ipsa declaratio, et propositio Ecclesiae careat omni suspicione, et fallibilitate, alias semper dubitaremus, an ita contineatur in Scriptura."

[43] R. R. Reno, "The Evangelical Significance of the Historic Episcopate," in *Inhabiting Unity: Theological Perspectives on the Proposal Lutheran-Episcopal Concordat,* ed. Ephraim Radner and R. R. Reno (Grand Rapids, MI: Eerdmans, 1995), 90, emphasis added.

St. Thomas Aquinas has the same concern, and expresses it with a general principle. When he asks why God actually chooses some sacraments—which are not purely spiritual—for the transmission of salvation, he gives

> three reasons. The first is taken from the condition of human nature which is such that it has to be led by things corporeal and sensible to things spiritual and intelligible. Now *it belongs to Divine providence to provide for each one according as its condition requires.* Divine wisdom, therefore, fittingly provides man with means of salvation, in the shape of corporeal and sensible signs that are called sacraments.[44]

This principle is a sign of divine love, as it could be a sign of human politeness not to address others as if they were more than they are. We are earthly, physical beings. It is our nature, given to us by the Creator. God addresses us according to what we are. This is why there are all these earthly realities in the Church: sacraments, ministers, preachers who make mistakes, and so on. Because God loves us for what we are, he pulls us to him using created means as vehicles for his divine grace.

The Formal Object of Faith and the Nature of Christian Unity

Speaking about faith, St. Thomas makes a distinction that can be very useful for theological ecumenical dialogues:

> Accordingly if we consider, in faith, the *formal aspect* of the object, it is nothing else than the First Truth. *For the faith of which we are speaking, does not assent to anything, except because it is revealed by* God. Hence the mean on which faith is based is the Divine Truth. If, however, we consider *materially* the things to which faith assents, they include not only God, but also many other things, which, nevertheless, do not come under the assent of faith, except as bearing some relation to God.[45]

Faith is always therefore about God, but in two ways: not only because its content is God or what relates to him (like the humanity of Christ, the Church, the Bible, the sacraments . . .), but also because something belongs to faith only because it is revealed by God, at least implicitly. This implies

---

[44] *ST* III, q. 61, a. 1, emphasis added. The other reasons explained at the same place are the healing of our corporeal activities (that can lead to sin) and the giving of material practices that would not be superstitious.

[45] *ST* II–II, q. 1, a. 1, emphasis added.

for Thomas a unique importance of Sacred Scripture in theology,[46] although he makes clear that the content of the Bible can be understood always more deeply and expressed in different terms.[47]

---

[46] Cf. *ST* I, q. 1, a. 8, ad 2: "Sacred doctrine makes use also of the authority of philosophers in those questions in which they were able to know the truth by natural reason, as Paul quotes a saying of Aratus: 'As some also of your own poets said: For we are also his offspring' (Acts 17:28). Nevertheless, sacred doctrine makes use of these authorities as extrinsic and probable arguments; but properly uses the authority of the canonical Scriptures as an incontrovertible proof, and the authority of the doctors of the Church as one that may properly be used, yet merely as probable. For our faith rests upon the revelation made to the apostles and prophets who wrote the canonical books, and not on the revelations (if any such there are) made to other doctors. Hence Augustine says (*Epis. ad Hieron.* xix, 1): 'Only those books of Scripture which are called canonical have I learned to hold in such honor as to believe their authors have not erred in any way in writing them. But other authors I so read as not to deem everything in their works to be true, merely on account of their having so thought and written, whatever may have been their holiness and learning.'"

[47] Cf. *ST* II–II, q. 1, a. 7: "The articles of faith stand in the same relation to the doctrine of faith, as self-evident principles to a teaching based on natural reason. Among these principles there is a certain order, so that some are contained implicitly in others; thus all principles are reduced, as to their first principle, to this one: 'The same thing cannot be affirmed and denied at the same time,' as the Philosopher states (*Metaph.* iv, text. 9). In like manner all the articles are contained implicitly in certain primary matters of faith, such as God's existence, and his providence over the salvation of man, according to Hebrews 11: 'He that cometh to God, must believe that He is, and is a rewarder to them that seek Him.' For the existence of God includes all that we believe to exist in God eternally, and in these our happiness consists; while belief in his providence includes all those things which God dispenses in time, for man's salvation, and which are the way to that happiness: and in this way, again, some of those articles which follow from these are contained in others: thus faith in the Redemption of mankind includes belief in the Incarnation of Christ, his Passion and so forth. Accordingly we must conclude that, as regards the substance of the articles of faith, they have not received any increase as time went on: since whatever those who lived later have believed, was contained, albeit implicitly, in the faith of those Fathers who preceded them. But there was an increase in the number of articles believed explicitly, since to those who lived in later times some were known explicitly which were not known explicitly by those who lived before them. Hence the Lord said to Moses (Ex 6:2, 3): 'I am the God of Abraham, the God of Isaac, the God of Jacob [*Vulg.: 'I am the Lord that appeared to Abraham, to Isaac, and to Jacob'] . . . and My name Adonai I did not show them': David also said (Ps 118:100): 'I have had understanding above ancients': and the Apostle says (Eph 3:5) that the mystery of Christ, 'in other generations was not known, as it is now revealed to his holy apostles and prophets.'" Cf. also *ST* I, q. 29, a. 3, ad 1: "Although the word person is not found applied to God in Scripture, either in the Old or New Testament, nevertheless what the word signifies is

The importance of the formal aspect of faith—namely, divine revelation—is such that Thomas says that whoever denies one article of faith, if that person is informed and conscious, implicitly denies all articles of faith.[48] The reason for such a strong statement is that whoever refuses what the Church presents as revealed by God (this presupposes what has been said above about the meaning of Church authority in the preaching of faith) accepts other articles of faith on the basis of an argument similar to the argument that leads that person to reject one article. The argument becomes the personal opinion, and then theological statements are reduced to the level of philosophical arguments.

That we understand this theology of faith matters for at least two reasons in an ecumenical perspective:

1. because it helps understand the typical situation of the Catholic Church (the importance of a mutual understanding implies that Catholics try to clarify their own position), and

---

found to be affirmed of God in many places of Scripture; as that He is the supreme self-subsisting being, and the most perfectly intelligent being. If we could speak of God only in the very terms themselves of Scripture, it would follow that no one could speak about God in any but the original language of the Old or New Testament. The urgency of confuting heretics made it necessary to find new words to express the ancient faith about God. Nor is such a kind of novelty to be shunned; since it is by no means profane, for it does not lead us astray from the sense of Scripture. The Apostle warns us to avoid 'profane novelties of words' (1 Tim 6:20)."

48 Cf. *ST* II–II, q. 5, a. 3: "Neither living nor lifeless faith remains in a heretic who disbelieves one article of faith. The reason of this is that the species of every habit depends on the formal aspect of the object, without which the species of the habit cannot remain. Now the formal object of faith is the First Truth, as manifested in Holy Writ and the teaching of the Church, which proceeds from the First Truth. Consequently whoever does not adhere, as to an infallible and Divine rule, to the teaching of the Church, which proceeds from the First Truth manifested in Holy Writ, has not the habit of faith, but holds that which is of faith otherwise than by faith. Even so, it is evident that a man whose mind holds a conclusion without knowing how it is proved, has not scientific knowledge, but merely an opinion about it. Now it is manifest that he who adheres to the teaching of the Church, as to an infallible rule, assents to whatever the Church teaches; otherwise, if, of the things taught by the Church, he holds what he chooses to hold, and rejects what he chooses to reject, he no longer adheres to the teaching of the Church as to an infallible rule, but to his own will. Hence it is evident that a heretic who obstinately disbelieves one article of faith, is not prepared to follow the teaching of the Church in all things; but if he is not obstinate, he is no longer in heresy but only in error. Therefore it is clear that such a heretic with regard to one article has no faith in the other articles, but only a kind of opinion in accordance with his own will."

2. because it puts the theological dialogue at the only level that can fit the purpose of ecumenism.

Aquinas's theology helps us understand the typical elements of the Catholic position, particularly delicate in an ecumenical context, that are the dogmas. Words such as the ones used in 1950 by Pope Pius XII when he defined the dogma of the Assumption sound hard or incomprehensible to ecumenical ears:

> If anyone, which God forbid, should dare willfully to deny or to call into doubt that which we have defined, let him know that he has fallen away completely from the divine and Catholic Faith.[49]

The idea expressed is actually St. Thomas's idea: An article of faith, which is "based on Sacred Scripture,"[50] should not be received first on the basis of a personal opinion, but on the basis of divine revelation. And we cannot have a sure access to divine revelation without the Church: Even the nature and the content of the Bible (its canon) would then be uncertain. Of course theologians who accept a dogma as dogma keep the duty to understand and explain it better, and in that regard their studies can help the understanding of the dogma by all faithful.[51]

---

[49] Pius XII, apostolic constitution *Munificentissimus Deus* (November 1, 1950), Denzinger, no. 3904, cf. *The Christian Faith*, no. 715. Cf. also part of the dogma of the Immaculate Conception by Pius IX, bull Ineffabilis Deus (December 8, 1854), Denzinger, no. 2804, cf. *The Christian Faith*, no. 709: "If, therefore, any person shall dare to think—which God forbid—otherwise than as has been defined by us, let them clearly know that they stay condemned by their own judgment; that they have made shipwreck in their faith and fallen from the unity of the Church."

[50] Pius XII, apostolic constitution *Munificentissimus Deus* (November 1, 1950), Denzinger, no. 3902, cf. *The Christian Faith*, no. 714.

[51] Cf. Karl Rahner, "Scripture and Tradition," in *Theological Investigations*, vol. 6, *Concerning Vatican II* (London and New York: Darton, Longman & Todd, The Seabury Press, 1969), 109: "It does indeed go without saying for any Catholic theologian that, if the Church's actual consciousness of faith as it is today testifies and firmly holds to a truth as really believed with divine faith and as an apostolic tradition and declares it to be such by an infallible pronouncement by a pope or a council, then in virtue of the indefectibility of the faith of the Church this conviction must be true even when the individual theologian or believer has not yet proved this truth historically and has not yet made it explicit. Yet even in the case of such a dogmatic evaluation of the present state of the Church's doctrinal proclamation and hence of oral tradition, the Catholic theologian obviously still retains the right and beyond this the duty to show historically how the Church's dogma as believed today has come down to us from the apostolic age in a genuine, historical tradition and development."

When Vatican II's Decree on Ecumenism introduced the idea of the hierarchy of truths,[52] the commission in charge of explaining the text to the bishops before their vote clarified that "[a]lthough without doubt all revealed truths must be held with the same divine truth, their importance and 'weight' is different because of their link to Salvation history and to the mystery of Christ."[53]

The affirmation that anything that is revealed must be accepted is also mentioned in the explanation of the hierarchy of truths published in 1990 by the Joint Working Group between the Roman Catholic Church and the World Council of Churches.[54] All Christians can agree that faith cannot be founded upon anything other than divine revelation; the question is to know how to recognize that revelation, which leads us back to the Montreal conference's search for a criterion.

What seems a typically Catholic concern is actually central to ecumenical dialogue, if the purpose of ecumenism is full unity of Christians. Must ecumenical agreements have the form of consensus among theologians, or should they be covered with the authority of divine revelation? Theological consensus is not unanimous and does not last. Do we want a partial and not lasting Christian unity? If so, we are already there, and ecumenism is only a way to organize a peaceful life among different communities.

Conclusion

Martin Luther's theology was based on the reading of Scripture. Still, because any approach to a text is influenced by the culture of the reader, Luther read the biblical text with the presuppositions of his culture influenced by the latest trends in scholastic theology. As Pope John Paul II said, "Were theologians to refuse the help of philosophy, they would run the risk of doing philosophy

---

[52] Cf. Vatican Council II, Decree on Ecumenism, *Unitatis Redintegratio,* no. 11.

[53] Secretariat for Christian Unity, "Explanation of modus 49" (November 11, 1964), in *Acta Synodalia,* vol. III, pt. VII, 419, my translation: "Quamvis procul dubio omnes veritates revelatae eadem fide divina tenendae sint, momentum et 'pondus' earum differt pro nexu earum cum historia salutis et mysterio Christi."

[54] Cf. Joint Working Group Between the Roman Catholic Church and the World Council of Churches, *The Notion of "Hierarchy of Truths": An Ecumenical Interpretation, A Study Document Commissioned and Received by the Joint Working Group,* Faith and Order paper no. 150 (Geneva: World Council of Churches Publications, 1990), no. 17: "Certainly all revealed truths demand the same acceptance of faith, but according to the greater or lesser proximity that they have to the basis of the revealed mystery, they are variously placed with regard to one another and have varying connections among themselves" (this text quotes a 1970 document by the Secretariat for Promoting Christian Unity).

unwittingly and locking themselves within thought-structures poorly adapted to the understanding of faith."[55] This is at least what Cardinal Cajetan suspected when he prepared his 1518 meetings with Luther, and which was confirmed by later writings of the Reformer (most clearly by his 1525 *De servo arbitrio*). Luther always felt obliged to state that if a human being (for instance, the minister of a sacrament) claims to do something that is related to salvation, this means that God does not act completely. The same mindset can be found in John Calvin's works and in many of the Protestant answers to Faith and Constitution's *Baptism, Eucharist, Ministry*, in the 1980s. The impact of such views about the relationship between divine action and human actions on the understanding of the Church is very deep. This is part of the reason why even the 1999 Catholic-Lutheran Joint Declaration on Justification had to leave many questions for further study. Out of any polemical context linked to the Reformation, Thomas Aquinas had already addressed the question of the relation between divine and created actions, and did not see any problem in stating what Cajetan will later say about Lutheran views: There is no reason why God and a creature could not accomplish the same act, both simultaneously and completely, quite as a writer and his pen both write simultaneously 100 percent of a text. The key to this point is Thomas's analogy of being (instead of Scotus's univocity that Luther had unconsciously in mind): Two men cannot both claim to have accomplished 100 percent of the same action, because they are beings of the same level. But between beings of different levels, like the writer and his pen, or God and human beings, attributing an action to one does not mean not attributing it also fully to another one, the action of the lower one depending on the action of the higher one. That God also acts through our causality does not mean that he could not do everything alone, but that his love leads him to give us the dignity of causes. Thomism can here have an important contribution to the clarification of some important presuppositions of the Reformation and of contemporary Protestant theology. It can also help contemporary Protestant theologians who look for some way to understand why the Gospel requires human actions of all types, or how the Bible can have God and human beings as authors.

All Christians agree on the necessity of preaching the Word of God, so that the world can believe. But what does that mean? The 1963 Faith and Order Assembly in Montreal accepted the necessity of the long debated concept of *Tradition*, because ecumenical dialogue itself shows how all our readings of Scripture are influenced by our different traditions, even in the churches whose tradition is not to have any tradition. . . . Still, the Montreal

---

[55] John Paul II, *Fides et Ratio* (September 14, 1998), no. 77.

conference could not find a final criterion for the sometimes necessary discernment among the different traditions that claim to present Christ to the different situations of the contemporary world. This question is central to ecumenism: Without such a criterion Christian preaching is less credible and Christian unity cannot be achieved. Aquinas and his school ask similar questions. Thomas says that one condition of faith is that it must be announced as coming from God, but by human preachers. Cajetan will show that human (or angelic) preaching is the weakest point of the transmission of revelation, because creatures can lie or err; therefore God—who knows our weaknesses—provided a human ministry able to prevent final errors in the transmission of the Gospel. Without such a ministry later generations would be so unsure of what is preached to them—as constant disagreements show through history—that divine revelation could seem to have been useless. But God is neither reluctant nor unable to help us with our own help in the authority of the Church.

This Thomistic analysis of preaching does not only contribute to the ecumenical search for a criterion of discernment between different traditions, it also helps us understand the ecumenical question raised by Catholic dogmas. How can Pius XII say, in 1950, that who refuses the dogma of the Assumption of Mary has lost divine faith? And what does it say about non-Catholic Christians? The main point there is to see that in faith there is not only what Thomas calls a "material" element, namely a content (articles of faith), but also a "form." The form is what gives its identity to the content, and it is divine revelation. The reason I believe, for example, that Jesus is the Son of the living God (one aspect of the "material object" of faith) is not my own opinion (flesh and blood), but that the Father has revealed it. I can be sure of that thanks only to the transmission of divine revelation (also of its implicit content, progressively understood throughout the centuries), with the assistance of the Holy Spirit, within the Church. This is why there have been definitions of faith in the Ancient Church, and there are still some nowadays. Not only such a "formal" understanding of faith helps clarify the Catholic position, it is also a contribution of ecumenism as such. If unity in faith cannot be declared among previously divided Christians in a clearly perceived way assisted by God and received as such (this is the "formal" aspect of faith), then ecumenism cannot do more than look for a consensus among theologians, and such a consensus is usually partial and temporary.

CHAPTER 11

The Coming Middle Ages

EDWARD T. OAKES, S.J.

FOR ALL the technical mastery Father Matthew Lamb has shown in his work as a theologian (and for all of his laments at the *lack* of technical mastery in so many theologians today!), to me one of his greatest virtues as a theologian is his ability to see "the big picture," how contemporary movements fit into the much larger history of the Great Tradition of the Church's theological tradition. For that reason, I thought I could offer no better tribute to him than to offer my own views of the framework in which theology shall be operating in the next few centuries, speculative as my prognostications must of course remain.

In order to see some objects more clearly (especially if they are very large), it often pays to step back from them. Think of Impressionist or Pointillist paintings, for example. Up close, they do not look like pictures of water lilies or Sunday-afternoon strollers along La Grande Jatte: No, seen too near, they look to be just smeared daubs of paint or minute dots of color. In fact, anyone can transform his private, subjective field of vision into a personal Impressionist canvas, as it were, just by blurring the focus of his eyes. This technique of blurring one's eyes to get a better impression of the whole also works, I maintain, for intellectual history: paradoxical as that might sound, one sometimes gets a clearer picture of the history of human thought by blurring one's focus, if only for a few moments.

Take, for instance, the case of philosophy. Everyone knows that the history of philosophy is far too vast to include in a one-semester course, and so most philosophy departments divide their courses in the history of philosophy into three (or sometimes four) discrete periods: ancient, medieval, and modern (with contemporary philosophy usually given separate treatment). Nor is this rough-and-ready division entirely arbitrary. There does really seem to be something quite uniquely different in ethos, style, and doctrine in the ancient philosophy done from Thales to Plotinus, in the medieval philosophy pursued from Boethius to William of Ockham, and in the distinctly modern outlook inaugurated by René Descartes and culminating in Bertrand Russell. And finally (although this last point is disputed) that modern habit of mind seems somehow not to capture very well the peculiar "postmodern" style that was first adumbrated by Friedrich Nietzsche and then passed to Ludwig Wittgenstein and Martin Heidegger and is now culminating (so far) in Richard Rorty, Jacques Derrida, and a host of others.[1]

But anyone who takes a survey course in the history of philosophy, however that course is divided up, and then starts reading the original classical texts supposedly being described by that survey, immediately realizes how blunt an instrument a survey course really is. Needless to say, I do not wish to dispute the necessity of these once-over-lightly courses; nor is it a surprise that historiography gravitates toward a periodization of history under the tripartite rubric of ancient, medieval, and modern. In any event, the human mind tends to categorize the world into threes. From nursery rhymes like the Three Bears, Three Blind Mice, or the Three Little Maids That Went to School, all the way up to Hegel's thesis, antithesis, and synthesis, the number three accompanies us. So it does not surprise us to learn that all of history, and not just Caesar's Gaul, is divided (like human life itself) into three parts: old, middle-aged, and new. Unfortunately, time marches on, and what was once fresh and recent soon turns gray, so that the modern (meaning "new") no longer looks so modern, and sad reality leaves us stuck with calling our own age, rather unhelpfully and oxymoronically, "postmodern," as if anything could ever be "post"-new.[2]

---

[1] Nor can it be accidental that these divisions roughly coincide with the principle languages used in each period of philosophy: from Thales to Plotinus, most philosophers wrote in Greek; from Boethius to Ockham most philosophy was written in Latin; and from Descartes to the present most philosophers wrote (and still write) in their native vernacular (although Descartes, Spinoza, and Newton wrote some, but not all, of their major works in Latin). Of course, so-called "postmodern" philosophers still write in their native tongue too; but nowadays, if their works never get translated into English, their influence does not reach very far (whereas Kant's influence, for example, hardly depended on his three *Critiques* first getting translated into English). Take the case of Derrida: He seems more influential in the United States than in France, an influence that would have been impossible had he never been translated into English. So will English become the new *lingua franca* for philosophy the way Latin was for the Middle Ages? I suspect it will.

[2] By concentrating on the periodization of the history of Western philosophy I do not wish to claim that historians of philosophy were the first to invent this tripartite division. In fact it began as an interpretation of the civilization of the West by certain figures in the Renaissance who saw their era as a new "rebirth" of classical traditions that

In this article I wish to treat the question of "secularization and the Church in the twenty-first century" under a different kind of rubric than that normally suggested by the tripartite division of civilization and Western thought outlined above (with the additional "barnacle" of "post"-modernism added as a kind of excrescence to the schema). What I wish to point out is that postmodernism represents, at least in some of its aspects, not a further *advance* into the future but a kind of *doubling-back* into the Middle Ages. Moreover, if I am right, this will mean that the issue of secularization has been fundamentally misconceived.

Admittedly, my own schema of doubling-back has to fight against the linear view of history bequeathed to us by the Bible and St. Augustine's *City of God.* Is not time, after all, still marching forward; and is not history for that reason getting closer and closer to the Eschaton—when the heavenly Jerusalem will descend, when every tear will be wiped away, and when God will be all in all? Does not a doubling-back represent a reversion both to a dead past and to the cyclical view of history that Augustine had supposedly vanquished?

Abandonment of the linear view of history would certainly be costly, for the conflict between a cyclical and a linear view of history is actually rooted in a more fundamental conflict between polytheism and monotheism. Despite what a superficial glance at the etymology of these two words might at first seem to indicate, the real conflict between polytheism and monotheism is not really a question of number, with pagans thinking there are "many" gods, while monotheists insist there is but "one" (otherwise understandable, graspable) "god."

No, what is crucial is *why* polytheists believe in many gods: because they are *born.* As the great historian of Hebrew Bible Yehezkel Kaufmann puts it in his influential study of Israelite religion, if the gods are born, then they must be born out of a prior substance, which he calls the "meta-divine" realm. Now across the spectrum of pre-biblical mythology this meta-divine realm can be described variously as the cosmic egg, the confluence of world rivers, the tree at the center of the world, and so forth, all of which served as the proto-natural world out of which the gods of mythology are born. But for Kaufmann, the key is this:

> All of these embodiments involve one idea which is the distinguishing
> mark of pagan thought: the idea that there exists a realm of being prior
> to the gods and above them, upon which the gods depend, and whose

---

had fallen into desuetude during that period that these self-styled "reborn" thinkers saw as the "middle" period intervening between the "light" of classical civilizations and their own.

decrees they must obey. Deity belongs to, and is derived from, a primordial realm. This realm is conceived of variously—as darkness, water, spirit, earth, sky, and so forth—but always as the womb in which the seeds of all being are contained. This is to say that in the pagan view, the gods are not the source of all that is, nor do they transcend the universe.[3]

Precisely because this primordial realm is prior to the gods, it is cyclical, for it starts off as, so to speak, *predifferentiated*: that is, it already has a male and female principle; it already has light and darkness as part of its components; it already has a movement of seasons, a diurnal movement of day to night and night to day, prior to the emergence of the self-conscious and quasi-human gods. This too follows from the fact that the gods are born. Often the gods who are worshipped are of the second or third generation (or more), who overthrow their parents for the suzerainty of the world. But where did these parents themselves come from? As the theogony is traced back, the genealogy of the gods continues to go back along the "family tree" from "gods" to "titans" (as in Greek mythology) and then finally to some more abstractly named principle (as in Greek mythology, where the titans owe their existence to Ouranos and Gaia, words that literally mean "sky" and "earth," with the former being a masculine principle and the latter feminine).[4] The relationship between these two principles is a cyclical one and, above all, impersonal.

Quite different is the view of the God-world relationship in Israel. With the opening line of Genesis, "In the beginning God created the heavens and the earth" (Gen 1:1), the mythological worldview was undercut at a stroke. For the word "created" is drawn above all from the world of art, where the artist has control over his creation, which can be regarded as fundamentally a product of his *will*. For the author of Genesis, God is most basically a deciding, willing, creating Being, who owes his existence to nothing outside of himself. And this emerges most obviously in the fact that the God of Israel knows no theogony. As Kaufmann says, "Israel's God has no pedigree, fathers no generations; He nether inherits nor bequeaths his authority. He does not die and is not resurrected. He has no sexual qualities or desires and shows no need of or dependence upon powers outside Himself."[5]

---

[3] Yehezkel Kaufmann, *The Religion of Israel: From Its Beginnings to the Babylonian Exile,* trans. Moshe Greenberg (Chicago: University of Chicago Press, 1960), 21–22.

[4] In Greek mythology the Ouranos and Gaia in their turn come from Chaos. Thus out of Chaos there simply emerges the pre-differentiated world of Father Sky and Mother Earth, the alternation of seasons, rain, fructification of the earth, and so forth.

[5] Kaufmann, *The Religion of Israel,* 60–61.

But if creation is fundamentally an act of will in monotheism, in polytheism both the emergence of the world and the birth of the gods are primarily matters of *fate* (who chooses to be born?). Thus the real conflict between monotheism and polytheism is, as we have said, not a conflict of number but of the nature of the deity. In the mythological worldview, fate is fundamental and all-determinative, whereas in monotheism God's will trumps all. (Not for nothing are the flags of India and South Korea symbols of the cyclical view: The former is a wheel and the latter shows the famous Yin/Yang principles moving in an endless cycle.)

I mention these observations, which have become standard for quite some time now in the field of comparative religion, only to highlight how much a linear view of history is part and parcel of the monotheistic religions, whereas polytheism leads ineluctably to a cyclical view of history. But it shall be my contention in this article that the linear view of history is now bumping up against some real dilemmas. Or let me put in this way: When I look out into the future, I do not see anything "new" or "modern," still less do I see anything, except in the most obvious and literal sense, *post*modern. What I see (and this could be, I admit, a completely idiosyncratic view) is, as my title indicates, a *coming Middle Ages*.

What do I mean? Well, first, at the most obvious level, I am thinking of that still-unpaid bill left over from the accounts of the Middle Ages, the conflict with Islam. It is quite remarkable how much the history of modernity depends on regarding Islam as "dispatched" into (to borrow that most shopworn of all linear terms of Marxist historiography) the "dustbin of history." Modernity likes to tell a tale of itself as one of progressive liberation from medieval darkness, a habit first picked up from the Renaissance and then brought to fullest self-expression in Immanuel Kant's programmatic essay "What is Enlightenment?" Little wonder, then, that the world of Western civilization was caught off guard by the Ayatollah Khomeni's *fatwa* ordering the execution of a British novelist, Salman Rushdie, and even more by the revanchist attacks of Muslim jihadists against the World Trade Center and the Pentagon on September 11, 2001, just as it continues to be baffled by the irrational nihilism of suicide bombings, the imposition of traditional Islamic law in the Sudan, Pakistan, northern Nigeria, and other areas. If progress is ineluctable, why is Islam proving so susceptible to these "medieval" reversions?

But this is only one aspect of what I am trying to say. For, the "signs of the times" I have pointed to so far only allude to obscurantist politics and terrorist nihilism of Islamists; and that very way of phrasing things could still fit into the story modernity tells of itself: According to the secularist mindset, Islam is obscurantist because it is still, in contradiction to Christianity (at least as it is practiced in the West), a living religion; and since to the Enlightened secular mind religion is inherently obscurantist, little wonder that a living religion would prove so threatening to rationality.[6]

Actually my title predicting a "Coming Middle Ages" wishes to point not just to the medieval revanchism of radical versions of Islam; my thesis also wants to point to something more positive as well: The signs are as yet embryonic, but I believe one can detect a reversion to medieval values *inside the West,* a recuperation of resources that will prove baffling to the Enlightenment outlook on history.

I am thinking here especially of philosophical trends in the West that seem to be pointing to, at least in my estimation, a return to medieval ways of thinking. A philosopher at the University of St. Thomas in Houston, John Deely, brought this home to me when I read his remarkable new history of philosophy, *Four Ages of Understanding.*[7] Accepting the standard division of philosophical historiography into ancient, medieval, modern, and postmodern philosophy (hence the title of his book), he then asks if there is anything in the internal development of each era that would justify such a periodization beyond mere convenience. Yes, he answers. In fact, he dares to

---

6 One sign of the nonplussed puzzlement of the secular mind to the resurgence of Islam is the way writers in the elite secular media will equate "fundamentalist" Muslims with "fundamentalist" Christians (a term that in journalistic parlance lazily refers not to the properly so-called Christian fundamentalists, who hold to the inerrancy of the Bible in its every verse, but to *any* Christian denomination that fights secular morality regarding abortion, gay marriage, and the like). A good example of this journalistic sloth can be seen in this bizarre passage from a newspaper of the British left: "Puritanical yet wealthy, convinced of their God-given mission to the rest of the world, sure of a divinely inspired history—Saudi Arabia and the United States are surprisingly similar in their mixture of religion, politics, and interference in other countries' affairs. Saudi Arabia has Wahhabi Islam, Middle America has evangelical Christianity. Historically, they hate each other. Yet both see themselves as exponents of the purest version of their faith. Both are suspicious of modernity. Both see no distinction between politics and religion" (Cristina Odone, "Faith Invaders," *New Statesman,* April 18, 2005, A1). As Phillip Johnson rightly notes of this preposterous conflation, "Such relativism sees little difference between the religious tyranny of the Wahhabi-backed Saudi monarchy, which violently oppresses not only non-Islamic religions but other forms of Islam, and the thriving religious pluralism of the United States, where Muslims have far more freedom than they have in Arabia, and where formerly bitter religious differences, such as the chasm that once separated Protestants and Catholics, have become more like amiably held differences of opinion." Phillip E. Johnson, "Religious War and Peace," *Touchstone: A Journal of Mere Christianity* 18 (2005): 11.

7 John Deely, *Four Ages of Understanding: The First Postmodern Survey of Philosophy from Ancient Times to the Turn of the Twenty-First Century* (Toronto: University of Toronto Press, 2001).

characterize each era by one overriding concern that preoccupies each age in contradistinction to the other periods. According to him, ancient philosophy focused, above all else, on the question of *substance*, medieval philosophy on *being*, modern philosophy on the *idea* (in the Cartesian sense of private cognition or the Lockean sense of subjective sensory impression), and the postmodern age on the *sign*.

Now if such an assertion were just to be left standing there without an accompanying analysis, such a schema might seem merely a gimmick. But in Deely's hands it works because of the massive amount of documentation he brings to his analysis, the sheer scope of his erudition, and the delightful intelligence and verve of his writing. It works.[8] Of course, to be convinced of his thesis will come with a price, and I am not just referring to the size of the book or its hefty price tag of $110.[9] This large tome is, in fact, a liberal education in itself.

The argument, to put it as briefly as possible, works like this: Everyone knows that the pre-Socratics set themselves the task of finding the ultimate substrate of the world, whether it be earth, air, fire, water, whatever. Parmenides brought a real advance to this debate by showing that there was a further substrate that all of these various substances had in common, the sheer fact that they exist at all. In other words, the various substances of earth, air, fire, and water share in the ultimate substrate, being itself. But he got caught in his own too-literalistic view of being: As a substance itself, being simply is. But that means being cannot be caused, for if it were caused, that cause would first have to be, and so that cause would therefore have to partake of being, which means the cause could not bring into being what already was. Nor could being go out of existence, for that too would have to be caused by a being already in being. But if being cannot come to be nor go out of being, then the world of becoming cannot be either; for in the world of becoming beings are coming into existence and going out of existence all the time: That is what "becoming" means. This conclusion seems on the face of it absurd, which is why Heraclitus posited fire—the least substantial of all substances, so to speak—as the ultimate substance. For him only becoming "is," not being itself.

---

[8] As he rightly says, "Every general statement risks oversimplification, yet without general statements, made as responsibly as we can make them, there can be no intellectual advance. . . . Moreover, general statements, unlike categorical, universal assertions, are not falsified but illustrated by true exceptions" (Deely, *Four Ages of Understanding*, 217). In other words Deely is painting the history of philosophy Impressionistically. He blurs his focus to make some features stand out more clearly.

[9] However, the author dedicates his book to anyone who manages to read its every word, so that those who have never had a book dedicated to them can claim, by sheer dint of industry, the honor of finally becoming the dedicatee of a book!

Both Plato and Aristotle inherited these two prongs of a seemingly insoluble antinomy, and both chose—tellingly—a way out that still privileged the notion of substance. Plato gave the Ideas[10] a more substantial reality, whereas Aristotle stressed the reality of what he called (and doesn't this terminology say it all?) "substantial form."

St. Thomas Aquinas's great innovation on Aristotle was a renewed focus on Parmenidean being, but with the benefit of hindsight bequeathed to him by Aristotle. He brilliantly saw where Parmenides was right (being underlies all other substances), but *he denied that being itself is a substance*; rather, it is an *act*. Or as Deely says:

> What was original with Aquinas was the singling out of existence as such . . . as itself an effect to be accounted for as effect, and not simply presupposed to the action of various other types of causes explaining this or that formal effect in the order of finite beings. . . . So as an effect existence is a *universal effect*, the one effect without which there are no other effects.[11]

In other words, Parmenides got it wrong: Being is not just there, but is an effect—crucially a *created* effect—of Subsistent Being Itself, of Pure Act, whom all men call God.

But when Descartes turned away from this hard-won achievement and sought to prove the existence of God through "clear and distinct ideas" located in the indubitably existing human mind, the Thomistic view of being was lost. True, Descartes saw his methodological doubt as a liberation from a supposedly dead scholastic past, a liberation meant, among other things, to liberate science from the stultifying effects of a top-heavy scholasticized Aristotle, and such was the story modernity told of itself thereafter: Just as ancient philosophy saw itself as the liberation of philosophy from mythology, and medieval philosophy saw itself as the liberation of philosophy from theology, modernity tells the story of itself as the liberation of science from both theology and philosophy.[12]

---

10 "Ideas" here should not connote what Descartes and Locke meant, which for them were mental representations, not objective realities beyond the ephemeral world of becoming.

11 Deely, *Four Ages of Understanding*, 292–93, emphasis added.

12 "As one of the main achievements of the Latin Age can be said to be the establishment of the distinction and boundary between dogmas of religious orthodoxy and the doctrinal exercise of human understanding in theology as formally distinct from philosophy, so the modern period can be said to have achieved an establishment of the distinction and boundary between even philosophical doctrines and the formally distinct experimental exercise of understanding in the formation and testing of

But as the old saying goes, be careful what you wish for, since it might come true. Experimental science was no doubt liberated to study nature head-on, without the intermediary of authoritative texts, either from the classical or medieval past. Unfortunately, as history would later prove, only *science* was liberated, not philosophy.[13] For Descartes had liberated science from philosophy through his notion of clear and distinct ideas, which soon proved to be itself a very unclear and indistinct idea. For Descartes had assumed—and Benedict Spinoza, Gottfried Leibniz, John Locke, Bishop Berkeley, and David Hume all followed him in this same presupposition as well—that ideas (as items of subjective vision and logical analysis) were

hypotheses properly called 'scientific' in contrast to philosophy and theology alike, as well as to religious belief or faith. What in the time of Augustine was yet one grand mélange of reason, faith, and politics was gradually being sorted out in the intellectual culture of the developing civilization [of the Middle Ages] into distinct if compenetrating spheres of theology, philosophy, and science in the cognitive order and the distinct if compenetrating spheres of church (religious authority) and state (civil authority) in the practical order of the organization of everyday life. *Part and parcel of this separation of science from both philosophy and religion, however, was the larger rejection of the study of written texts as a proper way to acquire knowledge about the world.* The writings of Aristotle, which the religious authorities had met with condemnations and attempts to suppress as heretical when they were first introduced into the Latin West in the twelfth century, had been turned by the time of Galileo into an authority of almost intolerable dimensions. . . . By the time of Galileo, the commentary tradition had transformed itself into a series of independent works on special topics. . . . The founding fathers of modern philosophy showed their appreciation [of these commentaries] by deferring to the authority of Suarez on all questions of what the Latins taught in philosophy, while turning their own attention to the exciting new project of establishing the study of the world independently of an exegesis of texts, sacred as well as secular. It was the death of Latin scholasticism, for textual exegesis was the method by which scholasticism as a distinct historical form had been defined and created." Deely, *Four Ages of Understanding,* 498–500, emphasis added.

13 No wonder philosophy finds itself exhausted. Consider these assertions from Heidegger's aptly titled book, *The End of Philosophy*: "The decline of the truth of beings occurs necessarily, and indeed as the completion of metaphysics. The decline occurs through the collapse of the world characterized by metaphysics, and at the same time through the desolation of the earth stemming from metaphysics. . . . The decline has already taken place. The consequences of this occurrence are the events of world history in this century. They are merely the course of what has already ended" (Martin Heidegger, *The End of Philosophy,* trans. Joan Stambough [New York: Harper & Row, 1973], 86). Heidegger's notorious membership in the Nazi Party might make it seem that he is hardly one to talk; but his political follies actually point to the truth of the exhaustion he was talking about, as well as to the failure of his own philosophical response to the emptiness he diagnosed. Accurate diagnosis does not guarantee a genuinely therapeutic prognosis!

immediately present to the mind, and certainly more immediate than the objects "out there" *causing* the ideas.

But if external objects might well be not as clear to us as our mental representations of them are, still they have to be causally connected if solipsism is to be refuted. As Deely says, "All moderns hold the view that ideas as representations and the objects we directly experience are one and the same."[14] True, the modern philosophers radically differed on the ontological status of those objects of experience, and the inability of those allegedly clear and distinct ideas to give a clear and distinct idea of what those objects "really" are forced philosophy against the shoals of solipsism again and again, despite all its best intentions. As Deely wittily says:

> Students of philosophy today can hardly see or hear the word "philosophy" without associating it with people who wonder if they are really there and who can't tell whether they are dreaming or experiencing others. What these same students don't realize is that this seemingly inevitable association is actually a product mainly of modern philosophy, a consequence that is inevitable only in light of the modern doctrine that ideas are self-representing objects.[15]

Obviously something was going to have to give, for philosophy was starting to turn itself into a joke, a mockery to the very empirical science that it helped to midwife: "So came about one of history's great ironies: that modern empiricism, introduced to vindicate the views of the 'plain man of common sense' against the dream of Descartes, ended up, of all the philosophies in history, the one most removed from and contemptuous of 'common sense.'"[16]

One of the most fascinating features of postmodern philosophy is its refusal to take this bizarre outcome on its own terms. The scandal of solipsism is only a scandal if one accepts Descartes's terms of the debate. But this is just what the postmodern "linguistic turn" refuses to do. For language—whatever else it is—is a web of relations. As Deely says, "signification does

---

[14] Deely, *Four Ages of Understanding*, 501.

[15] Ibid., 528. One has only to think of the knotty problem of primary and secondary sense qualities to see the madness into which modern philosophy let itself fall: "The modern distinction between secondary and primary qualities begs the question of which qualities are the comparatively more fundamental by ignoring the role of sensation in experience and supposing straight off that we can say in advance what is real and what is not—precisely the point on which Berkeley called the early-modern bluff to devastating effect. Instead of showing what was real and what ideal, the modern approach gave away the game by having adopted a standpoint consistent with showing everything in sensation to be ideal." Ibid., 530.

[16] Ibid., 552.

not occur as an isolated act, but as something sustained by a vast network, a network that will prove as vast ultimately as the universe itself."[17] This is a point that no one could possibly be in a position to deny (for one thing, the denial would have to be expressed in a mutually understandable language), but unless the focus is set on language, the significance of signification will be lost, especially when the focus is instead on the epistemological obsessions of the moderns.[18]

Even a layman's glance at linguistics (above all, semiotics) would show up such a monadic view of human subjectivity for the absurdity it is. No doubt, what passes under the banner of "postmodernity" can include a lot of nonsense of its own; but following Deely, I am referring to those linguistic turns in philosophy first adumbrated by Charles Sanders Peirce and Ferdinand de Saussure and then brought to fruition by Ludwig Wittgenstein and Martin Heidegger (this lumping-together of these figures of course ignores the very substantial disagreements among them, just as the characterization of the other periods of philosophy must ignore the differences between Plato and Aristotle among the Greeks, between Thomas Aquinas and Duns Scotus among the medievals, and between Descartes and Kant, or Berkeley and Hume, among the moderns). What Deely really means by "postmodernity" is this:

> By postmodernism, or postmodernity, I do not mean that collection of quintessentially idealist writings which revel in deconstruction and Hermetic drift. I mean quite simply the development of the consequences for human thought of the demonstration that ideas as signs do not and cannot consist in being the direct objects of experience and apprehension, as the moderns assumed.[19]

But why do I call this trend not so much an *advance* as a *reversion*? Since when did the medievals focus on semiotics? Actually, they did (or at least the later ones), but the memory of that development was effaced by the Cartesian

---

[17] Ibid., 385.

[18] One has only to think of Kant in this context, who completely missed the connection between signification and mental representations: "Since every self-sufficient being," he says, "contains within itself the complete source of all its determinations, it is not necessary for its existence that it stand in relation to other things. Substances can therefore exist, and yet have no other relation to things, nor stand in any actual connection with them." Kant, "Thoughts on the True Estimation of Living Forces" (1747), in *Kant's Inaugural Dissertation and Early Writings on Space*, trans. John Handyside and Norman Kemp Smith (Chicago: Open Court Publishing Co., 1929), 8.

[19] Deely, *Four Ages of Understanding*, 691.

revolution. Consider this important line from Thomas Aquinas: *"By as much as an effect is posterior, so much the more does it have the rationale of a sign."*[20]

It is not the purpose of this article to interrogate medieval philosophy of language, merely to show how the recent linguistic turn of philosophy represents, at least to some extent, a resumption of late-medieval achievements that were lost when science was freed from the tutelage of philosophy in early modernity. According to Deely, "all thought takes place in signs," and this apothegm could well serve as the motto for postmodernity—just as *cogito, ergo sum* has done for modern philosophy; and *this postmodern motto is itself a medieval theme*. As Deely says, this postmodern mantra returns us

> to the fork in the road where the moderns began their trek down the way of ideas, and follows rather the way previously less taken, the way of signs. By taking up where Latin thought left off on this point, semiotic consciousness constitutes a definitive break with modernity and, at the same time, manifests a continuity to philosophical tradition and history, something that had been lost for three hundred years in the wake of Descartes.[21]

The narrative I have told here bears significant similarities with the story of philosophy also told by Etienne Gilson,[22] Jacques Maritain,[23] and (to some extent) Jacques Barzun.[24] But only Deely, I think, has seen the deep "elective

---

[20] Thomas Aquinas, *De veritate*, q. 4, ad 7, emphasis added: "Quanto effectus est posterior, tanto magis habet rationem signi."

[21] Deely, *Four Ages of Understanding*, 692.

[22] For example,: "Granted that a concept is but a particular sign that stands for several individuals, it does not follow that reality is exclusively individual; otherwise, how could several individuals be signified by the same sign? Granted that our knowledge of causality is but an association of ideas, it does not follow that effects are not intrinsically related to their causes; otherwise why should there be, in their succession, that regularity which makes our associations of ideas possible? Psychologism consists in demanding that psychology answer philosophical questions. Psychology is a science, psychologism is a sophism; it substitutes the definition for the defined, the description for the described, the map for the country. . . . Scientists themselves can afford such blunders; faith in science being what they live by, they have no need of reality." Etienne Gilson, *The Unity of Philosophical Experience* (San Francisco: Ignatius Press, 1937, 1999), 72.

[23] For example, "It is certainly moving to see a philosopher struggle to break the fetters of his own prejudices in the effort to re-establish certain rudimentary truths rejected by colleagues who are sunk even more deeply than he in the empiricist mire." Jacques Maritain, *Moral Philosophy: An Historical Survey of the Great Systems* (New York: Charles Scribner's Sons, 1964), 407.

[24] From one point of view, Barzun's marvelous history *From Dawn to Decadence* can be interpreted in the Deely manner, as showing the cultural exhaustion of contemporary

affinities" between late-medieval and early postmodern developments. More crucially, I think his perspective can throw new and unexpected light on the vexed question of the future of the Church in an industrial world grown increasingly secular and in a wider world characterized more and more by a "clash of civilizations."

So here, in conclusion, is my thesis in a nutshell: (1) the resolution of the different worldviews of Islam and the Christian civilizations of the West and the Orthodox East remains as the last one "unpaid bill" of the last millennium; (2) as an external reality, this as-yet unachieved resolution will force history (at least in the West) back upon the very medieval resources that the "story of modernity" had thought it had shucked; and (3) finally, internal philosophical and cultural trends within the West have forced (or will soon force) modern citizens of democratic civilizations back to reconsider medieval resources, precisely because of wrong turns taken by modernity when it abandoned the medieval synthesis. Secularization, in other words, is losing its steam and becoming increasingly jejune, unable to address external threats and internal contradictions. By way of summary, let us take each of these theses in turn.

1. *The unpaid bill of Islam.* Just consider the Iranian revolution of 1979 (when the pro-Western shah of Iran was overthrown and the government was assumed by an Islamic theocracy); the *fatwa* against the British postmodern (and, crucially, post-Muslim) novelist Salman Rushdie in 1984; the terrorist assaults on the cities of Rome, Paris, New York, and London in the 1990s, culminating in the wanton attacks against New York and Washington in September of 2001, against Madrid in 2003, and against London in 2005—I presume that it can now be taken as proven that there is an unpaid bill in arrears here.

But what is unique in this age-old contrast and conflict between Islam and the West is the worrisome fact that our secular and relativist

---

civilization (as the title itself implies), although Barzun does not explicitly hearken back to medieval models to point the way out (but he does salute American pragmatism, as does Deely—who goes even further and insists that Peirce completes the unfinished agenda of the late medievals). But Barzun does spot this one telling reversion to the Middle Ages: teacher-evaluations handed out at the end of each course! "[Professors'] authority, whether conferred by scholarship or the title itself, is now held in check by practices reminiscent of the Middle Ages. Students now give their teachers good or bad marks annually, and these are used in determining salary and promotion." Jacques Barzun, *From Dawn to Decadence: 500 Years of Western Cultural Life, 1500 to the Present* (New York: HarperCollins, 2000), 766.

value-system (in short a civil liberties-based liberalism) cannot seem to see the true contours of the contrast.[25]

---

25 There is no need to belabor the obvious here, except that because of secular relativism, the obvious is no longer obvious. So I shall rely here on the basics of the conflict as discussed by the lucid commentator, Victor Davis Hanson: "Failed states in the Middle East—autocratic, statist, unfree, intolerant of women and other religions—blame the West for their self-inflicted miseries. Sometimes they are theocratic, like the late Taliban or the current Iranian mullahs. But more often they are dictatorial like the Syrians, Pakistanis, Saudis, or Egyptians, who all, in varying degrees and in lieu of reform, have come to accommodations with the terrorists to shift popular anguish onto the West and the Jews.

"That is the Petri dish of Islamic fascism, an evil that will only disappear when the dictatorships that allow it or nourish it do as well. Whether the jihadists are in Iraq, the United States, or Europe, they all share a sick notion that someone else (the decadent Western oppressor and unbeliever) is responsible for their own poverty and backwardness rather than the fundamentalism, corruption, bias, and intolerance endemic to the Middle East. . . . To criticize Islamic fascism is supposedly to be unfair to Islam, so we allow on our own shores mullahs and madrassas to spread hatred and intolerance, as part of our illiberal acceptance of 'not offending Islam.'

"It is not that we don't believe in Western values as much as we don't even know what they are anymore. The London bombings [of July 7, 2005] were only a reification of what goes on daily with impunity blocks away in the mosques and Islamist schools of London. The enemy knows that and thrives on it. That refuge in religion is why imams shout that 'Islam doesn't condone such things'—even as bin Laden has become a folk hero on the Arab Street. Jihadists sense that even here at home more Americans are more concerned about a flushed Koran at Guantánamo Bay than five Americans fighting for the Iraqi jihadists or Taliban sympathizers in Lodi, California. . . .

"Finally Western self-loathing and guilt is essential: A fascist agenda of the jihadist—religious persecution, gender apartheid, racism, militarist autocracy, and xenophobia—all that must be embedded deeply within the postmodern landscape of the oppressed. A non-Christian and non-Western 'other' can mask his venom only through victim status, grafting his cause to the same exploited groups that seek from Western society benefaction and compensation. The jihadists expect that Westerners will slink out of the Middle East, allowing fascist fundamentalists to gain control of half the world's oil and thus buy enough weapons to blackmail their way back to the caliphate.

"Destroying Israel, killing Christians in Africa, running Westerners out of the Middle East, Pakistan, Indonesia, or Bali, all that is mere relish. In Europe, the goal for the unhinged is the creation of another al Andalus [the Arabic name for Spain under the Caliphate]; for the more calculating it is enough intimidation and terror to carve out zones of Muslim sanctuary, where millions can live parasite-like, within the largess of Western society, but without its bothersome liberal agenda of freedom and equality, in hopes of implanting the universal law of sharia. So here we are. Even though the killers profess revenge equally for Afghanistan (the so-called 'right' war), they expect Westerners to scream 'Iraq.' Even though such bombings are predicated on infiltration, careful

2. *External forces compelling the West to medieval reversions.* If my analysis is correct, then secular strategies for dealing with this world-wide challenge will prove unavailing; in fact, they will only exacerbate the problem, and perhaps lead to the demise of Western European civilization in the next fifty to one hundred years, as both Bernard Lewis and George Weigel are now warning us. A society that does not believe in itself cannot last. This dawning realization, I believe, constitutes the real significance of the election of Joseph Cardinal Ratzinger to become Pope Benedict XVI; for approximately a year before his election, he warned Europe in just these terms:

> Europe, precisely in this its hour of maximum success, seems to have become empty inside, paralyzed in a certain sense by a crisis in its circulatory system, a crisis that puts its life at risk, resorting, as it were, to transplants that cannot but eliminate its identity. To this interior failure of its fundamental spiritual powers corresponds the fact that, even ethnically, Europe appears to be on the way out. There is a strange lack of desire for a future. Children, who are the future, are seen as a threat for the present; the idea is that they take something away from our life. They are not felt as a hope, but rather as a limitation of the present. We are forced to make comparisons with the Roman Empire at the time of its decline: it still worked as a great historical framework, but in practice it was already living off those who would dissolve it, since it had no more vital energy.[26]

---

stealthy reconnaissance, and long sojourns within London, expect cries of anguish and worrying about the stereotyping of Middle Eastern males. Look for the same scripted crocodile tears and 'concern' from the Middle East's illegitimate leaders, even as much of the Islamic Street takes a secret delight in the daring of the jihadists, and the governments sense relief that the target was Westerners and not themselves. Anticipate Western leaders condemning the terrorists in the same breath as they call for 'eliminating poverty' and 'bringing them to justice'—as if the jihadists and their patrons are mere wayward and impoverished felons.

"In the short term, Bush and Blair will appear as islands in the storm amid an angry and anguished public. But as 7/7 fades, as did 9/11, expect them to become even more unpopular, as the voices of appeasement assure us that if they just go away, maybe so will the terrorists.

"It is our task, each of us according to our station, to speak the truth to all these falsehoods, and remember that we did not inherit a wonderful civilization just to lose it to the Dark Ages." Victor Davis Hanson, "The Same Old, Same Old . . ." *National Review Online,* July 8, 2005, www.nationalreview.com/hanson/hanson200507080811.asp.

[26] Joseph Cardinal Ratzinger, "If Europe Hates Itself," Avvenire, May 14, 2004, www.comunioneliberazione.org/articoli/eng/RatzAvv140504.htm.

Fine, but exactly how are we to recover that lost energy? At first, then-Cardinal Ratzinger's solution might sound quintessentially modern and Enlightened, for he insists that only a universal recognition of the universal rights of man will ensure that Europe can be saved from its own headlong rush into empty nihilism. But on closer examination, he shows that such rights can only be grounded in a view of the person as directly created by God and that all secular attempts to guard the sanctity of the person are bound to fail, as headlines almost daily remind us:

> Thus we are faced with the question: how are things to go ahead? In the violent turbulence of our time, is there a European identity that has a future and for which we can commit ourselves with our whole being? I am not prepared to enter into a detailed discussion on the future European Constitution. I would just like to indicate briefly the fundamental moral elements, which to my mind should not be missing, [above all] the "unconditionality" with which human dignity and human rights must be presented as values that precede any jurisdiction on the part of the State. These basic rights are not created by the legislator, nor conferred on the citizens, but rather exist in their own right, are always to be respected by the legislator, are given previously to him as values of a superior order. This validity of human dignity, prior to every political action and to every political decision, refers back ultimately to the Creator: only He can establish values that are founded on the essence of man and that are intangible. That there be values that cannot be manipulated by anyone is the real, true guarantee of our freedom and of man's greatness; Christian faith sees in this the mystery of the Creator and of the condition of the image of God that He conferred upon man.[27]

3. *Internal dynamics calling the West back to medieval resources.* The problem will be to get from here to there. The road will certainly be long and hard. Since I am no prophet, I cannot claim to know how the Church is to face the challenges ahead in the twenty-first century, nor am I particularly optimistic about the outcome.[28] But *if* there is to be a way out, it

---

27 Ibid. This quote disproves, in my opinion, the claim made by Tracey Rowland, Joseph Komonchak, and others, that Pope Benedict XVI is more Augustinian than Thomist in his approach. While there is a certain amount of mild (very mild) truth to the claim, it can be exaggerated to the point that it will end up distorting the pope's views on secularism, civil liberties, and his Thomistic defense of the sacredness of the human person.

28 In that regard, the one-sidedness of the Second Vatican Council is becoming increasingly evident, just as the one-sidedness of the First Vatican Council had become increasingly evident in the decades leading up to Vatican II. I am referring here not

will, I maintain only be found by returning to the resources of the medieval synthesis, modified by the stress made by Charles Sanders Peirce on the sign as the mode of "openness of inquiry" that is necessary for a community of committed thinkers to arrive at the truth.[29]

Openness, I think, is the key. In a way, the entire history of human thought can be gauged by using the mantra "openness to inquiry" as the hermeneutical key. From the Galileo affair, to the anti-Catholic pogroms during the French Revolution, to the concentration camps and Gulags of twentieth-century totalitarianism, and finally now to Muslim *fatwas* against novelists (I am referring above all to what Midge Decter tartly calls the "Rushdiad"), civilizations rise and fall by their commitment to openness, as Deely spends a very large tome explaining, especially in this marvelous passage:

> Such an affair [Deely is referring here to the Rushdiad] needs to be seen as a symptom of a profound philosophical and cultural problem rooted in the failure of some major currents of contemporary civilizations to recognize the coming of age of human understanding on its own ground of experience. . . . But above all should it be understood that what is at stake here is not an issue of "diversity", but a structural issue of the formation within civilization of institutions capable of sustaining inquiry, which is a matter quite distinct from psychological and sociological diversity and "individual preferences." . . . [But] there is not only the problem of [a self-styled Islamicist] faith seeking to dominate or suppress reason; there is also [he refers here to the case of the Soviet Union] the problem of reason seeking to eliminate even legitimate possibilities of belief. The thought-control mentality can operate through secular institutions no less than through religious ones, and this "secular inversion" of the mentality represents in the early twenty-first

---

just to the anodyne attitude taken by the council toward Islam, but also to its neglect of scholastic and medieval resources. According to Bernard Lonergan, "in the Second Vatican Council we find that the adjective 'Scholastic' had become a term of reproach. What was Scholastic certainly was not pastoral and had no place in a pastoral council; and so when a bishop wished to disparage effectively a certain type of proposal or amendment, he would tend to refer to it as 'Scholastic.'" Bernard Lonergan, S.J., "The Scope of Renewal," lecture delivered at Trinity College, University of Toronto, November 15, 1973, in *Collected Works of Bernard Lonergan: Philosophical and Theological Papers, 1965–1980*, ed. Robert C. Croken and Robert M. Doran (Toronto: University of Toronto Press, 2004), 283. Again, be careful what you wish for!

[29] For my own appreciation of Charles Sander Peirce as a quintessentially scholastic thinker, see "Discovering the American Aristotle," *First Things* 38 (1993): 24–33.

century a greater challenge to the delicate experiment of balancing or "separating" church and state than does the religious original which inspired the Enlightenment experiment to begin with.[30]

So here we are, "knocked down, but not defeated; taken for dead men, and yet we live." I think part of what makes me hearken to the Middle Ages for inspiration in these dark times is the fact that the Catholic Church at that time in history was actually (although perhaps unbeknownst to the medievals themselves) a rather exiguous presence on the stage of history. Seen on the world stage with the benefit of hindsight, medieval Catholicism did not represent a terribly large area of the globe. Yet unlike our times, it was a civilization confident of itself—at least before the plagues and wars of the fourteenth century began a process of despair, decline, and dissolution, resulting in the break-up of the unity of the Church and the later aggressions against the Christian religion in the name of secular reason. These aggressions continue to this very day.[31] But these desperate attacks by jejune secularists on the Church

---

30 Deely, *Four Ages of Understanding*, 191–92. In other words, militant secularism can be its own threat to free religious inquiry and practice. But, for now, Islamism is the much greater threat. For Deely, this is precisely what makes the Rushdiad so disturbing, for it draws on traditions that choked off intellectual inquiry in the House of Islam in some of its earliest stages: "In a word, the abdication in principle and in detail of all judgment to the religious interpreters of sacred texts, for which Islam as a civilization opted after the twelfth century, left no room for the development in its tradition of the way of thinking called in postmodern times 'pragmaticism.' . . . In 1150 the caliph at Baghdad had burned all the philosophical writings of Averroës under his power. In 1194 the emir at Seville did the same, adding a ban on the study of philosophy and urging his subjects to burn whatever books of philosophy they might find whenever they might find them. Among the Latins the recondite commentaries of Averroës on Aristotle were prized and influential. But among his own people he became a prophet without honor. Al-Ghazali had won a victory for which Islam continues to pay the price. For after him the civilization that had carried the torch of learning and speculation while Europe went dark, and which had passed that torch back to Europe at the cresting of the Latins' so-called dark age, itself went dark. The hermeneutics of Hadith and the Koran indulged that singular capacity of mind-dependent being to multiply relations upon relations in the justification of positions literally unjustifiable, just because they happened to occur in a context considered sacred by the people of the book and therefore to be adhered to literally, at whatever cost, by the device of an infinite semiosis in the service of closing, rather than opening, the mind." Ibid., 188–89.

31 Again the story is familiar enough that it only needs to be summarized, as was recently done in, of all places, the liberal *Tablet*: "One of the most obvious examples of this [secular aggressiveness] is Spain, where the socialist government, which came to power in the wake of the Madrid bombings, has clashed over and over

are also now, I maintain, in their last stages (which last stages will themselves result either in the disappearance of Western civilization in Europe or its revival based on a *new* rebirth of open inquiry based on medieval examples).

No wonder, then, that Alasdair McIntyre concluded his famous book *After Virtue* by looking forward to a new, but doubtlessly very different, St. Benedict!

again with the country's Catholic bishops. Plans to relax abortion laws, to legalize gay unions, and to reform religious education have all invoked the fury of the Spanish hierarchy. . . . Today a more aggressive mood appears to be developing, and not just in secular society, which, rather than providing a neutral place for the separation of matters temporal and spiritual, increasingly seems hostile to the Church. This aggression seems contagious." Catherine Pepinster, "The Darkening Continent," *Tablet* 259.8591 (2005): 14.

CHAPTER 12

What Use Is Kant for Theology?

GIOVANNI B. SALA, S.J.

A Body of Philosophical Thought that Must Be Taken into Account

THIS IS NOT the place to repeat the story of Kant's fortunes (and misfortunes) in the Catholic culture of the past two centuries. I will only recall that in the last years of Kant's life there was already a notable interest in this new philosophy in the Catholic regions of South Germany. One of its outstanding propagators was the Benedictine Maternus Reuss (1751–1798). But the superficiality of this first reception explains its brief duration. Better known and closer to us are the reception and transformation connected with the name of Joseph Maréchal, S.J. (1878–1944), who in 1926 published "Le thomisme devant la philosophie critique," the fifth of his *cahiers* on "Le point de départ de la métaphysique." In it the author proposed to overcome "Kant's agnosticism from his own principles."[1] From Maréchal's proposal a significant movement originated among the Neo-Scholastic thinkers of the time, particularly among German Jesuits, called "Transcendental Thomism." This current of thought was playing itself out by the end of the 1960s.

Kant's relevance for Catholic theology has no doubt been considerable, in the first place because in the last two centuries his thought has been a basic influence both on culture in general and on philosophy in particular. Now any influence on philosophy is in itself an influence on theology, since

---

Translated from the Italian by Dr. Donald E. Buzzelli, Washington, DC.

[1] J. Maréchal, *Le point de départ de la métaphysique,* Cahier V (Brussels: L'Edition Universelle, 1949), 34. One should not overlook the fact that, while Maréchal judged Kant's "transcendental" perspective to be legitimate and fruitful, he believed that Kant had ended in a kind of agnosticism.

theology cannot operate without calling upon a battery of conceptual and argumentative instruments that are philosophical in nature. Careful consideration of the present-day cultural situation will show that beneath conceptions, valuations, and practices that are commonly accepted today stand ideas advocated by Kant or derived from him, even when this dependence is not obvious.

Kant had proposed to bring into unity the two philosophical currents of his time: the rationalist-dogmatic current and the sensist-skeptical current. But in reality, his synthesis proved to be only an external juxtaposition, so that the two currents have been able to continue operating separately by dint of the error proper to each one. Theology's task is to mediate between the Christian faith and the culture in which the faithful live their faith. It is therefore necessary for theologians, to whom the Church's task of reflecting on the Christian faith falls most directly, to know the cultural elements that can favor the announcement and reception of the Gospel as well as the elements that tend to impede it.

The present article seeks to aid the theologian in performing this work of discernment with regard to the philosophy of Kant. To this end my examination will concentrate on his principal work, the *Critique of Pure Reason*, which I believe can be said to be much more admired (and feared) than studied and understood. The aura of almost superhuman profundity that surrounds it results in his positions sometimes being received in the Catholic camp as settled achievements, so that it is no longer possible to go back to an earlier position if one wants to keep up with progress in philosophy. Because of this kind of "prejudice" not a few Catholic theologians have abandoned the fonts of a rational tradition that let itself be challenged and at the same time aided by the superrational truth of Revelation. They have drawn instead from "broken cisterns" (Jer 2:13), whose value consists above all in conforming to the "spirit of the times," but which in my opinion do not stand up to a rational examination based on what our mind is and how it in fact operates. This criterion seems to be accepted by Kant himself. In his polemic against the Wolffian Johann August Eberhard, he wrote: "What is right in philosophy cannot and must not be learned from Leibniz [the great authority of the time!]; the criterion that is near to both the one and the other [of the disputants] is the human reason that is common to all; hence classical authors do not exist in philosophy."[2]

---

[2] I. Kant, *Über eine Entdeckung, nach der alle neue Kritik der reinen Vernunft durch eine ältere entbehrlich gemacht werden soll,* VIII, 218f. For the works of Kant, I refer to pages in the respective original editions (A or B), and/or in the Academy edition (Roman numerals indicate the volume). In citations without an indication of the work, but only with an A or B, the reference is to the *Critique of Pure Reason*.

A Halfway Turn to the Subject

Kant is considered to be the one who brought to completion the turn to the subject that has been present in "Western" culture since the Renaissance. What interests us here is this turn in the realm of philosophy, more precisely in the realm of the theory of knowledge and of reality. Kant speaks of it in the introduction to the *Critique of Pure Reason*, designating it by the term "transcendental knowledge": "I entitle *transcendental* all knowledge which is occupied not so much with objects as with the mode of our *knowledge of objects* insofar as this mode of knowledge is to be possible a priori" (B 25; Norman Kemp Smith translation; emphasis added). Kant wishes to know how we can (a) a priori (b) know objects. This is the problem that he had posed in his famous letter of February 21, 1772, to Marcus Herz: How can we explain the relation of conformity between a representation that is present in us before the action of things on our senses and the things themselves? The formulation of the problem in 1772 and the definition of transcendental knowledge in 1781 are comprehensible in terms of the rationalistic premise that Kant expressed in the same introduction, that is, that "we are in possession of certain modes of a priori knowledge" (B 3).[3] By virtue of these a priori components the theoretical sciences provide universal and necessary knowledge.

The turn to the subject within the theory of knowledge is thus an inquiry (which Kant calls transcendental)[4] into our "scientific" knowledge of objects. Here the subject is studied not directly in its subjectivity, but *from the point of view of the object*. Thus the true point of departure for Kant's inquiry is the object, the object of mathematics and the sciences of nature. From there Kant ascends to the subject and finds, or rather *postulates*, in it content-providing (object-related) elements that are meant to explain the properties that he believes characterize the object of science, that is, universality and necessity.

---

[3] This is not knowledge in the primary and full sense of the word (knowledge of objects as being), but the formal, object-related components of this knowledge of objects (that is, the formal components of the intuitions of the sensibility and the concepts of the understanding).

[4] In Kant the word "transcendental" takes on various meanings (cf. Vaihinger, *Kommentar zu Kants Kritik der reinen Vernunft* [1881], vol. 1, 467–74). But one can state that the basic meaning is (a) the a priori character of the formal, object-related elements present in the subject, (b) to these is attributed a *constitutive function* with regard to the object to be known. Cf. in the *Prolegomena* the note to A 204 = IV 373f., where the two terms "transcendental" and "transcendent" are clearly defined and distinguished (except for the fact that Kant often speaks of the "transcendental" when he wishes to indicate what is "transcendent" and thus unknowable).

The solution to the problem of "conformity" formulated in 1772 is that we can know objects a priori because we ourselves are the "author[s] [constructors] of the experience in which [the] objects are found" (B 127). Their being therefore consists in being represented or thought. We are not interested here in the phenomenalist and idealist outcome of Kant's position on knowledge and reality; rather, we are interested in bringing out the way Kant turned his attention not directly to the subject, but to the subject viewed in terms of the known object. As a result, any shortcomings or errors in his conception of the object lead inevitably to an insufficient or erroneous knowledge of what the subject is and what it does when it knows.

A real turn to the subject requires, rather, that the subject be considered directly in its subjectivity. And this is possible because in the performance of knowing (as also in the performance of willing) not only does the subject know objects (what it perceives through the senses, what it thinks, what it affirms) but also, in the same act by which it knows (or tends toward) an object, it is present to itself as subject, that is, as the one that experiences, understands, and judges. This presence of the subject to itself precisely as the subject of its own acting is called consciousness. It thus is possible to thematize this conscious activity and thereby explicitly recognize what the subject does when it knows: what operations it performs, on the basis of what norms immanent in the subject itself it performs them, and what the objects are of these operations. In this way we come to recognize what the capabilities are of the cognitive instrument that we humans possess.[5]

Before I set out to show how Kant conceives the way of knowing proper to man and thus how he conceives the reality known, I will briefly indicate the corresponding doctrine in St. Thomas (who in turn goes back to and goes beyond Aristotle).[6] The core of Thomas's position lies in the correlativity between the cognitive dynamism of our spirit and the reality that we can know: "Intellectus respicit suum obiectum secundum communem rationem entis, ed quod intellectus possibilis est 'quo est omnia fieri.' "[7]

The (possible) intellect can "become all things" in the sense that, while it has no innate knowledge, it is still capable of an intentional assimilation of all of reality. This capability extends to all sensible reality (the world) by virtue of the agent intellect's ability to probe that reality with its questions

---

[5] Cf. B. Lonergan, S.J., *Method in Theology* (London: Longman, Darton & Todd, 1972), 25.

[6] The immediate sources for my discussion are the following works by Bernard Lonergan, S.J., *Verbum: Word and Idea in Aquinas* (Toronto: University of Toronto Press, 1997); idem, *Insight. A Study of Human Understanding* (London: Longmans, Green and Co., 1957); idem, *Method in Theology.*

[7] *Summa theologiae* I, q. 79, a. 7, emphasis added.

(capax "omnia facere?"). These are intelligent questions—*quid sit*—directed toward understanding what has been given to us, ultimately, by the senses, and rational questions—*an sit*—directed toward ascertaining whether this understanding is correct. Now to assert a correlativity between an *unlimited* cognitive dynamism and all that toward which it tends is to recognize that being is intrinsically intelligible, just because it is known through answers to questions posed in search of the intelligible. *A fortiori,* this intrinsic intelligibility must be recognized in the reality that transcends the range of our experience. We ask about this reality because material reality proves not to have in itself a sufficient explanation for its own existence. Material reality thus appears not to be intelligible and thus not to be knowable through intelligent questions—which is contrafactual. Therefore there must be an absolutely intelligible reality that is able to explain its own existence as well as the existence of the world.

The Sensism of Kant's Position on Knowing and Being

It is precisely the recognition of the intrinsic intelligibility of being that is missing in Kant's philosophy, and this is because of his incorrect analysis of the cognitive process. Although Kant's theory of knowledge has an obscurity seldom equaled in the history of philosophical writing, its core is presented in the first two paragraphs of the "Transcendental Aesthetic" with a clarity that leaves nothing to be desired, all the more so since what is said there is repeated innumerable times throughout the book. Kant writes: "In whatever manner and by whatever means a mode of knowledge may relate to objects, *intuition* is that through which it is in immediate relation to them, and to which all thought as a means is directed" (A 19).

In other words, among the many and diverse acts that we perform when we know, intuition is the only one that is truly cognitive. This is because only *Anschauung* is able to reach cognitively the things to be known. If beyond that there is also a *Denken* (thinking), then this, as a "means," will be in the service of intuition. The introductory text of the "Transcendental Aesthetic" permits us to draw the following conclusion: There are several operations that contribute to the formation of human knowledge in its various characteristics, but if we ask: "What brings it about that knowledge is knowledge of an object, and therefore truly is knowledge?," we must answer: "Intuition." Whatever mediate relations the other operations are able to establish with the object, there must be one operation that is capable by its nature of throwing a bridge between the knower and the known, and that is intuition. Knowing is essentially a kind of "seeing"; knowing consists in the duality that is grounded in and at the same time overcome by the movement of extroversion characteristic of the senses, and in particular of sight. The appropriate category for indicating the thing known is therefore the word "object" *(ob-iectum, Gegen-stand)*, that which stands outside the knower and in front of him, not the word "being" (since the senses know nothing about what "is").

To speak of knowledge in terms of "seeing" is to employ a metaphor that is spontaneous and, in itself, innocent. But it becomes misleading when it is used in a philosophical context to *explain* how man succeeds in knowing reality. In that case one passes easily from analogy to explanation, not by examining (introspectively) the operations we perform when we know, but by *deducing* from the metaphor what an operation *must* be in order to really be knowing: It must be a grasping of what stands out there(!), and thus an instance of the movement of extroversion proper to seeing. The objection that this seeing is spiritual does not at all change what is constitutive of the metaphor, namely extroversion.

The formulation of the general principle that says what knowledge consists in is followed by the specification of that principle with regard to human knowledge: The intuition that we humans possess is only a sensible intuition. But if only that which affects our senses can become an object of our knowledge, then human knowledge is inescapably confined within the "limits of possible experience" (A 131, 644; B xxx, 423, etc.). We have here that sensist determination of the limits of human knowledge that is one of the goals of Kant's *Critique of Pure Reason.* Kant's gnoseology must be characterized as fundamentally sensist.

Connected with this sensist *Grenzbestimmung* is the irrational conception of reality: The reality that we can know is correlative to our *sensible* intuition. Kant also speaks of an intellectual intuition (which we do not have!) to which the reality of the "thing in itself" that is unknowable to us would be correlative. But how does Kant conceive this intellectual intuition that he denies to man and attributes only to God (cf. B 71)? He recognizes, in his way, an intelligence and a rationality in man. They are treated in the "Transcendental Analytic" and the "Transcendental Dialectic." If, therefore, he denies an intellectual intuition to man, this intuition cannot be an operation with the characters of intelligence and rationality. In fact man does exercise these operations, even according to Kant! Therefore he cannot conceive intellectual intuition except in terms of the extroversion proper to sense even if, as an intuition of the intellect, it is "spiritual." This means that man understands and reasons, but that with these operations he does not succeed in knowing reality, for the simple reason that reality is not intrinsically intelligible and rational. It is completely disparate from our intelligence.

What Kant writes at the opening of the first critique takes up—giving it the dignity of a philosophical doctrine—the naïve realism to which everyone is spontaneously inclined when he sets out to reflect on the obvious fact of knowledge. In Kant naïve realism becomes a sensist philosophical realism that he, in contrast to common sense, limits to the world of appearances because he recognizes that sense cannot know an object as being.

St. Thomas: The Concept Expresses an Intelligible Content Grasped by the Intellect

In the cognitive process, the stage of sensation is followed by the intellectual stage, in which two moments must be distinguished: the moment of understanding and conceiving, and the moment of judging. I now intend to examine the first moment, at the center of which, according to St. Thomas, lies the act of understanding. As we shall see, the act of understanding is missing in Kant. A concept is the internal expression *(verbum mentis)* of an intelligible content grasped by the intellect, (ultimately) in what the senses present to it. Without the act of understanding, the external word *(verbum oris)* that expresses the concept would be a *flatus vocis* devoid of meaning.

Precisely because it expresses an intelligibility, every human concept is universal, that is it can be realized in an indefinite number of cases. This does not hinder the use of universal concepts to refer to singular realities, for example, in the judgment "This is a book." Such a use is based on the fact that the universal concept was formed as the result of understanding a concrete thing. In the subsequent judgment we are able to attribute that concept to the same thing as indicated to us by sense. What is said here has general validity; that is, it is valid also in cases where the understanding from which the concept proceeds is no longer referred to immediate data of sense, but to concepts and items of knowledge already acquired, whose intelligibility is taken up into a more comprehensive act of understanding. One thinks of concepts like "progress," "economy," "happiness," and the like.

The *intelligere in sensibili* is the key to St. Thomas's theology, which is entirely addressed to understanding the saving truth revealed to us by God. The fundamental discovery by which Aristotle had succeeded in overcoming the impasse of the Platonic ideas was that *ta eide to noetikon en tois phantasmasi noei.*[8] This discovery holds first place among the philosophical instruments with which the medieval master was able to give systematic unity and speculative depth to the theological reflections of the Patristic Age and of the Scholastic doctors who followed.

---

[8] Aristotle, *De anima* III, 7: "understanding grasps the intelligibles in phantasms."

What is at issue, writes St. Thomas, is an act that is *proprius eius [animae humanae], perfecte demonstrans virtutem eius et naturam.*[9] It is so far from being esoteric that he repeatedly emphasizes its experienceable nature: *hoc quilibet in seipso experiri potest.*[10] Our internal experience shows that our understanding is always referred to data that were provided by sense, and then elaborated by the internal sense that is the imagination, in order to present the intellect with an appropriate image *(phantasma)* in which the intellect can grasp those relations among the various components that give intelligible unity to the material datum. On the basis of this experience St. Thomas states that our intellect is naturally *conversus ad phantasma,*[11] that is, oriented to the sensibility, without which it can understand nothing.

St. Thomas's gnoseology is closely connected to his conception of man. While he distinguishes clearly between body and soul, matter and spirit, he recognizes their unity in a single essence. This unity extends to their operations, so that the *modus intelligendi per conversionem ad phantasmata est animae naturalis, sicut et corpori uniri.*[12] His attention to the typically human act of understanding allowed him to recognize that all our concepts originate from the collaboration of sensibility and intelligence. Consequently they are empirical and intelligent at the same time.

Kant: A Gnoseology Without the *Intelligere*

Kant is very far from being a pure sensist. The text quoted above (A 19f), after describing the role of the *Anschauung,* continues by examining the intellect, to which is attributed the task of thinking, through its concepts, that which the senses have enabled us to know. Where do these concepts come from? The answer is found in the "Transcendental Analytic," where Kant presents a table of twelve a priori concepts ("categories") that for him constitute the natural endowment of the intellect.

By what right do we apply these concepts to the content of empirical intuition in order to know things? The answer to this question, which touches on the *articulus stantis et cadentis* of the *Critique of Pure Reason,* is given in the "Transcendental Deduction of the Pure Concepts of Understanding": Our a priori concepts have objective validity with regard to things because they themselves constitute those things in their formal and therefore knowable component (A 128f). This is a "subjective objectivity," as critics

---

[9] *ST* I, q. 88, a. 2, ad 3.
[10] *ST* I, q. 84, a. 7, emphasis added; q. 89, a. 1; q. 88, a. 1.
[11] *ST* I, q. 84, a. 7; q. 86, a. 1.
[12] *ST* I, q. 89, a. 1.

have objected from the beginning.[13] It is an objectivity based on the thetic (from *tithemi*: to put, construct) character of our knowledge that Kant emphasized with special vigor in the preface to the second edition (B ix–xviii), and in accordance with which he writes "the understanding . . . is itself the lawgiver of nature" (A 126), since with its categories it "prescribe[s] laws a priori to . . . nature" (B 163).

Kant stood in a long conceptualist tradition going back at least as far as Duns Scotus. Scotus had denied the Aristotelian *noein en tois phantasmasi,* replacing it with an unconscious process, a kind of metaphysical abstracting machine that produces a universal object. Only after this activity, according to him, does the properly cognitive psychic activity begin, with an act of intellection that knows, that is, that "looks at"(!), the universal object. From there the intellect can proceed to "understand," which for Scotus means grasping the nexus between concepts *(intelligere in conceptibus)*, not grasping relations and thus an intelligible unity in the content provided by sense. Now Kant dropped any such metaphysical theory of abstraction. Lacking the act of understanding that connects the intellect with the sensible ground of all our knowledge, he explained the growth and at the same time the universality of our knowledge by introducing his synthetic a priori judgments, and to support these he postulated twelve universal a priori concepts.[14]

But as to how these "categories" can confer true universality on the generalizations that—according to Kant (B 3f)—are our empirical concepts, he has not a word to say. On the other hand, Kant was not willing to accept completely an idealism that would have made useless the experimentation that is characteristic of the modern sciences of nature. Therefore he limited the thetic activity of the intellect to the "transcendental" or very general laws, while for "particular" (B 165) or "empirical" (A 127f) laws it is necessary to have recourse to experience. Now such an assertion means not only restricting, but totally eliminating the presupposition of the "Copernican revolution" that no knowledge that has a universal character can come from experience.[15]

---

[13] In the *Critique of Pure Reason* "objectivity" means validity for all men (cf. *Prolegomena,* A 78f = IV 298), since all are equipped with the same formal a priori elements. It does not mean correspondence to reality.

[14] Cf. Lonergan, *Verbum: Word and Idea in Aquinas,* 39.

[15] Cf. Friedrich Paulsen, *I. Kant. Sein Leben und seine Lehre* (Stuttgart: Frommans Verlag, 1920, 173 [originally published in 1898]; and G. Sala, "Ein experimentum crucis der Transzendentalphilosophie: Kants Erkenntnis des Besonderen," in *Kant, Lonergan und der christliche Glaube. Ausgewählte philosophische Beiträge zum 75. Geburtstag,* eds. von Ulrich Lehner and Ronald Tacelli (Nordhausen: Bautz, 2005), 203–20.

Vatican Council I Recovered the intelligere

Six centuries after St. Thomas, Vatican Council I left behind the heavy conceptualism that in the meantime had overlain the Anselmian-Augustinian-Thomist tradition, and retrieved the notion of understanding in a text that justly has been called the "magna charta" of theology.

> Reason, illustrated by faith, when it zealously, piously, and soberly seeks, attains with the help of God some understanding of the mysteries, and that a most profitable one [*aliquam . . . mysteriorum* intelligentiam[16] *eamque fructuosissimam*], not only from the analogy of those things which it knows naturally, but also from the connections of the mysteries among themselves and with the last end of man; nevertheless it is never capable of perceiving those mysteries in the way it does the truths that constitute its own proper object.[17]

"Understanding" in the Augustinian and Anselmian "crede ut *intelligas*" does not mean "Believe that you may judge," since belief already is a judgment. It does not mean "Believe that you may demonstrate," for the truths of faith do not admit human demonstration (in spite of ambiguities in the case of St. Anselm!). The Augustinian and Anselmian precept luminously means "Believe that you may understand," for the truths of faith make sense to a believer and they seem to be nonsense to an unbeliever.[18]

The understanding in question is not an understanding of a universal, as the conceptualists would have it. Indeed, the realities of the order of salvation are singular realities. It is not an understanding of something necessary.

---

[16] It is astonishing that both the Latin-German edition of *Denzinger* (Freiburg: Herder, 1991) and the Latin-Italian collection of the decrees of the ecumenical councils (Bologna: 1973, 1991) have translated the word *intelligere* as *Erkenntnis/conoscenza* [knowledge]. One wants to ask: Does not the theologian, like the simple believer, *already* know the mysteries hidden in God, through Revelation and faith? Human knowledge is a structure of several acts, each of which is not knowledge in the primary and proper sense but a component of it, so that each, taken by itself, is knowledge only in a "diminished" sense. Until one has seen this clearly, one cannot grasp exactly what the council intended when it denied to the human mind the capacity to *know* (*DS* 3015) the mysteries of God and attributed to it the capacity for some *understanding* of them. It belongs to the theologian to build up a systematic understanding that goes beyond the common-sense or "catechetical" understanding of the simple believer, without which the act of faith would have no meaning.

[17] *DS* 3016, in *The Sources of Catholic Dogma*, trans. Roy J. Deferrari, from the 30th ed. of Henry Denzinger's *Enchiridion Symbolorum* (Binghamton, NY: B. Herder, 1957), 447.

[18] Cf. Lonergan, *Method in Theology*, 335f.

Indeed, except for the mystery of the intimate life of God, the history of salvation is a history of contingent realities that follow from the wise plan of God to save humanity by sending down to earth his only begotten Son to perform the work of redemption and to institute the Church.

The ideal of science that St. Thomas had inherited from the Aristotelian tradition of the "Posterior Analytics" was that science is *de universalibus et necessariis.* Such a conception objectively could have been an obstacle to the work of the theologian. St. Thomas was able to overcome this obstacle only in his concrete practice, that is, by doing what the material he was dealing with in fact permitted him to do. In other words, between the strictly deductivist logical ideal for science in the "Posterior Analytics" and the theological practice of St. Thomas, there are notable adaptations, made *via facti,* without a revision in principle of the very ideal of science. Only later, with the birth of experimental science and then of the historical and interpretive sciences, was it possible to develop a conception of science that was more suited to the science of theology.

In conclusion, we can say that in St. Thomas the *intelligere* has an applicability to the work of the theologian that the Kantian gnoseology based on the a priori does not possess. It does not possess it because an a priori with a fixed content cannot be connected to the a posteriori data that the theologian must reflect on, nor, because of its fixed and immutable character, does it have the adaptability that characterizes understanding. "The mind," Lonergan writes, "is not just a factory with a set of fixed processes; rather it is a universal machine tool that erects all kinds of factories, keeps adjusting and improving them, and eventually scraps them in favor of radically new designs."[19] It would be interesting to know how the theologians who plead for a broader use of transcendental philosophy would manage the task of theology today with Kant's conceptual arsenal. This task requires examining the Christian tradition as it has passed through various cultures and then, on that basis, building up an understanding of the faith that, while it recovers what is normative (including concepts and terms!) in the Church's understanding of that faith, rethinks it and expresses it in *Denkformen* comprehensible to today's culture.

The *Intellectus Fidei* Is Neither True nor False

The *intellectus fidei* that the theologian seeks occurs at the level of the first operation of the mind. Though our mind is directed toward knowledge of reality, it reaches that knowledge only in the next operation, which is judgment. In the affirmation of judgment, the mind recognizes as true what it has understood in the data and expressed in the concept, and so arrives at a

---

[19] Lonergan, *Insight,* 406.

knowledge of reality. All cognitive processes directed at the reality proportioned to our way of knowing begin with pure data provided by experience, whereas the theologian's reflection begins with what he as a believer recognizes as true since he assents to Revelation. Thus he begins with knowledge of supernatural reality. He has no need to pass from what he has understood of Revelation to a judgment about its truth, since he is already in the truth and thus in the knowledge of (supernatural) reality.[20]

The theologian's task is not to arrive at knowledge of the truths of faith, but rather to understand them for the sake of humanly announcing and appropriating them in the context of diverse and changing cultures. Such understanding, in itself, is neither true nor false. The question, rather, is to what extent it is suitable for the appropriation of the divine mysteries in relation to a certain culture. That depends on several factors: (a) on the created reality taken as a point of departure for the analogical understanding of revealed reality; (b) on the context of revealed truths to which, as Vatican I says (*DS* 3016), a certain mystery is referred in order to be understood through those relations; and (c) on the cultural context in which the theologian works and in service to which he reflects on Revelation. The degree of suitability of a certain understanding may in fact turn out to be unsuitability. This happens primarily when the proposed *intellectus fidei*, either in itself or in its logical consequences, contradicts a revealed truth. Not all philosophical and rational tools are suitable for mediating an understanding of faith. For example, a philosophical system would be unsuitable if it had human knowledge inescapably confined to the world of sense experience and declared it unable to arrive at truth in the sense of correspondence to what "is."

What has been said about the *intellectus fidei* is based on a very precise premise, namely on the distinction between understanding and judging. Now it is precisely this distinction, as we shall see below, that Kant ignored.

Theology and History

One of the greatest challenges that theology has had to face since the rise of historical consciousness in recent centuries is the integration of history into theological reflection. This historical consciousness in turn is connected to the birth and development of the historical-interpretive human sciences. These investigate the human world, the world that (a) man is creating with meanings originating from his intelligent and rational dynamism that are

---

[20] A judgment about the "truth" of the *intellectus fidei* is not even possible, since it would concern truths that exceed our minds and that we therefore can know only by the authority of God who has revealed them. Cf. *DS* 3008.

implemented in corresponding actions, institutions, and objects, and that (b) is motivated by the values that the same dynamism in its moral dimension discovers and pursues.

The human world has a community dimension, where communities result from a multiplicity of individuals sharing a common field of experience, having common or complementary understandings, having judgments shared by all, and pursuing common goals. This human world also has a historical dimension, since experiences, meanings, knowledge, and values develop and change, but also decline and cease to be shared. The achievements of the human world in turn lay down the conditions that will influence the subsequent community, which will carry forward its meanings and values, but will also correct and enrich them, or else impoverish and disfigure them until one culture is exhausted and makes way for another.

But the world men live in is not merely human. God too has come to take part in it through his Revelation and his economy of salvation. The task of theology is to work out an understanding of the saving truth so that it can be communicated to men at all times and in all cultures. Such a truth is essentially historical, since it was revealed by God at a certain time and in a certain culture, was concluded with the final and definitive word of Jesus Christ, and is transmitted by the Church, within various cultures, in a tradition that stands under the guidance of the Holy Spirit.

The truth, and thus the definitiveness, of the Christian faith, together with the historical growth in our understanding of it,[21] imposes on the theologian the question (a) how it has been possible to have an evolution in Christian doctrine, which has grown in its understanding of the truth, while at the same time changes have occurred in the concepts by which this growing understanding has been expressed; and (b) how the theologian can recover the objective meaning of expressions from the past in order to take this meaning into account in understanding the truths that he has the task of elaborating.

In his theory of knowledge St. Thomas did not confront the problem of the exegesis of texts belonging to different cultures, or the more general problem of historical knowledge. But what I quoted at the beginning of the present essay, namely the correlation that he pointed out between the dynamism of our spirit and our knowledge of being, contains in germ the solution to the problem of how it is possible to know objectively the meanings, truths, and values of other times and cultures.

Indeed, the transcendental notions of our intentional dynamism that permits us to know being through a true judgment, also allow us to recover the intelligibilities, the truths, and the values that have been realized in the

---

[21] *DS* 3020; *Lumen Gentium,* no. 12; *Dei Verbum,* no. 8b.

human world throughout the centuries. As intelligent, the intentional dynamism anticipates every possible intelligible; as rational it anticipates all truth and all being; as moral it anticipates all good as an object of the will. The intentionality of the human spirit with its transcendental, that is, all-inclusive, notions is the normative invariant that is the source of all the categorial and variable elements that enter into the various cultures.

Intentionality provides the "universal viewpoint" that embraces every particular viewpoint, all the *Denkformen* that characterize individuals and cultures. This is why it is possible, in principle—if sufficient data on the past exist—to reconstruct the peculiar character of an epoch or culture, within which its writings and monuments have their specific meaning. At least up to a certain point, it is possible to reconstruct the dialectical chain of events that gave birth to a certain constellation of meanings, truths, and values, and in this way to arrive at an understanding of them. The analysis of intentionality is able to indicate to the theologian the means that he has at his disposal for integrating modern historical consciousness with a "traditional" truth that has reached him in a historical series of expressions and implementations.

It is just this analysis that is missing in Kant. His theory of knowledge was developed largely by a regressive argument that moves from the *object* of natural science to the conditions of its possibility in the subject. It thus fails to take into account the performance of knowing and willing in its various configurations (*one* of which is experimental science) and also in its transcultural structure. Where Kant believes he has reached the highest point on which depends all the synthetic activity of the intuition and the intellect (B 134), the "transcendental apperception" (A 106f), he still can only note the "obscurity in matters which are by their very nature deeply veiled" (A 88).

The *Denken* that Kant confined to twelve forms, fixed once and for all, proves inadequate for explaining the manifold ways in which humans know and the many and diverse configurations of human life and culture, as well as for grounding an objective knowledge of history. Not a few students have noted the rigid and anti-historical character of a transcendental philosophy of the Kantian type, and have sought to overcome it within a gnoseology and metaphysics that maintain the basis laid down by Kant.

Richard Schaeffler, an author who repeatedly has spoken in favor of utilizing the transcendental philosophy in Catholic theology, has advanced the possibility of connecting transcendental reflection to historical reflection. To this end he proposes that Kant's transcendental structures be considered not as ultimate foundations of our cognitive abilities, but as "phenomena that themselves need to be explained."[22] They would be conceived as "historical-

---

22 R. Schaeffler, *Glaubensreflexion und Wissenschaftslehre. Thesen zur Wissenschaftstheorie und Wissenschaftsgeschichte der Theologie* (Freiburg i.B.: Herder, 1980), 122.

contingent quantities."[23] Schaeffler's considerations move in a direction that has already been pointed out by Kantians of the strict observance.[24] But if "the structures of consciousness and the forms of the relation with objects" that guarantee the subjective-objectivity of our knowledge (that is, its universality) are in turn thought of as "subjected to historical change,"[25] the result is a radicalization of Kant's relativistic conception. The guarantors of the truth of the "appearances" would themselves be variable.

Judgment and the Christian Faith

Kant: Judgment Is a Synthesis of Subject and Predicate

In judgment, Kant writes, "the relation of a subject to the predicate is thought" (A 6). His attention is especially concentrated on synthetic a priori judgments, the real theme of the *Critique of Pure Reason*, since they are the basis of the universal and necessary knowledge that characterizes every science.

What interests us in our study of the possible use of the *Critique of Pure Reason* in theology is that for Kant judgment is essentially a synthesis of subject and predicate. Consequently, at the beginning of the "Analytic of Concepts," in the section titled "The Logical Employment of the Understanding" (A 67–69), we find a series of variations on the thesis, which derives from the reduction of judgment to synthesis, that thinking and judging are the same activity. "The only use which the understanding can make of . . . concepts is to judge by means of them" (A 68). "All judgments are functions of unity [synthesis!] among our representations" (A 69). And again, "We can reduce all acts of the understanding to judgments, and the *understanding* may therefore be represented as a *faculty of judgment*. For, as stated above, the understanding is a *faculty of thought*. Thought is knowledge by means of concepts" (A 69).

On the basis of these affirmations, and from the fact that with the "Transcendental Aesthetic" (sense knowledge) and the "Transcendental Analytic" (inquiry into the a priori concepts and the principles based on them) Kant's theory of knowledge is complete, Vaihinger's criticism seems justified when he reproaches Kant for having blurred the difference between concept and judgment.[26] This is confirmed by the first two pages of the "Transcendental

---

23 Ibid., 126.

24 Gottfried Martin, *Immanuel Kant. Ontologie und Wissenschaftstheorie* (Cologne: Kölner Universitätsverlag 1960), 97.

25 R. Schaeffler, *Einführung in die Geschichtsphilosophie* (Darmstadt: Wissenschaftliche Buchgesellschaft, 1973), 217.

26 Vaihinger, *Kommentar zu Kants Kritik der reinen Vernunft*, vol. 1, 352.

Analytic," which in various wordings repeat the thesis that "intuition and concepts constitute . . . the elements of all our knowledge" (A 50).

At the beginning of the third part of the *Critique of Pure Reason*, the "Dialectic," Kant discusses at length an element of our cognitive intentionality that he has not spoken of at all in working out his theory of knowledge in the first two parts. This is our tendency toward the unconditioned (A 307, where the term appears for the first time). Kant connects this tendency to the syllogism, which he considers the characteristic process of reason. By the syllogism reason moves from a conditioned to its condition, and from this to the condition of the condition, et cetera, without the mind ever arriving in this way at a truly unconditioned reality.

But by virtue of this tendency toward the unconditioned our knowledge, which is the result of the synthesis of the object of sense and the concept of the understanding, can have order conferred on it by the mind's subordinating one item of knowledge to another. This is the "regulative use" of the idea of the unconditioned, which is our mind's a priori.[27] Believing that our mind can reach a truly unconditioned reality is the "natural and inevitable" illusion that afflicts our mind and that Kant intends to expose in the "Dialectic."[28]

Later, in the preface to the second edition of the *Critique of Pure Reason*, Kant speaks still more incisively of the mind's dynamism toward the unconditioned or absolute: "For what necessarily forces us to transcend the limits of experience and of all appearances is the *unconditioned*, which reason, by necessity and by right, demands . . . to complete the series of conditions" (B xx). But here too the unconditioned is declared unreachable; it is to be met with "in things . . . only so far as we do not know them" (ibid.). Kant is entirely consistent with his thesis that our knowledge cannot reach something that "is," where the "is" does not have any conditions, when he states that no unconditioned element whatever enters into the formation of our knowledge. If judgment is only a synthesis of subject and predicate, then the concept of the understanding will only be able to confer intelligibility on what the sensibility has known. Now sense obviously is not able to know anything absolute and real.

---

[27] Kant speaks of three transcendental ideas of reason—the I, the world, and God—that represent the three directions in which the systematization of our knowledge proceeds. He derives them from the three forms of the syllogism: the categorical, the hypothetical, and the disjunctive. But this is only an artifice for obtaining three ideas that can be used to criticize *metaphysica specialis* in its three parts: psychology, cosmology, and theology. The real a priori of reason is the idea of the unconditioned, of which Kant writes in a "Reflection": "The unconditioned is the only theoretical idea of reason" (R 6414: XVIII, 709).

[28] *Critique of Pure Reason*, A 297.

Judgment in St. Thomas

The conception of judgment as a synthesis of subject and predicate, which corresponds to the grammatical form in which a judgment is expressed, goes back to Plato and Aristotle. This inadequate definition of judgment was then taken up by medieval Scholasticism, for which judgment is a *compositio* (the affirmative judgment) or a *divisio* (the negative judgment). St. Thomas regularly uses this definition.

There is some value in such a characterization in that there indeed is an element of synthesis in the judgment. For example, in the judgment "Peter is prudent," prudence is thought in relation to the subject as its property. This synthesis arises from a development of understanding and consists in the fact that two acts of understanding (what I intend by the subject "Peter" and what I intend by the predicate "prudent") have been fused into a single, more comprehensive act of understanding. But until this synthesis is unconditionally affirmed, there is lacking that verification of the synthesis that enables it to refer to an existing object.[29]

St. Thomas's use of traditional terminology obscures to some extent the explicit analysis that he makes in some places of the *proprium* of the judgment. He speaks of a *via iudicii* to indicate the reflective moment of the cognitive process, the mind's critical return to sense-experience and to naturally known principles, so as to judge the correctness of its intellectual synthesis.[30] By virtue of the unconditioned affirmation of what at first was only thought, there emerges truth, that is, knowledge of the correspondence of the mental synthesis to reality. To indicate this characteristic element of the judgment, St. Thomas sometimes uses the term *assensus*.[31]

---

[29] Judgment adds to the synthesis borrowed from the level of understanding the *est* of affirmation. It is just this act of positing the synthesis intentionally that makes the judgment the third and final phase of the cognitive process, a phase distinct from understanding-conceiving.

[30] Cf. *ST* I, q. 79, aa. 8 and 12. Lonergan in *Insight* has specified further what this reflective-critical moment in the structure of our knowledge consists in. It is a return to the direct understanding in order to examine whether the connection it has established between the content of experience and the concept actually exists. The question, in other words, is whether all the data relevant to the understanding that is expressed in the concept actually are present in the object of sense, and whether there are other data that have not been taken into consideration that might bring into question the correctness of that understanding. This verification of the conditions of the conditioned (the thought intelligible) provides the unconditioned element (the "virtually unconditioned") that is the basis of the unconditioned affirmation of the judgment. Through the *intentional being* of the affirmation we know the *real being* of things. Cf. *ST* I, q. 3, a. 4, ad 2; *Summa contra Gentiles* I, 12, 78.

[31] *De veritate,* q. 14, a. 1; *De malo,* q. 6, a. 1, ad 14.

The Realism of the Act of Faith

The judgment of faith has characteristics that distinguish it from judgments immanently generated by man's intelligence and rationality: It begins with true knowledge revealed by God and is justified by God's authority. Common to both types of judgment is that through them we cognitively gain access to reality, but faith accesses the supernatural while the other accesses the natural reality. In this sense I speak of a realism of the judgment. The reflections that follow are intended to show that in Western culture, the culture that has carried on the heritage of classical Greece, the realism of the Christian faith has contributed to the explicit recognition within philosophy of the thesis *ens iudicio vero cognoscitur.* This thesis is the core of "critical realism," the realism that is based on the introspective examination of the operations that we perform when we know.[32]

Study of the long debate that led from the New Testament to the dogma of Nicea concerning the consubstantiality of the Son with the Father can help us recognize the influence of the Christian faith in clarifying the philosophical problem of our mind's ability to know reality. According to Athanasius, the council fathers wanted to say with the term "consubstantial" that *"eadem de Filio quae de Patre dicuntur, Patris excepto nomine."*[33] This means that (a) we know what or who God is through true predications about God—whether they are predicates known by reason or predicates known through Revelation; (b) these predicates are to be attributed to the Son as well as to the Father; and (c) exception is to be made for "Father" and "Son," since the latter is to be attributed only to Jesus while the former is attributed to the divine person from whom the Son proceeds. The "rule" of Athanasius is therefore a proposition about propositions: All propositions that are true of the Father are also true of the Son, except that the Father is the Father and not the Son, and the Son is the Son and not the Father. The reality of the Father and of the Son, together with their consubstantiality, is disclosed to the believer in an act of faith that conforms to this rule. Although the rule is formulated directly with regard to the dogma of Nicea, it is correspondingly valid for every other dogma, because a dogma is always a true proposition to which the believer gives his assent.

---

[32] On the subject of this section cf. B. Lonergan, *De Deo Trino.,* I. Pars, *Dogmatica* (Roma: Gregorian University Press, 1964), 104–12; idem, "The Origins of Christian Realism" (1961), in *Philosophical and Theological Papers: 1958–1964,* vol. 6 of *Collected Works of Bernard Lonergan* (1996), 80–93. Different from but with the same title as the latter is the lecture of 1972 in *A Second Collection* (London: Darton, Longman & Todd, 1974), 239–61; cf. also "The Dehellenization of Dogma," in ibid., 11–31.

[33] Athanasius, "Oratio tertia contra Arianos," *MG* 26, 329 A.

The dogma of Nicea, far from having been a "Hellenization" of Revelation, actually signals the overcoming of Hellenism. In particular, it overcame a Stoic ontology compromised by materialism and the Platonic ontology of the ideas, both of which had shown themselves inadequate for mediating an understanding of the revealed mystery. This is not to deny, however, that the Hellenistic context contributed to the formulation of the Nicene faith. The Greek miracle consisted in the discovery of the propositional nature of truth, so that to assent to the truth of a proposition is to know the reality signified by that proposition. By this discovery Greek thought was able to move from myth to logos.

We saw above that the philosophical thought employed by the medieval theologians contains a serious ambiguity regarding the nature of judgment. It is serious since the act of faith that Revelation requires cannot be understood as adding to a subject the further intelligibility of a predicate that our mind has grasped by examining the very nature of the subject. The revealed mysteries are not accessible to our understanding. Rather, the judgment of Christian faith (for example, "Jesus is God") turns out to consist in an *affirmation*, in a "yes" with respect to a synthesis that we know only from Revelation and that we can understand only remotely by an analogy, which is insufficient for judgment.

It is not unreasonable to suppose that the philosophical conception implied in the act of faith led philosophical reflection to recognize the *proprium* of judgment, namely that it goes beyond thinking by means of a concepts. This seems even more plausible if one notes that we spontaneously consider that we know something whenever we pronounce the yes of judgment in connection with our natural beliefs, which are an unrenounceable part of our cognitive heritage. Certainly a difference remains between the act of supernatural faith and a natural belief. The latter kind of knowledge, and not the knowledge of supernatural faith, is in principle reachable by a cognitive process that one can carry out personally. But in spite of this difference, both kinds of knowledge come under the basic epistemological principle that only in affirmation does one know reality.

The *est* of the judgment of faith led Western thought to the philosophy of being. It thus led to an overcoming of the most serious limitation of Greek philosophy, the essentialism of a theory of knowledge based, in Plato, on the ideas as participations in the highest intelligibles and, in Aristotle, on the judgment as a synthesis of intelligibles.

The realism of the act of faith is a *dogmatic* realism in the sense that it is not the result of philosophical reflection on truth as mediating our knowledge of reality; rather, it is implied in the act of accepting the word revealed by God and announced by the Church. It is an *implicit* realism in that believers did not know about the mediation that intentional being performs with regard to real being. Therefore they did not pose the philosophical question of realism, nor did they deduce from their assent to the truth the epistemological and metaphysical consequences that objectively derive from that assent.

It has been the task of philosophical reflection to accept the challenge of the Word of God and the pronouncements of the Church and work out a theory of knowledge and of being that is consonant with the assent of faith. The believer rightly considers that this assent can and should stand up to his own reason since "the truth can never contradict the truth" (*DS* 3017). "Critical realism" on the one hand corresponds to the requirements of a faith (a) that has access to (supernatural) reality by way of assent to revealed truth, and (b) by which created reality becomes intelligible because it has come from the creative act of God, who is intelligibility itself. On the other hand, (c) critical realism is directly based on an inquiry that thematizes the performance of knowing in common sense, in the sciences of nature, and in the human sciences. Each of these involves a knowledge in which an unlimited intelligent and rational intentionality is at work. This intentionality is indeed turned to the senses, but it is also able to go beyond the range of the sensibility so as to ask about a transcendent being and answer that question positively.

Critical realism leaves behind both the sensist realism of the infrastructure of the *Critique of Pure Reason* and the transcendental idealism of its superstructure. It takes into account both the senses privileged by the former and the concepts recognized by the latter. It goes beyond both to the unconditioned affirmation of the judgment, in which sense and intellect bring their contribution to a knowledge of what is singular, intelligible, and existent.

Conclusion

The *Critique of Pure Reason*'s analysis of the human subject as a knower is seriously deficient.

1. The sensibility is elevated to the sole properly cognitive activity: It alone is in immediate relation with the reality to be known. From this follows (a) the merely phenomenal character of what man knows. Subsequent intellectual activity is completely in the service of this knowledge of "appearances"; (b) the exclusion of any knowledge beyond the range of the senses.

2. The understanding is capable only of adding to sense knowledge the intelligibility of the twelve a priori concepts. Kant's gnoseology misses the typical human act of grasping an intelligibility in the sensible—the

act by which the theologian can develop an (analogical) understanding of revealed truths.

3. Reason's tending toward the unconditioned does not have any constitutive role in the genesis of our knowledge of reality, but only a regulative and systematizing role with regard to knowledge already reached through the synthesis of intuition and concept. The judgment is missing, in the sense of an absolute affirmation of what, at first, is only thought. Consequently the presupposition is missing for the act of faith that is an unconditioned affirmation of the revealed truth. Moreover, the absence of the act of understanding and the act of affirming does not allow any explanation of how it is possible to reconcile growth in our understanding of the faith with the definitiveness and unsurpassability of the truth believed.

Appendix: Kant's Ethics and Moral Theology

What use is Kant's ethics ("Foundations of the Metaphysics of Morals" and "Critique of Practical Reason") for moral theology? I will limit myself to simple assertions.[34] There are two fundamental characteristics of Kant's ethics.

First, it is a merely formal ethics: The criterion that governs moral action is the universality of the maxim to which one's actions conform. Thereby, in addition to the impossibility of deducing concrete norms from a formal principle, Kant has eliminated the object of the action. Now it is precisely on this object, from the perspective of the person who knows and values it, that the primary and fundamental moral specification of an action depends.[35] In Kant an adequate theory of action is almost completely lacking.

Second, it is an ethics that is autonomous in an absolute sense. For Kant autonomy is the foundation, measure, and end of morality, so that he can write: "A categorical imperative . . . commands neither more nor less than this very autonomy."[36] In Kant's ethics there is a clear tendency to divinize man as a moral being, which in the *Opus Postumum* sometimes finds explicit formulation: "God is the practico-moral reason that is legislator to itself" (XXI 145; also 149).

Kant believed that with his moral proof or postulate he had recovered the knowledge of God that he had denied to speculative reason (B xxx). But in reality, that is impossible on the basis of his formalistic and autonomous

---

[34] For a development of what I only hint at here cf. G. Sala, *Kants "Kritik der praktischen Vernunft". Ein Kommentar* (Darmstadt: Wissenschaftliche Buchgesellschaft, 2004).

[35] Cf. Pope John Paul II, *Veritatis Splendor,* no. 78.

[36] "Foundations of the Metaphysics of Morals," A88 (cf. footnote 2).

conception of morality. Because of these premises his proof results in a pen-dulum movement between a morality that is meaningful (in that it leads to a goal that is adequate for good behavior) but no longer autonomous, and a morality that is autonomous but absurd (in that it would lead to nothing),[37] the pendulum cannot reach a definitive position. Moreover, it should be noted that the "faith" in God to which the proof leads is "no objective teach-ing as to the reality" of God,[38] but means "to act . . . as though *[als ob]* such a world-government were real."[39]

Kant's morality is marked by a profound dualism between practical rea-son and the sensible and spiritual dynamisms (inclinations) with which man is endowed.[40] These are not integrated into the subject that acts under the guidance of reason, but are considered principles of immoral action. Hence the rigorism of Kantian ethics.

---

[37] Cf. "Critique of Judgment," B 428: "Nichtigkeit."

[38] "What real progress has metaphysics made in Germany since the time of Leibniz and Wolff?" XX 298, *The Cambridge Edition of the Works of Immanuel Kant, Theo-retical Philosophy after 1781* (Cambridge: Cambridge University Press, 2002), 387.

[39] "On a Recently Prominent Superior Tone in Philosophy," VIII 397 (ibid., 438).

[40] Cf., to the contrary, St. Thomas, for whom the *inclinationes naturales* are part of the *lex naturalis*: *ST* I–II, q. 91, a. 2; q. 94, a. 2.

CHAPTER 13

A Speyrian Anthropology:
The Expansion of Human Liberty
to the "Measure" of the Divine

MICHELE M. SCHUMACHER

THE REASONABLENESS of the Christian faith does not lessen the apparent contradictions contained therein, as expressed in the Lord's invitation to life precisely by sacrificing one's life (Mk 8:34–35). These contradictions cannot be obliterated, for the mystery expressed thereby is redemptive revelation for us today, just as certainly as it was for the disciples to whom these words were first addressed. As the Lord did not spare them the contradictions and difficulties contained in his words, neither does he spare us. Instead, we receive "the whole burden with which they [and we] must come to terms. 'This is a hard saying.' 'Let him understand it who can.'" Indeed, "the Lord accommodates his teaching as little as possible to mankind, so that those who follow him will not have the impression that they are equal to it."[1]

The Christian challenge, as Father Matthew Lamb has demonstrated throughout his fruitful theological mission, is not to measure up, as it were, but simply to follow; not to trust in one's own goodness, but in the power of grace; not to control, but simply to surrender—not in defeat, but in love— and thus ultimately to live one's freedom as obedience in imitation of Christ himself. In an effort to better understand this challenge and the paradox that it entails, this essay will draw upon the profound mystical and biblically inspired insights of a figure of keen interest to Father Lamb and one whose own works demonstrate a common origin with his (namely, the inspiration that arises out of prayer): the Swiss physician and mystic Adrienne von Speyr (1902–67), who is perhaps best known for her extraordinary influence upon

I wish to express my gratitude to Father Jacques Servais for his very helpful suggestions and to the National Swiss Scientific Foundation for their generous financial support.

[1] Adrienne von Speyr, *The Christian State of Life* (San Francisco: Ignatius Press, 1986), 182. Unless otherwise specified, all references are to Adrienne's works.

the renowned theologian Hans Urs von Balthasar. Because Adrienne's insights are scattered in an unsystematic manner throughout her very large corpus of more than sixty volumes of mystical theology, the task of bringing together her thoughts on any particular theme are a rather daunting one, which may explain why so few students of Balthasar explicitly treat Adrienne,[2] despite his insistence upon the unity of their theological missions.[3]

---

[2] There are notable exceptions. See, for example, the authors contributing to the Roman colloquium (September 27–29, 1985) on Adrienne's ecclesial mission, *Adrienne von Speyr und ihre kirchliche Sendung* (Einsiedeln: Johannes Verlag, 1986), many of whom are well-respected disciples of Balthasar, including Angelo Scola, Antonio Sicari, Georges Chantraine, Marc Ouellet, and Joseph Fessio. Both Elio Guerriero and Raymond Gawronski dedicate an entire chapter to Adrienne in their respective works on Balthasar. See Guerriero's *Hans Urs von Balthasar* (Paris: Desclée, 1993); and Gawronski's *Word and Silence: Hans Urs von Balthasasr and the Spiritual Encounter Between East and West* (Edinburgh: T&T Clark, 1995). See also Johann Roten, "The Two Halves of the Moon: Marian Anthropological Dimensions in the Common Mission of Adrienne von Speyr and Hans Urs von Balthasar," in *Hans Urs von Balthasar: His Life and Work,* ed. David L. Schindler (San Francisco: Communio Books/Ignatius Press, 1991), 65–86; Peter Henrici, "A Sketch of Von Balthasar's Life" in ibid., 7–43; Jacques Servais, "The Ressourcement of Contemporary Spirituality Under the Guidance of Adrienne von Speyr and Hans Urs von Balthasar," *Communio: International Catholic Review* 26 (1999): 343–57. Even the Holy Father has acknowledged that "Hans Urs von Balthasar is inconceivable without Adrienne von Speyr." "Das Problem der christlichen Prophetie, Neils Christian Hvidt im Gespräch mit Joseph Kardinal Ratzinger," in *Internationale katholische Zeitschrift "Communio"* 28 (1999): 182–83.

[3] "The greater part of so much of what I have written," explains Balthasar, "is a translation of what is present in more immediate, less technical fashion in the powerful work of Adrienne von Speyr, only part of which has been published." He goes on to explain that Adrienne's opus, which was almost entirely dictated to him, represents "about a third of the books written with my own hand. . . . It was Adrienne von Speyr who showed the way in which Ignatius is fulfilled by John and therewith laid the basis for most of what I have published since 1940. Her work and mine are neither psychologically nor philologically to be separated; two halves of a single whole, which has as its center a unique foundation." (*My Work: In Retrospect* [San Francisco: Ignatius Press/Communio Books, 1993], 105, 107, 89; cf. 20.) In *Our Task: A Report and a Plan* (San Francisco: Ignatius Press, 1981), 13, Balthasar explains: "This book has one chief aim: to prevent any attempt being made after my death to separate my work from that of Adrienne von Speyr." In the same work (72–73), he argues that "my own ideas and way of thinking were not extinguished but rather enriched by what I received from Adrienne. It is quite pointless to try to disentangle what is hers from what is mine in these later works." Similarly, in Balthasar, *First Glance at Adrienne von Speyr* (San Francisco: Ignatius Press, 1981), 13, he argues: "On the whole I received far more from her, theologically, than she from me, though, of course, the exact proportion can never be calculated. . . . Today, after her death, her work appears far more important to me than mine, and the

Hence, another aim of this essay is simply to serve those students of Balthasar (and thus also, perhaps, certain students of Father Lamb), who would appreciate a synthetic overview of her Christian anthropology,[4] especially in that which concerns the paradoxical relation between freedom and obedience, nature and grace, divine action and human cooperation, which is also the reason for the many references herein.

To these ends, I will begin by presenting her understanding of the human person as realized in divine communion (part I) and more specifically in the dynamic of Christ's own life and mission and thus also of Christ's growing presence in the Christian (part II). This will become the basis for my development (in part III) of Adrienne's presentation of nature and grace in terms of the mutual indwelling of Christ and the Christian. Human nature will be further treated (in part IV) as mysteriously surpassing its own limitations through Christ's dwelling within the Christian. A similar phenomenon will be studied (in part V) with the presentation of the expansion of the Christian's assent within Christ's own obedient love for the Father. In part VI, the reader who is already familiar with Balthasar's Christian anthropology will recognize

---

publication of her still unpublished writings takes precedence over all personal work of my own." See also, Angelo Scola, *Test Everything, Hold Fast to What is Good, An Interview with Hans Urs von Balthasar* (Ignatius Press: San Francisco, 1989), 88–90.

[4] Elsewhere I have provided a similar synthesis of one particular aspect of her anthropology, namely, her theology of the body, and I have argued, in another article, that hers is an existential theology. See Michele M. Schumacher, "A Speyrian Theology of the Body," in *The Virgin Mary and Theology of the Body*, ed. Donald H. Calloway, M.I.C. (Stockbridge, MA: Marian Press, 2005), 243–78; and idem, "Leben in der Begegnung der Gaben. Die existentielle Theologie Adriennes von Speyr," *Internationale katholische Zeitschrift Communio* 6 (2003): 601–14. Well worth noting is Barbara Albrecht's two-volume anthology of Adrienne: *Eine Theologie des Katholischen: Einführung in das Werk Adriennes von Speyr,* vol. 1, *Durchblick in Texten* (Einsiedeln: Johannesverlag, 1972); vol. 2, *Darstellulng* (1973), as well as that of Balthasar himself: *Kostet und seht* (Einsiedeln: Johannesverlag, 1988). A general exposition of Adrienne's existential theology has been treated by Paola Ricci Sindoni, *Adrienne von Speyr. Storia di una esistenza teologica* (Torino: Socità editrice internazionale, 1996); and four doctoral dissertations have, to date, been written on Adrienne: Johannes Shiettecatte, *Disponiblité aimante. L'attitude d'amour johannique chez Adrienne von Speyr à la lumière de l'exégèse contemporaine* (Rome: Pontifical Theology Faculty "Teresianum," 1998); Justin Matro, *Christian Suffering in the Spiritual Writings off Adrienne von Speyr* (Rome: Pontifical Gregorian University, 1999); William Schmitt, *The Sacrament of Confession as a "Sequela Christi" in the Writings of A. von Speyr* (Rome: Pontifical Lateran University, Pontifical John Paul II Institute of Studies on Marriage and Family, 1999); Blaise R. Berg, *Christian Marriage According to Adrienne von Speyr* (Rome: Pontifical Lateran University, Pontifical John Paul II Institute of Studies on Marriage and Family, 2003).

in Adrienne's presentation of Mary the silhouette of what Balthasar calls a theological person. Mary is presented here—as in Balthasar's *Theo-drama*[5]—as the exemplar Christian, who is realized through her obedient and loving participation in Christ's mission. Finally, I will conclude with the Speyrian challenge to the Christian to accept Mary's maternity as a means of expanding his own surrender to the "measure" of God's gift in Christ-Jesus.

Human Perfection in Divine Communion

The central concern of self-realization, so prevalent in Western society since Descartes, has been relegated by the Thomistic tradition and Catholic theology as a whole to its place within the much broader question of God's governance of the world and the universe. God governs all things, Thomas teaches, according to their natures, whereby they are "naturally" orientated to their proper ends; and since man has a rational nature, God governs man through his (man's) capacity to govern himself. Having the capacity to know the truth and to choose the good, man is naturally orientated to the true and the good, and supernaturally orientated to the True and the Good, that is to say, to God himself. His *exitus* from the hands of the Creator, in whose image he is created, is organically related to his *reditus*: his return to the Creator by the effective realization of this image, that is to say, through his voluntary adherence to God as to his last end. Within this schema, the human person—so focal to the rugged individualism of contemporary Western civilization—is necessarily decentralized; for his accomplishment, or self-realization, and thus his happiness is not achieved through his own, isolated action, but in union with other actors, both human and divine. These communitarian and self-perfecting actions are, moreover, orientated towards communion, as that in which his perfection consists. His is an ecstatic nature, for his own good consists in the common good and his own perfection is organically related to the good of all: the subjection of all beings to Christ as Head, who himself is perfectly subject to the Father. Indeed, rather than the isolated human person, it is the divine person of Christ who is ultimately responsible for the human being's perfection; for Christ is both the instrumental and final cause of this perfection: instrumental—because it is through Christ and in Christ, the one mediator between God and man (cf. 1 Tim 2:5), that the latter is accorded the grace of redemption and sanctification whereby the image of God is perfected in him—and final, because it is to Christ, the Omega, that the human person tends as to his own perfec-

---

[5] See most especially, vol. 3, *Dramatis Personae: Persons in Christ* (San Francisco: Ignatius Press, 1992). Theological persons are treated in part 3, 263–461.

tion: We are sons in the Son, in whose image we were created (the Alpha and predecessor of Adam).

In the theology of Adrienne von Speyr, this Catholic presentation of human perfection is both upheld and advanced, particularly in its profoundly biblical focus, which takes Christ as its starting point. Preempting, so to speak, the Christological inspiration of the conciliar document *Gaudium et Spes*, whereby "Christ shows man to himself and makes known his most high calling,"[6] Adrienne reasons in a manner opposite the traditional metaphilosophical one: Rather than proceeding from general, abstract, or universal human nature to its particular concretization in any one individual human being, she, like the council after her, proceeds from the concrete, individual human nature of the man-God, Jesus Christ, who manifests the universal significance of human nature within his own privileged relationship with the Father. "Jesus is not 'anyone,' nor is he 'everyone': he is himself. And precisely as such a particular person is he the way to the Father."[7] His uniqueness *(Das Einmalige)* is the foundation of his universality.[8] Through the manifestation of the truly human by the eternal Son of God, the human person is introduced, Adrienne explains, into "the incomprehensible dimension of the Father,"[9] wherein consists his own properly spiritual dimension. This spiritual dimension, in turn, cannot be separated from the revelation of sonship in the form of obedient love. Like Christ, who reveals his divine filiation in the form of obedient love, the Christian, Adrienne reasons, lives his divine adoption in the form of loving obedience. Christ's surrender of his life to us—throughout his entire earthly mission and ultimately on the Cross—is an expression and revelation of the eternal Trinitarian communion, "whereby each divine person, in his exchange of love with the others, surrenders himself unlimitedly, surpassingly."[10] The

---

[6] Vatican II, Pastoral Constitution on the Church in the Modern World, *Gaudium et Spes,* no. 22.

[7] *They Followed His Call: Vocation and Asceticism* (San Francisco: Ignatius Press, 1986), 67.

[8] *Der erste Korintherbrief* (Einsiedeln: Johannesverlag), 323. Similarly, Balthasar argues: "For Christology (as sketched in its outlines by Chalcedon) gives an account of an event that cannot be made subject to any universal law but that subjects all other laws (regulating the relationship between God and the creature, that is) to its own uniqueness." (Hans Urs von Balthasar, *Theo-Logic* II: *Truth of God* [San Francisco: Ignatius Press, 2004], 311) Cf. idem, *A Theology of History* (San Francisco: Ignatius Press, 1994), especially 18–19, 21, 70–71.

[9] Adrienne von Speyr, *John II: The Discourses of Controversy. Meditations on John 6–12,* vol 2 (San Francisco: Ignatius Press, 1993), 78–79.

[10] *Das Wort und die Mystik* II: *Objektive Mystik* (Einsiedeln: Johannesverlag, 1970), 523. Cf. Hans Urs von Balthasar, *Theo-Drama* II, 256 and idem, *Theo-Drama* III: *Dramatis Personae: Persons in Christ* (San Francisco: Ignatius Press, 1992), 22.

Christian, in turn, receives the wealth of this surrender through his own surrender, whereby he is, so to speak, equipped to surrender himself as "bread for the world," in imitation of the Eucharist. Indeed, the Eucharist is, as we shall see, illustrative of the mysterious "expansion" of human nature within the infinite dimension of divine life. Hence, the Christian who has eaten of the flesh of the Lord is impelled by a single and insatiable desire: "the striving, in intensifying yearning, to assimilate himself totally to the life of the Lord."[11]

This assimilation is in no way foreign to human persons, for Christ is presented by Adrienne as the measure of our humanity; he is "perfect and complete," unlike we, who are "barely indicated."[12] We have being only in the form of *becoming*, Adrienne explains, which is to say that we must " 'become' what God 'is.' "[13] This does not mean that the Christian's movement toward God is simply a movement toward more being; nor is it simply a movement toward the source and goal of his being, except when this is understood as *a movement toward communion*: the accomplishment of the human person through his or her participation in Christ's own filial relation with the Father by the Holy Spirit. This, in turn, means that the human person realizes himself—and thus his human potential—by entering into the divine communion *precisely by means that are characteristic of this divine communion*: the loving—and thus willing—surrender of the self as a gift for others. This participation is thus subjectively experienced as a participation in Christ's obedience by the same Holy Spirit.[14] Hence the dynamic of Adrienne's theological anthropology is not so much that of the human being advancing toward God, who is presented as the term of his search for happiness, as it is that of God descending toward the human being to take him up into his own Trinitarian life.

In this regard, Adrienne's perspective does not greatly differ from that of the theological tradition inspired by the Church Fathers and continued by Thomas Aquinas and his disciples. The "becoming," which constitutes the dynamism of the Christian life, is—for Adrienne, as for the theological tradition as a whole—conceived as a continuation of the act of creation involving the human person not only as the object of the divine creative action,

---

[11] *Discourses of Controversy,* 67.

[12] *John I: The Word Becomes Flesh. Meditations on John 1–5* (San Francisco: Ignatius Press, 1994), 40. See also ibid., 27.

[13] *Das Wort und die Mystik,* II, 105.

[14] See *The Word Becomes Flesh,* 63. Similarly, Balthasar reasons that because God is "personified handing-over," one can "know" and "possess" him "only when one is oneself expropriated and handed over." *Glory of the Lord VII: Theology: The New Covenant* (San Francisco: Ignatius Press, 1989), 400. See also *Theo-Drama* II, 258, 259. On the Holy Spirit's role in mediating Christ's obedience to the Christian, who is said to participate therein, see idem, *Theo-Drama* V: *The Last Act* (San Francisco: Ignatius Press, 1998), 259.

but also as an acting subject: "Coming from him, we are his handiwork, so that, returning to him, we may do good works"; works whose purpose is "to help us remain on the path that leads to God."[15] Because God created us to participate in his divinity, our "being here" is, Adrienne reasons, the beginning of our being with God.[16]

From this perspective, the dynamic of human fulfillment is not understood as a discovery of the self from within the depths of his own soul, unless these "depths" are understood as a place of encounter. The "Yes" of faith is initially directed, Adrienne explains, "to a being that is before me, above me, beside me. That is how we imagine the Son. . . . But our Yes is hardly uttered before it takes an altogether unexpected turn, it turns inward, it enters into us." By this, Adrienne explains that the Lord makes us thereby aware of his presence within us, "hidden in our inmost I."[17] It is not narcissism, therefore, that renders one fully human, in Adrienne's presentation, but communion within the "unity" of God, a unity which comprehends our own unity. It follows that the interiorization symbolic of self-discovery is directed in Adrienne's theology toward an exteriorization: an ecstatic movement "out" of one's own self toward the divine Other, who is always the first to surrender himself. "It is when we forget ourselves and rise above ourselves that we discover God's grace," Adrienne teaches, which is to say that grace is possessed only when one is confidently abandoned to it.[18] So too with redemption: This gift is never really "possessed" outside of the act of receiving it, which is to say that "we receive it continually as something new."[19] It is therefore not surprising that Adrienne presents the path to divine communion as more spiral than linear. Constantly mounting to higher vantage points, it simultaneously and continuously returns to the same reference point, or "overview," in contemplation.[20]

---

[15] *The Letter to the Ephesians* (San Francisco: Ignatius Press, 1996), 92. Similarly, Thomas Aquinas interprets Augustine's famous phrase, "He who created you without you will not justify you without you" to mean: "not without you in some way disposing yourself for grace." *De veritate* q. 28, a. 8, ad. 6.

[16] *Der erste Korintherbrief,* 378.

[17] *The Word Becomes Flesh,* 101. Cf. Balthasar, *Glory of the Lord* I: *Seeing the Form* (San Francisco: Ignatius Press, 1982), 430.

[18] On the other hand, "the more we concern ourselves with our being and our self, the further it eludes our grasp." Ibid., 41. For Balthasar, this means that "the creature, man, suspended in the medium of God's freedom, is anchored—objectively—solely in God's truthfulness and subjectively—in his own attitude of trust." (*Theo-Drama* II, 253)

[19] *The Letter to the Ephesians,* 38; cf. 30. See also *Discourses of Controversy,* 64.

[20] *Discourses of Controversy,* 304. Assured thereby is the possibility not only of an overview, but also and especially "of giving everything back and handing it over to God." Ibid., 305.

The "action" of human perfection is thus primarily *contemplative* action, with primacy being awarded not so much to self-consciousness as to love: a loving awareness of the divine Other in virtue of whom one comes to know oneself within a loving communion of persons, and thus as beloved and as lover. Knowledge of oneself is no longer important for the one who truly loves, however, for love drives him toward what Adrienne calls anonymity. Whoever takes himself—his own honor, his own "principles," and so on—as the criterion of his relation with another, does not really love him, Adrienne argues.[21] Not unlike the Lord's call to find one's life by losing it, Adrienne teaches that the fullness of life that he wishes to give us is not that "of *our* life, of our person, of our character, but unity in him." That which we regard as "our own unity, and perhaps endeavor to attain, can be won only be moving toward his unity."[22] Similarly, Adrienne recognizes as appropriately Christian the attitude of promoting God rather than oneself. Contrary to the natural tendency of human beings to let their light shine, to make their mark in the world, and to manifest their own personalities, the Christian is challenged by Adrienne's biblically inspired insight, to hide his own light, in imitation of Christ. Precisely by concealing his light "in the Father," Christ reveals both the Father and himself to the world, for this is precisely how he reveals his love for the Father, which is the meaning of his entire life, mission and person.[23] It follows that we ought not to compel God to shed his light into our obscurity, "but allow his

---

[21] *Discourses of Controversy,* 102. See also *Theologie der Geschlechter* (Einsiedeln: Johannesverlag, 1969), 114. See also Balthasar, "Action and Contemplation" in *Explorations in Theology I: The Word Made Flesh* (San Francisco: Ignatius Press, 1989): 227–240, and idem, *Love Alone is Credible* (San Francisco: Ignatius Press, 2004), especially 108–10.

[22] *Discourses of Controversy,* 72. See also Adrienne's commentary on the passage from Mk 8:35 in *Markus* (Einsiedeln: Johannesverlag, 1971), 379. This is the thesis of Balthasar's book entitled *A Theological Anthropology* (New York: Sheed and Ward, 1967).

[23] *The Word Becomes Flesh,* 69; cf. Jn 1: 6–8. The references to the same in Balthasar's opus are so numerous that one has good reason to believe that it is one of the most important themes of his theology. Christ's obedience is "the kenotic translation" of the Son's eternal love for the Father. *Mysterium Paschale: The Mystery of Easter* (Edinburgh: T&T Clark, 1990), 90–91. Hence "Jesus does not live in order to exhibit himself as the highest example of the human species but solely to fulfil the Father's will." *Theo-Drama* III, 225. "[T]his man, who is obeying even as he 'makes' himself into a God, is a God who is obeying even as he makes himself into a man." *Glory of the Lord* I, 479. See also his *The Christian State of Life,* 37 (not to be confused with Adrienne's book by the same title) and his chapter entitled "Existence as Receptivity" in *A Theology of History,* 29–40. This important insight of both Adrienne and Balthasar is more profoundly Johannine as Ignace de la Potterie points. See his: *La vérité dans Saint Jean II: Le croyant et la vérité,* Analecta Biblica Investigationes Scientificae in Res Biblicas, no. 74 (Rome: Biblical Institute Press, 1977), 769–70.

love to create clarity in us." Rather than suppose that God should receive us as we are, we should "let happen" so as "not to be, but to become."[24]

Christ's Life as an Existence in Exchange

This radically Christological—and therefore Trinitarian—perspective, so characteristic of Adrienne's theology, preserves the dynamic of human self-realization within the principal and primary dynamic of Christ's own continuous incarnation within the Church and thus also within Christians. The thirty-three years of the Lord's terrestrial life are thus described by Adrienne as his continuous terrestrial becoming, wherein is manifest "the mystery of our becoming within the becoming of the Lord."[25] This means that the entire earthly existence of Christ is in service of our incorporation into his eternal life, with the result that we might be said to have life from him and even "to live and progress in him."[26] This new life in Christ is so real and so radical that once it is received, "Christ means life." Christ, Adrienne specifies, as he is objectively and not as we imagine him to be: Christ, active and present in the Church, distributing his grace in the sacraments and revealing, through his teaching, the path to life, the path that leads to the Father.[27] On the other hand, Christ is both life and *resurrection*, which means that his life cannot even be considered apart from heaven. The Lord did not become man so as simply to raise all of mankind up with him, Adrienne explains. He sought also thereby to reveal a divine life within the mortal condition, and the resurrected life that he accords us from heaven might be understood as a manifestation of this truth.[28]

Given the radicalism of the Christian's life in Christ, it is not surprising that Adrienne presents our growth in faith, hope, and charity as a growing participation in the perfected virtue of Christ. The theological virtues are, more specifically, presented by our author—following the lead of St. John the Evangelist—in terms of a bidirectional movement between heaven and earth, a movement that is "nothing other than the Son himself." It is precisely this reality that explains why, Adrienne continues, the evangelist presents the "living

---

24 *Theologie der Geschlechter*, 70. Cf. Balthasar's *Theo-Drama* V, 512.

25 *Die Katholischen Briefe II: Die Johannesbriefe* (Einsiedeln: Johannesverlag, 1961), 203. Similarly she argues that "the curve of man's life is enclosed within the curve of the Word made man." *The Word Becomes Flesh*, 34.

26 *The Letter to the Colossians* (San Francisco: Ignatius Press, 1998), 71. See also, ibid., 37; *Discourses of Controversy*, 70; and *Victory of Love: A Meditation on Romans 8* (San Francisco: Ignatius Press, 1990), 23.

27 *Deinst der Freude* (Einsiedeln: Johannesverlag, 1951), 35. On Balthasar's development of this insight, especially with regard to the Spirit's role therein, see his *A Theology of History*.

28 *The Mystery of Death* (San Francisco: Ignatius Press, 1988), 67–68.

bread" as leading to eternal life.[29] Similarly, the Swiss mystic argues—in a manner altogether compatible with the Christian tradition[30]—that God did not create the human person once and for all, but that He continuously generates him anew, by nourishing him with the Eucharist.[31] Indeed, the Lord is at the origin of the Church "as the one Eucharistically distributed,"[32] whereby it is possible to speak of a "one flesh" union (cf. Eph 5:32; Gen 2:24; Mk 10:8) of Christ and the Church, and thus also of Christ and the Christian. This fundamental and pivotal insight of Christianity, which Adrienne refers to as its "greatest mystery," is also the meaning that she attributes to the Lord's entire terrestrial mission, including his whole passion and ascension to the Father.[33] Even as a child he was realizing this mystery, Adrienne reasons, because his entire terrestrial existence is lived as an exchange between himself and those to whom he is sent. It is thus impossible that he might exist without the Church, which comes forth from him. It is already present, Adrienne notes, in the form of the holy family.[34] Similarly, she explains that the real humanity of Christ is particularly evident in that he does not construct the Church alone but in association with Mary and the other saints, in whom, she adds, "there can also be something of the non-saintly."[35]

To clarify the idea of Christ's existence in exchange—a concept not unlike that of the *admirabile commercium* of salvation described by the Church fathers as the "exchange" effected by Christ, who offers us his divinity, while taking on our sinful humanity[36]—Adrienne describes the development in John's Gospel from the presentation of Christ as having "all life" *in himself* to that of our having "all life" *through him*. It follows that the Christian life is not static but occurs within the dynamic of the Son's movement to the Father. From the perspective of our author, Christ is this movement and the life that he himself promises, whereby he is also this movement and this life "in those who believe in him, love him and hope in him."[37] His being, received by us, brings about our becoming,[38] but always in him, with the result that our *becoming* is also rightfully described—as in John's Gospel—as *remaining*.

---

[29] *Discourses of Controversy*, 64; cf. Jn 6:51; cf. *The Letter to the Ephesians*, 18–19.

[30] See the final encyclical of John Paul II, *Ecclesia de Eucharistia* (April 17, 2003), in which this rich tradition is magnificently exposed.

[31] See *The Letter to the Ephesians*, 104–5.

[32] *The Passion from Within* (San Francisco: Ignatius Press, 1998), 45.

[33] *The Letter to the Ephesians*, 240, 241.

[34] *Theologie der Geschlecter*, 99.

[35] *The Countenance of the Father* (San Francisco: Ignatius Press, 1997), 99.

[36] The references are bountiful, as Balthasar notes. See his *Theo-Drama*, vol. III, 237–45.

[37] *Discourses of Controversy*, 66; cf. *The Letter to the Colossians*, 32.

[38] *The Letter to the Colossians*, 71. The reception, Adrienne specifies, is by way of his word and the sacraments, especially that of the Eucharist.

To remain means: to remain in movement, to hunger and to be fed, to thirst and to be given drink, to feel all the needs of the spirit and to experience their satisfaction, and all of this in a continuously intensifying sense, so that each satisfaction awakens a greater hunger, because it broadens out the soul, and love becomes ever more urgent and more burning.[39]

This biblical image of remaining in Christ opens still another dimension of the one mystery of our becoming (divinization) within the Lord's "becoming" (Incarnation, Ascension and all that follows therefrom): the fact that Christ's dwelling within us—as is evident in our Eucharistic communions and in his teaching received by us—cannot be separated from our dwelling within him.[40] The latter is a revealed reality that Adrienne admits is much more difficult to understand and visualize. Both of these mysteries of indwelling, common to Johannine and Pauline theology alike—Christ's dwelling in us and our dwelling in him—are, moreover, so much a part of Christ's "essence," Adrienne explains, that they cannot be separated one from the other. Concretely this means that the emphasis in Adrienne's theology is not upon Christ over and above the Christian, but upon the Christian within the total reality of Christ who dominates both her anthropological and theological vision. He is everything, whereas we are "nothing." "And yet his Everything would not be complete if we were not in him." By this Adrienne means that we are not only possessed by him, but also that we are "comprehended in his person," so as to be taken with him "everywhere that he is."[41]

This idea of being "in his person," is assuredly very difficult to justify philosophically, but the insight is more biblical than philosophical. The divine person of Christ, as revealed in John's Gospel, "constitutes himself in the mission and through the mission," from the Father, Adrienne observes, which is to say that he "is a Person in the mission."[42] This does not mean that the

---

[39] *Discourses of Controversy*, 70–71. See also *The Holy Mass* (San Francisco: Ignatius Press, 1999), 73, where reference is made to persevering in love.

[40] See Balthasar's treatment of the Pauline concept "En Christoi" in his *Theo-Drama* III, 245–50. Cf. Balthasar, *Theo-Drama* V, 520 and 528. For Balthasar's commentary on the "exchangeable formulae" of Paul, who says both that "Christ lives in me" or "in us" (Gal 2:19f; 4:19; Rm 8:9–11; 2 Cor 4:16; 13:2–5) and that we are, or live or are found "in Christ" (Rm 8:1; Gal 3:2b; Phil 3:9; etc.), see *Glory of the Lord* VII, 407, 411.

[41] *John III: The Farewell Discourses, Meditations on John 13–17* (San Francisco: Ignatius Press, 1987), 128. See also ibid., 129; and *The Letter to the Colossians*, 71.

[42] *The Discourses of Controversy*, 372. See also ibid., 71; *The Word becomes Flesh*, 68, 106; and idem, *The Letter to the Ephesians*, 32. The references to the same in Balthasar's works are almost too numerous to mention. Perhaps the most important reference is in his *Theo-Drama* III, 149–229.

essence of personhood as revealed by Christ is to be understood primarily in terms of action, for the concept of mission is itself presented foremost in terms of *obedience*, from which proceed actions characteristic of the person.[43] Obedience, in turn, points to the essentially *relational quality of the divine Person*: "The Son is nothing more, and wishes to be nothing more, than the pure act of proceeding from the Father. He does not wish to be Son in anything other than this; and he thanks the Father for permitting him to be this."[44]

Within this context of the person-mission identity of Christ, Adrienne recognizes the possibility of a certain acquired perfection of the God-man. Beyond his growth "in wisdom and in stature, and in favor with God and man" (Lk 2: 52), she notes a certain "fullness" attributable to Christ in virtue of his mission.[45] It is "his own self in fullness," that he offers the Father with the completed mission.[46] The mission, in turn, is achieved when his Incarnation is achieved, or effected, *in us*: by way of the Eucharist. The "infinite dissemination" of the Lord in an unimaginable number of Hosts serves our unity in him, Adrienne explains, and the dissemination is complete when all of his members have effectively received him. At that point his unity is again realized.[47] From this perspective, "the fullness of Christ" referred to by Paul (cf. Eph 1:23) is the Church, present in each of her members. She is his Body and Bride; he, her Bridegroom, "who does not leave his Bride when he returns to heaven."[48]

> The Son, who founded the Church, has this Church as his body and thus takes her fullness into himself, in order to let her be filled up in him. Thus, in the likeness of the body, the other likeness, that of bride and bridegroom, makes its appearance: the bridegroom is over the bride but draws her to himself, in order thereby to fill her up in himself: that he might fill himself up in her by pouring out his entire energy into her.[49]

---

43 On this, see Balthasar's forward to Adrienne's *The Mission of the Prophets* (San Francisco: Ignatius Press, 1996), 7–9; and *The Letter to the Colossians*, 59.

44 *The Discourses of Controversy*, 372.

45 Of notable correspondence is the development of this theme in Balthasar's *Theo-Drama* III, 154–63. For Adrienne's commentary of Lk 2:52, see *Handmaid of the Lord* (San Francisco: Ignatius Press, 1985), 87–92.

46 *The Farewell Discourses*, 373.

47 *The Word Becomes Flesh*, 123.

48 *The Mystery of Death*, 73.

49 *The Letter to the Ephesians*, 74–75; cf. Eph 1:23: "She is his body, the fullness of him who is fulfilled in all through all." In a similar manner, Balthasar writes: "The Church as a whole is not set over against him as *another* subject; she is his Body, animated and governed by his Spirit." *A Theology of History*, 114. See also idem, "Who is the Church?" in *Explorations in Theology II: Spouse of the Word* (San Francisco: Ignatius Press, 1991), 143–91; idem, *A Theological Anthropology* (New York: Sheed and Ward, 1967), 310–14.

From Adrienne's perspective, it thus possible to address the Church as the fullness of Christ, on the one hand, and the Church as fulfilled in Christ, on the other. The same may be said of the relationship between Christ and the Christian, as we shall see; for the Church, as presented by Adrienne, "embodies" Christ's power as it is "efficacious and operative in us."[50]

The Christian's Fulfillment in the Dynamic of Christ's Life

It is possible to discern in the foregoing analysis of Adrienne's theology the patristic theme of the continuous Incarnation of Christ: his assumption, throughout the long history of the Church and of mankind, so as present us to the Father *in himself*.[51] Although the Incarnation is achieved without the Christian's willing it, the incarnate Son of God offers to each of us the real possibility of becoming, precisely as his members, one body with him, and in this is also realized his mission of recapitulating all of creation, and thus all of humanity, in himself.[52]

From within this perspective, the classic theological debate over the paradoxical relation between nature and grace—guided, to some extent, by the Aristotelian principle, *ordo essendi est ordo agendi*—is presented in terms of the relationship of mutual immanence between Christ and the Christian, which follows upon the mutual immanence, or internal reciprocity, of the Father and the Son;[53] hence the pivotal role assumed by the complementary concepts of mission and obedience. As Christ is "fulfilled" in the obedient realization of

---

[50] Ibid., 150.

[51] Irenaeus, for example, argues that "The Word of God became man so as to accustom man to seize God and to accustom God to live in man" (*Verbum Dei* quod habitauit in homine et Filius hominis factus est, ut adsuesceret hominem percipere Deum et adsuesceret Deum habitare in homine secundum placitum Patris). *Adversus Haereses* III, 20, 2; *Sources chrétiennes*, no. 211, 390–92. Much more recently, Cardinal Journet Charles Journet has presented the Church as the continuous incarnation of the Son. See his two-volume work: *L'Église du Verbe Incarné* (St. Maurice: Saint Augustine, 1998–99).

[52] See *Der erste Korintherbrief*, 390; and *The Letter to the Ephesians*, 48.

[53] As there is "no boundary" in Christ "between his possessing the Father and his being possessed by the Father," (See *Farewell Discourses*, 104) so also (that is, analogically: allowing for difference on the level of substance) our reception of the Son and his reception of us "can no longer be clearly distinguished: the border between the one received and the one receiving is obliterated." (*The Word Becomes Flesh*, 102; see also *Die Johannesbriefe*, 179.) Similarly in the theology of Balthasar: The mediating role that St. Thomas Aquinas assigns to Christ's humanity—as the instrument of his divinity, it is both sanctified and sanctifying (cf. *Summa theologiae* III, q. 34, a. 1, ad. 3; and a. 3; q. 48, a. 1; and I–II, q. 114, a. 6)—the Swiss theologian attributes to the divine personality of Christ: He is "the middle term of a double relation of reciprocal

his mission from the Father to draw all things to himself as Head (cf. Eph 1:22–23; Col 1:18), the Christian is fulfilled in his effective participation in this same mission—the universal mission of Christ—by means of this same obedience: a participated obedience.[54]

> We cannot be children of God in the Lord without simultaneously being assigned a task and a corresponding empowerment. Otherwise our status as children would not be active, it would not really belong to us; it would be a mere title, not a truth. Implicit in our state of grace is a mission. But as the former has its place in the Son, so too our mission as children of God cannot be situated anywhere else but in the mission of the Son, in participation in it.[55]

Similarly, the sacraments are conceived by Adrienne as linking the Christian to the Cross in that they not only share, but also give a share, in the Son's

---

immanence [namely, his primary and fundamental relationship with the Father in the unity of the Holy Spirit and his relationship—for love of the Father—with the Church and mankind in the unity of the same Spirit]." (Hans Urs von Balthasar, *Does Jesus Know Us? Do We Know Him?* [San Francisco: Ignatius Press, 1983], 52). Hence, the teaching of Chalcedon—the union in Christ of the two natures (divine and human) in the one (divine) person—many not pay "sufficient attention," Balthasar argues, "to the fact that his divine person can, as such, exist only in a (trinitarian) relation." ("On the Concept of Person," *Communio* 13 [1986]: 21–22.) Hence the union of nature and grace within the mystery of Christ, who is the "concrete analogy of being" as Balthasar is fond of saying: "Just as Christ did not leave the Father when he became man to bring creation in all its spheres to fulfillment, so also the Christian," Balthasar reasons, "does not need to step outside the center, Christ, to mediate Christ to the world, to understand his relation to the world, to build the bridge between revelation and nature, between philosophy and theology." ("Theology and Sanctity," in *The World Made Flesh* [San Francisco: Ignatius Press, 1989], 195). With regard to Christ as the concrete analogy of being, Balthasar explains that he "constitutes in himself, in the unity of his divine and human natures, the proportion of every interval between God and man." *A Theology of History* (San Francisco: Ignatius Press/Communio Books, 1994), 69–70, n. 5.

54 Christ's being "Lord" is, Adrienne explains, an expression of his obedience to the Father, who wishes that the Son exercise lordship. See *The Letter to the Ephesians*, 23; and *The Cross, Word and Sacrament*, 46. On the Christian's participation in Christ's obedience, see *The Letter to the Ephesians* (225), where Adrienne explains that every Christian "lives by the Lord's obedience toward the Father in order to obey him, the Lord." See also *The Word Becomes Flesh*, 103; and *Das Buch vom Gehorsam*: (Einsiedeln: Johannes Verlag, 1966), 19–20; *Colossians*, 37; *The Victory of Love*, 22; *They Followed His Call*, 67.

55 *The Letter to the Ephesians*, 31. See also, *They Followed His Call*, 129; and *Theologie der Geschlechter*, 130.

mission.[56] Hence, the believer communicates grace not in the manner of a sacrament—that is to say, as a simple "canal"—but as something that is actually *in* him or her without being *of* him or her.[57] Beyond the dialectic of nature or grace, Adrienne thus proposes the authentically Catholic unity of nature *and* grace, or—more true to the thought of Adrienne—of the Christian *and* Christ. This formula in turn, to be more accurately accorded with Adrienne's thought, might be presented as the mystery of Christ *in* the Christian and the Christian *in* Christ. The Christian acts together with Christ, so as to act "with grace and by merit."[58] This means, on the one hand, that the Christian must have an active faith ("merit") if he is to authentically experience the "grace of faith" *(Glaubensgnade)* in his life.[59] On the other hand, Adrienne recognizes that the Lord "needs" our works to fully "round off" his own.[60]

It is in this sense that we might understand Adrienne's insistence upon the Lord forming "for himself a Church who suits him," a suitability that does not admit that every humiliation assumed by him in his incarnation be also realized in her (for we must allow, Adrienne reasons, the distinction between God and his creature). Rather, the Church—precisely as a "womb" receptive of his grace—is said to *participate in his elevation*. Such, for example, is the relationship between Christ and Mary: "The Son remains God despite his abasement to mankind; Mary remains fully human despite the extraordinary grace of her pre-redemption." She also assumes, moreover, the closest possible fellowship with her Son, in accord with his own desire, whereby she "stands before his distinct and immediate mystery: his being

---

56 *The Cross: Word and Sacrament* (San Francisco: Ignatius Press, 1983), 10.

57 See *Erde und Himmel. Ein Tagebuch*, I (Einsiedeln: Johannesverlag, 1975), 82. On the other hand, Adrienne insists that: "Grace comes solely from God; it is something we can never compare ourselves to, something we can only receive and that never becomes our own property, that we can transmit but never possess as our substance. Grace is always with God, even though we transmit it, so that in spite of us it is he who transmits it. We never communicate it as we communicate our knowledge or a truth we have understood." *The Word Becomes Flesh*, 121.

58 *Victory of Love*, 23. Merit, understood as a human striving after God, is always a response to a divine grace, Adrienne explains. See *Das Wort und die Mystik*, II, 529.

59 The saint, Adrienne explains, is a "graced human being" *(ein Gnadenmensch)*, whose works contain the characteristics of both the human being and grace. See *Der Mensch vor Gott* (Einsiedeln: Johannesverlag, 1966), 9.

60 *Theologie der Geschlechter*, 234. Similarly, he needs the Church's fullness to manifest his own. See *Ephesians*, 73–74. See also *Der erste Korintherbrief*, 389, where Adrienne argues that included in the mystery of Christians being one body *(Mit-Leib-Seins)* with the Lord is that of a "co-working" *(eine Witwirkens)* of the members together with the body, with its highest expression in the "co-redemption" of Mary.

begotten by the Father and his direct vision of the Father." Hence, she is also integrated—through her prayer—into the unapproachable mystery of his own prayer: "The Son in prayer does not give as a simple man; nor does he, as such, simply receive what God gives; rather he gives as God-Man. He receives what God gives him, but he simultaneously gives himself as God and also receives as God."[61] Like Mary, who is integrated into Christ's prayer and obedience to the Father, the so-called ordinary Christian must live from the "center" of himself that has been so occupied by the Word of God, that it can no longer be possessed by him: "I do not live; he lives in me. He must grow, I diminish."[62] Contrary to appearances, however, the believer's life in Christ is "infinitely more active," Adrienne insists, than the life that is not lived explicitly for Christ. Our "part" does not consist in simply allowing Christ to work in us, for we are called at each particular moment "to the most intense, most vital participation."[63]

In virtue of this participation, it is possible to speak of a certain *community of action*, whereby Christ's activity and ours form *a single action*, a "synergy of God's power with ours."[64] Through his presence within us, the Lord enables us to participate in his power and its possibilities. He does not, in other words, overcome the limitations of our nature from without—pushing us to excel beyond what we deem possible—but from within: by his power at work in us, that is to say, by faith and love, which he plants in our soul with the intention that they grow therein. In commenting upon Paul's letter to the Ephesians, Adrienne explains this phenomenon not so much in terms of grace and merit, as in the activity of man meeting the activity of God. Unlike the Son of God, who is eternally one with the Father, we must learn to become increasingly one with him. In so doing, we have the help of the Son, who assumes the most important part of our activity: from within us, he meets the Father "halfway."[65] Indeed, Christ's action is decisive in the reciprocal collaboration between Christ and the Christian, with the result that our merit consists in readiness or availability for grace.

It is in this sense that Adrienne presents the grace of the Mass as "measured and proportioned to the individual believer," in virtue of which it is a real drama, moving "from person to person, from life to life."[66] Though the

---

61 *Das Wort und die Mystik* I, *Subjektive Mystik* (Einsiedeln: Johannesverlag, 1970), 20, 21.

62 *Theologie der Geschlechter*, 89; cf. Gal 2:20.

63 *The Word Becomes Flesh*, 104.

64 *The Letter to the Ephesians*, 149.

65 Ibid., 22. See, for what follows, *The Letter to the Colossians*, 56–57; *Das Wort und die Mystik*, II, 413.

66 *The Word Becomes Flesh*, 46.

Mass, each individual Christian is given the grace to make of his life and suffering a part of the Lord's own life and suffering, and to the extent that he or she thus effectively participates in the Eucharistic mysteries—offering his life and sufferings—the Mass may be considered more perfect and complete, all in remaining an act of God.[67] This participation is reckoned by Adrienne as part of the Church's faith, which is required of her in the celebration of the Eucharist; for it corresponds to the will of the Lord that he be received in faith, in virtue of which we may be said to live in him rather than in ourselves. Hence the efficacy of sacramental grace is determined, humanly speaking, by the extent of the believer's consent.[68]

By way of further explanation, Adrienne refers to the scene of the Cross, from whence she explains—like the Church fathers before her—the sacraments originate. The Lord desires, she continues, that those witnessing his crucifixion take in and grasp as much as possible of what they observe and hear. His passion is not meant to be simply an *opus operatum*, happening to them in the absence of their knowledge. Rather, they are taken seriously in their humanity, by which she means that they are expected to accept his self-surrender, and to the extent that they do so, Christ's life is effectively taken from him, so as to be given to them.[69] The unity between Christ's life-*giving* surrender and our own life-*receiving* surrender is, as we shall see, the Eucharist, which mediates between the finiteness of sin and infinity of Trinitarian life and love, and thus also between nature and grace.

Breaking Boundaries from Within

The Expansion of Human Nature by Christ in the Christian

In explaining the union of nature and grace within the mystery of the mutual indwelling of Christ and the Christian, Adrienne refers to a certain "expansion" of nature by grace. Already on the conceptual level, Adrienne invites her reader to extend the nature-grace balance beyond the limits imposed by our fragile intellects; for the measure of this balance is not the finite powers of

---

[67] Our suffering does not, Adrienne specifies, lighten in any way the Lord's suffering, but "feeds" his joy: his joy present at the Resurrection and Ascension, when he presents the perfection of his work to the Father. Our co-suffering is, Adrienne reasons, a sign and fruit of his work. See *Erde und Himmel. Ein Tagebuch*, II (Einsiedeln: Johannesverlag, 1975), 249.

[68] See *The Holy Mass*, 84; *Das Wort und die Mystik*, II, 497–98.

[69] *The Cross: Word and Sacrament*, 10. On the patristic theme of the sacraments of the Church coming forth from the side of Cross, asleep on the Cross, see *Catechism of the Catholic Church*, n. 766 and Balthasar, "Who is the Church?", 146.

human nature, but the infinite power of God, surpassing the limitations otherwise imposed by human nature and sin.[70] When human understanding is not continually nourished by divine meaning, it is dulled: Certain limitations are automatically constructed by us precisely where God had spoken an infinite word. What God "can" say is then, as it were, measured by human comprehension, for the infinite is thereby subject to, or measured by, the finite. In conceiving a thought, for example, we tend automatically to create a certain boundary: in acknowledging that an object is "so and thus," we simultaneously acknowledge that it is "not otherwise." When, in contrast, by an act of faith we acknowledge that something is "so," no negation is implied therein: "not because it is simultaneously so and otherwise, but because this 'so' lies open within the Lord's infinity." Faith is, for Adrienne, simply enough "stretching to God's measure," which is to say, no measure.[71]

The phenomenon of faith is, on the other hand, just one example of how human nature is stretched beyond its own (natural) limits by the incarnate Son of God. This is not to admit, however, that the mysterious overcoming of nature's limitations by grace is a de facto consequence of the Incarnation, whereby the God-Man accomplishes divine actions as a man and human actions as God, or whereby the unlimited henceforth exists within the realm of the limited.[72] Rather, or most especially, the Incarnation is presented by Adrienne as a source of grace for all humanity precisely in that all of humanity is thereby drawn into Trinitarian love.[73]

To be sure, Adrienne concentrates upon the dialogue of love between the Father and the incarnate Son, who loves the Father from within the world, so as to offer the world's response of praise and thanksgiving for the gift of the Father's love.[74] In virtue of the same, he realizes God's image in the human being: He makes of his body a response of infinite love to the Father whose

---

[70] "It is sin," Adrienne teaches, "that sharply shows up the limitations of creatureliness. It separates human consciousness from God and isolates it in itself." *The Passion from Within*, 44.

[71] *Das Wort und die Mystik*, 26. See also 42–43; and *The Letter to the Ephesians*, 149.

[72] It bears mentioning that these elements are not, however, absent in Adrienne's theology. See, for example, *The Farewell Discourses*, 311; *Gebetserfahrung* (Einsiedeln: Johannesverlag, 1965), 11; and *Der Mensch vor Gott*, 11–12.

[73] In this, there is a continuum with the theological tradition. Although St. Thomas, for example, argued that the grace of union is reserved to Christ alone (*ST* III, q. 2, a. 10), it is the source of every other grace. See also *ST* III, q. 6, a. 6; q. 7, a. 13. Similarly, the saint argues that the grace of redemption, which is given to all who receive Christ in faith, follows upon the grace that filled his human soul. (*ST* III, q. 8, a. 5; cf. *De veritate*, q. 29, a. 5). See also Pope John Paul II, encyclical letter "The Holy Spirit in the Life of the Church and the World," *Dominum et vivificatem*, no. 50.

[74] See *The Letter to the Ephesians*, 33.

act of creation is also a pure act of love and, as such, a work of surrender.[75] Hence, unlike Thomas Aquinas, who presents Christ's humanity as the instrument of his divinity, Adrienne recognizes in the human body of Christ, the instrument *(Werkzeug)* of his obedient love for the Father.[76] The Son, who is the only human being to understand the depths of paternal love from which this creation precedes, offers in the Eucharist his most perfect surrender and also "the full response of the world to the Father's extravagant love."[77] The Eucharist, however, is the fulfillment of the Incarnation, precisely in that it gives us a share in his response to the Father's love. It is "seed" bringing forth the fruit of good works, love in return for love. It is thus also the Eucharist that mediates between the infinite love of God and the finite love of man, which is nevertheless called to perfection in the Lord's infinity.

To help clarify the mode of this mediation, Adrienne calls again upon the illustrative analogy of sexual love. Commenting, more specifically, upon the aforementioned passage from Mark 10:8,[78] in which reference is made to Genesis 2:24—"So they are no longer two but one"—Adrienne recognizes the original unity of man and woman in God's creative plan as an analogy for the fruitful union between Christ and the Church, or Christ and the Christian: a union in virtue of which it is no longer possible for the latter to distinguish between that which is properly his (and thus human) and that which is supernaturally received, between what is attributable to nature and what is attributable to grace. In the mutual gift of self (surrender) between man and woman in the marital act, "the boundaries between yours and mine disappear; the I being led, without realizing it, into the You." Adrienne reasons that it is no longer possible to determine whether the act takes form in the *I* or in the *You*, "because the boundaries have fallen,"[79] and, in fact, the one bears fruit in the other. Similarly, there is no clear boundary between the handing over *(Übergabe)* and taking on *(Übernahme)* of grace, between grace as given and grace as received, between the consent and the exchange of absolute love.[80] This

---

[75] Adrienne explains that as such it contains "a moment of sacrifice," which, she specifies, is "not necessarily painful." It is the "spending (Abgabe) of love." *Das Wort und die Mystik*, II, 522; see also 50.

[76] See *Theologie der Geschlechter*, 183; and *The Letter to the Ephesians*, 156. See also Thomas Aquinas, *ST* III, q. 34, a. 1, ad. 3.

[77] *Das Wort und die Mystik*, II, 523. See also ibid., 101, 502; and *Theologie der Geschlechter*, 133. Through the work of redemption, the Son "wants to bring the Father a love from the world that is greater than the insult it has offered him." *Farewell Discourses*, 311.

[78] See above, the text corresponding to note 34.

[79] *Theologie der Geschlechter*, 98. See also 104, 100.

[80] See *Der Mensch vor Gott*, 53–54. See also *The World of Prayer* (San Francisco: Ignatius Press, 1985), 4; and *Theologie der Geschlechter*, 140.

exchange is effected by the indiscriminate manner in which the Lord hands himself over to the Church, such that it is no longer possible to distinguish between what the Lord gives and what the Church receives and gives back by way of her response.[81] She is simply drawn into the Lord's "open space" with the result that his openness becomes hers.[82] Giving and receiving are "one in love,"[83] which also means that love's expression is inspired by both the lover and the beloved in an "interplay of fulfillment and expectation."[84] For this same reason, Adrienne reasons that one cannot address Christ as active with regard to the Church, who is passive; both are simultaneously active and passive, although the Lord is also the first to initiate.[85]

In applying this same sexual analogy to the relationship between Christ and the Christian, Adrienne teaches us that grace really is actualized by means of our cooperation, which is to say that we really do surrender ourselves to the Lord, who—it bears repeating—is always the first to surrender himself to us. In virtue of the Lord's fullest possible surrender in the Eucharist, the surrender of every man to his wife in the marital act is elevated.[86] Henceforth the man assumes a certain primacy in the marital act: He initiates the act "by surrendering and losing himself."[87] The woman who is, in the first instance, receptive of his gift—her own surrender to him assuming the form of receptivity—is, on the other hand, more strongly affected by the marital embrace than is the man, Adrienne argues. While he remains—at least physiologically—as he was prior to the act, she is "indelibly" and perceptibly marked thereby: The virgin is transformed, as it were, into "a woman" by her reception of the man's self-surrender.[88] This change within her is due to a certain "impressing power" *(eine Prägungskraft)* that the man exercises in her regard

---

81 *The Letter to the Ephesians*, 230–31.

82 *The Farewell Discourses*, 364.

83 *Der erste Korintherbrief*, 427.

84 *The World of Prayer*, 40.

85 *Theologie der Geschlechter*, 132. Cf. Balthasar, *Theo-Drama* V, 85–91.

86 Ibid., 133, 132. Within Adrienne's perspective, the full meaning of creation and thus also of sexuality lies in Christ (see *Theologie der Geschlechter*, 155) and ultimately in the Trinity (see *Der erste Korintherbrief*, 319–320). Indeed, the Father created the world, Adrienne teaches, "after the primordial image of the Son." *The Letter to the Colossians*, 32; cf. *Das Wort und die Mystik*, II, 52. On this theme in the Catholic tradition, see: Michele M. Schumacher, "An Inseparable Connection: The Fruitfulness of Conjugal Love and the Divine Norm," English edition of *Nova et Vetera* (Fall 2003): 137–58.

87 *The World of Prayer*, 41. Even in the period of their courtship, Adrienne acknowledges that the man must risk a certain humiliation—revealed by Christ's relationship with the Church—which spares the woman of the same. *The Letter to the Ephesians*, 239.

88 *Der erste Korintherbrief*, 390.

during the sexual act: a power, whose effect is first of all physiological but potentially spiritual as well, affecting the whole of her person.[89] This power—especially in that which concerns the more spiritual transformation of the woman—is largely dependent upon her own surrender to the man, which entails the whole dimension of her person.[90] Indeed, the woman's surrender is decisive not only with regard to her own transformation, but also with regard to the power itself. Although the man has this power from the Creator, Adrienne explains, his act is realized in the woman, who, so to speak, "liberates" his power. Adam needed Eve in this sense to experience his own masculinity, or, as Adrienne puts it, "to prove himself a man."[91] Analogically,[92] Adrienne presents the Church as a second Eve in her relationship to Christ, the New Adam. If, accordingly, the Church were to receive the Eucharistic Lord with an openness matching his surrender to her, she would be "entirely impressed with the Lord's meaning."[93]

This challenge to the Church to prepare for her bridal encounters with the Lord might serve to explain why Adrienne recognizes the mystery of confession as included within the Eucharistic mystery: It is the Lord's surrender of himself to the Church in the Eucharist that also "opens" her to him in the readiness of love. The Church's openness, in turn, is comparable to that of confession, an openness that Adrienne regards as a sort of "nakedness," not unlike that of spouses mutually offering themselves in the marital act.[94]

---

[89] Adrienne argues that when the sexual act occurs "in God," the man is granted "an unheard of power of impression" *(eine unerhörte Prägungskraft)* vis-à-vis the woman, not only in the physiological sense, but also in the whole of her humanity *(im gesamtmenschlichen Vorgang)*. See *Das Hohelied* (Einsiedeln: Johannesverlag, 1972), 43.

[90] Adrienne mourns girls who fornicate more than she mourns boys, because she recognizes that in the case of the young man, the surrender is almost always sexual alone. In the case of the woman, on the other hand, "it is always also a total surrender." See *Kreuz und Hölle*, vol. I, *Die Passionen* (Einsiedeln: Johannesverlag, 1966), 39.

[91] *Theologie der Geschlechter*, 33, see also 32.

[92] Strictly speaking, one could admit more than an analogy, since Adrienne teaches that the sacrament of marriage "is first of all a supernatural thing, the corporal being included within the spiritual. The spiritual fecundity is primary and remains greater than the corporal." For this reason, one must "know the world of grace (openness to God, to faith) so as to be able to properly correspond with his body." (*Theologie der Geschlechter*, 117) On the analogical value of the comparison, see ibid., 140.

[93] *Das Hohelied*, 43.

[94] See *Theologie der Geschlechter*, 82–83, 109; *Das Wort und die Mystik*, II, 514. Similarly, Adrienne presents the "confessional attitude" as one of "pure openness and readiness" (Balthasar's introduction to Adrienne's *Das Allerheiligenbuch* I [Einsiedeln: Johannes Verlag, 1966, 30]). See also *Confession* (San Francisco: Ignatius Press, 1985). With regard to confession included in the Eucharist, see *Das Hohelied*, 43.

"Only a naked soul can be fruitful,"[95] Adrienne insists, for every soul must and can be possessed entirely by the Lord, so as to be "pure devotion, pure surrender" in his regard.[96] "By impregnating a soul, the Lord renders it virginal," Adrienne explains, by which she suggests not only that the soul belongs henceforth to the Lord—as a bride belongs to her bridegroom—but also that the Lord renders the beloved soul "unconditionally ready" to do all that he demands. Consequently, the soul is "fecund from his fecundity."[97] The freedom of the human person is so great, however, that he effectively has the power to determine whether he will be fecund or sterile vis-à-vis God who, on the other hand, "allows no seed to go to waste; he binds himself" to the chosen soul, "like a faithful husband to his wife."[98]

The Expansion of the Christian's Consent to the Proportion of God's Surrender

In the foregoing it is apparent that the authentic gift of self proper to the divine persons is not only revealed by Christ in his self-surrender to the Church but is also *communicated* to us thereby—as a fruit of redemption—so as also to be really *required* of us. Grace works in such a way as to render us capable of responding to God with a purity corresponding to the divine love.[99] The strength of the Lord's power within us does not, however, lessen the force of his demands *(Forderungen)* upon us, which often appear as exorbitant or excessive *(Überforderungen)*, Adrienne explains, because they do not account for the limitations of our nature.[100] Hence, when the Lord says to his

---

[95] *Theologie der Geschlechter,* 123.

[96] *Farewell Discourses,* 364, cf. *Letter to the Ephesians,* 225; and *Das Wort und die Mystik,* II, 27.

[97] *Theologie der Geschlechter,* 136.

[98] Ibid., 131; cf. *Das Wort und Mystik,* I, 28. "The Spirit lies in the Word-Seed," Adrienne explains, but the question of its diffusion "can only be clarified when the Church receives the Spirit of the mission and is thus receptively disposed for God's seed." (Ibid., 135.) With regard to the question of "fecundity" and "sterility," Adrienne explains the consequences of a call that is not answered: "The hindering or omission of a decision regarding one's state of life cannot but have its effect on the Church: positions that should be filled remain empty, and there is a dearth of individuals ready, within the structure of the Church, to serve the interests of the Church and of the Lord. The living harmony among the states of life and within each separate state is disturbed and suffers." Ultimately: "A plan made in heaven will be thwarted on earth." (Von Speyr, *The Christian State of Life,* 174, 175.) On the absolute fidelity of God, on the other hand, see *Der erste Korintherbrief,* 23, 287–88.

[99] See *The Letter to the Ephesians,* 33–34.

[100] See *Mary in the Redemption,* 100; and *They Followed His Call,* 16. On the other hand, Adrienne explains that the Lord's demands "never come in a moment," because the

disciples that for man it is impossible to be saved (cf. Mk 10:26), Adrienne insists with even greater intensity: "Complete impossibility, a human salvation," even (or especially) when one acts according to "the rules" as, for example, are set forth by the commandments (cf. Mk 10:19–20). Adrienne invites her reader to remember that life on earth is a sort of exclusion, not only with regard to time, but also with regard to the limitations of being, acting, and possibilities *(Könnens)*.[101] For the Lord, on the other hand, these limitations pose no difficulty: For him every miracle is possible, not just the great ones, but also those that concern the minor details of our lives. Adrienne believes that we are too theoretical in our thoughts concerning God's omnipotence. We disregard or fail to see the power that he has to change our lives, so that they might be useful for him; to affect our acts so that they might really witness to his divine power; and to inform each of our thoughts, so that they accord with his all-powerful will. Far from leading us to despair, the acknowledgment that we are incapable of saving ourselves should lead us to salvation by encouraging us to live wholly by his grace.[102] When we, like Martha, respond affirmatively to the ultimate question of faith—"Do you believe?" namely, that Christ is the "resurrection and the life" (cf. Jn 11:26–27)—then our life, like hers, "will be taken up into his life," with the result that "every anxiety we have, every attempt we make, every calculation—all is taken up into him and dissolved."[103] Henceforth, it is His "ever-more" *(Je-mehr)*[104] that is determinative of our "limits." These he stretches from within us, so that the openness thereby accorded might match the extent of his unlimited grace: "His grace knows no barriers in itself, and therefore none in us."[105]

Simply speaking, this means that the Lord will not adapt to our "measures."[106] Indeed, when the Lord gives himself, Adrienne reasons, he gives himself entirely, without restrictions, including those that would hinder our

---

individual's "Yes" cannot be expected so quickly, and is sought by the Lord only after a certain preparation. In this sense, Adrienne refers to "a beginning of the surrender" in which the individual "stands up, or does the necessary, to open the door." (*Das Hohelied*, 60.) On Adrienne's own experience of these "excessive demands," see Balthasar, *First Glance at Adrienne von Speyr*, 45.

[101] As if to stress the point, she adds that the human being should feel as if he lives "in a prison." Markus, 473. This is an important theme developed in Balthasar's *A Theology of History*.

[102] See ibid., 473.

[103] *The Mystery of Death*, 66–67. Similarly, Adrienne explains that the Lord transforms our love, our expectations, and our efforts within his own "until what is ours simply dissolves in what is his." *The Farewell Discourses*, 364.

[104] See *Mary in the Redemption*, 100.

[105] *The Farewell Discourses*, 364.

[106] Ibid., 164.

capacity to receive him. He is "ready for everything."[107] Coming to meet us in the annihilation *(anéantissement)* of the Eucharist—which is itself the fruit of his unlimited suffering[108]—he awaits a corresponding response from us in faith. As he, more specifically, "annihilates himself in the host," we must in turn "annihilate ourselves in him in order to receive him worthily and in faith."[109]

Communion with the Eucharistic Lord does not only suppose this openness, or "emptiness," in us, however; it also creates it. Every Communion is an exchange whereby we both receive the Lord, so as to approach him more closely, and simultaneously give him what he wishes to receive from us. Precisely as an exchange, it is not inhibited by our limitations, by our meager readiness for him, but breaks down the boundaries of our resistance according to the magnitude of the Father's love.[110] Here there can be no question of our measuring up, so to speak, "for the content [of his gift] far surpasses the container [whom we are]."[111] Because, on the other hand, his overabundant generosity really does provide for what is lacking in us, the Lord will permit nothing less than an unlimited engagement from us: an engagement matching, as it were, the extent of his own engagement in our lives and history. What is required of us, in other words, is an authentic and unconstrained Yes, a perfectly generous consent: one, which is so faithfully given that it can never be withdrawn, but which can and must, on the other hand, be expanded to meet the growing demands of the Lord, who continually draws us more deeply into his own mission. "One can remain open for God only in a once-for-all total assent, not in a tentative, limited, cautious Yes."[112]

Adrienne takes this "Yes" so seriously that she will admit of no "third state" of life in the structure of the Church. The disciple of the Lord cannot

---

[107] *Das Hohelied,* 70; cf. *The Farewell Discourses,* 67: "It is a love that is ready to take everything on itself, even the Cross."

[108] "The hour proceeds, the suffering goes beyond all measure, the Son himself renounces all 'measure.'" *The Cross: Word and Sacrament,* 10.

[109] *The Holy Mass,* 71. See also *Das Hohelied,* 70.

[110] See *The Discourses of Controversy,* 73–74. "Communion is the overflowing answer of God's love to the barely indicated love of man," Adrienne explains. *The Word Becomes Flesh,* 83.

[111] *The Word Becomes Flesh,* 102. She adds: "the vessel becomes an unimportant adjunct to the content." (Ibid.) Balthasar, in a similar manner, argues that grace makes and fills the *fiat* which receives it, which is to say that the divine "outpouring" of love prepares the "womb" for its own coming. See *The Glory of the Lord: A Theological Aesthetics,* vol. 1, *Seeing the Form* (San Francisco: Ignatius Press, 1982), 114; and *Love Alone: The Way of Revelation* (London: Sheed and Ward, 1968), 63.

[112] *The Farewell Discourses,* 261. On the demands of this Yes, from the first instant of the call, see *Das Wort und die Mystik,* vol. I, *Subjektive Mystik* (Einsiedeln: Johannesverlag, 1970), 26.

do otherwise than to give himself absolutely and thus irrevocably, whether in an indissoluble marriage or in the consecrated life, which is "as a matter of principle, equally irrevocable."[113] Those, on the other hand, who have already given of themselves once and for all must nonetheless guard against complacency. Faith, Adrienne teaches, must be constantly exercised as something new, something living; it must be newly embraced every day in such a way as to allow for no monotony, for it corresponds to the vitality of God's Word, who is the Lord himself.[114]

In this way von Speyr cautions her reader against assuming for himself the ultimate responsibility for his own fidelity. Recognizing that we are all really "unfit to dispose of our own Yes," she encourages us to surrender it to God in prayer, so as to live no longer in ourselves "but in his word."[115] This word, in whom we should strive to live, is also the word who lives in us: "the objective word which is proposed to my faith" and "the subjective word which prays in me."[116] Thus guiding and ruling us from within and from without, the Word of God—who, in this capacity, is also the Spirit of God—is particularly efficacious in taking on our opposition to him; and taking on our opposition is no small matter, for the Lord's "possibility" of changing us—of rendering us like himself—is, Adrienne maintains, also determined by our openness to him.[117] This is not to deny that our openness to him is always very limited: Our "Yes"

---

[113] Balthasar, *First Glance and Adrienne von Speyr*, 54. See also *Das Hohelied*, 61. Balthasar maintains the same in his own *Christian State of Life* (San Francisco: Ignatius Press, 1983), not to be confused with the book of the same title by Adrienne. He explains (in *Our Task*, 99) that "Adrienne's doggedly maintained opinion" about there being no third state had a certain influence upon this work of his.

[114] Von Speyr, *The Christian State of Life*, 146–47. Not surprisingly, the Son of God is presented by Adrienne as an example, par excellence: "It would be a mistake . . . to want to find obedience only at the Cross. Whoever wishes to be obedient must be so as much on the good days as on the difficult ones, and he must not be troubled if obeying comes easily to him. Even though the Son knew exactly the kind of Cross that awaited him, we cannot say that he let its shadow cast a gloom over every moment of his life. There was his childhood, the thirty years of the hidden life, the feasts and other joyful events of the public life, each of them with the appropriate atmosphere even though they were all a part of the way of the Cross." *They Followed His Call*, 65.

[115] *The Word Becomes Flesh*, 36.

[116] *The World of Prayer*, 282. Indeed, Adrienne explains that God does not merely address us, but is also understood and received by us through his Holy Spirit. See *The Word Becomes Flesh*, 27, 63. On the cooperation between the Holy Spirit and the Son, who is also God's Word, see *Theologie der Geschlechter*, 135. Cf. Balthasar, *Prayer* (San Francisco: Ignatius Press, 1986), 35–36.

[117] On the efficiency of the Word in taking on our opposition, see *Die Schöpfung* (Einsiedeln: Johannesverlag, 1972), 44; and on our openness as determinant, see *Die Johannesbriefe*, 179.

to him is never full-hearted, Adrienne notes, and our reception of him is always tainted by selfishness. He must, therefore, constantly fight to destroy the boundaries we set up. The enemy here is us, Adrienne explains, with the result that the Lord "must continually be killing us to make us living in God, until we have grasped that it is not we who bring him to God, but he us."[118] He must, more specifically fight for the entire space of our soul, and he prunes us from himself whenever we "apply measuring rods" and seek to "survey the whole."[119] Cutting away, in fact, all that is not generous, unaccountable gift in us, the Lord clears not just a space for himself within us, but every space. Because the new life that he wishes to give us really does require every space within us, "every space must be emptied for it."[120] Thrusting aside all that he considers incompatible with his presence, he converts our half-hearted "Yes" into "a whole" resounding "Yes." Thus no matter how feeble and uncertain our "Yes" might be in its origin, when it is really given to the Lord so as to be deposed in him, it is henceforth contained within the Lord's own superabundant "Yes" to us, so as to be carried, nourished, and fortified by him to the full stature of Christian faithfulness, the full surrender of the resurrected life.[121]

Even the most obedient of God's human creatures—and Adrienne calls upon the example of Mary and Joseph to bring clarity to the matter—lack something of the completeness required by God, a completeness for which he is ultimately responsible. Hence, the meaning of their obedience lies in their willingness to hand over their obedience, as it were, to entrust it to the Lord, who fills in "the empty spaces." They must, more specifically, be obedient "without strings attached" so as to be dispossessed of their own obedience. They must surrender it—along with every aspect of their persons—to God: as an act of love, of course, but also for his safekeeping, whereby the surren-

---

[118] *The Farewell Discourses,* 129–30. Similarly, Adrienne explains, "I thought I could surrender myself to him just as I pleased. But he drives me out of myself, expelling everything that does not serve his purpose." *The Word Becomes Flesh,* 101–2.

[119] *Farewell Discourses,* 164. The context here is Jn 15:2: "Every branch of mine that bears no fruit, he takes away. . . ."

[120] *The Victory of Love,* 22. See also *Theologie der Geschlechter,* 89.

[121] See *The Word Becomes Flesh,* 103. "To be faithful in the Lord means to live in a sort of permanent state in which the image of the Lord remains steadily before one's eyes and determines everything. In this 'fidelity in the Lord,' it is the Lord who is the faithful one, and those who believe attempt to adapt themselves to this faithfulness and out of his fidelity to do what is asked of them. The fidelity of the Lord, which in man becomes fidelity in the Lord, is something given, just like grace." (*The Letter to the Ephesians,* 18–19.) Similarly: "if he is there for us as the one who brings us the always-more of faith, love and hope." *John IV: The Birth of the Church* (San Francisco: Ignatius Press, 1991), 77. On the full surrender in the life of the resurrection, see *Markus,* 561.

der is also an act of faith.[122] This mystery of our surrender to God's power over our lives is also explained by Adrienne as the act of depositing our "Yes" with God in prayer, whereby it is actually *his* word more than our own. In giving it to him, we no longer have rights over it: "We do not say it of ourselves, by ourselves or in ourselves." Having thus objectively surrendered it, moreover, we must subjectively grow into it, or be made—"by purgatorial fire"[123]—to correspond to it: the word in which we were created, which is also God's image of each individual human being, present in him from before all time. In the final analysis, Christian obedience is thereby transformed from a subjective gift of the human person *offered to* God to an objective gift *accepted by* God, in virtue of which it is also perfected, as if by fire. In the one who dares to say "Yes" to God, the perfect assent of Christ is "only imperfectly fulfilled." When, however, his "Yes" is received and accepted by God, "it is fulfilled to utmost perfection in God."[124] His is a word of affirmation for which God himself offers the guarantee. It is an assent that is "formed from the very substance of his obedience to the Father."[125]

Mary–Church: Person as Response

This mysterious encounter of grace and faith, of God's faithfulness and our assent, of his invitation and our response, and ultimately of the Spirit who is God's objective gift to us and the same Spirit who is "the subject within our

---

[122] A similar thing happens, Adrienne explains, when the Lord surrenders his Spirit on the Cross. "Weakness and death merely keep him from continuing to exercise an active kind of obedience, and in order to preserve it whole and total the Son hands it over to the Father. It is somewhat like a mother who is carrying her child in her arms and who, on stumbling and feeling she is about to fall, instinctively first looks to the safety of the child. The giving back of the spirit guarantees that Christ's obedience will remain intact." (*They Followed His Call,* 64.) It would seem, from the example of Christ, that Christian obedience is purified by fire (or death, although this death is perhaps more spiritual than physical, without necessarily excluding the latter), as it were, so as to pass from a stage of active obedience, to passive obedience.

[123] *The Word Becomes Flesh,* 36, 37. "There in fire, he will lay aside his irresolution and his vacillation and conform to God's thought; he will have to learn to love through the painful expansion of love until he becomes one with his word deposited in God." (Ibid., 37.) On the image of this purifying fire, see also ibid., 26–27.

[124] *They Followed His Call,* 62.

[125] Ibid., 67. See also ibid., 122 with regard to sacramental grace as a partaking of Christ's obedience. On God's guarantee of our obedience, see *The Mission of the Prophets,* 123. For an example of the perfection achieved by the Lord in a human being, who surrenders himself in loving confidence to the Lord, see the example of St. John the Evangelist as presented by Adrienne in *The Word Becomes Flesh,* 7–14. On this theme in Balthasar, see, for example, *Glory of the Lord* I, 253f.

subject that receives him,"[126] reaches a sort of climactic center in Adrienne's presentation of the Church as a person in response to the person of the Lord. Anticipating Balthasar's presentation of a "theological person"[127] by three decades and the Second Vatican Council's presentation of the human person as finding himself in giving himself by two decades,[128] Adrienne presents a dialogical model of human fulfillment: "The word addressed by the Lord is the mission, and the response of the one commissioned to it is the 'person.'"[129] The project of self-realization from the Speyrian perspective thus consists, almost ironically, of being so depersonalized that one exists in total expectation and readiness for the Lord, whose grace is given in the form of a mission and more properly as a participation in his mission, which in turn is the constitutive element of his person, as we have seen.[130]

---

[126] *The Word Becomes Flesh,* 63. See above, the text corresponding to note 117.

[127] This concept which, in name, is attributable to him, is undoubtedly inspired by Adrienne's presentation thereof in her *Theologie der Geschlechter,* 130: "The Church is in fact only a person insofar as she is *response* to the person of the Lord." This work, although published in 1969 after Adrienne's death, was actually dictated in 1946 and 1947. Balthasar's four-volume *Theo-Drama* was published between 1973 and 1983. In volume three dedicated to "Persons in Christ" *(Dramatis personae)* (Einsiedeln: Johannesverlag, 1978; English trans. Ignatius Press, San Francisco, 1992), Balthasar explains: "In the acting area opened up by Christ, created conscious subjects can become persons of theological relevance, coactors in theo-drama. They cannot enter this acting area of their own accord; even less, once they are admitted, can they choose their own theological role. . . . But, . . . if man freely affirms and accepts the election, vocation and mission which God, in sovereign freedom, offers him, he has the greatest possible chance of becoming a person, of laying hold of his own substance, of grasping that most intimate idea of his own self—which otherwise would remain undiscoverable." (English ed., 263) On the dialogical aspect of human fulfillment based upon the relation between the sexes, for example, see *Theo-Drama* III, 284–87. See also 267 where he explains the distinction between vocation and mission. The "grace" of the Christian's calling, Balthasar explains, "contains within itself the demand for an answer, for a way of life that befits the state to which he has been elected and called." (Balthasar, *The Christian State of Life,* 141.) "He is the living God, 'bodily' present with and for man, and so he calls for an 'embodied' response: man, in the entirety of his existence as a hearer and answerer of the word." (Balthasar, *Prayer* [San Francisco: Ignatius Press, 1986], 36.) For an overview of his theology of mission, see Marc Ouellet, *L'existence comme mission: l'anthropologie théologigique de Hans Urs von Balthasar* (Ph.D. diss., Rome: Pontifical Gregorian University, 1983).

[128] See the Pastoral Constitution on the Church in the Modern World, *Gaudium et Spes* (December 7, 1965), no. 22.

[129] *Theologie der Geschlechter,* 130.

[130] See above, note 43. It is perhaps important to add, as Adrienne does, that precisely as obedient, Christ "does not become impersonal, since even in being obedient he is

The most obvious model of this mystery lies in the person of Mary, whose entire existence is presented by Adrienne in terms of her all-encompassing and constantly expanding consent to the Lord.[131] Mary puts all the potentialities of her nature at God's disposal, without consciously or even unconsciously holding anything back.[132] In thus remaining open and continuously ready for the Son, to whom she is given to be used as he deems necessary for the accomplishment of his mission, she also realizes herself as God has intended that she be.[133] Having no particular image of herself, she concentrates all her energies upon the task of love, without wasting time reflecting upon the question of her own self accomplishment.[134] She simply "lets happen" according to God's will so as to participate in the Son's mission as none other participates.[135]

---

both God and Person, and together with the Father he effects the procession of the Holy Spirit. Nor does the pliancy of his human nature before his divine Person make that nature impersonal." (*They Followed His Call*, 66.) "Being fully ecclesial means: to be so depersonalized *(entpersönlicht)* that one is as a whole readiness for the Lord." (*Theologie der Geschlechter*, 130.) In a similar manner, Balthasar explains that "it is a fundamental characteristic of all those who thus step onto the theological stage *en Christoi* that, in contrast to Christ, there is no identity between their (eternal) election and their (temporal) vocation and mission." (*Theo-Drama* III, 263.) So too: "our 'acting' in the acting area, that is, Christ, consists in bringing our innate non-identity into an ever-closer approximation to perfect identity. This is the purpose of our 'following of Christ,' in whom identity reigns. In other words, we are to assimilate our own 'I' more and more completely to our God-given mission and to discover in this mission our own identity, which is both personal and social." *Theo-Drama* III, 270–71.

131 Thus begins Adrienne's portrait of Mary in her book, *Handmaid of the Lord*: "As a sheaf of grain is tied together in the middle and spreads out at either end, so Mary's life is bound together by her assent" (7). To describe the nature of this assent Adrienne uses a series of negations: "She sets no conditions, she makes no reservations . . . no wish, no preference, no demands which must be taken into consideration. She enters into no contract with God. . . . She knows no calculation, no guarantee, no hint of reservation." (Ibid., 9.) Adrienne also explains that Mary's "Yes," as it is accepted by the Lord, is the model of the "express obedience of the vows" to religious life. See *They Followed His Call*, 16–17, 64. See also Balthasar's *First Glance at Adrienne von Speyr*, 51.

132 See *Handmaid of the Lord*, 9; see also *Das Wort und die Mystik*, I, 19, 23, 26.

133 *Mary in the Redemption*, 37.

134 *Das Wort und die Mystik* II, 517.

135 On this, see *The Mission of the Prophets*, 123; and *Farewell Discourses*, 266. On Adrienne's use of the term *Geschehenlassen* (letting happen), see Jacques Servais, "The *ressourcement* of contemporary spirituality under the guidance of Adrienne von Speyr and Hans Urs von Balthasar," *Communio: International Catholic Review* 26 (1999): 343–57.

In harmony with the constant tradition of the Church, Adrienne explains that all of Mary's extraordinary graces, including most especially her Immaculate Conception, are granted in view of her extraordinary mission to be the Mother of the Lord and thus also in some way to her human assent.[136] Beyond this, or rather as part of the same, Adrienne explains that her assent is itself a grace. Hers is not simply a human answer to God's invitation. It is such a tremendous grace that it is also "the divine answer to her entire life."[137] Her "Yes" is, then, not only *her word-gift to God*—the determination of her own free will—it is also and more profoundly still *God's gift-Word to her*: the Word of God as faith and the Word of God in the most supreme sense, namely, the Son of God.[138] Ultimately this means that Mary's

---

[136] Mary's assent is "unconditional," Adrienne explains, "because the Lord had redeemed her in advance, having chosen her from all eternity and found her to be worthy" (*They Followed His Call*, 70). Adrienne understands Mary's life as a "miracle" originating, like all miracles, from the eternal, "perfect love between the Father and the Son, which also includes the decision of the Incarnation." (*The Farewell Discourses*, 288.) Balthasar presents for himself the task of seeing "the privilege of the Immaculate Conception in the context of Mary's twofold mission: As a Mother, she has to mediate—in the requisite purity—everything human that her Child needs; as her Son's 'companion' and 'bride,' she must be able to share in his sufferings in a way appropriate to her, and what most fits her for this task is her utter purity, which means that she is profoundly exposed and vulnerable." Hence, "her privilege (which is demanded by her mission) only deepens her solidarity with mankind. Sin brings about isolation and thwarts effective solidarity . . . , whereas innocence makes it possible to be open to suffering with others and to be ready, in love, to embrace such suffering." *Theo-Drama* III, 323, 324. As for the doctrine of the Church, the Immaculate Conception was solemnly declared by Pope Pius IX on December 8, 1849 accordingly: "We declare, pronounce, and define: the doctrine which holds that the most Blessed Virgin Mary was, from the first moment of her conception, by a singular grace and privilege granted by Almighty God and in view of the merits of Jesus Christ, the Saviour of the human race, preserved immune from all stain of original sin, is a doctrine revealed by God and therefore to be believed and firmly and constantly by all the faithful." (Bull *Ineffabilis Deus, DS* 2803)

[137] *Handmaid of the Lord*, 8. Indeed, her entire life is, as Adrienne sees it, united in her assent, which "accompanies her at every moment of her existence." From it, "her life receives its meaning and form and unfolds toward past and future." (Ibid., 7.) "So completely was she enclosed in God from the very beginning," Adrienne explains, "that no other destiny could have been reserved for her than that of her assent." (*Farewell Discourses*, 266). See also *Das Wort und die Mystik*, II, 19.

[138] *Mary in the Redemption*, 24. See also *Theologie der Geschlechter*, 99; and *The Mission of the Prophets*, 123. Balthasar argues that because Mary is "pure readiness for the Word of God" so as to be its "graced, gifted prerequisite," this Word "can become not only 'spirit' (as, for example, in the Psalms) but also 'flesh'." "Maria und der Geist," *Geist und Leben* 56 (1983), 175.

assent to the angel is also realized by the Spirit, who is present at the Annunciation not only in overshadowing her but also within her. It is He "who will extend the Yes of her spirit to an assent of her body."[139] On the other hand, from within its enclosure within the Spirit's "Yes," Mary's assent "becomes a true, free and independent word of her own spirit."[140]

This mystery of encounter, orchestrated by the Spirit, is perhaps best understood in terms of a common and participated obedience: the obedience of Mary, who gives herself, body and soul, to the Father to do with as he will (and thus to the Son as a Mother) and the obedience of the Son, who gives himself to the Father for the world's salvation in the event of the Incarnation, and thus as a Son to the Mother.[141]

The resulting relationship between Mother and Son becomes the paradigm for Adrienne of the mysterious tension between flesh and spirit, nature and grace, divine action and human cooperation, as they are united in any project of "self"-realization. In this exemplar relationship it is hardly possible—nor necessary, Adrienne tells us—to determine at what point the Mother receives the Son and at what point the Son receives the Mother. The whole is a constant, mysterious, reciprocal relationship in which it is equally impossible to ascertain who accomplishes what. Granted, Christ gives more to his mother than she gives to him, but we must not attempt, Adrienne

---

[139] *Handmaid of the Lord,* 8. Similarly Adrienne explains that Mary's pregnancy "is a token of how great the surrender of her contemplation is" (*Handmaid of the Lord,* 157). See also *They Followed His Call,* 63. Despite this reference to the primacy of Mary's contemplation, Adrienne also insists upon the importance of the corporal aspect of her maternity: "If Christianity did not need the concrete, then Mary would somehow have given birth, conceived, and been pregnant in the spirit, so as to be able spiritually to bear the Son of the Spirit. But what actually happened was that, although she was overshadowed by the Spirit, Mary had to bear and give birth in a human way to the incarnate Son. She had to feel his weight in her body and, after his birth, in her arms" (*Mary in the Redemption,* 67). St. Augustine of Hippo argues in a similar manner that the Virgin conceives Christ in her faith before she conceives him in her womb (*Christum prius mente quam ventre concipiens, Sermo* 215, 4: *In redditione symboli,* PL 38, 1074). Hence, "By faith she believes; by faith she conceives" (*fide credidit, fide concepit).* Idem, *Sermo* 25, 7: PL 46, 937.

[140] *Handmaid of the Lord,* 8.

[141] Adrienne explains that the Mother participates in the Son's obedience. See *Handmaid of the Lord,* 33; and *Mary in the Redemption,* 13 and 16. On the other hand, Adrienne recognizes that the Son's terrestrial mission is fulfilled in Mary's Yes, "for she is pre-redeemed and has received the grace and dignity to join in uttering the valid word, in the Son, that he himself will utter *[fiat].* He has fulfilled himself in this word just as she has fulfilled herself through it." *The Boundless God* (San Francisco: Ignatius Press, 2004), 151.

warns us, "to reduce the mystery to a transparent proportion."[142] When Mary gives her assent, she gives herself entirely, body and soul, without attempting to determine how much she surrenders and how much God will take from her, nor how much he will give to her in return.[143] To speculate about such matters would, Adrienne explains, be potentially "deleterious to divine grace,"[144] for no earthly standard can be applied here; "the Spirit himself holds the standard in his hands."[145]

Similarly, it would be "perverse" to think of everything in Mary as attributable to a special grace, for Christ recognizes in his mother an authentic human good: a whole-hearted willingness to be united to him. This is, more specifically, "the human good that conforms to, nourishes, and, above all, makes possible his human form."[146] This is so much the case that Christ learns as a child to know love in the form in which his mother loves him, with the result that his love for the disciples is wholly penetrated with his Mother's love. In this love, the divine and the human "are inseparably mingled. It is love that is heavenly as well as earthly, masculine as well as feminine."[147] As for Mary, she subjectively experiences her obedience as constant and living, with the result that she discovers therein "more far-reaching consequences and more energetic and inexhaustible life than she had suspected."[148] Hers is, under the Spirit's guidance, a "living, self-fulfilling perfection,"[149] as is manifest in the "perfect unity and harmony" between what Mary accomplishes in her mediation and what God accomplishes through her mediation.[150]

The mysterious meeting of liberties at the Annunciation is, therefore, the beginning of a dynamic relationship not only between the Mother and the Son, but also between Mary and the Spirit. Mary receives the Spirit at the Annunciation, Adrienne teaches, in a twofold manner: *for the Son,* who lives in her—and in this sense, she receives the Spirit so as to become his vessel—and

---

[142] *Mary in the Redemption,* 38. On the question of Mary's merit in relation to the grace she has received, see *Das Wort und die Mystik,* II, 430.

[143] See *Das Wort und die Mystik,* I, 23; and *They Followed His Call,* 73.

[144] *The Mission of the Prophets,* 124.

[145] "This standard has its visible effects both in the Mother's spirit and in her body, but this visibility itself bears the signs of its origin in the Spirit. It is a standard that disappears into God's invisible standard" (*They Followed His Call,* 63).

[146] *Mary in the Redemption,* 38.

[147] *The Farewell Discourses,* 67.

[148] *They Followed His Call,* 61. An obvious example given by Adrienne is the loss of the child in the temple.

[149] *Farewell Discourses,* 266.

[150] This unity and harmony is, Adrienne explains, ultimately founded in her graced participation in the Trinitarian life. See *Mary in the Redemption,* 45.

for herself; namely, so that she might become the Church, Christ's Bride.[151] All of this is possible because her assent is so unlimited, "a malleable material out of which God can make whatever he will."[152] Indeed, even her virginity is interpreted by Adrienne in this sense: a "letting happen, even into her inner-most flesh."[153] Through her faith, her body is willing, and as a result, she is the first human being to experience the Trinity both corporally and spiritually.[154]

Ultimately this means not only that the Mother (actively) realizes herself, or her person, in and through her mission, but also and more profoundly that she is (passively but willingly) *realized* in her mission. She does not fulfill her mission simply in that she becomes the Son's "vessel." More profoundly still, "she herself becomes fruit;"[155] for "God's action in her gradually outweighs her own action."[156] This more passive, or obedient, form of self-realization points, moreover, to the fact that it is not so much *her mission* that is of sig-nificance, but rather *Christ's mission*, wherein she participates. This in turn means that the living Mother-Son relationship is a paradigm for the various tensions present in human fulfillment—those, especially, between nature and grace, spirit and flesh, the divine and human actions, and so on—most espe-cially as the merging of missions. Mary's mission "loses itself in, and is rounded off by, the Son's mission," Adrienne explains. Christ's mission as the Son of Man, on the other hand, is fulfilled "by merging with the Mother's mission."[157] If, in fact, it were to be severed from hers, it would be as it if he were severed from himself, Adrienne explains.[158] In the merging of their mis-sions, the Lord "simultaneously fulfils his Mother," Adrienne continues, "and from that moment on, there exists an immutable state of being reciprocally

---

[151] See ibid., 107. Balthasar presents Mary as the "archetypical Bride of Christ" ("Maria und der Geist," 174), "the symbol and more than the symbol of this bride, her irre-trievable origin and her final goal." *Mary for Today* (San Francisco: Ignatius Press, 1988), 53. Hence, her personal election as a "theological person" (her unique role as the mother of Christ) cannot be separated from the election of the Church as a whole. See his *Theo-Drama* III, 272–73, 299. She is, he argues, both "the part" and "the whole" of the Church. See his *Threefold Garland* (San Francisco: Ignatius Press, 1982), 129, 21 and *Test Everything Hold Fast to What is Good* (San Francisco: Ignatius Press, 1989), 82–83.

[152] *Handmaid of the Lord*, 8.

[153] *Bereitschaft. Dimensionen Christlichen Gehorsams* (Einsiedeln: Johannesverlag, 1975), 68.

[154] See *Der erste Korintherbrief*, 323; *The Handmaid of the Lord*, 8; and *Das Themenheft* (Einsiedeln: Johannesverlag, 1977), 11.

[155] *Theologie der Geschlechter*, 99. Adrienne explains that being fruit here means both that she becomes the Lord's Mother and that she becomes his Bride (ibid., 100).

[156] *The Farewell Discourses*, 265.

[157] *The Mission of the Prophets*, 124.

[158] *Mary in the Redemption*, 76.

bound together—the Mother to the Son and the Son to the Mother—which also provides the point of departure for all Christian missions."[159] Drawn into Christ's mystery in this way, she becomes a significant part therein and actually helps him to accomplish it.[160] In receiving him, into her womb, she simultaneously receives his mission; in carrying him, she also carries his mission; in praying, she carries his prayer; and in determining the hour of his public ministry, she gives birth to him again "into his mission."[161] Accompanying him thereafter in her contemplation, she becomes his companion in the Spirit, in whom and through whom he accomplishes his every action,[162] and in this capacity of helpmate, she "bears his fruit."[163] Her mission throughout his public ministry is, in other words, conceived by Adrienne as "one extended pregnancy," impelling her toward the Cross, "the hour of birth."[164] In this sense, she lives toward the Cross, together with her Son, but Adrienne also presents Mary as living most especially *from* the Cross: "[H]er whole destiny as a mother is sealed and consummated in conceiving."[165]

Although one would perhaps recognize in these words a reference to the Immaculate Conception—the fruit of Christ's redemption being at the origin of her maternal mission—Adrienne refers thereby to the assent of Mary as uniting the events of Nazareth, Bethlehem, and Golgotha with the result that the latter sacrifice is already implicit in the former.[166] This means also

---

[159] *The Mission of the Prophets,* 124, von Speyr, *The Christian State of Life.* See also *The Farewell Discourses,* 265: "the entire mission of the Son and her own mission grow together into a developing unity." Cf. Balthasar's *Theo-Drama* III, 304–5.

[160] *Handmaid of the Lord,* 38.

[161] *The Word Becomes Flesh,* 167. See also *Mary in the Redemption,* 76, 103, 122; and *Theologie der Geschlechter,* 118.

[162] See *The Word Becomes Flesh,* 166; and *Mary in the Redemption,* 87. On contemplation as Mary's "new form" of accompanying her Son, see *Handmaid of the Lord,* 99; and *Mary in the Redemption,* 104.

[163] *The Handmaid of the Lord,* 37.

[164] *The Farewell Discourses,* 265.

[165] *The Word Becomes Flesh,* 53.

[166] "At the foot of the Cross is the *Mother of the Lord,* who participates in the sacrifice. Though in her case the sequence is lived in the reverse order. She gives her consent at the foot of the Cross; the birth of the child in Bethlehem is the consummation of the sacrifice; and when the child was conceived in Nazareth she was already the victim, given to God. This reversal of the order reveals her very being as woman: her end is already in her beginning. Her whole destiny as a mother is sealed and consummated in conceiving: she lives *from* the Cross, while Christ, being man, lives in the opposite direction, *toward* the Cross." Ibid., 53. Cf. Hans Urs von Balthsar, *Mary For Today,* 62; idem, *Unless You Become Like This Child* (San Francisco: Ignatius Press, 1991); idem, "O Vierge, Mère et fille de ton Fils" in *Marie, première Église* (Paris and Montreal: Apostolat des editions and Editions paulines, 1981), 54.

that the Cross lies constantly in the shadows of the Mother's mind: Every manifestation of his glory and every task accomplished leads him ever closer and inevitably to the Cross.[167] It is there that she becomes the Mother of all those for whom Christ gives his life, those who are entrusted to her in the person of John.[168]

It is within this context of Mary's universal maternity effected on the Cross that Adrienne recognizes her as having the express mission, and thus also the grace, to educate and nourish our assent to the Lord. This she does by leading us along the paths of our lives—paths of joy and suffering—that she has already walked with her Son and in his Spirit. The strength of her faith encourages ours, even to the extent that her faith actually becomes *our* faith. By this is meant not only that the deposit of faith imparted to us by the Church and mediated by the apostles is first of all the faith of Mary, the faith of she who shared most closely in the redemptive mysteries.[169] More profoundly still, it means that Mary's all-encompassing and unfailing assent strengthens and encourages our only too feeble assents. For our part, accepting Mary as our mother does not mean that we can simply resign ourselves to the power of her "Yes," but that we must actually appropriate it as our own by generously surrendering and entrusting ourselves "to these powers of growth which carry" us.[170] In so doing, we have Adrienne's assurance that this Mother lends her help to expand our limited "Yes" to the measure of the Lord's task, or mission, for us.

The manner in which Mary accomplishes this mystery of her maternity in our regard is as mysterious as is the unity of her mission in the mission of Christ, but it is precisely therein (in the mystery of their united mission) that the mystery of her maternity is illuminated. Already at the scene of the Annunciation, for example, Adrienne recognizes Mary's assent as the prototype for

---

[167] Ibid., 166.

[168] *The Birth of the Church*, 124. "Just as the eternal and unique devotion between Father and Son flows out into the temporal and unbounded devotion of the Eucharist, so the unique virginal relation between Mother and Son flows out into the endless bestowal of her spiritual motherhood." (ibid.) See also *Handmaid of the Lord*, 165–66.

[169] In the prayer of the rosary, for example, Adrienne explains that "the Mother, through her concreteness, prepares the understanding for the hidden truths of the Son." (*Handmaid of the Lord*, 158, see also 84.) Similarly, Balthasar remarks that in keeping "all these things in her heart" (cf. Lk 2:51), Mary "lets them grow in her bosom in order afterward to pass them on to the Church and her hierarchical institution as being the archetypal Christian experience and wisdom." *The Threefold Garland*, 67.

[170] *Handmaid of the Lord*, 164. Henceforth: "If anyone keeps faith with her, she will keep everlasting faith with him." Ibid, 171.

every reception of the Lord in Holy Communion.[171] Every reception of Communion, in turn, actually *participates in her reception* of the Lord at the Annunciation.[172] This is the case, Adrienne argues, because, first of all, her "Yes" is subjectively so comprehensive that it includes not only *everything* that the Lord might ask of her, but also everyone who wants to believe and to offer their assistance to the Lord in the accomplishment of his mission.[173] Furthermore, her "Yes" is objectively so comprehensive that she becomes a "vessel for the whole of belief,"[174] and even a "mediatrix of self-surrender."[175] The unity of the subjective and objective elements of her faith—realized in both cases by the intervention of the Holy Spirit—are apparent in that her "private" "Yes" is, as Adrienne sees it, transformed by God into a "Catholic" one, so as to become "the cradle of all Christianity."[176]

---

[171] On this, see *Das Wort und die Mystik*, II, 127.

[172] *Handmaid of the Lord*, 153. For precisely this reason, the communicant need not be concerned with the worthiness of his soul, for ultimately his communion should be entrusted to hers (ibid). And indeed, she is indifferent to no Eucharistic communion, but attends at each and every one. "Each and every Communion is for her like a feast of remembrance of her own reception of the Lord, a feast that makes present what has been in a supra-temporal way" (*Mary in the Redemption*, 119). Similarly, Balthasar, in his meditation of the first joyful mystery of the rosary (the Annunciation) writes: "The sinful Church—we ourselves—receives the Lord's Body Eucharistically. But none of us receives him wholly, according to his intention of giving himself to us. This is why, behind each of our communions, there stands the *Ecclesia immaculate*, the spotless Church who completes our imperfect assent. Only the Church in us communicates perfectly in Christ's Body, and this is one more reason to be thankful to her and adhere to her Spirit." *The Threefold Garland*, 34.

[173] *Mary in the Redemption*, 11. Her fiat is "the original vow out of which arises every form of definitive Christian commitment to God and in God." Balthasar, *First Glance at Adrienne von Speyr*, 51.

[174] *The Birth of the Church*, 255. This is also apparent in that, as Adrienne teaches, it was—in virtue of its pure openness—able to "correspond to the manifestation of God." *Handmaid of the Lord*, 66–67.

[175] *Handmaid of the Lord*, 170. See also *They Followed His Call*, 72–73; and *Mary in the Redemption*, 12.

[176] Ibid., 66–67. It possesses the qualities of being "internally substitutive, social and Eucharistic," Adrienne adds (ibid., 67). Similarly, Balthasar maintains: "The Marian fiat, unequalled in its perfection, is the all-inclusive, protective and directive form of all ecclesial life. It is the interior form of *communion*, insofar as this is an unlimited mutual acceptance, far more than a human 'getting along together' or fraternization. The space and time limitations of the human condition remain external to this (ideally) unlimited receptivity." *The Office of Peter and the Structure of the Church* (San Francisco: Ignatius Press, 1986), 208.

Conclusion

The example of the Mother of God demonstrates how anyone who surrenders himself to the Lord may be drawn into his mission and may even help him realize it.[177] At the same time, the example of the Virgin manifests how personal fulfillment is achieved precisely therein: by means of a real participation in Christ's universal mission and thus also in his obedience. As God's gift, Mary's assent—to continue the example—is the highest grace; as a human response it is "the highest achievement made possible by grace: unconditional, definitive self-surrender."[178] It is thus not surprising that in Adrienne's theology the most personal and personalizing activity of the human being is not primarily of his own doing, but of his *allowing* to be done to him *(geschehen lassen)*. Requiring—contrary to appearances—an extraordinary exercise of the free will, such "actions" of allowing God to determine the direction of one's own accomplishment by grace consist primarily in the continued and generous perseverance of readiness and expectation. Like the fiat of the Blessed Virgin, this act of self-realization is, in other words, an act of obedience: a willing surrender of self—Adrienne uses the term *Hingabe*, denoting both surrender and devotion—which precisely as *willed* constitutes the highest form of personal freedom.[179]

It is certainly not in opposition to our freedom, then, that we should conceive of human perfection as being "burst apart,"[180] so as to die perfectly open to, and thus fully receptive of, the Lord. Created in order to be fulfilled in communion with the triune God, the human being is realized in a living relationship with God, Adrienne teaches, and more specifically, in a state of constant readiness to receive God according to God's desire to give of himself. This remaining flexible,[181] this allowing oneself to be formed by God, is that which constitutes the "unity" of the human being, the Swiss mystic tells us. In Mary, the new Eve, who remains fully open to God, permitting him to work within her as he pleases, it is perfectly realized: both in her complete readiness, or openness, which is already grace, and in the fulfillment of this

---

[177] *Handmaid of the Lord*, 32; cf. *They Followed His Call*, 59.

[178] Balthasar, *First Glance at Adrienne von Speyr*, 51.

[179] "Mary is totally dependent upon God and completely directed towards him, and, at the side of her Son, she is *the most perfect image of freedom and of the liberation* of humanity and of the universe." (Congregation for the Doctrine of the Faith, *Instruction on Christian Freedom and Liberation* (March 22, 1986), no. 97. The citation also appears in John Paul II's encyclical letter *The Mother of the Redeemer*, *Redemptoris mater* (March 25, 1987), no. 37. Cf. Balthasar, *Theo-Drama* III, 299.

[180] See *The Birth of the Church*, 77; and *The Word Becomes Flesh*, 103.

[181] Adrienne calls it, "keeping fluid," and she specifies: "within his essence and being." *Mary in the Redemption*, 35.

readiness, that is to say, in her maternal mission: in the enfleshment of God's Word (and grace) within her.

> God the Father's place in man is represented bodily by the Son in the Mother. Mary's genuine being and becoming is fulfilled through her acceptance of the Son. Even though she bears the Son within her and allows herself to be formed through him, she does not thereby alienate herself from other people or from herself; she experiences and performs her prime personal mission; she fulfils her task and adheres to becoming what God intended for her. Her unity is crowned by the Son.[182]

Like Mary, the Christian is challenged to let the Lord determine the conditions of his fulfillment by grace, with the result that it is the surrender itself that is decisive, humanly speaking, for the Christian's perfection. Just as the Lord's unlimited self-surrender on the Cross is the fulfillment of his life of love whereby death itself is destroyed and transformed into life, our own self-surrender to the Lord is that whereby our lives participate in the mystery of his ongoing incarnation and thus also in his redemptive mission, which continues in the Church. It follows that our reception of the Lord and his reception of us—not unlike Mary's reception of Christ and his of her—cannot be clearly distinguished: "the border between the one received and the one receiving is obliterated."[183] To receive the Lord means quite simply to be received by him.[184] Consequently the boundaries between objective and subjective redemption are also blurred. Ultimately, Adrienne's presentation of these mysteries only leads to more mystery, but such is perhaps the determinative sign of its authenticity. Such paradoxes "mirror something of the fullness and the incomprehensibility of God."[185]

---

[182] Ibid.

[183] To clarify: "one can no longer say who received and who is received, where receiving begins and where being received ends." *The Word Becomes Flesh,* 102.

[184] *The Letter to the Colossians,* 71.

[185] Balthasar, *First Glance at Adrienne von Speyr,* 49.

CHAPTER **14**

The Augustinian Foundations
of a Nuptial Theology of the Body:
"He Who Created Both Sexes
Will Restore Both"

LAWRENCE J. WELCH

Embodied Nuptial Sexuality: Does It Matter?

THE PLACE and importance of nuptial sexuality in Christian revelation is greatly questioned today. By nuptial sexuality I mean the reciprocity between man and woman whereby in their sexual existence each one of them is placed in relation to the other in a special way. What special way? I mean in the way that both man and woman experience the other as a different personal embodiment of human identity; in that man is made for woman and woman for man.[1] What some dispute, including some theologians, is whether this nuptial ordering of sexuality is of any importance for Christian revelation.

Two Contemporary Views

For example, the well-known theologian Elizabeth Johnson thinks that nuptial sexuality has very little theological significance.[2] For one thing, Johnson

---

[1] This reciprocity is asymmetrical in the sense that the sexual difference of the other can never be overcome or transcended by me. In other words, the reciprocal relation between the sexes is between two beings each of whom has a certain irreducible identity. There can be a union between the two ways of being in the body as man or woman but this union is not an absorption of one into the other or a union into a third way of being in a body. The other always remains "other" for me. On this point see Angelo Scola, "The Nuptial Mystery at the Heart of the Church," *Communio* 25 (1998): 630–62, at 645.

[2] Elizabeth Johnson, *She Who Is* (New York: Crossroad, 1993), 154–55. Johnson also objects to what she calls the "prevailing dualistic model" that imagines each sex as

353

argues that we need to go beyond an idea of a human nature that is polarized on the basis of sex in favor of "one human nature celebrated in a multiplicity of differences"[3] of which sex is one among many. Being a male or female is no more important than many other things that are said to be part of a person's identity. It is "short-sighted" to think of sexuality as more important and more fundamental than the elements of race, of culture, and of politics as well as a whole host of other elements said to be intrinsic to personal identity. Sexuality is one among many essential anthropological elements that makes up the identity of a human person. For Johnson what is important about sexuality is not that it has an enduring theological determination or meaning in Christian revelation but that it is a part of set of combinations that make up and celebrate the one human nature. According to Johnson only if sexuality is conceived as integrated into a holistic vision as one anthropological element among many, will sexuality avoid being distorted as a "touchstone of personal identity."[4]

Another theologian, Fr. David Power, has argued that sexuality is part of the limiting condition of our human enfleshment that the Risen Christ now somehow transcends.[5] Thus Power distinguishes between "a historical Jesus from the past," who was sexually determined, from the risen Christ, who is not. At the resurrection, Christ overcame the negative and limiting conditions of human existence including that of maleness and entered into solidarity with the whole human race. Transformed in the resurrection by the power of the Spirit, Christ takes body in the Church-communion where there is no male or female, Greek or Jew. Power therefore proposes that it is more fitting to see Christ as the renewed human rather than "as the male unit of a renewed male-female unity in one body." Here again nuptial sexuality is judged to have little if any lasting importance for Christian revelation.

The theological significance of the fact that human persons are created in two different bodily incarnations has been disputed for some time in the history of Christian thought. Already in the fourth and fifth centuries a common

---

"bearing unique characteristics from which the other sex is excluded." She rejects any idea of the complementarity of the sexes as rigidly determining the qualities and roles each should cultivate and play and as functioning as a "smoke screen for the subordination of women."

[3] Ibid., 155. At least here Johnson does not seem to make much of a distinction between "nature" and "person."

[4] Ibid., 156. Johnson explains that the sexuality of Jesus is important for his personal and historical identity, "but is not theologically determinative for his identity as the Christ nor normative for the identity of Christian community."

[5] See, for example, David Power, O.M.I., "Representing Christ in Community and Sacrament," in *Being a Priest Today*, ed. Donald Goergan (Collegeville, MN: Michael Glazier, 1992), 97–123, at 116.

view among many of the Fathers of the Church was that sexual differentiation was something God in his mercy gave to a humanity threatened by death because of the Fall of Adam. Some of the Fathers thought that originally Adam and Eve, were sexless angelic-like creatures who had no need of reproduction as we know it now. Sexuality after the Fall was important for one reason and one reason only: that the human race might continue to live and that God's command "Be fruitful and multiply" might be obeyed. The role sexuality played in the cosmic drama was temporary and instrumental. This was, albeit with some variation, the view of Ambrose,[6] Gregory of Nyssa,[7] and Jerome.[8]

An Impermanent Reality: Gregory of Nyssa

Gregory of Nyssa was particularly insistent about the temporary nature of sexuality. In his interpretation of the creation of humanity in the Genesis accounts, Gregory distinguished between an ideal, angelic-like humanity and an actual humanity. In his original design, God saw humanity as collective whole destined for Christ in whom there is neither male or female. In a process unknown to us, humanity would have grown and multiplied in an angelic way, rather than through bodily sexual union. Why then an actual creation of humanity as male and female? Gregory explains that God foresaw that humanity as a whole would sin against its spiritual nature by turning away from God and toward material realities. The human race, no longer existing in an angelic way, would have stopped reproducing and would have faced extinction. Therefore God in his mercy divided humanity into male and female with garments of skin, in order that they might multiply by way of carnal generation like the animals. Thus, for Gregory sexual differentiation is secondary and temporary. Sexuality and procreation serve God's original design for humanity but only because they prevent the extinction of a sinful humanity.[9] While Gregory believes that humanity is created in the image of

---

[6] Ambrose, *Exhortation on Virginity,* 6, 36 (*Exhortatio uirginitatis,* PL, 16, 197–244; E. Cazzaniga, *Sancti Ambrosii De Virginibus,* Turin, 1948). For an English translation, see *On Virginity, by Ambrose, Bishop of Milan,* trans. Daniel Callam (Toronto: Peregrina, 1980).

[7] Gregory of Nyssa, *On the Making of Man,* 17 (*De opifico hominis,* PG, 44, 125–256; SC, 6 [1943]); for an English translation *A Select Library of the Nicene and Post-Nicene Fathers,* Gregory of Nyssa, *On the Making of Man,* ed. P. Schaff and H. Wace, 2/5 (Grand Rapids, MI: Eerdmans, 1994 [reprint]). Hereafter referred to as *NPNF.*

[8] See Jerome, *Against Jovinian,* 1, 29 (*Adversus Jovinianum,* PL, 23, 211–338). For an English translation, see *NPNF,* 2/6, Jerome, *Against Jovinianus.*

[9] The following account is taken from the work *On the Making of Man,* 16–17. See also the Oration "On Those Who Have Fallen Asleep," 9.63 (*Gregory Nysseni*

God, he argues that the creation of humanity as *male and female* in no way pertains to the divine image and likeness.[10] He holds that in the resurrection we will all be one in Christ and that our risen bodies will be divested of all signs of sexual differentiation.[11] In the resurrected state we will leave behind all that we have received with the garment of skin—all those things that we share with the nature of irrational animals. The ideal humanity of God's original design will be fulfilled eschatologically. Ultimately, sexuality is something alien to both the original divine design and the final definition of humanity.

Opera, W. Jaeger et al.ed. (Leiden: E.J. Brill, 1960), where Gregory repeats his opinion that the differences between the sexes were given solely for the purpose of procreation. Gregory's views proved to be influential for some of the Greek Fathers that followed him. For instance, Hans Urs von Balthasar cites this interesting passage from Maximus the Confessor: "I repeat what the great Gregory of Nyssa taught me: the first thing to happen when man fell from perfection was that *pathe* were introduced, growing up in the irrational part of man's nature; only then did that manner of procreation enter into human existence that is connected to fleshly pleasure, on the one hand and death on the other." See *Maximus, Questiones ad Thalassium* 1 (PG, 90, 296A), quoted in Hans Urs von Balthasar, *Theo-Drama*, trans. Graham Harrison, vol. 2 (San Francisco: Ignatius Press, 1990), 380.

[10] In his *On the Making of Man*, 16.14, Gregory claims that the distinction between male and female "has no reference to the Divine Archetype, but, as we have said, is an approximation to the less rational nature." See 16.7 where he makes reference to Galatians 3:28 in support of this claim:

> We must, then, examine the words carefully: for we find, if we do so, that that which was made "in the image" is one thing, and that which is now manifested in wretchedness is another. "God created man," it says; "in the image of God created He him." There is an end of the creation of that which was made "in the image": then it makes a resumption of the account of creation, and says, "male and female created He them." I presume that every one knows that this is a departure from the Prototype: for "in Christ Jesus," as the apostle says, "there is neither male nor female." Yet the phrase declares that man is thus divided.

For Gregory man, male and female, shares the likeness of animals. See *On the Making of Man*, 17.5. For a helpful summary of Gregory of Nyssa's understanding of sexuality, see Verna E. F. Harrison, "Male and Female in Cappadocian Theology," *Journal of Theological Studies* 41 (1990): 441–71, at 465–71. Harrison points out that "For Gregory, this second likeness includes a whole complex of non-rational and biological characteristics—gender and the corresponding mode of reproduction, childhood and old age, nutrition and elimination, passions such as desire and aggressiveness, and mortality itself" (467).

[11] For example, see his discussion in the dialogue *On the Soul and Resurrection*, trans. Virginia Woods Callahan, in *Saint Gregory of Nyssa, Ascetical Works* (Washington, DC: Catholic University Press of America Press, 1967), 264–71, especially 266. For Gregory the resurrection will be the return of human nature to its original form, that is, before its division into male and female.

The common element between these theologians, both ancient and modern, is that nuptial sexuality is disconnected from the order of redemption insofar as it is considered to be without any real theological significance in Christian revelation. Whether one thinks of nuptial sexuality as temporary, or a limitation, or just another part of a socially constructed identity, it is supposed that Christ and the redemption he brings has very little to say about something that is important to embodied human existence. Surely this is something of a problem. For instance, if as the Christian tradition teaches us about the resurrection, our whole bodies will rise and not just some part of our bodies, then, our risen bodies will be masculine and feminine. If we will be raised as men and women, then sexuality is in some way a redeemed reality. If sexuality is a redeemed reality, it must bear some theological meaning. Surely, it is the case that at least someone among the Fathers saw this and thought about it. I believe there is someone, but oddly enough someone that many people might least suspect.

Augustine of Hippo. Sexual Differentiation: A Sacramental Reality

An important exception to the understanding in his day of sexuality as a temporary and instrumental remedy against death and therefore of little or no theological meaning was Augustine of Hippo. He saw the sexual differentiation of the first couple as a part of God's original creative plan and as something that foreshadowed the unity between Christ and the Church. The idea that Augustine has anything to say of importance to us today about sexuality may strike some as rather odd. After all, we often hear, wrongly I might add, that it was Augustine who taught that sexual relations between a husband and wife always involved at least a venial sin.[12]

The real Augustine is far more complicated. As one of his twentieth-century biographers reminds us: We should not demonize Augustine on the issue of sexuality.[13] Peter Brown has pointed out, rightly I believe, that Augustine's

---

[12] Augustine actually held that intercourse for the purpose of procreation is not sinful. He thought that when married couples engaged in intercourse beyond the need for generation it was venially sinful. This may be rigorist but it is not the same thing as saying all intercourse between married men and women is a venial sin. See *On the Good of Marriage*, 5.6 and *On Marriage and Concupiscence*, 1.12.13. For an excellent discussion of this issue, see John Hugo, *Augustine on Nature, Sex, and Marriage* (Chicago: Scepter, 1969), 109–15.

[13] Peter Brown, *Augustine of Hippo* (Los Angeles: University of California, 1967, 2000), 502. See also his *The Body and Society* (New York: Columbia University Press, 1988), 399–408.

thought on sexuality evolved and developed over time—the result of a long inner journey that the North African saint underwent. I believe that we can learn something today from Augustine's journey, particularly as it touches on the theological significance of the creation of human persons as sexually differentiated. It shows us that the context for thinking about the place and meaning of nuptial sexuality in Christian anthropology is sacramental. Augustine saw that if marriage is in some sense a sacrament, and if the union between Christ and the Church is understood nuptially, then sexuality cannot be regarded simply as given for biological survival. It has a significance intrinsic to our salvation. I believe that Augustine's journey anticipated, in a way, today's struggle over the sacramental meaning of sexuality.

Augustine's insights to be sure are incomplete. Nevertheless he grasped, with unusual perceptivity something about how nuptial sexuality is a central part of human existence that is really addressed by divine revelation, really addressed by Christ. In terms of contributing to the current discussion about the significance of nuptial sexuality in Christian revelation, Augustine's journey shows us that to think of it as theologically neutral is to put in question the sacramentality of marriage and the nature of the relationship between Christ and the Church. It is to put in question sacramental realism; it is to put in question the belief that the sacramental acts of the Church reflect and correspond to the truth of existence as effected by God.

At the same time that Augustine explained the married unity of couples as a sacrament of Christ and the Church, he was also explaining how the unity between Christ and his Church should be understood as a personal unity like that of marriage. There is a real relation between Augustine's theology of marriage and his ecclesiology. Thanks to a number of factors, Augustine's thought was sharpened over time. His rethinking of the significance of the sexuality of Adam and Eve in paradise, as well as his explanation of the relationship between Christ and the Church as a nuptial reality, is an intellectual journey that is instructive for us today.

In what follows I will sketch in broad strokes this journey of Augustine. Of course I will have to be brief. I make no pretense of giving a comprehensive description of Augustine's complicated views on human sexuality. Still, I believe that Augustine can show us some important things.

My presentation will unfold in four parts. In the first part, I will give a brief overview of Augustine's early attempt to articulate the sacramentality of marriage in the history of salvation. He saw that understanding marriage as a sacrament inevitably raised questions about the role of nuptial sexuality in God's plan of creation even prior to the Fall. In the second part, I will describe how Augustine rethought his views on the place and importance of the sexual differentiation of the first couple in paradise and how he came to the conclusion that the first man and woman foreshadowed the future reality of Christ and the Church. So strongly did Augustine connect nuptial sexuality to the order of redemption that he insisted that the unity between Christ and the Church should be understood in terms of personal unity like that of marriage. Thus in the third part, I will give a brief overview of how Augustine described Christ and the Church as joined in a bodily union as bridegroom and bride. In the fourth and final section of my presentation I will indicate how I believe Augustine's thought is helpful for the contemporary discussion about theological significance of nuptial sexuality.

Augustine and the Sacramentality of Marriage

In 401 Augustine wrote a treatise titled *On The Good of Marriage*.[14] In his *Retractions*, Augustine says that he wrote the work in response to the heresy of the monk Jovinian. The writings of Jovinian rejected the doctrine that the merit of virginity was superior to the merit of marriage. Jovinian argued that to hold virginity as superior to marriage involved a negative, Manichean understanding of marriage. These views of Jovinian were very influential and persuaded some nuns in Rome to give up celibacy for marriage. Jovinian's teachings commanded a following even after they were condemned in 393 by a Roman Synod headed by Pope Siricus and by a synod in Milan headed by Ambrose.

Augustine tells us that the supporters of Jovinian bragged that he could only be answered by censuring marriage, not by praising it. Augustine disagreed. For this reason he wrote *On Good of Marriage*. But there was also another reason. He tells us that there were previous unsuccessful attempts to refute Jovinian. One that Augustine may have in mind was an infamous treatise by Jerome, *Against Jovinian*. Jerome, perhaps the most accomplished Christian polemicist of all time, was so harsh and negative in his rhetoric that his response to Jovinian was rightly regarded by many as an attack on marriage itself. Some of Jerome's friends tried to have copies of his treatise withdrawn from circulation.

---

[14] All quotes are taken from the English translation, *Marriage and Virginity: The Excellence of Marriage, Holy Virginity, The Excellence of Widowhood, Adulterous Marriages, Continence,* trans. Ray Kearney, ed. David Hunter, in *The Works of Saint Augustine,* ed. John E. Rotelle, vol. 1/9 (Hyde Park, NY: New City Press, 1999), 33–61. Although I make use of this translation in this paper, I have chosen not to follow its translation of the title *De bono conjugali* into the *Excellence of Marriage.* I prefer to translate the title *De bono conjugali into On the Good of Marriage.* This has been the more common way of translating *De bono conjugali* in earlier and familiar English translations. For the Latin texts see *De bono conjugali,* PL, 40, 373–96; *CSEL,* 41.

Augustine's treatise *On the Good of Marriage* is an effort to sail a middle way between the claim of Jovinian that gift of virginity is in no way superior to marriage and Jerome's belittling of marriage. Augustine argued on the one hand, that the gift of virginity is of greater merit than the married state and, on the other hand, that marriage was good, holy, and instituted by God.[15] He presented marriage as a form of friendship and "the first natural bond of human society."[16] In defense of marriage, Augustine identified three goods destined to become classic for the Catholic theology of marriage: off-spring,[17] mutual fidelity,[18] and the *sacramentum* or the sacramental bond.[19]

It is this third good that is of particular interest for the present purposes because the holiness of the *sacramentum* is something specific to the marriage of Christians. While we should be careful not to read back into Augustine's thought a later and more developed understanding of sacraments and sacra-mental causality, it should be remembered that Augustine's theology of the sacraments was quite advanced for its time and proved to be very influential. He understood sacraments broadly as visible signs that corresponded to an invisible sacred reality.[20] He could also make more precise distinctions with

---

15 Augustine believed that virginity was of higher merit because of its intense eschato-logical character. Virginity anticipated the life of the world to come. In *On Holy Virginity*, Augustine could describe it as a sharing in the life of the angels (13). Vir-gins, Augustine contends, preserve in their bodies that spiritual integrity that the whole Church preserves in the faith, imitating the Mother of the Lord. At the same time Augustine said that those who have the gift of virginity needed sound instruc-tion so that they might be humble and not become puffed up with pride so that love might not be offended against. He also points out that the gift of martyrdom is even higher than the gift of virginity (46.46–47).

16 *On the Good of Marriage,* 1.1.

17 Ibid., 1.1; 6; 24, 32. Thanks to children, who are the worthy fruit of the union of man and wife, human persons are held together in society not only by similarity of race but also of the bond of kinship.

18 Ibid., 4.4; 24, 32. This good of marriage referred to that power of authority each spouse has over the body of his or her partner. A husband or wife was not to abstain from sexual relations except with the approval of their spouse. The violation of fidelity of course is adultery. Augustine understood husband and wife as giving one another the mutual service of sustaining each other in weakness for the avoidance of illicit sexual union.

19 Ibid., 18.21; 24, 32.

20 See Letter 138 (*Epistula* 138; *CSEL,* 44.131): "It would take too long to discuss adequately the variety of signs which are called sacraments when they applied [per-tinent] to divine things" (Fathers of the Church, vol. 20, trans. Sr. Wilfrid Parsons [New York: Fathers of the Church, Inc.], 40). Cf. *City of God,* 10, 5: "A sacrifice, therefore, is the visible sacrament or sacred sign of an invisible sacrifice." All quota-tions of the *Civitas Dei* (PL, 41; *CSEL,* 40) are taken from *The City of God,* trans. Marcus Dods (New York: The Modern Library, 1950).

regard to the sacraments such as Baptism and Eucharist. Augustine could distinguish between the sacramental sign itself *[sacramentum tantum]* and the effect of the sacrament or the *res sacramenti*. Water, for example washes the body and signifies what occurs in the soul.[21] Moreover, Augustine argued that sacraments are not arbitrary sacred signs. They have a likeness to the reality that they signify.[22]

Augustine could also speak of a sacrament in terms of a binding oath or sacred religious commitment. In *On the Good of Marriage* Augustine seems to understand the *sacramentum* of marriage in this way although he sees it too as symbol capable of signifying a plurality of sacred realities. He could even speak of the polygamous marriages of the Old Testament patriarchs as *sacramentum*. They signified "the plurality of people who would one day be subject to God in all nations of the earth."[23] The many wives of the patriarchs also signified the future churches arising from all nations subject to one husband, Christ. What made the *sacramentum* of monogamous marriages in the Christian dispensation different had to with the fact that indissolubility was fundamental to it. The holiness or sanctity of the *sacramentum* of Christian marriage did not permit divorce and remarriage even in the case of adultery on the part of one of the spouses or for reason of sterility.

Augustine thought that the Christian signification of marriage brought about an indissoluble bond that was more binding than the bond of non-Christian marriage.[24] What brings about this *sacramentum*, this indissoluble bond? Augustine takes it almost for granted that it comes from Christ in his union with the Church. Although he does not explicitly cite Ephesians 5:31–32—where the one flesh union of Genesis 2:24 is said to be a great mystery in reference to Christ and the Church—this passage lurks in the background of Augustine's discussion of the indissolubility of Christian marriage. Augustine supposes that Christ and the Church is the great *sacramentum* that contains the holiness of indissolubility. This can be seen in a fascinating and often overlooked passage in the eighteenth chapter of *On the Good of Marriage* where Augustine makes an interesting argument from the

---

[21] See *Tractates on the First Letter of John*, 6.3.11 in *NPNF*, 1/7 (*In epistulam Ioannis ad Parthos*, PL, 35; SC, 75). "Consequently, the water of the sacrament is one thing: another, the water which betokens the Spirit of God. The water of the sacrament is visible: the water of the Spirit invisible. That washes the body, and betokens that which is done in the soul. By this Spirit the soul itself is cleansed and fed."

[22] For example, Letter 98 (*Epistula* 98, *CSEL*, 34.520) in Fathers of the Church, vol. 18, 137–38. "If the sacred rites had no resemblance to the things which they represent, they would not be sacred rites; they generally take their names from the mysteries they represent."

[23] *On the Good of Marriage*, 18.21.

[24] Ibid., 24, 32.

liturgical practice of the Church of his day comparing holy orders to marriage.[25] He explains that after our pilgrimage on earth there will be a perfection of human unity in heaven where there will be a city of people with a single heart and soul turned toward God. For this reason, he thinks that with the coming of Christ, marriage has been restored to a union of one man and one woman to the extent that a man who has been married more than once should not be ordained. A presiding priest *[antiste]* who is able to symbolize the union of all nations in submission to Christ is a man who has had only one wife or who has not been married at all. Augustine argues that a man who has married more than once, even though he has not sinned, has lost a certain standard or prerequisite for the seal of ordination. He seems to think of him as unable to symbolize the great *sacramentum*, the indissoluble union of Christ and the Church.

It is not too surprising that Augustine almost as a matter of fact assumes in *On the Good of Marriage* that the unity of all nations or the Church with Christ is a nuptial kind of unity. In earlier works Augustine had already spoken of the church as a wife created from the side of Christ[26] and of "the marriage of the catholic Church to the Lord."[27]

Augustine goes on to say in the chapter 18 of *On the Good of Marriage* that this unity of all nations in submission to Christ will be perfected in the future. The sacrament of monogamous marriage, he claims, symbolically signifies this future reality in the heavenly city. But Augustine seems to suppose

---

[25] Augustine also compares the bond of marriage to the permanency of ordination. See ibid. He makes the point there are times when one of the purposes of marriage is not achieved and yet the sacrament remains. Something like this can happen with the sacrament of ordination as well. Ordination, the Bishop of Hippo says, is given for the purpose of forming the community of the faithful. Nevertheless, sometimes communities fall apart or cannot be formed. Still, the sacrament of ordination remains. So, too, in the cases where an ordained man is dismissed from the clerical state. The Lord's sacrament still remains, although the unworthy man must answer for his wrongdoing at the judgment. Similarly, if a man or woman divorces his or her spouse and marries another the marriage bond is not broken. The Lord's sacrament is still intact and will remain so until the death of one of the marriage partners. Augustine's comments show that he had some idea that the sacrament of marriage brought about a bond that had certain kind of sacramental objectivity to it.

[26] *On Genesis Against the Manichees*, 2.24.11 (*De Genesi contra Manichaeos, libri II*, PL 34, 173–220; *CSEL* 91). For an English translation, see *Two Books on Genesis Against the Manichees*, trans. Roland J. Teske, in *Fathers of the Church*, vol. 84, (Washington, DC: CUA Press, 1991). This early work was written from 388–89. See also *Reply to Faustus the Manichean*, 15.3 (*Contra Faustum Manicheum*, PL, 42; *CSEL*, 25.1). For an English translation see *NPNF*, 1/4. This theme appears in later works of Augustine as well. For instance, *The City of God*, 22.17.

[27] *Reply to Faustus the Manichean*, 15.5.

too that marriage is able to signify this reality because it signifies the indissolubility of Christ and the Church and in a way participates in it. Augustine thinks of the symbolic signification of Christian marriage in more than one way but always in reference to the Christ-Church unity.[28] That the *sacramentum* of Christian marriage signifies this nuptial reality is an idea that Augustine will return to again in his later works.

Rethinking the Place of Embodied Sexuality in Paradise

A keen interpreter of Augustine's thought once observed that it would have never occurred to Augustine, who was biblical to his fingertips, to use any other basis for evaluating marriage other than the history of salvation in its eschatological movement.[29] For eschatological things cast light on first things. This approach also prods Augustine into raising a question in *On the Good of Marriage* that he answers only in a later work. The question had to do with whether the begetting of children by means of sexual intercourse was a part of God's original plan for the first man and the first woman even if they had not sinned. A number of Church Fathers, as I mentioned earlier, asked the same question and answered it in the negative. Bodily reproduction was thought to be tied up with being a fallen creature. Augustine was not so sure and left the question open in *On the Good of Marriage* only to answer it later in an important way in another work, *On the Literal Interpretation of Genesis*. Augustine began this commentary on Genesis around 401, soon after he had completed *On the Good of Marriage*. He did not finish his commentary on Genesis until about 415. In this work there is an important shift in his understanding of marriage and sexuality, a shift that put Augustine in stark contrast with some prominent Christian thinkers up to that time. The shift in Augustine's thinking in this work is an important moment in the intellectual movement of his thought about marriage and sexuality.

In an earlier commentary on Genesis prior to 401, Augustine gave a highly spiritualized interpretation of Adam and Eve in paradise. In his commentary *On Genesis Against the Manichees*, written around 389, Augustine was more interested in what the first man and woman spiritually symbolize than he was in the meaning of the first couple's corporeal reality. For instance

---

[28] One scholar of Augustine has remarked, rightly, that while Augustine "never draws the explicit conclusion that matrimony is a grace-giving sacrament of the New Law, as subsequently has become defined Catholic doctrine, but everything he says on this point has sacramental connotations, and makes such a conclusion almost inevitable." See Augustine Regan, "The Perennial Value of Augustine's Theology of the Goods of Marriage," *Studia Moralia* 21 (1983): 351–76, at 358.

[29] Ibid., 353.

in one passage, Augustine seems to say that prior to the Fall, human souls had no need for spoken words but drank directly from the Word of God, the fountain of truth.[30] Commenting on the creation of woman (Gen 2:22) Augustine was less interested in the bodily reality of the first man and woman and more interested in how as male and female they symbolized certain parts of the soul and how these parts are related to one another. The first woman illustrates how the soul's appetites should be subject to the virile mind.[31] The command in Genesis 1:28 to be fruitful and multiply according to Augustine refers to a spiritual, not a corporeal union, which would produce the fruit of good works.[32] Prior to the Fall the first man and woman would not have produced children in a carnal, fleshy way in keeping with their quasi-angelic condition. Sexual reproduction was something that happened only after Adam and Eve had incurred the penalty of death for their sin.

But in his *Literal Interpretation of Genesis* Augustine embarked upon a very different reading. He admitted that his interpretation in *On Genesis Against the Manichees* was overly allegorical and did not explain the text according to its proper historical meaning.[33] Augustine now insists that paradise must not be interpreted in an exclusively spiritual sense. It should be taken to refer to a spiritual and a literal, corporeal sense.[34] He explicitly rejected the opinion of some authors who thought that history properly speaking did not begin until Adam and Eve sinned, fell into tunics of skin, were joined in sexual union, and bore children.[35]

This new approach to reading Genesis allows Augustine to take up the question he had previously left unanswered in *On the Good of Marriage*: whether the begetting of children through sexual intercourse was a part of God's original plan for the first man and woman even if they had not sinned. Augustine now explains that Adam and Eve were fully physical, sexual, and social human beings before the Fall. The bodies of Adam and Eve, although unlike ours and not subject to death, would have been earthly ones, not heavenly, angelic like ones.[36]

---

[30] *On Genesis Against the Manichees*, 2.4.5. Even in his *Confessions*, XIII, 24, 37, he interprets Gen 1:28 as referring to the spiritual production of thoughts produced by the mind.

[31] *On Genesis Against the Manichees*, 2.11.15.

[32] Ibid., I, 19, 30.

[33] *On the Literal Interpretation of Genesis*, 8.2.5 (*De Genesi ad litteram libri* XII, PL, 34, 245 ≠ 486; *CSEL*, 28, 1). For an English translation see *The Literal Meaning of Genesis*, trans. John Hammond Taylor, 2 vols., in *Ancient Christian Writers* (New York: Newman Press, 1992).

[34] Ibid., 8.1.1.

[35] Ibid., 8.1.2.

[36] Ibid., 9.10.17.

Augustine acknowledged that there was no actual sexual union before the Fall of the first couple, but he insisted there was nothing in paradise that would have forbidden it. He contended that Adam and Eve chose to sin before they had a chance to know the corporeal union of sexual intercourse.[37] Had they avoided sin, the intercourse they could have enjoyed would have been free from any lust or compulsion. They would not have known of that inner struggle that the Apostle Paul wrote about between the law in our members and the law of our minds making us captive to the law of sin.[38] Childbirth would have been free from any pain and labor. Children would have been born not to make up for dead parents but for the purpose of populating the City of God. Once a certain determined number of people were born, they all would have been given an additional gift: the transformation of their bodies into a new higher, heavenly form of bodily existence without having to first pass through death, the punishment for sin.[39] Far from being asexual souls who fell from an angelic state into a physical one, Augustine now presented Adam and Eve as physical, sexual, and social creatures whom God placed in paradise to establish a people for the City of God. This vision of God's original plan for man before the Fall was a bold one and very different from the ascetic interpretation of Genesis in which marriage and sexuality were basically alien to the man's original state.

Augustine continues to champion the goodness of marital sexual relations and procreation in paradise in his famous work, the *City of God.* In Book XIV, written around 418–419, shortly after he completed *On the Literal Interpretation of Genesis,* he argues that it is absurd to think that were it not for sin there would be no need for sexual relations and procreation. This is tantamount, he objects, to asserting that sin is necessary to complete the number of saints. No, marriage and children were worthy of the happiness of paradise. Rejecting an over-spiritualized interpretation of God's creation of humanity as male and female as described in the book of Genesis, Augustine continues to insist that sexuality, the gift of marriage, and procreation were all instituted by God before Adam and Eve sinned. As proof for this claim he appeals to Christ's reply to the Pharisees concerning divorce: "Have you not read that He who made them from beginning made them male and female and said, For this reason shall a man leave father and mother, and shall cleave to his wife, and they shall be no longer two but one flesh."[40]

Augustine goes on to a discussion of what sexual relations between Adam and Eve would have been like had there been no sin and no Fall. He

---

[37] Ibid., 9.3.5.
[38] Ibid., 9.10.16.
[39] Ibid., 9.3.5; 9.6.10.
[40] *City of God,* 14.22.

argues that there would have been a complete harmony between the bodies and souls of Adam and Eve. They would have enjoyed a calmness of mind and integrity of body. There would have been an absence not only of lust but of impotence as well. Augustine draws a picture of the first couple with a freedom, a freedom for the good; that is, a greater freedom where spontaneity is not divorced from the mind. This is something Augustine thinks is largely unknown to us. We know only fallen freedom weighed down by concupiscence, disordered desire.[41]

For Augustine, the sexual existence of humanity as male and female was not limited to the original state and the fallen state. In Book 22 of the *City of God* Augustine contends that although there will be no marriage and procreation in heaven, nevertheless, those just men and women who are risen with Christ will keep their sexuality. In chapter 17, "Whether the bodies of women shall retain their own sex in the resurrection,"[42] Augustine refutes those who thought that because Romans 7:29 spoke of human creatures as being "Conformed to the image of the Son" it must mean women would rise as men. Against this idea, Augustine says that the trouble is not that there exist women but that there is lust. He says, "For before they sinned, the man and the woman were naked, and were not ashamed."[43] The woman is a part of the good creation as is the man and her creation from man expresses that God intends a unity between them. Furthermore, Augustine explains that the creation of woman foreshadowed Christ and the Church. For just as the woman was made from the side of Adam as he slept, so the Church was created from the side of Christ who was asleep in death on the cross. Augustine goes on to claim that "He, then, who created both sexes will restore both." In other words, if risen bodies were asexual they would not be the resurrection of *our* bodies, the bodies that God made in the good creation.

Augustine has gone far beyond his earlier, highly spiritualized interpretation of the original state of Adam and Eve in *On Genesis Against the Manichees*. The contrast with his earlier views could not be more striking. Augustine now presents Adam and Eve in the original plan of God as fully embodied sexual beings who are to procreate and raise up citizens for the City of God. Sexual reproduction is something God intended prior to the Fall. Therefore it is not something that can be simply understood as a merciful remedy against death. Augustine, in affirming sexuality and procreation not only as compatible with paradise but as a part of it, detached sexuality and procreation from any necessary link with the Fall. Human sexuality and procreation now had a meaning independent from the Fall and its conse-

---

[41] Ibid., 14.23.

[42] Ibid., 22.17.

[43] Ibid.

quences. While marriage and procreation do not constitute the eschatological future of humanity, nevertheless masculinity and femininity—part of God's good creation—will not pass away in the risen life.

Augustine continues this line of thought in another work, *On Marriage and Concupiscence,* written around 419–420. This work was addressed to Valerius, an officer of the Imperial court. In the first book of this work, Augustine repeats his claim that marriage is good and was instituted in paradise prior to the Fall and that sexual reproduction could have taken place. Marriage after the Fall labors under the burden of concupiscence. This is illustrated by the fact that the sexual organs are not completely obedient to fallen man whether in the case of compulsive copulation or in the case of impotence.[44] Augustine answers his Pelagian opponents who accused him of teaching, in effect, that marriage was sinful because it produced children who inherit the fallen condition of Adam. Against these opponents he is adamant about the fact that even though marriage produces children who have been corrupted by the sin of Adam and need to be reborn in baptism, marriage is nevertheless good. The three goods of offspring, mutual fidelity, and the sacramental bond still mark marriage after the Fall. At one point, Augustine rhetorically interrogates the three goods to show that sin does not arise from them but that they would have been more secure in marriage had sin not wounded them. What is of particular interest for my purpose is what Augustine says about the sacramental bond:

> And then this will be the answer of the sacramental bond of marriage,—the third good: Of me was that word spoken in paradise before the entrance of sin: "A man shall leave his father and his mother, and shall cleave unto his wife; and the two shall become one flesh." This the apostle applies to the case of Christ and of the Church, and calls it then "a great sacrament." What, then, in Christ and in the Church is great, in the instances of each married pair it is but very small, but even then it is the sacrament of an inseparable union.[45]

This passage shows that for Augustine the great nuptial mystery is the one flesh union of Christ and the Church. The full meaning and significance of the "small" one flesh union between man and woman is known from the "great" one flesh union of Christ and his Church. It is the paradigm for the nuptial union between the sexes. This is the reason for the indissolubility of Christian marriage. In another passage, Augustine explains that married

---

[44] *On Marriage and Concupiscence,* 1.6.7 (*De Nuptiis et Concupiscentia;* PL, 44; *CSEL,* 42). All quotations are taken from *NPNF,* 1/5.
[45] Ibid., 1.23.21

believers as members of the Body of Christ are never permitted to divorce and remarry. Just as there can be no separation or divorce in the case of Christ and the Church, so there can be no separation between married believers while both are still alive. Augustine compares the marriage bond with the sacrament of baptism. Just as the apostate retains his baptism after his apostasy, so the marriage partners retain their marriage bond even if one or both of them sins or divorces and remarries. Clearly, for Augustine marriage between believers involves a participation in the nuptial union of Christ and the Church, which in turn creates an indissoluble bond between the partners. But again, Christ, the Bridegroom, and his Bride function as the norm and paradigm for marriage.

In the second book of *On Marriage and Concupiscence*, Augustine makes a short comment about marriage prior to the Fall that builds on this point.[46] It occurs in the course of his answer to his Pelagian opponent Julian of Eclanum who accused him of teaching that marriage after the Fall was changed into something evil. In defense of his views, Augustine argues again that what is changed after the sin of Adam and Eve is not the nature of marriage but the nature of humanity. He says that marriage was instituted by God in paradise and that marriage remains something instituted by God even after sin. At one point in this explanation, Augustine makes an additional claim about marriage in paradise. He says that the marriage instituted in paradise was a figure of the great mystery between Christ and the Church. Now an important part of the holiness and goodness of Adam and Eve in their nuptial union is that they are a figure of a reality that is to come.[47] The

---

[46] Ibid., 2.54.32.

[47] It is true that in *On Genesis Against the Manichees*, 2.24.37 he says what was fulfilled as history in Adam and the woman signifies as prophecy Christ in his one flesh union with the Church. The important difference between this affirmation and the one in *On Marriage and Concupiscence* is that in *On Genesis Against the Manichees* Adam and Eve prophesied Christ and the Church not from the very beginning but only after sin. In 1.19.30 Augustine, commenting on Gen 1:28, "Increase be fruitful and multiply," claims that the bodily union between Adam and Eve occurred only after the first sin. Prior to sin there would have been a union of virile reason and a lower part of the soul that would have brought forth spiritual children. It would seem then that Adam and Eve did not prophesy Christ and the Church until their one flesh bodily union and thus after the first sin. This is what Augustine refers to as "what was fulfilled in history in Adam." At least in *On Genesis Against the Manichees*, Augustine saw a link between bodily union and procreation and the first sin. On the other hand, this notion is completely absent in *On Marriage and Concupiscence* where there could have been a bodily union prior to sin and where nuptial relationship between Adam and Eve even before sin prefigured the mystery of Christ and the Church.

goodness of marriage and sexuality, far from being something alien in paradise, is most fitting because it is a figure of how man and woman will be further blessed in Christ.[48] It seems too that here again for Augustine, Christ and the Church is the nuptial union par excellence, the one flesh union, and the paradigm for every nuptial union.

Totus Christus: *A Nuptial Reality*

There is strong evidence that shows while Augustine rethought his views on sexuality in paradise he was also thinking more deeply about the nuptial union between Christ and the Church. Over 50 percent of the occurrences of the term *sponsa Christi*, referring to the Church as spouse of Christ, are found in works that Augustine wrote between 401 and 420.[49] For instance in his homilies on the first epistle of John written around 406–407, Augustine proclaimed: "For all the Church is Christ's Bride, of which the beginning and first fruits is the flesh of Christ: there was the Bride joined to the Bridegroom in the flesh."[50] In a passage from *Tractates on the Gospel According to John*, also dated from around 406–407, Augustine says that the marriage at Cana is a reflection of the virginal marriage between Christ and the Church.[51] Thus even women who vow virginity have a share in marriage,

---

[48] In several of his other works written after *On Marriage and Concupiscence*, Augustine continues to proclaim the presence of marriage in paradise. For instance, there is a letter discovered only in 1975, known as Letter 6* (*CSEL*, 88.32–38) in which Augustine wrote to Atticus of Constantinople defending his understanding of marriage and sexuality. Not only does Augustine affirm that marriage and sexuality were a part of God's original plan he tries to imagine what sexual intercourse might have been like in paradise. Sexual desire in paradise would have been different from sexual desire as man now knows it as there would have been absent any sort of compulsiveness.

[49] A search of the entire corpus of Augustine run on the database *Cetedoc Library of Christian Texts* shows 23 out 44 occurrences of *sponsa Christi* occur in works written between 401 and 420.

[50] *Tractates on the First Letter of John,* 2.2, in *NPNF*, 1/7. Omnis enim Ecclesia sponsa Christi est, cujus principium et primitae caro Christi est: ibi iuncta est sponsa sponso in carne.

[51] *Tractates on the Gospel According to John,* 9.2.2 (*In Johannis evangelium tractus;* PL, 35; CCL, 36). "Nor are those women who vow virginity to God, although they hold a higher place of honor and sanctity in the Church, without marriage. For they too, together with the whole Church, attain to a marriage, a marriage in which Christ is the Bridegroom. And for this cause, therefore, did the Lord, on being invited, come to the marriage, to confirm conjugal chastity, and to show forth the sacrament of marriage. For the bridegroom in that marriage, to whom it was said, 'Thou hast kept the good wine until now,' represented the person of the Lord. For the good wine—namely, the gospel—Christ has kept until now."

"For they too, together with the whole Church, attain to a marriage, a marriage in which Christ is the Bridegroom."[52]

Still more telling at this time is how Augustine appealed to the nuptial, marital relation to explain the nature of unity between the head and body of the *totus Christus*. Earlier in this paper I asserted my belief that there is a real relation between Augustine's theology of marriage and his ecclesiology. At the center of Augustine's doctrine of the Church is the *totus Christus*, the whole Christ, which encompasses the head and body. The eternal Son of God made man is the head, while the body is made up of the baptized who are the members. Together the head and body is the *totus Christus*. After his death and resurrection, Christ the head is present and embodied on earth in the body that is the Church. The head and the body are always united and are never apart or divided. The union of the body with the head is a unity that is freely chosen out of love. Tarcisius van Bavel observes that this unity for Augustine is a personal unity like that of a bridegroom and bride:[53] Christ the head is to the body as bridegroom is to bride.

Van Bavel notices that Augustine makes the point repeatedly in his writings that the head and body seem to be two but they are also one, one flesh that is. There is a certain unity through identification but not an identity between the Church and Christ. For instance, in a commentary on Psalm 30 probably written around 411 Augustine says:

> I want you to understand that the Head and body together are called one Christ. To make this quite clear he [the Lord] says, when speaking of marriage, *They will be two in one flesh; so they are two no longer, but one flesh* (Mt 19:5–5) But perhaps it might be thought that he only means this to apply to any ordinary marriage? No, because listen to what Paul tells us: They shall be two in one flesh, he says. *This is a great mystery, but I am referring it to Christ and the Church* (Eph 5:31–32). So

---

[52] Ibid. In addition to these passages there are also three sermons which speak of the wedding contracts *(tabulae matrimoniales)* between Christ and the Church: Sermon 238.1 (PL, 38:1125), Sermon 183.11 (PL, 38:992), Sermon 340A.11 (*MA*, 1:573). On this see David Hunter, "Augustine and the Making of Marriage in Roman North Africa," *Journal of Early Christian Studies* 11 (2003): 63–85. Hunter has pointed out that the argument Augustine makes in all three sermons is the same: "Since Christ is the Bridegroom and the Church is the Bride, their wedding contracts will reveal their true identity and the true nature of their union" (82). The gospels according to Augustine are these wedding contracts and Lk 24.46–47 contains the essentials of these *tabulae matrimoniales*: "Thus it is written the Messiah would suffer and rise from the dead on the third day. . . ."

[53] S.v. "Church," in *Augustine Through the Ages*, ed. Alan Fitzgerald (Grand Rapids, MI: Eerdmans, 1999) 169–79, at 171.

out of two, one single person comes to be, the Head and body, Bride-groom and Bride.[54]

In another sermon that Augustine preached around 417, he explains that Christ can be understood in the scriptures as named in three ways. The first way is before his assumption of the flesh as according to the divine nature in which he is God coeternal with Father. The second way is after the Son assumed flesh and became the mediator and head of the Church. Augustine says about the third way:

> The third way is how the whole Christ is predicted with reference to the Church, that is as head and body. . . . Where do we find this, that head and body form one Christ, that is, the body together with its head? In Isaiah he is speaking as if in the singular, [and it is one and the same speaking] and see what is said: "As for a bridegroom he has bound a turban on my head, and as for a bride he has decked me out with ornaments." (Isa 61:10) As bridegroom and bride; he calls one and the same bridegroom with reference to the head, bride with reference to the body. They are seen as two, and are one. [55]

---

[54] *Exposition of the Psalms*, 30.2, 4 (*Ennarrationes in Psalmos;* PL, 36–37; CCL, 38–40). All quotations are taken from the English translations in *The Works of Saint Augustine: a translation of the 21 century*, ed. J. E. Rotelle, vol. 3, 14–17 (New York: New City Press, 1990), hereafter *WSA*. The translation above is from *WSA*, 3/15. I have also slightly reworked it eliminating the word "people" where it does not appear in the Latin original. This is Augustine's second commentary on Psalm 30. Augustine's commentary on the Psalms can be hard to date. On the basis of internal evidence, scholars believe that Augustine possibly preached this commentary at a church near Carthage possibly in 411. See *WSA*, 3/15, 324.

[55] Sermon 341, 19 (Dolbeau, 22); *WSA*, 3/11. This nuptial understanding of the Head-Body relationship leads Augustine to propose the principle of the one flesh, one voice that highlights the unity hidden in the distinction between the Head and the Body. For instance, in a commentary composed sometime around 414, Augustine wrote about Psalm 34:

> We hear Christ's voice in it: the voice, that is of Christ, Head and body. When you hear Christ mentioned never divorce Bridegroom from Bride, but recognize the great sacrament, they will be two in one flesh (Eph 5:31; Gen 2:24). If there are two in one flesh, why not two in one voice? (*Exposition of the Psalms*, 34.2; WSA, 3/16)

Similarly commenting on Psalm 30: "Let Christ speak, then, because in Christ the Church speaks, and in the Church Christ speaks, and the body speaks in the Head, and the Head in the body" (*Exposition of the Psalms*, 30.2.4; WSA, 3/15). We see again how important the nuptial reality is not only for Augustine's ecclesiology and for his interpretation of the psalms as well.

Augustine goes on to say later in the same sermon: "So whether I say head and body, or whether I say bridegroom and bride, you must understand the same thing."[56]

What is of interest for the present purpose is that some of the most profound texts in which Augustine explained the Head-Body relationship in nuptial terms occur around the same time he claimed that marriage was part of God's original plan, and insisted upon its sacramentality. It may well be that as Augustine thought about and explained the eschatological reality of Christ and the Church as nuptial, he was stirred to think about the place of marriage and sexuality in God's original plan. Whatever the case may be, Augustine's claim that the sexual differentiation of created humanity[57] is something that is a part of the eschatological reality of Christ and the Church is absolutely indispensable for Augustine's understanding of the sacramentality of marriage. Sacramental signs for Augustine were not arbitrary. They have a likeness to the reality that they signify. Augustine once explained to a puzzled bishop that "[I]f the sacred rites had no resemblance to the things which they represent, they would not be sacred rites; they generally take their names from the mysteries they represent."[58] The logic of Augustine's thought leads to the conclusion that unless the union between Christ and his Church is in some sense nuptial, unless the bipolarity of man and woman is in some way a part of the Christ-Church relationship, marriage would not be a sacrament.

If we look back over Augustine's intellectual journey, from his early work *On Genesis Against the Manichees* to his later work *On Marriage and Concupiscence*, we see that his thought evolved from a disinterest in sexuality in the original plan of God to a profound affirmation of the religious significance of the masculine-feminine bipolarity of sexuality that embraces the order of creation and the order of redemption. His thinking about the sacramentality of marriage inevitably raised the question about the place of nup-

---

56 Ibid., 20. Augustine also argues that the one flesh union spoken of Gen 2:24 applies to Christ and the Church. We should also understand Christ as referring Gen 2:24 to the one flesh union between himself and the Church in Mt 19:5–6 where Christ says, "They shall be two in one flesh; they are not now two, but there is one flesh."

57 By bipolarity I mean what Angelo Scola means when he writes about a "constitutive polarity": "The reciprocity that springs from sexual difference thus shows that the 'I' emerges into existence from within a kind of constitutive polarity. In order to be able to say 'I' in the fullest sense, I need to take the other into account; I have the possibility of (that is, the resource for) taking the other into account" (Scola, "The Nuptial Mystery at the Heart of the Church," 643). See also Hans Urs von Balthasar, *Theo-Drama* II, 346–94.

58 Letter 98 [*Epistula* 98; *CSEL*, 34.520] in *Fathers of the Church*, v.18, 137–38. Augustine writes to Boniface, the bishop.

tial sexuality in God's original plan of creation. For Augustine, the complete meaning of the one flesh union of man and woman written about in Genesis 2:24 is found in the one flesh union of Christ and his Church (Eph 5:32). Nuptial sexuality is thus sacramental. Ultimately, the truth of sexuality, the truth of masculine-feminine bipolarity of the good creation, is a matter of mystery that is best known and discovered in the light of the eschatological relationship of Christ and his Church. This means, of course, that the masculine-feminine distinction is something intrinsic to the New Covenant, the new creation in Christ. Finally, by insisting on the created goodness and permanency of sexuality, Augustine could not avoid the conclusion that human persons will enjoy the full perfection of sexuality in heaven that is in the perfected unity of Christ and the Church. Nuptial sexuality is therefore a supernaturally redeemed reality. Augustine, unlike Gregory of Nyssa, could not regard sexuality as instrumental and temporary and as a mere remedy for death.

Embodied Nuptial Sexuality: A Redeemed Reality

What conclusions might be drawn from Augustine's intellectual journey for the current discussion about the theological significance or insignificance of nuptial sexuality? First and foremost, Augustine's thought points us in the direction of sacramental realism. Marriage as a sacrament tells us something real and true about our salvation. If marriage is a sacrament in which the union of one man and one woman *really and truly* signifies and participates in the unity between Christ and his Church, then it communicates the truth that the union between Christ and the Church is a nuptial one. It means, as Augustine knew, that the masculinity and femininity of created humanity is a redeemed reality and ultimately an eschatological reality because its exemplar, its archetype is Christ, the Bridegroom, and the Church, his Bride.

If on the other hand, as some contemporary theologians have proposed, we should think of the unity between Christ and the Church as beyond all masculinity and femininity, then the nuptial relation of man and woman cannot signify it, or any other intrinsically differentiated symbol for that matter. There would be nothing of intrinsic significance in nuptial sexuality with its masculine-feminine bipolarity that would be capable of really and truly signifying a Christ-Church unity that is beyond sexuality, that is not nuptial. The only signification of such a Christ-Church relation would be nominalist one at best. One theologian has pointed out that fallen humanity would have nothing to say to such a Christ-Church union, the most complete union it would presumably know, because it is utterly transcended by it. This theologian remarks: "Sacramental signs have been reduced to programmatic gesturing, of some real social and psychological value but without any intrinsic relation to our salvation. . . ."[59]

In other words, there has been for nearly two millennia the sacramental worship of marriage. What would it mean to repudiate nearly two millennia of worship? But this is what we would have to do if we would think that sexuality is simply one "anthropological element" like race, politics, or culture that makes up human identity or if masculinity and femininity is some limitation that is overcome in the resurrection. On the contrary, if the man-woman relation in Christian marriage is a sacramentally real and true sign of a heavenly, eschatological reality, then it has a greater meaning and theological importance than the racial, the cultural, and the political.

Close attention to Augustine's journey shows us that if human sexuality with its masculine feminine bipolarity has no intrinsic relation to the Christ-Church union and therefore no intrinsic relation to our salvation, then sexuality is indeed temporary and instrumental as Gregory of Nyssa in a more innocent age than ours envisioned it. On the other hand, if the masculine-feminine bipolarity is of the good creation and if the meaning of it is given and found in the one flesh union of Christ and the Church, then embodied nuptial sexuality is not only of prime significance for Christian revelation, but its full splendor will be manifested and made known when, in the words of the Second Vatican Council, "that mystical marriage established by God" will be "fully revealed" in the future resurrection.[60]

---

[59] Donald Keefe, "Sacramental sexuality and the Ordination of Women," *Communio* 3 (1978): 228–51, at 240.

[60] "Decree on the Ministry and Life of Priests," no. 16.

CHAPTER 15

Finality, History, and Grace: General and Special Categories in Lonergan's Theory of History

JEREMY D. WILKINS

JESUS CHRIST, St. Paul reminds us, is the summit and goal of all history. This theme—*pantôn anakephalaiôsis,* the recapitulation of all things in Christ—was the title of one of Bernard Lonergan's earliest essays on the theology of history and a leitmotif throughout his career. For Lonergan, a theory of history would supply the formal element of a treatise on the Mystical Body of Christ,[1] and bring out the intelligibility of the twofold mission of Word and Spirit.[2] Matthew Lamb has ceaselessly called attention to theology's vocation as an attunement to the order wisely and lovingly imprinted on creation by its divine Author, and he has long been convinced of the importance of Lonergan's achievement in setting theology on the level of our time. In this spirit, though without Fr. Lamb's erudition, the present study aims to highlight how Lonergan's theory of finality, history, and grace forges a new synthesis of philosophical and theological wisdom on the level of our time.

One of the heavy debits against Lonergan's influence on theology is the fact that his celebrated English works are overwhelmingly philosophical and methodological, while most of his actual theology is cocooned away in Neo-Scholastic Latin tractates he himself regarded as relics of a bygone era. While the publication of the Collected Works has begun to present these texts to a wider audience, the context in which they were composed no longer exists and a new context for their reception has yet to be created on a significant scale. I hope this modest study can contribute something to that end by simply bringing out some connections between the general categories for a theory

---

[1] Bernard Lonergan, *Collected Works of Bernard Lonergan,* vol. 3, *Insight: A Study of Human Understanding,* ed. Frederick E. Crowe and Robert M. Doran (Toronto: University of Toronto, 1992), 764.

[2] Bernard Lonergan, *De Deo Trino,* vol. 2 (Rome: Gregorian University 1964), 244–48.

of history developed in *Insight* and elements of Lonergan's specifically theological work on grace. The basic coherence of the categories is analogical: the economy of grace stands to history—the general field of human process—as history itself stands to finality in the natural order, the directedness of natural process. As human collaboration and achievement transforms and sublates the processes of subhuman nature, so too the order of grace transforms and sublates human history.

The study moves from the most general categories—finality and history—to the specifically theological categories of grace and providence.[3] After a brief glance at the precursors to *Insight*, the study turns to *Insight* itself to explore how Lonergan brought metaphysics into conversation with modern science. A third section places this consideration of natural and historical process within the context of God's transcendent dominion, while a fourth shows how human and historical finality is transformed by the supernatural gift of participation in the divine life. The study concludes by outlining a heuristic perspective on human history as the dialectical unfolding of finality, sin, and redemptive grace.

The Way To *Insight*: Grappling With Modern Science

The notion of finality has to do with the "directedness" of beings. In his 1943 article "Finality, Love, Marriage,"[4] Lonergan distinguishes absolute, horizontal, and vertical finality. Absolute and horizontal finality are complementary, distinct aspects of all appetition and process. Materially, the good is a motive for the response of an appetite, or a term for the orientation of a process. But the formal constituent of any end is the good, not as motive or term, but as final cause. Absolutely, the motive and term of all appetition and process is God's intrinsic goodness.[5] This absolute finality "is hypothetically necessary, for if there is anything to respond to motive or to proceed to term, then its response or tendency can be accounted for ultimately only by the one self-sufficient good."[6] But beings are of different kinds, and though all seek God, each does so according to its own mode of perfection; "accordingly, one has to think of the universe as a series of horizontal strata; on each level reality responds to God as absolute motive and tends to him as absolute

---

[3] On the distinction between "general" and "special" theological categories, see Bernard Lonergan, *Method in Theology* (New York: Herder, 1972), 281–93.

[4] Bernard Lonergan, "Finality, Love, Marriage," in *Collected Works of Bernard Lonergan*, vol. 4, *Collection*, ed. Frederick E. Crowe and Robert M. Doran (Toronto: University of Toronto, 1988), 17–52.

[5] Ibid., 19–20.

[6] Ibid., 22.

term; but on each level it does so differently" according to the proportion of its proper nature.[7]

Besides absolute and horizontal finality, there is vertical finality, and it is formulated, not from concrete instances, but from a general conception of world order.[8] It is characterized as "a vertical dynamism and tendency, an upthrust from lower to higher levels of appetition and process."[9] Vertical finality is the principle, in a hierarchical universe, by which lower grades of being subserve higher grades, either instrumentally or participatively. Because the higher order effects are disproportionate to the natures of their lower causes, the notion of vertical finality cannot be attained by a metaphysical analysis of natures. Rather, it operates "through the fecundity of a concrete plurality."[10] Thus while horizontal finality is in the field of "natural law," vertical finality is "not from the isolated instance but from the conjoined plurality; and it is in the field . . . of statistical law."[11]

Part of what is at stake in the notion of finality is the tension between modern science and classical teleology.[12] Now if, in the context of proportionate being, absolute and horizontal finalities are instances of final causality, the *finis qui* and the *finis quo* of natural process, respectively,[13] in the same context vertical finality is not simply final causality. For final causality enjoys the determinacy of intrinsic good and abstract essence, but vertical finality exhibits the indeterminacy of statistical probability. Again, the final cause is extrinsic, but vertical finality denotes an immanent intelligibility, an intrinsic cause. Its content as the fertility of a concrete plurality of lower processes for the emergence of the higher finds its verification not in metaphysics but in the natural (statistical) and human sciences.

In "Finality," Lonergan distinguishes four modalities of vertical finality. Three are general: the subservience of an instrument to a higher agent (for example, using a computer to write); the disposition of lower events toward higher (experiencing the effects disposes to understanding the cause); the material participation of lower processes in a higher-order unity (for example,

---

[7] Ibid., 20.

[8] Ibid., 19.

[9] Ibid., 18.

[10] Ibid., 21.

[11] Ibid., 22. The connection between vertical finality and statistical law is iterated at 22, n. 16, which draws attention to "a noteworthy affinity between modern statistical law and the *contingens ut in maiori parte*, between modern 'chance variation' and the *contingens ut in minori parte*" in connection with organic evolution; and at 38.

[12] See Lonergan, "Finality," 52; Patrick H. Byrne, "Teleology, Modern Science and Verification," in *Lonergan Workshop* 10, ed. Fred Lawrence (Boston: Boston College, 1994), 1–47.

[13] Lonergan, "Finality," 19–20.

chemical reactions in a biological organism).[14] Specific to theology is the vertical finality by which an incarnate human spirit may be raised to participation in the very life of God:

> a concrete plurality of rational beings have the obediential potency to receive the communication of God himself: such is the mystical body of Christ with its head in the hypostatic union, its principal unfolding in the inhabitation of the Holy Spirit by sanctifying grace, and its ultimate consummation in the beatific vision which Aquinas explained on the analogy of the union of soul and body.[15]

Notice that the obediential potency is predicated, not of individual rational beings, but of "a concrete plurality of rational beings," that is, of humanity "not [as] an abstract essence nor a concrete individual but [as] the concrete aggregate of all men at all times."[16] For

> just as there is a human solidarity in sin with a dialectical descent deforming knowledge and perverting will, so also there is a divine solidarity in grace which is the mystical body of Christ; as evil performance confirms us in evil, so good edifies us in our building unto eternal life; and as private rationalization finds support in fact, in common teaching, in public approval, so also the ascent of the soul towards God is not merely a private affair but rather a personal function of an objective common movement in that body of Christ which takes over, transforms, and elevates every aspect of human life.[17]

A few years later, in "The Natural Desire to See God,"[18] Lonergan argues that the subjective ground of obediential potency is the natural desire to understand whose range is all that is, even God.[19] But while the metaphysics of pro-

---

[14] Ibid., 20–22.

[15] Ibid., 20–21.

[16] Ibid., 38.

[17] Ibid., 27.

[18] Bernard Lonergan, "The Natural Desire to See God," in Crowe and Doran, *Collection,* 81–91, originally 1949. Lonergan devoted a thesis to the obediential potency and the natural desire to see God in his 1946 course on grace (thesis four of *De ente supernaturali: Supplementum schematicum,* ed. Frederick E. Crowe, Conn O'Donovan, and Giovanni Sala (Toronto: Regis College, 1973, available in photocopy; originally notes for students, College of the Immaculate Conception, Montreal, 1946), and had been considering the problem at length at least since the early 1940s: see Frederick Crowe's editorial introduction, in Crowe and Doran, *Collection,* 268.

[19] Lonergan, "Natural Desire," 82–83. Compare idem, *Verbum,* 65–66; and index at "Being the object of intellect."

portionate being can affirm a natural desire to understand whose range is unrestricted, it can affirm neither the possibility nor the fact of its fulfillment in the vision of God's essence. For intellectual desire can be properly fulfilled only by

> an act of understanding in virtue of a form proportionate to the object; hence proper knowledge of God must be in virtue of an infinite form, in virtue of God himself. . . . A philosopher operating solely in the light of natural reason could not conceive that we might understand God properly; for understanding God properly is somehow being God; and somehow being God is somehow being infinite.[20]

Hence, "only the theologian can affirm a natural desire to see God; a philosopher has to be content with [the] paradox" of finite intellect oriented toward infinite understanding.[21]

"Natural Desire" repeats a theme sounded in "Finality": A universe marked by vertical finality cannot be adequately conceived merely as a collection of autonomous parts whose order derives from their interaction. Rather, the concrete order of the universe is prior to its parts, "an intelligible unity mirroring forth the glory of God."[22] The task of discerning this dynamic order pertains to wisdom, "for the wise man contemplates the universal scheme of things and sees each in the perspective of its causes right up to the ultimate cause."[23] Human goodness consists in recognizing and embracing this order that entails the subordination of reason to God and the reasonable ordering of all the lower goods that contribute to the human good.[24] By distinguishing between extrinsic and intrinsic subordination,[25] Lonergan highlights the basic difference between instrumental and other types of vertical finality: an instrument as such is extrinsic, does not participate in the perfection of the higher end to which it is applied. In the supernatural economy, by contrast, human persons participate in the higher unity of the universe not only extrinsically, as instruments,[26] but also intrinsically by "a created communication of the divine nature."[27]

---

[20] Lonergan, "Natural Desire," 83.

[21] Ibid., 84. See also 87; and Lonergan, *Verbum,* 100.

[22] Lonergan, "Natural Desire," 85; compare idem, "Finality," 22.

[23] Lonergan, *Verbum,* 79; see ibid., 78–87. On wisdom in Lonergan's thought, see Ivo Coelho, *Hermeneutics and Method: The "Universal Viewpoint" in Bernard Lonergan* (Toronto: University of Toronto, 2001), esp. 21–28.

[24] Lonergan, "Natural Desire," 86.

[25] See ibid., 85; compare idem, "Finality," 21–22.

[26] See "On God and Secondary Causes" (1946).

[27] Lonergan, *De ente,* Thesis 1. The matter is revisited in Lonergan's much later article "Mission and the Spirit," in *A Third Collection,* ed. Frederick E. Crowe (New York:

380 WISDOM AND HOLINESS, SCIENCE AND SCHOLARSHIP

Finality and Emergent Probability:
The Achievement of *Insight*

Lonergan's "Finality, Love, Marriage" drew attention to a notable connection between horizontal finality and natural (that is, classical) law, on the one hand, and vertical finality and statistical law, on the other.[28] "The Natural Desire to See God" highlighted the implications of this interplay for conceiving the world order. In *Insight* this dynamic perspective on world order is named "emergent probability."[29]

Lonergan formulates the notion of emergent probability by observing that scientific investigation uses both classical and statistical heuristic structures in a complementary way, that is, both statistical expectations (probabilities) and classical correlations (for example, the "laws" of physics) are relevant to understanding the data of the natural world. This suggests that the natural order is an assembly of conditioned schemes of recurrence that emerge and survive according to probabilities.[30]

> What is probable, sooner or later occurs. When it occurs, a probability of emergence is replaced by a probability of survival; and as long as the scheme survives, it is in its turn fulfilling conditions for the possibility of still later schemes in the series. Such is the general notion of emergent probability.[31]

The notion of emergent probability illuminates the evolutionary significance of space, time, and absolute numbers. Since later schemes in a series can only emerge where earlier schemes are in place, there is successive narrowing of the spatial and numerical bases for the more complex schemes, and large initial numbers and volumes of space gradually yield importance to long intervals of time. Further, the distinction between probabilities of emergence and probabilities of survival has selective significance and gives rise to the

---

Paulist, 1985), 23–34 at 24 (original publication, *Concilium* 9 [1976]: 69–78). On Lonergan's early writings on grace and world order, the magisterial treatment is J. Michael Stebbins, *The Divine Initiative: Grace, World Order, and Human Freedom in the Early Writings of Bernard Lonergan* (Toronto: University of Toronto, 1995) ch. 2, esp. 43–47.

28 Lonergan, "Finality," 22; see also 22, n. 6; 38; and passim.

29 Compare Lonergan, *Insight*, 144–51 and 470–76.

30 Lonergan, *Insight*, 144–45. For a more extended discussion of issues treated cursorily here, see Kenneth R. Melchin, *History, Ethics, and Emergent Probability: Ethics, Society and History in the Work of Bernard Lonergan,* 2nd ed. (Lanham, MD: University Press of America, 1987, 1999), chs. 3 and 4; and Philip McShane, *Randomness, Statistics, and Emergence* (Dublin: Gill and Macmillan, 1970).

31 Lonergan, *Insight*, 145.

possibility of conflict between stability and development, since more stable schemes tend to preclude the chance variations from which later schemes can emerge, while less stable schemes will compromise the survival of later schemes whose conditions they meet, unless the later schemes include some provision for the endurance of the earlier.[32]

In "Finality" Lonergan articulated a vision of the universe of proportionate being as a series of horizontal strata, not isolated, but hierarchically integrated so that the lower are made to subserve the higher and the higher, conversely, extend and perfect the capacities of the lower. With *Insight*'s deployment of the notion of the "flexible circle of schemes of recurrence" occurring at different levels,[33] this understanding of world order can be elaborated in a fully modern scientific context. The basic insight into explanatory genera has been available to the reader of *Insight* since the introduction of the notion of the higher viewpoint in mathematics in the very first chapter.[34] Now it is expanded to reveal fuller implications of emergent probability as the order, the immanent intelligibility, of the universe. Just as successive orders of mathematics are developed to account for features unintelligible from the standpoint of some lower math, so in the universe of proportionate being each successive genus systematizes conjugates and schemes that are merely coincidental in the lower genera. Moreover, the hierarchical structure of the universe of proportionate being is isomorphic to the series of higher viewpoints that constitute the several distinct sciences; in proportionate being as in viewpoints the higher organizes, without negating, the lower. A lower viewpoint, which can only regard as coincidental what in fact is systematic, is not yet adequate, and the actual emergence of higher order conjugates and schemes as constituting a regular system justifies the introduction of the higher viewpoint.[35]

Emergent probability thus provides a heuristic structure for the hierarchical integration of the sciences and, isomorphically, of the ordered totality of proportionate being, and this integration is an extension of notion of the higher viewpoint formulated from an analysis of cognitional structure.[36] The methodological priority afforded to cognitional theory is still more pronounced in Lonergan's realignment of metaphysics. The metaphysical elements of potency, form, and act are grounded on the basis of the conscious

---

[32] Ibid., 146. Compare 195.

[33] Ibid., 494. The first two paragraphs of chapter fifteen, sec. 7.4 (494–95) are illuminating.

[34] Ibid., 40–42, 282.

[35] Ibid., 281.

[36] See Matthew L. Lamb, "Towards a Synthetization of the Sciences," *Philosophy of Science* 32 (1965): 182–91.

self-appropriation of the compound structure of human knowing in presentations ("experience"), understanding, and judgment.[37]

Insight is first a pedagogy, so it is not surprising that it should find the paradigm for finality in the orientation of presentations to understanding and understanding to judgment, relationships each reader is meant to progressively discover for herself. Presentations–understanding–judgment themselves are specific and conscious instances of the orientation of potency to form and form to act, and the order among potency–form–act is isomorphic to presentations–understanding–judgment. As cognitional process moves from presentations to insights to judgments in such a way that the ground of its development lies on the level of presentations, so too world process moves from potency to form to act, in such a way that both its limitations and its upward dynamism are grounded in potency, and ultimately in prime potency. The metaphysical elements in the ontological order represent the basic and irreducible instance of finality,

> a theorem of the same generality as the notion of being. This theorem affirms a parallelism between the dynamism of the mind and the dynamism of proportionate being. It affirms that the objective universe is not at rest, not static, not fixed in the present, but in process, in tension, fluid. . . . As what is to be known becomes determinate only through knowing, so what is to be becomes determinate only through its own becoming. But as present knowing is not just present knowing but also a moment in process towards fuller knowing, so also present reality is not just present reality but also a moment in process to fuller reality.[38]

Finality denotes more than merely passive potency; it is a positive disposition, an orientation of what is toward what will be ("what is probable, sooner or later occurs").[39] It is "an upward but indeterminately directed dynamism," the general disposition of proportionate being to move from less to fuller completeness, from lower to higher integrations, from less to greater explanatory differentiation.[40]

In the natural order there are higher integrations whenever a thing of a higher order takes up processes of a lower order; this becomes the basis for Lonergan to work out the notions of explanatory genera and species. With

---

[37] See Lonergan, *Verbum*, 24; idem, "*Insight:* Preface to a Discussion," in Crowe and Doran, *Collection*, 142–45. On isomorphism in St. Thomas, see Frederick E. Crowe, "St Thomas and the Isomorphism of Human Knowing and Its Proportionate Object," in idem, *Three Thomist Studies* (Boston: Lonergan Workshop Institute, 2000).

[38] Lonergan, *Insight*, 470–71.

[39] Ibid., 145.

[40] Ibid., 688.

each higher genus of thing, the importance of inner conditions for development increases, and the relevance of outer conditions decreases.[41] This is increasingly the case for successive genera. Thus the successive genera of living beings exhibit an increasing independence from the lower manifolds they integrate and, correspondingly, are able to exercise increasing levels of control over their environments.

In this framework the human mind is related to sensitive process as sensitive process is to organic process. "As sensitive appetite and perception are a higher system of the organic, so inquiry and insight, reflection and judgment, deliberation and choice are a higher system of sensitive process" and indeed, "a perennial source of higher systems, so that human living has its basic task in reflecting on systems and judging them, deliberating on their implementation and choosing between possibilities."[42] These higher systems are, for human beings, the solution to the further problems of living that, in the case of animals and plants, would be met by the emergence of new species.[43] The judgment and implementation of higher systems of human living is a collaborative, normatively cumulative enterprise, an enterprise not of the individual but of the community, and their very conception is itself the result of the fruitful cross-fertilization of scientific and scholarly conversation.

As statistical method is deployed to study emergence in the general case of world process, so genetic method is deployed to meet the specific cases of emergence that are organic, psychic, intellectual, and human development. It is this notion of specifically developmental emergence that transposes the not yet fully explanatory notion of horizontal finality employed in "Finality, Love, Marriage." Lonergan explicitly draws attention to its continuity with the Aristotelian notion of nature, *physis*, the immanent principle of movement and of

---

[41] See ibid., 290. Compare Lonergan, "The Mediation of Christ in Prayer," in *Collected Works of Bernard Lonergan*, vol. 6, *Philosophical and Theological Papers*, ed. Robert C. Croken et al. (Toronto: University of Toronto, 1996), 160–82, esp. 167–74.

[42] Lonergan, *Insight*, 291.

[43] Lonergan's work in macroeconomics is an effort to promote a higher system in that aspect of human living, and is therefore a clue to the kind of thing he has in mind here. For his earlier efforts, see *Collected Works of Bernard Lonergan*, vol. 21, *For a New Political Economy*, ed. Philip McShane (Toronto: University of Toronto, 1999); for his later efforts see *Collected Works of Bernard Lonergan*, vol. 15, *Macroeconomic Analysis: An Essay in Circulation Dynamics* (Toronto: University of Toronto, 1999). For an introduction to Lonergan's economic thought, see Philip McShane, *Economics for Everyone* (Halifax, Nova Scotia: Axial, 1998). For its integral relationship to his theory of history and his understanding of praxis, see Michael Shute, "Economic Analysis within Redemptive Praxis: An Achievement of Lonergan's Third Decade," *Lonergan Workshop* 14, ed. Fred Lawrence (Boston: Boston College, 1998), 243–64, esp. 243–57.

rest.[44] Development "may be defined as a flexible, linked sequence of dynamic and increasingly differentiated higher integrations that meet the tension of successively transformed underlying manifolds through successive applications of the principles of correspondence and emergence."[45] The tension lies in the principle of finality, the "upwardly but indeterminately directed dynamism."[46] The principle of correspondence iterates that form emerges only from potency as principle of limitation: "Inasmuch as the goal of the genetic sequence is fixed by the initial manifold, only oaks from acorns grow."[47] The initial manifold ineluctably conditions the possibilities for future development.

> Each higher genus is limited by the preceding lower genus. On the one hand, it must not interfere with the autonomy of the lower order, for if it were to do so, it would destroy its own foundation. On the other hand, the higher genus is a systematization of manifolds that would be coincidental on the lower level; and a higher systematization is limited by the manifolds it systematizes.[48]

At the same time, the principle of emergence asserts that form emerges from potency not only as principle of limitation but also of finality: "Otherwise coincidental manifolds of lower conjugate acts *invite* the higher integration effected by higher conjugate forms."[49] Here again, the paradigm of development (in the way of discovery) is human intelligence moving from data to insights to further questions and so on.[50]

As in the objective field there is a principle of correspondence and a principle of emergence, so genetic method endeavors to specify both an integrator and an operator[51] and acknowledges in human development both a law of limitation and transcendence[52] and a law of genuineness.[53] The integrator is any given stage of development as the accomplished fact of higher integration. The operator is the higher system as dynamically oriented to and preparing for transition to some further integration. The laws of limitation and transcendence and of genuineness are extensions of these basic insights into the realm of integral human development, which is a compound process

---

44 Lonergan, *Insight*, 476.
45 Ibid., 479.
46 Ibid., 477.
47 Ibid., 480.
48 Ibid., 468.
49 Ibid., 477, emphasis added.
50 Ibid., 483.
51 Ibid., 489–90.
52 Ibid., 497–99.
53 Ibid., 499–504.

of organic, psychic, and intellectual maturation. These three levels of human development "are not three independent processes. They are interlocked, with the intellectual providing a higher integration of the psychic and the psychic providing a higher integration of the organic."[54]

There is yet a further aspect, and it is intimated by the introduction of the law of genuineness. For human living is ever a precarious integration of organic, psychic, and spiritual demands, and human knowing is ever caught in a tension between the extroversion of biological sensitivity and the fully human knowing of intellectual self-transcendence.[55] To be genuine is to consciously strive for the integration of one's spirit and psyche, to admit into the full light of consciousness both what one in fact is and also what one is called to become, to face the tension between one's accomplished integration and one's further growth.[56] This genuineness has its sanction, for "to fail in genuineness is not to escape but to displace the tension between limitation and transcendence. Such displacement is the root of the dialectical phenomena of scotosis in the individual, of the bias of common sense, of basic philosophical differences, and of their prolongation" in every field of human endeavor.[57] The inherent tensions of human development, therefore, because they are open to a sequence of positions that are not intelligibly related, require the deployment of a dialectical method no less than of a genetic method. The dialectical method differentiates sharply between the positional and the counterpositional, between explanation and description, between the proper unfolding of the detached, disinterested desire to know and love integrally with other desires and its disintegrated surrender to biased knowing and disordered loving.[58] Through self-appropriation dialectical method grounds the reorientation not only of the sciences but also of common sense.[59]

For Lonergan, "explicit metaphysics is the conception, affirmation, and implementation of the integral heuristic structure of proportionate being."[60] This task founds itself upon the appropriation of the normative structure immanent in human cognitional acts,[61] and consequently the way "to explicit

---

[54] Ibid., 494; see 648, 762.

[55] Ibid., 498.

[56] Ibid., 501–2.

[57] Ibid., 503. On bias see chs. 6 and 7, esp. 214–20, 244–67. See also Robert M. Doran, *Theology and the Dialectics of History* (Toronto: University of Toronto, 1990), esp. 177–210, 355–86, 500–526.

[58] Lonergan, *Insight,* 560–65. The integral unfolding of the dynamism of the human spirit requires not only a cognitional but also volitional and sensitive appropriations of truth: see ibid., 581–85.

[59] Ibid., 425.

[60] Ibid., 416.

[61] Ibid., 420–21.

metaphysics is primarily a process to self-knowledge."[62] The structure of cognition "provides the relations by which unknown contents of the acts [of cognition] can be defined heuristically,"[63] and this heuristic anticipation in turn provides a fourfold battery of methods:[64]

> The anticipation of a constant system . . . grounds classical method; the anticipation of an intelligibly related sequence of systems grounds genetic method; the anticipation that data will not conform to system grounds statistical method; and the anticipation that the relations between the successive stages of changing system will not be directly intelligible grounds dialectical method.[65]

Explicit metaphysics, then, is grounded on the appropriation of the normatively recurring patterns of the self-transcending eros of the human mind.

Finally, this movement includes human decision and commitment no less than human knowing, and so ethics can be conceived as the extension of metaphysics into the domain of human action.[66] For being is intelligible and good,[67] and so

> intelligible orders and their contents, as objects of rational choice, are values; but the universal order which is generalized emergent probability conditions and penetrates, corrects and develops every particular order; and rational self-consciousness cannot consistently choose the conditioned and reject the condition, choose the part and reject the whole, choose the consequent and reject the antecedent.[68]

Commitment to intelligence, reason, responsibility, then, is commitment to a universal order, the situation of oneself, one's community, and one's living within the context of universal finality.

> The obligatory structure of our rational self-consciousness (1) finds its materials and its basis in the products of universal finality, (2) is itself finality on the level of intelligent and rational consciousness, and (3) is

---

62 Ibid., 422; see 558–60.

63 Ibid., 420.

64 Ibid., 708.

65 Ibid., 509; see 630. On the dialectical criticism of subjects in ethics, see ibid., 626–28.

66 Ibid., 618; 626–28.

67 Ibid., 619–30.

68 Ibid., 629.

finality confronted with the alternative of choosing either development and progress or decline and extinction.[69]

So freedom itself is an emergence and a finality in human consciousness,[70] effective only in the measure that the human spirit successfully integrates the laws and schemes of the psyche.[71]

The overarching import of this account of finality in the metaphysics of proportionate being is that the dynamism of the human spirit is but an instance of a world process characterized by finality, and therefore essentially open-ended. "Indeed, since cognitional activity is itself but a part of this universe, so its heading to being is but the particular instance in which universal striving towards being becomes conscious and intelligent and reasonable."[72] All of proportionate being, and especially the human spirit, has a dynamic orientation that points it ever beyond itself into the unknown.[73] So it is that

> man's spirit, his mind and his heart, is an active power, an eros, for self-transcendence; consequently, the subject is related intrinsically and indeed, constitutively to the object towards which it transcends itself; finally, knowledge, morality, and religion are the three distinct phases in which such self-transcendence is realized.[74]

So it is, at length, that there is a natural finality of the human spirit to the vision of God in the face of which mere philosophy is reduced to silence.[75]

Finality and Transcendence

On the question of finality and emergent probability, Lonergan's thought matured as he brought the achievement of Thomas Aquinas into conversation with modern science to affirm a dynamic and open world order. As noted above, from early on Lonergan realized that the intelligible unity of the world order is prior to the individual beings constituted in that order. He also realized that the fundamental analogue for divine eternity is the act

---

[69] Ibid., 626.

[70] Ibid., 640–41.

[71] Ibid., 632.

[72] Ibid., 470.

[73] Ibid., 557–58; 569–70.

[74] Lonergan, "Natural Knowledge of God," 130.

[75] Lonergan, *Insight*, 662.

of insight that transcends the limitations of space and time.[76] This explains why Lonergan was never tempted by mental fashions like process theology or "open theism." His position on God's transcendent causality remained constant (at least) from the time of his doctoral work forward.[77]

In his study of operative grace in Thomas Aquinas, Lonergan noticed that for St. Thomas, individual things have a participation in the divine design that goes beyond their proper essences, because of their involvement in a dynamic contingent order that enables them to operate.[78] He calls this Thomas's "analogy of operation," whereby God's agency operates on a higher level in the operation of every contingent agent: "the causation of the created cause is itself caused; . . . it is a procession that is made to proceed; . . . an operation in which another operates."[79] From the perspective of transcendent causality, every contingent agent is an instrument in the hands of the divine artisan.[80]

This conjunction of transcendent efficient and final causality is the Thomist doctrine of "application." In *Grace and Freedom*, after rescuing the Aristotelian concept of premotion from the "metaphysical mystery"[81] propounded by Bañez and his followers,[82] Lonergan argues that St. Thomas's theory of application adds a new level of complexity to the Aristotelian concept.[83] Aristotelian premotion means simply that causation in time depends not only on the essence of agent and patient but also their being in some appropriate proximity to each other, and this proximity is a function of world order. A fire only burns what is combustible, but a particular fire burns, not every combustible, but only those that are appropriately proximate in space and time. In the context of his theological reorientation of Aristotle, St. Thomas calls this causal relationship "application." It is corollary to the metaphysical affirmation, *quicquid movetur ab alio movetur*, and

---

[76] See Matthew Lamb, "Eternity and Time," in *Gladly to Learn and Gladly to Teach: Essays in Honor of Ernest Fortin*, ed. M. Foley and D. Kreis (New York: Lexington, 2002), 195–214.

[77] See Lonergan, "On God and Secondary Causes," in Crowe and Doran, *Collection*, 53–65; idem, *Grace and Freedom*, 64 and n. 6; idem, *De ente*, nos. 103–106; idem, *De scientia atque voluntate Dei: Supplementum schematicum* (notes for students, Regis College, Toronto, 1950) 80, 90, 218; Stebbins, *Divine Initiative*, 224–45.

[78] See Lonergan, *Grace and Freedom*, 83.

[79] Ibid., 88.

[80] Lonergan, *Insight*, 687.

[81] Lonergan, *Grace and Freedom*, 77.

[82] Ibid., 63–71, esp. 71. See Stebbins, *Divine Initiative*, ch. 6 on the debate between Bañez and Molina on divine efficacy (the *de auxiliis* controversy), which forms the background to Lonergan, *Grace and Freedom*.

[83] Lonergan, *Grace and Freedom*, 72–80.

leads inexorably back to a first, unmoved mover, for it implies a "successive dependence [that] does not cease until one arrives ultimately at God; therefore, it necessarily follows that God moves and applies every agent."[84]

Since for Thomas, unlike Aristotle, it was necessary to account not only for the systematic but also for the coincidental in world process, the content of application is more than simply premotion. It is premotion precisely as "a mediated execution of divine providence,"[85] premotion as affirming an ordering of causes dependent upon God's transcendent causality as

> the cause of all cases [sic]: the mover moves the moved if the pair are in the right mutual relation, disposition, proximity; the mover does not, if any other cause prevents the fulfillment of this condition; but both the combinations that result in motion and the interferences that prevent it must ultimately be reduced to God who is universal cause, and therefore divine providence cannot be frustrated.[86]

What Thomist application adds to Aristotelian premotion is the causal certitude of divine providence that brings about necessary things necessarily and contingent things contingently.

Universal application implies universal instrumentality, which adds the possibility that as an instrument, a cause of a lower order may be rendered proportionate to an ontologically superior effect.

> An instrument is a lower cause moved by a higher so as to produce an effect within the category proportionate to the higher; but in the cosmic hierarchy all causes are moved but the highest and every effect is at least in the category of being; therefore, all causes except the highest are instruments.[87]

For the rest of his life, Lonergan insisted that universal instrumentality grounds the possibility of an evolutionary world order:

> For it is only as an instrument operating beyond its own proportion that the lower, as long as it is lower, can bring about and participate in the constitution of the higher; and it is only the cause of the whole universe that from lower species can bring about the emergence of successive higher species.[88]

---

[84] Ibid., 73.
[85] Ibid.
[86] Ibid., 76–77.
[87] Ibid., 81.
[88] Lonergan, "Mission," 24.

Although "Finality, Love, Marriage" had introduced four distinct types of vertical finality, in terms of the operation of divine providence all finality is instrumental.

The significance assigned to finality as the instrument of divine governance underscores the priority of world order to individual beings. For Lonergan, universal finality is the instrument of providence precisely as the intelligible unity of proportionate being. God is uniquely the principal author of every cause, existence, or occurrence because he alone is the author of the whole order.[89] Only the cause of the whole order of the universe can be the sufficient ground for the occurrence of any event; further, since every development and every emergence depends on a complex of events, only the cause of the order of the universe can be the sufficient ground for any development or emergence.[90]

This points to an important difference between Lonergan's approach to the question of God in *Insight*, and the movement called "Intelligent Design."[91] Intelligent Design arguments typically assert that particular adaptive systems are irreducibly complex and can only be explained by postulating an intelligent designer.[92] Lonergan, however, sees particular instances of adaptation as evidence for the immanent intelligible order of the whole universe, which is an evolutionary order, a "generalized emergent probability."[93] It is generalized emergent probability—the whole order of the universe in time as well as in space—that explains the complexity of individual entities and the occurrence of individual events. But this order itself is an intelligible unity that nevertheless is contingent. If there are no ultimate brute matters of fact, no ultimate unexplained contingencies, then the intelligible order of the universe invites and indeed requires the affirmation of God. Thus Lonergan's strategy in *Insight* is to move from the whole order of the universe to the intelligible ground and transcendent cause of that order.

---

[89] Lonergan, *Insight*, 686–87; see idem, *De ente*, no. 179; idem, *De scientia*, nos. 89, 97.

[90] Lonergan, *Insight*, 687.

[91] See Patrick H. Byrne, "Evolution, Randomness, and Divine Purpose: A Reply to Cardinal Schönborn," *Theological Studies* 67 (2006): 653–65.

[92] The basic form of the Intelligent Design argument seems to be: If there is a design, there must be a designer; but there are entities so well adapted, or so complex, that they must have been designed; therefore, there must be a designer [God]. The basic form of Lonergan's argument is something like this: There are no brute matters of fact (that is, no ultimate, unexplainable contingencies). But the whole universe is a contingent intelligible unity. Therefore, there must be a transcendent cause of the whole order of the universe. I am indebted to Patrick Byrne for helping me appreciate this point.

[93] Lonergan, *Insight*, 532; see idem, "Finality," 22; and idem, *Grace and Freedom*, 76–80.

This strategy unfolds through an extrapolation from restricted to unrestricted understanding, that is, from the dynamic openness and finite achievement of human intelligence to the conception of God as the "idea of being," *ipsum intelligere,* the infinite act of understanding that grasps everything about everything.[94] Once this question is broached, there is "a transformation of metaphysics as we have conceived it. For the metaphysics of proportionate being becomes a subordinate part of a more general metaphysics that envisages the transcendent idea of being."[95] If the complete intelligibility of being involves us in affirming the existence of God as *ipsum intelligere*, it is no longer adequate to affirm the fact of finality merely as "an upward but indeterminately directed dynamism."[96] This earlier statement had been adequate within a metaphysics of proportionate being and within the unfolding pedagogy of *Insight*. Considered "from below," solely as a heuristic framework for understanding proportionate being, finality is indeed indeterminate. However, "from above,"

> from the viewpoint of unrestricted understanding, the nonsystematic vanishes to yield place to a fully determinate and absolutely efficacious plan and intention. It follows that finality is to be conceived more accurately. Instead of an upward but indeterminately directed dynamism, there is the intended ordination of each potency for the form it receives, of each form for the act it receives, of each manifold of lower acts for the higher unities and integrations under which they are subsumed.[97]

What "from below" seems merely intelligible probability is in fact intelligent ordination by a wise and sovereign God. Finality, then, is not merely an aspect of an evolutionary world order, but in fact a manifestation and a means of divine governance.[98]

The affirmation of *ipsum intelligere*, then, effects the integration of finality with final causality, not by collapsing two properly distinct notions, but by acknowledging the ordination of finality to the final cause as to its summit (the absolute finality affirmed in "Finality, Love, Marriage").[99] Finality is related to the final cause as *finis quo* to *finis qui*.[100] The complete intelligibility and goodness of contingent being is found in an infinite loving insight, and

---

[94] Lonergan, *Insight,* 665–99.

[95] Ibid., 688.

[96] Ibid.

[97] Ibid.

[98] See Lonergan, *Grace and Freedom,* 84.

[99] Lonergan, *Insight,* 687.

[100] Compare Lonergan, "Finality," 19–22.

realized according to an historically unfolding order of contingent probabilities brought about by the free agency of the Creator utterly without conditions and capable in freedom of effecting anything else that can be.

Finality and Grace

In the pedagogy of *Insight*, the dynamism of the human mind provides the basic instance for formulating the notions of finality and transcendence. "Initially, transcendence is the common experience of raising further questions."[101] Initially, finality is the indeterminate directedness of asking and answering questions. But the vast implications of asking and answering questions, brushing aside obscurantism, ground the basic position that being is completely intelligible. The experience of asking and answering questions supplies the analogy for conceiving and affirming God as the transcendent Idea of being, *ipsum intelligere,* limitless insight. This affirmation, in turn, means that human beings are not only free and intelligent architects of their own destiny, but also, at the very same time, instruments in the hands of a higher Artisan. Moreover, analogical knowledge of God is incapable of fully satisfying the open-ended quest(ions) of the human spirit.

It is this peculiar conjunction of limitation and transcendence in the human constitution that Lonergan means by "obediential potency," the human capacity to receive God's self-communication in love. In order to grasp what is at stake here, it is important to notice that God's intervention in history responds to a twofold exigency in the human condition. On the one hand, there is the problem of sin in human history, which can only be overcome through a divinely initiated collaboration. On the other hand, there is the natural human openness to transcendence, which can only be adequately fulfilled by the immediate vision of God who is all in all. For the sake of exposition, I will treat the desire to see God in this section and the problem of sin in the next.

In his early treatise on grace, *De ente supernaturali,* Lonergan affirms that obediential potency is an instance of dispositive potency, which is, in the human creature, the self-same potency to natural beatitude.

> [N]atural potency and obediential potency are the same inasmuch as they are intrinsically one and the same human potency, differing only by reason of the causal agent proportionate to their actuation, since a finite agent is proportionate to actuating a natural potency, but only an

---

101 See Matthew Lamb, "The Exigencies of Meaning and Meta-Science: A Prolegomenon to the God-Question," in *Trinification of the World,* ed. T. A. Dunne and J.-M. Laporte (Toronto: Regis College, 1978), 34.

infinite agent is proportioned to actuating an obediential potency; and from this extrinsic diversity arises the diversity in ends for which the potency exists.[102]

The natural openness of the human spirit that reaches out to know and love the whole universe of being is itself the radical capacity of human beings to receive, by unmerited grace, the divine self-gift and so enjoy a fulfillment surpassing the possibilities of every created nature. Like every created agency, human agency too is transcendentally an exercise of divine instrumental causality, whether or not it is ordered, as obediential potency, to the absolutely supernatural.

Hence when obediential potency is affirmed to be a unique instance of vertical finality in human agents, it is not to be inferred that it represents the only manner in which human agents are instruments of the divine Artisan. It is, however, to assert that the "advent of the absolutely supernatural solution to man's problem of evil adds to man's biological, psychic, and intellectual levels of development a fourth level that includes the higher conjugate forms of faith, hope, and charity."[103] There is in the actual ordering of this universe a finality for human beings that surpasses without destroying the capacities of their nature and takes them up into the higher unity of the Mystical Body of Christ in which they share, by incommensurable gift, in the very life of the Triune God.[104]

In his later work, Lonergan appeals to the ineluctable orientation of human beings toward knowledge and love of the whole universe of being to supply the basic meaning of religion.[105] In *Method in Theology*, the problem

---

[102] Lonergan, *De ente*, no. 75; see also no. 69; and Lonergan, "Natural Desire," 81–84, 87.

[103] Lonergan, *Insight*, 762. See 718–19 on the continuity of grace and nature.

[104] Lonergan, *De ente*, thesis 1, on which see Stebbins, *Divine Initiative*, ch. 2. See also Lonergan, *De Deo Trino*, vol. 2 (Rome: Gregorian University Press, 1964), 232–37, esp. 234; Lonergan, "Mission," 26; idem, *Insight*, 746–47. See too Matthew L. Lamb, "An Analogy for the Divine Self-Gift," in *Lonergan Workshop Journal* 14, ed. Fred Lawrence (1998), 115–54.

[105] This whole trajectory of thought is already intimated in the fertile discussion of the "ascent from nature to beatific vision" in Lonergan, "Finality" (see 28–37); as well as in such early articles as 1949's "The Natural Desire to See God," in Crowe and Doran, *Collection*, 81–91; and especially in the short but provocative 1961 paper "Openness and Religious Experience," in Crowe and Doran, *Collection*, 185–87. Among later writings, see for instance "Prolegomena to the Study of the Emerging Religious Consciousness of Our Time," in Crowe, *Third Collection*, 55–73; the three "Lectures on Religious Studies and Theology," in Crowe, *Third Collection*, 113–65; and for a review of the development in the emphases of Lonergan's thought, see Frederick E. Crowe, "Lonergan's Universalist View of Religion," *Method: Journal* 12 (1994): 147–79, esp. 148–58.

of God is generalized in terms of the whole human orientation to transcendence: "an orientation to transcendent mystery . . . provides the primary and fundamental meaning of the name, God,"[106] and the appropriate "response to transcendent mystery is adoration."[107] This orientation to transcendent mystery includes the specifically intellectual pattern in which the question of God was raised in *Insight*, but also makes more explicit how the question of God is implicated at every level of our being and so faces more expressly the Enlightenment temptation to restrict transcendence to the moral and cognitive realms and so subordinate the cosmic order to ourselves rather than ourselves to the cosmic order, as Matthew Lamb has prophetically decried:

> With the gusto of Prometheus unbound in a new world, modern man affirmed his dedication to the *quest* for knowledge, wealth, comfort, justice, rather than to any particular achievements. Science and technology provided the model for this exhilarating experience of "transcendence without a Transcendent" (E. Bloch) in their promise of an exponential growth-without-end of knowledge, material progress, and economic benefits.[108]

By connecting more emphatically the question of God with the movement to adoration, Lonergan's later writings underscore with greater existential urgency the primacy of love in the economy of grace. The passionateness of the human spirit is oriented radically to "the point beyond . . . being-in-love, a dynamic state that sublates all that goes before, a principle of movement at once purgative and illuminative, and a principle of rest in which union is fulfilled."[109] The finality of the human spirit is ultimately to the radical surrender of one's very self:

> Being in love with God, as experienced, is being in love in an unrestricted fashion. All love is self-surrender, but being in love with God is being in love without limits or qualifications or reservations. Just as unrestricted questioning is our capacity for self-transcendence, so being in love in an unrestricted fashion is the proper fulfillment of that capacity.[110]

---

106 Lonergan, *Method*, 341. Compare "Bernard Lonergan Responds," *Language, Truth, and Meaning*, 306–12, at 309.

107 Lonergan, *Method*, 344.

108 Lamb, ibid., 35; see 34–37.

109 Lonergan, "Natural Right and Historical Mindedness," in Crowe, *Third Collection*, 175.

110 Lonergan, *Method*, 105–6.

This radical commitment of ourselves to the whole of being is our free, reasonable, and loving participation in the finality of the whole universe. It involves the supreme self-displacement that acknowledges a cosmic order to which each individual is entirely subordinate.

The utter gratuity of God's gift, on the one hand, and the relentless finality of the human spirit that God's gift perfects, on the other, mean that there is a transformation of our being "from above" even as there is a striving "from below."[111] Frederick Crowe has aptly summarized this twofold dynamic: "[W]e are in the grip of two complementary forces. On one side there is the gift of God's love," a gift beyond the capacity of our knowledge and choice, a gift that occupies and perhaps even sublates the highest level of our being,[112]

> the effect of which, prior to all images and reflection, is orientation to mystery, the response to which is adoration. On the other side there is the spontaneous intentionality of human spirit, starting from experience, asking endless questions, and seeking a good beyond criticism, intentionality therefore as human capacity for religion reaching up toward love of God.[113]

The gift of God's love flooding our hearts is both free and prior to—indeed the very condition of—our entering into personal communion with God.[114] In this broader context, then, *Insight's* definition of faith as a higher, conjugate form in the intellect needs qualification. First there is God's gift of love, which transforms one's whole horizon, effecting an antecedent willingness.[115] Then

---

111 See, for instance, Lonergan, "Healing and Creating in History," in Crowe, *Third Collection,* 100–109, at 106; idem, "Natural Right," 180–81.

112 See Lonergan, *Method,* 106–7; idem, "Philosophy and the Religious Phenomenon," 134; idem, *Philosophy of God, and Theology: The Relationship between Philosophy of God and the Functional Specialty, Systematics* (Philadelphia: Westminster, 1973), 38. See too Robert M. Doran, "Consciousness and Grace," *Method: Journal* 11 (1993): 51–75; Michael Vertin, "Lonergan on Consciousness: Is There a Fifth Level?" *Method: Journal* 12 (1994): 1–36; Robert M. Doran, "Revisiting 'Consciousness and Grace,'" *Method: Journal* 13 (1995): 151–59; and now especially "'Complacency and Concern' and a Basic Thesis on Grace," in *Lonergan Workshop* 13, ed. Fred Lawrence (Boston, Boston College, 1997), 57–78.

113 "Lonergan's View of Religion," 155.

114 See Lonergan, *Method,* 283, 340–41; idem, *Philosophy of God, and Theology,* 50–51. The position of Lonergan, *Grace and Freedom,* is remarkably resonant: "The first act [of operative grace] does not presuppose any object apprehended by the intellect; God acts directly on the radical orientation of the will" (124).

115 Lonergan, *Method,* 105–7. See "Openness and Religious Experience," esp. the section "Openness as Gift."

there is faith, the knowledge born of love,[116] which in *Insight*'s terms is the apprehension of the truthfulness of God,[117] grounding the assent of belief.[118]

In "Finality, Love, Marriage," Lonergan observed that obediential potency, like every instance of vertical finality, pertains not to the abstract essence but to the concrete plurality; that is, not to individual human beings but rather to a community of human beings. The transformation of human living that is the self-communication of God is a being-in-love with absolute love, and "being-in-love is properly itself, not in the isolated individual, but only in a plurality of persons that disclose their love to one another."[119] Fully human living requires community not only for collaborative action but above all for the very possibility of self-donation, which in human beings constitutes the highest possibility of their nature, and it is this inter-subjective character of human self-transcendence that participation in the trinitarian life of God perfects and sublates. Even more than human love, the gift of divine love is a call to a total self-donation, a disposing of oneself that is never simply once and for all, but always worked out in the concrete context in which the demands of a universal finality make themselves felt in one's life and the communities to which one belongs.[120]

God's gift of love is prior to our cognitive apprehension and is its basis; it is the cause of our orientation to the unknown, to transcendent mystery, and this orientation is "the main source of man's search for God."[121] Still, as inner word it demands objectification in the outer word of a religious tradition, and such traditions are many.[122] Because the inner gift is transcendent mystery, it defies adequate expression even in all that is authentic in religious traditions; only the very incarnation of the Word of God can definitively and adequately express the reality of God's gift of love.[123] The incarnate

---

[116] Lonergan, *Method,* 115.

[117] Lonergan, *Insight,* 741–42, 729–32.

[118] Lonergan, *Method,* 118–19. Compare idem, *Insight,* 731.

[119] Lonergan, *Method,* 283. Echoes of this theme are all over Lonergan's later writings: see for example, ibid., 112–13; idem, "Theology in Its New Context," in *Second Collection,* 55–67, at 66; idem, "Response of the Jesuit as Priest and Apostle in the Modern World," in *Second Collection,* 165–87, at 173–74.

[120] See, for example, Lonergan, "Finality," 33–34; idem, "The Mediation of Christ in Prayer," 172. These concerns extend to Lonergan's earliest writings: see R. Michael Clark, "Byway of the Cross: The Early Lonergan and Political Order," in *Lonergan Workshop* 12, ed. Fred Lawrence (Boston: Boston College, 1996), 27–44.

[121] Lonergan, "Bernard Lonergan Responds," 309.

[122] See the discussion of the dialectic of religious development in Lonergan, *Method,* 110–12 (and a related discussion 138–40); see too idem, "Religious Experience," in Crowe, *Third Collection,* 115–28.

[123] Lonergan, *Method,* 119.

Word alone provides the adequate interpretation of the mysteries of grace, of the gift of the Spirit; for in this Word was conceived the plan of God before all ages; and in this Word we shall one day know as we are known.

Grace and Sin

In human beings the finality of the created universe takes rational possession of itself, but the course of human history is not a uniform movement to God. If there is a particular relevance of genetic method for the study of human development, still there is also the law of genuineness and the fact of sin, and hence the necessity to the human sciences of a further, dialectical method that takes its stand on the inverse insight that grasps the absence of intelligible correlation. For if human beings are rational and free, they are also characterized by a notable lack of personal integration and, more profoundly, by the simple refusal of reason and responsibility. The concrete unfolding of history, then, is dialectical.[124]

The fact of evil adds a further dimension to universal finality from which the earlier discussion of finality and divine transcendence largely prescinded. If it is affirmed that God, as the cause of the whole universe, is the principal author of every event, still it is not to be inferred that God is the author of sin. Basic evil is a defect of intelligibility, to be distinguished from physical privations, which attend naturally to a world order characterized by emergent probability.[125] The former possess a certain intelligibility, inasmuch as a dynamic universe is in potency to its perfection. Because the world order is a dynamic whole moving from incompleteness to fuller completeness through emergent probability, there are evolutionary failures as well as evolutionary breakthroughs, and there are extinct species quite apart from the disastrous effects of human shortsightedness. For instance, the short-term destruction of a forest by fire can be for the long-term health of its ecosystem.

In the case of basic sin and moral evil, however, there is no intelligibility to be grasped. By basic sin Lonergan denotes an utter and unaccountable failure of human reasonableness or willingness, "the root of the irrational in man's rational self-consciousness."[126] Basic sin is an unreasonable, inexplicable non-act of intelligence or will—either the refusal to engage further questions or the refusal to act responsibly. Further questions can be refused

---

124 On this whole section see Melchin, *History, Ethics,* ch. 7; Doran, *Theology and the Dialectics of History,* ch. 3; and Gerald K. Whelan, *The Development of Lonergan's Notion of the Dialectic of History.*

125 Lonergan, *Insight,* 689–91.

126 Ibid., 689.

unconsciously, by the refusal of the pertinent images (dramatic bias), or consciously, by the restriction of questions to what is directly relevant to me (individual bias), to us (group bias), or to the omnicompetence of common sense (general bias). In short, sin and bias constitute a failure to situate oneself and one's action in the context of a universal finality. By moral evil he indicates the consequences of basic sin in the human situation, concrete acts of omission or commission stemming from failure of will or willing of failed intelligence. Because evil is essentially a defect of being, it cannot be said to have a proper cause. What is caused is being; the fact that being is defective follows upon a failure of causality, a failure that is properly ascribed to free, secondary, human agency, agency that as truly free can also disobey even unto self-destruction.[127]

History, as we have seen, is the concrete unfolding of schemes of recurrence that are solutions to the problem of human living.[128] Concretely, human beings are always involved with attachments, interestedness, sensitivity, and intersubjectivity, and these are in themselves both good and necessary for "the mass and momentum" of human living.[129] Nevertheless, they are in tension and potential conflict with the detachment and disinterestedness required for human beings to discover what is true and love what is good. Inevitably this tension erupts in the field of individual consciousness and spills over into the community, with compounding consequences.

There is an objectification of the personal struggle in society and culture, resulting in a bipolar dialectic of progress and decline.[130] The conjunction of progress and decline does not represent a temporal sequence; both are permanent aspects of the human situation.[131] However, the metaphysical axiom that nothing reduces itself from potency to act has a kind of relevance to the succession of human situations. It points up the human problem, namely, that the wisdom required for successful living is only obtained through successful living, that virtue is only acquired through the exercise of

---

[127] For Lonergan's position on evil as objective surd and non-being, see Lonergan, *De ente,* nos. 128–29, 138–41, 143; idem, *De scientia,* nos. 58–62, 65; idem, *Grace and Freedom,* 112–15; idem, *Verbum,* 209; idem, *Insight,* 690–91, 709–15; idem, *De Verbo incarnate* (Rome: Gregorian University Press, 1964), thesis 17, scholion 2 (589–93). On evil as potency for good, idem, *Insight,* 688–90; idem, *De Verbo incarnato,* thesis 16, conclusion 6; thesis 17 conclusions 1–3.

[128] See Melchin, *History, Ethics,* ch. 5

[129] Lonergan, *Method,* 30.

[130] Lonergan, *Insight,* ch. 7, and 711–15. See idem, "Natural Right," 176–82; idem, "The Dialectic of Authority," in Crowe, *Third Collection,* 5–12.

[131] See, for instance, *Collected Works of Bernard Lonergan,* vol. 10, *Topics in Education: The Cincinnati Lectures of 1959 on the Philosophy of Education,* ed. R. M. Doran and F. E. Crowe (Toronto: University of Toronto 1993), 69.

virtue.[132] Accordingly, though a priori there would seem to obtain a kind of equilibrium in the tension between progress and decline, between the pure desire for truth and goodness and the myriad conflicting selfish desires, as a matter of fact the cumulative consequences of decline exceed the power of human efforts to meet them.

> Within each man there are both the attachment and interestedness of subjectivity and intersubjectivity and, on the other hand, the detachment and disinterestedness of the pure desire to know. From this conjunction of opposites there follow (1) the interference of the lower level with the unfolding of inquiry and reflection, of deliberation and decision, (2) the consequent unintelligibility of situations, and (3) the increasing irrelevance of intelligence and reasonableness to the real problem of human living.[133]

As practical, commonsense intelligence raises questions and effects courses of action only with respect to the data at hand, concerned only with an immediate palpable difference and ill-suited to seeking the inverse insight or envisaging long-term consequences, new unintelligible situations are produced out of old unintelligible situations. Human history is marred by an increasing absurdity, a heightening of the tension between limitation and transcendence. The fact of sin becomes the reign of sin, and "the reign of sin . . . is the expectation of sin."[134]

Such, then, is the bipolar dialectic, the gradual collapse of human history under the weight of human sin. But human decline is a disruption of the universal order in which "God is the first agent of every event and emergence and development."[135] Sin, therefore, is not merely a fact but also a problem that sets for us the further task of discerning "what God is or has been doing about the fact of evil."[136] Through this discernment the bipolar dialectic of progress and decline is understood to be the dialectic of pure nature, and in the concretely existing universe, there is no pure nature. For though the problem of evil is a human problem, it cannot be resolved by the native capacities of men and women. Thus every possible solution is either relatively or strictly supernatural. "When this problem of evil is met by a supernatural solution, human perfection itself becomes a limit to be transcended, and then the dialectic is transformed from a bipolar to a tripolar

---

[132] Lonergan, *Insight,* 711–15.

[133] Ibid., 749. See Lonergan, "Natural Right," 183.

[134] Lonergan, *Insight,* 715.

[135] Ibid., 709.

[136] Ibid.; see 715–18.

conjunction and opposition."[137] Moreover, since the actual solution is strictly supernatural, an invitation to a sharing in God's inner life that no creature could possibly claim for itself, the healing and restoration of human integrity and human history from the reign of sin is for the purpose of the elevation of human finality to an end infinitely beyond its natural capacities.

> For if the humanist is to stand by the exigencies of his own unrestricted desire, if he is to yield to the demands for openness set by every further question, then he will discover the limitations that imply man's incapacity for sustained development, he will acknowledge and consent to the one solution that exists, and if that solution is supernatural, his very humanism will lead beyond itself.[138]

The fact of sin and decline means that the gift of divine grace confronts humanity with a radical decision that can be neither ignored nor transferred. If human achievement cannot reverse the dizzying spiral of decline, neither can it daringly ignore the fact of grace without by that very gesture placing itself resolutely on the side of decline and so becoming its own undoing.

The course of human history, then, is the outworking of a tension, not merely between all that we would be and all that we fail to become, but pre-eminently between all that we are offered and all that we refuse. It is the history of grace drawing men and women beyond the narrow sphere of their self-interest and attaching them to what is best and truest, to the Good that surpasses every other. In the apprehension of transcendent value lies the very possibility of redemption, the recovery, through the self-displacement of love, of values betrayed. But the apprehension of transcendent value is the gift of faith, and it moves the whole scale of values into a new context, the context of a universal finality in which God, not the human subject, is recognized as the originating value. Now the question of God is not a question for intelligence and reason but a question for decision. "Without faith the originating value is man and the terminal value is the human good man brings about. But in the light of faith, originating value is the divine light and love, while terminal value is the whole universe,"[139] the universal finality that God has wisely ordered and lovingly chosen.

---

[137] Ibid., 749. The notion of a tripolar dialectic structuring history was consistently a major theme in Lonergan's thought. See, for instance, the very early essays Lonergan, "Analytic Concept of History," *Method: Journal* 11 (1993): 5–35; idem, *"Pantôn Anakephalaiôsis," Method: Journal* 9 (1991): 139–72.

[138] Lonergan, *Insight,* 749.

[139] Lonergan, *Method,* 116. See idem, "Natural Right," 173; and idem, *Method,* 30–40, esp. 30–31.

Not only is there the tension between what is offered on God's part and what is accepted on ours; there is a further, related tension as our acceptance of God's free gift is played out in the course of human history. Because grace strikes at the root of sin, there is

> a heightening of the tension that . . . arises whenever the limitations of lower levels are transcended. Moreover, when the higher integration is emergent in consciousness, not only is the tension itself conscious as an inner opposition and struggle but also it is objectified socially and culturally in the dialectical unfolding of human living and human history. For the supernatural solution not only meets a human problem but also goes beyond it to transform it into the point of insertion into human life of truths beyond human comprehension, of values beyond human estimation, of an alliance and a love that, so to speak, brings God too close to man.[140]

The tripolar dialectic consists not only in the tension between those who would receive grace and those who would reject it, but also among and within those who accept the gift, between their gratuitous receiving and their imperfect responding.

"Thus, the historical realization of the mystical body of Christ is also the instrument by which divine love brings about the healing of human history,"[141] a healing that embraces that history in its every aspect. For even in the face of sin God's gift will be

> not only a renovation of will that matches intellectual detachment and aspiration, not only a new and higher collaboration of intellects through faith in God, but also a mystery that is at once symbol of the uncomprehended and sign of what is grasped and psychic force that sweeps living human bodies, linked in charity, to the joyful, courageous, wholehearted, yet intelligently controlled performance of the tasks set by a world order in which the problem of evil is not suppressed but transcended.[142]

Between grace and sin the intelligibility of human history is cruciform: the transformation of human evil into the highest good of kenotic love through the just and mysterious Law of the Cross.[143] The Law of the Cross manifests

---

[140] Lonergan, *Insight,* 747. Compare idem, "Mission," 33.
[141] Stebbins, *Divine Initiative,* 141.
[142] Lonergan, *Insight,* 744–45.
[143] See Lonergan, *De Verbo incarnato,* 552, thesis 17.

not a drama of abandonment within God, but rather the drama of divine love entering the field of a history distorted by the absurdity of sin.[144]

Conclusion

In this little study of finality, history, and grace in the thought of Bernard Lonergan I have tried to sketch the main features from his early appropriation of St Thomas, through his adaptation and refinement of the notion of finality in an explicit metaphysics and a fully scientific world view, to the significance of this notion for his understanding of human history and human destiny, of "the concrete universal that is mankind in the concrete and cumulative consequences of the acceptance or rejection of the Gospel."[145] In this procedure we have been moving from general to specifically theological categories, from the heuristic structure of generalized emergent probability to the genetic sublation of human progress and the dialectical transformation of human decline by the free gift of divine love.

Pierre Hadot, in his stimulating exploration of classical philosophy, describes the quest for a wisdom that "is nothing more than the vision of things as they are, the vision of the cosmos as it is in the light of reason, and . . . the mode of being and living that should correspond to this vision."[146] It might be tempting to interpret Lonergan's project in just such terms. Yet Lonergan's is a profoundly Christian vision, conforming not only to the most rigorous demands of reason but also perceived in the light of faith and so under the judgment of the Gospel. Concretely, men and women in this world must choose between escalating the cycle of violence and domination or grace-filled joyous victory over evil through the just and mysterious Law of the Cross; between the pathological self-indulgence that mistakes pleasure for fulfillment and so production for transcendence,[147] or the "implementation" of metaphysics that is self-appropriation grounding attentive, intelligent, reasonable, responsible, and loving commitment to the universal finality, natural and supernatural, by which God brings all things to their recapitulation in Christ.

---

[144] Lonergan, *Insight,* 688–90; idem, *De Verbo incarnato,* 543–44, 568–71.

[145] Lonergan, *Insight,* 64.

[146] Pierre Hadot, *Philosophy as a Way of Life,* ed. A. I. Davidson, trans. M. Case (Cambridge, MA: Blackwell, 1995), 58.

[147] See Matthew Lamb, "Exigencies of Meaning and Metascience," 40.

General Index

academic freedom, 73–107
    CDF *Instruction* on. *See Instruction on the Ecclesial Vocation of the Theologian* (CDF) and academic freedom
    Ex Corde Ecclesiae on. *See under Ex Corde Ecclesiae*
    political correctness and, 77*n*9
    as a priori power, 82–83
    realist approach to, 73, 77–82, 98–101
    of theologians, 83–97
        authority of Magisterium, 74–75, 87–97
        complementary roles of theologians and Magisterium, 96–97
        critical regard for Magisterium by, 105–7
        higher wisdom, act of faith flowing from, 99–101
        "loyal dissent," concept of, 95–96, 104
        mandatum, 94–96
        obedience, 91–94, 98–104
        revealed truth as objective of, 83–85
        will, role of, 104–5

truth
    Magisterium and, 85–86
    search for, 79–80
    theologians, as objective of, 83–85
    voluntarist view of, 73, 75–77, 82–83, 98–99
Acts
    ecclesial structure evidenced in, 151, 155
    Trinity in, 181
Alan of Lille, 205
Alberic of Monte Cassino, 120
Albrecht, Barbara, 317*n*4
Alfonso VIII of Castile, 39
Allen, Prudence, 28*n*20
Ambrose of Milan, 139, 227*n*49, 356
Annunciation, 345–46, 349, 350
Anselm of Canterbury, 70, 302
anthropology
    personalism, 223*n*41, 241*n*84, 313
    Speyrian. *See* Speyr, Adrienne von, anthropology of
Apollinarius, 135
application, Thomist doctrine of, 388–89
Aquinas. *See* Thomas Aquinas

Arians, 53
Aristotle
    creation as revelatory and, 234,
        237–38, 240
    Kant's knowledge theory and, 299,
        301, 303, 309
    Philippians, Thomist commentary
        on, 120, 123–26, 127n48
    postmodern philosophy and, 280,
        281n12, 283
    on premotion, 388–89
    university education, Davies on
        Thomist concept of, 54
    on wisdom, 62, 65
Arius, 134
ars dictaminis or letter writing, Pauline
    corpus as exemplar of, 120–23
Assumption, 268
Athanasius, 184, 200, 310
atheism, modern rise of, 233–35
Augustine of Hippo
    anthropology of, 321n15
    on canonical scripture, 266n46
    on concepts and understanding, 302
    on habitus, 127n48, 133n77
    Lamb and, x, 17, 45
    on Mary, 345n139
    Monica and, 14
    on nuptial sexuality, 357–74
        Christ and Church, 366–73
        prelapsarian existence of sexuality,
            363–69
        sacramental nature of marriage,
            358, 359–63, 372
    on revelatory nature of creation,
        243–44
    Rule of, 17–18, 33
    sacraments, theology of, 360–61
    on search for truth, 79
    on spiritual beauty, 17–18
    theological system of, 70
    tractates on Gospel of John, 130n64
    on Trinity in Scripture, 174–75,
        176–77, 181, 182, 183, 198,
        200–201, 203n87
authority of Magisterium and academic
    freedom, 74–75
Avicenna, 54

Bach, J. S., 92
Baglow, Christopher, 109n1, 110
Balthasar, Hans Urs von
    on creation as revelatory, 232n64,
        237n72, 247n106
    on hierarchy of Church authority,
        157–58n51
    on nuptial sexuality, 356n9, 372n56
    Speyrian anthropology and, x,
        316–18. See also Speyr, Adrienne
        von, anthropology of
    on Trinity in Scripture, 175–76
    on wisdom, 70
Bañez, Domingo, 388n82
Barr, Colin, 3
Barth, Karl, 217, 256
Baruch
    on wisdom, 189
Barzun, Jacques, 284–85n24
Bauerschmidt, Frederick Christian,
    146n16
Bavel, Tarcisius van, 370
Bea, Augustine, 256–57
Beauchamp, Paul, 192n59
beauty, spiritual, 17–20, 33–34
Becker, Joseph, 25
Bedouelle, Guy, 32n26, 34, 41
Behm, J., 123n37
Behr, John, 178n27, 183n40, 186n44
being
    creation as foundation for
        understanding of, 238–46
    Kant on. See under Kant
Benedict of Nursia, 18, 22, 30, 45, 290
Benedict XVI. See also Ratzinger, Joseph
    on academic freedom, 93, 106n67
    on consecrated life, 28, 30, 33

on hierarchy in Church authority, 147*n*17
on postmodern world, 287, 288*n*27
on wisdom, 60
Benoit, Pierre, 117
Berg, Blaise R., 317*n*4
Berkeley, George, 281, 282*n*15, 283
Bernadot, M.-V., 44*n*46
Bernard of Clairvaux, 45
Bernstein, Leonard, 92
Bianchi, Eugene C., 147*n*17
Bible. *See also* individual biblical books, e.g. Romans
    authoritative character for Thomas, 52–53, 265–69
    creation as revelatory in biblical tradition, 207–33
        Hebrew Bible, narrative and prayer in, 207–12
        New Testament. *See under* Pauline corpus
        wisdom literature, 212, 213–17, 228–30
    as divinely inspired, 256–57
    theological discipline of biblical studies, 68–69
    Thomist commentaries on, 109–10
    Trinity in. *See* Trinity in Scripture
birth control, 98, 99, 101, 103
bishops, vii, 19, 147–48*n*17. *See also* hierachical authority of Church
Blair, Tony, 286*n*25
blueprint ecclesiology, 143*n*1
Boethius, 227, 274
Bonaventure, 70, 110, 206*n*3
Boniface VIII, 145, 147
Boulanger, Nadia, 92
Boulding, Maria, 200
Bouyer, Louis, 178*n*28, 188*n*50
Boyle, John F., 116–17
Brettler, Marc Zvi, 247*n*105
Briel, Don, x, 1–16
Brown, Peter, 357

Brown, Raymond, 149–51, 154, 155, 192*n*58
Buber, Martin, 241, 246*n*103
Buckley, Michael, 235
Burns, J. Patout, 177*n*22
Burtchaell, James, 149, 151–54, 155, 156
Bush George W., 286*n*25
Byrne, Patrick H., 377*n*12

Cajetan, Thomas de Vio, 253–54, 263, 270
Callahan, Virginia Woods, 356*n*11
Calvin, John, 250–51, 270
Cameron, J. M., 1
Cameron, Peter John, 34
Caparello, Adriana, 125*n*44
Carey, Ann, 26, 27
Cathars, 37
Catherine of Siena, 35–36, 42
Catholic Church. *See* Church
Catholic Theological Society of America (CTSA), 84*n*29
Catholic universities. *See* entries at university
Cessario, Romanus, x, 17–45, 75*n*5, 76*n*6, 78*n*11, 83*n*25
Chalcedonian Christology and Speyrian anthropology, 328*n*53
Chantraine, Georges, 316*n*2
Chaput, Charles J., vii, x, 19, 34
chastity
    in consecrated life, 30–31
    in early Christianity, 359–60
    eschatological character of, 360*n*15
    marriage between Christ and Church and, 369–70
Chavannes, Henry, 256
Childs, Brevard, 114*n*16, 173*n*2
Christocentrism *vs.* theocentrism in Dominican spirituality and Thomism, 37–38

Christological perspective of Speyrian anthropology, 323–27

Christus Dominus, 34*n*30

Church

academic freedom and authority of Magisterium, 74–75, 87–97

Augustine on marital union of Christ and, 366–74. *See also* nuptial sexuality in theology

complementary roles of theologians and Magisterium, 96–97

critical regard for Magisterium by theologians, 105–7

ecumenism and Church authority. *See under* ecumenism, Thomistic contributions to

eschatological, 144–45

hierarchical authority of. *See* hierarchical authority of Church

infallibility

academic freedom and, 83, 87–90, 100–102, 106

Newman on, 11, 12

revealed truth and Magisterium, 85–86

in Speyrian anthropology, 341–42, 347

university, Newman on relationship to, 4–5, 11–16

Cicero, 54, 120, 123

Cizewski, Wanda, 109*n*1

Clark, R. Michael, 396*n*120

Clarke, Walter Norris, 220*n*36–37, 239, 240

1 Clement, 154

Clement of Rome, 151

Clericis laicos, 145

Colish, Marcia L., 110*n*6

Communion. *See* Eucharist

community

history and theology, 305

individualism and, 30

Newman on university as, 7

concepts

Kant on, 300–301

Thomas Aquinas on, 299–300

Vatican I on, 302–3, 304

Congar, Yves, 183*n*39

consecrated life, 17–45

chastity in, 30–31

of Dominicans. *See* Dominicans

education and, 23–24

homosexuality and, 28, 31, 38

objective superiority of, 29

original genius of founder, importance of following, 34

pastoral care for, 29–30

poverty, 31–32

present-day state of decline, 20–34

causal factors, 23–29

challenges faced, 29–33

Vatican II and, 21–25, 26–28

spiritual beauty and, 17–20, 33–34

theology of, 29

Vatican II and

Dominican General Chapter held in response to Vatican II, 43

original genius of founder, 34

present-day state of, 21–25, 26–28

virtue of religion and, 24, 32

Constitution for Europe, 33

contemplative life of Dominicans, 37, 41

contraception, 98, 99, 101, 103

Copeland, Aaron, 92

1 Corinthians

hierarchical authority of Church in, 157–65

Thomas on, 110, 111, 112–13

Trinity in, 190, 191

2 Corinthians

Thomas on, 111, 113*n*13, 128

corruption and power in Church, 145–47

Council of Major Superiors of Women Religious, 23, 32

creation, revelatory nature of, 205–47
  in biblical tradition, 207–33
    Hebrew Bible, narrative and
      prayer in, 207–12
    New Testament. *See under*
      Pauline corpus
    wisdom literature, 212, 213–17,
      228–30
  Dei Verbum on, 206–7
  failure to glorify God, 228–30
  in history, 242–45
  homosexuality, 226*n*47, 232*n*63
  idolatry, 230–32
  language, 236, 245–46
  in modern Jewish and Christian
    thought, 233–46
    being, understanding of, 238–46
    closed systems, opening, 236–37
    foundational nature of revelation,
      237–38
    transcendence, loss of, 233–36
  subjectivity of person, 240–42
  Thomas Aquinas on
    modern thought and, 238*n*77,
      240, 241*n*84, 245
    Pauline commentaries and
      biblical tradition, 218,
      219–27, 232–33*n*65, 233
  truth, suppression and manifestation
    of, 219–27
  what can be known about God
    in Christian tradition, 217–19,
      228
    in narrative and prayer in
      Hebrew Bible, 207–12
    in wisdom literature, 212,
      213–17
Crowe, Frederick E., 393*n*105, 395
CTSA (Catholic Theological Society of
  America), 84*n*29
Culpepper, Gary, 73*n*1, 76*n*7, 98*n*55
Curran, Charles, 104
Curtius, Ernst Robert, 205*n*2

cyclical vs. linear views of history,
  274–77
Cyril of Alexandria, 177*n*22

Dauphinais, Michael A., x, xi, 47–58
Davies, Brian. *See* university education,
  Brian Davies' interpretation of
  Thomas Aquinas on
Dawson, Christopher, 15
Day, Dorothy, ix
D'Costa, Gavin, 82*n*22, 89*n*40
de la Potterie, Ignace, 322*n*23
Decter, Midge, 289
Deely, John, 278–84, 285*n*24, 289–90
Dei Verbum, 70*n*13, 85–88, 206–7,
  256*n*21, 305*n*21
democratization of Church, arguments
  for, 143–49. *See also* hierarchical
  authority of Church
Derrida, Jacques, 237, 274, 274*n*1
Descartes, René, 235, 274, 279–83,
  318
Deutero-Isaiah, 207
Diego de Acebo, 39
Dilthey, Wilhelm, ix
"dispensation," Dominican practice of,
  40, 44
Divine Providence, Dominican
  dependence on, 38–40
dogmatic theology, 60, 69
Dominic de Guzmán
  Catherine of Siena on, 35–36
  contemplation, devotion to, 37
  humor, sense of, 44
  individualism and community for,
    30
  on John of Navarre, 40
  Lamb and, 45
  original genius of, 34
  on poverty, 32
  Providence and grace, reliance on,
    38, 40
  sin, mindfulness of, 42

vocation, failed diplomatic mission
as catalyst of, 39
Dominicans, 34–45
Catherine of Siena on, 35–36
contemplative life, 37
"dispensation" for, 40, 44
humor, importance of, 44
Marian devotion of, 44–45
mercy of God, mindfulness of,
42–43
obedience, devotion to, 43–44
Providence and grace, dependence
on, 38–40
realism of, 34–38
Rule of St. Augustine, 17–18
theocentrism vs. Christocentrism in
spirituality of, 37–38
Thomas Aquinas on, 19
truth and, 35, 37, 40–42, 43
virtue-centered life of, 41–42
Doran, Robert M., 395n112, 397n124
dualism, 37, 314, 353–54n2
Dulles, Avery, x, 59–71
Duns Scotus, 70, 256, 301
Dupont, Jacques, 215n24
Dupré, Louis, 235n70, 243n91
Duquoc, Christian, 78n10
Durkheim, Emile, 24

Eberhard, Johann August, 294
ecclesiology. *See* Church; hierarchical
authority of Church
ecumenism, Thomistic contributions
to, 249–71
Church authority, 257–69
ecumenical dialogues, tradition
in, 257–61
human character of and divine
love in, 261–62
revealed truth and, 265–69
theology of faith in Thomas,
261–64, 265–69

divine action and human action,
relationship between, 250–57
Protestant questions regarding,
250–52
Thomist answers, 253–57
divine inspiration of Scripture,
256–57
justification by faith, 252
Penance, 250, 253
education
at Catholic universities. *See* entries at
university
religious vocation and, 23–24
Egan, Robert J., 76–77n8, 94n47
Eliot, T. S., 14
emergent probability, 380–87, 390
Emery, Gilles, 176n20, 182n34
Engberg-Pedersen, Troels, 165n55
Ephesians
Thomas's commentary on, 109–10,
122, 173–74
epic ecclesiology, 143–44, 147–48, 150
epistemology. *See* knowledge
Erasmus, 250
eschatological character of chastity,
360n15
eschatological Church, 144–45
eschatological reality of marriage of
Christ and Church, 366–69, 372
Eucharist
in blueprint ecclesiologies, 143n1
Catholic ignorance about, 24
in Dominican spirituality, 42
in Speyrian anthropology, 330–31,
333, 335, 338, 350
Thomas Aquinas on, 40
Europe, Constitution for, 33
Eutyches, 135
evidentialism, 98–99, 101–2
evil, sin, and grace, Lonergan on,
397–402

Ex Corde Ecclesiae
  on academic freedom, 73, 74, 107
    authority of Magisterium, 86, 90,
      91
    critical response to, 76
    mandatum, 94*n*47
    realist approach, 78, 79, 81
  on Catholic universities, 16
  wisdom as unifying force in
    university curriculum and, 47, 54

Fabro, Cornelio, 239*n*80
Fagin, Gerald M., 177*n*22
faith and reason
  Davies' interpretation of Thomas
    Aquinas on *scientia* and *fides,*
    49–50, 51, 53, 57–58
  intellectus fidei and Kantian
    knowledge theory, 303–4
  judgment of faith, realism of,
    310–12
  Newman on complementarity of,
    4–5, 16
  obedience and intellectual
    engagement, 101–4
  theological wisdom and, 64–66
  wisdom, act of faith flowing from
    higher order of, 99–101
faith, ecumenical dialogue on Church
  authority and Thomist theology of,
  261–64
family life and consecrated life, 30
Farley, Margaret, 26
feminism, 27, 28, 29, 77*n*9
Fessio, Joseph, 316*n*2
Festugière, André-Jean, 224*n*45
Fides et Ratio, 60–61, 270*n*55
finality, history, and grace, Lonergan's
  theory of, 375–402
  absolute, horizontal, and vertical
    finality, 376–79
  emergent probability, 380–87, 390
  evil, sin, and grace, 397–402

  genuineness, 385
  Intelligent Design, 389–92
  knowledge, 385–87
  obediential potency, 392–97
  transcendence, 387–92
Finland and Nordic Way, 103
First Vatican Council. *See* Vatican I
Flores, Daniel E., 179*n*29, 195*n*64,
  201*n*81
Fra Angelico (Giovanni da Fiesole), 37
fragmentation of university curriculum.
  See university curriculum, wisdom as
  source of unity for
Francis of Assisi, 30, 33, 35–36
Franciscans, 35–36
free will
  divine and human action,
    relationship between, 250–57
    Protestant questions regarding,
      250–52
    Thomist answers, 253–57
  faith, Thomist theology of, 261–64
freedom, academic. *See* academic
  freedom
Frei, Hans, 173
Freud, Sigmund, 235
Friedman, Maurice S., 241*n*84
Friedrowicz, Michael, 200
fundamentalism in Islam and
  Christianity, 278*n*6

Galatians
  Thomas on, 111
  Trinity in, 190
Galileo, 281*n*12, 289
Gallagher, Michael Paul, 224*n*44
Gallin, Alice, 78*n*10
Garrigou-Lagrange, Reginald, 39, 70
Gaudium et Spes, 319, 342*n*128
Gawronski, Raymond, 316*n*2
Genesis
  Augustine's commentary on, 363–64

gentlemen, Newman on university
  education as creation of, 5, 9–10
genuineness, Lonergan on, 385
Gilson, Etienne, 284
Giovanni da Fiesole (Fra Angelico), 37
Glendon, Mary Ann, 27
Gondreau, Paul, x, 73–107
Grabowski, John, 75n5
grace
  Dominican dependence on, 38–40
  free will and (relationship between
    divine and human action),
    250–57
    Protestant questions regarding,
      250–52
    Thomist answers, 253–57
  in history. See finality, history, and
    grace, Lonergan's theory of
  Speyr on expansion of nature by
    grace in mutual indwelling of
    Christ and Christian, 331–36
Gregory of Nyssa, 70, 355–57, 373,
  374
Gregory the Great, 19–20, 244n100
Grignon de Montfort, Louis, 44
Groupe de Dombes, 260–61
Guerriero, Elio, 316n2

Haberman, Joshua, 238n74
Hadot, Pierre, 402
Hanson, Victor Davis, 286–87n25
Harrison, Verna E. F., 356n10
Hart, David Bentley, 221n39, 241n86,
  242n89
Hays, Richard B., 185n43,
  191n56–57, 201n80
Healy, Nicholas M., 143–47, 150, 171
Hebrews
  Thomas on, 111
  Trinity in, 180, 182, 193
Hegel, Georg Wilhelm Friedrich, 235,
  237, 242

Heidegger, Martin, 237, 239n78, 242,
  274, 281n13, 283
Hengel, Martin, 190n54, 192
Henrici, Peter, 316n2
Heraclitus, 279
Herz, Marcus, 295
Heschel, Abraham J., 238
hierarchical authority of Church,
  143–72
  arguments against, 143–49
  in 1 Corinthians, 157–65
  ecumenism and. See under
    ecumenism, Thomistic
    contributions to
  historical accounts of early Church
    and, 149–57
  in Matthew, 165–71
  power and corruption associated
    with, 145–47
  self-subordination, importance of,
    172
  synagogues compared, 152–54
historical theology, 69
history
  cyclical vs. linear views of, 274–77
  Lonergan on. See finality, history,
    and grace, Lonergan's theory of
  periodization of, 273–74
  revelatory nature of creation in,
    242–45
  theology and, 304–7
Holmes, Jeremy, x, 109–41
Holy Name societies, 38
Holy Spirit
  knowledge of Trinity derived from,
    179–80
  as speaker in Scripture, 177, 182–83
  wisdom as gift of, 67–68, 70
homosexuality
  consecrated life and, 28, 31, 38
  creation, revelatory nature of,
    226n47, 232n63

Hoye, William J., 75*n*4
Hugh of St. Victor, 245*n*101
Hugo, John, 357*n*12
Hugo of Bologna, 120
Humanae Vitae, 99, 100, 102, 103
Hume, David, 281, 283
humility *vs.* modesty, Newman on,
    9–10
humor, Dominican sense of importance
    of, 44
Hunter, David, 370*n*52

Idea of a University, The (Newman). *See*
    university, education, Newman on
idolatry and revelatory nature of
    creation, 230–32
Ignatius of Antioch, 151
Ignatius of Loyola, 98
Immaculate Conception, 344
individualism and community life, 30
infallibility
    academic freedom and, 83, 87–90,
        100–102, 106
    Newman on, 11, 12
Insight. See finality, history, and grace,
    Lonergan's theory of
*Instruction on the Ecclesial Vocation of
    the Theologian* (CDF) and academic
    freedom, 73, 107
    on authority of Magisterium, 86, 90
    on complementary roles of
        theologians and Magisterium,
        96–97
    on *mandatum*, 95, 96
    on obedience, 92*n*44, 93*n*45–46
    reactions to, 77–78*n*8
    realist view of, 78, 79, 81*n*20
    on truth as objective of theology,
        85*n*30
    on voluntarism, 75*n*3, 76*n*6, 83,
        102
intellectus fidei, 303–4
Intelligent Design, 389–92

intentionality, Kant's failure to account
    for, 305–7
Iraq, pronouncements on military
    intervention in, 105–6
Ireland, failed Catholic University of,
    3–5
Irenaeus of Lyons, 183*n*38, 230–31,
    232*n*65, 327*n*51
Isaiah
    Trinity in, 179
Islam, continuing conflict with,
    277–78, 285–86, 289, 290*n*30

James 2:19, 140–41
Jandel, Vincent Alexander, 43
Jerome, 356, 359
Jesuits, 25–26
Jewish synagogues, hierarchical
    authority in, 152–54
Jewish thought, creation as revelatory
    in. *See under* creation, revelatory
    nature of
Job
    Thomas's commentary on, 110
John (Gospel)
    Thomas's commentary on, 110,
        141*n*112, 195–99
    Trinity in, 175, 191–93, 195–99
1 John (Epistle)
    Hosea and, 229
John Chrysostom, 231*n*61
John of Navarre, 40
John of St. Thomas, 263–64
John of Vercelli, 38
John Paul II. *See also* Wojtyla, Karol
    on academic freedom, 73, 74
    on Catholic universities, 16
    on consecrated life, 21*n*9, 29*n*22, 30
    on fragmentation of knowledge,
        60–61
    on Mary, 351*n*179
    on moral theology, 69–70, 313*n*35

"papal maximalization" under,
147n17
on philosophy and theology, 269–70
Speyrian anthropology and, 332n73
Johnson, Elizabeth, 353–54
Johnson, Philip, 278n6
Jordan of Saxony, 39n40
Josephites (Sisters of St. Joseph), 24
Josephus, 216, 217
Journet, Charles, 145, 327n51
Jovinian, 359–60
Jubilees, 216n26, 217
Judaism and hierarchical authority,
152–54
Judaism, revelatory nature of creation
in. *See under* creation, revelatory
nature of
judgment in Kant and St. Thomas,
307–12
Julian of Eclanum, 368
Julian the Apostate, 10
justification by faith, 252

Kant, Immanuel, 293–314
Catholic theology, relevance to,
293–94
Catholic university education and,
48
creation as revelatory and, 235, 237
on ethics and moral theology,
313–14
intellectus fidei and, 303–4
on knowledge, being, and reality
concepts, understanding of,
300–301
deficiencies of, 312–13
direction of modern philosophy
turned towards, 295–97
intellectus fidei and, 303–4
intentionality, failure to account
for, 305–7
judgment, 307–8
sensism of, 297–99

postmodern world as new Middle
Ages and, 237, 274n1, 277, 283
Thomas Aquinas and, 293, 296,
299–303, 305, 309
Karris, Robert J., 110n7
Käsemann, Ernst, 228n52
Kasper, Walter, 233n66
Kaufmann, Yehezkel, 275–76
Keating, James F., 73n1, 98n55
Keefe, Donald, 374n59
Keller, Paul, 73n1
Kennedy, George A., 120n27
Ker, Ian, 3, 11, 88n38, 106n67
Khomeni, Ayatollah, 277
knowledge
concepts
Kant on, 300–301
Thomas Aquinas on, 299–300
Vatican I on, 302–3, 304
Davies' interpretation of Thomas
Aquinas on, 49–50, 51, 53,
57–58
faith and. *See* faith and reason
intentionality, 305–7
judgment, 307–12
Kant on. *See under* Kant, Immanuel
Lonergan on, 385 87
Newman on, 3
Thomas Aquinas on, 299–303, 305,
309
Kowalczyk, Stanislaw, 223

Lacordaire, Henry Dominic, 43
Lacroix, Jean, 244
Lafont, Ghislain, 147n17, 148n17
Lakeland, Paul, 147–48n17
Lamb, Matthew, vii, ix–xi
consecrated life and, 17–20, 26–27,
28n20, 34, 45
on emergent probability, 381n36
on fragmentation of university
curriculum, 59

on history and revelatory nature of
creation, 243*n*90
Lonergan and, ix, xi, 275, 381*n*36,
388*n*76, 392*n*101, 393*n*104,
394, 402*n*147
on Thomist commentaries on
Pauline epistles, 109–10, 116,
173–74, 179*n*30
language
periodization of history and, 274*n*1
postmodern philosophical trends
and, 283–85
revelatory nature of creation and,
236, 245–46
Larcher, Fabian R., 126
Leadership Conference of Women
Religious (LCWR), 23
Leibniz, Gottfried, 281, 294
Letter of Aristeas, 216, 228
letter writing or *ars dictaminis,* Pauline
corpus as exemplar of, 120–23
Levenson, Jon D., 208*n*10, 212*n*18
Levering, Matthew, x, xi, 28*n*20,
143–72
Levinas, Emmanuel, 241, 246*n*103,
247*n*106
Leviticus 16, 188
Lienhard, Joseph T., 69*n*11
Lightfoot, J. B., 124
Lindbeck, George, 260
linear *vs.* cyclical views of history,
274–77
Locke, John, 279, 280*n*10, 281
Lohfink, Norbert, 210*n*15
London bombings of 2005, 285,
286–87*n*25
Lonergan, Bernard J. F.
on finality, history, and grace. *See*
finality, history, and grace,
Lonergan's theory of
on genuineness, 385
Kant and, 296*n*5–6, 301*n*14,
302*n*18, 303, 310*n*32

on knowledge, 385–87
on macroeconomics, 383*n*43
postmodern period as new Middle
Ages and, 289*n*28
on Trinity in Scripture, 176*n*17
Lubac, Henri de, 50*n*12, 70, 104,
178*n*27, 224*n*45
Luke
Trinity in, 186–89, 202*n*85
Lumen Gentium
academic freedom and, 86, 87, 91,
92*n*44, 102
consecrated life and, 34*n*30
on hierarchical authority of Church,
155
on history and theology, 305*n*21
Luther, Martin, 250, 253, 269–70
Lyonnet, Stanislaus, 219*n*33, 232*n*64

MacIntyre, Alasdair, 290
macroeconomics, Lonergan on, 383*n*43
Magisterium. *See* entries under Church
Maguire, Daniel, 76*n*8, 83*n*24, 94*n*47
Maimonides, 54, 57, 225–26, 226*n*47,
237–38
Malachi 4:5, 185
male religious. *See* consecrated life
Malloy, Edward A., 77*n*8, 94*n*47
mandatum for professors of Catholic
theology, 54, 94–96
Manichees, 53, 359
Mansini, Guy, x, 173–203, 207*n*5,
226*n*47
Maréchal, Joseph, 293
Maritain, Jacques, 79*n*12, 222*n*40, 284
Mark
Trinity in, 184–85, 190
marriage. *See* nuptial sexuality in
theology
Martin, Francis, x, 205–47
Martin, Gottfried, 307*n*24
Martin, Ralph P., 124*n*39, 124*n*43
Martin, Raymond M., 38

Marx, Karl, 235, 277
Mary
    Augustine on virginity of, 360n15
    Dominican devotion to, 44–45
    in Speyrian anthropology, 329–30,
        340, 343–50, 351–52
Matro, Justin, 317n4
Matthew
    on hierarchical authority of Church,
        165–71
    Thomas on, 110, 128
    Trinity in, 185, 186–90
Maximus the Confessor, 356n9
McShane, Philip, 380n30, 383n43
Melchin, Kenneth R., 380n30,
    397n124, 398n128
mercy of God, Dominican mindfulness
    of, 42–43
Metz, John Baptist, ix
Mews, Constant J., 205n1
Meyer, Ben F., 185n42, 187, 188n48,
    188n50
Middle Ages, coming. See postmodern
    world as new Middle Ages
modesty vs. humility, Newman on,
    9–10
Möhler, Johann Adam, 70
Molina, Luis de, 388n82
Monan, J. Donald, 77n8, 94n47
Monica, 14
monotheism and polytheism, different
    views of history in, 274–77
Montfort, Louis Grignon de, 44
moral theology, 69–70, 313–14
morality generally. See virtue/morality
Morerod, Charles, x, 146n16, 249–71
Murphy, James J., 120n28, 121n30,
    122n33
Murphy-O'Connor, Jerome, 113n14
Muslim world, continuing conflict
    with, 277–78, 285–86, 289, 290n30

natural law
    academic freedom and, 105
    chastity and, 30
    Humanae Vitae on natural moral
        law, 100
    religion as natural-law relationship
        to God, 33
nature. See creation, revelatory nature of
Neoscholasticism, 293
Nestorius and Nestorians, 53, 134–35
Newman, John Henry
    on faith and reason, 4–5, 16, 99
    on Magisterium, 88, 106
    on rationalism, 65
    on revelation, 66
    theological system of, 70
    on university education. See
        university education, Newman on
    on wisdom, 61n4, 67
Newton, Isaac, 274n1
Nicene creed, 310–11
Nietzsche, Friedrich, 48, 76, 77, 235,
    242, 274
nominalism, 83
Nordic Way, 103
Novak, David, 217
Numbers 11:25, 183
nuptial sexuality in theology, 353–74
    Augustine of Hippo on, 357–74
        Christ and Church, 366–73
        prelapsarian existence of sexuality,
            363–69
        sacramental nature of marriage,
            358, 359–63, 372
    defined, 353
    Gregory of Nyssa and, 355–57, 373,
        374
    modern resistance to concept of,
        353–54, 357
    Patristic controversy regarding,
        354–57

sacramental nature of marriage and, 358, 359–63, 372, 373–74
Speyrian anthropology and, 333–36

Oakes, Edward T., x, 273–91
Oates, Edward, 232n64
obedience
    academic freedom and, 91–94, 98–104
    Dominican devotion to, 43–44
    Lonergan on obediential potency, 392–97
    in Speyrian anthropology, 339n114, 340–41
O'Brien, Mary Judith, 28n20
O'Brien, Peter T., 115n18, 124n39, 124n41, 124n43
O'Connor, Flannery, ix
Odone, Christina, 278n6
O'Keefe, John J., 173n2
O'Malley, Seán Patrick, 22n10, 22n12
ontology
    creation as foundation for understanding of being, 238–46
    Kant on knowledge, being, and reality. See under Kant
Orange, Second Council of, 70n13
Order of Preachers. See Dominicans
Ordinatio Sacerdotalis, 99, 102, 103, 104
ordination
    Augustine on marriage and, 362
    of women, 98, 99, 101, 103, 104
Origen, 140, 176n15, 194n62, 230
Orsay, Ladislas, 78n10
Ouellet, Marc, 316n2, 342n127

papacy. See Church, and specific popes, e.g. Benedict XVI
Parmenides, 280
Pater, Walter, 1
Patristic theology, 69

Paul VI, 102n61
Pauline corpus. See also specific letters, e.g. Romans
    creation as revelatory in, 217–33
        failure to glorify God, 228–30
        idolatry, 231–32
        suppression of truth, 219
        truth, suppression and manifestation of, 219–17
        what can be known about God, 217–19, 228
    divisio of, 110–15
    letter writing or ars dictaminis, Pauline corpus as exemplar of, 120–23
    Trinity in, 190–91
Paulsen, Friedrich, 301n15
Peirce, Charles Sanders, 283, 289
Pelagians, 262, 368
Penance and ecumenism, 250, 253
Pepinster, Catherine, 290–91n31
Perfectae caritatis, 34n31
periodization of history, 273–74
Perkins, Pheme, 165n55
personalism, 223n41, 241n84, 313. See also Speyr, Adrienne von, anthropology of
Pesch, Otto Herman, 109n1, 112, 123
1 Peter
    ecclesial structure evidenced in, 155
Peter Lombard, 133n77
Philemon, Thomas on, 111
Philippians
    hierachical authority of Church evidenced in, 151
Philippians, commentary of St. Thomas on, 109–41
    Aristotelian assumptions regarding use of μορφη (forma), 123–26
    internal divisio of letter, 114–19
    Latin translations, Thomas's reliance on, 125–26

letter writing or *ars dictaminis*, Pauline corpus as exemplar of, 120–23
Pauline corpus as a whole, Thomas's treatment of, 110–15
rhetorical analysis of, 117–20
translation notes, 126
translation of commentary on 2:5–11, 127–41
Philo Judaicus, 213, 215, 232n63
philosophy
    Benedict XVI on, 60
    Kantian. *See* Kant, Immanuel
    limitations of, 63
    postmodern trends, 278–85
    Thomist. *See* Thomas Aquinas
    university education, Davies' interpretation of Thomas Aquinas on, 50–51
    wisdom, philosophical, 61–63
Photinus, 134
Pinckaers, Servais, 42, 75n5, 78n11, 82n23
Pius IX, 344n136
Pius XII, 268
Plato, 54, 234, 240, 280, 283, 309
Plotinus, 240, 274
Polanyi, Michael, 223
political correctness and academic freedom, 77n9
polytheism and monotheism, different views of history in, 274–77
Pope, Hugh, 125n44
Pope, Stephen J., 147n17
popes. *See* specific popes, e.g. Benedict XVI
"popularizers," post-conciliar theology of, 26–27
Porter, Jean, 90–91n41, 94n47
positivism, 83, 102
postmodern world as new Middle Ages, 273–91

external forces leading to, 287–88
internal dynamics leading to, 288–90
Islam, continuing conflict with, 277–78, 285–86, 289, 290n30
language and linguistic theory, 283–85
linear *vs.* cyclical views of history, 274–77
periodization of history, 273–74
philosophical trends, 278–85
Potterie, Ignace de la, 322n23
poverty and consecrated life, 31–32
power and corruption in Church, 145–47
Power, David, 354
pre-Socratic philosophy, 279
premotion, Aristotelian concept of, 388–89
priesthood, hierarchical. *See* hierarchical authority of Church
probabilistic evidence, 98–99, 101–2
professional skill and liberal knowledge, Newman on, 7–9
Proverbs
    Trinity in, 179
Providence, Dominican dependence on, 38–40
Psalms
    Trinity in, 200–202
Pseudo-Cicero, 121n32

Quinn, John R., and Quinn Commission, 21, 22, 24, 32
Quintillian, 121n32

Rad, Gerhard von, 210n14–15
Rahner, Karl, ix, 144, 180n32, 215n24, 220n37, 268n51
Ramirez, Santiago, 36
Rashi, 212
rationalism in theology, dangers of, 64–65

Ratzinger, Joseph. *See also* Benedict XVI
on academic freedom, 75, 91,
93*n*46, 105
on creation as revelatory, 236*n*72
on hierarchy of Church authority,
164
Newman on university education
and, 15
on postmodern world, 287–88
on Speyr and Balthasar, 316*n*2
Raymond of Capua, 42*n*44
realism
academic freedom and, 73, 77–82,
98–101
of Dominican spirituality, 34–38
of judgment of faith, 310–12
reality, Kant on. *See under* Kant,
Immanuel
reason. *See* faith and reason; knowledge
Redemptoris mater, 351*n*179
reductionism
rationalism in theology, dangers of,
64–65
university education and tendency
towards, Newman on, 12–13, 15
Reese, James, 215
Regan, Augustine, 363*n*28
Regimini Ecclesiae, 102*n*61
Reginald of Orleans, 45
relativism and fragmentation of
theology as discipline, 59–61
religious life and religious institutes. *See*
consecrated life
Reno, R. R., 173*n*2, 264
Reuss, Maternus, 293
revelation
authoritative character of divine
revelation for Thomas, 52–53,
265–69
creation as form of. *See* creation,
revelatory nature of
Magisterium and, 85–86

theologians, revealed truth as
objective of, 83–85
Ricoeur, Paul, 239*n*78
Rocca, Gregory, 239*n*80
Rockinger, Ludwig, 120–21*n*29–31
Roman Catholic Church. *See* Church
Romans
Thomas's commentary on, 110, 111,
112–13, 114, 131*n*69
Trinity in, 190–91
Rorty, Richard, 274
Rosenzweig, Franz, 238, 246*n*103
Roten, Johann, 316*n*2
Rousseau, Jean-Jacques, 76
Rowe, C. Kavin, 202*n*85
Ruddy, Christopher, 147*n*17
Ruether, Rosemary Radford, 147*n*17
Rushdie, Salman, 277, 285, 289
Russell, Bertrand, 274

sacra doctrina
university education, Brian Davies'
interpretation of Thomas Aquinas
on, 49, 50, 53–54, 57
as wisdom, 65
sacraments. *See also* Eucharist
Augustinian theology of, 360–61
marriage, 358, 359–63, 372,
373–74. *See also* nuptial sexuality
in theology
ordination
Augustine on marriage and, 362
of women, 98, 99, 101, 103, 104
Penance and ecumenism, 250, 253
saints. *See* specific names of saints, e.g.
Augustine of Hippo
Sala, Giovanni B., xi, 293–14
Salvation Army, 251
1 Samuel 10:10, 183
Sapientia Christiana, 74, 84*n*26, 91,
94*n*47
Sarna, Nahum, 212*n*19

Saussure, Ferdinand de, 283
Schaeffler, Richard, 306–7
Scheeben, Matthias Joseph, 70
Schindler, David, 236n72
Schmitt, William, 317n4
Schmitz, Kenneth, 236n72, 243n90
Schumacher, Bernard, 82n23
Schumacher, Michele, x, 315–52
Schute, Michael, 383n43
Scola, Angelo, 316n2, 317n3, 353n1, 372n56
Scriptures. *See* Bible
Second Vatican Council. *See* Vatican II
secularism in postmodern world. *See* postmodern world as new Middle Ages
Seitz, Christopher, 190n55
sensism of Kant's theory of knowledge and being, 297–99
September 11, 2001 terrorist attacks, 277, 285, 286n25
Servais, Jacques, 315n1, 316n2
sexuality. *See* chastity; homosexuality; nuptial sexuality in theology
Shaw, George Bernard, 48
Shepherd of Hermas, 155
Shiettecatte, Johannes, 317n4
Sicari, Antonio, 316n2
sign, postmodern philosophical focus on, 279–85
Simonetti, Manlio, 176n15
Simonides, 62
sin, evil, and grace, Lonergan on, 397–402
Sindoni, Paola Ricci, 317n4
Sirach
Trinity in, 179
Siricus (pope), 359
Sisters of St. Joseph (Josephites), 24
68ers, 28
social utility view of religion, 24
sociocritical hermeneutics, 236

Sokolowski, Robert, 175, 176n18, 178n26, 182, 183n37–38, 214n22, 243n91
Spaemann, Robert, 236n72
Speyr, Adrienne von, anthropology of, x, 315–52
  Christological perspective, 323–27
  Church as person in response to person of Christ, 341–42, 347
  divine communion, realization of human person in, 318–23
  Eucharist in, 330–31, 333, 335, 338, 350
  gracious expansion of nature in mutual indwelling, 331–36
  limitations of human nature expanded by divine communion, 336–41
  Mary as theological person, 329–30, 340, 343–50, 351–52
  nuptial sexuality in, 333–36
  obedience, 339n114, 340–41
Spinoza, Benedict, 274n1, 281
spiritual beauty and consecrated life, 17–20, 33–34
St. John, Ambrose, 2
Stebbins, Michael, 380n27, 388n77, 388n82, 393n104, 401n141
Steiner, George, 246
Steinheim, Salomon Ludwig, 238
Stendahl, Krister, 188n49
Suarez, Francisco, 281n12
subjectivity of person, 240–42
Sullivan, Francis
  on academic freedom, 75n4, 77n8, 78n10, 88n38, 91n41, 97n52, 102n61
  on hierarchical authority in early Church, 149, 154–56
Suso, Henry, 38
Swierzawski, Waclaw, 109n1, 141n111
synagogues, hierarchical authority in, 152–54

Synave, Paul, 117n24
systematic theology, 60, 69

Thales, 274
theocentrism *vs.* Christocentrism in
   Dominican spirituality and
   Thomism, 37–38
theodramatic ecclesiology, 143–44,
   147–48
theology, theologians, and theological
   dissent. *See also under* academic
   freedom
   bishops and theologians, vii
   differences between contemporary
     and mid-19th century situations,
     1–2
   different theological systems, use of,
     70
   fragmentation of theology as
     discipline, 59–61
   history and theology, 304–7
   Kant's relevance to, 293–94. *See also*
     Kant, Immanuel
   nuptial sexuality and. *See* nuptial
     sexuality in theology
   "popularizers," post-conciliar
     theology of, 26–27
   revealed truth as objective of, 83–85
   unity, recovery of, 68–71
   wisdom, theological, 63–66, 70–71
1 Thessalonians
   Thomas on, 111
2 Thessalonians, Thomas on, 111
Thiselton, Anthony C., 236n71
Thomas Aquinas
   application, doctrine of, 388–89
   argumentative texts, fondness for, 110
   authoritative character of divine
     revelation for, 52–53, 265–69
   on authority of Magisterium, 87, 88,
     105
   biblical commentaries of, 109–10

on biblical interpretation, 116
Catherine of Siena on, 36
on contemplation, 41
on creation as revelatory
   modern thought and, 238n77,
     240, 241n84, 245
   Pauline commentaries and
     biblical tradition, 218,
     219–27, 232–33n65, 233
on Dominicans, 19
ecclesiology of, 146n16
ecumenism and thought of. *See*
   ecumenism, Thomistic
   contributions to
on Eucharist, 40
faith, theology of, 261–64
on first principles, 95
on judgment, 309
Kant and, 293, 296, 299–303, 305,
   309
knowledge theory of, 299–303, 305,
   309
Lamb's training in, ix
on language, 245
mandatum and, 96
moral theology of, 314n40
Pauline corpus, treatment of,
   110–14
on Philippians. *See* Philippians,
   commentary of St. Thomas on
postmodern philosophical trends
   and, 280, 283, 284
as realist, 79n13, 80–81
Speyrian anthropology and, 318,
   320–21, 327n51, 332n73, 333
on spiritual beauty, 18, 20
theocentrism *vs.* Christocentrism, 37
theological system of, 70
Transcendental Thomism, 293
on Trinity in Scripture, 177n23–24,
   179n29–30, 180–81, 182n34,
   182n36, 195–99, 201n81, 202,
   203

on truth, 79n12–13, 80, 83n25,
84n27–28
on university education. *See*
university education, Brian
Davies' interpretation of Thomas
Aquinas on
on viewing everthing in God, 44
on will and faith, 104
on wisdom, 61–62, 65–66, 67, 99,
100n57, 100n59, 245
Thompson, James W., 157n50
threes, human tendency to categorize
things into, 274
Tillard, Jean-Marie, 143n1, 146,
147n17
1 Timothy
Thomas on, 111
2 Timothy
Thomas on, 111
Titus
Thomas on, 111
Torrell, Jean-Pierre, 112
tradition in ecumenical dialogues,
257–61
transcendence
finality and transcendence,
Lonergan's theory of, 387–92
Kant's concept of transcendental
knowledge, 295. *See also* Kant,
Immanuel
modern loss of, 233–36
Thomism, Transcendental, 293
Trinity in Scripture, 173–203
authorship, 177–78
discourse on Trinity in Scripture,
178–79, 194–96
God the Father as speaker, 174,
175–76, 178 81, 194 96
Holy Spirit as speaker, 177, 182–83
issues related to, 174–80
Jesus as Second
Person/Word/incarnate son
discourse on, 178–79, 194–96

in Hebrews, 180, 182, 193
in John's Gospel, 191–93,
195–99
in Pauline epistles, 190–91
in Psalms, 200–202
in Revelation, 193
as speaker, 176–77, 181–83,
196–99
in Synoptic Gospels, 184–90
speakers, identity of, 174–77,
180–83
wisdom, 189–90
truth
academic freedom and
Magisterium and, 85–86
search for, 79–80
theologians, as objective of,
83–85
Dominicans and, 35, 37, 40–42, 43
intellectus fidei and, 303–4
supression/manifestation of, 219–27

Unam sanctam, 145
Unitatis redintegratio, 82n22
university curriculum, wisdom as
source of unity for, 59–71
different theological systems, use of,
70
fragmentation of theology as
discipline, 59–61
Holy Spirit, wisdom as gift of,
67–68, 70
philosophical wisdom, 61–63
recovery of unity, 68–71
theological wisdom, 63–66, 70–71
university education, Brian Davies'
interpretation of Thomas Aquinas
on, 47–58
antinomial relationship between
search for and possession of
knowledge, 47–48
authoritative character of divine
revelation for Thomas, 52–53

critique of, 52–57
disagreement, learning from, 56–58
faith and knowledge, 49–50, 51, 53, 57–58
implications for modern teachers, 51–56, 58
major premises of, 49–52
mandatum, omission of, 54
philosophy, student engagement with, 50–51
sacra doctrina, 49, 50, 53–54, 57
university education, Newman on, 1–16
　Church's relationship to university, 4–5, 11–16
　community, university as, 7
　differences between contemporary and mid-19th century situations, 1–3
　faith and reason, complementarity of, 4–5, 16
　gentleman, education as creation of, 5, 9–10
　humility *vs.* modesty, 9–10
　knowledge as good, assertions regarding, 3
　professional skill and liberal knowledge, 7–9
　reductionism, tendency towards, 12–13, 15
　theology, inclusion of, 5
　virtue/morality and liberal education, 5–7, 10, 15
　wisdom, role of, 61n4
university professors, academic freedom of. *See* academic freedom

Vaihinger, Hans, 295n4, 307
Valentinus, 135
Valerius, 367
van Bavel, Tarcisius, 370

Vatican I
　on concepts and understanding, 302–3, 304
　creation, revelatory nature of, 206, 233
　doctrine of papal infallibility declared at, 106
　on faith and reason, 66
　one-sidedness of, 288n28
Vatican II. *See also* specific documents
　consecrated life
　　Dominican General Chapter held in response to Vatican II, 43
　　original genius of founder, 34
　　present-day state of, 21–25, 26–28
　creation, revelatory nature of, 233
　on divine inspiration of Scripture, 256–57
　ecumenism, decree on, 269
　on nuptial sexuality in theology, 374
　one-sidedness of, 288–89n28
　Speyrian anthropology and, 342
Verardo, R. A., 180n33
Veritatis Splendor, 69–70, 313n35
Vertin, Michael, 395n112
Vicaire, M.-H., 34n32, 44n47
Vigilius (pope), 201n81
virginity. *See* chastity
virtue/morality
　Dominicans and, 41–42
　Humanae Vitae on natural moral law, 100
　Kant on ethics and moral theology, 313–14
　moral theology, 69–70, 313–14
　religion, virtue of, 24, 32
　university education, Newman on, 5–7, 10, 15
vocations. *See* consecrated life
voluntarism
　in academic freedom, 73, 75–77, 82–83, 98–99
　Dominican rejection of, 42

von Balthasar, Hans Urs. *See* Balthasar, Hans Urs von
von Speyr, Adrienne. *See* Speyr, Adrienne von, anthropology of
Vonier, Anscar, 182

Waldstein, Michael, 114n15, 136n92
Watson, Duane F., 117, 118, 119, 121
Weber, Max, 24
Weigel, George, 287
Weisheipl, James A., 128–29n56
Welch, Lawrence J., xi, 226n47, 353–74
Westermann, Claus, 208, 210n13
Whelan, Gerald K., 397n124
White, Victor, 49n8
Wilken, Robert, 232n65
Wilkin, Robert Louis, 177n22
Wilkins, Jeremy, xi, 375–402
will and academic freedom of theologians, 104–5
William of Ockham, 75n5, 83n24, 234, 274
Winston, David, 213n20, 214n21, 215
wisdom
    act of faith flowing from higher order of, 99–101
    creation as revelatory, wisdom literature on, 212, 213–17, 228–30
    as source of unity for university curriculum. *See* university curriculum, wisdom as source of unity for
    Trinity in Scripture and, 189–90
Wisdom (biblical book)
    Trinity in, 189–90
Witherington, Ben, III, 186n45, 189n52, 190n53
Wittgenstein, Ludwig, 274, 283
Wojtyla, Karol, 223n41, 241n84. *See also* John Paul II
Wolff, Hans Walter, 229n54
women
    feminism, 27, 28, 29, 77n9
    marginalization by Church, 146
    marriage and sexuality, theological understanding of. *See* nuptial sexuality in theology
    ordination of, 98, 99, 101, 103, 104
    in religious life. *See* consecrated life

Zenger, Erich, 210n15
Zizioulas, John D., 236n72

Index of Scriptural Citations

Genesis
  1, 174, 175, 180,
    196, 211, 212
  1:1, 276
  1:1–2:3, 209
  1:28, 364, 368n47
  2, 174, 180
  2:22, 364
  2:24, 185, 333, 361,
    371n55, 372n56,
    373
  3, 180
  3:5, 130
  12:1, 217
  14:19, 22, 208n8
  18, 174
  33, 174

Exodus
  3, 174
  3:6, 185
  6:2, 3, 266n47
  12, 188
  16, 192
  16:4, 192
  19:4–6, 247n104
  20:11, 209n11

  24, 188
  33:19, 131

Deuteronomy
  5:15, 209n11
  24:1–4, 185
  25:5, 185

Job
  7:17, 211
  22:29, 137
  26:6–14, 208
  28, 213
  32:8, 199
  35:11, 219
  38:4–11, 209

Psalms
  6:9, 201n82
  8, 180n31, 211, 212
  8:2, 138
  8:3, 201n82
  15, 179n29, 201
  15:10, 190n55
  17:45, 128
  19, 212
  19:2–7, 213

  19:9b, 212
  21, 180n31, 184,
    201, 201n82
  24, 211n16
  30, 370, 371n55
  33:8–10, 211
  33:9, 128
  39, 201n82
  42:3, 220
  44, 180n31
  68:5, 130
  69, 201n82
  74:12–17, 208
  77, 188
  78:21, 201n82
  85:9, 140
  89:9–14, 208
  94, 180n31, 182
  96:7, 140
  99:33, 131
  101, 180n31
  104, 211, 212
  104:1, 212
  104:4, 212
  106:20, 231
  109, 180n3, 184,
    185, 201

117, 184
117:16, 137
117:26, 187, 201n82
118:100, 266n47
144:3, 212
177:16ff, 138

Proverbs
  2, 213
  8, 193, 202
  8:12, 192
  8:22–36, 213
  9, 213
  9:5, 192
  21:28, 136

Song of Songs
  1:3, 128
  1:6, 203n87
  5:2, 202
  6:3, 40

Wisdom
  1:1, 215
  2:20, 137
  7:25–26, 193
  8:2, 213
  8:4, 215
  8:21, 215
  9, 193
  13:1–14:31, 213–15
  13:8, 228
  13:10–14:11, 214
  14:12–14, 214
  14:27, 214
  16, 192
  18:15, 192

Sirach
  1:10, 220, 232n65
  3:17(18), 135
  6:17–18, 189
  6:26, 195

7:27, 189
9:9, 189
10–11, 189
17:1–24, 213n20
18:8, 212
24, 189, 192
24:1–23, 213
24:8, 192
24:14–10, 213
24:19, 190
24:23, 189
24:33, 189
42:15ff, 189
43, 189
44–50, 189
51:17, 190
51:26, 190

Isaiah
  5, 185
  7:14, 188
  8, 180n31
  14:14, 130
  33:17, 128
  40:5, 141
  40:12, 21–22, 209
  42:1, 131
  45:22–25, 207n6
  45:24, 140
  51:9, 208
  52, 187
  53, 184
  55:1–3, 213
  55:10–11, 192
  56, 185
  61, 187
  61:1, 183

Jeremiah
  2:13, 192, 294
  2:20, 190
  3:14, 226
  5:5, 190

18:18, 181n33
22:5, 187
22:16, 229
27:5, 207n6
31, 180n31, 182
31:25, 190

Baruch
  3:9ff, 192
  3:38, 132, 196

Ezekiel
  2:2, 183
  7:26, 181n33
  28:11–19, 208
  36:24–28, 230

Daniel
  7, 184, 185n43
  12, 185n43

Hosea
  2:2, 229
  2:14, 199
  2:22, 230
  4:1, 229
  6:2, 190n55
  6:3, 229
  6:6, 229
  8:2, 229n56
  8:4, 229n57
  9:7, 229n56
  13:4, 229

Amos
  3:2, 229n57

Zechariah
  13:7, 184

2 Maccabees
  7:28, 209n12

Matthew
  1:18, 183
  1:23, 188
  4:18, 166
  4:20, 168
  4:22, 168
  5:17, 184, 190
  5:18, 187
  7:23, 201*n*82
  7:24, 190
  7:29, 53
  8:11–12, 187
  8:26, 168
  9:21, 128
  10, 181
  10:19–20, 167
  10:20, 182
  11:12–13, 187
  11:19, 190
  11:25–27, 168
  11:28, 190
  11:29, 135
  12:42, 190
  13:10, 185, 186
  13:34, 201*n*82
  13:35, 188
  13:36–39, 167
  14:26, 170
  14:31, 167
  15:36, 166
  16:16, 167
  16:17, 167
  16:18, 170, 188
  16:18–19, 167
  16:23, 167
  17:1–7, 169
  17:20, 168
  18:3–4, 148, 165
  19:5–6, 372*n*56
  19:28, 168
  19:29, 168
  20:25–28, 148, 166
  21:16, 201*n*82

  23:8, 10, 190
  23:29–31, 186
  23:34–36, 186
  23:37–39, 187
  23:39, 201*n*82
  25:41, 140
  26:26–28, 166
  26:33–35, 169
  26:39, 136
  26:61, 188
  27:5, 169
  28, 181
  28:18–20, 166
  28:20, 166, 167, 171

Mark
  1:5, 192
  1:15, 185
  6:2, 189
  8:34–35, 315
  8:35, 322*n*22
  9:11, 185
  10:2–9, 185
  10:8, 333
  10:19–20, 337
  10:26, 337
  10:45, 184
  11, 185
  12, 185
  12:10, 184
  12:18–27, 185*n*43
  12:24, 185
  12:26–27, 185
  12:28, 185
  12:35, 185
  13, 184
  14:27, 184
  14:62, 184, 201
  15:37, 184, 201

Luke
  1:35, 183
  2:51, 349*n*169

  5:6, 171
  5:8, 171
  5:10, 171
  10:24, 186
  11:47–51, 186
  12:8, 189, 192
  13:25–27, 187
  13:28–29, 187
  13:34–35, 187
  16:16–17, 187
  16:29–31, 185
  24, 184, 188
  24:45, 195

John
  1:10, 233*n*65
  1:14, 133, 192
  2:13–22, 201*n*82
  2:46, 192
  3:12, 192
  4:14, 192
  5, 129*n*61
  5:18, 130
  5:23, 141
  5:24, 192
  5:26, 138
  5:37*ff*, 191
  5:39, 184
  5:46, 192
  6, 192
  7:16, 198*n*69, 199*n*75
  7:38–39, 192
  8:32, 170
  8:51, 192
  8:56, 192
  11, 185
  11:26–27, 337
  12:41, 192
  13:13, 199*n*74
  14:3, 192
  14:6, 85
  14:23–25, 192

14:24, 197
14:25, 196
14:26, 177, 198, 199
14:27, 170
15:2, 340n119
16:12, 195
17:3, 191
17:5, 141
17:26, 199n74
18:13, 192
18:37, 196

Acts
2:14–36, 188n51
2:25, 31, 201
2:31, 179n29
2:36, 139
3:18, 22, 24, 188
3:24, 179n29
7:2–53, 188n51
7:52, 186n46, 188
7:56, 180
8:25, 188n51
10:19–20, 182
10:43, 188
13:2, 182
13:27, 188n51
13:27–29, 32, 188
14:15, 170
14:15–17, 225n46
17:22–25, 224–25n46
26:6, 22, 188
28:23, 188

Romans
1:2, 191
1:3, 138
1:4, 138
1:18–23, 218
1:20, 206n4, 233n65
1:22–23, 64, 231
1:24–31, 219
1:25, 231

1:28, 232n62
2:14–16, 224
5, 190
5:19, 136
6:9, 137
7:29, 366
8, 190
8:4, 191
8:26, 183
9:28, 131n69, 184, 197
10:4, 191
10:6–8, 191
10:15, 262
30:12f, 191

1 Corinthians
1:1, 157n51, 158
1:2, 157
1:5, 157
1:7, 157
1:8, 157
1:9, 158n51
1:12, 158
1:13, 158
1:17, 157, 158, 159
1:21, 228, 232n65
1:23–24, 158
1:24, 185
1:26–29, 64
1:30, 157
2:2, 158
2:4, 64
2:5, 158
2:6–7, 64, 65
2:7, 157, 191
2:12–13, 158
2:16, 158
3:5–7, 159
3:11, 161
4:1, 159
4:9–13, 163
4:15, 161

4:16, 164
4:17, 161
5:3–5, 159
5:7, 161
5:19–20, 159
5:20, 159
5:21, 159
6:17, 67
8:4–6, 217–18
9:26–27, 163
10:14, 194
10:16, 158n51, 159
10:17, 160
10:18, 160
10:21, 160
10:33, 161
11:1, 164
11:20, 160
11:23–26, 160
12:4–7, 162
12:12–13, 161
12:14, 161
12:15, 161
12:20, 161
12:22, 161
12:24–25, 161
12:26, 162
12:27–28, 162
12:29–30, 162
12:31, 162
13:1–3, 162
14:36, 163
14:37–38, 163
14:38, 166
15:1–3, 190
16:10–11, 157n51, 163
16:12, 163
16:15–16, 163
16:18, 163

2 Corinthians
1:20, 184, 191

2:4, 195
3:1–6, 191*n*57
3:14, 184
3:18, 128
7:15, 158*n*51
8:23, 157*n*51
13:3–4, 165*n*55
13:14, 158*n*51
38:16, 157*n*51

Galatians
2:20, 330*n*62

Ephesians
1:1–2, 122
1:3–23, 122
1:20*ff*, 138
1:22–23, 328
2:20, 191
3:5, 266*n*47
3:8–9, 56
4:1–6:9, 122
4:13, 71
4:17–19, 230
5:31, 371*n*55
5:31–32, 361, 370
5:32, 373
6:10–24, 122

Philippians
1:1, 122
1:1–2, 114, 117, 118
1:3–4, 118
1:3–11, 114
1:3–26, 117–18
1:5, 118
1:6–7, 118
1:8–11, 118
1:12–17, 118
1:12–24, 114
1:12*ff*, 118
1:18, 118
1:19–21, 118

1:19*ff*, 118
1:22–24, 118
1:25–26, 114, 119
1:25*ff*, 118
1:27–30, 114, 115,
    118, 119
2, 119
2:1–3:21, 118
2:1–4, 119
2:1–11, 118
2:5, 124*n*42, 125
2:5–11, 115, 119,
    123, 127–41
2:5–18, 115
2:6, 115, 123–26
2:6–7, 130*n*67,
    133*n*77, 141*n*112
2:7, 125, 130*n*65,
    131–32*n*72,
    132*n*74, 136*n*92
2:8, 139*n*104, 172
2:8–9, 139*n*104
2:9, 172
2:11, 124
2:12–18, 118, 119
2:19, 119
2:19–30, 115, 118
3, 115, 119
3:1–3, 119
3:1–21, 118
3:2, 118
3:3, 119
3:3–21, 118
3:4*ff*, 119
4, 119
4:1–3, 119
4:1–6:9, 122
4:1–9, 115, 118
4:1–20, 118
4:4–9, 119
4:10–18, 119
4:10–20, 118
4:10–23, 115

4:10*ff*, 119
4:19, 119, 122*n*35

Colossians
1:18, 328
1:28, 35
2:8, 64
3:11, 35

1 Thessalonians
1:9–10, 225*n*46

1 Timothy
6:20, 267*n*47

2 Timothy
3:15, 191

Titus
1:5, 157*n*51

Hebrews
1:3, 129
1:8–9, 180*n*31
1:10–12, 180*n*31
1:13, 180*n*31
2:5–8, 180*n*31
2:12, 180*n*31,
    201*n*82
2:13, 180*n*31
2:17, 131–32
3:3, 193
3:7–11, 180*n*31
4:15, 132
7:11–18, 193
7:19, 193
8:6, 193
9:12, 193
9:14, 196
9:24, 193
10:5–7, 180*n*31
10:5–7, 201*n*82
10:16–17, 180*n*31,
    182

11, 266n47
13:8, 68
94, 4:7–11

1 Peter
  1:10–11, 193
  1:11, 193
  1:12, 193
  3:18, 137
  3:18–22, 193n61

2 Peter
  1:19, 193
  1:21, 177

1 John
  2:4, 229n56
  4:20, 170
  5:20, 128

Revelation
  1:11, 193
  2:1, 193
  5:1–5, 193
  14:1, 193
  14:13, 182, 193
  17:8, 193
  19:9, 193
  21:6, 193
  22:13, 193
  22:17, 182